T0218796

Lecture Notes in Computer Science 13966

The series Lecture Notes in Computer Science (LNCS), including its subseries Lecture Notes in Artificial Intelligence (LNAI) and Lecture Notes in Bioinformatics (LNBI), has established itself as a medium for the publication of new developments in computer science and information technology research, teaching, and education.

LNCS enjoys close cooperation with the computer science R & D community, the series counts many renowned academics among its volume editors and paper authors, and collaborates with prestigious societies. Its mission is to serve this international community by providing an invaluable service, mainly focused on the publication of conference and workshop proceedings and postproceedings. LNCS commenced publication in 1973.

Constantin Enea · Akash Lal

Editors

Computer Aided Verification

35th International Conference, CAV 2023
Paris, France, July 17–22, 2023
Proceedings, Part III

 Springer

Editors
Constantin Enea
LIX, Ecole Polytechnique, CNRS and Institut
Polytechnique de Paris
Palaiseau, France

Akash Lal
Microsoft Research
Bangalore, India

ISSN 0302-9743   ISSN 1611-3349 (electronic)
Lecture Notes in Computer Science
ISBN 978-3-031-37708-2   ISBN 978-3-031-37709-9 (eBook)
https://doi.org/10.1007/978-3-031-37709-9

Preface

It was our privilege to serve as the program chairs for CAV 2023, the 35th International Conference on Computer-Aided Verification. CAV 2023 was held during July 19–22, 2023 and the pre-conference workshops were held during July 17–18, 2023. CAV 2023 was an in-person event, in Paris, France.

CAV is an annual conference dedicated to the advancement of the theory and practice of computer-aided formal analysis methods for hardware and software systems. The primary focus of CAV is to extend the frontiers of verification techniques by expanding to new domains such as security, quantum computing, and machine learning. This puts CAV at the cutting edge of formal methods research, and this year's program is a reflection of this commitment.

CAV 2023 received a large number of submissions (261). We accepted 15 tool papers, 3 case-study papers, and 49 regular papers, which amounts to an acceptance rate of roughly 26%. The accepted papers cover a wide spectrum of topics, from theoretical results to applications of formal methods. These papers apply or extend formal methods to a wide range of domains such as concurrency, machine learning and neural networks, quantum systems, as well as hybrid and stochastic systems. The program featured keynote talks by Ruzica Piskac (Yale University), Sumit Gulwani (Microsoft), and Caroline Trippel (Stanford University). In addition to the contributed talks, CAV also hosted the CAV Award ceremony, and a report from the Synthesis Competition (SYNTCOMP) chairs.

In addition to the main conference, CAV 2023 hosted the following workshops: Meeting on String Constraints and Applications (MOSCA), Verification Witnesses and Their Validation (VeWit), Verification of Probabilistic Programs (VeriProP), Open Problems in Learning and Verification of Neural Networks (WOLVERINE), Deep Learning-aided Verification (DAV), Hyperproperties: Advances in Theory and Practice (HYPER), Synthesis (SYNT), Formal Methods for ML-Enabled Autonomous Systems (FoMLAS), and Verification Mentoring Workshop (VMW). CAV 2023 also hosted a workshop dedicated to Thomas A. Henzinger for this 60th birthday.

Organizing a flagship conference like CAV requires a great deal of effort from the community. The Program Committee for CAV 2023 consisted of 76 members—a committee of this size ensures that each member has to review only a reasonable number of papers in the allotted time. In all, the committee members wrote over 730 reviews while investing significant effort to maintain and ensure the high quality of the conference program. We are grateful to the CAV 2023 Program Committee for their outstanding efforts in evaluating the submissions and making sure that each paper got a fair chance. Like recent years in CAV, we made artifact evaluation mandatory for tool paper submissions, but optional for the rest of the accepted papers. This year we received 48 artifact submissions, out of which 47 submissions received at least one badge. The Artifact Evaluation Committee consisted of 119 members who put in significant effort to evaluate each artifact. The goal of this process was to provide constructive feedback to tool developers and help make the research published in CAV more reproducible. We are also very grateful to the Artifact Evaluation Committee for their hard work and dedication in evaluating the submitted artifacts.

CAV 2023 would not have been possible without the tremendous help we received from several individuals, and we would like to thank everyone who helped make CAV 2023 a success. We would like to thank Alessandro Cimatti, Isil Dillig, Javier Esparza, Azadeh Farzan, Joost-Pieter Katoen and Corina Pasareanu for serving as area chairs. We also thank Bernhard Kragl and Daniel Dietsch for chairing the Artifact Evaluation Committee. We also thank Mohamed Faouzi Atig for chairing the workshop organization as well as leading publicity efforts, Eric Koskinen as the fellowship chair, Sebastian Bardin and Ruzica Piskac as sponsorship chairs, and Srinidhi Nagendra as the website chair. Srinidhi, along with Enrique Román Calvo, helped prepare the proceedings. We also thank Ankush Desai, Eric Koskinen, Burcu Kulahcioglu Ozkan, Marijana Lazic, and Matteo Sammartino for chairing the mentoring workshop. Last but not least, we would like to thank the members of the CAV Steering Committee (Kenneth McMillan, Aarti Gupta, Orna Grumberg, and Daniel Kroening) for helping us with several important aspects of organizing CAV 2023.

We hope that you will find the proceedings of CAV 2023 scientifically interesting and thought-provoking!

June 2023   Constantin Enea
                                                                              Akash Lal

Organization

Conference Co-chairs

Constantin Enea	LIX, École Polytechnique, France
Akash Lal	Microsoft Research, India

Artifact Co-chairs

Bernhard Kragl	Amazon Web Services, USA
Daniel Dietsch	Qt Group/University of Freiburg, Germany

Workshop Chair

Mohamed Faouzi Atig	Uppsala University, Sweden

Verification Mentoring Workshop Organizing Committee

Ankush Densai	AWS CA, USA
Eric Koskinen	Stevens Institute of Technology, USA
Burcu Kulahcioglu Ozkan	TU Delft, The Netherlands
Marijana Lazic	TU Munich, Germany
Matteo Sammartino	Royal Holloway, University of London, UK

Fellowship Chair

Eric Koskinen	Stevens Institute of Technology, USA

Website Chair

Srinidhi Nagendra	Université Paris Cité, CNRS, IRIF, France and Chennai Mathematical Institute, India

Sponsorship Co-chairs

Sebastian Bardin   CEA LIST, France
Ruzica Piskac   Yale University, USA

Proceedings Chairs

Srinidhi Nagendra   Université Paris Cité, CNRS, IRIF, France and
                                Chennai Mathematical Institute, India
Enrique Román Calvo   Université Paris Cité, CNRS, IRIF, France

Program Committee

Aarti Gupta   Princeton University, USA
Abhishek Bichhawat   IIT Gandhinagar, India
Aditya V. Thakur   University of California, USA
Ahmed Bouajjani   University of Paris, France
Aina Niemetz   Stanford University, USA
Akash Lal   Microsoft Research, India
Alan J. Hu   University of British Columbia, Canada
Alessandro Cimatti   Fondazione Bruno Kessler, Italy
Alexander Nadel   Intel, Israel
Anastasia Mavridou   KBR, NASA Ames Research Center, USA
Andreas Podelski   University of Freiburg, Germany
Ankush Desai   Amazon Web Services
Anna Slobodova   Intel, USA
Anthony Widjaja Lin   TU Kaiserslautern and Max-Planck Institute for
                                Software Systems, Germany
Arie Gurfinkel   University of Waterloo, Canada
Arjun Radhakrishna   Microsoft, India
Aws Albarghouthi   University of Wisconsin-Madison, USA
Azadeh Farzan   University of Toronto, Canada
Bernd Finkbeiner   CISPA Helmholtz Center for Information
                                Security, Germany
Bettina Koenighofer   Graz University of Technology, Austria
Bor-Yuh Evan Chang   University of Colorado Boulder and Amazon,
                                USA
Burcu Kulahcioglu Ozkan   Delft University of Technology, The Netherlands
Caterina Urban   Inria and École Normale Supérieure, France
Cezara Dragoi   Amazon Web Services, USA

Christoph Matheja	Technical University of Denmark, Denmark
Claudia Cauli	Amazon Web Services, UK
Constantin Enea	LIX, CNRS, Ecole Polytechnique, France
Corina Pasareanu	CMU, USA
Cristina David	University of Bristol, UK
Dirk Beyer	LMU Munich, Germany
Elizabeth Polgreen	University of Edinburgh, UK
Elvira Albert	Complutense University, Spain
Eunsuk Kang	Carnegie Mellon University, USA
Gennaro Parlato	University of Molise, Italy
Hossein Hojjat	Tehran University and Tehran Institute of Advanced Studies, Iran
Ichiro Hasuo	National Institute of Informatics, Japan
Isil Dillig	University of Texas, Austin, USA
Javier Esparza	Technische Universität München, Germany
Joost-Pieter Katoen	RWTH-Aachen University, Germany
Juneyoung Lee	AWS, USA
Jyotirmoy Deshmukh	University of Southern California, USA
Kenneth L. McMillan	University of Texas at Austin, USA
Kristin Yvonne Rozier	Iowa State University, USA
Kshitij Bansal	Google, USA
Kuldeep Meel	National University of Singapore, Singapore
Kyungmin Bae	POSTECH, South Korea
Marcell Vazquez-Chanlatte	Alliance Innovation Lab (Nissan-Renault-Mitsubishi), USA
Marieke Huisman	University of Twente, The Netherlands
Markus Rabe	Google, USA
Marta Kwiatkowska	University of Oxford, UK
Matthias Heizmann	University of Freiburg, Germany
Michael Emmi	AWS, USA
Mihaela Sighireanu	University Paris Saclay, ENS Paris-Saclay and CNRS, France
Mohamed Faouzi Atig	Uppsala University, Sweden
Naijun Zhan	Institute of Software, Chinese Academy of Sciences, China
Nikolaj Bjorner	Microsoft Research, USA
Nina Narodytska	VMware Research, USA
Pavithra Prabhakar	Kansas State University, USA
Pierre Ganty	IMDEA Software Institute, Spain
Rupak Majumdar	Max Planck Institute for Software Systems, Germany
Ruzica Piskac	Yale University, USA

Sebastian Junges	Radboud University, The Netherlands
Sébastien Bardin	CEA, LIST, Université Paris Saclay, France
Serdar Tasiran	Amazon, USA
Sharon Shoham	Tel Aviv University, Israel
Shaz Qadeer	Meta, USA
Shuvendu Lahiri	Microsoft Research, USA
Subhajit Roy	Indian Institute of Technology, Kanpur, India
Suguman Bansal	Georgia Institute of Technology, USA
Swarat Chaudhuri	UT Austin, USA
Sylvie Putot	École Polytechnique, France
Thomas Wahl	GrammaTech, USA
Tomáš Vojnar	Brno University of Technology, FIT, Czech Republic
Yakir Vizel	Technion - Israel Institute of Technology, Israel
Yu-Fang Chen	Academia Sinica, Taiwan
Zhilin Wu	State Key Laboratory of Computer Science, Institute of Software, Chinese Academy of Sciences, China

Artifact Evaluation Committee

Alejandro Hernández-Cerezo	Complutense University of Madrid, Spain
Alvin George	IISc Bangalore, India
Aman Goel	Amazon Web Services, USA
Amit Samanta	University of Utah, USA
Anan Kabaha	Technion, Israel
Andres Noetzli	Cubist, Inc., USA
Anna Becchi	Fondazione Bruno Kessler, Italy
Arnab Sharma	University of Oldenburg, Germany
Avraham Raviv	Bar Ilan University, Israel
Ayrat Khalimov	TU Clausthal, Germany
Baoluo Meng	General Electric Research, USA
Benjamin Jones	Amazon Web Services, USA
Bohua Zhan	Institute of Software, Chinese Academy of Sciences, China
Cayden Codel	Carnegie Mellon University, USA
Charles Babu M.	CEA LIST, France
Chungha Sung	Amazon Web Services, USA
Clara Rodriguez-Núñez	Universidad Complutense de Madrid, Spain
Cyrus Liu	Stevens Institute of Technology, USA
Daniel Hausmann	University of Gothenburg, Sweden

Daniela Kaufmann	TU Wien, Austria
Debasmita Lohar	MPI SWS, Germany
Deivid Vale	Radboud University Nijmegen, Netherlands
Denis Mazzucato	Inria, France
Dorde Žikelić	Institute of Science and Technology Austria, Austria
Ekanshdeep Gupta	New York University, USA
Enrico Magnago	Amazon Web Services, USA
Ferhat Erata	Yale University, USA
Filip Cordoba	Graz University of Technology, Austria
Filipe Arruda	UFPE, Brazil
Florian Dorfhuber	Technical University of Munich, Germany
Florian Sextl	TU Wien, Austria
Francesco Parolini	Sorbonne University, France
Frédéric Recoules	CEA LIST, France
Goktug Saatcioglu	Cornell, USA
Goran Piskachev	Amazon Web Services, USA
Grégoire Menguy	CEA LIST, France
Guy Amir	Hebrew University of Jerusalem, Israel
Habeeb P.	Indian Institute of Science, Bangalore, India
Hadrien Renaud	UCL, UK
Haoze Wu	Stanford University, USA
Hari Krishnan	University of Waterloo, Canada
Hünkar Tunç	Aarhus University, Denmark
Idan Refaeli	Hebrew University of Jerusalem, Israel
Ignacio D. Lopez-Miguel	TU Wien, Austria
Ilina Stoilkovska	Amazon Web Services, USA
Ira Fesefeldt	RWTH Aachen University, Germany
Jahid Choton	Kansas State University, USA
Jie An	National Institute of Informatics, Japan
John Kolesar	Yale University, USA
Joseph Scott	University of Waterloo, Canada
Kevin Lotz	Kiel University, Germany
Kirby Linvill	CU Boulder, USA
Kush Grover	Technical University of Munich, Germany
Levente Bajczi	Budapest University of Technology and Economics, Hungary
Liangcheng Yu	University of Pennsylvania, USA
Luke Geeson	UCL, UK
Lutz Klinkenberg	RWTH Aachen University, Germany
Marek Chalupa	Institute of Science and Technology Austria, Austria

Mario Bucev	EPFL, Switzerland
Mário Pereira	NOVA LINCS—Nova School of Science and Technology, Portugal
Marius Mikucionis	Aalborg University, Denmark
Martin Jonáš	Masaryk University, Czech Republic
Mathias Fleury	University of Freiburg, Germany
Matthias Hetzenberger	TU Wien, Austria
Maximilian Heisinger	Johannes Kepler University Linz, Austria
Mertcan Temel	Intel Corporation, USA
Michele Chiari	TU Wien, Austria
Miguel Isabel	Universidad Complutense de Madrid, Spain
Mihai Nicola	Stevens Institute of Technology, USA
Mihály Dobos-Kovács	Budapest University of Technology and Economics, Hungary
Mikael Mayer	Amazon Web Services, USA
Mitja Kulczynski	Kiel University, Germany
Muhammad Mansur	Amazon Web Services, USA
Muqsit Azeem	Technical University of Munich, Germany
Neelanjana Pal	Vanderbilt University, USA
Nicolas Koh	Princeton University, USA
Niklas Metzger	CISPA Helmholtz Center for Information Security, Germany
Omkar Tuppe	IIT Bombay, India
Pablo Gordillo	Complutense University of Madrid, Spain
Pankaj Kalita	Indian Institute of Technology, Kanpur, India
Parisa Fathololumi	Stevens Institute of Technology, USA
Pavel Hudec	HKUST, Hong Kong, China
Peixin Wang	University of Oxford, UK
Philippe Heim	CISPA Helmholtz Center for Information Security, Germany
Pritam Gharat	Microsoft Research, India
Priyanka Darke	TCS Research, India
Ranadeep Biswas	Informal Systems, Canada
Robert Rubbens	University of Twente, Netherlands
Rubén Rubio	Universidad Complutense de Madrid, Spain
Samuel Judson	Yale University, USA
Samuel Pastva	Institute of Science and Technology Austria, Austria
Sankalp Gambhir	EPFL, Switzerland
Sarbojit Das	Uppsala University, Sweden
Sascha Klüppelholz	Technische Universität Dresden, Germany
Sean Kauffman	Aalborg University, Denmark

Shaowei Zhu	Princeton University, USA
Shengjian Guo	Amazon Web Services, USA
Simmo Saan	University of Tartu, Estonia
Smruti Padhy	University of Texas at Austin, USA
Stanly Samuel	Indian Institute of Science, Bangalore, India
Stefan Pranger	Graz University of Technology, Austria
Stefan Zetzsche	Amazon Web Services, USA
Sumanth Prabhu	TCS Research, India
Sumit Lahiri	Indian Institute of Technology, Kanpur, India
Sunbeom So	Korea University, South Korea
Syed M. Iqbal	Amazon Web Services, USA
Tobias Meggendorfer	Institute of Science and Technology Austria, Austria
Tzu-Han Hsu	Michigan State University, USA
Verya Monjezi	University of Texas at El Paso, USA
Wei-Lun Tsai	Academia Sinica, Taiwan
William Schultz	Northeastern University, USA
Xiao Liang Yu	National University of Singapore, Singapore
Yahui Song	National University of Singapore, Singapore
Yasharth Bajpai	Microsoft Research, USA
Ying Sheng	Stanford University, USA
Yuriy Biktairov	University of Southern California, USA
Zafer Esen	Uppsala University, Sweden

Additional Reviewers

Azzopardi, Shaun
Baier, Daniel
Belardinelli, Francesco
Bergstraesser, Pascal
Boker, Udi
Ceska, Milan
Chien, Po-Chun
Coglio, Alessandro
Correas, Jesús
Doveri, Kyveli
Drachsler Cohen, Dana
Durand, Serge
Fried, Dror
Genaim, Samir
Ghosh, Bishwamittra
Gordillo, Pablo

Guillermo, Roman Diez
Gómez-Zamalloa, Miguel
Hernández-Cerezo, Alejandro
Holík, Lukáš
Isabel, Miguel
Ivrii, Alexander
Izza, Yacine
Jothimurugan, Kishor
Kaivola, Roope
Kaminski, Benjamin Lucien
Kettl, Matthias
Kretinsky, Jan
Lengal, Ondrej
Losa, Giuliano
Luo, Ning
Malik, Viktor

Markgraf, Oliver
Martin-Martin, Enrique
Meller, Yael
Perez, Mateo
Petri, Gustavo
Pote, Yash
Preiner, Mathias
Rakamaric, Zvonimir
Rastogi, Aseem
Razavi, Niloofar
Rogalewicz, Adam
Sangnier, Arnaud
Sarkar, Uddalok
Schoepe, Daniel
Sergey, Ilya

Stoilkovska, Ilina
Stucki, Sandro
Tsai, Wei-Lun
Turrini, Andrea
Vafeiadis, Viktor
Valiron, Benoît
Wachowitz, Henrik
Wang, Chao
Wang, Yuepeng
Wies, Thomas
Yang, Jiong
Yen, Di-De
Zhu, Shufang
Žikelić, Đorđe
Zohar, Yoni

Contents – Part III

Probabilistic Systems

A Flexible Toolchain for Symbolic Rabin Games under Fair and Stochastic
Uncertainties 3
   Rupak Majumdar, Kaushik Mallik, Mateusz Rychlicki,
   Anne-Kathrin Schmuck, and Sadegh Soudjani

Automated Tail Bound Analysis for Probabilistic Recurrence Relations 16
   Yican Sun, Hongfei Fu, Krishnendu Chatterjee,
   and Amir Kafshdar Goharshady

Compositional Probabilistic Model Checking with String Diagrams
of MDPs 40
   Kazuki Watanabe, Clovis Eberhart, Kazuyuki Asada, and Ichiro Hasuo

Efficient Sensitivity Analysis for Parametric Robust Markov Chains 62
   Thom Badings, Sebastian Junges, Ahmadreza Marandi, Ufuk Topcu,
   and Nils Jansen

MDPs as Distribution Transformers: Affine Invariant Synthesis for Safety
Objectives 86
   S. Akshay, Krishnendu Chatterjee, Tobias Meggendorfer,
   and Đorđe Žikelić

Search and Explore: Symbiotic Policy Synthesis in POMDPs 113
   Roman Andriushchenko, Alexander Bork, Milan Češka,
   Sebastian Junges, Joost-Pieter Katoen, and Filip Macák

Security and Quantum Systems

AUTOQ: An Automata-Based Quantum Circuit Verifier 139
   Yu-Fang Chen, Kai-Min Chung, Ondřej Lengál, Jyun-Ao Lin,
   and Wei-Lun Tsai

Bounded Verification for Finite-Field-Blasting: In a Compiler for Zero
Knowledge Proofs 154
   Alex Ozdemir, Riad S. Wahby, Fraser Brown, and Clark Barrett

Formally Verified EVM Block-Optimizations 176
  Elvira Albert, Samir Genaim, Daniel Kirchner,
  and Enrique Martin-Martin

SR-SFLL: Structurally Robust Stripped Functionality Logic Locking 190
  Gourav Takhar and Subhajit Roy

Symbolic Quantum Simulation with Quasimodo 213
  Meghana Sistla, Swarat Chaudhuri, and Thomas Reps

Verifying the Verifier: eBPF Range Analysis Verification 226
  Harishankar Vishwanathan, Matan Shachnai, Srinivas Narayana,
  and Santosh Nagarakatte

Software Verification

Automated Verification of Correctness for Masked Arithmetic Programs 255
  Mingyang Liu, Fu Song, and Taolue Chen

Automatic Program Instrumentation for Automatic Verification 281
  Jesper Amilon, Zafer Esen, Dilian Gurov, Christian Lidström,
  and Philipp Rümmer

Boolean Abstractions for Realizability Modulo Theories 305
  Andoni Rodríguez and César Sánchez

Certified Verification for Algebraic Abstraction 329
  Ming-Hsien Tsai, Yu-Fu Fu, Jiaxiang Liu, Xiaomu Shi, Bow-Yaw Wang,
  and Bo-Yin Yang

Complete Multiparty Session Type Projection with Automata 350
  Elaine Li, Felix Stutz, Thomas Wies, and Damien Zufferey

Early Verification of Legal Compliance via Bounded Satisfiability Checking . . . 374
  Nick Feng, Lina Marsso, Mehrdad Sabetzadeh, and Marsha Chechik

Formula Normalizations in Verification 398
  Simon Guilloud, Mario Bucev, Dragana Milovančević, and Viktor Kunčak

Kratos2: An SMT-Based Model Checker for Imperative Programs 423
  Alberto Griggio and Martin Jonáš

Making IP = PSPACE Practical: Efficient Interactive Protocols for BDD
Algorithms 437
  Eszter Couillard, Philipp Czerner, Javier Esparza, and Rupak Majumdar

Ownership Guided C to Rust Translation 459
  Hanliang Zhang, Cristina David, Yijun Yu, and Meng Wang

R2U2 Version 3.0: Re-Imagining a Toolchain for Specification, Resource
Estimation, and Optimized Observer Generation for Runtime Verification
in Hardware and Software 483
  *Chris Johannsen, Phillip Jones, Brian Kempa, Kristin Yvonne Rozier,
  and Pei Zhang*

Author Index 499

Probabilistic Systems

A Flexible Toolchain
for Symbolic Rabin Games
under Fair and Stochastic Uncertainties

Rupak Majumdar[1], Kaushik Mallik[2($\boxtimes$)], Mateusz Rychlicki[3],
Anne-Kathrin Schmuck[1], and Sadegh Soudjani[4]

[1] MPI-SWS, Kaiserslautern, Germany
{rupak,akschmuck}@mpi-sws.org
[2] ISTA, Klosterneuburg, Austria
kaushik.mallik@ist.ac.at
[3] School of Computing, University of Leeds, Leeds, UK
scmkry@leeds.ac.uk
[4] Newcastle University, Newcastle upon Tyne, UK
Sadegh.Soudjani@newcastle.ac.uk

Abstract. We present a flexible and efficient toolchain to *symbolically* solve (standard) Rabin games, fair-adversarial Rabin games, and 2¹/₂-player Rabin games. To our best knowledge, our tools are the first ones to be able to solve these problems. Furthermore, using these flexible game solvers as a back-end, we implemented a tool for computing correct-by-construction controllers for stochastic dynamical systems under LTL specifications. Our implementations use the recent theoretical result that all of these games can be solved using the same symbolic fixpoint algorithm but utilizing different, domain specific calculations of the involved predecessor operators. The main feature of our toolchain is the utilization of two programming abstractions: one to separate the symbolic fixpoint computations from the predecessor calculations, and another one to allow the integration of different BDD libraries as back-ends. In particular, we employ a multi-threaded execution of the fixpoint algorithm by using the multi-threaded BDD library Sylvan, which leads to enormous computational savings.

1 Introduction

Piterman and Pnueli [17] derived the currently best known symbolic algorithm for solving two-player Rabin games over finite graphs with a theoretical complexity of $O(n^{k+1}k!)$ in time and space, where n is the number of states and k is the number of pairs in the winning condition. This work did not provide an

---

Authors ordered alphabetically. R. Majumdar and A.-K. Schmuck are partially supported by DFG project 389792660 TRR 248-CPEC. A.-K. Schmuck is additionally funded through DFG project (SCHM 3541/1-1). K. Mallik is supported by the ERC project ERC-2020-AdG 101020093. M. Rychlicki is supported by the EPSRC project EP/V00252X/1. S. Soudjani is supported by the following projects: EPSRC EP/V043676/1, EIC 101070802, and ERC 101089047.

C. Enea and A. Lal (Eds.): CAV 2023, LNCS 13966, pp. 3–15, 2023.
https://doi.org/10.1007/978-3-031-37709-9_1

implementation. In a series of papers [3,4,15,16], Mallik et al. showed that this symbolic algorithm can be extended to solve different automated design questions for reactive hardware, software, and cyber-physical systems under fair or stochastic uncertainties. The main contribution of their work is to show that these extensions only require a very mild syntactic change of the Piterman-Pnueli fixed-point algorithm (with very little effect on its overall complexity) and domain-specific realizations of two types of predecessor operators used therein.

Using this insight, we present a *toolchain* for the *efficient symbolic solution of different extensions of Rabin games*. We have created three inter-connected libraries for solving different parts of the problem from different levels of abstraction. The first library, called Genie, offers a set of virtual classes to implement the fixpoint algorithm—abstractly, leaving open (i.e. virtual) the predecessor computation. Alongside, we created two other libraries, called FairSyn and Mascot-SDS, where FairSyn solves fair-adversarial [4] and $2\frac{1}{2}$-player Rabin games [3], while Mascot-SDS solves abstraction-based control problems [15,16]. FairSyn and Mascot-SDS use the optimized fixpoint computation provided by Genie, with domain specific implementations of the predecessor operations.

The flexibility of our toolchain comes from two different programming abstractions in Genie. Firstly, Genie offers multiple high-level optimizations for solving the Rabin fixpoint, such as parallel execution (requires a thread-safe BDD library like Sylvan) and an acceleration technique [13], while abstracting away from the low-level implementations of the predecessor functions. As a result, any synthesis problem using the core Rabin fixpoint of Genie can use the optimizations without spending any extra implementation effort. We used these optimizations from FairSyn and Mascot-SDS, and achieved remarkable computational savings. Secondly, Genie offers easy portability of codes from one BDD library to another, which is important as different BDD libraries have different pros and cons, and the choice of the best library depends on the needs. We empirically showed how switching between the two BDD libraries Sylvan and CUDD impacts the performance of FairSyn and CUDD: overall, the Sylvan-based experiments were significantly faster, whereas the CUDD-based experiments consumed considerably lower amount of memory. Using the combined power of multi-threaded BDD operations using Sylvan and the optimizations offered by Genie, Mascot-SDS was between one and three orders of magnitude faster than the state-of-the-art tool in our experiments.

Comparison with Existing Tools: We are not aware of any available tool to directly solve (normal or stochastic) Rabin games *symbolically*. However, it is well-known how to translate *stochastic* Rabin games into (standard) Rabin games [5], and Rabin games into parity games, for which efficient solvers exist, e.g. oink [9]. Yet, efficient solutions of stochastic Rabin games via parity games are difficult to obtain, because: (i) the translation from a stochastic Rabin game to a Rabin game involves a quadratic blow-up, and the translation from a Rabin game to a parity game results in an exponential blow-up in the size of the game, (ii) symbolic fixpoint computations become cumbersome very fast for parity games, as the number of vertices and/or colors in the game graph increases, leading to high computation times in practice, and (iii) the only known algorithms capable of handling fair and stochastic uncertainties efficiently are all *symbolic* in nature, while most of the efficient parity game solvers are non-symbolic. Additionally, unlike the Rabin fixpoint, the nesting of the parity fixpoint does not enable parallel execution.

While it is well known that for normal parity games, computational tractability can be achieved by different non-symbolic algorithms, such as Zielonka's algorithm [22], tangle learning [8] or strategy-improvement [19], implemented in oink [9], it is currently unclear if and how these algorithms allow for the efficient handling of fair or stochastic uncertainties. We are therefore unable to compare our toolchain to the translational workflow via parity games in a fair manner.

In the area of temporal logic control of stochastic systems, Mascot-SDS has two powerful features: (a) it can handle synthesis for the rich class of omega-regular (infinite-horizon) specifications, and (b) it provides both over- and under-approximations of the solution, thus enabling a quantitative refinement loop for improving the precision of the approximation. The features of Mascot-SDS is compared with other tools in the stochastic category of the recent ARCH competition (see the report [1] for the list of participating tools). As concluded in the report of the competition, other state-of-the-art tools in stochastic category are either limited to a fragment of ω-regular specifications or do not provide any indication of the quality of the involved approximations. The only tool [10] that supports ω-regular specifications uses a different alternate non-symbolic approach, against which Mascot-SDS fares significantly well in our experiments (see Sect. 4.2). Even if we leave stochasticity aside, our tool implements a new and orthogonal heuristic for multi-threaded computation of Rabin fixpoints, which is not considered by other controller synthesis tools [11].

2 Theoretical Background

We briefly state the synthesis problems our toolchain is solving. We follow the same (standard) notation for two-player game graphs, winning regions, strategies and μ-calculus formulas, as in [4].

2.1 Solving Rabin Games Symbolically

Given a game graph $G = (V, V_0, V_1, E)$, a Rabin game is specified using a set of Rabin pairs $\mathcal{R} = \{(Q_1, R_1), \ldots, (Q_k, R_k)\}$, with $Q_i, R_i \subseteq V$ for every $i \in [1; k]$, and $\varphi := \bigvee_{i \in [1;k]} (\lozenge \square \neg R_i \wedge \square \lozenge Q_i)$ being the Rabin acceptance condition. Piterman and Pnueli [17] showed that the winning region of a Rabin game can be computed using the μ-calculus expression given in (2), where the set transformers $Cpre : 2^V \to 2^V$ and $Apre : 2^V \times 2^V \to 2^V$ are defined for every $S, T \subseteq V$ as:

$$Cpre(S) := \{v \in V_0 \mid \exists v' \in S \,.\, (v, v') \in E\}$$
$$\cup \{v \in V_1 \mid \forall v' \in V \,.\, (v, v') \in E \implies v' \in S\}, \quad \text{(1a)}$$
$$Apre(S, T) := Cpre(T). \quad \text{(1b)}$$

Fair-Adversarial Rabin Games. A Rabin game is called *fair-adversarial* when there is an additional fairness assumption on a set of edges originating from

The symbolic fixpoint algorithm for solving Rabin games with $\mathcal{R} = \{(Q_1, R_1), \ldots, (Q_k, R_k)\}$ and $K = [1; k]$:

$$\nu Y_{p_0}.\mu X_{p_0}. \bigcup_{p_1 \in K} \nu Y_{p_1}.\mu X_{p_1}. \bigcup_{p_2 \in K \setminus \{p_1\}} \nu Y_{p_2}.\mu X_{p_2}. \quad \ldots \quad \bigcup_{p_k \in K \setminus \{p_1, \ldots, p_{k-1}\}} \nu Y_{p_k}.\mu X_{p_k}. \left[\bigcup_{j=0}^{k} \mathcal{C}_{p_j} \right], \quad (2)$$

where

$$\mathcal{C}_{p_j} := \left(\bigcap_{i=0}^{j} \overline{R_{p_i}} \right) \cap \left[(Q_{p_j} \cap Cpre(Y_{p_j})) \cup (Apre(Y_{p_j}, X_{p_j})) \right],$$

and the definitions of *Cpre* and *Apre* are problem specific.

Player 1 vertices in G. Let $E^\ell \subseteq E \cap (V_1 \times V)$ be a given set of edges, called the *live edges*. Given E^ℓ and a Rabin winning condition φ, we say that *Player* 0 wins the *fair-adversarial Rabin game* from a vertex v if *Player* 0 wins the (normal) game for the modified winning condition $\varphi^\ell := \left(\bigwedge_{e=(v,v') \in E^\ell} (\Box \Diamond v \implies \Box \Diamond e) \right) \implies \varphi$. Based on the results of Banerjee et al. [4], fair-adversarial Rabin games can be solved via (2), by defining for every $S, T \subseteq V$

$$Cpre(S) := \{v \in V_0 \mid \exists v' \in S . (v, v') \in E\}$$
$$\cup \{v \in V_1 \mid \forall v' \in V . (v, v') \in E \implies v' \in S\}, \quad (3a)$$
$$Apre(S, T) := Cpre(T) \cup \{v \in Cpre(S) \cap V_1 \mid \exists v' \in T . (v, v') \in E^\ell\}. \quad (3b)$$

We see that (3) coincides with (1) if E^ℓ is empty.

$2^1/_2$-**Player Rabin Games.** A $2^1/_2$-player game is played on a game graph (V, V_0, V_1, V_r, E), and the only difference from a 2-player game graph is the additional set of vertices V_r which are called the *random* vertices. The sets V_1, V_2, and V_r partition V. Based on the results of [3] $2^1/_2$-Player rabin games can be solved via (2) by defining for all $S, T \subseteq V$

$$Cpre(S) := \{v \in V_0 \mid \exists v' \in S . (v, v') \in E\}$$
$$\cup \{v \in V_1 \cup V_r \mid \forall v' \in V . (v, v') \in E \Rightarrow v' \in S\}, \quad (4a)$$
$$Apre(S, T) := Cpre(T) \cup \{v \in Cpre(S) \cap V_r \mid \exists v' \in T . (v, v') \in E\}. \quad (4b)$$

2.2 Computing Symbolic Controllers for Stochastic Dynamical Systems

A discrete-time stochastic dynamical system S is represented using a tuple (X, U, W, f), where $X \subseteq \mathbb{R}^n$ is a *continuous* state space, U is a *finite* set of control inputs, $W \subset \mathbb{R}^n$ is a *bounded* set of disturbances, and $f : X \times U \to X$ is the nominal dynamics. If $x^k \in X$ and $u^k \in U$ are the state and control input of S at some time $k \in \mathbb{N}$, then the state at the next time step is given by:

$$x^{k+1} = f(x^k, u^k) + w^k, \quad (5)$$

where w^k is the disturbance at time k which is sampled from W using some (possibly unknown) distribution. Without loss of generality we assume that W

is centered around the origin, which can be easily achieved by shifting f if needed. A *path* of S originating at $x^0 \in X$ is an infinite sequence of states $x^0 x^1 \ldots$ for a given infinite sequence of control inputs $u^0 u^1 \ldots$, such that (5) is satisfied.

Let φ be a given Rabin specification—called the *control objective*—defined using a finite set of predicates over X. For every controller $C \colon X \to U$, the domain of C, written $Dom(C)$, is the set of states from where the property φ can be satisfied with probability 1. For a fixed φ, a controller $\hat{C}$ is called *optimal* if $Dom(\hat{C})$ contains the domain of every other controller C. The problem of computing such an optimal controller for the system in (5) is in general undecidable. Following [15], we compute an approximate solution instead.

This approximate solution is obtained by a discretization of the state space. For this, we assume that the state space X is a closed and bounded subset of the n-dimensional Euclidean space $\mathbb{R}^n$ for some $n > 0$, and use the notation $[\![a, b)\!)$ to denote the set $\prod_{i \in [1;n]} [a_i, b_i)$. Now, consider a grid-based discretization $\widehat{X}$ of X, where $\widehat{X} = \{[\![a, b)\!) \mid a, b \in \mathbb{R}^n = X\}$. One of the key ingredients of our abstraction process is a function $\widehat{f}$ providing hyper-rectangular over-approximation of the one-step reachable set of the nominal dynamics f of the system S: for every grid element $\widehat{x} \in \widehat{X}$, we have $\widehat{f}(\widehat{x}, u) = [\![a', b')\!) \supseteq \{x' \in X \mid \exists x \in \widehat{x} . x' = f(x, u)\}$. The function $\widehat{f}$ is known to be available for a wide class of commonly used forms of the function f, and in our implementation we assumed that f is mixed-monotone and $\widehat{f}$ is the so-called decomposition function (see standard literature for details [7]).

Given the over-approximation of the nominal dynamics obtained through $\widehat{f}$, we define, respectively, the over- and the under-approximation of the *perturbed* dynamics as $\overline{g}(\widehat{x}, u) := W \oplus \widehat{f}(\widehat{x}, u)$ and $\underline{g}(\widehat{x}, u) := W \ominus (-\widehat{f}(\widehat{x}, u))$, where $\oplus$ and $\ominus$ respectively denote the Minkowski sum and the Minkowski difference. Next, we transfer $\overline{g}$ and $\underline{g}$ to the abstract state space $\widehat{X}$ to obtain, respectively, the over- and the under-approximation in terms of the *abstract transition* function[1], i.e., $\overline{h}(\widehat{x}, u) := \left\{ \widehat{x}' \in \widehat{X} \mid \overline{g}(\widehat{x}, u) \cap \widehat{x}' \neq \emptyset \right\}$ and $\underline{h}(\widehat{x}, u) := \left\{ \widehat{x}' \in \widehat{X} \mid \underline{g}(\widehat{x}, u) \cap \widehat{x}' \neq \emptyset \right\}$. With $\overline{h}$ and $\underline{h}$ available, it was shown by Majumdar et al. [16] that the over-approximation of the optimal controller can be solved by using the fixpoint algorithm in (2), where the predecessor operators are defined for every $S, T \subseteq \widehat{X}$ as

$$Cpre(S) := \left\{ \widehat{x} \in \widehat{X} \mid \exists u \in U . \overline{h}(\widehat{x}, u) \subseteq S \right\} \tag{6a}$$

$$Apre(S, T) := \left\{ \widehat{x} \in \widehat{X} \mid \exists u \in U . \overline{h}(\widehat{x}, u) \subseteq S \wedge \underline{h}(\widehat{x}, u) \cap T \neq \emptyset \right\}. \tag{6b}$$

3   Implementation Details

We develop three interconnected tools, `Genie`, `FairSyn`, and `Mascot-SDS`, which work in close harmony to implement efficient solvers for the solution of (2) with

---

[1] Here we assume that $\widehat{f}(\widehat{x}, u) \subseteq X$; otherwise we need to take some extra steps. Details can be found in the work by Majumdar et al. [16].

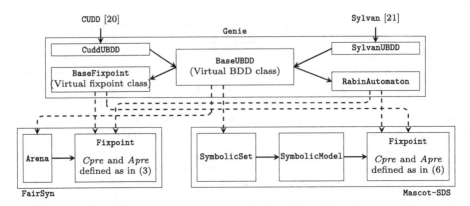

Fig. 1. A schematic diagram of interaction among the three tools. Each block represents one class in the respective tool, and an arrow from class A to class B denotes that B depends on A. The dependency within each tool is shown using solid arrows, while the dependencies of Mascot-SDS and FairSyn on Genie is shown using dashed arrows.

pre-operators defined via (3), (4) and (6), respectively. The tools use binary decision diagrams (BDD) to symbolically manipulate sets of vertices/states of the underlying system, and to manage the BDDs, we offer the flexibility to choose between two of the well-known existing BDD libraries, namely CUDD [20] and Sylvan [21]. The two libraries have their own merits: while CUDD has significantly lower memory footprint, Sylvan offers superior computation speed through multi-threaded BDD operations. Thus, the optimal choice of the library depends on the size of the problem, the computational time limit, and the memory budget, and through our implementation it is possible to choose one or the other by, in some cases, changing only a single line of code and, in the other cases, changing the value of just one flag. Moreover, we expect that integrating other BDD libraries having the same basic BDD operations in our tools will be easy and seamless—thanks to the programming abstraction offered by Genie. Such extensions will possibly bring more diverse set of computational strengths for solving the fundamental synthesis problems that we address.

The tools are primarily written using C++, with some small python scripts implementing parts of visualizations of outputs. The main classes of the three tools and their interactions are depicted in Fig. 1. We briefly describe the core functionalities of the tools in the following.

3.1 Genie

Genie implements the fixpoint algorithm (2) in the class BaseFixpoint through two layers of abstraction. One abstraction is through the virtual definitions of the *Cpre* and *Apre* operators, whose concrete implementations are provided in the front-end synthesis tools (in our case FairSyn and Mascot-SDS). Using this abstraction, we implemented two different optimizations for the efficient iterative computation of the Rabin fixpoint in (2)—independently from the actual implementations of the *Apre* and *Cpre* operators. The first optimization is a multi-threaded computation of the Rabin fixpoint, exploiting the fixpoint's inherent parallel structure due to the independence among different sequences of $(p_1, p_2, \ldots)$ used to compute $\bigcup_{j=0}^{k} \mathcal{C}_{p_j}$. The second optimization is an accelerated computation of the Rabin fixpoint, achieved through bookkeeping of intermediate values of the BDD variables. The core of the acceleration procedure for general μ-calculus fixpoints was proposed by Long et al. [13], and the details specific to the fixpoint in (2) can be found in the paper by Banerjee et al. [4].

The other abstraction in `Genie` is the set of virtually defined low-level BDD operations in the auxiliary class `BaseUBDD`, which enable us to easily switch between different off-the-shelf BDD libraries. The virtual BDD operations in `BaseUBDD` are concretely realized in the classes `CuddUBDD` and `SylvanUBDD`, which work as interfaces between, respectively, the CUDD and the Sylvan BDD libraries. Support for additional BDD libraries can be easily built by creating new interface classes. More details on the functionalities of `Genie` can be found in the longer version of this paper [14].

3.2 FairSyn

The core of `FairSyn` is written as a header-only library, which offers the infrastructure to solve (2) with pre-operators defined via (3) and (4). The main component of `FairSyn` is the class `Fixpoint`, which derives from the class `BaseFixpoint` from `Genie`, and implements the concrete definitions of *Cpre* and *Apre* in (3) and (4).

How to Use: For computing the winning region and the winning strategy in a fair-adversarial Rabin game (resp. a $2^{1}/2$-player Rabin game) using `FairSyn`, one needs to write a program to create the game as a `Fixpoint` object. One possible way of constructing a `Fixpoint` object is through a synchronous product of a game graph (an object of class `Arena`) and a specification Rabin automaton (an object of class `RabinAutomaton`) with an input alphabet of sets of nodes of the `Arena` object. Following is a snippet:

```
// typedef Genie::CuddUBDD UBDD; // use this for CUDD
typedef Genie::SylvanUBDD UBDD; // use this for Sylvan
UBDD base;
...
Arena<UBDD> A(base, vars, nodes, sys_nodes, env_nodes, edges,
    live_edges); // the game graph
RabinAutomaton<UBDD> R(base, vars, inp_alphabet, filename); // the
    specification automaton
Fixpoint<UBDD> Fp(base, "under", A, R); // the synchronous product
// UBDD strategy = Fp.Rabin(true, 20, Fp.nodes_, 0); // sequential
    fixpoint solver
UBDD strategy = Fp.Rabin(true, 20, Fp.nodes_, 0,
    Genie::ParallelRabinRecurse); // parallel fixpoint solver
...
```

where `vars` is a (possibly initially empty) set of integers which will contain the set of newly created BDD variables, `nodes`, `sys_nodes`, and `env_nodes` are, respectively, vectors of indices of various types of vertices, `edges` and `live_edges` are, respectively, vectors of the respective types of edges, `inp_alphabet` is a `std::map` object that maps input symbols of the Rabin automaton to the respective BDDs representing sets of nodes in the `Arena`, and `filename` is the name of the file in which the Rabin automaton is stored (using the standard HOA format [2]). The game is solved by calling `Fp.Rabin`, a member function of the `Genie::BaseFixpoint` class (see Sect. 3.1).

3.3   Mascot-SDS

The core of `Mascot-SDS` is also written as a header-only library. It is built on top of the well-known tool called `SCOTS` [18], with several classes of `Mascot-SDS` still retaining their original identities from `SCOTS`, owing to the close similarity of the basic uniform grid-based abstraction used in both tools. The main difference between the two tools is that `Mascot-SDS` synthesizes controllers for *stochastic* systems, while `SCOTS` synthesizes controllers for only *non-stochastic* systems.

The two main classes of `Mascot-SDS` are called `SymbolicSet` and `SymbolicModel`, which respectively model the abstract spaces obtained through uniform grid-based discretizations (like $\widehat{X}$ in Sect. 2.2) and the abstract transition relations ($\overline{h}$ and $\underline{h}$ in Sect. 2.2). The abstract transition relations are computed using an auxiliary class called `SymbolicModelMonotonic` (not shown in Fig. 1). Notice that we offer the flexibility to use both CUDD and Sylvan while creating objects from `SymbolicSet` and `SymbolicModel`. A `Fixpoint` object is a child of the class `BaseFixpoint` from `Genie`, which is created by taking a synchronous product between a `SymbolicModel` object and a `RabinAutomaton` object specifying the control objective given as user input. The class `Fixpoint` implements the concrete definitions of the *Cpre* and *Apre* operator according to (6).

How to Use: For ease of use, we have written a pair of tools called `Synthesize` and `Simulate` using the library of `Mascot-SDS`. `Synthesize` synthesizes controllers for stochastic dynamical systems whose nominal dynamics is mixed-monotone, and `Simulate` visualizes simulated closed-loop trajectories using the synthesized controller. The inputs to `Synthesize` include the dynamic model of the system and the control objective; the latter can be specified either in LTL or using a Rabin automaton. To use `Synthesize`, simply use the following syntax:

```
<path-to-Synthesize binary>/Synthesize <path-to-input-file>/<input.cfg>
    <sylvan/cudd flag>
```

where the `<input.cfg>` is an input configuration file containing all the inputs, and the `<sylvan/cudd flag>` is either 1 or 0 depending on whether the parallel version using `Sylvan` is to be run or the sequential version using `CUDD`.

Some of the main ingredients in the `input.cfg` file are: (a) the description of the dynamical system's variable spaces (like state space, input space, etc.) including their discretization parameters, (b) the file where the decomposition function of the nominal dynamics of the system is stored, (c) the absolute value of maximum disturbance, and (d) the specification either as an LTL formula or as the filename where a Rabin automaton is stored (in HOA format [2]). The decomposition function is required to be given as a C-compatible header file so that `Synthesize` can link to (use) this function at runtime (see the `mascot-sds/examples/` directory for examples). When the specification is given as a Rabin automaton (over a labeling alphabet of the system states), the automaton needs to be stored in a file in the HOA format. Alternatively, an LTL specification can be given, along with a mapping between the atomic predicates and the states of the system. In that case `Synthesize` uses `Owl` [12] to convert the LTL specification to a Rabin automaton.

The output of `Synthesize` is a folder called `data` that contains pieces of the controller encoded in BDDs and stored in binary files as well as various metadata information stored in text files. These files can be processed by `Simulate` to visualize simulated closed-loop trajectories of the system. The usage of `Simulate` is similar to `Synthesize`:

```
<path-to-Simulate binary>/Simulate <path-to-input-file>/<input.cfg>
    <sylvan/cudd flag>
```

where the `input.cfg` file should, in this case, contain information that are required to simulate the closed-loop, like simulation time steps, the python script that will plot the state space predicates (see the examples), etc.

4   Examples

We present experimental results, showcasing practical usability of our tools and comparing performances with the state of the art. All the experiments were run on a computer with Intel Xeon E7-8857 v2 48 core processor and 1.5 TB RAM.

4.1   Synthesizing Code-Aware Resource Mangers Using `FairSyn`

We consider a case study introduced by Chatterjee et al. [6]. In this example, there are two bounded FIFO queues, namely the broadcast and output queues, which interact among each other and transmit and receive data packets through a common network. The two queues are implemented using separate threads running on a single CPU. For this multi-threaded program, we consider the problem of synthesizing a code-aware resource manager, whose task is to grant different threads accesses to different shared synchronization resources (mutexes and counting semaphores). The specification is deadlock freedom across all threads at all time while assuming a fair scheduler (scheduling every thread always eventually) and fair progress in every thread (i.e., taking every existing execution branch always eventually). The resource-manager is code-aware, and has knowledge about the require and release characteristics of all threads for different resources. This enables us to avoid deadlocks more effectively than the case when the resource-manager does not have access to the code. Chatterjee et al. [6] showed that the synthesis problem (of the resource manager) can be reduced to the problem of computing the winning strategy in a $2^1/_2$-player game, which we solved using FairSyn.

Table 1 compares the computational resources for the CUDD and Sylvan-based implementations of FairSyn; more details can be found in our earlier work [4]. It can be observed that the Sylvan-based implementation is significantly faster, although it consumes much more memory.

Table 1. Performance of FairSyn; code-aware resource management benchmark.

Broadcast and Output Queue Capacities	Number of BDD variables	Computation Time (seconds)		Peak Memory Usage	
		CUDD	Sylvan	CUDD	Sylvan
(1, 1)	25	255.33	11.40	292 MiB	671 MiB
(2, 1)	27	957.99	29.20	310 MiB	681 MiB
(3, 1)	27	903.01	31.13	310 MiB	973 MiB
(1, 2)	27	1308.09	39.57	315 MiB	682 MiB
(1, 3)	27	1249.37	41.76	309 MiB	681 MiB
(2, 2)	29	5127.93	111.62	342 MiB	685 MiB
(3, 2)	29	5104.20	114.30	339 MiB	975 MiB
(2, 3)	29	5644.09	118.12	341 MiB	975 MiB
(3, 3)	29	6156.57	137.56	339 MiB	975 MiB

4.2 Synthesizing Controllers for Stochastic Dynamical Systems Using Mascot-SDS

We use Mascot-SDS to synthesize controllers for two different applications.

A Bistable Switch. First, we compare our tool's performance against the state-of-the-art tool called StochasticSynthesis (abbr. SS) [10] on a benchmark example that was proposed by the authors of SS. In this example, there is a 2-dimensional nonlinear bistable switch that is perturbed with bounded stochastic noise. There are two synthesis problems with two different control objectives: one, a safety objective, and, two, a Rabin objective with two Rabin pairs. The model of the system and the control objectives can be found in the original paper [10].

The tool SS uses graph theoretic techniques to solve the controller synthesis problem, which is an alternative approach that is substantially different from our symbolic fixpoint based technique. In Table 2, we summarize the performance of Mascot-SDS powered by CUDD and Sylvan, alongside the performance of SS. Both

Table 2. Performance comparison between `Mascot-SDS` and StochasticSynthesis (abbreviated as SS) [10] on the bistable switch. Col. 1 shows the specifications and the respective numbers of Rabin pairs, Col. 2 shows the approximation error ranges (smaller error means more intense computation), Col. 3, 4, and 5 Col. 6, 7, and 8 compare the peak memory footprint (as measured using the "time" command) for `Mascot-SDS` with CUDD, `Mascot-SDS` with `Sylvan`, and SS respectively. "TO" stands for timeout (5 h of cutoff time).

Spec.	upper bound on approx. error	Total running time			Peak memory footprint		
		Mascot-SDS		SS [10]	Mascot-SDS		SS [10]
		CUDD	Sylvan		CUDD	Sylvan	
φ_1 (1 Rabin pair)	20%–30%	11 s	<2 s	27 s	351 MiB	79 MiB	223 MiB
	10%–20%	9 s	2 s	43 s	351 MiB	105 MiB	290 MiB
	5%–10%	14 s	4 s	1 h 49 min	405 MiB	251 MiB	25 GiB
	0%–5%	48 s	10 s	TO	553 MiB	759 MiB	TO
φ_2 (2 Rabin pairs)	20%–30%	21 s	<2 s	21 s	324 MiB	40 MiB	202 MiB
	10%–20%	26 s	2 s	25 s	371 MiB	80 MiB	203 MiB
	5%–10%	37 s	4 s	1 min 17 s	436 MiB	242 MiB	490 MiB
	0%–5%	2 min 24 s	13 s	TO	573 MiB	761 MiB	TO

Table 3. Performance of `Mascot-SDS` with CUDD and `Sylvan` for the table-serving robot experiment.

	CUDD	Sylvan
Comp. time	1 h 3 min	2 min 55 s
Peak memory	673 MiB	1.1 GiB

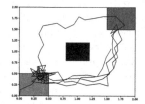

Fig. 2. Closed-loop trajectories for 100 time steps with *kitchen* (green), *table* (blue), and *obstacle* (black). (Color figure online)

`Mascot-SDS` and SS compute controllers whose domains under-approximate the optimal controller domains. The second column of Table 2 shows a measure of the approximation error. For every comparable approximation error bound, both versions of `Mascot-SDS` significantly outperformed SS, both time and memory-wise. In fact, `Mascot-SDS` with `Sylvan` was at least an order of magnitude faster in all instances. This is particularly astonishing, since SS uses a sophisticated *lazy* abstraction refinement technique, whereas `Mascot-SDS` uses a plain *uniform* abstraction which is typically computationally expensive. This shows the immense potential of our toolchain; we plan to extend `Mascot-SDS` with lazy gridding, an orthogonal optimization, in a future release to make further computational savings. For `Mascot-SDS` itself, as expected, `Sylvan` was significantly faster than CUDD. On the other hand, though `Sylvan` used less memory than CUDD in the simpler setups (the ones with more error), the memory requirement of `Sylvan` quickly grew and surpassed that of CUDD for the more complicated setup.

Table-Serving Robot. We consider the controller synthesis problem for a table-serving robot that needs to satisfy the following specification: $\square\lozenge kitchen \wedge$ $\square\neg obtsacle \wedge (\square\lozenge request \leftrightarrow \square\lozenge table)$, where *table, kitchen, obstacle*, and *request* are predicates over the state space. The robot itself is modeled as the discrete-time abstraction of the standard 3-dimensional Dubins vehicle [15] with an additional (i.e., 4th) dimension that records if a *request*, which is controlled by the environment, is pending. In Table 3, we summarize the computational resources, and, in Fig. 2, we show a simulated closed-loop trajectory that was plotted using our tool `Simulate`. We observe that `Sylvan` was much faster, but `CUDD` consumed much less memory.

References

1. Abate, A., et al.: ARCH-COMP21 category report: stochastic models. In: 8th International Workshop on Applied Verification of Continuous and Hybrid Systems, pp. 55–89 (2021)
2. Babiak, T., et al.: The Hanoi omega-automata format. In: Kroening, D., Păsăreanu, C.S. (eds.) CAV 2015. LNCS, vol. 9206, pp. 479–486. Springer, Cham (2015). https://doi.org/10.1007/978-3-319-21690-4_31
3. Banerjee, T., Majumdar, R., Mallik, K., Schmuck, A.-K., Soudjani, S.: A direct symbolic algorithm for solving stochastic Rabin games. In: TACAS 2022. LNCS, vol. 13244, pp. 81–98. Springer, Cham (2022). https://doi.org/10.1007/978-3-030-99527-0_5
4. Banerjee, T., Majumdar, R., Mallik, K., Schmuck, A.K., Soudjani, S.: Fast symbolic algorithms for omega-regular games under strong transition fairness. TheoretiCS (to appear) (2023). arXiv preprint arXiv:2202.07480
5. Chatterjee, K., de Alfaro, L., Henzinger, T.A.: The complexity of stochastic Rabin and Streett games. In: Caires, L., Italiano, G.F., Monteiro, L., Palamidessi, C., Yung, M. (eds.) ICALP 2005. LNCS, vol. 3580, pp. 878–890. Springer, Heidelberg (2005). https://doi.org/10.1007/11523468_71
6. Chatterjee, K., De Alfaro, L., Faella, M., Majumdar, R., Raman, V.: Code aware resource management. Formal Methods Syst. Des. **42**(2), 146–174 (2013)
7. Coogan, S., Arcak, M.: Efficient finite abstraction of mixed monotone systems. In: Proceedings of the 18th International Conference on Hybrid Systems: Computation and Control, pp. 58–67 (2015)
8. Dijk, T.: Attracting tangles to solve parity games. In: Chockler, H., Weissenbacher, G. (eds.) CAV 2018. LNCS, vol. 10982, pp. 198–215. Springer, Cham (2018). https://doi.org/10.1007/978-3-319-96142-2_14
9. Dijk, T.: Oink: an implementation and evaluation of modern parity game solvers. In: Beyer, D., Huisman, M. (eds.) TACAS 2018. LNCS, vol. 10805, pp. 291–308. Springer, Cham (2018). https://doi.org/10.1007/978-3-319-89960-2_16
10. Dutreix, M., Huh, J., Coogan, S.: Abstraction-based synthesis for stochastic systems with omega-regular objectives. Nonlinear Anal. Hybrid Syst **45**, 101204 (2022)
11. Geretti, L., et al.: ARCH-COMP20 category report: continuous and hybrid systems with nonlinear dynamics. In: Proceedings of the 7th International Workshop on Applied Verification of Continuous and Hybrid Systems, pp. 49–75 (2020)

12. Křetínský, J., Meggendorfer, T., Sickert, S.: Owl: a library for ω-words, automata, and LTL. In: Lahiri, S.K., Wang, C. (eds.) ATVA 2018. LNCS, vol. 11138, pp. 543–550. Springer, Cham (2018). https://doi.org/10.1007/978-3-030-01090-4_34
13. Long, D.E., Browne, A., Clarke, E.M., Jha, S., Marrero, W.R.: An improved algorithm for the evaluation of fixpoint expressions. In: Dill, D.L. (ed.) CAV 1994. LNCS, vol. 818, pp. 338–350. Springer, Heidelberg (1994). https://doi.org/10.1007/3-540-58179-0_66
14. Majumdar, R., Mallik, K., Rychlicki, M., Schmuck, A.K., Soudjani, S.: A flexible toolchain for symbolic Rabin games under fair and stochastic uncertainties (2023). https://kmallik.github.io/assets/pdf/cav23-toolpaper.pdf
15. Majumdar, R., Mallik, K., Schmuck, A.K., Soudjani, S.: Symbolic qualitative control for stochastic systems via finite parity games. IFAC-PapersOnLine **54**(5), 127–132 (2021)
16. Majumdar, R., Mallik, K., Soudjani, S.: Symbolic controller synthesis for büchi specifications on stochastic systems. In: Proceedings of the 23rd International Conference on Hybrid Systems: Computation and Control, pp. 1–11 (2020)
17. Piterman, N., Pnueli, A.: Faster solutions of Rabin and Streett games. In: 21st Annual IEEE Symposium on Logic in Computer Science (LICS'06), pp. 275–284. IEEE (2006)
18. Rungger, M., Zamani, M.: Scots: a tool for the synthesis of symbolic controllers. In: Proceedings of the 19th International Conference on Hybrid Systems: Computation and Control, pp. 99–104 (2016)
19. Schewe, S.: An optimal strategy improvement algorithm for solving parity and payoff games. In: Kaminski, M., Martini, S. (eds.) CSL 2008. LNCS, vol. 5213, pp. 369–384. Springer, Heidelberg (2008). https://doi.org/10.1007/978-3-540-87531-4_27
20. Somenzi, F.: Cudd: CU decision diagram package release 3.0.0 (2015). https://github.com/ivmai/cudd
21. van Dijk, T., van de Pol, J.: Sylvan: multi-core decision diagrams. In: Baier, C., Tinelli, C. (eds.) TACAS 2015. LNCS, vol. 9035, pp. 677–691. Springer, Heidelberg (2015). https://doi.org/10.1007/978-3-662-46681-0_60
22. Zielonka, W.: Infinite games on finitely coloured graphs with applications to automata on infinite trees. Theor. Comput. Sci. **200**(1), 135–183 (1998). https://doi.org/10.1016/S0304-3975(98)00009-7, https://www.sciencedirect.com/science/article/pii/S0304397598000097

Automated Tail Bound Analysis
for Probabilistic Recurrence Relations

Yican Sun[1], Hongfei Fu[2(✉)], Krishnendu Chatterjee[3],
and Amir Kafshdar Goharshady[4]

[1] School of Computer Science, Peking University, Beijing, China
`sycpku@pku.edu.cn`
[2] Department of Computer Science and Engineering, Shanghai Jiao Tong University,
Shanghai, China
`fuhf@cs.sjtu.edu.cn`
[3] Institute of Science and Technology, Klosterneuburg, Austria
`krishnendu.chatterjee@ist.ac.at`
[4] Department of Computer Science and Engineering, Hong Kong University of
Science and Technology, Hong Kong, Hong Kong SAR, China
`goharshady@cse.ust.hk`

Abstract. Probabilistic recurrence relations (PRRs) are a standard formalism for describing the runtime of a randomized algorithm. Given a PRR and a time limit κ, we consider the tail probability $\Pr[T \geq \kappa]$, i.e., the probability that the randomized runtime T of the PRR exceeds κ. Our focus is the formal analysis of tail bounds that aims at finding a tight asymptotic upper bound $u \geq \Pr[T \geq \kappa]$. To address this problem, the classical and most well-known approach is the cookbook method by Karp (JACM 1994), while other approaches are mostly limited to deriving tail bounds of specific PRRs via involved custom analysis.

In this work, we propose a novel approach for deriving the common exponentially-decreasing tail bounds for PRRs whose preprocessing time and random passed sizes observe discrete or (piecewise) uniform distribution and whose recursive call is either a single procedure call or a divide-and-conquer. We first establish a theoretical approach via Markov's inequality, and then instantiate the theoretical approach with a template-based algorithmic approach via a refined treatment of exponentiation. Experimental evaluation shows that our algorithmic approach is capable of deriving tail bounds that are (i) asymptotically tighter than Karp's method, (ii) match the best-known manually-derived asymptotic tail bound for QuickSelect, and (iii) is only slightly worse (with a $\log \log n$ factor) than the manually-proven optimal asymptotic tail bound for QuickSort. Moreover, our algorithmic approach handles all examples (including realistic PRRs such as QuickSort, QuickSelect, DiameterComputation, etc.) in less than 0.1 s, showing that our approach is efficient in practice.

Due to different academic norms, authors in Mainland China are ordered by contribution, whereas authors in Austria and Hong Kong SAR are ordered alphabetically. The code and benchmarks are available at https://github.com/boyvolcano/PRR.

C. Enea and A. Lal (Eds.): CAV 2023, LNCS 13966, pp. 16–39, 2023.
https://doi.org/10.1007/978-3-031-37709-9_2

1   Introduction

Probabilistic program verification is a fundamental area in formal verification [3]. It extends the classical (non-probabilistic) program verification by considering randomized computation in a program and hence can be applied to the formal analysis of probabilistic computations such as probabilistic models [14], randomized algorithms [2,9,28,30], etc. In this line of research, verifying the time complexity of probabilistic recurrence relations (PRRs) is an important subject [9,30]. PRRs are a simplified form of recursive probabilistic programs and extend recurrence relations by incorporating randomization such as randomized preprocessing and divide-and-conquer. They are widely used in analyzing the time complexity of randomized algorithms (e.g., QuickSort [16], QuickSelect [17], and DiameterComputation [26, Chapter 9]). Compared with probabilistic programs, PRRs abstract away detailed computational aspects, such as problem-specific divide-and-conquer and data-structure manipulations, and include only key information on the runtime of the underlying randomized algorithm. Hence, PRRs provide a clean model for time-complexity analysis of randomized algorithms and randomized computations in a general sense.

In this work, we focus on the formal analysis of PRRs and consider the fundamental problem of tail bound analysis that aims at bounding the probability that a given PRR does not terminate within a prescribed time limit. In the literature, prominent works on tail bound analysis include the following. First, Karp proposed a classic "cookbook" formula [21] similar to Master Theorem. This method is further improved, extended, and mechanized by follow-up works [5,13,30]. While Karp's method has a clean form and is easy to use and automate, the bounds from the method are known to be not tight (see e.g. [15,25]). Second, the works [25] and resp. [15] performed ad-hoc custom analysis to derive asymptotically tight tail bounds for the PRRs of QuickSort and resp. QuickSelect, respectively. These methods require manual effort and do not have the generality to handle a wide class of PRRs.

From the literature, an algorithmic approach capable of deriving tight tail bounds over a wide class of PRRs is a major unresolved problem. Motivated by this challenge, we have the following contributions to this work:

- Based on Markov's inequality, we propose a novel theoretical approach to derive exponentially-decreasing tail bounds, a common type for many randomized algorithms. We further show that our theoretical approach can always derive an exponentially-decreasing tail bound at least as tight as Karp's method under mild assumptions.
- From our theoretical approach, we propose a template-based algorithmic approach for a wide class of PRRs that have (i) common probability distributions such as (piecewise) uniform distribution and discrete probability distributions and (ii) either a single call or a divide-and-conquer for the form of the recursive call. The technical novelties in our algorithm lie in a refined treatment of the estimation of the exponential term arising from our theoretical approach via integrals, suitable over-approximation, and the monotonicity of the template function.

– Experiments show that our algorithmic approach derives asymptotically tighter tail bounds when compared with Karp's method. Furthermore, the tail bounds derived from our approach match the best-known bound for QuickSelect [15], and are only slightly worse by a $\log \log n$ factor against the optimal manually-derived bound for QuickSort [25]. Moreover, our algorithm synthesizes each of these tail bounds in less than 0.1 s and is efficient in practice.

A limitation of our approach is that we do not consider the transformation from a realistic implementation of a randomized algorithm into its PRR representation. However, such a transformation would require examining a diversified number of randomization patterns (e.g., randomized divide-and-conquer) in randomized algorithms and thus is an orthogonal direction. In this work, we focus on the tail bound analysis and present a novel approach to address this problem. Due to space limitations, we relegate some details in the extended version [29].

2   Preliminaries

Below we present necessary background in probability theory and the tail bound analysis problem we consider.

A *probability space* is a triple $(\Omega, \mathcal{F}, \Pr)$ such that Ω is a non-empty set termed as the *sample space*, $\mathcal{F}$ is a *σ-algebra* over Ω (i.e., a collection of subsets of Ω that contains the empty set $\emptyset$ and is closed under complement and countable union), and $\Pr(\cdot)$ is a *probability measure* on $\mathcal{F}$ (i.e., a function $\mathcal{F} \to [0, 1]$ such that $\Pr(\Omega) = 1$ and for every pairwise disjoint set-sequence $A_1, A_2, \ldots$ in $\mathcal{F}$, we have that $\sum_{i \geq 1} \Pr(A_i) = \Pr\left(\bigcup_{i \geq 1} A_i\right)$.

A *random variable* X from a probability space $(\Omega, \mathcal{F}, \Pr)$ is an $\mathcal{F}$-measurable function $X : \Omega \to \mathbb{R}$, i.e., for every $d \in \mathbb{R}$, we have that $\{\omega \in \Omega \mid X(\omega) < d\} \in \mathcal{F}$. We denote $\mathbb{E}[X]$ as its expected value; formally, we have $\mathbb{E}[X] := \int X \, d\Pr$. A *discrete probability distribution* (DPD) over a countable set U is a function $\eta : U \to [0, 1]$, such that $\sum_{u \in U} \eta(u) = 1$. The *support* of the DPD is defined as $\mathrm{supp}(\eta) := \{u \in U \mid \eta(u) > 0\}$. We abbreviate finite-support DPD as FSDPD.

A *filtration* of probability space $(\Omega, \mathcal{F}, \Pr)$ is an infinite sequence of $\{\mathcal{F}_n\}_{n \geq 0}$ of σ-algebra over Ω such that $\mathcal{F}_n \subseteq \mathcal{F}_{n+1} \subseteq \mathcal{F}$ for every $n \geq 0$. Intuitively, it models the information at the n-th step. A *discrete-time stochastic process* is an infinite sequence $\Gamma = \{X_n\}_{n \geq 0}$ of random variables from the probability space $(\Omega, \mathcal{F}, \Pr)$. The process Γ is *adapted* to a filtration $\{\mathcal{F}_n\}_{n \geq 0}$ if for all $n \geq 0$, X_n is $\mathcal{F}_n$-measurable. Given a filtration $\{\mathcal{F}_n\}_{n \geq 0}$, a *stopping time* is a random variable $\tau : \Omega \to \mathbb{N}$, such that for every $n \geq 0$, $\{\omega \in \Omega \mid \tau(\omega) \leq n\} \in \mathcal{F}_n$.

A discrete-time stochastic process $\Gamma = \{X_n\}_{n \in \mathbb{N}}$ adapted to a filtration $\{\mathcal{F}_n\}_{n \in \mathbb{N}}$ is a *martingale* (resp. *supermartingale*) if for every $n \in \mathbb{N}$, $\mathbb{E}[|X_n|] < \infty$ and it holds a.s. that $\mathbb{E}[X_{n+1} \mid \mathcal{F}_n] = X_n$ (resp. $\mathbb{E}[X_{n+1} \mid \mathcal{F}_n] \leq X_n$). Intuitively, a martingale (resp. supermartingale) is a discrete-time stochastic process in which for an observer who has seen the values of $X_0, \ldots, X_n$, the expected value at the next step, i.e. $\mathbb{E}[X_{n+1} \mid \mathcal{F}_n]$, is equal to (resp. no more than) the last observed value X_n. Also, note that in a martingale, the observed values for

$X_0, \ldots, X_{n-1}$ do not matter given that $\mathbb{E}\left[X_{n+1} \mid \mathcal{F}_n\right] = X_n$. In contrast, in a supermartingale, the only requirement is that $\mathbb{E}\left[X_{n+1} \mid \mathcal{F}_n\right] \leq X_n$ and hence $\mathbb{E}\left[X_{n+1} \mid \mathcal{F}_n\right]$ may depend on $X_0, \ldots, X_{n-1}$. Also, note that $\mathcal{F}_n$ might contain more information than just the observations of X_i's.

Example 1. Consider the classical gambler's ruin: a gambler starts with Y_0 dollars of money and bets continuously until he loses all of his money. If the bets are unfair, i.e. the expected value of his money after a bet is less than its expected value before the bet, then the sequence $\{Y_n\}_{n \in \mathbb{N}_0}$ is a supermartingale. In this case, Y_n is the gambler's total money after n bets. On the other hand, if the bets are fair, then $\{Y_n\}_{n \in \mathbb{N}_0}$ is a martingale.   □

We refer to standard textbooks (such as [6,34]) for a detailed treatment of all the concepts illustrated above.

2.1   Probabilistic Recurrence Relations

In this work, we focus on probabilistic recurrence relations (PRRs) that describe the runtime behaviour of a single recursive procedure. Instead of having a direct syntax for a PRR, we propose a mini programming language *LRec* that captures a wide class of PRRs that have common probability distributions such as (piecewise) uniform distributions and discrete probability distributions, and whose recursive call consists of either a procedure call or two procedure calls in a divide-and-conquer style. We present the grammar of *LRec* in Fig. 1.

$$
\begin{aligned}
\textbf{(PRR)} \quad & \text{proc} ::= \textbf{def } p(n; c_p) = \{\text{comm}\} \\
\textbf{(Command)} \quad & \text{comm} ::= \textbf{sample } v \leftarrow \text{dist in } \{\text{body}\} \mid \bigoplus_{i=1}^{k} c_i : \text{comm}_i \\
\textbf{(Recursive Body)} \quad & \text{body} ::= \textbf{pre}(\text{expr}); \textbf{invoke call} \\
\textbf{(Recurive Call)} \quad & \text{call} ::= p(v); p(\text{size} - v) \mid p(v) \mid p(\text{size} - v) \\
& \quad (\text{where size is either } \lfloor \tfrac{n}{b} \rfloor + c \text{ or } \lceil \tfrac{n}{b} \rceil + c) \\
\textbf{(Distribution)} \quad & \text{dist} ::= \texttt{uniform}(n) \mid \texttt{muniform}(n) \mid \texttt{discrete} \mid \ldots \\
\textbf{(Expression)} \quad & \text{expr} ::= v \mid v^{-1} \mid \ln v \mid n \mid \ln n \mid n^{-1} \mid c \\
& \quad \mid \text{expr} + \text{expr} \mid \text{expr} - \text{expr} \mid \text{expr} \times \text{expr}
\end{aligned}
$$

Fig. 1. The Grammar of *LRec*

In the grammar, we have two positive-integer valued variables n, v which stand for the input size and the sampled value in the randomization of the passed size to the recursive calls of a procedure, respectively. We use $b > 0, c, c_p$ to denote integer constants, and use p to denote the name of the single procedure in the PRR. We consider arithmetic expressions expr as polynomials over $v, v^{-1}, \ln v$ and $n, n^{-1}, \ln n$ (which we call *pseudo-polynomials* in this work) and common probability distributions, including (i) the uniform distribution $\texttt{uniform}(n)$ over $\{0, 1, \ldots, n-1\}$, (ii) the piecewise uniform distribution $\texttt{muniform}(n)$ that returns $\max\{i, n-i-1\}$ where i observes the uniform distribution $\texttt{uniform}(n)$, and (iii) any FSDPD (indicated by discrete) whose probabilities and values are constants and pseudo-polynomials, respectively. We also support other piecewise uniform distribution, e.g., the distribution that each $v \in \{0, \ldots, n/2\}$ has probability $\frac{2}{3n}$ and each $v \in \{n/2+1, \ldots, n-1\}$ has probability $\frac{4}{3n}$.

The nonterminal proc generates the PRR in the form def $p(n; c_p) = \{\text{comm}\}$, for which c_p is an integer constant as the threshold of recursion, meaning that the procedure halts immediately when $n < c_p$, and comm is the function body of the procedure. The nonterminal comm generates all statements with one of the two forms as follows.

– A sampling statement (indicated by sample) followed by first a special expression pre(expr) that stands for the preprocessing time of expr amount, then the recursive calls generated by the nonterminal call.
– A probabilistic choice in the form $\bigoplus_{i=1}^{k} c_i$:comm$_i$ where each statement comm$_i$ is executed with probability c_i.

We restrict the recursive calls to be either a single recursive call $p(v)$ or $p(\text{size} - v)$, or a divide-and-conquer composed of two consecutive recursive calls $p(v)$ and $p(\text{size} - v)$, for which we consider a general setting that the relevant overall size size is in the form of the input size n divided by some positive integer b with possibly an offset c. Choosing $b = 1, c = -1$ means the normal situation that the overall size is $n - 1$, i.e., removing one element from the original input.

Given a PRR p, we use func(p) to represent its function body.

We always assume that the given PRR is *well-formed*, i.e., every c_i in a probabilistic choice is within $[0, 1]$ and every random passed size (e.g. v, size $- v$) falls in $[0, n]$. Below, we present two examples for PRRs.

Example 2 (QuickSelect). Consider the problem of finding the d-th smallest element in an unordered array of n distinct elements. A classical randomized algorithm for solving this problem is QuickSelect [17] with $O(n)$ expected running time. We model the algorithm as the following PRR:

$$\text{def } p(n; 2) = \{\text{sample } v \leftarrow \text{muniform}(n) \text{ in } \{\text{pre}(n); \text{ invoke } p(v); \}\}$$

Here, we use $p(n; 2)$ to represent the number of comparisons performed by Quick-Select over an input of size n, and v is the variable that captures the size of the remaining array that has to be searched recursively. It observes as the value $\max\{i, n-1-i\}$ where the value of i is sampled uniformly from $\{0, \ldots, n-1\}$, we use muniform(n) to represent this distribution.   □

Example 3 (QuickSort). Consider the classical problem of sorting an array of n distinct elements. A well-known randomized algorithm for solving this problem is QuickSort [16]. We model the algorithm as the following PRR.

$$\text{def } p(n; 2) = \{\text{sample } v \leftarrow \text{uniform}(n) \text{ in } \{\text{pre}(n); \text{ invoke } p(v); p(n-1-v); \}\}$$

Here, v and $n - 1 - v$ capture the sizes of the two sub-arrays.   □

Below we present the semantics of a PRR in a nutshell. Consider a PRR generated by *LRec* with the procedure name p, a *configuration* σ is a pair $\sigma =$

$(comm, \widehat{n})$ where $comm$ represents the current statement to be executed and $\widehat{n} \geq c_p$ is the current value for the variable n. A *PRR state* μ is a triple $\langle \sigma, C, \mathbf{K} \rangle$ for which:

- σ is either a configuration, or halt for the termination of the whole PRR.
- $C \geq 0$ records the cumulative preprocessing time so far.
- $\mathbf{K}$ is a stack of configurations that remain to be executed.

We use emp to denote an empty stack, and say that a PRR state $\langle \sigma, C, \mathbf{K} \rangle$ is *final* if $\mathbf{K} =$ emp and $\sigma =$ halt. Note that in a final PRR state $\langle$halt, $C,$ emp$\rangle$, the value C represents the total execution runtime of the PRR. The semantics of the PRR is defined as a discrete-time Markov chain whose state space is the set of all PRR states and whose transition function $\mathbf{P}$, where $\mathbf{P}(\mu, \mu')$ is the probability that the next PRR state is μ' given the current PRR state is $\mu = ((comm, \widehat{n}), C, \mathbf{K})$. The probability is determined by the following cases.

- For final PRR states μ, $\mathbf{P}(\mu, \mu) := 1$ and $\mathbf{P}(\mu, \mu') := 0$ for other $\mu' \neq \mu$. This means that the PRR stays at termination once it terminates.
- In the divide-and-conquer case $comm =$ sample $v \leftarrow dist$ in $\{$pre(e); invoke $p(v); p(s-v)\}$, we first sample v from the distribution $dist$. Then, with probability $dist(v)$, we accumulate the preprocessing time e into the cumulative processing time C. We recursively invoke $p(v)$ and push the remaining task $p(s - v)$ into the stack. The probability for the single recursion case is defined analogously. The only difference is that there is no need to push some recursive call into the stack in the single recursion case.
- In the case $comm = \bigoplus_{i=1}^{k} c_i : comm_i$, we have that $\mathbf{P}(\mu, \mu_i) = c_i$ for each $1 \leq i \leq k$ for which we have $\mu_i := ((comm_i, \widehat{n}), C, \mathbf{K})$.

With an initial PRR state $((\text{func}(p), n^*), 0, \text{emp})$ where $n^* \geq c_p$ is the input size, the Markov chain induces a probability space where the sample space is the set of all infinite sequences of PRR states, the σ-algebra is generated by all *cylinder sets* over infinite sequences of PRR states, and the probability measure is uniquely determined by the transition function $\mathbf{P}$. We refer to [3] for details. We use $\Pr_{n^*}$ for the probability measure where $n^* \geq c_p$ is the input size.

We further define the random variable τ such that for any infinite sequence of PRR states $\rho = \mu_0, \mu_1, \ldots, \mu_t, \ldots$ with each $\mu_t = ((comm_t, \widehat{n}_t), C_t, \mathbf{K}_t)$, $\tau(\rho)$ equals the first moment that the sequence reaches a final PRR state, i.e., $\tau(\rho) = \inf\{t \mid$ the PRR state μ_t is final$\}$, for which $\inf \emptyset = \infty$. We will always ensure that τ is almost-surely finite, i.e., $\Pr_{n^*}(\tau < \infty) = 1$. Note that the random cumulative processing time C_τ in the PRR state $\mu_\tau \in \rho$ is the total execution time of the given PRR.

We formulate the tail bound analysis over PRRs as follows. Given a time limit $\alpha \cdot \kappa(n^*)$ symbolic in the initial input n^* and the coefficient α, the goal of tail bound analysis is to infer an upper bound $u(\alpha, n^*)$ symbolic in n^* and α such that for every input size n^* and plausible value for α, we have that

$$\Pr_{n^*}[C_\tau \geq \alpha \cdot \kappa(n^*)] \leq u(\alpha, n^*). \tag{1}$$

As tails bounds are often evaluated asymptotically, we focus on deriving tight $u(\alpha, n^*)$ when α, n^* are sufficiently large. To compare the magnitude of two tail bounds, we follow the straightforward way that first treats α as a fixed constant and compares the bounds over n^*, and then if the magnitude over n^* is identical, we take a further comparison over the magnitude on the coefficient α.

Example 4 (Our result on QuickSelect). Continue with Example 2, suppose the user is interested in the tail bound $\Pr[C_\tau \geq \alpha \cdot n^*]$, where C_τ is the running time of the QuickSelect algorithm over an array with length n^*. Then, Karp's method produces the symbolic tail bound as follows.

$$\Pr[C_\tau \geq \alpha \cdot n^*] \leq \exp(1.15 - 0.28 \cdot \alpha)$$

However, our method can produce the following tail bound.

$$\Pr[C_\tau \geq \alpha \cdot n^*] \leq \exp(2 \cdot \alpha - \alpha \cdot \ln \alpha)$$

Note that our method produces tail bounds with a better magnitude on α. □

Example 5 (Our result on QuickSort). Continue with Example 3, consider the tail bound $\Pr[C_\tau \geq \alpha \cdot n^* \cdot \ln n^*]$, where C_τ is the running time of QuickSort over a length-n^* array. Then, Karp's method produces the symbolic tail bound as:

$$\Pr[C_\tau \geq \alpha \cdot n^* \cdot \ln n^*] \leq \exp(0.5 - 0.5 \cdot \alpha),$$

while our method can produce the bound as:

$$\Pr[C_\tau \geq \alpha \cdot n^* \cdot \ln n^*] \leq \exp((4 - \alpha) \cdot \ln n^*)$$

Note that our method produces tail bounds with a better magnitude on n^*. □

3   Exponential Tail Bounds via Markov's Inequality

In this section, we demonstrate our theoretical approach for deriving exponentially decreasing tail bounds based on Markov's inequality.

Before illustrating our approach, we first translate a PRR in the language *LRec* with the single procedure p into the canonical form as follows.

$$p(n; c_p) = \texttt{pre}(S(n)); \texttt{invoke } p(\text{size}_1(n)); \ldots; p(\text{size}_r(n)) \tag{2}$$

where (i) $S(n)$ is a random variable related to the input size n that represents the randomized pre-processing time and observes a probability distribution resulting from a discrete probability choice of piecewise uniform distributions, and (ii) $\texttt{invoke } p(\text{size}_1(n)); \ldots; p(\text{size}_r(n))$ is a statement that is either a single recursive call $p(\text{size}_1(n))$ or a divide-and-conquer $p(\text{size}_1(n)); p(\text{size}_2(n))$ upon the resolution of the randomization. For the latter, we use a random variable r (which is either 1 or 2) to represent the number of recursive calls.

The translation can be implemented by a straightforward recursive procedure $\mathsf{Tf}(n, Prog)$ that takes on input a positive integer n (as the input size) and a statement $Prog$ (generated by the nonterminal comm) to be processed, Note that the procedure $\mathsf{Tf}(n, Prog)$ outputs the *joint* distribution of the random value $S(n)$ and the recursive call $p(\mathsf{size}_1(n)); \ldots; p(\mathsf{size}_r(n))$ with randomized input size. These random variables may be dependent.

Our theoretical approach then works directly on the canonical form (2). It consists of two major steps to derive an exponentially-decreasing tail bound. In the first step, we apply Markov's inequality and reduce the tail bound analysis problem to the over-approximation of the moment generating function $\mathbb{E}[\exp(t \cdot C_\tau)]$ where C_τ is the cumulative pre-processing time defined previously and $t > 0$ is a scaling factor that aids the derivation of the tail bound. In the second step, we apply Optional Stopping Theorem (a classical theorem in martingale theory) to over-approximate the expected value $\mathbb{E}[\exp(t \cdot C_\tau)]$. Below we fix an PRR with procedure p in the canonical form (2), and a time limit $\alpha \cdot \kappa(n^*)$.

Our first step applies Markov's inequality. Our approach relies on the well-known exponential form of Markov's inequality below.

Theorem 1. *For every random variable X and any scaling factor $t > 0$, we have that $\Pr[X \geq d] \leq \mathbb{E}[\exp(t \cdot X)]/\exp(t \cdot d)$.*

The detailed application of Markov's inequality to tail bound analysis requires to choose a scaling factor $t := t(\alpha, n)$ symbolic in α and n. After choosing the scaling factor, Markov's inequality gives the following tail bound:

$$\Pr[C_\tau \geq \alpha \cdot \kappa(n^*)] \leq \mathbb{E}[\exp(t(\alpha, n^*) \cdot C_\tau)]/\exp(t(\alpha, n^*) \cdot \alpha \cdot \kappa(n^*)). \quad (3)$$

The role of the scaling factor $t(\alpha, n^*)$ is to scale the exponent in the term $\exp(\kappa(\alpha, n^*))$, and this is in many cases necessary as a tail bound may not be exponentially decreasing directly in the time limit $\alpha \cdot \kappa(n^*)$.

An unsolved part in the tail bound above is the estimation of the expected value $\mathbb{E}[\exp(t(\alpha, n^*) \cdot C_\tau)]$. Our second step over-approximates the expected value $\mathbb{E}[\exp(t(\alpha, n^*) \cdot C_\tau)]$. To achieve this goal, we impose a constraint on the scaling factor $t(\alpha, n)$ and an extra function $f(\alpha, n)$ and show that once the constraint is fulfilled, then one can derive an upper bound for $\mathbb{E}[\exp(t(\alpha, n^*) \cdot C_\tau)]$ from $t(\alpha, n)$ and $f(\alpha, n)$. The theorem is proved via Optional Stopping Theorem. The theorem requires the almost-sure termination of the given PRR, a natural prerequisite of exponential tail bound. In this work, we consider PRRs with finite termination time that implies the almost-sure termination.

Theorem 2. *Suppose we have functions $t, f : [0, \infty) \times \mathbb{N} \to [0, \infty)$ such that*

$$\mathbb{E}[\exp(t(\alpha, n) \cdot \mathsf{Ex}(n \mid f))] \leq \exp(t(\alpha, n) \cdot f(\alpha, n)) \quad (4)$$

for all sufficiently large $\alpha, n^* > 0$ and all $c_p \leq n \leq n^*$, where

$$\mathsf{Ex}(n \mid f) := S(n) + \sum_{i=1}^r f(\alpha, \mathsf{size}_i(n)).$$

Then for $t_*(\alpha, n^*) := \min_{c_p \leq n \leq n^*} t(\alpha, n)$, *we have that*

$$\mathbb{E}[\exp(t_*(\alpha, n^*) \cdot C_\tau)] \leq \mathbb{E}[\exp(t_*(\alpha, n^*) \cdot f(\alpha, n^*))].$$

Thus, we obtain the upper bound $u(\alpha, n^*) := \exp(t_*(\alpha, n^*) \cdot (f(\alpha, n^*) - \alpha \cdot \kappa(n^*)))$ *for the tail bound in (1).*

Proof Sketch. We fix a procedure p, and some sufficiently large α and n^*. In general, we apply the martingale theory to prove this theorem. To construct a martingale, we need to make two preparations.

First, by the convexity of $\exp(\cdot)$, substituting $t(\alpha, n)$ with $t_*(\alpha, n^*)$ in (4) does not affect the validity of (4).

Second, given an infinite sequence of the PRR states $\rho = \mu_0, \mu_1, \ldots$ in the sample space, we consider the subsequence $\rho' = \mu'_0, \mu'_1, \ldots$ as follows, where we represent μ'_i as $((\mathsf{func}(p), \hat{n}'_i), C'_i, \mathbf{K}'_i)$. It only contains states that are either final or at the entry of p, i.e., $comm = \mathsf{func}(p)$. We define $\tau' := \inf\{t : \mu'_t \text{ is final}\}$, then it is straightforward that $C'_{\tau'} = C_\tau$. We observe that μ'_{i+1} represents the recursive calls of μ'_i. Thus, we can characterize the conditional distribution $\mu'_{i+1} \mid \mu_i$ by the transformation function $\mathsf{Tf}(\hat{n}, \mathsf{func}(p))$ as follows.

– We first draw $(S, \mathsf{size}_1, \mathsf{size}_2, r)$ from $\mathsf{Tf}(\hat{n}'_i, \mathsf{func}(p))$.
– We accumulate S into the global cost. If there is a single recursion ($r = 1$), we invoke this sub-procedure. If there are two recursive calls, we push the second call $p(\mathsf{size}_2)$ into the stack and invoke the first one $p(\mathsf{size}_1)$.

Now we construct the super-martingale as follows. For each $i \geq 0$, we denote the stack as $\mathbf{K}'_i$ for μ'_i as $(\mathsf{func}(p), \mathsf{s}_{i,1}) \cdots (\mathsf{func}(p), \mathsf{s}_{i,q_i})$, where q_i is the stack size. We prove that another process $y_0, y_1, \ldots$ that forms a super-martingale, where $y_i := \exp\left(t_*(\alpha, n^*) \cdot \left(C'_i + f(\alpha, \hat{n}'_i) + \sum_{j=1}^{q_i} f(\alpha, \mathsf{s}_{i,j})\right)\right)$. Note that $y_0 = \exp(t_*(\alpha, n^*) \cdot f(\alpha, n^*))$, and $y_{\tau'} = \exp(t_*(\alpha, n^*) \cdot C'_{\tau'}) = \exp(t_*(\alpha, n^*) \cdot C_\tau)$. Thus we informally have that $\mathbb{E}\left[\exp(t_*(\alpha, n^*) \cdot C_\tau)\right] = \mathbb{E}[y_{\tau'}] \leq \mathbb{E}[y_0] = \exp(t_*(\alpha, n^*) \cdot f(\alpha, n^*))$ and the theorem follows.   □

It is natural to ask whether our theoretical approach can always find an exponential-decreasing tail bound over PRRs. We answer this question by showing that under a difference boundedness and a monotone condition, the answer is yes. We first present the difference boundedness condition (A1) and the monotone condition (A2) for a PRR Δ in the canonical form (2) as follows.

(A1) Δ is *difference-bounded* if there exist two real constants $M' \leq M$, such that for every $n \geq c_p$, and every possible value $(V, s_1, \ldots, s_k)$ in the support of the probability distribution $\mathsf{Tf}(n, \mathsf{func}(p))$, we have that

$$M' \cdot \mathbb{E}[S(n)] \leq V + (\sum_{i=1}^{k} \mathbb{E}[p(s_i)]) - \mathbb{E}[p(n)] \leq M \cdot \mathbb{E}[S(n)].$$

(A2) Δ is *expected non-decreasing* if $\mathbb{E}[S(n)]$ does not decrease as n increases.

In other words, (A1) says that for any possible concrete pre-processing time V and passed sizes $s_1, \ldots, s_k$, the difference between the expected runtime before and after the recursive call is bounded by the magnitude of the expected pre-processing time. (A2) simply specifies that the expected pre-processing time be monotonically non-decreasing.

With the conditions (A1) and (A2), our theoretical approach guarantees a tail bound that is exponentially decreasing in the coefficient α and the ratio $\mathbb{E}[p(n^*)]/\mathbb{E}[S(n^*)]$. The theorem statement is as follows.

Theorem 3. *Let Δ be a PRR in the canonical form (2). If Δ satisfies (A1) and (A2), then for any function $w : [1, \infty) \to (1, \infty)$, the functions f, t given by*

$$f(\alpha, n) := w(\alpha) \cdot \mathbb{E}[p(n)] \quad and \qquad t(\alpha, n) := \frac{\lambda(\alpha)}{\mathbb{E}[S(n)]}$$

$$with \qquad \lambda(\alpha) := \frac{8(w(\alpha) - 1)}{w(\alpha)^2 (M_2 - M_1)^2}$$

fulfill the constraint (4) in Theorem 2. Furthermore, by choosing $w(\alpha) := \frac{2\alpha}{1+\alpha}$ in the functions f, t above and $\kappa(\alpha, n^*) := \alpha \cdot \mathbb{E}[p(n^*)]$, one obtains the tail bound

$$\Pr[C_\tau \geq \alpha \mathbb{E}[p(n^*)]] \leq \exp\left(-\frac{2(\alpha - 1)^2}{\alpha(M_2 - M_1)^2} \cdot \frac{\mathbb{E}[p(n^*)]}{\mathbb{E}[S(n^*)]}\right).$$

Proof Sketch. We first rephrase the constraint (4) as

$$\mathbb{E}\left[\exp\left(t(\alpha, n) \cdot \left(S(n) + \sum_{i=1}^{r} f(\alpha, \mathsf{size}_i(n)) - f(\alpha, n)\right)\right)\right] \leq 1$$

Then we focus on the exponent in the $\exp(\cdot)$, by (A1), the exponent is a bounded random variable. By further calculating its expectation and applying Hoeffding's Lemma [18], we obtain the theorem above.   □

Note that since $\mathbb{E}[p(n)] \geq \mathbb{E}[S(n)]$ when $n \geq c_p$, the tail bound is at least exponentially-decreasing with respect to the coefficient α. This implies that our theoretical approach derives tail bounds that are at least as tight as Karp's method when (A1) and (A2) holds. When $\mathbb{E}[p(n)]$ is of a strictly greater magnitude than $\mathbb{E}[S(n)]$, our approach derives asymptotically tighter bounds.

Below, we apply the theorem above to prove tail bounds for Quickselect (Example 2) and Quicksort (Example 3).

Example 6. For QuickSelect, its canonical form is $p(n; 2) = n + p(\mathsf{size}_1(n))$, where $\mathsf{size}_1(n)$ observes as $\mathsf{muniform}(n)$. Solving the recurrence relation, we obtain that $\mathbb{E}[p(n)] = 4 \cdot n$. We further find that this PRR satisfies (A1) with two constants $M' = -1, M = 1$. Note that the PRR satisfies (A2) obviously. Hence, we apply Theorem 3 and derive the tail bound for every sufficiently large α:

$$\Pr[C_\tau \geq 4 \cdot \alpha \cdot n^*] \leq \exp\left(-\frac{2(\alpha - 1)^2}{\alpha}\right).$$

On the other hand, Karp's cookbook has the tail bound

$$\Pr[C_\tau \geq 4 \cdot \alpha \cdot n^*] \leq \exp\left(1.15 - 1.12 \cdot \alpha\right).$$

Our bound is asymptotically the same as Karp's but has a better coefficient. □

Example 7. For QuickSort, its canonical form is $p(n; 2) = n + p(\text{size}_1(n)) + p(\text{size}_2(n))$, where $\text{size}_1(n)$ observes as $\texttt{muniform}(n)$ and $\text{size}_2(n) = n - 1 - \text{size}_1(n)$. Similar to the example above, we first calculate $\mathbb{E}[p(n)] = 2 \cdot n \cdot \ln n$. Note that this PRR also satisfies two assumptions above with two constants $M' = -2 \log 2, M = 1$. Hence, for every sufficiently large α, we can derive the tail bound as follows:

$$Pr[C_\tau \geq 2 \cdot \alpha \cdot n^* \cdot \ln n^*] \leq \exp\left(-\frac{0.7(\alpha - 1)^2}{\alpha} \cdot \ln n^*\right).$$

On the other hand, Karp's cookbook has the tail bound

$$Pr[C_\tau \geq 2 \cdot \alpha \cdot n^* \cdot \ln n^*] \leq \exp\left(-\alpha + 0.5\right).$$

Note that our tail bound is tighter than Karp's with a $\ln n$ factor.   □

From the generality of Markov's inequality, our theoretical approach can handle to general PRRs with three or more sub-procedure calls. However, the tail bounds derived from Theorem 3 is still not tight since the theorem only uses the expectation and bound of the given distribution. For example, for QuickSelect, the tightest known bound $\exp(-\Theta(\alpha \cdot \ln \alpha))$ [15], is tighter than that derived from Theorem 3. Below, we present an algorithmic approach that fully utilizes the distribution information and derives tight tail bounds that can match [15].

4   An Algorithmic Approach

In this section, we demonstrate an algorithmic implementation for our theoretical approach (Theorem 2). Our algorithm synthesizes the functions t, f through template and a refined estimation on the exponential terms from the inequality (4). The estimation is via integration and the monotonicity of the template. Below we fix a PRR $p(n; c_p)$ in the canonical form (2) and a time limit $\alpha \cdot \kappa(n^*)$.

Recall that to apply Theorem 2, one needs to find functions t, f that satisfy the constraint (4). Thus, the first step of our algorithm is to have pseudo-monomial template for $f(\alpha, n)$ and $t(\alpha, n)$ in the following form:

$$f(\alpha, n) := c_f \cdot \alpha^{p_f} \cdot \ln^{q_f} \alpha \cdot n^{u_f} \cdot \ln^{v_f} n \tag{5}$$

$$t(\alpha, n) := c_t \cdot \alpha^{p_t} \cdot \ln^{q_t} \alpha \cdot n^{u_t} \cdot \ln^{v_t} n \tag{6}$$

In the template, we have $p_f, q_f, u_f, v_f, p_t, q_t, u_t, v_t$ are given integers, and $c_f, c_t > 0$ are unknown positive coefficients to be solved. For several compatibility reasons (see Proposition 1 and 2 in the following), we require that $u_f, v_f \geq 0$ and

$u_t, v_t \leq 0$. We say that the concrete values $\overline{c_f}, \overline{c_t}$ for the unknown coefficients $c_f, c_t > 0$ are *valid* if the concrete functions $\overline{f}, \overline{t}$ obtained by substituting $\overline{c_f}, \overline{c_t}$ for c_f, c_t in the template (5) and (6) satisfy the constraint (4) for every sufficiently large $\alpha, n^* \geq 0$ and all $c_p \leq n \leq n^*$.

We consider the pseudo-polynomial template since the runtime behavior of randomized algorithms can be mostly captured by pseudo-polynomials. We choose monomial templates since our interest is the asymptotic magnitude of the tail bound. Thus, only the monomial with the highest degrees matter.

Our algorithm searches the values for $p_f, q_f, u_f, v_f, p_t, q_t, u_t, v_t$ by an enumeration within a bounded range $\{-B, \ldots, B\}$, where B is a manually specified positive integer. To avoid exhaustive enumeration, we use the following proposition to prune the search space.

Proposition 1. *Suppose that we have functions $t, f : [0, \infty) \times \mathbb{N} \to [0, \infty)$ that fulfill the constraint (4). Then it holds that (i)*
$(p_f, q_f) \leq (1, 0)$ *and* $(p_t, q_t) \geq (-1, 0)$*, and (ii)*
$f(\alpha, n) = \Omega(\mathbb{E}[p(n)])$, $f(\alpha, n) = O(\kappa(n))$ *and* $t(\alpha, n) = \Omega(\kappa(n)^{-1})$ *for any fixed $\alpha > 0$, where we write $(a, b) \leq (c, d)$ for the lexicographic order, i.e., $(a \leq c) \wedge (a = c \to b \leq d)$.*

Proof. Except for the constraint that $f(\alpha, n) = \Omega(\mathbb{E}[p(n)])$, the other constraints simply ensure that the tail bound is exponentially-decreasing. To see why $f(\alpha, n) = \Omega(\mathbb{E}[p(n)])$, we apply Jensen's inequality [27] to (4) and obtain $f(n) \geq \mathbb{E}[\mathsf{Ex}(n|f)] = \mathbb{E}[S(n) + \sum_{i=1}^{r} f(\mathsf{size}_i(n))]$. Then we imitate the proof of Theorem 2 and derive that $f(n) \geq \mathbb{E}[p(n)]$. □

Proposition 1 shows that it suffices to consider (i) the choice of u_f, v_f that makes the magnitude of f to be within $\mathbb{E}[p(n)]$ and $\kappa(n)$, (ii) the choice of u_t, v_t that makes the magnitude of t^{-1} within $\kappa(n)$, and (iii) the choice of p_f, q_f, p_t, q_t that fulfills $(p_f, q_f) \leq (1, 0), (p_t, q_t) \geq (-1, 0)$. Note that an over-approximation of $\mathbb{E}[p(n)]$ can be either obtained manually or derived from automated approaches [9].

Example 8. Consider the quickselect example (Example 2), suppose we are interested in the tail bound $\Pr[C_\tau \geq \alpha \cdot n]$, and we enumerate the eight integers in the template from -1 to 1. Since $\mathbb{E}[p(n)] = 4 \cdot n$, by the proposition above, we must have that $(u_f, v_f) = (1, 0), (u_t, v_t) \geq (-1, 0), (p_t, q_t) \geq (-1, 0), (p_f, q_f) \leq (1, 0)$. This reduces the number of choices for the template from 1296 to 128, where these numbers are automatically generated by our implementation. A choice is $f(\alpha, n) := c_f \cdot \alpha \cdot (\ln \alpha)^{-1} \cdot n$ and $t(\alpha, n) := c_t \cdot \ln \alpha \cdot n^{-1}$. □

In the second step, our algorithm solves the unknown coefficients c_t, c_f in the template. Once they are solved, our algorithm applies Theorem 2 to obtain the tail bound. In detail, our algorithm computes $t_*(\alpha, n^*)$ as the minimum of $t(\alpha, n)$ over $c_p \leq n \leq n^*$, and by $u_t, v_t \leq 0$, $t_*(\alpha, n^*)$ is simply $t(\alpha, n^*)$, so that we obtain the tail bound $u(\alpha, n^*) = \exp(t(\alpha, n^*) \cdot (f(\alpha, n^*) - \alpha \cdot \kappa(n^*)))$.

Example 9. Continue with Example 8. Suppose we have successfully found that $\overline{c_f} = 2, \overline{c_t} = 1$ is a valid concrete choice for the unknown coefficients in the template. Then $t_*(\alpha, n^*)$ is $t(\alpha, n^*) = \ln \alpha \cdot (n^*)^{-1}$, and we have the tail bound $u(\alpha, n^*) = \exp(2 \cdot \alpha - \alpha \cdot \ln \alpha)$, which has better magnitude than the tail bound by Karp's method and our Theorem 3 (See Example 6). □

Our algorithm follows the guess-and-check paradigm. The guess procedure explores possible values $\overline{c_f}, \overline{c_t}$ for c_f, c_t and invokes the check procedure to verify whether the current choice is valid. Below we present the guess procedure in Sect. 4.1, and the check procedure in Sect. 4.2.

4.1 The Guess Procedure Guess(f, t)

The pseudocode for our guess procedure Guess(f, t) is given in Algorithm 1. In detail, it first receives a positive integer M as the doubling and halving number (Line 1), then iteratively enumerates possible values for the unknown coefficients c_f and c_t by doubling and halving for M times (Line 3 – Line 4), and finally calls the check procedure (Line 5). It is justified by the following theorem.

Theorem 4. *Given the template for $f(\alpha, n)$ and $t(\alpha, n)$ as in (5) and (6), if $\overline{c_f}, \overline{c_t}$ are valid choices, then (i) for every $k > 1$, $k \cdot \overline{c_f}, \overline{c_t}$ remains to be valid, and (ii) for every $0 < k < 1$, $\overline{c_f}, k \cdot \overline{c_t}$ remains to be valid.*

Algorithm 1: Guess Procedure

Input : Template for $f(\alpha, n)$ and
$t(\alpha, n)$ as in (5) and (6)
Output: $\overline{c_f}, \overline{c_t} > 0$ for (5) and (6)
1 **Parameter:** M for the maximum steps
of doubling and halving.
2 **Procedure** Guess(f, t):
3 　for $\overline{c_t} := 1, 2^{-1}, \ldots, 2^{-M}$ **do**
4 　　for $\overline{c_f} := \frac{1}{2}, 1, 2, \ldots, 2^{M-1}$ **do**
5 　　　if CheckCond($\overline{c_f}, \overline{c_t}$) **then**
6 　　　　Return ($\overline{c_f}, \overline{c_t}$)

By Theorem 4, if the check procedure is sound and complete (i.e., CheckCond always terminates and $\overline{c_f}, \overline{c_t}$ fulfills the constraint (4) iff CheckCond($\overline{c_f}, \overline{c_t}$) returns true), then the guess procedure guarantees to find a solution $\overline{c_f}, \overline{c_t}$ (if it exists) when the parameter M is large enough.

Example 10. Continued with Example 8, suppose $M = 2$, we enumerate $\overline{c_f}$ from $\{\frac{1}{2}, 1, 2\}$, and $\overline{c_t}$ from $\{1, \frac{1}{2}, \frac{1}{4}\}$. We try every possible combination, and we find that CheckCond$(2, 1)$ returns true. Thus, we return $(2, 1)$ as the result. In Sect. 4.2, we will show how to conclude that CheckCond$(2, 1)$ is true. □

4.2 The Check Procedure CheckCond($\overline{c_f}, \overline{c_t}$)

The check procedure takes as input the concrete values $\overline{c_f}, \overline{c_t}$ for the unknown coefficients in the template, and outputs whether they are valid. It is the most involved part in our algorithm due to the difficulty to tackle the validity of the constraint (4) that involves the composition of polynomials, exponentiation and logarithms. The existence of a sound and complete decision procedure for such validity is extremely difficult and is a long-standing open problem [1, 33].

To circumvent this difficulty, the check procedure first strengthens the original constraint (4) into a canonical constraint with a specific form, so that a decision algorithm that is sound and complete up to any additive error applies. Below we fix a PRR with procedure p in the canonical form (2). We also discuss possible extensions for the check procedure in Remark 1.

The Canonical Constraint. We first present the canonical constraint $Q(\alpha, n)$ and how to decide the canonical constraint. The constraint is given by (where $\forall^\infty$ means "for all sufficiently large α" or formally $\exists \alpha_0.\forall \alpha \geq \alpha_0$)

$$Q(\alpha, n) := \forall^\infty \alpha.\forall n \geq c_p. \left[\sum_{i=1}^{k} \gamma_i \cdot \exp(f_i(\alpha) + g_i(n)) \leq 1 \right] \quad (7)$$

subject to:

(C1) For each $1 \leq i \leq k$, we have $\gamma_i > 0$ is a positive constant, $f_i(\alpha)$ is a pseudo-polynomial in α, and $g_i(n)$ is a pseudo-polynomial in n.
(C2) For each $1 \leq i \leq k$, the exponents for n and $\ln n$ in $g_i(n)$ are non-negative.

We use $Q_L(\alpha, n)$ to represent the summation term $\sum_{i=1}^{k} \gamma_i \cdot \exp(f_i(\alpha) + g_i(n))$ in (7). Below we show that this can be checked by the algorithm *Decide* up to any additive error. We present an overview of this algorithm. We also present its pseudo-code in Algorithm 2.

The algorithm *Decide* requires an external function $\mathsf{NegativeLB}(P(n))$ that takes on input a pseudo-polynomial $P(n)$ and outputs an integer T_n^* such that $P(n) \leq 0$ for every $n \geq T_n^*$, or output $+\infty$ for the absence of T_n^*. The idea of this function is to apply the monotonicity of pseudo-polynomials. With the function $\mathsf{NegativeLB}(P(n))$, the algorithm *Decide* consists of two steps as follows.

First, we can change the bound of n from $[c_p, \infty)$ into $[c_p, T_n]$, where T_n is a constant, without affecting the soundness and completeness. This is achieved by the observation that either: (i) we can conclude $Q(\alpha, n)$ does not hold, or (ii) there is an integer T_n such that $Q_L(\alpha, n)$ is non-increasing when $n \geq T_n$. Hence, it suffices only to consider $c_p \leq n \leq T_n$. Below we show how to compute T_n by case analysis of the limit M_i of $g_i(n)$ as $n \to \infty$, for each $1 \leq i \leq k$.

- If $M_i = +\infty$, then $\exp(g_i(n) + f_i(\alpha))$ could be arbitrarily large when $n \to \infty$. As a result, we can conclude that $Q(\alpha, n)$ does not hold.
- Otherwise, by (C2), either $g_i(n)$ is a constant function, or $M_i = -\infty$. In both cases, $g_i(n)$ is non-increasing for every sufficiently large n. More precisely, there exists L_i such that $g_i'(n) \leq 0$ for every $n \geq L_i$, where $g_i'(n)$ is the derivative of $g_i(n)$. Moreover, we can invoke $\mathsf{NegativeLB}(g_i'(n))$ to get L_i.

Finally, we set T_n as the maximum of L_i's and c_p.

Second, for every integer $c_p \leq \overline{n} \leq T_n$, we substitute n with $\overline{n}$ to eliminate n in $Q(\alpha, n)$. Then, each exponent $f_i(\alpha) + g_i(\overline{n})$ becomes a pseudo-polynomial solely over α. Since we only concern sufficiently large α, we can compute the limit $R_{\overline{n}}$ for $Q_L(\alpha, \overline{n})$ as $\alpha \to \infty$. We decide based on the limit $R_{\overline{n}}$ as follows.

- If $R_{\overline{n}} < 1$ for every $c_p \leq \overline{n} \leq L$, we conclude that $Q(\alpha, n)$ holds.
- If $R_{\overline{n}} \geq 1$ for some $c_p \leq \overline{n} \leq L$, we conclude that $Q(\alpha, n)$ does not hold to ensure soundness.

Algorithm 2: The Decision procedure for canonical constraints

---

Input : A canonical constraint $Q(\alpha, n)$ in the form of (7)
Output: Decide whether $Q(\alpha, n)$ holds.
1 **Procedure** $Decide(Q(\alpha, n))$:
2      $T_n := c_p$;   // ◁ The first step
3   **for** $i := 1, 2, \ldots, k$ **do**
4          $M_i :=$ The limit of $g_i(n)$ as $n \to \infty$.
5   **if** $M_i = +\infty$ **then**
6   **Return** False
7   **else**
8              $g'_i(n) :=$ the derivative of $g_i(n)$
9              $T_n := \max\{T_n, \mathsf{NegativeLB}(g'_i(n))\}$
10   **for** $\overline{n} := c_p, \ldots, T_n$ **do**   // ◁ The second step
11         $R := 0$
12   **for** $i := 1, 2, \ldots, k$ **do**
13             $\Delta :=$ the limit of $f_i(\alpha) + g_i(\overline{n})$ as $\alpha \to \infty$.
14   **if** $\Delta = +\infty$ **then**
15   **Return** False
16   **else**
17                 $R := R + \gamma_i \cdot \exp(\Delta)$
18   **if** $R \geq 1$ **then Return** False
19   **Return** True

Algorithm *Decide* is sound, and complete up to any additive error, as is illustrated by the following theorem.

Theorem 5. *Algorithm Decide has the following properties:*

- *(Completeness) If $Q(\alpha, n)$ does not hold for infinitely many α and some $n \geq c_p$, then the algorithm returns false.*
- *(Soundness) For every $\varepsilon > 0$, we have that if $Q_L(\alpha, n) \leq 1 - \varepsilon$ for all sufficiently large α and all $n \geq c_p$, then the algorithm returns true.*

The Strengthening Procedure. Then we show how to strengthen the constraint (4) into the canonical constraint (7), so that Algorithm *Decide* applies. We rephrase (4) as

$$\mathbb{E}\left[\exp(t(\alpha, n) \cdot \left(S(n) + \sum_{i=1}^{r} f(\alpha, \mathsf{size}_i(n)) - f(\alpha, n)\right)\right] \leq 1 \qquad (8)$$

and consider two functions $\overline{f}, \overline{t}$ obtained by substituting the concrete values $\overline{c_f}, \overline{c_t}$ for unknown coefficients into the template (5) and (6). We observe that the joint-distribution of the random quantities $S(n), r \in \{1, 2\}$ and $\mathsf{size}_1(n), \ldots, \mathsf{size}_r(n)$ in the canonical form (2) over PRRs can be described by several probabilistic branches $\{c_1 : B_1, \ldots, c_k : B_k\}$, which corresponds to the probabilistic choice commands in the PRR. Each probabilistic branch B_i has a constant probability c_i, a deterministic pre-processing time $S_i(n)$, a fixed number of subprocedure calls r_i, and a probability distribution for the variable v. The strengthening first handles each probabilistic branch, and then combines the strengthening results of every branch into a single canonical constraint.

The strengthening of each branch is an application of a set of rewriting rules. Intuitively, each rewriting step over-approximates and simplifies the expectation term in the LHS of (8). Through multiple steps of rewriting, we eventually obtain the final canonical constraint. Below we present the details of the strengthening for a single probabilistic branch with the single recursion case. The divide-and-conquer case follows a similar treatment, see the extended version for details.

Consider the single recursion case $r = 1$ where a probabilistic branch has deterministic pre-processing time $S(n)$, distribution dist for the variable v and passed size $H(v, n)$ for the recursive call. We have a case analysis on the distribution dist as follows.

— *Case I*: dist is a FSDPD `discrete`$\{c'_1 : \mathsf{expr}_1, \ldots, c'_k : \mathsf{expr}_k\}$, where v observes as expr_i with probability c'_i. Then the expectation in (8) is exactly:

$$\sum_{i=1}^{k} c'_i \cdot \exp\left(t(\alpha, n) \cdot S(n) + t(\alpha, n) \cdot f(\alpha, H(\mathsf{expr}_i, n)) - t(\alpha, n) \cdot f(\alpha, n)\right)$$

Thus it suffices to over-approximate the exponent $X_i(\alpha, n) := t(\alpha, n) \cdot S(n) + t(\alpha, n) \cdot f(\alpha, H(\mathsf{expr}_i, n)) - t(\alpha, n) \cdot f(n)$ into the form subject to (C1)–(C2). For this purpose, our strengthening repeatedly applies the following rewriting rules (R1)–(R4) for which $0 < a < 1$ and $b > 0$:

(R1) $f(\alpha, H(\mathsf{expr}_i, n)) \le f(\alpha, n)$

(R2) $\ln(an - b) \le \ln n + \ln a \quad \ln(an + b) \le \ln n + \ln(\min\{1, a + \frac{b}{c_p}\})$

(R3) $0 \le n^{-1} \le c_p^{-1} \quad 0 \le \ln^{-1} n \le \ln^{-1} c_p$ (R4) $\lfloor \frac{n}{b} \rfloor \le \frac{n}{b} \quad \lceil \frac{n}{b} \rceil \le \frac{n}{b} + \frac{b-1}{b}$

(R1) follows from the well-formedness $0 \le H(\mathsf{size}_i, n) \le n$ and the monotonicity of $f(\alpha, n)$ with respect to n. (R2)–(R4) are straightforward. Intuitively, (R1) can be used to cancel the term $f(\alpha, H(\mathsf{size}_i, n)) - f(\alpha, n)$, (R2) simplifies the subexpression in ln, (R3) is used to remove floors and ceils, and (R4) to remove n^{-c} and $\ln^{-c} n$ to satisfy the restriction (C2) of the canonical constraint. To apply these rules, we consider two strategies below.

(S1-D) Apply (R1) and over-approximate $X_i(\alpha, n)$ as $t(\alpha, n) \cdot S(n)$. Then, we repeatedly apply (R3) to remove terms n^{-c} and $\ln^{-c} n$.

(S2-D) Substitute f and t with the concrete functions $\overline{f}, \overline{t}$ and expand $H(\mathsf{expr}_i, n)$. Then we first apply (R4) to remove all floors and ceils, and repeatedly apply (R2) to replace all occurrences of $\ln(an + b)$ with $\ln n + \ln C$ for some constant C. By the previous replacement, the whole term $X_i(\alpha, n)$ will be over-approximated as a pseudo-polynomial over α and n. Finally, we eagerly apply (R3) to remove all terms n^{-c} and $\ln^{-c} n$.

Our algorithm first tries to apply (S2-D), if it fails to derive a canonical constraint, then we apply the alternative (S1-D) to the original constraint. If both the strategies fails, we report failure and exit the check procedure.

Example 11. Suppose v observes as $\{0.5 : n - 1, 0.5 : n - 2\}, S(n) := \ln n, t(\alpha, n) := \frac{\ln \alpha}{\ln n}, f(\alpha, n) := 4 \cdot \frac{\alpha}{\ln \alpha} \cdot n \cdot \ln n, H(v, n) := v$. We consider applying both strategies to the first term $\mathtt{expr}_1 := n - 1$ and $X_1(\alpha, n) := t(\alpha, n) \cdot (S(n) + f(\alpha, n - 1) - f(\alpha, n))$. If we apply (S1-D) to X_1, it will be approximated as $\exp(\ln \alpha)$. If we apply (S2-D) to X_1, it will be first over-approximated as $\frac{\ln \alpha}{\ln n} \cdot (\ln n + 4 \cdot \frac{\alpha}{\ln \alpha} \cdot v \cdot \ln n - 4 \cdot \frac{\alpha}{\ln \alpha} \cdot n \cdot \ln n)$, then we substitute $v = n - 1$ and derive the final result $\exp(\ln \alpha - 4 \cdot \alpha)$. Hence, both the strategies succeed. □

— *Case II*: dist is $\mathtt{uniform}(n)$ or $\mathtt{muniform}(n)$. Note that $H(v, n)$ is linear with respect to v, thus $H(v, n)$ is a bijection over v for every fixed n. Hence, if v observes as $\mathtt{uniform}(n)$, then

$$\mathbb{E}[\exp(t(\alpha, n) \cdot f(\alpha, H(v, n)))] \leq \frac{1}{n} \sum_{v=0}^{n-1} \exp(t(\alpha, n) \cdot f(\alpha, v)) \qquad (9)$$

If v observes as $\mathtt{muniform}(n)$, a similar inequality holds by replacing $\frac{1}{n}$ with $\frac{2}{n}$. Since $f(\alpha, v)$ is a non-decreasing function with respect to v, we further over-approximate the summation in (9) by the integral $\int_0^n \exp(t(\alpha, n) \cdot f(\alpha, v)) dv$.

Example 12. Continue with Example 10, we need to check $\bar{t}(\alpha, n) = \frac{\ln \alpha}{n}$ and $\overline{f}(\alpha, n) = \frac{2 \cdot \alpha}{\ln \alpha} \cdot n$. By the inequality (9), we expand the constraint (8) into $\frac{2}{n} \cdot \exp(\ln \alpha - 2 \cdot \alpha) \cdot \sum_{v=0}^{n-1} \exp(\frac{2 \cdot \alpha \cdot i}{n})$. By integration, it is further over-approximated as $\frac{2}{n} \cdot \exp(\ln \alpha - 2 \cdot \alpha) \cdot \int_0^n \exp(\frac{2 \cdot \alpha \cdot v}{n}) dv$. □

Note that we still need to resolve the integration of an exponential function whose exponent is a pseudo-monomial over α, n, v. Below we denote by d_v the degree on the variable v and by ℓ_v the degree of $\ln v$. We first list the situations where the integral can be computed exactly.

- If $(d_v, \ell_v) = (1, 0)$, then the exponent could be expressed as $W(\alpha, n) \cdot v$, where $W(\alpha, n)$ is a pseudo-monomial over α and n. We can compute the integral as $\frac{\exp(n \cdot W(\alpha, n)) - 1}{W(\alpha, n)}$ and over-approximate it as $\frac{\exp(n \cdot W(\alpha, n))}{W(\alpha, n)}$ by removing -1 in the numerator.
- If $(d_v, \ell_v) = (0, 1)$, then the exponent is of the form $W(\alpha, n) \cdot \ln v$. We follow a similar procedure with the case above and obtain the over-approximation $\frac{n \cdot \exp(\ln n \cdot W(\alpha, n))}{W(\alpha, n)}$.
- If $(d_v, \ell_v) = (0, 0)$, then the result is trivially $n \cdot \exp(W(\alpha, n))$.

Then we handle the situation where the exact computation of the integral is infeasible. In this situation, the strengthening further over-approximates the integral into simpler forms by first replacing $\ln v$ with $\ln n$, and then replacing v with n to reduce the degrees ℓ_v and d_v. Eventually, the exponent in the integral bows down to one of the three situations (where the integral can be computed exactly) above, and the strengthening returns the exact value of the integral.

Example 13. Continue with Example 12. We express the exponent as $\frac{2 \cdot \alpha}{n} \cdot v$. Thus, we can plug $\frac{2 \cdot \alpha}{n}$ into $W(\alpha, n)$ and obtain the integration result $\frac{\exp(2 \cdot \alpha)}{2 \cdot \alpha/n}$. Furthermore, we can simplify the formula in Example 12 as $\frac{\exp(\ln \alpha)}{\alpha}$. □

In the end, we move the term $\frac{1}{n}$ (or $\frac{2}{n}$) that comes from the `uniform` (or `muniform`) distribution and the coefficient term $W(\alpha, n)$ into the exponent. If we move these terms directly, it may produce $\ln \ln n$ and $\ln \ln \alpha$ that comes from taking the logarithm of $\ln n$ and $\ln \alpha$. Hence, we first apply $\ln c_p \leq \ln n \leq n$ and $1 \leq \ln \alpha \leq \alpha$ to remove all terms $\ln n$ and $\ln \alpha$ outside the exponent (e.g., $\frac{\ln \alpha}{\ln n}$ is over-approximated as $\frac{\alpha}{\ln c_p}$). After the over-approximation, the terms outside the exponentiation form a polynomial over α and n, we can trivially move these terms into the exponent by taking the logarithm. Finally, we apply (R4) in Case I to remove n^{-c} and $\ln^{-c} n$. If we fail to obtain the canonical constraint, the strengthening reports failure.

Example 14. Continue with Example 13, we move the term α into the exponentiation and simplify the over-approximation result as $\exp(\ln \alpha - \ln \alpha) = 1$. As a result, we over-approximate the LHS of (8) as 1 and we conclude that `CheckCond(2, 1)` holds. □

The details of the divide-and-conquer case are similar and omitted. Furthermore, we present how to combine the strengthening results for different branches into a single canonical constraint. Suppose for every probabilistic branch B_i, we have successfully obtained the canonical constraint $Q_{L,i}(\alpha, n) \leq 1$ as the strengthening of the original constraint (8). Then, the canonical constraint for the whole distribution is $\sum_{i=1}^{k} c_i \cdot Q_{L,i}(\alpha, n) \leq 1$. Intuitively, there is probability c_i for the branch B_i, thus the combination follows by simply expanding the expectation term.

A natural question is to ask whether our algorithm can always succeed to obtain the canonical constraint. We have the proposition as follows.

Proposition 2. *If the template for t has a lower magnitude than $S(n)^{-1}$ for every branch, then the rewriting always succeeds.*

Proof. We first consider the single recursion case. When `dist` is FSDPD, we can apply (S1-D) to over-approximate the exponent as $t(\alpha, n) \cdot S(n)$. Since $t(\alpha, n)$ has a lower magnitude than $S(n)^{-1}$, by further applying (R3) to eliminate n^{-c} and $\ln^{-c} n$, we obtain the canonical constraint. If `dist` is `uniform(n)` or `muniform(n)`, we observe that the over-approximation result for the integral is either $\frac{\exp(f(\alpha,n))}{f(\alpha,n)\cdot t(\alpha,n)}$ (when $d_v > 0$) or $\frac{\ln n \cdot \exp(f(\alpha,n))}{f(\alpha,n)\cdot t(\alpha,n)}$ (when $d_v = 0$). Thus, we can cancel the term $f(\alpha, n)$ in the exponent and obtain the canonical constraint by the subsequent steps. The proof is the same for the divide-and-conquer case. □

By Proposition 2, we restrict $u_t, v_t \leq 0$ in the template to ensure our algorithm never fails.

Remark 1. Our algorithm can be extended to support piecewise uniform distributions (e.g. each of $0, \ldots, n/2$ with probability $\frac{2}{3n}$ and each of $n/2+1, \ldots, n-1$ with probability $\frac{4}{3n}$) by handling each piece separately.

5   Experimental Results

In this section, we evaluated our algorithm over classical randomized algorithms such as QuickSort (Example 3), QuickSelect (Example 2), DiameterComputation [26, Chapter 9], RandomizedSearch [24, Chapter 9], ChannelConflictResolution [22, Chapter 13], examples such as Rdwalk and Rdadder in the literature [7], and four manually-crafted examples (MC1 – MC4). For each example, we manually compute its expected running time for the prunning.

We implemented our algorithm in C++. We choose $B = 2$ (as the bounded range for the template), $M = 4$ (in the guess procedure), $Q = 8$ (for the number of parts in the integral), and prune the search space by Theorem 1. All results were obtained on an Ubuntu 18.04 machine with an 8-Core Intel i7-7900x Processor (4.30 GHz) and 40 GB of RAM.

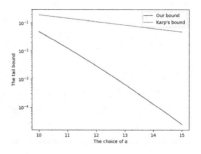

Fig. 2. Plot for QuickSelect

We report the tail bound derived by our algorithm in Table 1, where "Benchmark" lists the benchmarks, "$\alpha \cdot \kappa(n^*)$" lists the time limit of interest, "Our bound" lists the tail bound by our approach, "Time(s)" lists the runtime (in seconds) of our approach, and "Karp's bound" lists the bounds by Karp's method. From the table, our algorithm constantly derives asymtotically tighter tail bounds than Karp's method. Moreover, all these bounds are obtained in a few seconds, demonstrating the efficiency of our algorithm. Furthermore, our algorithm obtains bounds with tighter magnitude than our completeness theorem (Theorem 3) in 9 benchmarks, and bounds with the same magnitude as the others.

For an intuitive comparison, we also report the concrete bounds and their plots of our method and Karp's method. We choose three concrete choices of α and n^* and plot the concrete bounds over $10 \leq \alpha \leq 15, n^* = 17$. For concrete bounds, we also report the ratio $\frac{\text{Karp's Bound}}{\text{Our Bound}}$ to show the strength of our method. Due to space limitations, we only report the results for QuickSelect (Example 2) in Table 2 and Fig. 2.

Table 1. Experimental Result

Benchmark	$\alpha \cdot \kappa(n^*)$ in (1)	Our bound	Time(s)	Karp's bound
QuickSelect	$\alpha \cdot n^*$	$\exp(2 \cdot \alpha - \alpha \cdot \ln \alpha)$	0.03	$\exp(1.15 - 0.28 \cdot \alpha)$
QuickSort	$\alpha \cdot n^* \cdot \ln n^*$	$\exp((4 - \alpha) \cdot \ln n^*)$	0.02	$\exp(0.5 - 0.5 \cdot \alpha)$
L1Diameter	$\alpha \cdot n^*$	$\exp(\alpha - \alpha \cdot \ln \alpha)$	0.03	$\exp(1.39 - 0.69 \cdot \alpha)$
L2Diameter	$\alpha \cdot n^* \cdot \ln n^*$	$\exp(\alpha - \alpha \cdot \ln \alpha)$	0.03	$\exp(1.39 - 0.69 \cdot \alpha)$
RandSearch	$\alpha \cdot \ln n^*$	$\exp((2 \cdot \alpha - \alpha \cdot \ln \alpha) \cdot \ln n^*)$	0.03	$\exp(-0.29 \cdot \alpha \cdot \ln n^*)$
Channel	$\alpha \cdot n^*$	$\exp((8 - \alpha) \cdot n^*)$	0.05	$\exp(1 - 0.37 \cdot \alpha)$
Rdwalk	$\alpha \cdot n^*$	$\exp((0.5 - \alpha) \cdot n^*)$	0.05	$\exp(0.60 - 0.41 \cdot \alpha)$
Rdadder	$\alpha \cdot n^*$	$\exp((4 - 0.5 \cdot \alpha) \cdot n^*)$	0.04	Not applicable
MC1	$\alpha \cdot \ln n^*$	$\exp((\alpha - \alpha \cdot \ln \alpha) \cdot \ln n^*)$	0.03	$\exp(-0.69 \cdot \alpha \cdot \ln n^*)$
MC2	$\alpha \cdot \ln^2 n^*$	$\exp((\alpha - \alpha \cdot \ln \alpha) \cdot \ln n^*)$	0.03	$\exp(-0.69 \cdot \alpha \cdot \ln n^*)$
MC3	$\alpha \cdot n^* \cdot \ln^2 n^*$	$\exp(\alpha - \alpha \cdot \ln \alpha)$	0.03	$\exp(1.15 - 0.28 \cdot \alpha)$
MC4	$\alpha \cdot n^*$	$\exp(2 \cdot \alpha - \alpha \cdot \ln \alpha)$	0.04	Not applicable

Table 2. Concrete Bounds for QuickSelect

Concrete choice	Our bound	Karp's Bound	Ratio
$\alpha = 10; n^* = 13$	0.0485	0.192	3.96
$\alpha = 11; n^* = 15$	0.0126	0.145	11.6
$\alpha = 12; n^* = 17$	0.00297	0.110	36.9

6 Related Work

Karp's Cookbook. Our approach is orthogonal to Karp's cookbook method [21] since we base our approach on Markov's inequality, and the core of Karp's method is a dedicated proof for establishing that an intricate tail bound function is a prefixed point of the higher order operator derived from the given PRR. Furthermore, our automated approach can derive asymptotically tighter tail bounds than Karp's method over all 12 PRRs in our benchmark. Our approach could also handle randomized preprocessing times, which is beyond the reach of Karp's method. Since Karp's proof of prefixed point is ad-hoc, it is non-trivial to extend his method to handle the randomized cost. Nevertheless, there are PRRs (e.g., Coupon-Collector) that can be handled by Karp's method but not by ours. Thus, our approach provides a novel way to obtain asymptotically tighter tail bounds than Karp's method.

The recent work [30] extends Karp's method for deriving tail bounds for parallel randomized algorithms. This method derives the same tail bounds as Karp's method over PRRs with a single recursive call (such as QuickSelect) and cannot handle randomized pre-processing time. Compared with this approach, our approach derives tail bounds with tighter magnitude on $11/12$ benchmarks.

Custom Analysis. Custom analysis of PRRs [15,25] has successfully derived tight tail bounds for QuickSelect and QuickSort. Compared with the custom analysis that requires ad-hoc proofs, our approach is automated, has the generality from Markov's inequality, and is capable of deriving bounds identical or very close to the tail bounds from the custom analysis.

Probabilistic Programs. There are also relevant approaches in probabilistic program verification. These approaches are either based on martingale concentration inequalities (for exponentially-decreasing tail bounds) [7,10–12,19], Markov's inequality (for polynomially-decreasing tail bounds) [8,23,31], fixed-point synthesis [32], or weakest precondition reasoning [4,20]. Compared with these approaches, our approach is dedicated to PRRs (a light-weight representation of recursive probabilistic programs) and involves specific treatment of common recursive patterns (such as randomized pivoting and divide-and-conquer) in randomized algorithms, while these approaches usually do not consider common recursion patterns in randomized algorithms. Below we have detailed technical comparisons with these approaches.

- Compared with the approaches based on martingale concentration inequalities [7,10–12,19], our approach has the same root as them, since martingale concentration inequalities are often proved via Markov's inequality. However, those approaches have more accuracy loss since these martingale concentration inequalities usually make further relaxations after applying Markov's inequality. In contrast, our automated approach directly handles the constraint after applying Markov's inequality by having a refined treatment of exponentiation and hence has better accuracy in deriving tail bounds.
- Compared with the approaches [8,23,31] that derive polynomially-decreasing tail bounds, our approach targets the sharper exponentially-decreasing tail bounds and hence is orthogonal.
- Compared with the fixed-point synthesis approach [32], our approach is orthogonal as it is based on Markov's inequality. Note that the approach [32] can only handle $3/12$ benchmarks.
- Compared with weakest precondition reasoning [4,20] that requires first specifying the bound functions and then verifying the bound functions by proof rules related to fixed-point conditions, mainly with manual efforts, our approach can be automated and is based on Markov's inequality rather than fixed point theorems. Although Karp's method is also based on a particular tail bound function as a prefixed point and can thus be embedded into the weakest precondition framework, Karp's proof of prefixed point requires deep insight, which is beyond existing proof rules. Moreover, even a slight relaxation of the tail bound function into a simpler form in Karp's method no longer keeps the bound function to be a prefixed point. Hence, the approach of the weakest precondition may not be suitable for deriving tail bounds.

Acknowledgement. We thank Prof. Bican Xia for valuable information on the exponential theory of reals. The work is partially supported by the National Natural Science Foundation of China (NSFC) with Grant No. 62172271, ERC CoG 863818 (ForM-SMArt), the Hong Kong Research Grants Council ECS Project Number 26208122, the HKUST-Kaisa Joint Research Institute Project Grant HKJRI3A-055 and the HKUST Startup Grant R9272.

References

1. Achatz, M., McCallum, S., Weispfenning, V.: Deciding polynomial-exponential problems. In: Sendra, J.R., González-Vega, L. (eds.) Symbolic and Algebraic Computation, International Symposium, ISSAC 2008, Linz/Hagenberg, Austria, July 20–23, 2008, Proceedings, pp. 215–222. ACM (2008). https://doi.org/10.1145/1390768.1390799
2. Aguirre, A., Barthe, G., Hsu, J., Kaminski, B.L., Katoen, J.P., Matheja, C.: A pre-expectation calculus for probabilistic sensitivity. Proc. ACM Program. Lang. **5**(POPL) (2021). https://doi.org/10.1145/3434333
3. Baier, C., Katoen, J.P.: Principles of Model Checking. MIT Press, Cambridge (2008)
4. Batz, K., Kaminski, B.L., Katoen, J.P., Matheja, C., Verscht, L.: A calculus for amortized expected runtimes. Proc. ACM Program. Lang. **7**(POPL), 1957–1986 (2023). https://doi.org/10.1145/3571260
5. Bertot, Y., Castéran, P.: Interactive Theorem Proving and Program Development - Coq'Art: The Calculus of Inductive Constructions. Texts in Theoretical Computer Science. An EATCS Series, Springer, Heidelberg (2004). https://doi.org/10.1007/978-3-662-07964-5
6. Billingsley, P.: Probability and Measure, 3rd edn. Wiley, New York (1995)
7. Chakarov, A., Sankaranarayanan, S.: Probabilistic program analysis with martingales. In: CAV, pp. 511–526 (2013)
8. Chatterjee, K., Fu, H.: Termination of nondeterministic recursive probabilistic programs. CoRR abs/1701.02944 (2017)
9. Chatterjee, K., Fu, H., Murhekar, A.: Automated recurrence analysis for almost-linear expected-runtime bounds. In: Majumdar, R., Kunčak, V. (eds.) CAV 2017. LNCS, vol. 10426, pp. 118–139. Springer, Cham (2017). https://doi.org/10.1007/978-3-319-63387-9_6
10. Chatterjee, K., Fu, H., Novotný, P., Hasheminezhad, R.: Algorithmic analysis of qualitative and quantitative termination problems for affine probabilistic programs. TOPLAS **40**(2), 7:1-7:45 (2018)
11. Chatterjee, K., Goharshady, A.K., Meggendorfer, T., Zikelic, D.: Sound and complete certificates for quantitative termination analysis of probabilistic programs. In: Shoham, S., Vizel, Y. (eds.) CAV 2022. LNCS, vol. 13371, pp. 55–78. Springer, Cham (2022). https://doi.org/10.1007/978-3-031-13185-1_4
12. Chatterjee, K., Novotný, P., Žikelić, Đ.: Stochastic invariants for probabilistic termination. In: POPL 2017, pp. 145–160 (2017)
13. Chaudhuri, S., Dubhashi, D.P.: Probabilistic recurrence relations revisited. Theoret. Comput. Sci. **181**(1), 45–56 (1997)
14. Goodman, N.D., Mansinghka, V.K., Roy, D., Bonawitz, K., Tenenbaum, J.B.: Church: a language for generative models. In: UAI 2008, pp. 220–229. AUAI Press (2008)
15. Grübel, R.: Hoare's selection algorithm: a Markov chain approach. Journal of Applied Probability **35**(1), 36–45 (1998). http://www.jstor.org/stable/3215544
16. Hoare, C.A.R.: Algorithm 64: quicksort. Commun. ACM **4**(7), 321 (1961)
17. Hoare, C.A.R.: Algorithm 65: find. Commun. ACM **4**(7), 321–322 (1961)
18. Hoeffding, W.: Probability inequalities for sums of bounded random variables. J. Am. Stat. Assoc. **58**(301), 13–30 (1963)
19. Huang, M., Fu, H., Chatterjee, K.: New approaches for almost-sure termination of probabilistic programs. In: APLAS, pp. 181–201 (2018)

20. Kaminski, B.L., Katoen, J., Matheja, C., Olmedo, F.: Weakest precondition reasoning for expected runtimes of randomized algorithms. J. ACM **65**(5), 30:1-30:68 (2018). https://doi.org/10.1145/3208102
21. Karp, R.M.: Probabilistic recurrence relations. J. ACM **41**(6), 1136–1150 (1994)
22. Kleinberg, J.M., Tardos, É.: Algorithm Design. Addison-Wesley (2006)
23. Kura, S., Urabe, N., Hasuo, I.: Tail probabilities for randomized program runtimes via martingales for higher moments. In: Vojnar, T., Zhang, L. (eds.) TACAS 2019. LNCS, vol. 11428, pp. 135–153. Springer, Cham (2019). https://doi.org/10.1007/978-3-030-17465-1_8
24. McConnell, J.J. (ed.): The Analysis of Algorithms: An Active Learning Approach. Jones & Bartlett Learning (2001)
25. McDiarmid, C., Hayward, R.: Large deviations for quicksort. J. Algorithms **21**(3), 476–507 (1996)
26. Motwani, R., Raghavan, P.: Randomized Algorithms. Cambridge University Press, Cambridge (1995)
27. Rudin, W.: Real and Complex Analysis, 3rd edn. McGraw-Hill Inc, USA (1987)
28. Smith, C., Hsu, J., Albarghouthi, A.: Trace abstraction modulo probability. Proc. ACM Program. Lang. **3**(POPL) (2019). https://doi.org/10.1145/3290352
29. Sun, Y., Fu, H., Chatterjee, K., Goharshady, A.K.: Automated tail bound analysis for probabilistic recurrence relations. CoRR (2023). http://arxiv.org/abs/2305.15104
30. Tassarotti, J., Harper, R.: Verified tail bounds for randomized programs. In: ITP, pp. 560–578 (2018)
31. Wang, D., Hoffmann, J., Reps, T.W.: Central moment analysis for cost accumulators in probabilistic programs. In: Freund, S.N., Yahav, E. (eds.) PLDI 2021: 42nd ACM SIGPLAN International Conference on Programming Language Design and Implementation, Virtual Event, Canada, June 20–25, 2021, pp. 559–573. ACM (2021). https://doi.org/10.1145/3453483.3454062
32. Wang, J., Sun, Y., Fu, H., Chatterjee, K., Goharshady, A.K.: Quantitative analysis of assertion violations in probabilistic programs. In: Freund, S.N., Yahav, E. (eds.) PLDI, pp. 1171–1186. ACM (2021)
33. Wilkie, A.J.: Schanuel's conjecture and the decidability of the real exponential field. In: Hart, B.T., Lachlan, A.H., Valeriote, M.A. (eds.) Algebraic Model Theory. NATO ASI Series, vol. 496 pp. 223–230. Springer, Dordrecht (1997). https://doi.org/10.1007/978-94-015-8923-9_11
34. Williams, D.: Probability with Martingales. Cambridge University Press, Cambridge (1991)

Compositional Probabilistic Model Checking with String Diagrams of MDPs

Kazuki Watanabe[1,2]([✉]) , Clovis Eberhart[1,3] , Kazuyuki Asada[4] , and Ichiro Hasuo[1,2]

[1] National Institute of Informatics, Tokyo, Japan
{kazukiwatanabe,eberhart,hasuo}@nii.ac.jp
[2] The Graduate University for Advanced Studies (SOKENDAI), Hayama, Japan
[3] Japanese-French Laboratory of Informatics, 3527 CNRS, Tokyo, Japan
[4] Tohoku University, Sendai, Japan
kazuyuki.asada.b6@tohoku.ac.jp

Abstract. We present a compositional model checking algorithm for Markov decision processes, in which they are composed in the categorical graphical language of *string diagrams*. The algorithm computes optimal expected rewards. Our theoretical development of the algorithm is supported by category theory, while what we call decomposition equalities for expected rewards act as a key enabler. Experimental evaluation demonstrates its performance advantages.

Keywords: model checking · compositionality · Markov decision process · category theory · monoidal category · string diagram

1 Introduction

Probabilistic model checking is a topic that attracts both theoretical and practical interest. On the practical side, probabilistic system models can naturally accommodate uncertainties inherent in many real-world systems; moreover, probabilistic model checking can give quantitative answers, enabling more fine-grained assessment than qualitative verification. Model checking of Markov decision processes (MDPs)—the target problem of this paper—has additional practical values since it not only verifies a specification but also synthesizes an optimal control strategy. On the theoretical side, it is notable that probabilistic model checking has a number of efficient algorithms, despite the challenge that the problem involves continuous quantities (namely probabilities). See e.g. [1].

However, even those efficient algorithms can struggle when a model is enormous. Models can easily become enormous—the so-called *state-space explosion*

The authors are supported by ERATO HASUO Metamathematics for Systems Design Project (No. JPMJER1603), JST. K.W. is supported by the JST grant No. JPMJFS2136.

C. Enea and A. Lal (Eds.): CAV 2023, LNCS 13966, pp. 40–61, 2023.
https://doi.org/10.1007/978-3-031-37709-9_3

problem—due to the growing complexity of modern verification targets. Models that exceed the memory size of a machine for verification are common.

Among possible countermeasures to state-space explosion, one with both mathematical blessings and a proven track record is *compositionality*. It takes as input a model with a compositional structure—where smaller *component* models are combined, sometimes with many layers—and processes the model in a divide-and-conquer manner. In particular, when there is repetition among components, compositional methods can exploit the repetition and reuse intermediate results, leading to a clear performance advantage.

Focusing our attention to MDP model checking, there have been many compositional methods proposed for various settings. One example is [14]: it studies probabilistic automata (they are only slightly different from MDPs) and in particular their *parallel composition*; the proposed method is a compositional framework, in an assume-guarantee style, based on multi-objective probabilistic model checking. Here, *contracts* among parallel components are not always automatically obtained. Another example is [11], where the so-called *hierarchical model checking* method for MDPs is introduced. It deals with *sequential composition* rather than parallel composition; assuming what can be called *parametric homogeneity* of components—they must be of the same shape while parameter values may vary—they present a model-checking algorithm that computes a guaranteed interval for the optimal expected reward.

In this work, inspired by these works and technically building on another recent work of ours [20], we present another compositional MDP model checking algorithm. We compose MDPs in *string diagrams*—a graphical language of category theory [15, Chap. XI] that has found applications in computer science [3, 8, 17]—that are more sequential than parallel. Our algorithm computes the optimal expected reward, unlike [11].

One key ingredient of the algorithm is the identification of compositionality as the *preservation of algebraic structures*; more specifically, we identify a compositional solution as a "homomorphisms" of suitable *monoidal categories*. This identification guided us in our development, explicating requirements of a desired compositional semantic domain (Sect. 2).

Another key ingredient is a couple of *decomposition equalities* for reachability probabilities, extended to expected rewards (Sect. 3). Those for reachability probabilities are well-known—one of them is *Girard's execution formula* [7] in linear logic—but our extension to expected rewards seems new.

The last two key ingredients are combined in Sect. 4 to formulate a compositional solution. Here we benefit from general categorical constructions, namely the Int *construction* [10] and *change of base* [5, 6].

We implemented the algorithm (it is called CompMDP) and present its experimental evaluation. Using the benchmarks inspired by real-world problems, we show that 1) CompMDP can solve huge models in realistic time (e.g. 10^8 positions, in 6–130 s); 2) compositionality does boost performance (in some ablation experiments); and 3) the choice of the degree of compositionality is important. The last is enabled in CompMDP by the operator we call *freeze*.

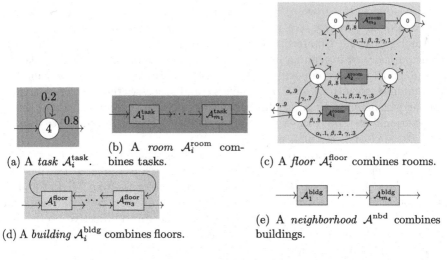

(a) A *task* $\mathcal{A}_i^{\mathrm{task}}$.

(b) A *room* $\mathcal{A}_i^{\mathrm{room}}$ combines tasks.

(c) A *floor* $\mathcal{A}_i^{\mathrm{floor}}$ combines rooms.

(d) A *building* $\mathcal{A}_i^{\mathrm{bldg}}$ combines floors.

(e) A *neighborhood* $\mathcal{A}^{\mathrm{nbd}}$ combines buildings.

Fig. 1. String diagrams of MDPs, an example (the Patrol benchmark in Sect. 5).

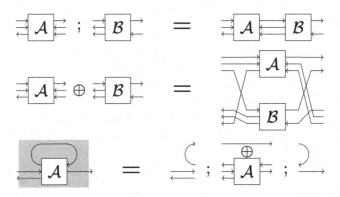

Fig. 2. Sequential composition ;, sum $\oplus$, and loops of MDPs, illustrated.

Compositional Description of MDPs by String Diagrams. The calculus we use for composing MDPs is that of *string diagrams*. Figure 1 shows an example used in experiments. String diagrams offer two basic composition operations, *sequential composition* ; and *sum* $\oplus$, illustrated in Fig. 2. The rearrangement of wires in $\mathcal{A} \oplus \mathcal{B}$ is for bundling up wires of the same direction. It is not essential.

We note that *loops* in MDPs can be described using these algebraic operations, as shown in Fig. 2. We extend MDPs with open ends so that they allow such composition; they are called *open MDPs*.

The formalism of string diagrams originates from category theory, specifically from the theory of *monoidal categories* (see e.g. [15, Chap. XI]). Capturing the mathematical essence of the algebraic structure of arrow composition $\circ$ and tensor product $\otimes$—they correspond to ; and $\oplus$ in this work, respectively—monoidal categories and string diagrams have found their application in a wide variety of scientific disciplines, such as quantum field theory [12], quantum mechanics and computation [8], linguistics [17], signal flow diagrams [3], and so on.

Our reason for using string diagrams to compose MDPs is twofold. Firstly, string diagrams offer a rich metatheory—developed over the years together with its various applications—that we can readily exploit. Specifically, the theory covers *functors*, which are (structure-preserving) homomorphisms between monoidal categories. We introduce a *solution functor* $\mathcal{S}\colon \mathbf{oMDP} \to \mathbb{S}$ from a category $\mathbf{oMDP}$ of open MDPs to a semantic category $\mathbb{S}$ that consists of solutions. We show that the functor $\mathcal{S}$ preserves two composition operations, that is,

$$\mathcal{S}(\mathcal{A}\,;\mathcal{B}) = \mathcal{S}(\mathcal{A})\,;\mathcal{S}(\mathcal{B}), \quad \mathcal{S}(\mathcal{A}\oplus\mathcal{B}) = \mathcal{S}(\mathcal{A})\oplus\mathcal{S}(\mathcal{B}), \tag{1}$$

where ; and $\oplus$ on the right-hand sides are *semantic composition* operations on $\mathbb{S}$. The equalities (1) are nothing but *compositionality*: the solution of the whole (on the left) is computed from the solutions of its parts (on the right).

The second reason for using string diagrams is that they offer an expressive language for composing MDPs—one that enables an efficient description of a number of realistic system models—as we demonstrate with benchmarks in Sect. 5.

Granularity of Semantics: A Challenge Towards Compositionality Now the main technical challenge is the design of a semantic domain $\mathbb{S}$ (it is a category in our framework). We shall call it the challenge of *granularity of semantics*; it is encountered generally when one aims at compositional solutions.

– The coarsest candidate for $\mathbb{S}$ is the original semantic domain; it consists of solutions and nothing else. This coarsest candidate is not enough most of the time: when components are composed, they may interact with each other via a richer interface than mere solutions. (Consider a team of two people. Its performance is usually not the sum of each member's, since there are other affecting factors such as work style, personal character, etc.)
– Therefore one would need to use a finer-grained semantic domain as $\mathbb{S}$, which, however, comes with a computational cost: in (1), one will have to carry around bigger data as intermediate solutions $\mathcal{S}(\mathcal{A})$ and $\mathcal{S}(\mathcal{B})$; their semantic composition will become more costly, too.

Therefore, in choosing $\mathbb{S}$, one should find the smallest enrichment[1] of the original semantic domain that addresses all relevant interactions between components and thus enables compositional solutions. This is a theoretical challenge.

In this work, following our recent work [20] that pursued a compositional solution of parity games, we use category theory as guidance in tackling the above challenge. Our goal is to obtain a solution functor $\mathcal{S}\colon \mathbf{oMDP} \to \mathbb{S}$ that preserves suitable algebraic structures (see (1)); the specific notion of algebra of our interest is that of *compact closed categories (compCC)*.

– The category $\mathbf{oMDP}$ organizes open MDPs as a category. It is a compCC, and its algebraic operations are defined as in Fig. 2.

---

[1] *Enrichment* here is in the natural language sense; it has nothing to do with the technical notion of *enriched category*.

- For the solution functor $\mathcal{S}$ to be compositional, the semantic category $\mathbb{S}$ *must itself be a compCC*, that is, $\mathbb{S}$ has to be enriched so that the compCC operations (; and $\oplus$) are well-defined.
- Once such a semantic domain $\mathbb{S}$ is obtained, choosing $\mathcal{S}$ and showing that it preserves the algebraic operations are straightforward.

Specifically, we find that $\mathbb{S}$ must be enriched with *reachability probabilities*, in addition to the desired solutions (namely expected rewards), to be a compCC. This enrichment is based on the *decomposition equalities* we observe in Sect. 3.

After all, our semantic category $\mathbb{S}$ is as follows: 1) an object is a pair of natural numbers describing an interface (how many entrances and exits); 2) an arrow is a collection of "semantics," collected over all possible (memoryless) schedulers τ, which records the expected reward that the scheduler τ yields when it traverses from each entrance to each exit. The last "semantics" is enriched so that it records the reachability probability, too, for the sake of compositionality.

Related Work. Compositional model checking is studied e.g. in [4,19,20]. Besides, probabilistic model checking is an actively studied topic; see [1, Chap. 10] for a comprehensive account. We shall make a detailed comparison with the works [11,14] that study compositional probabilistic model checking.

The work [14] introduces an assume-guarantee reasoning framework for parallel composition $\|$, as we already discussed. Parallel composition is out of our current scope; in fact, we believe that compositionality with respect to $\|$ requires a much bigger enrichment of a semantic domain $\mathbb{S}$ than mere reachability probabilities as in our work. The work [14] is remarkable in that its solution to this granularity problem—namely by assume-guarantee reasoning—is practically sensible (domain experts often have ideas about what contract to impose) and comes with automata-theoretic automation. That said, such contracts are not always automatically synthesized in [14], while our algorithm is fully automatic.

The work [11] is probably the closest to ours in the type of composition (sequential rather than parallel) and automation. However, the technical bases of the two works are quite different: theirs is the theory of *parametric MDPs* [18], which is why their emphasis is on parametrized components and interval solutions; ours is monoidal categories and some decomposition equalities (Sect. 3).

We note that the work [11] and ours are not strictly comparable. On the one hand, we do not need a crucial assumption in [11], namely that a locally optimal scheduler in each component is part of a globally optimal scheduler. The assumption limits the applicability of [11]—it practically forces each component to have only one exit. The assumption does not hold in our benchmarks Patrol and Wholesale (see Sect. 5). Our algorithm does not need the assumption since it collects the semantics of all relevant memoryless schedulers.

On the other hand, unlike [11], our algorithm is not parametric, so it cannot exploit the similarity of components if they only differ in parameter values. Note that the target problems are different, too (interval [11] vs. exact here).

Notations. For natural numbers m and n, we let $[m, n] := \{m, m + 1, \ldots, n - 1, n\}$; as a special case, we let $[m] := \{1, 2, \ldots, m\}$ (we let $[0] = \emptyset$ by convention). The disjoint union of two sets X, Y is denoted by $X + Y$.

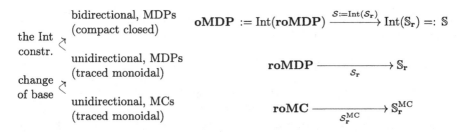

Fig. 3. Categories of MDPs/MCs, semantic categories, and solution functors.

2 String Diagrams of MDPs

We introduce our calculus for composing MDPs, namely *string diagrams of MDPs*. Our formal definition is via their *unidirectional* and *Markov chain (MC)* restrictions. This apparent detour simplifies the theoretical development, allowing us to exploit the existing categorical infrastructure on (monoidal) categories.

2.1 Outline

We first make an overview of our technical development. Although we use some categorical terminologies, prior knowledge of them is not needed in this outline.

Figure 3 is an overview of relevant categories and functors. The verification targets—*open MDPs*—are arrows in the compact closed category (compCC) **oMDP**. The operations ;, ⊕ of compCCs compose MDPs, as shown in Fig. 2. Our semantic category is denoted by $\mathbb{S}$, and our goal is to define a solution functor **oMDP** → $\mathbb{S}$ that is compositional. Mathematically, such a functor with the desired compositionality (cf. (1)) is called a *compact closed functor*.

Since its direct definition is tedious, our strategy is to obtain it from a unidirectional *rightward* framework $\mathcal{S}_{\mathbf{r}} \colon \mathbf{roMDP} \to \mathbb{S}_{\mathbf{r}}$, which canonically induces the desired bidirectional framework via the celebrated Int *construction* [10]. In particular, the category **oMDP** is defined by **oMDP** = Int(**roMDP**); so are the semantic category and the solution functor ($\mathbb{S} = \mathrm{Int}(\mathbb{S}_{\mathbf{r}})$, $\mathcal{S} = \mathrm{Int}(\mathcal{S}_{\mathbf{r}})$).

Going this way, a complication that one would encounter in a direct definition of **oMDP** (namely potential loops of transitions) is nicely taken care of by the Int construction. Another benefit is that some natural equational axioms in **oMDP**—such as the associativity of sequential composition ;—follow automatically from those in **roMDP**, which are much easier to verify.

Mathematically, the unidirectional framework $\mathcal{S}_{\mathbf{r}} \colon \mathbf{roMDP} \to \mathbb{S}_{\mathbf{r}}$ consists of *traced symmetric monoidal categories (TSMCs)* and *traced symmetric monoidal functors*; these are "algebras" of unidirectional graphs. The Int construction turns TSMCs into compCCs, which are "algebras" of bidirectional graphs.

Yet another restriction is given by *(rightward open) Markov chains (MCs)*. See the bottom row of Fig. 3. This MDP-to-MC restriction greatly simplifies our semantic development, freeing us from the bookkeeping of different schedulers. In fact, we can introduce (optimal memoryless) schedulers systematically by the categorical construction called *change of base* [5,6]; this way we obtain the semantic category $\mathbb{S}_\mathbf{r}$ from $\mathbb{S}_\mathbf{r}^{MC}$.

2.2   Open MDPs

We first introduce *open MDPs*; they have open ends via which they compose. They come with a notion of *arity*—the numbers of open ends on their left and right, distinguishing leftward and rightward ones. For example, the one on the right is from $(2,1)$ to $(1,3)$.

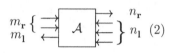

$$\tag{2}$$

Definition 2.1 (open MDP (oMDP)). *Let A be a non-empty finite set, whose elements are called* actions. *An* open MDP $\mathcal{A}$ *(over the action set A) is the tuple $(\overline{m}, \overline{n}, Q, A, E, P, R)$ of the following data. We say that it is from $\overline{m}$ to $\overline{n}$.*

1. *$\overline{m} = (m_\mathbf{r},\ m_\mathbf{l})$ and $\overline{n} = (n_\mathbf{r},\ n_\mathbf{l})$ are pairs of natural numbers; they are called the* left-arity *and the* right-arity, *respectively. Moreover (see (2)), elements of $[m_\mathbf{r} + n_\mathbf{l}]$ are called* entrances, *and those of $[n_\mathbf{r} + m_\mathbf{l}]$ are called* exits.
2. *Q is a finite set of* positions.
3. *$E : [m_\mathbf{r} + n_\mathbf{l}] \to Q + [n_\mathbf{r} + m_\mathbf{l}]$ is an entry function, which maps each entrance to either a position (in Q) or an exit (in $[n_\mathbf{r} + m_\mathbf{l}]$).*
4. *$P : Q \times A \times (Q + [n_\mathbf{r} + m_\mathbf{l}]) \to \mathbb{R}_{\geq 0}$ determines transition probabilities, where we require $\sum_{s' \in Q + [n_\mathbf{r} + m_\mathbf{l}]} P(s, a, s') \in \{0, 1\}$ for each $s \in Q$ and $a \in A$.*
5. *R is a reward function $R : Q \to \mathbb{R}_{\geq 0}$.*
6. *We impose the following "unique access to each exit" condition. Let* exits : $([m_\mathbf{r} + n_\mathbf{l}] + Q) \to \mathcal{P}([n_\mathbf{r} + m_\mathbf{l}])$ *be the* exit function *that collects all immediately reachable exits, that is, 1) for each $s \in Q$, exits$(s) = \{t \in [n_\mathbf{r} + m_\mathbf{l}] \mid \exists a \in A. P(s, a, t) > 0\}$, and 2) for each entrance $s \in [m_\mathbf{r} + n_\mathbf{l}]$, exits$(s) = \{E(s)\}$ if $E(s)$ is an exit and exits$(s) = \emptyset$ otherwise.*
   - *For all $s, s' \in [m_\mathbf{r} + n_\mathbf{l}] + Q$, if exits$(s) \cap$ exits$(s') \neq \emptyset$, then $s = s'$.*
   - *We further require that each exit is reached from an identical position by at most one action. That is, for each exit $t \in [n_\mathbf{r} + m_\mathbf{l}]$, $s \in Q$, and $a, b \in A$, if both $P(s, a, t) > 0$ and $P(s, b, t) > 0$, then $a = b$.*

Note that the unique access to each exit condition is for technical convenience; this can be easily enforced by adding an extra "access" position to an exit.

We define the semantics of open MDPs, which is essentially the standard semantics of MDPs given by expected cumulative rewards. In this paper, it suffices to consider memoryless schedulers (see Remark 2.1).

Definition 2.2 (path and scheduler). *Let $\mathcal{A} = (\overline{m}, \overline{n}, Q, A, E, P, R)$ be an open MDP. A (finite) path $\pi^{(i,j)}$ in $\mathcal{A}$ from an entrance $i \in [m_\mathbf{r} + n_\mathbf{l}]$ to an exit $j \in [n_\mathbf{r} + m_\mathbf{l}]$ is a finite sequence $i, s_1, \ldots, s_n, j$ such that $E(i) = s_1$ and for all $k \in [n]$, $s_k \in Q$. For each $k \in [n]$, $\pi_k^{(i,j)}$ denotes s_k, and $\pi_{n+1}^{(i,j)}$ denotes j. The set of all paths in $\mathcal{A}$ from i to j is denoted by $\mathrm{Path}^{\mathcal{A}}(i, j)$.*

A (memoryless) scheduler τ of $\mathcal{A}$ is a function $\tau : Q \to A$.

Remark 2.1. It is well-known (as hinted in [2]) that we can restrict to memoryless schedulers for optimal expected rewards, *assuming that* the MDP in question is almost surely terminating under any scheduler (†). We require the assumption (†) in our compositional framework, too, and it is true in all benchmarks in this paper. The assumption (†) must be checked only for the top-level (composed) MDP; (†) for its components can then be deduced.

Definition 2.3 (probability and reward of a path). *Let $\mathcal{A} = (\overline{m}, \overline{n}, Q, A, E, P, R)$ be an open MDP, $\tau : Q \to A$ be a scheduler of $\mathcal{A}$, and $\pi^{(i,j)}$ be a path in $\mathcal{A}$. The* probability $\mathrm{Pr}^{\mathcal{A},\tau}(\pi^{(i,j)})$ *of $\pi^{(i,j)}$ under τ is $\mathrm{Pr}^{\mathcal{A},\tau}(\pi^{(i,j)}) := \prod_{k=1}^{n} P(\pi_k^{(i,j)}, \tau(\pi_k^{(i,j)}), \pi_{k+1}^{(i,j)})$. The* reward $\mathrm{Rw}^{\mathcal{A}}(\pi^{(i,j)})$ *along the path $\pi^{(i,j)}$ is the sum of the position rewards, that is, $\mathrm{Rw}^{\mathcal{A}}(\pi^{(i,j)}) := \sum_{k \in [n]} R(\pi_k^{(i,j)})$.*

Our target problem on open MDPs is to compute the *expected cumulative reward* collected in a passage from a specified entrance i to a specified exit j. This is defined below, together with reachability probability, in the usual manner.

Definition 2.4 (reachability probability and expected (cumulative) reward of open MDPs). *Let $\mathcal{A}$ be an open MDP and τ be a scheduler, as in Definition 2.2. Let i be an entrance and j be an exit.*

The reachability probability $\mathrm{RPr}^{\mathcal{A},\tau}(i,j)$ *from i to j, in $\mathcal{A}$ under τ, is defined by $\mathrm{RPr}^{\mathcal{A},\tau}(i,j) := \sum_{\pi^{(i,j)} \in \mathrm{Path}^{\mathcal{A}}(i,j)} \mathrm{Pr}^{\mathcal{A},\tau}(\pi^{(i,j)})$.*

The expected (cumulative) reward $\mathrm{ERw}^{\mathcal{A},\tau}(i,j)$ *from i to j, in $\mathcal{A}$ under τ, is defined by $\mathrm{ERw}^{\mathcal{A},\tau}(i,j) := \sum_{\pi^{(i,j)} \in \mathrm{Path}^{\mathcal{A}}(i,j)} \mathrm{Pr}^{\mathcal{A},\tau}(\pi^{(i,j)}) \cdot \mathrm{Rw}^{\mathcal{A}}(\pi^{(i,j)})$. Note that the infinite sum here always converges to a finite value; this is because there are only finitely many positions in $\mathcal{A}$. See e.g. [1].*

Remark 2.2. In standard definitions such as Definition 2.4, it is common to either 1) assume $\mathrm{RPr}^{\mathcal{A},\tau}(i,j) = 1$ for technical convenience [11], or 2) allow $\mathrm{RPr}^{\mathcal{A},\tau}(i,j) < 1$, but in that case define $\mathrm{ERw}^{\mathcal{A},\tau}(i,j) := \infty$ [1]. These definitions are not suited for our purpose (and for compositional model checking in general), since we take into account multiple exits, to each of which the reachability probability is typically < 1, and we need non-∞ expected rewards over those exits for compositionality. Note that our definition of expected reward is not conditional (unlike [1, Rem. 10.74]): when the reachability probability from i to j is small, it makes the expected reward small as well. Our notion of expected reward can be thought of as a "weighted sum" of rewards.

2.3   Rightward Open MDPs and Traced Monoidal String Diagrams

Following the outline (Sect. 2.1), in this section we focus on (unidirectional) *rightward* open MDPs and introduce the "algebra" **roMDP** of them. The operations $;, \oplus, \mathrm{tr}$ of *traced symmetric monoidal categories (TSMCs)* compose rightward open MDPs in string diagrams.

$$(\mathcal{A} : l + m \to l + n)$$
$$\mapsto \left(\mathrm{tr}_{l;m,n}(\mathcal{A}) : m \to n \right), \qquad \text{as in}$$

Fig. 4. The trace operator.

Definition 2.5 (rightward open MDP (roMDP)). *An open MDP* $\mathcal{A} = (\overline{m}, \overline{n}, Q, A, E, P, R)$ *is* rightward *if all its entrances are on the left and all its exits are on the right, that is,* $\overline{m} = (m_{\mathbf{r}}, 0_{\mathbf{l}})$ *and* $\overline{n} = (n_{\mathbf{r}}, 0_{\mathbf{l}})$ *for some* $m_{\mathbf{r}}$ *and* $n_{\mathbf{r}}$. *We write* $\mathcal{A} = (m_{\mathbf{r}}, n_{\mathbf{r}}, Q, A, E, P, R)$, *dropping* 0 *from the arities.*

We say that a rightward open MDP $\mathcal{A}$ *is* from m to n, *writing* $\mathcal{A} : m \to n$, *if it is from* $(m, 0)$ *to* $(n, 0)$ *as an open MDP.*

We use an equivalence relation by *roMDP isomorphism* so that roMDPs satisfy TSMC axioms given in Sect. 2.4. See [21, Appendix A] for details.

We move on to introduce algebraic operations for composing rightward open MDPs. Two of them, namely *sequential composition* ; and *sum* $\oplus$, look like Fig. 2 except that all wires are rightward. The other major operation is the *trace operator* tr that realizes (unidirectional) loops, as illustrated in Fig. 4.

Definition 2.6 (sequential composition ; of roMDPs). *Let* $\mathcal{A} : m \to k$ *and* $\mathcal{B} : k \to n$ *be rightward open MDPs with the same action set* A *and with matching arities. Their* sequential composition $\mathcal{A}; \mathcal{B} : m \to n$ *is given by* $\mathcal{A}; \mathcal{B} := \left(m, n, Q^{\mathcal{A}} + Q^{\mathcal{B}}, A, E^{\mathcal{A};\mathcal{B}}, P^{\mathcal{A};\mathcal{B}}, [R^{\mathcal{A}}, R^{\mathcal{B}}] \right)$, *where*

- $E^{\mathcal{A};\mathcal{B}}(i) := E^{\mathcal{A}}(i)$ *if* $E^{\mathcal{A}}(i) \in Q^{\mathcal{A}}$, *and* $E^{\mathcal{A};\mathcal{B}}(i) := E^{\mathcal{B}}(E^{\mathcal{A}}(i))$ *otherwise (if the $\mathcal{A}$-entrance i goes to an $\mathcal{A}$-exit which is identified with a $\mathcal{B}$-entrance);*
- *the transition probabilities are defined in the following natural manner*

$$P^{\mathcal{A};\mathcal{B}}(s^{\mathcal{A}}, a, s') := \begin{cases} P^{\mathcal{A}}(s^{\mathcal{A}}, a, s') & \text{if } s' \in Q^{\mathcal{A}}, \\ \sum_{i \in [k]} P^{\mathcal{A}}(s^{\mathcal{A}}, a, i) \cdot \delta_{E^{\mathcal{B}}(i) = s'} & \text{otherwise (i.e. } s' \in Q^{\mathcal{B}} + [n]), \end{cases}$$

$$P^{\mathcal{A};\mathcal{B}}(s^{\mathcal{B}}, a, s') := \begin{cases} P^{\mathcal{B}}(s^{\mathcal{B}}, a, s') & \text{if } s' \in Q^{\mathcal{B}} + [n], \\ 0 & \text{otherwise,} \end{cases}$$

where δ *is a characteristic function (returning* 1 *if the condition is true);*
- *and* $[R^{\mathcal{A}}, R^{\mathcal{B}}] : Q^{\mathcal{A}} + Q^{\mathcal{B}} \to \mathbb{R}_{\geq 0}$ *combines* $R^{\mathcal{A}}, R^{\mathcal{B}}$ *by case distinction.*

Defining sum $\oplus$ of roMDPs is straightforward, following Fig. 2. See [21, Appendix A] for details.

The trace operator tr is primitive in the TSMC **roMDP**; it is crucial in defining bidirectional sequential composition shown in Fig. 2 (cf. Definition 2.9).

Definition 2.7 (the trace operator $\mathrm{tr}_{l;m,n}$ over roMDPs). *Let* $\mathcal{A} : l + m \to l + n$ *be a rightward open MDP. The* trace $\mathrm{tr}_{l;m,n}(\mathcal{A}) : m \to n$ *of* $\mathcal{A}$ *with respect to* l *is the roMDP* $\mathrm{tr}_{l;m,n}(\mathcal{A}) := \left(m, n, Q^{\mathcal{A}}, A, E, P, R^{\mathcal{A}} \right)$ *(cf. Fig. 4), where*

– The entry function E is defined naturally, using a sequence $i_0, \ldots, i_{k-1}$ of intermediate open ends (in $[l]$) until reaching a destination i_k.
Precisely, we let $i_0 := i + l$ and $i_j = E^{\mathcal{A}}(i_{j-1})$ for each j. We let k to be the first index at which i_k comes out of the loop, that is, 1) $i_j \in [l]$ for each $j \in [k-1]$, and 2) $i_k \in [l+1, l+n] + Q^{\mathcal{A}}$. Then we define $E(i)$ by the following: $E(i) := i_k - l$ if $i_k \in [l+1, l+n]$; and $E(i) := i_k$ otherwise.

– The transition probabilities P are defined as follows. We let $\mathrm{prec}(t)$ be the set of open ends in $[l]$—those which are in the loop—that eventually enter $\mathcal{A}$ at $t \in [l+1, n] + Q^{\mathcal{A}}$. Precisely, $\mathrm{prec}(t) := \{i \in [l] \mid \exists i_0, \ldots, i_k. i_0 = i, i_{j+1} = E(i_j) \text{(for each } j), i_k = t, i_0, \ldots, i_{k-1} \in [1, l], i_k \in [l+1, n] + Q^{\mathcal{A}}\}$. Using this,

$$P(q, a, q') := \begin{cases} P^{\mathcal{A}}(q, a, q' + l) + \sum_{i \in \mathrm{prec}(q'+l)} P^{\mathcal{A}}(q, a, i) & \text{if } q' \in [n], \\ P^{\mathcal{A}}(q, a, q') + \sum_{i \in \mathrm{prec}(q')} P^{\mathcal{A}}(q, a, i) & \text{otherwise, i.e. if } q' \in Q^{\mathcal{A}}. \end{cases}$$

Here $Q^{\mathcal{A}}$ and $[l]$ are assumed to be disjoint without loss of generality.

Remark 2.3. In string diagrams, it is common to annotate a wire with its type, such as $\xrightarrow{n}$ for $\mathrm{id}_n : n \to n$. It is also common to separate a wire for a sum type into wires of its component types, such as below on the left. Therefore the two diagrams below on the right designate the same mathematical entity. Note that, on its right-hand side, the type annotation 1 to each wire is omitted.

2.4   TSMC Equations Between roMDPs

Here we show that the three operations $;, \oplus, \mathrm{tr}$ on roMDPs satisfy the equational axioms of TSMCs [10], shown in Fig. 5. These equational axioms are not directly needed for compositional model checking. We nevertheless study them because 1) they validate some natural bookkeeping equivalences of roMDPs needed for their efficient handling, and 2) they act as a sanity check of the mathematical authenticity of our compositional framework. For example, the handling of open ends is subtle in Sect. 2.3—e.g. whether they should be positions or not—and the TSMC equational axioms led us to our current definitions.

The TSMC axioms use some "positionless" roMDPs as wires, such as identi-ties $\mathcal{I}_m$ ($\xrightarrow{m}$ in string diagrams) and swaps $\mathcal{S}_{m,n}$ ($\times$). See [21, Appendix A] for details. The proof of the following is routine. For details, see [21, Appendix B].

Theorem 2.1. *The three operations* $;, \oplus, \mathrm{tr}$ *on roMDPs, defined in Sect. 2.3, satisfy the equational axioms in Fig. 5 up-to isomorphisms (see [21, Appendix A] for details).*   □

Corollary 2.1 (a TSMC roMDP). *Let* roMDP *be the category whose objects are natural numbers and whose arrows are roMDPs over the action set A modulo isomorphisms. Then the operations* $;, \oplus, \mathrm{tr}, \mathcal{I}, \mathcal{S}$ *make* **roMDP** *a traced symmetric monoidal category (TSMC).*   □

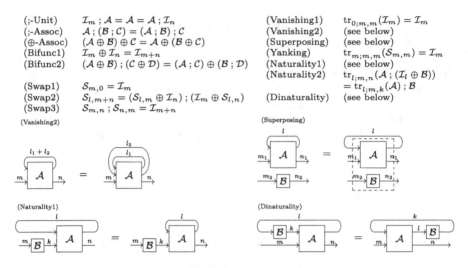

(;-Unit)	$\mathcal{I}_m \,;\, \mathcal{A} = \mathcal{A} = \mathcal{A}\,;\, \mathcal{I}_n$	(Vanishing1)	$\mathrm{tr}_{0;m,m}(\mathcal{I}_m) = \mathcal{I}_m$
(;-Assoc)	$\mathcal{A}\,;\,(\mathcal{B}\,;\,\mathcal{C}) = (\mathcal{A}\,;\,\mathcal{B})\,;\,\mathcal{C}$	(Vanishing2)	(see below)
(⊕-Assoc)	$(\mathcal{A}\oplus\mathcal{B})\oplus\mathcal{C} = \mathcal{A}\oplus(\mathcal{B}\oplus\mathcal{C})$	(Superposing)	(see below)
(Bifunc1)	$\mathcal{I}_m \oplus \mathcal{I}_n = \mathcal{I}_{m+n}$	(Yanking)	$\mathrm{tr}_{m;m,m}(\mathcal{S}_{m,m}) = \mathcal{I}_m$
(Bifunc2)	$(\mathcal{A}\oplus\mathcal{B})\,;\,(\mathcal{C}\oplus\mathcal{D}) = (\mathcal{A}\,;\,\mathcal{C})\oplus(\mathcal{B}\,;\,\mathcal{D})$	(Naturality1)	(see below)
		(Naturality2)	$\mathrm{tr}_{l;m,n}(\mathcal{A}\,;\,(\mathcal{I}_l \oplus \mathcal{B}))$
(Swap1)	$\mathcal{S}_{m,0} = \mathcal{I}_m$		$= \mathrm{tr}_{l;m,k}(\mathcal{A})\,;\,\mathcal{B}$
(Swap2)	$\mathcal{S}_{l,m+n} = (\mathcal{S}_{l,m}\oplus\mathcal{I}_n)\,;\,(\mathcal{I}_m \oplus \mathcal{S}_{l,n})$	(Dinaturality)	(see below)
(Swap3)	$\mathcal{S}_{m,n}\,;\,\mathcal{S}_{n,m} = \mathcal{I}_{m+n}$		

Fig. 5. The equational axioms of TSMCs, expressed for roMDPs, with some string diagram illustrations. Here we omit types of roMDPs; see [10] for details.

2.5   Open MDPs and "Compact Closed" String Diagrams

Following the outline in Sect. 2.1, we now introduce a bidirectional "compact closed" calculus of open MDPs (oMDPs), using the Int construction [10] that turns TSMCs in general into compact closed categories (compCCs).

The following definition simply says **oMDP** := Int(**roMDP**), although it uses concrete terms adapted to the current context.

Definition 2.8 (the category oMDP). *The category **oMDP** of open MDPs is defined as follows. Its objects are pairs $(m_\mathbf{r}, m_\mathbf{l})$ of natural numbers. Its arrows are defined by rightward open MDPs as follows:*

$$\frac{\textit{an arrow } (m_\mathbf{r}, m_\mathbf{l}) \longrightarrow (n_\mathbf{r}, n_\mathbf{l}) \textit{ in } \mathbf{oMDP}}{\textit{an arrow } \mathcal{A}\colon m_\mathbf{r} + n_\mathbf{l} \longrightarrow n_\mathbf{r} + m_\mathbf{l} \textit{ in } \mathbf{roMDP}, \textit{ i.e. an roMDP}} \qquad (3)$$

where the double lines $=$ *mean "is the same thing as."*

The definition may not immediately justify its name: no open MDPs appear there; only roMDPs do. The point is that we identify the roMDP $\mathcal{A}$ in (3) with the oMDP $\Psi(\mathcal{A})$ of the designated type, using "twists" in Fig. 6. See [21, Appendix A] for details.

We move on to describe algebraic operations for composing oMDPs. These operations come from the structure of **oMDP** as a compCC; the latter, in turn, arises canonically from the Int construction.

Definition 2.9 (; of oMDPs). *Let $\mathcal{A} : (m_\mathbf{r}, m_\mathbf{l}) \to (l_\mathbf{r}, l_\mathbf{l})$ and $\mathcal{B} : (l_\mathbf{r}, l_\mathbf{l}) \to (n_\mathbf{r}, n_\mathbf{l})$ be arrows in **oMDP** with the same action set A. Their sequential composition $\mathcal{A}\,;\,\mathcal{B} : (m_\mathbf{r}, m_\mathbf{l}) \to (n_\mathbf{r}, n_\mathbf{l})$ is defined by the string diagram in Fig. 7,*

Fig. 6. Turning oMDPs to roMDPs, and vice versa, via twists.

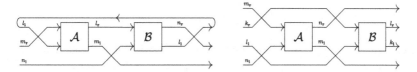

Fig. 7. String diagrams in **roMDP** for $\mathcal{A}\,;\mathcal{B}$, $\mathcal{A}\oplus\mathcal{B}$ in **oMDP**.

formulated in **roMDP**. *Textually the definition is* $\mathcal{A}\,;\mathcal{B} := \operatorname{tr}_{l_1;m_r+n_1,n_r+m_1}$
$\big((\mathcal{S}_{l_1,m_r}\oplus\mathcal{I}_{n_1})\,;(\mathcal{A}\oplus\mathcal{I}_{n_1})\,;(\mathcal{I}_{l_r}\oplus\mathcal{S}_{m_1,n_1})\,;(\mathcal{B}\oplus\mathcal{I}_{m_1})\,;(\mathcal{S}_{n_r,l_1}\oplus\mathcal{I}_{m_1})\big)$.

The definition of *sum* $\oplus$ of oMDPs is similarly shown in the string diagram in Fig. 7, formulated in **roMDP**. Definition of "wires" such as identities, swaps, *units* ($\subset$ in string diagrams) and *counits* ($\supset$) is easy, too.

Theorem 2.2 (oMDP is a compCC). *The category* **oMDP** *(Definition 2.8), equipped with the operations* $;, \oplus,$ *is a compCC.* ☐

3 Decomposition Equalities for Open Markov Chains

Here we exhibit some basic equalities that decompose the behavior of (rightward open) Markov chains. We start with such equalities on *reachability probabilities* (which are widely known) and extend them to equalities on *expected rewards* (which seem less known). Notably, the latter equalities involve not only expected rewards but also reachability probabilities.

Here we focus on *rightward open Markov chains (roMCs)*, since the extension to richer settings is taken care of by categorical constructions. See Fig. 3.

Definition 3.1 (roMC). *A* rightward open Markov chain (roMC) $\mathcal{C}$ *from* m *to* n *is an roMDP from* m *to* n *over the singleton action set* $\{\star\}$.

For an roMC $\mathcal{C}$, *its* reachability probability $\operatorname{RPr}^{\mathcal{C}}(i,j)$ *and* expected reward $\operatorname{ERw}^{\mathcal{C}}(i,j)$ *are defined as in Definition 2.4. The scheduler* τ *is omitted since it is unique.*

Rightward open MCs, as a special case of roMDPs, form a TSMC (Corollary 2.1). It is denoted by **roMC**.

The following equalities are well-known, although they are not stated in terms of open MCs. Recall that $\operatorname{RPr}^{\mathcal{C}}(i,k)$ is the probability of reaching the exit k from the entrance i in $\mathcal{C}$ (Definition 2.4). Recall also the definitions of $\mathcal{C}\,;\mathcal{D}$ (Definition 2.6) and $\operatorname{tr}_{l;m,n}(\mathcal{E})$ (Definition 2.7), which are essentially as in Fig. 2 and Fig. 4.

Proposition 3.1 (decomposition equalities for RPr). *Let* $\mathcal{C} : m \to l$, $\mathcal{D} : l \to n$ *and* $\mathcal{E} : l + m \to l + n$ *be roMCs. The following matrix equalities hold.*

$$\left[\mathrm{RPr}^{\mathcal{C};\mathcal{D}}(i,j)\right]_{i\in[m],j\in[n]} = \left[\mathrm{RPr}^{\mathcal{C}}(i,k)\right]_{i\in[m],k\in[l]} \cdot \left[\mathrm{RPr}^{\mathcal{D}}(k,j)\right]_{k\in[l],j\in[n]}, \quad (4)$$

$$\left[\mathrm{RPr}^{\mathrm{tr}_{l;m,n}(\mathcal{E})}(i,j)\right]_{i\in[m],j\in[n]} = \left[\mathrm{RPr}^{\mathcal{E}}(l+i,l+j)\right]_{i\in[m],j\in[n]} + \sum_{d\in\mathbb{N}} A \cdot B^d \cdot C. \quad (5)$$

Here $\left[\mathrm{RPr}^{\mathcal{C};\mathcal{D}}(i,j)\right]_{i\in[m],j\in[n]}$ *denotes the* $m \times n$ *matrix with the designated components; other matrices are similar. The matrices* A, B, C *are given by* $A := \left[\mathrm{RPr}^{\mathcal{E}}(l+i,k)\right]_{i\in[m],k\in[l]}$, $B := \left[\mathrm{RPr}^{\mathcal{E}}(k,k')\right]_{k\in[l],k'\in[l]}$, *and* $C := \left[\mathrm{RPr}^{\mathcal{E}}(k',l+j)\right]_{k'\in[l],j\in[n]}$. *In the last line, note that the matrix in the middle is the d-th power.* □

The first equality is easy, distinguishing cases on the intermediate open end k (mutually exclusive since MCs are rightward). The second says

which is intuitive. Here, the small circles in the diagram correspond to dead ends. It is known as *Girard's execution formula* [7] in linear logic.

We now extend Prop. 3.1 to expected rewards $\mathrm{ERw}^{\mathcal{C}}(i,j)$.

Proposition 3.2 (decomposition eq. for ERw). *Let* $\mathcal{C} : m \to l$, $\mathcal{D} : l \to n$ *and* $\mathcal{E} : l + m \to l + n$ *be roMCs. The following equalities of matrices hold.*

$$\begin{aligned}\left[\mathrm{ERw}^{\mathcal{C};\mathcal{D}}(i,j)\right]_{i\in[m],j\in[n]} &= \left[\mathrm{RPr}^{\mathcal{C}}(i,k)\right]_{i\in[m],k\in[l]} \cdot \left[\mathrm{ERw}^{\mathcal{D}}(k,j)\right]_{k\in[l],j\in[n]} \\ &\quad + \left[\mathrm{ERw}^{\mathcal{C}}(i,k)\right]_{i\in[m],k\in[l]} \cdot \left[\mathrm{RPr}^{\mathcal{D}}(k,j)\right]_{k\in[l],j\in[n]},\end{aligned} \quad (6)$$

$$\left[\mathrm{ERw}^{\mathrm{tr}_{l;m,n}(\mathcal{E})}(i,j)\right]_{i\in[m],j\in[n]} = \left[\mathrm{ERw}^{\mathcal{E}}(l+i,l+j)\right]_{i\in[m],j\in[n]} + \sum_{d\in\mathbb{N}} A \cdot B^d \cdot C. \quad (7)$$

Here A, B, C *are the following* $m \times 2l \times 2l \times 2l \times n$ *matrices.*

$$A = \left(\left[\mathrm{RPr}^{\mathcal{E}}(l+i,k)\right]_{i\in[m],k\in[l]} \quad \left[\mathrm{ERw}^{\mathcal{E}}(l+i,k)\right]_{i\in[m],k\in[l]}\right),$$

$$B = \begin{pmatrix} \left[\mathrm{RPr}^{\mathcal{E}}(k,k')\right]_{k\in[l],k'\in[l]} & \left[\mathrm{ERw}^{\mathcal{E}}(k,k')\right]_{k\in[l],k'\in[l]} \\ \left[0\right]_{k\in[l],k'\in[l]} & \left[\mathrm{RPr}^{\mathcal{E}}(k,k')\right]_{k\in[l],k'\in[l]} \end{pmatrix},$$

$$C = \begin{pmatrix} \left[\mathrm{ERw}^{\mathcal{E}}(k',l+j)\right]_{k'\in[l],j\in[n]} \\ \left[\mathrm{RPr}^{\mathcal{E}}(k',l+j)\right]_{k'\in[l],j\in[n]} \end{pmatrix}.$$

□

Proposition 3.2 seems new, although proving them is not hard once the statements are given (see [21, Appendix C] for details). They enable one to compute the expected rewards of composite roMCs $\mathcal{C};\mathcal{D}$ and $\mathrm{tr}_{l;m,n}\mathcal{E}$ from those of component roMCs $\mathcal{C}, \mathcal{D}, \mathcal{E}$. They also signify the role of reachability probabilities in such computation, suggesting their use in the definition of semantic categories (cf. granularity of semantics in Sect. 1).

The last equalities in Propositions 3.1 and 3.2 involve infinite sums $\sum_{d\in\mathbb{N}}$, and one may wonder how to compute them. A key is their characterization as *least fixed points* via the Kleene theorem: the desired quantity on the left side (RPr or ERw) is a solution of a suitable linear equation; see Proposition 3.3. With the given definitions, the proof of Propositions 3.1 and 3.2 is (lengthy but) routine work (see e.g. [1, Thm. 10.15]).

Proposition 3.3 (linear equation characterization for (5) and (7)). *Let* $\mathcal{E} : l + m \rightarrow l + n$ *be an roMC, and* $k \in [l + 1, l + n]$ *be a specified exit of* $\mathcal{E}$. *Consider the following linear equation on an unknown vector* $[x_i]_{i\in[l+m]}$:

$$\left[x_i\right]_{i\in[l+m]} = \left[\mathrm{RPr}^{\mathcal{E}}(i,k)\right]_{i\in[l+m]} + \left[\mathrm{RPr}^{\mathcal{E}}(i,j)\right]_{i\in[l+m],j\in[l]} \cdot \left[x_j\right]_{j\in[l]}. \quad (8)$$

Consider the least solution $[\tilde{x}_i]_{i\in[l+m]}$ *of the equation. Then its part* $[\tilde{x}_{i+l}]_{i\in[m]}$ *is given by the vector* $\left(\mathrm{RPr}^{\mathrm{tr}_{l;m,n}(\mathcal{E})}(i, k - l)\right)_{i\in[m]}$ *of suitable reachability probabilities.*

Moreover, consider the following linear equation on an unknown $[y_i]_{i\in[l+m]}$:

$$\begin{aligned}\left[y_i\right]_{i\in[l+m]} = &\left[\mathrm{ERw}^{\mathcal{E}}(i,k)\right]_{i\in[l+m]} + \left[\mathrm{ERw}^{\mathcal{E}}(i,j)\right]_{i\in[l+m],j\in[l]} \cdot \left[x_j\right]_{j\in[l]} \\ &+ \left[\mathrm{RPr}^{\mathcal{E}}(i,j)\right]_{i\in[l+m],j\in[l]} \cdot \left[y_j\right]_{j\in[l]},\end{aligned} \quad (9)$$

where the unknown $[x_j]_{j\in[l]}$ *is shared with* (8). *Consider the least solution* $[\tilde{y}_i]_{i\in[l+m]}$ *of the equation. Then its part* $[\tilde{y}_{i+l}]_{i\in[m]}$ *is given by the vector of suitable expected rewards, that is,* $[\tilde{y}_{i+l}]_{i\in[m]} = \left(\mathrm{ERw}^{\mathrm{tr}_{l;m,n}(\mathcal{E})}(i, k - l)\right)_{i\in[m]}$.

We can modify the linear Eqs. (8,9)—removing unreachable positions, specifically—so that they have unique solutions without changing the least ones. One can then solve these linear equations to compute the reachabilities and expected rewards in (5,7). This is a well-known technique for computing reachability probabilities [1, Thm. 10.19]; it is not hard to confirm the correctness of our current extension to expected rewards.

4   Semantic Categories and Solution Functors

We build on the decomposition equalities (Proposition 3.2) and define the semantic category $\mathbb{S}$ for compositional model checking. This is the main construct in our framework. Our definitions proceed in three steps, from roMCs to roMDPs to oMDPs (Fig. 3). The gaps between them are filled in using general constructions from category theory.

4.1   Semantic Category for Rightward Open MCs

We first define the semantic category $\mathbb{S}_r^{\mathrm{MC}}$ for roMCs (Fig. 3, bottom right).

Definition 4.1 (objects and arrows of $\mathbb{S}_r^{MC}$). *The category $\mathbb{S}_r^{MC}$ has natural numbers m as objects. Its arrow $f: m \to n$ is given by an assignment, for each pair (i, j) of $i \in [m]$ and $j \in [n]$, of a pair $(p_{i,j}, r_{i,j})$ of nonnegative real numbers. There pairs $(p_{i,j}, r_{i,j})$ are subject to the following conditions.*

- *(Subnormality) $\sum_{j \in [n]} p_{i,j} \leq 1$ for each $i \in [m]$.*
- *(Realizability) $p_{i,j} = 0$ implies $r_{i,j} = 0$.*

An illustration is in Fig. 8. For an object m, each $i \in [m]$ is identified with an open end, much like in **roMC** and **roMDP**. For an arrow $f: m \to n$, the pair $f(i, j) = (p_{i,j}, r_{i,j})$ encodes a reachability probability and an expected reward, from an open end i to j; together they represent a possible roMC behavior.

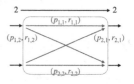

Fig. 8. An arrow $f: 2 \to 2$ in $\mathbb{S}_r^{MC}$.

We go on to define the algebraic operations of $\mathbb{S}_r^{MC}$ as a TSMC. While there is a categorical description of $\mathbb{S}_r^{MC}$ using a *monad* [16], we prefer a concrete definition here. See [21, Appendix D] for the categorical definition of $\mathbb{S}_r^{MC}$.

Definition 4.2 (sequential composition ; of $\mathbb{S}_r^{MC}$). *Let $f: m \to l$ and $g: l \to n$ be arrows in $\mathbb{S}_r^{MC}$. Their sequential composition $f ; g: m \to n$ of f and g is defined as follows: letting $f(i, j) = (p_{i,j}^f, r_{i,j}^f)$ and $g(i, j) = (p_{i,j}^g, r_{i,j}^g)$, then $f ; g(i) := (p_{i,j}^{f;g}, r_{i,j}^{f;g})_{j \in [n]}$ is given by*

$$\left[p_{i,j}^{f;g} \right]_{i \in [m], j \in [n]} = \left[p_{i,k}^f \right]_{i \in [m], k \in [l]} \cdot \left[p_{k,j}^g \right]_{k \in [l], j \in [n]},$$

$$\left[r_{i,j}^{f;g} \right]_{i \in [m], j \in [n]} = \left[p_{i,k}^f \right]_{i \in [m], k \in [l]} \cdot \left[r_{k,j}^g \right]_{k \in [l], j \in [n]} + \left[r_{i,k}^f \right]_{i \in [m], k \in [l]} \cdot \left[p_{k,j}^g \right]_{k \in [l], j \in [n]}$$

The sum $\oplus$ and the trace operator tr of $\mathbb{S}_r^{MC}$ are defined similarly. To define and prove axioms of the trace operator (Fig. 5), we exploit the categorical theory of *strong unique decomposition categories* [9]. See [21, Appendix D].

Definition 4.3 ($\mathbb{S}_r^{MC}$ as a TSMC). *$\mathbb{S}_r^{MC}$ is a TSMC, with its operations ;, $\oplus$, tr.*

Once we expand the above definitions to concrete terms, it is evident that they mirror the decomposition equalities. Indeed, the sequential composition ; mirrors the first equalities in Propositions 3.1 and 3.2. The same holds for the trace operator, too. Therefore, one can think of the above categorical development in Definition 4.2 and Definition 4.3 as a structured *lifting* of the (local) equalities in Propositions 3.1 and 3.2 to the (global) categorical structures, as shown in Fig. 3.

Once we found the semantic domain $\mathbb{S}_r^{MC}$, the following definition is easy.

Definition 4.4 ($\mathcal{S}_r^{MC}$). *The solution functor $\mathcal{S}_r^{MC}: \textbf{roMC} \to \mathbb{S}_r^{MC}$ is defined as follows. It carries an object m (a natural number) to the same m; it carries an arrow $\mathcal{C}: m \to n$ in $\textbf{roMC}$ to the arrow $\mathcal{S}_r^{MC}(\mathcal{C}): m \to n$ in $\mathbb{S}_r^{MC}$, defined by*

$$\mathcal{S}_r^{MC}(\mathcal{C})(i, j) := \left(\text{RPr}^{\mathcal{C}}(i, j), \text{ERw}^{\mathcal{C}}(i, j) \right), \tag{10}$$

using reachability probabilities and expected rewards (Definition 2.4).

Theorem 4.1 ($\mathcal{S}_\mathbf{r}^{\mathrm{MC}}$ is compositional). *The correspondence $\mathcal{S}_\mathbf{r}^{\mathrm{MC}}$, defined in (10), is a traced symmetric monoidal functor. That is, $\mathcal{S}_\mathbf{r}^{\mathrm{MC}}(\mathcal{C}\,;\mathcal{D}) = \mathcal{S}_\mathbf{r}^{\mathrm{MC}}(\mathcal{C})\,;$ $\mathcal{S}_\mathbf{r}^{\mathrm{MC}}(\mathcal{D})$, $\mathcal{S}_\mathbf{r}^{\mathrm{MC}}(\mathcal{C}\oplus\mathcal{D}) = \mathcal{S}_\mathbf{r}^{\mathrm{MC}}(\mathcal{C})\oplus\mathcal{S}_\mathbf{r}^{\mathrm{MC}}(\mathcal{D})$, and $\mathcal{S}_\mathbf{r}^{\mathrm{MC}}(\mathrm{tr}(\mathcal{E})) = \mathrm{tr}(\mathcal{S}_\mathbf{r}^{\mathrm{MC}}(\mathcal{E}))$. Here $;, \oplus, \mathrm{tr}$ on the left are from Sect. 2.3; those on the right are from Definition 4.3.* □

4.2 Semantic Category of Rightward Open MDPs

We extend the theory in Sect. 4.1 from MCs to MDPs (Fig. 3). In particular, on the semantics side, we have to bundle up all possible behaviors of an MDP under different schedulers. We find that this is done systematically by *change of base* [5,6]. We use the following notation for fixing scheduler τ.

Definition 4.5 (roMC $\mathrm{MC}(\mathcal{A},\tau)$ induced by $\mathcal{A},\tau$). *Let $\mathcal{A}: m \to n$ be a rightward open MDP and $\tau: Q^{\mathcal{A}} \to A$ be a memoryless scheduler. The rightward open MC $\mathrm{MC}(\mathcal{A},\tau)$ induced by $\mathcal{A}$ and τ is $(m, n, Q^{\mathcal{A}}, \{\star\}, E^{\mathcal{A}}, P^{\mathrm{MC}(\mathcal{A},\tau)}, R^{\mathcal{A}})$, where for each $s \in Q$ and $t \in ([n_\mathbf{r} + m_\mathbf{l}] + Q)$, $P^{\mathrm{MC}(\mathcal{A},\tau)}(s, \star, t) := P^{\mathcal{A}}(s, \tau(s), t)$.*

Much like in Sect. 4.1, we first describe the semantic category $\mathbb{S}_\mathbf{r}$ in concrete terms. We later use the categorical machinery to define its algebraic structure.

Definition 4.6 (objects and arrows of $\mathbb{S}_\mathbf{r}$). *The category $\mathbb{S}_\mathbf{r}$ has natural numbers m as objects. Its arrow $F: m \to n$ is given by a set $\{f_i: m \to n \text{ in} \mathbb{S}_\mathbf{r}^{\mathrm{MC}}\}_{i\in I}$ of arrows of the same type in $\mathbb{S}_\mathbf{r}^{\mathrm{MC}}$ (I is an arbitrary index set).*

The above definition of arrows—collecting arrows in $\mathbb{S}_\mathbf{r}^{\mathrm{MC}}$, each of which corresponds to the behavior of $\mathrm{MC}(\mathcal{A},\tau)$ for each τ—follows from the change of base construction (specifically with the powerset functor $\mathcal{P}$ on the category **Set** of sets). Its general theory gives sequential composition $;$ for free (concretely described in Definition 4.7), together with equational axioms. See [21, Appendix D]. Sum $\oplus$ and trace tr are not covered by general theory, but we can define them analogously to $;$ in the current setting. Thus, for $\oplus$ and tr as well, we are using change of base as an inspiration.

Here is a concrete description of algebraic operations. It applies the corresponding operation of $\mathbb{S}_\mathbf{r}^{\mathrm{MC}}$ in the elementwise manner.

Definition 4.7 ($;, \oplus, \mathrm{tr}$ in $\mathbb{S}_\mathbf{r}$). *Let $F: m \to l$, $G: l \to n$, $H: l+m \to l+n$ be arrows in $\mathbb{S}_\mathbf{r}$. Their sequential composition $F\,;G$ of F and G is given by $F\,;G := \{f\,;g \mid f \in F, g \in G\}$ where $f\,;g$ is the sequential composition of f and g in $\mathbb{S}_\mathbf{r}^{\mathrm{MC}}$. The trace $\mathrm{tr}_{l;m,n}(H): m \to n$ of H with respect to l is given by $\mathrm{tr}_{l;m,n}(H) := \{\mathrm{tr}_{l;m,n}(h) \mid h \in H\}$ where $\mathrm{tr}_{l;m,n}(h)$ is the trace of h with respect to l in $\mathbb{S}_\mathbf{r}^{\mathrm{MC}}$.*

Sum $\oplus$ in $\mathbb{S}_\mathbf{r}$ is defined analogously, applying the operation in $\mathbb{S}_\mathbf{r}^{\mathrm{MC}}$ elementwise. See [21, Appendix A] for details.

Theorem 4.2. *$\mathbb{S}_\mathbf{r}$ is a TSMC.* □

We now define a solution functor and prove its compositionality.

Definition 4.8 (S_r). *The* solution functor S_r: **roMDP** $\rightarrow$ S_r *is defined as follows. It carries an object $m \in \mathbb{N}$ to m, and an arrow $\mathcal{A}$: $m \rightarrow n$ in **roMDP** to $S_r(\mathcal{A})$: $m \rightarrow n$ in S_r. The latter is defined in the following elementwise manner, using S_r^{MC} in Definition 4.4.*

$$S_r(\mathcal{A}) := \left\{ S_r^{\mathrm{MC}}(\mathrm{MC}(\mathcal{A}, \tau)) \,\middle|\, \tau : Q^{\mathcal{A}} \rightarrow A \text{ a (memoryless) scheduler} \right\}. \quad (11)$$

Theorem 4.3 (compositionality). *The correspondence S_r: **roMDP** $\rightarrow$ S_r is a traced symmetric monoidal functor, preserving $;, \oplus, \mathrm{tr}$ as in Thm. 4.1.* □

Remark 4.1 (memoryless schedulers). Our restriction to memoryless schedulers (cf. Definition 2.2) plays a crucial role in the proof of Theorem 4.3, specifically for the trace operator (i.e. loops, cf. Fig. 4). Intuitively, a *memoryful* scheduler for a loop may act differently in different iterations. Its technical consequence is that the elementwise definition of tr, as in Definition 4.7, no longer works for memoryful schedulers.

4.3 Semantic Category of MDPs

Finally, we extend from (unidirectional) roMDPs to (bidirectional) oMDPs (i.e. from the second to the first row in Fig. 3). The system-side construction is already presented in Sect. 2.5; the semantical side, described here, follows the same Int construction [10]. The common intuition is that of twists, see Fig. 6.

Definition 4.9 (the semantic category S). *We define $S = \mathrm{Int}(S_r)$. Concretely, its objects are pairs (m_r, m_l) of natural numbers. Its arrows are given by arrows of S_r as follows:*

$$\frac{an \ arrow \ F: (m_r, m_l) \longrightarrow (n_r, n_l) \ in \ S}{an \ arrow \ F: m_r + n_l \longrightarrow n_r + m_l \ in \ S_r} \quad (12)$$

By general properties of Int, S is a compact closed category (compCC).

The Int construction applies not only to categories but also to functors.

Definition 4.10 (S). *The* solution functor S: **oMDP** $\rightarrow$ S *is defined by $S = \mathrm{Int}(S_r)$.*

The following is our main theorem.

Theorem 4.4 (the solution S is compositional). *The solution functor S: **oMDP** $\rightarrow$ S is a compact closed functor, preserving operations $;, \oplus$ as in*

$$S(\mathcal{A} ; \mathcal{B}) = S(\mathcal{A}) ; S(\mathcal{B}), \quad S(\mathcal{A} \oplus \mathcal{B}) = S(\mathcal{A}) \oplus S(\mathcal{B}). \quad □$$

We can easily confirm, from Definitions 4.4 and 4.8, that S computes the solution we want. Given an open MDP $\mathcal{A}$, an entrance i and an exit j, S returns the set

$$\left\{ \left(\mathrm{RPr}^{\mathrm{MC}(\mathcal{A}, \tau)}(i, j), \mathrm{ERw}^{\mathrm{MC}(\mathcal{A}, \tau)}(i, j) \right) \,\middle|\, \tau \text{ is a memoryless scheduler} \right\} \quad (13)$$

of pairs of a reachability probability and expected reward, under different schedulers, in a passage from i to j.

Remark 4.2 (synthesizing an optimal scheduler). The compositional solution functor $\mathcal{S}$ abstracts away schedulers and only records their results (see (13) where τ is not recorded). At the implementation level, we can explicitly record schedulers so that our compositional algorithm also synthesizes an optimal scheduler. We do not do so here for theoretical simplicity.

5   Implementation and Experiments

Meager Semantics. Since our problem is to compute optimal expected rewards, in our compositional algorithm, we can ignore those intermediate results which are *totally subsumed* by other results (i.e. those which come from clearly suboptimal schedulers). This notion of *subsumption* is formalized as an order $\leq$ between parallel arrows in $\mathbb{S}_{\mathbf{r}}^{MC}$ (cf. Definition 4.1): $(p_{i,j}, r_{i,j})_{i,j} \leq (p'_{i,j}, r'_{i,j})_{i,j}$ if $p_{i,j} \leq p'_{i,j}$ and $r_{i,j} \leq r'_{i,j}$ for each i, j. Our implementation works with this *meager semantics* for better performance; specifically, it removes elements of $\mathcal{S}_{\mathbf{r}}(\mathcal{A})$ in (11) that are subsumed by others. It is possible to formulate this meager semantics as categories and functors, compare it with the semantics in Sect. 4, and prove its correctness. We defer it to another venue for lack of space.

Implementation. We implemented the compositional solution functor $\mathcal{S} \colon \mathbf{oMDP} \to \mathbb{S}$, using the meager semantics as discussed. This prototype implementation is in Python and called CompMDP.

CompMDP takes a string diagram $\mathcal{A}$ of open MDPs as input; they are expressed in a textual format that uses operations $;, \oplus$ (such as the textual expression in Definition 2.9). Note that we are abusing notations here, identifying a string diagram of oMDPs and the composite oMDP $\mathcal{A}$ denoted by it.

Given such input $\mathcal{A}$, CompMDP returns the arrow $\mathcal{S}(\mathcal{A})$, which is concretely given by pairs of a reachability probability and expected reward shown in (13) (we have suboptimal pairs removed, as discussed above). Since different pairs correspond to different schedulers, we choose a pair in which the expected reward is the greatest. This way we answer the optimal expected reward problem.

Freezing. In the input format of CompMDP, we have an additional *freeze* operator: any expression inside it is considered monolithic, and thus CompMDP does not solve it compositionally. Those frozen oMDPs—i.e., those expressed by frozen expressions—are solved by PRISM [13] in our implementation.

Freezing allows us to choose how deep—in the sense of the nesting of string diagrams—we go compositional. For example, when a component oMDP $\mathcal{A}_0$ is small but has many loops, fully compositional model checking of $\mathcal{A}_0$ can be more expensive than (monolithic) PRISM. Freezing is useful in such situations.

We have found experimentally that the degree of freezing often should not be extremal (i.e. none or all). The optimal degree, which should be thus somewhere intermediate, is not known a priori.

However, there are not too many options (the number of layers in compositional model description), and freezing a half is recommended, both from our experience and for the purpose of binary search.

We require that a frozen oMDP should have a unique exit. Otherwise, an oMDP with a specified exit can have the reachability probability < 1, in which case PRISM returns ∞ as the expected reward. The last is different from our definition of expected reward (Remark 2.2).

Research Questions. We posed the following questions.

RQ1. Does the compositionality of CompMDP help improve performance?

RQ2. How much do we benefit from freezing, i.e., a feature that allows us to choose the degree of compositionality?

RQ3. What is the absolute performance of CompMDP?

RQ4. Does the formalism of string digrams accommodate real-world models, enabling their compositional model checking?

RQ5. On which (compositional) models does CompMDP work well?

Experiment Setting. We conducted experiments on Apple 2.3 GHz Dual-Core Intel Core i5 with 16 GB of RAM. We designed three benchmarks, called Patrol, Wholesale, and Packets, as string diagrams of MDPs. Patrol is sketched in Fig. 1; it has layers of *tasks, rooms, floors, buildings* and a *neighborhood.*

Wholesale is similar to Patrol, with four layers (*item, dispatch, pipeline, wholesale*), but their transition structures are more complex: they have more loops, and more actions are enabled in each position, compared to Patrol. The lowest-level component MDP is much larger, too: an *item* in Wholesale has 5000 positions, while a *task* in Patrol has a unique position.

Packets has two layers: the lower layer models a transmission of 100 packets with probabilistic failure. The upper layer is a sequence of copies of 2–5 variations of the lower layer—in total, we have 50 copies—modeling 50 batches of packets

For Patrol and Wholesale, we conducted experiments with varying *degree of identification (DI)*; this can be seen as an ablation study. These benchmarks have identical copies of a component MDP in their string diagrams; high DI means that these copies are indeed expressed as multiple occurrences of the same variable, informing CompMDP to reuse the intermediate solution. As DI goes lower, we introduce new variables for these copies and let them look different to CompMDP. Specifically, we have twice as many variables for DI-mid, and three (Patrol) or four (Wholesale) times as many for DI-low, as for DI-high.

For Packets, we conducted experiments with different degrees of freezing (FZ). FZ-none indicates no freezing, where our compositional algorithm digs all the way down to individual positions as component MDPs. FZ-all freezes everything, which means we simply used PRISM (no compositionality). FZ-int. (*intermediate*) freezes the lower of the two layers. Note that this includes the performance comparison between CompMDP and PRISM (i.e. FZ-all).

For Patrol and Wholesale, we also compared the performance of CompMDP and PRISM using their simple variations Patrol5 and Wholesale5. We did not use other variations (Patrol/Wholesale1–4) since the translation of the models to the PRISM format blowed up.

Table 1. Experimental results.

benchmark	$|Q|$	$|E|$	exec. time [s] DI-high	DI-mid	DI-low	benchmark	$|Q|$	$|E|$	exec. time [s] FZ-none	FZ-int.	FZ-all (PRISM)
Patrol1	10^8	10^8	21	42	83						
Patrol2	10^8	10^8	23	48	90	Packets1	$2.5\cdot10^5$	$5\cdot10^5$	TO	1	65
Patrol3	10^9	10^9	22	43	89	Packets2	$2.5\cdot10^5$	$5\cdot10^5$	TO	3	64
Patrol4	10^9	10^9	30	60	121	Packets3	$2.5\cdot10^5$	$5\cdot10^5$	TO	1	56
Wholesale1	10^8	$2\cdot10^8$	130	260	394	Packets4	$2.5\cdot10^5$	$5\cdot10^5$	TO	3	56
Wholesale2	10^8	$2\cdot10^8$	92	179	274	Patrol5	10^8	10^8	22	22	TO
Wholesale3	$2\cdot10^8$	$4\cdot10^8$	6	12	23	Wholesale5	$5\cdot10^7$	10^8	TO	14	TO
Wholesale4	$2\cdot10^8$	$4\cdot10^8$	129	260	393						

$|Q|$ is the number of positions; $|E|$ is the number of transitions (only counting action branching, not probabilistic branching); execution time is the average of five runs, in sec.; timeout (TO) is 1200 sec.

Results and Discussion. Table 1 summarizes the experiment results.

RQ1. A big advantage of compositional verification is that it can reuse intermediate results. This advantage is clearly observed in the ablation experiments with the benchmarks Patrol1–4 and Wholesale1–4: as the degree of reuse goes $1/2$ and $1/3$–$1/4$ (see above), the execution time grew inverse-proportionally. Moreover, with the benchmarks Packets1–4, Patrol5 and Wholesale5, we see that compositionality greatly improves performance, compared to PRISM (FZ-all). Overall, we can say that compositionality has clear performance advantages in probabilistic model checking.

RQ2. The Packets experiments show that controlling the degree of compositionality is important. Packet's lower layer (frozen in FZ-int.) is a large and complex model, without a clear compositional structure; its fully compositional treatment turned out to be prohibitively expensive. The performance advantage of FZ-int. compared to PRISM (FZ-all) is encouraging. The Patrol5 and Wholesale5 experiments also show the advantage of compositionality.

RQ3. We find the absolute performance of CompMDP quite satisfactory. The Patrol and Wholesale benchmarks are huge models, with so many positions that fitting their explicit state representation in memory is already nontrivial. CompMDP, exploiting their succinct presentation by string diagrams, successfully model-checked them in realistic time (6–130 s with DI-high).

RQ4. The experiments suggest that string diagrams are a practical modeling formalism, allowing faster solutions of realistic benchmarks. It seems likely that the formalism is more suited for *task compositionality* (where components are sub-*tasks* and they are sequentially composed with possible fallbacks and loops) rather than *system compositionality* (where components are sub-*systems* and they are parallelly composed).

RQ5. It seems that the number of locally optimal schedulers is an important factor: if there are many of them, then we have to record more in the intermediate solutions of the meager semantics. This number typically increases when more actions are available, as the comparison between Patrol and Wholesale.

References

1. Baier, C., Katoen, J.: Principles of Model Checking. MIT Press, Cambridge (2008)
2. Baier, C., Klein, J., Klüppelholz, S., Wunderlich, S.: Maximizing the conditional expected reward for reaching the goal. In: Legay, A., Margaria, T. (eds.) TACAS 2017. LNCS, vol. 10206, pp. 269–285. Springer, Heidelberg (2017). https://doi.org/10.1007/978-3-662-54580-5_16
3. Bonchi, F., Holland, J., Piedeleu, R., Sobocinski, P., Zanasi, F.: Diagrammatic algebra: from linear to concurrent systems. Proc. ACM Program. Lang. 3(POPL), 25:1–25:28 (2019). https://doi.org/10.1145/3290338
4. Clarke, E.M., Long, D.E., McMillan, K.L.: Compositional model checking. In: Proceedings of the Fourth Annual Symposium on Logic in Computer Science (LICS '89), Pacific Grove, California, USA, 5–8 June 1989, pp. 353–362. IEEE Computer Society (1989). https://doi.org/10.1109/LICS.1989.39190
5. Cruttwell, G.S.: Normed spaces and the change of base for enriched categories. Ph.D. thesis, Dalhousie University (2008)
6. Eilenberg, S., Kelly, G.M.: Closed categories. In: Eilenberg, S., Harrison, D.K., MacLane, S., Röhrl, H. (eds.) Proceedings of the Conference on Categorical Algebra: La Jolla 1965, pp. 421–562. Springer, Heidelberg (1966). https://doi.org/10.1007/978-3-642-99902-4_22
7. Girard, J.Y.: Geometry of interaction I: interpretation of System F. In: Studies in Logic and the Foundations of Mathematics, vol. 127, pp. 221–260. Elsevier (1989)
8. Heunen, C., Vicary, J.: Categories for Quantum Theory: An Introduction. Oxford University Press, Oxford (2019)
9. Hoshino, N.: A representation theorem for unique decomposition categories. In: Berger, U., Mislove, M.W. (eds.) Proceedings of the 28th Conference on the Mathematical Foundations of Programming Semantics, MFPS 2012, Bath, UK, 6–9 June 2012. Electronic Notes in Theoretical Computer Science, vol. 286, pp. 213–227. Elsevier (2012). https://doi.org/10.1016/j.entcs.2012.08.014
10. Joyal, A., Street, R., Verity, D.: Traced monoidal categories. Math. Proc. Cambridge Philos. Soc. 119(3), 447–468 (1996)
11. Junges, S., Spaan, M.T.J.: Abstraction-refinement for hierarchical probabilistic models. In: Shoham, S., Vizel, Y. (eds.) CAV 2022, Part I. LNCS, vol. 13371, pp. 102–123. Springer, Cham (2022). https://doi.org/10.1007/978-3-031-13185-1_6
12. Khovanov, M.: A functor-valued invariant of tangles. Algebraic Geom. Topol. 2(2), 665–741 (2002)
13. Kwiatkowska, M., Norman, G., Parker, D.: PRISM 4.0: verification of probabilistic real-time systems. In: Gopalakrishnan, G., Qadeer, S. (eds.) CAV 2011. LNCS, vol. 6806, pp. 585–591. Springer, Heidelberg (2011). https://doi.org/10.1007/978-3-642-22110-1_47
14. Kwiatkowska, M.Z., Norman, G., Parker, D., Qu, H.: Compositional probabilistic verification through multi-objective model checking. Inf. Comput. 232, 38–65 (2013). https://doi.org/10.1016/j.ic.2013.10.001
15. Mac Lane, S.: Categories for the Working Mathematician, 2nd edn. Springer, Heidelberg (1998). https://doi.org/10.1007/978-1-4757-4721-8
16. Moggi, E.: Notions of computation and monads. Inf. Comput. 93(1), 55–92 (1991). https://doi.org/10.1016/0890-5401(91)90052-4

17. Piedeleu, R., Kartsaklis, D., Coecke, B., Sadrzadeh, M.: Open system categorical quantum semantics in natural language processing. In: Moss, L.S., Sobocinski, P. (eds.) 6th Conference on Algebra and Coalgebra in Computer Science, CALCO 2015, 24–26 June 2015, Nijmegen, The Netherlands. LIPIcs, vol. 35, pp. 270–289. Schloss Dagstuhl - Leibniz-Zentrum für Informatik (2015). https://doi.org/10.4230/LIPIcs.CALCO.2015.270

18. Quatmann, T., Dehnert, C., Jansen, N., Junges, S., Katoen, J.-P.: Parameter synthesis for Markov models: faster than ever. In: Artho, C., Legay, A., Peled, D. (eds.) ATVA 2016. LNCS, vol. 9938, pp. 50–67. Springer, Cham (2016). https://doi.org/10.1007/978-3-319-46520-3_4

19. Tsukada, T., Ong, C.L.: Compositional higher-order model checking via ω-regular games over Böhm trees. In: Joint Meeting of the Twenty-Third EACSL Annual Conference on Computer Science Logic (CSL) and the Twenty-Ninth Annual ACM/IEEE Symposium on Logic in Computer Science (LICS), CSL-LICS '14, Vienna, Austria, 14–18 July 2014, pp. 78:1–78:10. ACM (2014)

20. Watanabe, K., Eberhart, C., Asada, K., Hasuo, I.: A compositional approach to parity games. In: Sokolova, A. (ed.) Proceedings 37th Conference on Mathematical Foundations of Programming Semantics, MFPS 2021, Hybrid: Salzburg, Austria and Online, 30 August–2 September 2021. EPTCS, vol. 351, pp. 278–295 (2021). https://doi.org/10.4204/EPTCS.351.17

21. Watanabe, K., Eberhart, C., Asada, K., Hasuo, I.: Compositional probabilistic model checking with string diagrams of MDPs (extended version) (2023), to appear in arXiv

Efficient Sensitivity Analysis
for Parametric Robust Markov Chains

Thom Badings[1]([✉])[iD], Sebastian Junges[1][iD], Ahmadreza Marandi[2][iD],
Ufuk Topcu[3][iD], and Nils Jansen[1][iD]

[1] Radboud University, Nijmegen, The Netherlands
thom.badings@ru.nl
[2] Eindhoven University of Technology, Eindhoven,
The Netherlands
[3] University of Texas at Austin, Austin, USA

Abstract. We provide a novel method for sensitivity analysis of parametric robust Markov chains. These models incorporate parameters and sets of probability distributions to alleviate the often unrealistic assumption that precise probabilities are available. We measure sensitivity in terms of partial derivatives with respect to the uncertain transition probabilities regarding measures such as the expected reward. As our main contribution, we present an efficient method to compute these partial derivatives. To scale our approach to models with thousands of parameters, we present an extension of this method that selects the subset of k parameters with the highest partial derivative. Our methods are based on linear programming and differentiating these programs around a given value for the parameters. The experiments show the applicability of our approach on models with over a million states and thousands of parameters. Moreover, we embed the results within an iterative learning scheme that profits from having access to a dedicated sensitivity analysis.

1 Introduction

Discrete-time Markov chains (MCs) are ubiquitous in stochastic systems modeling [8]. A classical assumption is that all probabilities of an MC are precisely known—an assumption that is difficult, if not impossible, to satisfy in practice [4]. Robust MCs (rMCs), or uncertain MCs, alleviate this assumption by using *sets of probability distributions*, e.g., intervals of probabilities in the simplest case [12,39]. A typical verification problem for rMCs is to compute upper or lower bounds on measures of interest, such as the expected cumulative reward, under *worst-case realizations* of these probabilities in the set of distributions [52,59]. Thus, verification results are *robust* against any selection of probabilities in these sets.

This research has been partially funded by NWO grant NWA.1160.18.238 (PrimaVera), the ERC Starting Grant 101077178 (DEUCE), and grants ONR N00014-21-1-2502 and AFOSR FA9550-22-1-0403.

C. Enea and A. Lal (Eds.): CAV 2023, LNCS 13966, pp. 62–85, 2023.
https://doi.org/10.1007/978-3-031-37709-9_4

Where to improve my model? As a running example, consider a ground vehicle navigating toward a target location in an environment with different terrain types. On each terrain type, there is some probability that the vehicle will slip and fail to move. Assume that we obtain a sufficient number of *samples* to infer upper and lower bounds (i.e., intervals) on the slipping probability on each terrain. We use these probability intervals to model the grid world as an rMC. However, from the rMC, it is unclear how our model (and thus the measure of interest) will change if we obtain more samples. For instance, if we take one more sample for a particular terrain, some of the intervals of the rMC will change, but how can we expect the verification result to change? And if the verification result is unsatisfactory, for which terrain type should we obtain more samples?

Parametric Robust MCs. To reason about how additional samples will change our model and thus the verification result, we employ a sensitivity analysis [29]. To that end, we use parametric robust MCs (prMCs), which are rMCs whose sets of probability distributions are defined as a function of a set of *parameters* [26], e.g., intervals with parametric upper/lower bounds. With these functions over the parameters, we can describe dependencies between the model's states. The assignment of values to each of the parameters is called an *instantiation*. Applying an instantiation to a prMC induces an rMC by replacing each occurrence of the parameters with their assigned values. For this induced rMC, we compute a (robust) value for a given measure, and we call this verification result the *solution* for this instantiation. Thus, we can associate a prMC with a function, called the *solution function*, that maps parameter instantiations to values.

Differentiation for prMCs. For our running example, we choose the parameters to represent the number of samples we have obtained for each terrain. Naturally, the *derivative of this solution function* with respect to each parameter (a.k.a. sample size) then corresponds to the expected change in the solution upon obtaining more samples. Such differentiation for parametric MCs (pMCs), where parameter instantiations yield one precise probability distribution, has been studied in [34]. For prMCs, however, it is unclear how to compute derivatives and under what conditions the derivative exists. We thus consider the following problem:

Problem 1 *(Computing derivatives).* Given a prMC and a parameter instantiation, compute the partial derivative of the solution function (evaluated at this instantiation) with respect to each of the parameters.

Our Approach. We compute derivatives for prMCs by solving a parameterized linear optimization problem. We build upon results from convex optimization theory for differentiating the optimal solution of this optimization problem [9,15]. We also present sufficient conditions for the derivative to exist.

Improving Efficiency. However, computing the derivative for every parameter explicitly does not scale to more realistic models with thousands of parameters. Instead, we observe that to determine for which parameter we should obtain more samples, we do not need to know *all partial derivatives explicitly*. Instead, it may suffice to know which parameters have *the highest* (or lowest, depending on the application) derivative. Thus, we also solve the following (related) problem:

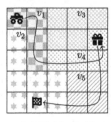

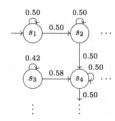

				Derivatives	
Par.	True	MLE	N	$\frac{\partial f}{\partial v_i}$	$\frac{\partial f^+}{\partial N_i}$
v_1	0.25	0.50	12	16.00	-2.74
v_2	0.40	0.42	36	2.93	-0.02
v_3	0.45	0.63	30	0.00	0.00
v_4	0.50	0.53	60	22.96	-0.07
v_5	0.35	0.41	22	8.59	-0.16

(a) Grid world.   (b) MLEs and derivatives.   (c) Portion of the MC.

Fig. 1. Grid world environment (a). The vehicle (🚗) must deliver the package (🎁) to the warehouse (🏁). We obtain the MLEs in (b), leading to the MC in (c).

Problem 2 *(k-highest derivatives).* Given a prMC with $|V|$ parameters, determine the $k < |V|$ parameters with the highest (or lowest) partial derivative.

We develop novel and efficient methods for solving Problem 2. Concretely, we design a linear program (LP) that finds the k parameters with the highest (or lowest) partial derivative without computing all derivatives explicitly. This LP constitutes a polynomial-time algorithm for Problem 2 and is, in practice, *orders of magnitude faster* than computing all derivatives explicitly, especially if the number of parameters is high. Moreover, if the concrete values for the partial derivatives are required, one can additionally solve Problem 1 for only the resulting k parameters. In our experiments, we show that we can compute derivatives for models with over a million states and thousands of parameters.

Learning Framework. Learning in stochastic environments is very data-intensive in general, and millions of samples may be required to obtain sufficiently tight bounds on measures of interest [43,47]. Several methods exist to obtain intervals on probabilities based on sampling, including statistical methods such as Hoeffding's inequality [14] and Bayesian methods that iteratively update intervals [57]. Motivated by this challenge of reducing the sample complexity of learning algorithms, we embed our methods in an iterative learning scheme that profits from having access to sensitivity values for the parameters. In our experiments, we show that derivative information can be used effectively to guide sampling when learning an unknown Markov chain with hundreds of parameters.

Contributions. Our contributions are threefold: (1) We present a first algorithm to compute partial derivatives for prMCs. (2) For both pMCs and prMCs, we develop an efficient method to determine a subset of parameters with the highest derivatives. (3) We apply our methods in an iterative learning scheme. We give an overview of our approach in Sect. 2 and formalize the problem statement in Sect. 3. In Sect. 4, we solve Problems (1) and (2) for pMCs, and in Sect. 5 for prMCs. Finally, the learning scheme and experiments are in Sect. 6.

2   Overview

We expand the example from Sect. 1 to illustrate our approach more concretely. The environment, shown in Fig. 1a, is partitioned into five regions of the same terrain type. The vehicle can move in the four cardinal directions. Recall that

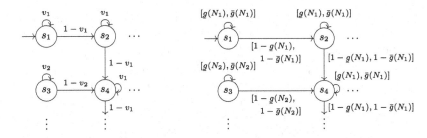

Fig. 2. Parametric MC.   **Fig. 3.** Parametric robust MC.

the slipping probabilities are the same for all states with the same terrain. The vehicle follows a dedicated route to collect and deliver a package to a warehouse. Our goal is to estimate the expected number of steps $f^\star$ to complete the mission.

Estimating Probabilities. Classically, we would derive maximum likelihood estimates (MLEs) of the probabilities by sampling. Consider that, using N samples per slipping probability, we obtained the rough MLEs shown in Fig. 1b and thus the MC in Fig. 1c. Verifying the MC shows that the expected travel time (called the solution) under these estimates is $\hat{f} = 25.51$ steps, which is far from the travel time of $f^\star = 21.62$ steps under the true slipping probabilities. We want to close this *verification-to-real gap* by taking more samples for one of the terrain types. For which of the five terrain types should we obtain more samples?

Parametric Model. We can model the grid world as a pMC, i.e., an MC with symbolic probabilities. The solution function for this pMC is the travel time $\hat{f}$, being a function of these symbolic probabilities. We sketch four states of this pMC in Fig. 2. The most relevant parameter is then naturally defined as the parameter with the *largest partial derivative of the solution function*. As shown in Fig. 1B, parameter v_4 has the highest partial derivative of $\frac{\partial \hat{f}}{\partial v_4} = 22.96$, while the derivative of v_3 is zero as no states related to this parameter are ever visited.

Parametric Robust Model. The approach above does not account for the uncertainty in each MLE. Terrain type v_4 has the highest derivative but also the largest sample size, so sampling v_4 once more has likely less impact than for, e.g., v_1. So, is v_4 actually the best choice to obtain additional samples for? The prMC that allows us to answer this question is shown in Fig. 3, where we use (parametric) intervals as uncertainty sets. The parameters are the sample sizes $N_1, \ldots, N_5$ for all terrain types (contrary to the pMC, where parameters represent slipping probabilities). Now, if we obtain one additional sample for a particular terrain type, how can we expect the uncertainty sets to change?

Derivatives for prMCs. We use the prMC to compute an upper bound f^+ on the true solution $f^\star$. Obtaining one more sample for terrain type v_i (i.e., increasing N_i by one) shrinks the interval $[\underline{g}(N_i), \bar{g}(N_i)]$ on expectation, which in turn decreases our upper bound f^+. Here, $\underline{g}$ and $\bar{g}$ are functions mapping sample sizes to interval bounds. The partial derivatives $\frac{\partial f^+}{\partial N_i}$ for the prMC are also shown in Fig. 1b and give a very different outcome than the derivatives for the pMC. In fact, sampling v_1 yields the biggest decrease in the upper bound f^+, so we ultimately decide to sample for terrain type v_1 instead of v_4.

Efficient Differentiation. We remark that we do not need to know all derivatives explicitly to determine where to obtain samples. Instead, it suffices to know *which parameter has the highest (or lowest) derivative.* In the rest of the paper, we develop efficient methods for computing either all or only the $k \in \mathbb{N}$ highest partial derivatives of the solution functions for pMCs and prMCs.

Supported Extensions. Our approaches are applicable to general pMCs and prMCs whose parameters can be shared between distributions (and thus capture dependencies, being a common advantage of parametric models in general [40]). Besides parameters in transition probabilities, we can handle parametric initial states, rewards, and policies. We could, e.g., use parameters to model the policy of a surveillance drone in our example and compute derivatives for these parameters.

3   Formal Problem Statement

Let $V = \{v_1, \ldots, v_\ell\}$, $v_i \in \mathbb{R}$ be a finite and ordered set of parameters. A parameter instantiation is a function $u \colon V \to \mathbb{R}$ that maps a parameter to a real valuation. The vector function $\mathbf{u}(v_1, \ldots, v_\ell) = [u(v_1), \ldots, u(v_\ell)]^\top \in \mathbb{R}^\ell$ denotes an ordered instantiation of all parameters in V through u. The set of polynomials over the parameters V is $\mathbb{Q}[V]$. A polynomial f can be interpreted as a function $f \colon \mathbb{R}^\ell \to \mathbb{R}$ where $f(\mathbf{u})$ is obtained by substituting each occurrence of v by $u(v)$. We denote these substitutions with $f[\mathbf{u}]$.

For any set X, let $pFun_V(X) = \{f \mid f \colon X \to \mathbb{Q}[V]\}$ be the set of functions that map from X to the polynomials over the parameters V. We denote by $pDist_V(X) \subset pFun_V(X)$ the set of *parametric probability distributions* over X, i.e., the functions $f \colon X \to \mathbb{Q}[V]$ such that $f(x)[\mathbf{u}] \in [0, 1]$ and $\sum_{x \in X} f(x)[\mathbf{u}] = 1$ for all parameter instantiations $\mathbf{u}$.

Parametric Markov Chain. We define a pMC as follows:

Definition 1 (pMC). *A pMC $\mathcal{M}$ is a tuple (S, s_I, V, P), where S is a finite set of states, $s_I \in Dist(S)$ a distribution over initial states, V a finite set of parameters, and $P \colon S \to pDist_V(S)$ a parametric transition function.*

Applying an instantiation $\mathbf{u}$ to a pMC yields an MC $\mathcal{M}[\mathbf{u}]$ by replacing each transition probability $f \in \mathbb{Q}[V]$ by $f[\mathbf{u}]$. We consider expected reward measures based on a state reward function $R \colon S \to \mathbb{R}$. Each parameter instantiation for a pMC yields an MC for which we can compute the solution for the expected reward measure [8]. We call the function that maps instantiations to a solution the *solution function.* The solution function is smooth over the set of graph-preserving instantiations [41]. Concretely, the solution function sol for the expected cumulative reward under instantiation $\mathbf{u}$ is written as follows:

$$\mathsf{sol}(\mathbf{u}) = \sum_{s \in S} \left(s_I(s) \sum_{\omega \in \Omega(s)} \mathrm{rew}(\omega) \cdot \mathrm{Pr}(\omega, \mathbf{u}) \right), \tag{1}$$

where $\Omega(s)$ is the set of paths starting in $s \in S$, $\text{rew}(\omega) = R(s_0) + R(s_1) + \cdots$ is the cumulative reward over $\omega = s_0 s_1 \cdots$, and $\Pr(\omega, \mathbf{u})$ is the probability for a path $\omega \in \Omega(s)$. If a terminal (sink) state is reached from state $s \in S$ with probability one, the infinite sum over $\omega \in \Omega(s)$ in Eq. (1) exist [53].

Parametric Robust Markov Chains. The convex polytope $T_{A,b} \subseteq \mathbb{R}^n$ defined by matrix $A \in \mathbb{R}^{m \times n}$ and vector $b \in \mathbb{R}^m$ is the set $T_{A,b} = \{p \in \mathbb{R}^n \mid Ap \leq b\}$. We denote by $\mathbb{T}_n$ the set of all convex polytopes of dimension n, i.e.,

$$\mathbb{T}_n = \{T_{A,b} \mid A \in \mathbb{R}^{m \times n}, b \in \mathbb{R}^m, m \in \mathbb{N}\}. \tag{2}$$

A robust MC (rMC) [54,58] is a tuple $(S, s_I, \mathcal{P})$, where S and s_I are defined as for pMCs and the uncertain transition function $\mathcal{P} \colon S \to \mathbb{T}_{|S|}$ maps states to convex polytopes $T \in \mathbb{T}_{|S|}$. Intuitively, an rMC is an MC with possibly infinite *sets of probability distributions*. To obtain robust bounds on the verification result for any of these MCs, an *adversary* nondeterministically chooses a precise transition function by fixing a probability distribution $\hat{P}(s) \in \mathcal{P}(s)$ for each $s \in S$.

We extend rMCs with polytopes whose halfspaces are defined by polynomials $\mathbb{Q}[V]$ over V. To this end, let $\mathbb{T}_n[V]$ be the set of all such *parametric polytopes*:

$$\mathbb{T}_n[V] = \{T_{A,b} \mid A \in \mathbb{Q}[V]^{m \times n}, b \in \mathbb{Q}[V]^m, m \in \mathbb{N}\}. \tag{3}$$

An element $T \in \mathbb{T}_n[V]$ can be interpreted as a function $T \colon \mathbb{R}^\ell \to 2^{(\mathbb{R}^n)}$ that maps an instantiation $\mathbf{u}$ to a (possibly empty) convex polytopic subset of $\mathbb{R}^n$. The set $T[\mathbf{u}]$ is obtained by substituting each v_i in T by $u(v_i)$ for all $i = 1, \ldots, \ell$.

Example 1. The uncertainty set for state s_1 of the prMC in Fig. 3 is the parametric polytope $T \in \mathbb{T}_2[V]$ with singleton parameter set $V = \{N_1\}$, such that

$$T = \big\{[p_{1,1}, p_{1,2}]^\top \in \mathbb{R}^2 \mid \underline{g}_1(N_1) \leq p_{1,1} \leq \bar{g}_1(N_1),$$
$$1 - \bar{g}_1(N_1) \leq p_{1,2} \leq 1 - \underline{g}_1(N_1), \quad p_{1,2} + p_{1,2} = 1\big\}.$$

We use parametric convex polytopes to define prMCs:

Definition 2 (prMC). *A prMC $\mathcal{M}_R$ is a tuple $(S, s_I, V, \mathcal{P})$, where S, s_I, and V are defined as for pMCs (Def. 1), and where $\mathcal{P} \colon S \to \mathbb{T}_{|S|}[V]$ is a parametric and uncertain transition function that maps states to parametric convex polytopes.*

Applying an instantiation $\mathbf{u}$ to a prMC yields an rMC $\mathcal{M}_R[\mathbf{u}]$ by replacing each parametric polytope $T \in \mathbb{T}_{|S|}[V]$ by $T[\mathbf{u}]$, i.e., a polytope defined by a concrete matrix $A \in \mathbb{R}^{m \times n}$ and vector $b \in \mathbb{R}^m$. Without loss of generality, we consider adversaries minimizing the expected cumulative reward until reaching a set of terminal states $S_T \subseteq S$. This minimum expected cumulative reward $\text{sol}_R(\mathbf{u})$, called the *robust solution* on the instantiated prMC $\mathcal{M}_R[\mathbf{u}]$, is defined as

$$\text{sol}_R(\mathbf{u}) = \sum_{s \in S} \Big(s_I(s) \cdot \min_{P \in \mathcal{P}[\mathbf{u}]} \sum_{\omega \in \Omega(s)} \text{rew}(\omega) \cdot \Pr(\omega, \mathbf{u}, P)\Big). \tag{4}$$

We refer to the function $\text{sol}_R \colon \mathbb{R}^\ell \to \mathbb{R}$ as the *robust solution function*.

Assumptions on pMCs and prMCs. For both pMCs and prMCs, we assume that transitions cannot vanish under any instantiation (graph-preservation). That is, for every $s, s' \in S$, we have that $P(s)[\mathbf{u}](s')$ (for pMCs) and $\mathcal{P}(s)[\mathbf{u}](s')$ (for prMCs) are either zero or strictly positive for all instantiations $\mathbf{u}$.

Problem Statement. Let $f(q_1, \dots, q_n) \in \mathbb{R}^m$ be a differentiable multivariate function with $m \in \mathbb{N}$. We denote the *partial derivative* of f with respect to q by $\frac{\partial x}{\partial q} \in \mathbb{R}^m$. The *gradient* of f combines all partial derivatives in a single vector as $\nabla_q f = [\frac{\partial f}{\partial q_1}, \dots, \frac{\partial f}{\partial q_n}] \in \mathbb{R}^{m \times n}$. We only use gradients $\nabla_{\mathbf{u}} f$ with respect to the parameter instantiation $\mathbf{u}$, so we simply write ∇f in the remainder.

The gradient of the robust solution function evaluated at the instantiation $\mathbf{u}$ is $\nabla \mathsf{sol}_R[\mathbf{u}] = \left[\left(\frac{\partial \mathsf{sol}_R}{\partial u(v_1)} \right)[\mathbf{u}], \dots, \left(\frac{\partial \mathsf{sol}_R}{\partial u(v_\ell)} \right)[\mathbf{u}] \right]$. We solve the following problem.

Problem 1. Given a prMC $\mathcal{M}_R$ and a parameter instantiation $\mathbf{u}$, compute the gradient $\nabla \mathsf{sol}_R[\mathbf{u}]$ of the robust solution function evaluated at $\mathbf{u}$.

Solving Problem 1 is linear in the number of parameters, which may lead to significant overhead if the number of parameters is large. Typically, it suffices to only obtain the parameters with the highest derivatives:

Problem 2. Given a prMC $\mathcal{M}_R$, an instantiation $\mathbf{u}$, and a $k \leq |V|$, compute a subset $V^\star$ of k parameters for which the partial derivatives are maximal.

For both problems, we present polynomial-time algorithms for pMCs (Sect. 4) and prMCs (Sect. 5). Section 6 defines problem variations that we study empirically.

4   Differentiating Solution Functions for pMCs

We can compute the solution of an MC $\mathcal{M}[\mathbf{u}]$ with instantiation $\mathbf{u}$ based on a system of $|S|$ linear equations; here for an expected reward measure [8]. Let $x = [x_{s_1}, \dots, x_{s_{|S|}}]^\top$ and $r = [r_{s_1}, \dots, r_{s_{|S|}}]^\top$ be variables for the expected cumulative reward and the instantaneous reward in each state $s \in S$, respectively. Then, for a set of terminal (*sink*) states $S_T \subset S$, we obtain the equation system

$$x_s = 0, \qquad\qquad \forall s \in S_T \tag{5a}$$

$$x_s = r_s + P(s)[\mathbf{u}]x, \quad \forall s \in S \backslash S_T. \tag{5b}$$

Let us set $P(s)[\mathbf{u}] = 0$ for all $s \in S_T$ and define the matrix $P[\mathbf{u}] \in \mathbb{R}^{|S| \times |S|}$ by stacking the rows $P(s)[\mathbf{u}]$ for all $s \in S$. Then, Eq. (5) is written in matrix form as $(I_{|S|} - P[\mathbf{u}])x = r$. The equation system in Eq. (5) can be efficiently solved by, e.g., Gaussian elimination or more advanced iterative equation solvers.

4.1   Computing Derivatives Explicitly

We differentiate the equation system in Eq. (5) with respect to an instantiation $u(v_i)$ for parameter $v_i \in V$, similar to, e.g., [34]. For all $s \in S_T$, the derivative

$\frac{\partial x_s}{\partial u(v_i)}$ is trivially zero. For all $s \in S \setminus S_T$, we obtain via the product rule that

$$\frac{\partial x_s}{\partial u(v_i)} = \frac{\partial P(s)x}{\partial u(v_i)}[\mathbf{u}] = (x^\star)^\top \frac{\partial P(s)^\top}{\partial u(v_i)}[\mathbf{u}] + P(s)[\mathbf{u}]\frac{\partial x}{\partial u(v_i)}, \tag{6}$$

where $x^\star \in \mathbb{R}^{|S|}$ is the solution to Eq. (5). In matrix form for all $s \in S$, this yields

$$\left(I_{|S|} - P[\mathbf{u}]\right)\frac{\partial x}{\partial u(v_i)} = \frac{\partial Px^\star}{\partial u(v_i)}[\mathbf{u}]. \tag{7}$$

The solution defined in Eq. (1) is computed as $\mathsf{sol}[\mathbf{u}] = s_I^\top x^\star$. Thus, the partial derivative of the solution function with respect to $u(v_i)$ in closed form is

$$\left(\frac{\partial \mathsf{sol}}{\partial u(v_i)}\right)[\mathbf{u}] = s_I^\top \frac{\partial x}{\partial u(v_i)} = s_I^\top \left(I_{|S|} - P[\mathbf{u}]\right)^{-1}\frac{\partial Px^\star}{\partial u(v_i)}[\mathbf{u}]. \tag{8}$$

Algorithm for Problem 1. Let us provide an algorithm to solve 1 for pMCs. 8 provides a closed-form expression for the partial derivative of the solution function, which is a function of the vector $x^\star$ in Eq. (5). However, due to the inversion of $(I_{|S|} - P[\mathbf{u}])$, it is generally more efficient to solve the system of equations in Eq. (7). Doing so, the partial derivative of the solution with respect to $u(v_i)$ is obtained by: (1) solving Eq. (5) with $\mathbf{u}$ to obtain $x^\star \in \mathbb{R}^{|S|}$, and (2) solving the equation system in Eq. (7) with $|S|$ unknowns for this vector $x^\star$. We repeat step 2 for all of the $|V|$ parameters. Thus, we can solve Problem 1 by solving $|V| + 1$ linear equation systems with $|S|$ unknowns each.

4.2 Computing k-Highest Derivatives

To solve Problem 2 for pMCs, we present a method to compute only the $k \leq \ell = |V|$ parameters with the highest (or lowest) partial derivative without computing all derivatives explicitly. Without loss of generality, we focus on the highest derivative. We can determine these parameters by solving a combinatorial optimization problem with binary variables $z_i \in \{0, 1\}$ for $i = 1, \ldots, \ell$. Our goal is to formulate this optimization problem such that an optimal value of $z_i^\star = 1$ implies that parameter $v_i \in V$ belongs to the set of k highest derivatives. Concretely, we formulate the following *mixed integer linear problem* (MILP) [60]:

$$\underset{y \in \mathbb{R}^{|S|},\, z \in \{0,1\}^\ell}{\text{maximize}} \quad s_I^\top y \tag{9a}$$

$$\text{subject to } \left(I_{|S|} - P[\mathbf{u}]\right) y = \sum_{i=1}^{\ell} z_i \frac{\partial Px^\star}{\partial u(v_i)}[\mathbf{u}] \tag{9b}$$

$$z_1 + \cdots + z_\ell = k. \tag{9c}$$

Constraint (9c) ensures that any feasible solution to Eq. (9) has exactly k nonzero entries. Since matrix $(I_{|S|} - P[\mathbf{u}])$ is invertible by construction (see, e.g., [53]), Eq.

(9) has a unique solution in y for each choice of $z \in \{0, 1\}^\ell$. Thus, the objective value $s_I^\top y$ is the sum of the derivatives for the parameters $v_i \in V$ for which $z_i = 1$. Since we maximize this objective, an optimal solution $y^\star, z^\star$ to Eq. (9) is guaranteed to correspond to the k parameters that maximize the derivative of the solution in Eq. (8). We state this correctness claim for the MILP:

Proposition 1. *Let $y^\star$, $z^\star$ be an optimal solution to Eq. (9). Then, the set $V^\star = \{v_i \in V \mid z_i^\star = 1\}$ is a subset of $k \leq \ell$ parameters with maximal derivatives.*

The set $V^\star$ may not be unique. However, to solve Problem 2, it suffices to obtain *a set* of k parameters for which the partial derivatives are maximal. Therefore, the set $V^\star$ provides a solution to Problem 2. We remark that, to solve Problem 2 for the k lowest derivatives, we change the objective in Eq. (9a) to minimize $s_I^\top y$.

Linear Relaxation. The MILP in Eq. (9) is computationally intractable for high values of ℓ and k. Instead, we compute the set $v^\star$ via a *linear relaxation* of the MILP. Specifically, we relax the binary variables $z \in \{0, 1\}^\ell$ to continuous variables $z \in [0, 1]^\ell$. As such, we obtain the following LP relaxation of Eq. (9):

$$\underset{y \in \mathbb{R}^{|S|},\, z \in \mathbb{R}^\ell}{\text{maximize}} \quad s_I^\top y \tag{10a}$$

$$\text{subject to } \left(I_{|S|} - P[\mathbf{u}]\right) y = \sum_{i=1}^{\ell} z_i \frac{\partial P x^\star}{\partial u(v_i)} [\mathbf{u}] \tag{10b}$$

$$0 \leq z_i \leq 1, \quad \forall i = 1, \dots, \ell \tag{10c}$$

$$z_1 + \cdots + z_\ell = k. \tag{10d}$$

Denote by y^+, z^+ the solution of the LP relaxation in Eq. (10). For details on such linear relaxations of integer problems, we refer to [36, 46]. In our case, every optimal solution y^+, z^+ to the LP relaxation with only binary values $z_i^+ \in \{0, 1\}$ is also optimal for the MILP, resulting in the following theorem.

Theorem 1. *The LP relaxation in Eq. (10) has an optimal solution y^+, z^+ with $z^+ \in \{0, 1\}^\ell$ (i.e., every optimal variable z_i^+ is binary), and every such a solution is also an optimal solution of the MILP in Eq. (9).*

Proof. From invertibility of $\left(I_{|S|} - P[\mathbf{u}]\right)$, we know that Eq. (9) is equivalent to

$$\underset{z \in \{0,1\}^\ell}{\text{maximize}} \sum_{i=1}^{\ell} z_i \left(s_I^\top \left(I_{|S|} - P[\mathbf{u}]\right)^{-1} \frac{\partial P x^\star}{\partial u(v_i)} [\mathbf{u}] \right) \tag{11a}$$

$$\text{subject to } z_1 + \cdots + z_\ell = k. \tag{11b}$$

The linear relaxation of Eq. (11) is an LP whose feasible region has integer vertices (see, e.g., [37]). Therefore, both Eq. (11) and its relaxation Eq. (10) have an integer optimal solution z^+, which constructs $z^\star$ in Eq. (9).   □

The binary solutions $z^+ \in \{0,1\}^\ell$ are the vertices of the feasible set of the LP in Eq. (10). A simplex-based LP solver can be set to return such a solution.[1]

Algorithm for Problem 2. We provide an algorithm to solve Problem 2 for pMCs consisting of two steps. First, for pMC $\mathcal{M}$ and parameter instantiation $\mathbf{u}$, we solve the linear equation system in Eq. (7) for $x^\star$ to obtain the solution $\mathsf{sol}[\mathbf{u}] = s_I^\top x^\star$. Second, we fix a number of parameters $k \leq \ell$ and solve the LP relaxation in Eq. (10). The set $V^\star$ of parameters with maximal derivatives is then obtained as defined in Proposition 1. The parameter set $V^\star$ is a solution to Proposition 2.

5   Differentiating Solution Functions for prMCs

We shift focus to prMCs. Recall that solutions $\mathsf{sol}_R[\mathbf{u}]$ are computed for the worst-case realization of the uncertainty, called the robust solution. We derive the following equation system, where, as for pMCs, $x \in \mathbb{R}^{|S|}$ represents the expected cumulative reward in each state.

$$x_s = 0, \qquad\qquad\qquad \forall s \in S_T \tag{12a}$$

$$x_s = r_s + \inf_{p \in \mathcal{P}(s)[\mathbf{u}]} \left(p^\top x \right), \qquad\qquad \forall s \in S \setminus S_T. \tag{12b}$$

Solving Eq. (12) directly corresponds to solving a system of nonlinear equations due to the inner infimum in Eq. (12b). The standard approach from robust optimization [12] is to leverage the dual problem for each inner infimum, e.g., as is done in [20,52]. For each $s \in S$, $\mathcal{P}(s)$ is a parametric convex polytope $T_{A,b}$ as defined in Eq. (3). The dimensionality of this polytope depends on the number of successor states, which is typically much lower than the total number of states. To make the number of successor states explicit, we denote by $\mathsf{post}(s) \subseteq S$ the successor states of $s \in S$ and define $T_{A,b} \in \mathbb{T}_{|\mathsf{post}(s)|}[V]$ with $A_s \in \mathbb{Q}^{m_s \times |\mathsf{post}(s)|}$ and $b_s[\mathbf{u}] \in \mathbb{Q}^{m_s}$ (recall m_s is the number of halfspaces of the polytope). Then, the infimum in Eq. (12b) for each $s \in S \setminus S_T$ is

$$\text{minimize } p^\top x \tag{13a}$$

$$\text{subject to } A_s[\mathbf{u}]p \leq b_s[\mathbf{u}] \tag{13b}$$

$$\mathbb{1}^\top p = 1, \tag{13c}$$

where $\mathbb{1}$ denotes a column vector of ones of appropriate size. Let $x_{\mathsf{post}(s)} = [x_s]_{s \in \mathsf{post}(s)}$ be the vector of decision variables corresponding to the (ordered) successor states in $\mathsf{post}(s)$. The dual problem of Eq. (13), with dual variables $\alpha \in \mathbb{R}^{m_s}$ and $\beta \in \mathbb{R}$ (see, e.g., [11] for details), is written as follows:

$$\text{maximize } -b_s[\mathbf{u}]^\top \alpha - \beta \tag{14a}$$

$$\text{subject to } A_s[\mathbf{u}]^\top \alpha + x_{\mathsf{post}(s)} + \beta \mathbb{1} = 0 \tag{14b}$$

$$\alpha \geq 0. \tag{14c}$$

---

[1] Even if a non-vertex solution y^+, z^+ is obtained, we can use an arbitrary tie-break rule on z^+, which forces each z_i^+ binary and preserves the sum in Eq. (10d).

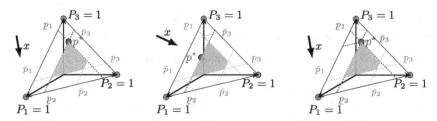

(a) Well-defined optimum. (b) Non-unique optimum. (c) Too many active constraints.

Fig. 4. Three polytopic uncertainty sets (blue shade), with the vector x, the worst-case points p^*, and the active constraints shown in red. (Color figure online)

By using this dual problem in Eq. (12b), we obtain the following LP with decision variables $x \in \mathbb{R}^{|S|}$, and with $\alpha_s \in \mathbb{R}^{m_s}$ and $\beta_s \in \mathbb{R}$ for every $s \in S$:

$$\text{maximize } s_I^\top x \tag{15a}$$

$$\text{subject to } x_s = 0, \qquad\qquad\qquad\qquad \forall s \in S_T \tag{15b}$$

$$x_s = r_s - \big(b_s[\mathbf{u}]^\top \alpha_s + \beta_s\big), \qquad \forall s \in S \setminus S_T \tag{15c}$$

$$A_s[\mathbf{u}]^\top \alpha_s + x_{\mathsf{post}(s)} + \beta_s \mathbb{1} = 0, \quad \alpha_s \geq 0, \qquad \forall s \in S \setminus S_T. \tag{15d}$$

The reformulation of Eq. (12) to Eq. (15) requires that $s_I \geq 0$, which is trivially satisfied because s_I is a probability distribution. Denote by x^*, α^*, β^* an optimal point of Eq. (15). The x^* element of this optimum is also an optimal solution of Eq. (12) [12]. Thus, the robust solution defined in Eq. (4) is $\mathsf{sol}_R[\mathbf{u}] = s_I^\top x^*$.

5.1 Computing Derivatives via pMCs (and When It Does Not Work)

Toward solving Problem 1, we provide some intuition about computing robust solutions for prMCs. The infimum in Eq. (12) finds the *worst-case* point p^* in each set $\mathcal{P}(s)[\mathbf{u}]$ that minimizes $(p^*)^\top x$. This minimization is visualized in Fig. 4a for an uncertainty set that captures three probability intervals $\underline{p}_i \leq p_i \leq \bar{p}_i$, $i = 1, 2, 3$. Given the optimization direction x (arrow in Fig. 4a), the point p^* (red dot) is attained at the vertex where the constraints $\underline{p}_1 \leq p_1$ and $\underline{p}_2 \leq p_2$ are active.[2] Thus, we obtain that the point in the polytope that minimizes $(p^*)^\top x$ is $p^* = [\underline{p}_1, \underline{p}_2, 1 - \underline{p}_1 - \underline{p}_2]^\top$. Using this procedure, we can obtain a worst-case point p_s^* for each state $s \in S$. We can use these points to convert the prMC into an induced pMC with transition function $P(s) = p_s^*$ for each state $s \in S$.

For small changes in the parameters, the point p^* in Fig. 4a changes smoothly, and its closed-form expression (i.e., the functional form) remains the same. As such, it feels intuitive that we could apply the methods from Sect. 4 to compute partial derivatives on the induced pMC. However, this approach does not always work, as illustrated by the following two corner cases.

---

[2] An inequality constraint $gx \leq h$ is active under the optimal solution x^* if $gx^* = h$ [15].

1. Consider Fig. 4b, where the optimization direction defined by x is parallel to one of the facets of the uncertainty set. In this case, the worst-case point $p^\star$ is not unique, but an infinitesimal change in the optimization direction x will force the point to one of the vertices again. Which point should we choose to obtain the induced pMC (and does this choice affect the derivative)?
2. Consider Fig. 4c with more than $|S| - 1$ active constraints at the point $p^\star$. Observe that decreasing $\bar{p}_3$ changes the point $p^\star$ while increasing $\bar{p}_3$ does not. In fact, the optimal point $p^\star$ changes *non-smoothly* with the halfspaces of the polytope. As a result, also the solution changes non-smoothly, and thus, the derivative is not defined. How do we deal with such a situation?

These examples show that computing derivatives via an induced pMC by obtaining each point $p_s^\star$ can be tricky or is, in some cases, not possible at all. In what follows, we present a method that directly derives a set of linear equations to obtain derivatives for prMCs (all or only the k highest) based on the solution to the LP in Eq. (15), which intrinsically identifies the corner cases above in which the derivative is not defined.

5.2   Computing Derivatives Explicitly

We now develop a dedicated method for identifying if the derivative of the solution function for a prMC exists, and if so, to compute this derivative. Observe from Fig. 4 that the point $p^\star$ is uniquely defined and has a smooth derivative only in Fig. 4a with two active constraints. For only one active constraint (Fig. 4b), the point is *underdetermined*, while for three active constraints (Fig. 4c), the derivative may *not be smooth*. In the general case, having exactly $n - 1$ active constraints (whose facets are nonparallel) is a sufficient condition for obtaining a unique and smoothly changing point $p^\star$ in the n-dimensional probability simplex.

Optimal Dual Variables. The optimal dual variables $\alpha_s^\star \geq 0$ for each $s \in S \setminus S_T$ in Eq. (15) indicate which constraints of the polytope $A_s[\mathbf{u}]p \leq b_s[\mathbf{u}]$ are active, i.e., for which rows $a_{s,i}[\mathbf{u}]$ of $A_s[\mathbf{u}]$ it holds that $a_{s,i}[\mathbf{u}]p^\star = b_s[\mathbf{u}]$. Specifically, a value of $\alpha_{s,i} > 0$ implies that the ith constraint is active, and $\alpha_{s,i} = 0$ indicates a nonactive constraint [15]. We define $E_s = [e_1, \ldots, e_{m_s}] \in \{0, 1\}^{m_s}$ as a vector whose binary values $e_i \, \forall i \in \{1, \ldots, m_s\}$ are given as $e_i = [\![\alpha_{s,i}^\star > 0]\!]$.[3] Moreover, denote by $\mathbf{D}(E_s)$ the matrix with E_s on the diagonal and zeros elsewhere. We reduce the LP in Eq. (15) to a system of linear equations that encodes only the constraints that are active under the worst-case point $p_s^\star$ for each $s \in S \setminus S_T$:

$$x_s = 0, \qquad\qquad\qquad\qquad\qquad \forall s \in S_T \tag{16a}$$

$$x_s = r_s - \left(b_s[\mathbf{u}]^\top \mathbf{D}(E_s)\alpha_s + \beta_s\right), \qquad\qquad \forall s \in S \setminus S_T \tag{16b}$$

$$A_s[\mathbf{u}]^\top \mathbf{D}(E_s)\alpha_s + x_{\text{post}(s)} + \beta_s \mathbb{1} = 0, \quad \alpha_s \geq 0, \qquad \forall s \in S \setminus S_T. \tag{16c}$$

Differentiation. However, when does Eq. (16) have a (unique) optimal solution? To provide some intuition, let us write the equation system in matrix form, i.e.,

---

[3] We use Iverson-brackets: $[\![x]\!] = 1$ if x is true and $[\![x]\!] = 0$ otherwise.

$C \begin{bmatrix} x & \alpha & \beta \end{bmatrix}^\top = d$, where we omit an explicit definition of matrix C and vector d for brevity. It is apparent that if matrix C is nonsingular, then Eq. (16) has a unique solution. This requires matrix C to be square, which is achieved if, for each $s \in S \setminus S_T$, we have $|\mathsf{post}(s)| = \sum E_s + 1$. In other words, the number of successor states of s is equal to the number of active constraints of the polytope plus one. This confirms our previous intuition from Sect. 5.1 on a polytope for $|\mathsf{post}(s)| = 3$ successor states, which required $\sum_{i=1}^{m_s} E_i = 2$ active constraints.

Let us formalize this intuition about computing derivatives for prMCs. We can compute the derivative of the solution $x^\star$ by differentiating the equation system in Eq. (16) through the product rule, in a very similar manner to the approach in Sect. 4. We state this key result in the following theorem.

Theorem 2. *Given a prMC $\mathcal{M}_R$ and an instantiation $\mathbf{u}$, compute $x^\star, \alpha^\star, \beta^\star$ for Eq. (15) and choose a parameter $v_i \in V$. The partial derivatives $\frac{\partial x}{\partial u(v_i)}$, $\frac{\partial \alpha}{\partial u(v_i)}$, and $\frac{\partial \beta}{\partial u(v_i)}$ are obtained as the solution to the linear equation system*

$$\frac{\partial x_s}{\partial u(v_i)} = 0, \qquad\qquad \forall s \in S_T \tag{17a}$$

$$\frac{\partial x_s}{\partial u(v_i)} + b_s[\mathbf{u}]^\top \mathbf{D}(E_s) \frac{\partial \alpha_s}{\partial u(v_i)} + \frac{\partial \beta_s}{\partial u(v_i)} = -(\alpha_s^\star)^\top \mathbf{D}(E_s) \frac{\partial b_s[\mathbf{u}]}{\partial u(v_i)}, \tag{17b}$$
$$\forall s \in S \setminus S_T$$

$$A_s[\mathbf{u}]^\top \mathbf{D}(E_s) \frac{\partial \alpha_s}{\partial u(v_i)} + \frac{\partial x_{\mathsf{post}(s)}}{\partial u(v_i)} + \frac{\partial \beta_s}{\partial u(v_i)} \mathbb{1} = -(\alpha_s^\star)^\top \mathbf{D}(E_s) \frac{\partial A_s[\mathbf{u}]}{\partial u(v_i)}, \tag{17c}$$
$$\forall s \in S \setminus S_T.$$

The proof follows from applying the product rule to Eq. (16) and is provided in [6, Appendix A.1]. To compute the derivative for a parameter $v_i \in V$, we thus solve a system of linear equations of size $|S| + \sum_{s \in S \setminus S_T} |\mathsf{post}(s)|$. Using Theorem 2, we obtain sufficient conditions for the solution function to be differentiable.

Lemma 1. *Write the linear equation system in Eq. (17) in matrix form, i.e.,*

$$C \left[\frac{\partial x}{\partial u(v_i)}, \frac{\partial \alpha}{\partial u(v_i)}, \frac{\partial \beta}{\partial u(v_i)} \right]^\top = d, \tag{18}$$

for $C \in \mathbb{R}^{q \times q}$ and $d \in \mathbb{R}^q$, $q = |S| + \sum_{s \in S \setminus S_T} |\mathsf{post}(s)|$, which are implicitly given by Eq. (17). The solution function $\mathsf{sol}_R[\mathbf{u}]$ is differentiable at instantiation $\mathbf{u}$ if matrix C is nonsingular, in which case we obtain $(\frac{\partial \mathsf{sol}_R}{\partial u(v_i)})[\mathbf{u}] = s_I^\top \frac{\partial x}{\partial u(v_i)}$.

Proof. The partial derivative of the solution function is $\frac{\partial \mathsf{sol}_R}{\partial u(v_i)}[\mathbf{u}] = s_I^\top \frac{\partial x^\star}{\partial u(v_i)}$, where $\frac{\partial x^\star}{\partial u(v_i)}$ is (a part of) the solution to Eq. (16). Thus, the solution function is differentiable if there is a (unique) solution to Eq. (16), which is guaranteed if matrix C is nonsingular. Thus, the claim in Lemma 1 follows. $\qquad\square$

Algorithm for Problem 1. We use Theorem 2 to solve Problem 1 for prMCs, similarly as for pMCs. Given a prMC $\mathcal{M}_R$ and an instantiation $\mathbf{u}$, we first solve

Eq. (15) to obtain $x^\star, \alpha^\star, \beta^\star$. Second, we use $\alpha_s^\star$ to compute the vector E_s of active constraints for each $s \in S \setminus S_T$. Third, for every parameter $v \in V$, we solve the equation system in Eq. (17). Thus, to compute the gradient of the solution function, we solve one LP and $|V|$ linear equation systems.

5.3   Computing k-Highest Derivatives

We directly apply the same procedure from Sect. 4.2 to compute the parameters with the $k \leq \ell$ highest derivatives. As for pMCs, we can compute the k highest derivatives by solving a MILP encoding the equation system in Eq. (17) for every parameter $v \in V$, which we present in [6, Appendix A.2] for brevity. This MILP has the same structure as Eq. (9), and thus we may apply the same linear relaxation to obtain an LP with the guarantees as stated in Theorem 1. In other words, solving the LP relaxation yields the set $V^\star$ of parameters with maximal derivatives as in Proposition 1. This set $V^\star$ is a solution to Problem 2 for prMCs.

6   Numerical Experiments

We perform experiments to answer the following questions about our approach:

1. Is it feasible (in terms of computational complexity and runtimes) to compute all derivatives, in particular compared to computing (robust) solutions?
2. How does computing only the k highest derivatives compare to computing all derivatives?
3. Can we apply our approach to effectively determine for which parameters to sample in a learning framework?

Let us briefly summarize the computations involved in answering these questions. First of all, computing the solution $\mathsf{sol}(\mathbf{u})$ for a pMC, which is defined in Eq. (1), means solving the linear equation system in Eq. (5). Similarly, computing the robust solution $\mathsf{sol}_R(\mathbf{u})$ for a prMC means solving the LP in Eq. (15). Then, solving Problem 1, i.e., computing all $|V|$ partial derivatives, amounts to solving a linear equation system for each parameter $v \in V$ (namely, Eq. (5) for a prMC and Eq. (17) for a prMC). In contrast, solving Problem 2, i.e., computing a subset $V^\star$ of parameters with maximal (or minimal) derivative, means for a pMC that we solve the LP in Eq. (10) (or the equivalent LP for a prMC) and thereafter extract the subset of $V^\star$ parameters using Proposition 1.

Problem 3: Computing the k-highest Derivatives. A solution to Problem 2 is a set $V^\star$ of k parameters but does not include the computation of the derivatives. However, it is straightforward to also obtain the actual derivatives $\left(\frac{\partial \mathsf{sol}}{\partial u(v)} \right) [\mathbf{u}]$ for each parameter $v \in V^\star$. Specifically, we solve Problem 1 for the k parameters in $V^\star$, such that we obtain the partial derivatives for all $v \in V^\star$. We remark that, for $k = 1$, the derivative follows directly from the optimal value $s_I^\top y^+$ of the LP in Eq. (10), so this additional step is not necessary. We will refer to computing the actual values of the k highest derivatives as *Problem 3*.

Setup. We implement our approach in Python 3.10, using Storm [35] to parse pMCs, Gurobi [31] to solve LPs, and the SciPy sparse solver to solve equation systems. All experiments run on a computer with a 4GHz Intel Core i9 CPU and 64 GB RAM, with a timeout of one hour. Our implementation is available at https://doi.org/10.5281/zenodo.7864260.

Grid World Benchmarks. We use scaled versions of the grid world from the example in Sect. 2 with over a million states and up to 10 000 terrain types. The vehicle only moves right or down, both with 50% probability (wrapping around when leaving the grid). Slipping only occurs when moving down and (slightly different from the example in Sect. 2) means that the vehicle moves *two cells instead of one*. We obtain between $N = 500$ and $1\,000$ samples of each slipping probability. For the pMCs, we use maximum likelihood estimation ($\frac{\bar{p}}{N}$, with $\bar{p}$ the sample mean) obtained from these samples as probabilities, whereas, for the prMCs, we infer probability intervals using Hoeffding's inequality (see Q3 for details).

Benchmarks from Literature. We also use several instances of parametric extensions of MCs and Markov decision processes (MDPs) from standard benchmark suits [33,44]. We also use pMC benchmarks from [5,23] as these models have more parameters than the traditional benchmarks. We extend these benchmarks to prMCs by constructing probability intervals around the pMC's probabilities.

Results. The results for all benchmarks are shown in [6, Appendix B, Tab. 2–3].

Q1. Computing Solutions vs. Derivatives

We investigate whether computing derivatives is feasible on p(r)MCs. In particular, we compare the computation times for computing derivatives on p(r)MCs (Problems 1 and 3) with the times for computing the solution for these models.

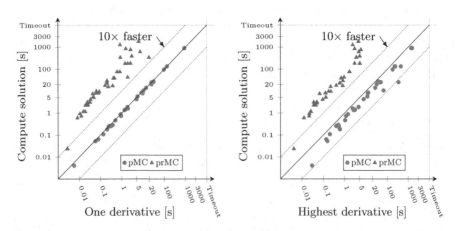

Fig. 5. Runtimes (log-scale) for computing a single derivative (left, Problem 1) or the highest derivative (right, Problem 3), vs. computing the solution $\mathsf{sol}[\mathbf{u}]/\mathsf{sol}_R[\mathbf{u}]$.

Table 1. Model sizes, runtimes, and derivatives for selection of grid world models.

Model statistics				Verifying		Problem 1	Problem 3		Derivatives	
Type	$|S|$	$|V|$	#trans	$\text{sol}_{(R)}[\mathbf{u}]$	Time [s]	All derivs. [s]	$k=1$ [s]	$k=10[s]$	Highest	Error %
pMC	5000	50	14995	5.07	1.39	3.32	2.64	2.69	1.54e+00	0.0
pMC	5000	100	14995	5.05	1.36	4.17	2.63	2.66	1.28e+00	0.0
pMC	5000	921	14995	4.93	1.87	19.92	4.52	2.87	1.20e+00	0.0
pMC	80000	100	239995	8.01	25.54	98.47	45.18	46.87	1.95e+00	0.0
pMC	80000	1000	239995	8.01	25.64	612.97	48.92	58.20	2.08e+00	0.0
pMC	80000	9831	239995	7.93	25.52	5,650.25	347.76	1,343.59	2.10e+00	0.0
pMC	1280000	100	3839995	12.90	902.52	4,747.43	1,396.51	1,507.77	3.32e+00	0.0
pMC	1280000	1000	3839995	12.79	902.67	37,078.12	1,550.45	1,617.27	3.18e+00	0.0
pMC	1280000	10000	3839995	Timeout[b]	—	—	—	—	—	—
prMC	5000	100	14995	136.07	23.46	3.55	0.60	1.58	-1.26e-02	-0.0
prMC	5000	921	14995	138.74	29.82	25.23	0.85	1.09	-4.44e-03	-0.0
prMC	20000	100	59995	1,276.43	15.68	2.40	2.70	-4.96e-01	-0.1
prMC	20000	1000	59995	2,258.41	339.96	159.70	3.53	4.09	-9.51e-02	-0.0
prMC	80000	100	239995	Timeout[b]	—	—	—	—	—	—

[a] Extrapolated from the runtimes for 10 to all $|V|$ parameters.
[b] Timeout (1 h) occurred for verifying the p(r)MC, not for computing derivatives.

In Fig. 5, we show for all benchmarks the times for computing the solution (defined in Eqs. (1) and (4)), versus computing either a single derivative for Problem 1 (left) or the highest derivative of all parameters resulting from Problem 3 (right). A point (x, y) in the left plot means that computing a single derivative took x seconds while computing the solution took y seconds. A line above the (center) diagonal means we obtained a speed-up over the time for computing the solution; a point over the upper diagonal indicates a 10× speed-up or larger.

One Derivative. The left plot in Fig. 5 shows that, for pMCs, the times for computing the solution and a single derivative are approximately the same. This is expected since both problems amount to solving a single equation system with $|S|$ unknowns. Recall that, for prMCs, computing the solution means solving the LP in Eq. (15), while for derivatives we solve an equation system. Thus, computing a derivative for a prMC is relatively cheap compared to computing the solution, which is confirmed by the results in Fig. 5.

Highest Derivative. The right plot in Fig. 5 shows that, for pMCs, computing the highest derivative is slightly slower than computing the solution (the LP to compute the highest derivative takes longer than the equation system to compute the solution). On the other hand, computing the highest derivative for a prMC is still cheap compared to computing the solution. Thus, if we are using a prMC anyways, computing the derivatives is relatively cheap.

Q2. Runtime Improvement of Computing only k Derivatives

We want to understand the computational benefits of solving Problem 3 over solving Problem 1. For Q2, we consider all models with $|V| \geq 10$ parameters.

An excerpt of results for the grid world benchmarks is presented in Table 1. Recall that, after obtaining the (robust) solution, solving Problem 1 amounts to solving $|V|$ linear equation systems, whereas Problem 3 involves solving a

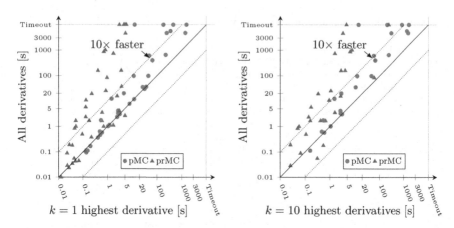

Fig. 6. Runtimes (log-scale) for computing the highest (left) or 10 highest (right) derivatives (Problem 3), versus computing all derivatives (Problem 1).

single LP and k equations systems. From Table 1, it is clear that computing k derivatives is orders of magnitudes faster than computing all $|V|$ derivatives, especially if the total number of parameters is high.

We compare the runtimes for computing all derivatives (Problem 1) with computing only the $k = 1$ or 10 highest derivatives (Problem 3). The left plot of Fig. 6 shows the runtimes for $k = 1$, and the right plot for the $k = 10$ highest derivatives. The interpretation for Fig. 6 is the same as for Fig. 5. From Fig. 6, we observe that computing only the k highest derivatives generally leads to significant speed-ups, often of more than 10 times (except for very small models). Moreover, the difference between $k = 1$ and $k = 10$ is minor, showing that retrieving the actual derivatives after solving Problem 2 is relatively cheap.

Numerical Stability. While our algorithm is exact, our implementation uses floating-point arithmetic for efficiency. To evaluate the numerical stability, we compare the highest derivatives (solving Problem 3 for $k = 1$) with an empirical approximation of the derivative obtained by perturbing the parameter by 1×10^3. The difference (column '*Error. %*' in Table 1 and [6, Appendix B, Table 2] between both is marginal, indicating that our implementation is sufficiently numerically stable to return accurate derivatives.

Q3. Application in a Learning Framework

Reducing the sample complexity is a key challenge in learning under uncertainty [43,47]. In particular, learning in stochastic environments is very data-intensive, and realistic applications tend to require millions of samples to provide tight bounds on measures of interest [16]. Motivated by this challenge, we apply our approach in a learning framework to investigate if derivatives can be used to effectively guide exploration, compared to alternative exploration strategies.

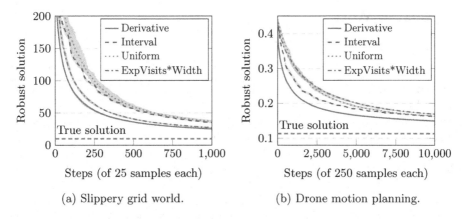

Fig. 7. Robust solutions for each sampling strategy in the learning framework for the grid world (a) and drone (b) benchmarks. Averages values of 10 (grid world) or 5 (drone) repetitions are shown, with shaded areas the min/max.

Models. We consider the problem of where to sample in 1) a slippery grid world with $|S| = 800$ and $|V| = 100$ terrain types, and 2) the drone benchmark from [23] with $|S| = 4\,179$ and $|V| = 1\,053$ parameters. As in the motivating example in Sect. 2, we learn a model of the unknown MC in the form of a prMC, where the parameters are the sample sizes for each parameter. We assume access to a model that can arbitrarily sample each parameter (i.e., the slipping probability in the case of the grid world). We use an initial sample size of $N_i = 100$ for each parameter $i \in \{1, \ldots, |V|\}$, from which we infer a $\beta = 0.9$ (90%) confidence interval using Hoeffding's inequality. The interval for parameter i is $[\hat{p}_i - \epsilon_i, \hat{p}_i + \epsilon_i]$, with $\hat{p}_i$ the sample mean and $\epsilon_i = \sqrt{\frac{\log 2 - \log(1-\beta)}{2N}}$ (see, e.g., [14] for details).

Learning Scheme. We iteratively choose for which parameter $v_i \in V$ to obtain 25 (for the grid world) or 250 (for the drone) additional samples. We compare four strategies for choosing the parameter v_i to sample for: 1) with highest derivative, i.e., solving Problem 3 for $k = 1$; 2) with biggest interval width ϵ_i; 3) uniformly; and 4) sampling according to the expected number of visits times the interval width (see [6, Appendix B.1] for details). After each step, we update the robust upper bound on the solution for the prMC with the additional samples.

Results. The upper bounds on the solution for each sampling strategy, as well as the solution for the MC with the true parameter values, are shown in Fig. 7. For both benchmarks, our derivative-guided sampling strategy converges to the true solution faster than the other strategies. Notably, our derivative-guided strategy accounts for both the uncertainty and importance of each parameter, which leads to a lower sample complexity required to approach the true solution.

7   Related Work

We discuss related work in three areas: pMCs, their extension to parametric interval Markov chains (piMCs), and general sensitivity analysis methods.

Parametric Markov Chains. pMCs [24,45] have traditionally been studied in terms of computing the solution function [13,25,28,29,32]. Much recent literature considers synthesis (find a parameter valuation such that a specification is satisfied) or verification (prove that all valuations satisfy a specification). We refer to [38] for a recent overview. For our paper, particularly relevant are [55], which checks whether a derivative is positive (for all parameter valuations), and [34], which solves parameter synthesis via gradient descent. We note that all these problems are (co-)ETR complete [41] and that the solution function is exponentially large in the number of parameters [7], whereas we consider a polynomial-time algorithm. Furthermore, practical *verification* procedures for uncontrollable parameters (as we do) are limited to less than 10 parameters. Parametric verification is used in [51] to guide model refinement by detecting for which parameter values a specification is satisfied. In contrast, we consider slightly more conservative rMCs and aim to stepwise optimize an objective. Solution functions also provide an approach to compute and refine confidence intervals [17]; however, the size of the solution function hampers scalability.

Parametric interval Markov Chains (piMCs). While prMCs have, to the best of our knowledge, not been studied, their slightly more restricted version are piMCs. In particular, piMCs have interval-valued transitions with parametric bounds. Work on piMCs falls into two categories. First, *consistency* [27,50]: is there a parameter instantiation such that the (reachable fragment of the) induced interval MC contains valid probability distributions? Second, parameter synthesis for quantitative and qualitative reachability in piMCs with up to 12 parameters [10].

Perturbation Analysis. Perturbation analysis considers the change in solution by any perturbation vector X for the parameter instantiation, whose norm is upper bounded by δ, i.e., $\|X\| \leq \delta$ (or conversely, which δ ensures the solution perturbation is below a given maximum). Likewise, [21] uses the distance between two instantiations of a pMC (called augmented interval MC) to bound the change in reachability probability. Similar analyses exist for stationary distributions [1]. These problems are closely related to the verification problem in pMCs and are equally (in)tractable if there are dependencies over multiple parameters. To improve tractability, a follow-up [56] derives asymptotic bounds based on first or second-order Taylor expansions. Other approaches to perturbation analysis analyze individual paths of a system [18,19,30]. Sensitivity analysis in (parameter-free) imprecise MCs, a variation to rMCs, is thoroughly studied in [22].

Exploration in Learning. Similar to Q3 in Sect. 6, determining where to sample is relevant in many learning settings. Approaches such as probably approximately correct (PAC) statistical model checking [2,3] and model-based reinforcement learning [47] commonly use optimistic exploration policies [48]. By contrast, we guide exploration based on the sensitivity analysis of the solution function with respect to the parametric model.

8   Concluding Remarks

We have presented efficient methods to compute partial derivatives of the solution functions for pMCs and prMCs. For both models, we have shown how to compute these derivatives explicitly *for all parameters*, as well as how to compute only the *k highest derivatives*. Our experiments have shown that we can compute derivatives for models with over a million states and thousands of parameters. In particular, computing the *k* highest derivatives yields significant speed-ups compared to computing all derivatives explicitly and is feasible for prMCs which can be verified. In the future, we want to support nondeterminism in the models and apply our methods in (online) learning frameworks, in particular for settings where reducing the uncertainty is computationally expensive [42,49].

References

1. Abbas, K., Berkhout, J., Heidergott, B.: A critical account of perturbation analysis of markov chains. arXiv preprint arXiv:1609.04138 (2016)
2. Agarwal, C., Guha, S., Kretínský, J., Muruganandham, P.: PAC statistical model checking of mean payoff in discrete- and continuous-time MDP. In: CAV (2). Lecture Notes in Computer Science, vol. 13372, pp. 3–25. Springer (2022). https://doi.org/10.1007/978-3-031-13188-2_1
3. Ashok, P., Křetínský, J., Weininger, M.: PAC statistical model checking for markov decision processes and stochastic games. In: Dillig, I., Tasiran, S. (eds.) CAV 2019. LNCS, vol. 11561, pp. 497–519. Springer, Cham (2019). https://doi.org/10.1007/978-3-030-25540-4_29
4. Badings, T., Simão, T.D., Suilen, M., Jansen, N.: Decision-making under uncertainty: beyond probabilities. Int. J. Softw. Tools Technol. Transf. (2023)
5. Badings, T.S., Cubuktepe, M., Jansen, N., Junges, S., Katoen, J., Topcu, U.: Scenario-based verification of uncertain parametric MDPs. Int. J. Softw. Tools Technol. Transf. 24(5), 803–819 (2022)
6. Badings, T.S., Junges, S., Marandi, A., Topcu, U., Jansen, N.: Efficient sensitivity analysis for parametric robust markov chains (extended version). Tech. rep., CoRR, abs/2305.01473 (2023)
7. Baier, C., Hensel, C., Hutschenreiter, L., Junges, S., Katoen, J., Klein, J.: Parametric markov chains: PCTL complexity and fraction-free gaussian elimination. Inf. Comput. 272, 104504 (2020)

8. Baier, C., Katoen, J.: Principles of model checking. MIT Press (2008)
9. Barratt, S.: On the differentiability of the solution to convex optimization problems. arXiv preprint arXiv:1804.05098 (2018)
10. Bart, A., Delahaye, B., Fournier, P., Lime, D., Monfroy, É., Truchet, C.: Reachability in parametric interval markov chains using constraints. Theor. Comput. Sci. **747**, 48–74 (2018)
11. Bazaraa, M.S., Jarvis, J.J., Sherali, H.D.: Linear programming and network flows. John Wiley & Sons (2011)
12. Ben-Tal, A., Ghaoui, L.E., Nemirovski, A.: Robust Optimization, Princeton Series in Applied Mathematics, vol. 28. Princeton University Press (2009)
13. Bortolussi, L., Milios, D., Sanguinetti, G.: Smoothed model checking for uncertain continuous-time markov chains. Inf. Comput. **247**, 235–253 (2016)
14. Boucheron, S., Lugosi, G., Massart, P.: Concentration Inequalities - A Nonasymptotic Theory of Independence. Oxford University Press, Oxford (2013)
15. Boyd, S.P., Vandenberghe, L.: Convex Optimization. Cambridge University Press, Cambridge (2014)
16. Buckman, J., Hafner, D., Tucker, G., Brevdo, E., Lee, H.: Sample-efficient reinforcement learning with stochastic ensemble value expansion. In: NeurIPS, pp. 8234–8244 (2018)
17. Calinescu, R., Ghezzi, C., Johnson, K., Pezzè, M., Rafiq, Y., Tamburrelli, G.: Formal verification with confidence intervals to establish quality of service properties of software systems. IEEE Trans. Reliab. **65**(1), 107–125 (2016)
18. Cao, X., Chen, H.: Perturbation realization, potentials, and sensitivity analysis of markov processes. IEEE Trans. Autom. Control **42**(10), 1382–1393 (1997)
19. Cao, X., Wan, Y.: Algorithms for sensitivity analysis of markov systems through potentials and perturbation realization. IEEE Trans. Control Syst. Technol. **6**(4), 482–494 (1998)
20. Chen, T., Feng, Y., Rosenblum, D.S., Su, G.: Perturbation analysis in verification of discrete-time markov chains. In: Baldan, P., Gorla, D. (eds.) CONCUR 2014. LNCS, vol. 8704, pp. 218–233. Springer, Heidelberg (2014). https://doi.org/10.1007/978-3-662-44584-6_16
21. Chonev, V.: Reachability in augmented interval markov chains. In: Filiot, E., Jungers, R., Potapov, I. (eds.) RP 2019. LNCS, vol. 11674, pp. 79–92. Springer, Cham (2019). https://doi.org/10.1007/978-3-030-30806-3_7
22. Cooman, G.D., Hermans, F., Quaeghebeur, E.: Sensitivity analysis for finite markov chains in discrete time. In: UAI, pp. 129–136. AUAI Press (2008)
23. Cubuktepe, M., Jansen, N., Junges, S., Katoen, J., Topcu, U.: Convex optimization for parameter synthesis in MDPs. IEEE Trans. Autom. Control **67**(12), 6333–6348 (2022)
24. Daws, C.: Symbolic and Parametric Model Checking of Discrete-Time Markov Chains. In: Liu, Z., Araki, K. (eds.) ICTAC 2004. LNCS, vol. 3407, pp. 280–294. Springer, Heidelberg (2005). https://doi.org/10.1007/978-3-540-31862-0_21

25. Dehnert, C., et al.: PROPhESY: a probabilistic parameter synthesis tool. In: Kroening, D., Păsăreanu, C.S. (eds.) CAV 2015. LNCS, vol. 9206, pp. 214–231. Springer, Cham (2015). https://doi.org/10.1007/978-3-319-21690-4_13

26. Delahaye, B.: Consistency for parametric interval markov chains. In: SynCoP. OASIcs, vol. 44, pp. 17–32. Schloss Dagstuhl - Leibniz-Zentrum für Informatik (2015)

27. Delahaye, B., Lime, D., Petrucci, L.: Parameter synthesis for parametric interval markov chains. In: Jobstmann, B., Leino, K.R.M. (eds.) VMCAI 2016. LNCS, vol. 9583, pp. 372–390. Springer, Heidelberg (2016). https://doi.org/10.1007/978-3-662-49122-5_18

28. Fang, X., Calinescu, R., Gerasimou, S., Alhwikem, F.: Fast parametric model checking through model fragmentation. In: ICSE, pp. 835–846. IEEE (2021)

29. Filieri, A., Tamburrelli, G., Ghezzi, C.: Supporting self-adaptation via quantitative verification and sensitivity analysis at run time. IEEE Trans. Softw. Eng. **42**(1), 75–99 (2016)

30. Fu, M.C., Hu, J.: Smoothed perturbation analysis derivative estimation for markov chains. Oper. Res. Lett. **15**(5), 241–251 (1994)

31. Gurobi Optimization, LLC: Gurobi optimizer reference manual (2023). https://www.gurobi.com

32. Hahn, E.M., Hermanns, H., Zhang, L.: Probabilistic reachability for parametric markov models. Int. J. Softw. Tools Technol. Transf. **13**(1), 3–19 (2011)

33. Hartmanns, A., Klauck, M., Parker, D., Quatmann, T., Ruijters, E.: The quantitative verification benchmark set. In: Vojnar, T., Zhang, L. (eds.) TACAS 2019. LNCS, vol. 11427, pp. 344–350. Springer, Cham (2019). https://doi.org/10.1007/978-3-030-17462-0_20

34. Heck, L., Spel, J., Junges, S., Moerman, J., Katoen, J.-P.: Gradient-descent for randomized controllers under partial observability. In: Finkbeiner, B., Wies, T. (eds.) VMCAI 2022. LNCS, vol. 13182, pp. 127–150. Springer, Cham (2022). https://doi.org/10.1007/978-3-030-94583-1_7

35. Hensel, C., Junges, S., Katoen, J.P., Quatmann, T., Volk, M.: The probabilistic model checker Storm. Softw. Tools Technol. Transf. (2021)

36. Hoffman, A.J., Kruskal, J.B.: Integral boundary points of convex polyhedra. In: Jünger, M., Liebling, T.M., Naddef, D., Nemhauser, G.L., Pulleyblank, W.R., Reinelt, G., Rinaldi, G., Wolsey, L.A. (eds.) 50 Years of Integer Programming 1958-2008, pp. 49–76. Springer, Heidelberg (2010). https://doi.org/10.1007/978-3-540-68279-0_3

37. Hoffman, A.J., Kruskal, J.B.: Integral boundary points of convex polyhedra. 50 Years of integer programming 1958–2008, p. 49 (2010)

38. Jansen, N., Junges, S., Katoen, J.: Parameter synthesis in markov models: a gentle survey. In: Principles of Systems Design. Lecture Notes in Computer Science, vol. 13660, pp. 407–437. Springer (2022). https://doi.org/10.1007/978-3-031-22337-2_20

39. Jonsson, B., Larsen, K.G.: Specification and refinement of probabilistic processes. In: LICS, pp. 266–277. IEEE Computer Society (1991)

40. Junges, S., et al.: Parameter synthesis for markov models. CoRR abs/1903.07993 (2019)

41. Junges, S., Katoen, J., Pérez, G.A., Winkler, T.: The complexity of reachability in parametric markov decision processes. J. Comput. Syst. Sci. **119**, 183–210 (2021)
42. Junges, S., Spaan, M.T.J.: Abstraction-refinement for hierarchical probabilistic models. In: CAV (1). Lecture Notes in Computer Science, vol. 13371, pp. 102–123. Springer (2022). https://doi.org/10.1007/978-3-031-13185-1_6
43. Kakade, S.M.: On the sample complexity of reinforcement learning. Ph.D. thesis, University of London, University College London (United Kingdom) (2003)
44. Kwiatkowska, M., Norman, G., Parker, D.: PRISM 4.0: verification of probabilistic real-time systems. In: Gopalakrishnan, G., Qadeer, S. (eds.) CAV 2011. LNCS, vol. 6806, pp. 585–591. Springer, Heidelberg (2011). https://doi.org/10.1007/978-3-642-22110-1_47
45. Lanotte, R., Maggiolo-Schettini, A., Troina, A.: Parametric probabilistic transition systems for system design and analysis. Formal Aspects Comput. **19**(1), 93–109 (2007)
46. Matousek, J., Gärtner, B.: Integer Programming and LP Relaxation, pp. 29–40. Springer, Berlin Heidelberg (2007). https://doi.org/10.1007/978-3-540-30717-4_3
47. Moerland, T.M., Broekens, J., Jonker, C.M.: Model-based reinforcement learning: a survey. CoRR abs/2006.16712 (2020)
48. Munos, R.: From bandits to monte-carlo tree search: The optimistic principle applied to optimization and planning. Found. Trends Mach. Learn. **7**(1), 1–129 (2014)
49. Neary, C., Verginis, C.K., Cubuktepe, M., Topcu, U.: Verifiable and compositional reinforcement learning systems. In: ICAPS, pp. 615–623. AAAI Press (2022)
50. Petrucci, L., van de Pol, J.: Parameter synthesis algorithms for parametric interval markov chains. In: Baier, C., Caires, L. (eds.) FORTE 2018. LNCS, vol. 10854, pp. 121–140. Springer, Cham (2018). https://doi.org/10.1007/978-3-319-92612-4_7
51. Polgreen, E., Wijesuriya, V.B., Haesaert, S., Abate, A.: Automated experiment design for data-efficient verification of parametric markov decision processes. In: Bertrand, N., Bortolussi, L. (eds.) QEST 2017. LNCS, vol. 10503, pp. 259–274. Springer, Cham (2017). https://doi.org/10.1007/978-3-319-66335-7_16
52. Puggelli, A., Li, W., Sangiovanni-Vincentelli, A.L., Seshia, S.A.: Polynomial-time verification of PCTL properties of MDPs with convex uncertainties. In: Sharygina, N., Veith, H. (eds.) CAV 2013. LNCS, vol. 8044, pp. 527–542. Springer, Heidelberg (2013). https://doi.org/10.1007/978-3-642-39799-8_35
53. Puterman, M.L.: Markov Decision Processes: Discrete Stochastic Dynamic Programming. Wiley Series in Probability and Statistics, Wiley (1994)
54. Sen, K., Viswanathan, M., Agha, G.: Model-checking markov chains in the presence of uncertainties. In: Hermanns, H., Palsberg, J. (eds.) TACAS 2006. LNCS, vol. 3920, pp. 394–410. Springer, Heidelberg (2006). https://doi.org/10.1007/11691372_26
55. Spel, J., Junges, S., Katoen, J.-P.: Finding provably optimal markov chains. In: TACAS 2021. LNCS, vol. 12651, pp. 173–190. Springer, Cham (2021). https://doi.org/10.1007/978-3-030-72016-2_10
56. Su, G., Feng, Y., Chen, T., Rosenblum, D.S.: Asymptotic perturbation bounds for probabilistic model checking with empirically determined probability parameters. IEEE Trans. Software Eng. **42**(7), 623–639 (2016)

57. Suilen, M., Simão, T.D., Parker, D., Jansen, N.: Robust anytime learning of markov decision processes. In: NeurIPS, vol. 35, pp. 28790–28802. Curran Associates, Inc. (2022)
58. Wiesemann, W., Kuhn, D., Sim, M.: Distributionally robust convex optimization. Oper. Res. **62**(6), 1358–1376 (2014)
59. Wolff, E.M., Topcu, U., Murray, R.M.: Robust control of uncertain markov decision processes with temporal logic specifications. In: CDC, pp. 3372–3379. IEEE (2012)
60. Wolsey, L.A.: Integer programming. John Wiley & Sons (2020)

MDPs as Distribution Transformers: Affine Invariant Synthesis for Safety Objectives

S. Akshay[1]([✉]) [iD], Krishnendu Chatterjee[2] [iD], Tobias Meggendorfer[2,3] [iD], and Đorđe Žikelić[2] [iD]

[1] Indian Institute of Technology Bombay, Mumbai, India
akshayss@cse.iitb.ac.in
[2] Institute of Science and Technology Austria (ISTA),
Klosterneuburg, Austria
{krishnendu.chatterjee,dzikelic}@ist.ac.at
[3] Technical University of Munich, Munich, Germany
tobias.meggendorfer@cit.tum.de

Abstract. Markov decision processes can be viewed as transformers of probability distributions. While this view is useful from a practical standpoint to reason about trajectories of distributions, basic reachability and safety problems are known to be computationally intractable (i.e., Skolem-hard) to solve in such models. Further, we show that even for simple examples of MDPs, strategies for safety objectives over distributions can require infinite memory and randomization.

In light of this, we present a novel overapproximation approach to synthesize strategies in an MDP, such that a safety objective over the distributions is met. More precisely, we develop a new framework for template-based synthesis of certificates as affine distributional and inductive invariants for safety objectives in MDPs. We provide two algorithms within this framework. One can only synthesize memoryless strategies, but has relative completeness guarantees, while the other can synthesize general strategies. The runtime complexity of both algorithms is in PSPACE. We implement these algorithms and show that they can solve several non-trivial examples.

Keywords: Markov decision processes · invariant synthesis · distribution transformers · Skolem hardness

1 Introduction

Markov decision processes (MDPs) are a classical model for probabilistic decision making systems. They extend the basic probabilistic model of Markov chains with non-determinism and are widely used across different domains and contexts. In the

This work was supported in part by the ERC CoG 863818 (FoRM-SMArt) and the European Union's Horizon 2020 research and innovation programme under the Marie Skłodowska-Curie Grant Agreement No. 665385 as well as DST/CEFIPRA/INRIA project EQuaVE and SERB Matrices grant MTR/2018/00074.

C. Enea and A. Lal (Eds.): CAV 2023, LNCS 13966, pp. 86–112, 2023.
https://doi.org/10.1007/978-3-031-37709-9_5

verification community, MDPs are often viewed through an automata-theoretic lens, as state transformers, with runs being sequences of states with certain probability for taking each run (see e.g., [9]). With this view, reachability probabilities can be computed using simple fixed point equations and model checking can be done over appropriately defined logics such as PCTL*. However, in several contexts such as modelling biochemical networks, queueing theory or probabilistic dynamical systems, it is more convenient to view MDPs as transformers of probability distributions over the states, and define objectives over these distributions [1,5,12,17,44,47]. In this framework, we can, for instance, easily reason about properties such as the probability in a set of states always being above a given threshold or comparing the probability in two states at some future time point. More concretely, in a chemical reaction network, we may require that the concentration of a particular complex is never above 10%. Such distribution-based properties cannot be expressed in PCTL* [12], and thus several orthogonal logics have been defined [1,12,44] that reason about distributions.

Unfortunately, and perhaps surprisingly, when we view them as distribution transformers even the simplest reachability and safety problems with respect to probability distributions over states remain unsolved. The reason for this is a number-theoretical hardness result that lies at the core of these questions. In [3], it is shown that even with just Markov chains, reachability is as hard as the so-called SKOLEM problem, and safety is as hard as the POSITIVITY problem [55, 56], the decidability of both of which are long-standing open problems in linear recurrence sequences. Moreover, synthesizing strategies that resolve the non-determinism in MDPs to achieve an objective (whether reachability or safety) is further complicated by the issue of how much memory can be allowed for the strategy. As we show in Sect. 3, even for very simple examples, strategies for safety can require infinite memory as well as randomization.

In light of these difficulties, what can one do to tackle these problems *in theory and in practice*? In this paper, we take an over-approximation route to approach these questions, not only to check existence of strategies for safety but also synthesize them. Inspired by the success of invariant synthesis in program verification, our goal is to develop a novel invariant-synthesis based approach towards strategy synthesis in MDPs, viewed as transformers of distributions. In this paper, we restrict our attention to a class of safety objectives on MDPs, which are already general enough to capture several interesting and natural problems on MDPs. Our contributions are the following:

1. We define the notion of *inductive distributional invariants* for safety in MDPs. These are sets of probability distributions over states of the MDP, that (i) contain all possible distributions reachable from the initial distribution, under all strategies of an MDP, and (ii) are closed under taking the next step.
2. We show that such invariants provide *sound and complete certificates* for proving safety objectives in MDPs. In doing so, we formalize the link between strategies and distributional invariants in MDPs. This by itself does not help us get effective algorithms in light of the hardness results above. Hence we then focus on synthesizing invariants of a particular *shape*.

3. We develop two algorithms for automated synthesis of *affine* inductive distributional invariants that prove safety in MDPs, and *at the same time*, synthesize the associated strategies.
   - The first algorithm is restricted to synthesizing memoryless strategies but is *relatively complete*, i.e., whenever a memoryless strategy and an affine inductive distributional invariant that witness safety exist, we are guaranteed to find them.
   - The second algorithm can synthesize general strategies as well as memoryless strategies, but is incomplete in general.

   In both cases, we employ a template-based synthesis approach and reduce synthesis to the existential first-order theory of reals, which gives a PSPACE complexity upper bound. In the first case, this reduction depends on Farkas' lemma. In the second case, we need to use Handelman's theorem, a specialized result for strictly positive polynomials.
4. We implement our approaches and show that for several practical and nontrivial examples, affine invariants suffice. Further, we demonstrate that our prototype tool can synthesize these invariants and associated strategies.

Finally, we discuss the generalization of our approach from affine to polynomial invariants and some variants that our approach can handle.

1.1 Related Work

Distribution-based Safety Analysis in MDPs. The problem of checking distribution-based safety objectives for MDPs was defined in [5] but a solution was provided only in the *uninitialized* setting, where the initial distribution is not given and also under the assumption that the target set is closed and bounded. In contrast, we tackle both initialized and uninitialized settings, our target sets are general affine sets and we focus on actually synthesizing strategies not just proving existence.

Template-based Program Analysis. Template-based synthesis via the means of linear/polynomial constraint solving is a standard approach in program analysis to synthesizing certificates for proving properties of programs. Many of these methods utilize Farkas' lemma or Handelman's theorem to automate the synthesis of program invariants [20,27], termination proofs [6,14,23,28,57], reachability proofs [8] or cost bounds [16,39,64]. The works [2,18,19,21,22,24,25,62,63] utilize Farkas' lemma or Handelman's theorem to synthesize certificates for these properties in probabilistic programs. While our algorithms build on the ideas from the works on template-based inductive invariant synthesis in programs [20,27], the key novelty of our algorithms is that they synthesize a fundamentally different kind of invariants, i.e. *distributional invariants* in MDPs. In contrast, the existing works on (probabilistic) program analysis synthesize *state* invariants. Furthermore, our algorithms synthesize distributional invariants *together* with MDP strategies. While it is common in controller synthesis to synthesize an MDP strategy for a *state* invariant, we are not aware of any previous work that uses template-based synthesis methods to compute MDP strategies for a *distributional* invariant.

Other Approaches to Invariant Synthesis in Programs. Alternative approaches to invariant synthesis in programs have also been considered, for instance via abstract interpretation [29,30,33,60], counterexample guided invariant synthesis (CEGIS) [7,10,34], recurrence analysis [32,42,43] or learning [35,61]. While some of these approaches can be more scalable than constraint solving-based methods, they typically do not provide relative completeness guarantees. An interesting direction of future work would be to explore whether these alternative approaches could be used for synthesizing distributional invariants together with MDP strategies more efficiently.

Weakest Pre-expectation Calculus. Expectation transformers and the weakest pre-expectation calculus generalize Dijkstra's weakest precondition calculus to the setting of probabilistic programs. Expectation transformers were introduced in the seminal work on probabilistic propositional dynamic logic (PPDL) [45] and were extended to the setting of probabilistic programs with non-determinism in [48,52]. Weakest pre-expectation calculus for reasoning about expected runtime of probabilistic programs was presented in [40]. Intuitively, given a function over probabilistic program outputs, the weakest pre-expectation calculus can be used to reason about the supremum or the infimum expected value of the function upon executing the probabilistic program, where the supremum and the infimum are taken over the set of all possible schedulers (i.e. strategies) used to resolve non-determinism. When the function is the indicator function of some output set of states, this yields the method for reasoning about the probability of reaching the set of states. Thus, weakest pre-expectation calculus allows reasoning about safety with respect to *sets of states*. In contrast, we are interested in reasoning about safety with respect to *sets of probability distribution over states*. Moreover, while the expressiveness of this calculus allows reasoning about very complex programs, its automation typically requires user input. In this work, we aim for a fully automated approach to checking distribution-based safety.

2   Preliminaries

In this section, we recall basics of probabilistic systems and set up our notation. We assume familiarity with the central ideas of measure and probability theory, see [13] for a comprehensive overview. We write $[n] := \{1, \ldots, n\}$ to denote the set of all natural numbers from 1 to n. For any set S, we use $\overline{S}$ to denote its complement. A *probability distribution* on a countable set X is a mapping $\mu : X \to [0,1]$, such that $\sum_{x \in X} \mu(x) = 1$. Its *support* is denoted by $\mathrm{supp}(\mu) = \{x \in X \mid \mu(x) > 0\}$. We write $\Delta(X)$ to denote the set of all probability distributions on X. An event happens *almost surely* (a.s.) if it happens with probability 1. We assume that countable sets of states S are equipped with an arbitrary but fixed numbering.

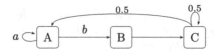

Fig. 1. Our running example MDP. It comprises three states $S = \{A, B, C\}$, depicted by rounded rectangles. In state A, there are two actions available, namely a and b. We have $\delta(A, a, A) = 1$ and $\delta(A, b, B) = 1$, indicated by arrows. States B and C have only one available action each, thus we omit explicitly labelling them.

2.1   Markov Systems

A *(discrete time) Markov chain (MC)* is a tuple $\mathsf{M} = (S, \delta)$, where S is a finite set of *states* and $\delta : S \to \Delta(S)$ a *transition function*, assigning to each state a probability distribution over successor states. A *Markov decision process (MDP)* is a tuple $\mathcal{M} = (S, Act, \delta)$, where S is a finite set of *states*, Act is a finite set of *actions*, overloaded to yield for each state s the set of *available actions* $Act(s) \subseteq Act$, and $\delta : S \times Act \to \Delta(S)$ is a *transition function* that for each state s and (available) action $a \in Act(s)$ yields a probability distribution over successor states. For readability, we write $\delta(s, s')$ and $\delta(s, a, s')$ instead of $\delta(s)(s')$ and $\delta(s, a)(s')$, respectively. By abuse of notation, we redefine $S \times Act := \{(s, a) \mid s \in S \wedge a \in Act(s)\}$ to refer to the set of state-action pairs. See Fig. 1 for an example MDP. This MDP is our running example and we refer to it throughout this work to point out some of the peculiarities.

An *infinite path* in an MC is an infinite sequence $\rho = s_1 s_2 \cdots \in S^\omega$, such that for every $i \in \mathbb{N}$ we have $\delta(s_i, s_{i+1}) > 0$. A *finite path* ϱ is a finite prefix of an infinite path. Analogously, infinite paths in MDP are infinite sequences $\rho = s_1 a_1 s_2 a_2 \cdots \in (S \times Act)^\omega$ such that $a_i \in Act(s_i)$ and $\delta(s_i, a_i, s_{i+1}) > 0$ for every $i \in \mathbb{N}$, and finite paths are finite prefixes thereof. We use ρ_i and ϱ_i to refer to the i-th state in the given (in)finite path, and IPaths_M and FPaths_M for the set of all (in)finite paths of a system M.

Semantics. A Markov chain evolves by repeatedly applying the probabilistic transition function in each step. For example, if we start in state s_1, we obtain the next state s_2 by drawing a random state according to the probability distribution $\delta(s_1)$. Repeating this ad infinitum produces a random infinite path. Indeed, together with an initial state s, a Markov chain M induces a unique probability measure $\mathsf{Pr}_{\mathsf{M},s}$ over the (uncountable) set of infinite paths [9].

This reasoning can be lifted to distributions over states, as follows. Suppose we begin in $\mu_0 = \{s_1 \mapsto 0.5, s_2 \mapsto 0.5\}$, meaning that initially we are in state s_1 or s_2 with probability 0.5 each. Then, $\mu_1(s') = \mu_0(s_1) \cdot \delta(s_1, s') + \mu_0(s_2) \cdot \delta(s_2, s')$, i.e. the probability to be in a state s' in the next step is 0.5 times the probability of moving from s_1 and s_2 there, respectively. For an initial distribution, we likewise obtain a probability distribution over infinite paths by setting $\mathsf{Pr}_{\mathsf{M},\mu_0}[S] := \sum_{s \in S} \mu_0(s) \cdot \mathsf{Pr}_{\mathsf{M},s}[S]$ for measurable $S \subseteq \mathsf{IPaths}_M$.

In contrast to Markov chains, MDPs also feature non-determinism, which needs be resolved in order to obtain probabilistic behaviour. This is achieved by *(path) strategies*, recipes to resolve non-determinism. Formally, a strategy on an MDP classically is defined as a function π : $\mathsf{FPaths}_\mathcal{M} \to \Delta(Act)$, which given a finite path $\varrho = s_0 a_0 s_1 a_1 \ldots s_n$ yields a probability distribution $\pi(\varrho) \in \Delta(Act(s_n))$ on the actions to be taken next. We write Π to denote the set of all strategies. Fixing any strategy π induces a Markov chain $\mathcal{M}^\pi = (\mathsf{FPaths}_\mathcal{M}, \delta^\pi)$, where for a state $\varrho = s_0 a_0 \ldots s_n \in \mathsf{FPaths}_\mathcal{M}$ the successor distribution is defined as $\delta^\pi(\varrho, \varrho a_{n+1} s_{n+1}) = \pi(\varrho, a_{n+1}) \cdot \delta(s_n, a_{n+1}, s_{n+1})$. (Note that the state space of this Markov chain in general is countably infinite.) Consequently, for each strategy π and initial distribution μ_0 we also obtain a unique probability measure $\mathsf{Pr}_{\mathcal{M}^\pi, \mu_0}$ on the infinite paths of $\mathcal{M}$. (Technically, the MC $\mathcal{M}^\pi$ induces a probability measure over paths in $\mathcal{M}^\pi$, i.e. paths where each element is a finite path of $\mathcal{M}$, however this can be directly projected to a measure over $\mathsf{IPaths}_\mathcal{M}$.)

A *one-step strategy* (also known as *memoryless* or *positional* strategy) corresponds to a fixed choice in each state, independent of the history, i.e. a mapping π : $S \to \Delta(Act)$. Fixing such a strategy induces a finite state Markov chain $\mathcal{M}^\pi = (S, \delta^\pi)$, where $\delta^\pi(s, s') = \sum_{a \in Act(s)} \pi(s)(a) \cdot \delta(s, a, s')$. We write Π_1 for the set of all one-step strategies.

A sequence of one-step strategies $(\pi_i) \in \Pi_1^\omega$ induces a general strategy which in each step i and state s chooses $\pi_i(s)$. Observe that aside from the state, such a strategy only depends on the current step, also called *Markov strategy*.

2.2   MDPs as Distribution Transformers

Probabilistic systems typically are viewed as "random generators" for paths, and we consequently investigate the (expected) behaviour of a generated path, i.e. path properties. However, in this work we follow a different view, and treat systems as *transformers of distributions*. Formally, fix a Markov chain M. For a given initial distribution μ_0, we can define the distribution at step i by $\mu_i(s) = \mathsf{Pr}_{\mu_0}[\{\rho \in \mathsf{IPaths}_M \mid \rho_i = s\}]$. We write $\mu_i = M(\mu_0, i)$ for the i-th distribution and $\mu_1 = M(\mu_0)$ for the "one-step" application of this transformation. Likewise, we obtain the same notion for an MDP $\mathcal{M}$ combined with a strategy π, and write $\mu_i = \mathcal{M}^\pi(\mu_0, i)$, $\mu_1 = \mathcal{M}^\pi(\mu_0)$. In summary, for a given initial distribution, a Markov chain induces a unique stream of distributions, and an MDP provides one for each strategy.

This naturally invites questions related to this induced stream of distributions. In their path interpretation, queries such as *reachability* or *safety*, i.e. asking the probability of reaching or avoiding a set of states, allow for simple, polynomial time solutions [9,58]. However, the corresponding notions already are surprisingly difficult in the space of distributions. Thus, we restrict to the *safety problem*, which we introduce in the following. Intuitively, given a *safe set* of distributions over states $H \subseteq \Delta(S)$, we are interested in deciding whether the MDP can be controlled such that the stream of distributions always remains inside H.

3   Problem Statement and Examples

Let $\mathcal{M} = (S, Act, \delta)$ be an MDP and $H \subseteq \Delta(S)$ be a safe set. A distribution μ_0 is called *H-safe under* π if $\mathcal{M}^\pi(\mu_0, i) \in H$ for all $i \geq 0$, and *H-safe* if there exists a strategy under which μ_0 is safe. We mention two variants of the resulting decision problem as defined in [5]:

- Initialized safety: Given an initial probability distribution μ_0 and safe set H, decide whether μ_0 is H-safe.
- Uninitialized safety: Given a safe set H, decide whether there exists a distribution μ which is H-safe.

Note that we have discussed neither the shape nor the representation of H, which naturally plays an important role for decidability and complexity.

One may be tempted to think that the initialized variant is simpler, as more input is given. However, this problem is known to be POSITIVITY-*hard*[1] already for simple cases and already when H is defined in terms of rational constants!

Theorem 1 ([3]). *The initialized safety problem for Markov chains and H given as linear inequality constraint ($H = \{\mu \mid \mu(s) \leq r, s \in S, r \in \mathbb{Q} \cap [0,1]\}$), is* POSITIVITY-*hard.*

Proof. In [3, Corollary 4], the authors show that the inequality version of the Markov reachability problem, i.e. deciding whether there exists an i such that $\mu_i(s) > r$ for a given rational r, is POSITIVITY-hard. The result follows by observing that safety is the negation of reachability.   □

Thus, finding a decision procedure for this problem is unlikely, since it would answer several fundamental questions of number theory, see e.g. [41,55,56]. In contrast, the uninitialized problem is known to be decidable for safe sets H given as closed, convex polytopes (see [5] for details and [1] for a different approach specific to Markov chains). In a nutshell, we can restrict to the potential fixpoints of $\mathcal{M}$, i.e. all distributions μ such that $\mu = \mathcal{M}^\pi(\mu, i)$ for some strategy π. It turns out that this set of distributions is a polytope and the problem – glossing over subtleties – reduces to checking whether the intersection of H with this polytope is non-empty. However, we note that the solution of [5] does not yield the witness strategy. In the following, we thus primarily focus on the initialized question. In Sect. 6, we then show how our approach, which also synthesizes a witness strategy, is directly applicable to the uninitialized case.

In light of the daunting hardness results for the general initialized problem, we restrict to *affine linear safe sets*, i.e. H which are specified by a finite set of affine linear inequalities. Formally, these sets are of the form $H = \{\mu \in \Delta(S) \mid \bigwedge_{j=1}^{N}(c_0^j + \sum_{i=1}^{n} c_i^j \cdot \mu(s_i)) \geq 0\}$, where $S = \{s_1, \ldots, s_n\}$, c_i^j are real-valued

---

[1] Intuitively, the POSITIVITY problem asks for a given rational (or integer or real) matrix M, whether $(M^n)_{1,1} > 0$ for all n [54]. This problem (and its many variants) has been the subject of intense research over the last 10–15 years, see e.g. [55]. Yet, quite surprisingly, it still remains open in its full generality.

constants and N is the number of affine linear inequalities that define H. Our problem formally is given by the following query.

Problem Statement Given an MDP $\mathcal{M}$, initial distribution μ_0, and affine linear safe set H, (i) decide whether μ_0 is H-safe, and (ii) if yes, then synthesize a strategy for $\mathcal{M}$ which ensures safety.

Note that the problem strictly subsumes the special case when H is defined in terms of rational constants, and our approach aims to solve both problems. Also, note that Theorem 1 still applies, i.e. this "simplified" problem is POSITIVITY-hard, too. We thus aim for a sound and *relatively complete* approach. Intuitively, this means that we restrict our search to a sub-space of possible solutions and within this space provide a complete answer. To give an intuition for the required reasoning, we provide an example safety query together with a manual proof.

Example 1. Consider our running example from Fig. 1. Suppose the initial distribution is $\mu_0 = \{A \mapsto \frac{1}{3}, B \mapsto \frac{1}{3}, C \mapsto \frac{1}{3}\}$ and (affine linear) $H = \{\mu \mid \mu(C) \geq \frac{1}{4}\}$. This safety query is satisfiable, by, e.g., choosing action b, as we show in the following. First, observe that the $i + 1$-th distribution is $\mu_{i+1}(A) = \frac{1}{2} \cdot \mu_i(C)$, $\mu_{i+1}(B) = \mu_i(A)$, and $\mu_{i+1}(C) = \mu_i(B) + \frac{1}{2}\mu_i(C)$. Thus, we cannot directly prove by induction that $\mu_i(C) \geq \frac{1}{4}$, we also need some information about $\mu_i(B)$ or $\mu_i(A)$ to exclude, e.g., $\mu_i = \{A \mapsto \frac{3}{4}, C \mapsto \frac{1}{4}\}$, where μ_{i+1} would violate the safety constraint. We invite the interested reader to try to prove that μ_0 is indeed H-safe under the given strategy to appreciate the subtleties.

We proceed by proving that $\mu_i(C) \geq \frac{1}{4}$ and additionally $\mu_i(A) \leq \mu_i(C)$ by induction. The base case follows immediately, thus suppose that μ_i satisfies these constraints. For $\mu_{i+1}(A) \leq \mu_{i+1}(C)$ observe that $\mu_{i+1}(A) = \frac{1}{2}\mu_i(C)$ and $\mu_{i+1}(C) = \frac{1}{2}\mu_i(C) + \mu_i(B)$. Since $\mu_i(B) \geq 0$, the claim follows. To prove $\mu_{i+1}(C) \geq \frac{1}{4}$ observe that $\mu_i(A) \leq \frac{1}{2}$ since $\mu_i(A) \leq \mu_i(C)$ by induction hypothesis and distributions sum up to 1. Moreover, $\mu_{i+1}(C) = \mu_i(B) + \frac{1}{2}\mu_i(C) = \frac{1}{2}\mu_i(B) + \frac{1}{2} - \frac{1}{2}\mu_i(A)$ by again inserting the fact that distributions sum up to 1. Then, $\mu_{i+1}(C) = \frac{1}{2} - \frac{1}{2}\mu_i(A) + \frac{1}{2}\mu_i(B) \geq \frac{1}{2} - \frac{1}{2}\mu_i(A) \geq \frac{1}{2} - \frac{1}{4} \geq \frac{1}{4}$. $\triangle$

Thus, already for rather simple examples the reasoning is non-trivial. To further complicate things, the structure of strategies can also be surprisingly complex:

Example 2. Again consider our running example from Fig. 1 with initial distribution $\mu_0 = \{A \mapsto \frac{3}{4}, B \mapsto \frac{1}{4}\}$ and safe set $H = \{\mu \mid \mu(B) = \frac{1}{4}\}$. This safety condition is indeed satisfiable, however the (unique) optimal strategy requires both infinite memory as well as randomization with arbitrarily small fractions! In step 1, we require choosing a with $\frac{2}{3}$ and b with $\frac{1}{3}$ to satisfy the safety constraint in the second step, getting $\mu_1 = \{A \mapsto \frac{1}{2}, B \mapsto \frac{1}{4}, C \mapsto \frac{1}{4}\}$. For step 2, we require choosing both a and b with probability $\frac{1}{2}$ each, yielding $\mu_2 = \{A \mapsto \frac{3}{8}, B \mapsto \frac{1}{4}, C \mapsto \frac{3}{8}\}$. Continuing this strategy, we obtain at step i that $\mu_i = \{A \mapsto \frac{1}{4} + \frac{1}{2^{i+1}}, B \mapsto \frac{1}{4}, C \mapsto \frac{1}{2} - \frac{1}{2^{i+1}}\}$ and action a is chosen with probability $1/(2^{i-1} + 1)$, converging to 1. $\triangle$

In the following, we provide two algorithms that handle both examples. Our first algorithm focusses on memoryless strategies, the second considers a certain type of infinite memory strategies. Essentially, the underlying idea is to automatically synthesize a strategy together with such inductive proofs of safety.

4   Proving Safety by Invariants

We now discuss our principled idea of proving safety by means of (inductive) invariants, taking inspiration from research on safety analysis in programs [20, 27]. We first show that considering strategies which are purely based on the current distribution over states are sufficient. Then, we show that inductive invariants are a *sound and complete* certificate for safety. Together, we obtain that an initial distribution is H-safe *if and only if* there exists an invariant set I and distribution strategy π such that (i) the initial distribution is contained in I, (ii) I is a subset of the safe set H, and (iii) I is inductive under π, i.e. if $\mu \in I$ then $\mathcal{M}^\pi(\mu) \in I$. In the following section, we then show how we search for invariants and distribution strategies *of a particular shape*.

4.1   Distribution Strategies

We show that *distribution strategies* $\pi : \Delta(S) \to \Pi_1$, yielding for each distribution over states a one-step strategy to take next, are sufficient for the problem at hand. More formally, we want to show that an H-safe distribution strategy exists if and only if there exists any H-safe strategy.

First, observe that distribution strategies are a special case of regular path strategies. In particular, for any given initial distribution, we obtain a uniquely determined stream of distributions as $\mu_{i+1} = \mathcal{M}^{\pi(\mu_i)}(\mu_i)$, i.e. the distribution μ_{i+1} is obtained by applying the one-step strategy $\pi(\mu_i)$ to μ_i. In turn, this lets us define the Markov strategy $\hat{\pi}_i(s) = \pi(\mu_i)(s)$. For simplicity, we identify distribution strategies with their induced path strategy.

Next, we argue that restricting to distribution strategies is sufficient.

Theorem 2. *An initial distribution μ_0 is H-safe if and only if there exists a distribution strategy π such that μ_0 is H-safe under π.*

Proof (Sketch). The full proof can be found in [4, Sec. 4.1]. Intuitively, only the "distribution" behaviour of a strategy is relevant and we can sufficiently replicate the behaviour of any safe strategy by a distribution strategy.   □

In this way, each MDP corresponds to a (uncountably infinite) transition system $\mathcal{T}_\mathcal{M} = (\Delta(S), T)$ where $(\mu, \mu') \in T$ if there exists a one-step strategy π such that $\mu' = \mathcal{M}^\pi(\mu)$. Note that $\mathcal{T}_\mathcal{M}$ is a purely non-deterministic system, without any probabilistic behaviour. So, our decision problem is equivalent to asking whether the induced transition system $\mathcal{T}_\mathcal{M}$ can be controlled in a safe way. Note that $\mathcal{T}_\mathcal{M}$ is uncountably large and uncountably branching.

4.2 Distributional Invariants for MDP Safety

We now define distributional invariants in MDPs and show that they provide sound and complete certificates for proving initialized (and uninitialized) safety.

Distributional Invariants in MDPs. Intuitively, a distributional invariant is a set of probability distributions over MDP states that contains all probability distributions that can arise from applying a strategy to an initial probability distribution, i.e. the complete stream μ_i. Hence, similar to the safe set H, distributional invariants are also defined to be subsets of $\Delta(S)$.

Definition 1 (Distributional Invariants). *Let $\mu_0 \in \Delta(S)$ be a probability distribution over S and π be a strategy in $\mathcal{M}$. A set $I \subseteq \Delta(S)$ is said to be a distributional invariant for μ_0 under π if the sequence of probability distributions induced by applying the strategy π to the initial probability distribution μ_0 is contained in I, i.e. if $\mathcal{M}^\pi(\mu_0, i) \in I$ for each $i \geq 0$.*

A distributional invariant I is said to be inductive *under π, if we furthermore have that $\mathcal{M}^\pi(\mu) \in I$ holds for any $\mu \in I$, i.e. if I is "closed" under application of $\mathcal{M}^\pi$ to any probability distribution contained in I.*

Soundness and Completeness for MDP Safety. The following theorem shows that, in order to solve the initialized (and uninitialized) safety problem, one can equivalently search for a distributional invariant that is fully contained in H. Furthermore, it shows that one can without loss of generality restrict the search to inductive distributional invariants.

Theorem 3 (Sound and Complete Certificate). *Let $\mu_0 \in \Delta(S)$ be a probability distribution over S, π be a strategy in $\mathcal{M}$, and $H \subseteq \Delta(S)$ be a safe set. Then μ_0 is H-safe under π if and only if there exists an inductive distributional invariant I for μ_0 and π such that $I \subseteq H$.*

The proof can be found in [4, Sec. 4.2].

Thus, in order to solve the initialized safety problem for μ_0, it suffices to search for (i) a strategy π and (ii) an inductive distributional invariant I for μ_0 and π such that $I \subseteq H$. On the other hand, in order to solve the uninitialized safety problem, it suffices to search for (i) an initial probability distribution μ_0, (ii) strategy π, and (iii) an inductive distributional invariant I for μ_0 and π such that $I \subseteq H$. In the following, we provide a fully automated, sound and *relatively* complete method of deciding the existence of such an invariant and strategy.

5 Algorithms for Distributional Invariant Synthesis

We now present two algorithms for automated synthesis of strategies and inductive distributional invariants towards solving distribution safety problems in MDPs. The two algorithms differ in the kind of strategies they consider and, as a consequence of differences in the involved expressions, also in their completeness guarantees. For readability, we describe the algorithms in their basic form applied to the initialized variant of the safety problem and discuss further extensions in Sect. 6. In particular, our approach is also directly applicable to the uninitialized variant, as we describe there.

We say that an inductive distributional invariant is *affine* if it can be specified in terms of (non-strict) affine inequalities, which we formalize below. Both algorithms jointly synthesize a strategy and an affine inductive distributional invariant by employing a *template-based synthesis* approach. In particular, they fix symbolic templates for each object that needs to be synthesized, encode the defining properties of each object as constraints over unknown template variables, and solve the system of constraints by reduction to the existential first-order theory of the reals.

For example, a template for an affine linear constraint on distributions $\Delta(S)$ is given by $\mathsf{aff}(\mu) = (c_0 + c_1 \cdot \mu(s_1) + \cdots + c_n \cdot \mu(s_n) \geq 0)$. Here, the variables c_0 to c_n, written in grey for emphasis, are the *template variables*. For fixed values of these variables the expression aff is a concrete affine linear predicate over distributions. Thus, we can ask questions like "Do there exist values for c_i such that for all distributions μ we have that $\mathsf{aff}(\mu)$ implies $\mathsf{aff}(\mathcal{M}^\pi(\mu))$?". This is a sentence in the theory of reals – however with quantifier alternation. As a next step, template-based synthesis approaches then employ various quantifier elimination techniques to convert such expressions into equisatisfiable sentences in, e.g., the existential theory of reals, which is decidable in PSPACE [15].

Difference between the Algorithms. Our two algorithms differ in their applicability and the kind of completeness guarantees that they provide. In terms of applicability, the first algorithm only considers *memoryless* strategies, while the second algorithm searches for *distribution* strategies specified as fractions of affine linear expressions. (We discuss an extension to rational functions in Sect. 6.) In terms of completeness guarantees, the first algorithm is *(relatively) complete* in the sense that it is guaranteed to compute a memoryless strategy and an affine inductive distributional invariant that prove safety *whenever they exist*. In contrast, the second algorithm does not provide the same level of completeness.

Notation. In what follows, we write $\equiv$ to denote (syntactic) equivalence of expressions, to distinguish from relational symbols used inside these expressions, such as "$=$". For example $\Phi(x) \equiv x = 0$ means that $\Phi(x)$ is the predicate $x = 0$. Moreover, $(x_1, \ldots, x_n)$ denotes a symbolic probability distribution over the state space $S = (s_1, \ldots, s_n)$, where x_i is a symbolic variable that encodes the probability of the system being in s_i. We use boldface notation $\boldsymbol{x} = (x_1, \ldots, x_n)$ to denote the vector of symbolic variables. Thus, the above example would be written $\mathsf{aff}(\boldsymbol{x}) \equiv c_0 + c_1 \cdot x_1 + \cdots + c_n \cdot x_n \geq 0$. Since we often require vectors to represent a distribution, we write $\boldsymbol{x} \in \Delta(S)$ as abbreviation for the predicate $\bigwedge_{i=1}^n (0 \leq x_i \leq 1) \wedge (\sum_{i=1}^n x_i = 1)$.

Algorithm Input and Assumptions. Both algorithms take as input an MDP $\mathcal{M} = (S, Act, \delta)$ with $S = \{s_1, \ldots, s_n\}$. They also take as input a safe set $H \subseteq \Delta(S)$.

We assume that H is specified by a boolean predicate over n variables as a logical conjunction of $N_H \in \mathbb{N}_0$ *affine* inequalities, and that it has the form

$$H(\boldsymbol{x}) \equiv (\boldsymbol{x} \in \Delta(S)) \wedge \bigwedge_{i=1}^{N_H} (h^i(\boldsymbol{x}) \geq 0),$$

where the first term imposes that $\boldsymbol{x}$ is a probability distribution over S and $h^i(\boldsymbol{x}) = h_0^i + h_1^i \cdot x_1 + \cdots + h_n^i \cdot x_n$ is an affine expression over $\boldsymbol{x}$ with real-valued coefficients h_j^i for each $i \in [N_H]$ and $j \in \{0, \ldots, n\}$. (Note that h_j^i are not template variables but fixed values, given as input.) Next, the algorithms take as input an initial probability distribution $\mu_0 \in \Delta(S)$. Finally, the algorithms also take as input technical parameters. Intuitively, these describe the size of used *symbolic templates*, explained later. For the remainder of the section, fix an initialized safety problem, i.e. an $\mathcal{M}$, safe set H of the required form, and an initial distribution μ_0.

5.1   Synthesis of Affine Invariants and Memoryless Strategies

We start by presenting our first algorithm, which synthesizes memoryless strategies and affine inductive distributional invariants. We refer to this algorithm as AlgMemLess. The algorithm proceeds in the following four steps:

1. *Setting up Templates.* The algorithm fixes symbolic templates for the memoryless strategy π and the affine inductive distributional invariant I. Note that the values of the symbolic template variables at this step are *unknown* and are to be computed in subsequent steps.
2. *Constraint Collection.* The algorithm collects the constraints which encode that π is a (memoryless) strategy, that I contains the initial probability distribution μ_0, that I is an inductive distributional invariant with respect to π and μ_0, and that I is contained within H. This step yields a system of affine constraints over symbolic template variables that contain universal and existential quantifiers.
3. *Quantifier Elimination.* The algorithm eliminates universal quantifiers from the above constraints to reduce it to a system of purely existentially quantified system of polynomial constraints over the symbolic template variables. Concretely, the first algorithm achieves this by application of *Farkas' lemma*.
4. *Constraint Solving.* The algorithm solves the resulting system of constraints by using an off-the-shelf solver to compute concrete values for symbolic template variables specifying the strategy π and invariant I.

We now describe each step in detail.

Step 1: Setting up Templates. The algorithm sets templates for π and I as follows:

- Since this algorithm searches for memoryless strategies, the probability of taking an action a_j in state s_i is always the same, independent of the current distribution. Hence, our template for π consists of a symbolic template variable p_{s_i,a_j} for each $s_i \in S$, $a_j \in Act(s_i)$. We write $p_{s_i,\circ} = (p_{s_i,a_1}, \ldots, p_{s_i,a_m})$ to refer to the corresponding distribution in state s_i.

- The template of I is given by a boolean predicate specified by a conjunction of N_I affine inequalities, where N_I is the *template size* and is an algorithm parameter. In particular, the template of I looks as follows:

$$I(\boldsymbol{x}) \equiv (\boldsymbol{x} \in \Delta(S)) \wedge \bigwedge_{i=1}^{N_I} (a_0^i + a_1^i \cdot x_1 + \cdots + a_n^i \cdot x_n \geq 0).$$

The first predicate enforces that I only contains vectors that define probability distributions over S.

Step 2: Constraint Collection. We now collect the constraints over symbolic template variables which encode that π is a memoryless strategy, that I contains the initial distribution μ_0, that I is an inductive distributional invariant under π, and that I is contained in H.

- For π to be a strategy, we only need to ensure that each $p_{s_i,\circ}$ is a probability distribution over the set of available actions at every state s_i. Thus, we set

$$\Phi_{\text{strat}} \equiv \bigwedge_{i=1}^{n} \left(p_{s_i,\circ} \in \Delta(Act(s_i)) \right).$$

- For I to be a distributional invariant for π and μ_0 as well as to be inductive, it suffices to enforce that I contains μ_0 and that I is closed under application of π. Thus, we collect two constraints:

$$\Phi_{\text{initial}} \equiv I(\mu_0) \equiv \bigwedge_{i=1}^{N_I} (a_0^i + a_1^i \cdot \mu_0^1 + \ldots a_n^i \cdot \mu_0^n \geq 0), \text{ and}$$
$$\Phi_{\text{inductive}} \equiv (\forall \boldsymbol{x} \in \mathbb{R}^n.\ I(\boldsymbol{x}) \implies I(\text{step}(\boldsymbol{x}))),$$

where $\text{step}(\boldsymbol{x})(x_i) = \sum_{s_k \in S, a_j \in Act(s_k)} p_{s_k,a_j} \cdot \delta(s_k, a_j, s_i) \cdot x_j$ yields the distribution after applying one step of the strategy induced by Φ_{strat} to $\boldsymbol{x}$.
- For I to be contained in H, we enforce the constraint:

$$\Phi_{\text{safe}} \equiv (\forall \boldsymbol{x} \in \mathbb{R}^n.\ I(\boldsymbol{x}) \implies H(\boldsymbol{x})).$$

Step 3: Quantifier Elimination. Constraints Φ_{strat} and Φ_{initial} are purely existentially quantified over symbolic template variables, thus we can solve them directly. However, $\Phi_{\text{inductive}}$ and Φ_{safe} contain both universal and existential quantifiers, which are difficult to handle. In what follows, we show how the algorithm translates these constraints into equisatisfiable *purely existentially quantified* constraints. In particular, our translation exploits the fact that both $\Phi_{\text{inductive}}$ and Φ_{safe} can, upon splitting the conjunctions on the right-hand side of implications into conjunctions of implications, be expressed as conjunctions of constraints of the form

$$\forall \boldsymbol{x} \in \mathbb{R}^n.\ (\text{affexp}_1(\boldsymbol{x}) \geq 0) \wedge \cdots \wedge (\text{affexp}_N(\boldsymbol{x}) \geq 0) \implies (\text{affexp}(\boldsymbol{x}) \geq 0).$$

Here, each $\text{affexp}_i(\boldsymbol{x})$ and $\text{affexp}(\boldsymbol{x})$ is an affine expression over $\boldsymbol{x}$ whose affine coefficients are either concrete real values or symbolic template variables.

In particular, we use Farkas' lemma [31] to remove universal quantification and translate the constraint into an equisatisfiable existentially quantified system of constraints over the symbolic template variables, as well as fresh auxiliary variables that are introduced by the translation. For completeness, we briefly recall (a strengthened and adapted version of) Farkas' lemma.

Lemma 1 ([31,37]). *Let $\mathcal{X} = \{x_1, \ldots, x_n\}$ be a finite set of real-valued variables, and consider the following system of $N \in \mathbb{N}$ affine inequalities over $\mathcal{X}$:*

$$\Phi : \begin{cases} c_0^1 + c_1^1 \cdot x_1 + \cdots + c_n^1 \cdot x_n \geq 0 \\ \quad\vdots \\ c_0^N + c_1^N \cdot x_1 + \cdots + c_n^N \cdot x_n \geq 0 \end{cases}.$$

Suppose that Φ is satisfiable. Then Φ entails an affine inequality $\phi \equiv c_0 + c_1 \cdot x_1 + \cdots + c_n \cdot x_n$, i.e. $\Phi \implies \phi$, if and only if ϕ can be written as a non-negative linear combination of affine inequalities in Φ, i.e. if and only if there exist $y_1, \ldots, y_n \geq 0$ such that $c_1 = \sum_{j=1}^{N} y_j \cdot c_1^j, \ldots, c_n = \sum_{j=1}^{N} y_j \cdot c_n^j$.

Note that, for any implication appearing in $\Phi_{\text{inductive}}$ and Φ_{safe}, the system of constraints on the left-hand side is simply $I(\boldsymbol{x})$, and the satisfiability of $I(\boldsymbol{x})$ is enforced by Φ_{initial}. Hence, we may apply Farkas lemma to translate each constraint with universal quantification into an equivalent purely existentially quantified constraint. In particular, for any constraint of the form

$$\forall \boldsymbol{x} \in \mathbb{R}^n. (\text{affexp}_1(\boldsymbol{x}) \geq 0) \wedge \cdots \wedge (\text{affexp}_N(\boldsymbol{x}) \geq 0) \implies (\text{affexp}(\boldsymbol{x}) \geq 0),$$

we introduce fresh template variables $y_1, \ldots, y_N$ and translate it into the system of purely existentially quantified constraints

$$(y_1 \geq 0) \wedge \cdots \wedge (y_N \geq 0) \wedge (\text{affexp}(\boldsymbol{x}) \equiv_F y_1 \cdot \text{affexp}_1(\boldsymbol{x}) + \cdots + y_N \cdot \text{affexp}_N(\boldsymbol{x})).$$

Here, we use $\text{affexp}(\boldsymbol{x}) \equiv_F y_1 \cdot \text{affexp}_1(\boldsymbol{x}) + \cdots + y_N \cdot \text{affexp}_N(\boldsymbol{x})$ to denote the set of $n + 1$ equalities over the symbolic template variable and $y_1, \ldots, y_N$ which equate the constant coefficients as well as the linear coefficients of each x_i on two sides of the equivalence, i.e. exactly those equalities which we obtain from applying Farkas' lemma. We highlight that the expressions affexp are only affine linear for *fixed* existentially quantified variables, i.e. they are in general quadratic.

Step 4: Constraint Solving. Finally, we feed the resulting system of existentially quantified polynomial constraints over the symbolic template variables as well as the auxiliary variables introduced by applying Farkas' lemma to an off-the-shelf constraint solver. If the solver outputs a solution, we conclude that the computed invariant I is an inductive distributional invariant for the strategy π and initial distribution μ_0, and that I is contained in H. Therefore, by Theorem 3, we conclude that μ_0 is H-safe under π.

$$\Phi_{\text{init}} : c_0 + c_1 \cdot \tfrac{1}{3} + c_2 \cdot \tfrac{1}{3} + c_3 \cdot \tfrac{1}{3} \geq 0$$

$$\Phi_{\text{safe}} : (c_0 + c_1 \cdot A + c_2 \cdot B + c_3 \cdot C \geq 0) \Longrightarrow C \geq \tfrac{1}{4}$$

$$\Phi_{\text{inductive}} : \begin{array}{c} (c_0 + c_1 \cdot A + c_2 \cdot B + c_3 \cdot C \geq 0) \Longrightarrow \\ c_0 + c_1 \cdot (A \cdot p_{A,a_1} + \tfrac{1}{2} C) + c_2 \cdot A \cdot p_{A,a_2} + c_3 \cdot (B + \tfrac{1}{2} C) \geq 0 \end{array}$$

$$\Phi_{\text{strat}} : p_{A,a_1} \geq 0 \quad p_{A,a_2} \geq 0 \quad p_{A,a_1} + p_{A,a_2} = 1$$

Fig. 2. List of constraints generated in Step 2 for Example 1 with $N_I = 1$. The uppercase letters correspond to variables indicating the distribution in these states, i.e. A refers to $\mu(A)$. These also are the universally quantified variables, which will be handled by the quantifier elimination in Step 3. The template variables are written in grey. For readability, we omit the constraints required for state distributions $\mu \in \Delta(S)$, i.e. $A \geq 0$ etc. The actual query sent to the solver in Step 4 after quantifier elimination comprises 27 constraints with 21 variables.

Theorem 4. Soundness: *Suppose* AlgMemLess *returns a memoryless strategy* π *and an affine inductive distributional invariant* I. *Then,* μ_0 *is* H-safe *under* π.

Completeness: *If there exist a memoryless strategy* π *and an affine inductive distributional invariant* I *such that* $I \subseteq H$ *and* μ_0 *is* H-safe *under* π, *then there exists a minimal value of the template size* $N_I \in \mathbb{N}$ *such that* π *and* I *are produced by* AlgMemLess.

Complexity: *The runtime of* AlgMemLess *is in PSPACE in the size of the MDP, the encoding of the safe set* H *and the template size parameter* $N_I \in \mathbb{N}$.

The proof can be found in [4, Sec. 5.1]. We comment on the PSPACE upper bound on the complexity of AlgMemLess. The upper bound holds since the application of Farkas' lemma reduces synthesis to solving a sentence in the existential first-order theory of the reals and since the size of the sentence is polynomial in the sizes of the MDP, the encoding of the safe set H and the invariant template size N_i. However, it is unclear whether the resulting constraints could be solved more efficiently, and the best known upper bound on the time complexity of algorithms for template-based affine inductive invariant synthesis in programs is also PSPACE [8,27]. Designing more efficient algorithms for solving constraints of this form would lead to better algorithms both for the safety problem studied in this work and for template-based affine inductive invariant synthesis in programs.

Example 3. For completeness, we provide the constraints generated in Step 2 for Example 1 with $N_I = 1$ for readability, i.e. our running example Fig. 1 with $\mu_0 = \{A \mapsto \tfrac{1}{3}, B \mapsto \tfrac{1}{3}, C \mapsto \tfrac{1}{3}\}$ and $H = \{\mu \mid \mu(C) \geq \tfrac{1}{4}\}$, in Fig. 2.

To conclude this section, we emphasize that our algorithm *simultaneously* synthesizes both the invariant and the witnessing strategy, which is the key component to achieve relative completeness.

5.2 Synthesis of Affine Invariants and General Strategies

We now present our second algorithm, which additionally synthesizes *distribution strategies* (of a particular shape) together with an affine inductive distributional invariant. We refer to it as AlgDist. The second algorithm proceeds in the analogous four steps as the first algorithm, AlgMemLess. Hence, in the interest of space, we only discuss the differences compared to AlgMemLess.

Step 1: Setting up Templates. The algorithm sets up templates for π and I. The template for I is defined analogously as in Sect. 5.1. However, as we now want to search for a strategy π that need not be memoryless but instead may depend on the current distribution, we need to consider a more general template. In particular, the template for the probability p_{s_i,a_j} of taking an action a_j in state s_i is no longer a constant value. Instead, $p_{s_i,a_j}(\boldsymbol{x})$ is a function of the probability distribution $\boldsymbol{x}$ of the current state of the MDP, and we define its template to be a quotient of two affine expressions for each $s_i \in S$ and $a_j \in Act(s_i)$:

$$p_{s_i,a_j}(\boldsymbol{x}) \equiv \frac{\text{num}(s_i,a_j)(\boldsymbol{x})}{\text{den}(s_i)(\boldsymbol{x})} \equiv \frac{r_0^{i,j} + r_1^{i,j} \cdot x_1 + \cdots + r_n^{i,j} \cdot x_n}{s_0^i + s_1^i \cdot x_1 + \cdots + s_n^i \cdot x_n}.$$

(In Sect. 6, we discuss how to extend our approach to polynomial expressions for numerator and denominator, i.e. rational functions.) Note that the coefficients in the numerator depend both on the state s_i and the action a_j, whereas the coefficients in the denominator depend only on the state s_i. This is because we only use the affine expression in the denominator as a normalization factor to ensure that p_{s_i,a_i} indeed defines a probability.

Step 2: Constraint Collection. As before, the algorithm now collects the constraints over symbolic template variables which encode that π is a strategy, that I is an inductive distributional invariant, and that I is contained in H. The constraints Φ_{initial}, $\Phi_{\text{inductive}}$, and Φ_{safe} are defined analogously as in Sect. 5.1, with the necessary adaptation to step($\boldsymbol{x}$). For the strategy constraint Φ_{strat} we now need to take additional care to ensure that each quotient template defined above does not induce division by 0 and that these values indeed correspond to a distribution over the available actions. We ensure this by the following constraint:

$$\Phi_{\text{strat}} \equiv \forall \boldsymbol{x} \in \mathbb{R}^n.\, I(\boldsymbol{x}) \implies \bigwedge_{i=1}^{n} \left(\begin{array}{l} \bigwedge_{a_j \in Act(s_i)} \text{num}(s_i,a_j)(\boldsymbol{x}) \geq 0 \,\wedge \\ \text{den}(s_i)(\boldsymbol{x}) \geq 1 \,\wedge \\ \sum_{a_j \in Act(s_i)} \text{num}(s_i,a_j)(\boldsymbol{x}) = \text{den}(s_i)(\boldsymbol{x}). \end{array} \right).$$

The first two constraints ensure that all quantities are positive and we never divide by 0. The third means that the numerators sum up to the denominator. Together, this ensures the desired result, i.e. $p_{s_i,\circ}(\boldsymbol{x}) \in \Delta(Act(s_i))$ whenever $\boldsymbol{x} \in \Delta(S)$. Note that the ≥ 1 constraint for the denominator can be replaced by an arbitrary constant > 0, since we can always rescale all involved coefficients.

Step 3: Quantifier Elimination. The constraints Φ_{strat}, Φ_{initial}, and Φ_{safe} can be handled analogously to Sect. 5.1. In particular, by applying Farkas' lemma these can be translated into an equisatisfiable purely existentially quantified system of polynomial constraints, and our algorithm applies this translation.

However, the constraint $\Phi_{\text{inductive}}$ now involves quotients of affine expressions: Upon splitting the conjunction on the right-hand side of the implication in $\Phi_{\text{inductive}}$ into a conjunction of implications, the inequalities on the right-hand side of these implications contain templates for strategy probabilities $p_{s_i,a_j}(x)$. The algorithm removes the quotients by multiplying both sides of the inequality by denominators of each quotient. (Recall that each denominator is positive by the constraint Φ_{strat}.) This results in the multiplication of symbolic affine expressions, hence $\Phi_{\text{inductive}}$ becomes a conjunction of implications of the form

$$\forall x \in \mathbb{R}^n. \, (\text{affexp}_1(x) \geq 0) \wedge \cdots \wedge (\text{affexp}_N(x) \geq 0) \implies (\text{polyexp}(x) \geq 0).$$

Here, each $\text{affexp}_i(x)$ is an affine expression over x, but $\text{polyexp}(x)$ is now a polynomial expression over x. Hence we cannot apply a Farkas' lemma-style result to remove universal quantifiers.

Instead, we motivate our translation by recalling Handelman's theorem [38], which characterizes *strictly* positive polynomials over a set of affine inequalities. It will allow us to soundly translate $\Phi_{\text{inductive}}$ into an existentially quantified system of constraints over the symbolic template variables, as well as fresh auxiliary variables that are introduced by the translation.

Theorem 5 ([38]). *Let $\mathcal{X} = \{x_1, \ldots, x_n\}$ be a finite set of real-valued variables, and consider the following system of $N \in \mathbb{N}$ non-strict affine inequalities over $\mathcal{X}$:*

$$\Phi : \begin{cases} c_0^1 + c_1^1 \cdot x_1 + \cdots + c_n^1 \cdot x_n \geq 0 \\ \qquad\qquad \vdots \\ c_0^N + c_1^N \cdot x_1 + \cdots + c_n^N \cdot x_n \geq 0 \end{cases} .$$

Let $Prod(\Phi) = \{\prod_{i=1}^t \phi_i \mid t \in \mathbb{N}_0, \phi_i \in \Phi\}$ be the set of all products of finitely many affine expressions in Φ, where the product of 0 affine expressions is a constant expression 1. Suppose that Φ is satisfiable and that $\{y \mid y \models \Phi\}$, the set of values satisfying Φ, is topologically compact, i.e. closed and bounded. Then Φ entails a polynomial inequality $\phi(x) > 0$ if and only if ϕ can be written as a non-negative linear combination of finitely many products in $Prod(\Phi)$, i.e. if and only if there exist $y_1, \ldots, y_n \geq 0$ and $\phi_1, \ldots, \phi_n \in Prod(\Phi)$ such that $\phi = y_1 \cdot \phi_1 + \cdots + y_n \cdot \phi_n$.

Notice that we cannot directly apply Handelman's theorem to a constraint

$$\forall x \in \mathbb{R}^n. \, (\text{affexp}_1(x) \geq 0) \wedge \cdots \wedge (\text{affexp}_N(x) \geq 0) \implies (\text{polyexp}(x) \geq 0),$$

since the polynomial inequality on the right-hand-side of the implication is non-strict whereas the polynomial inequality in Handelman's theorem is strict. However, the direction needed for the soundness of translation holds even with the non-strict polynomial inequality on the right-hand side. In particular, it clearly holds that if polyexp can be written as a non-negative linear combination of finitely many products of affine inequalities, then polyexp is non-negative whenever all affine inequalities are non-negative. Hence, we may use the translation in Handelman's theorem to translate each implication in $\varPhi_{\text{inductive}}$ into a system of purely existentially quantified constraints.

As Handelman's theorem does not impose a bound on the number of products of affine expressions that might appear in the translation, we *parametrize* the algorithm with an upper bound K on the maximal number of affine inequalities appearing in each product. To that end, we define $\text{Prod}_K(\varPhi) = \{\prod_{i=1}^{t} \phi_i \mid 0 \leq t \leq K, \phi_i \in \varPhi\}$. Let $M_K = |\text{Prod}_K(\varPhi)|$ be the total number of such products and $\text{Prod}_K(\varPhi) = \{\phi_1, \ldots, \phi_{M_K}\}$. Then, for any constraint of the form

$$\forall \boldsymbol{x} \in \mathbb{R}^n. (\text{affexp}_1(\boldsymbol{x}) \geq 0) \wedge \cdots \wedge (\text{affexp}_N(\boldsymbol{x}) \geq 0) \implies (\text{polyexp}(\boldsymbol{x}) \geq 0),$$

we introduce fresh template variables $y_1, \ldots, y_{M_K}$ and translate it into the system of purely existentially quantified constraints

$$(y_1 \geq 0) \wedge \cdots \wedge (y_N \geq 0) \wedge (\text{polyexp}(\boldsymbol{x}) \equiv_H y_1 \cdot \phi_1(\boldsymbol{x}) + \cdots + y_{M_K} \cdot \phi_{M_K}(\boldsymbol{x})).$$

Here, $\text{polyexp}(\boldsymbol{x}) \equiv_H y_1 \cdot \phi_1(\boldsymbol{x}) + \cdots + y_{M_K} \cdot \phi_{M_K}(\boldsymbol{x})$ denotes the set of equalities over template variables and $y_1, \ldots, y_{M_K}$ which equate the constant coefficients as well as the coefficients of each monomial over $\{x_1, \ldots, x_k\}$ of degree at most K on two sides of the equivalence, as specified by Handelman's theorem.

While our translation into a purely existentially quantified constraints is not complete due to the non-strict polynomial inequality and due to the parametrization by K, Handelman's theorem justifies the translation as it indicates that the translation is "close to complete" for sufficiently large values of K.

Step 4: Constraint Solving. This step is analogous to Sect. 5.1 and we use an off-the-shelf polynomial constraint solver to handle the resulting system of purely existentially quantified polynomial constraints. If the solver outputs a solution, we conclude that the computed I is an inductive distributional invariant for the computed strategy π and initial distribution μ_0, and that I is contained in H. Therefore, by Theorem 3, we conclude that μ_0 is H-safe under π.

Theorem 6. Soundness: *Suppose* AlgDist *returns a strategy* π *and an affine inductive distributional invariant* I. *Then,* π *is* H-safe *for* μ_0.

Complexity: *For any fixed parameter* $K \in \mathbb{N}$, *the runtime of* AlgDist *is in PSPACE in the size of the MDP and the template size parameter* $N_I \in \mathbb{N}$.

The proof can be found in [4, Sec. 5.2].

6   Discussion, Extensions, and Variants

With our two algorithms in place, we remark on several interesting details and possibilities for extensions.

Polynomial Expressions. Our second algorithm can also be extended to synthesizing *polynomial* inductive distributional invariants, i.e. instead of defining the invariant I through a conjunction of affine linear expressions we could synthesize polynomial expressions such as $x_1^2 + x_2 \cdot x_3 \leq 0.5$. This can be achieved by using Putinar's Positivstellensatz [59] instead of Handelman's theorem in Step 3. This technique has recently been used for generating polynomial inductive invariants in programs in [20], and our translation in Step 3 can be analogously adapted to synthesize polynomial inductive distributional invariants up to a specified degree. In the same way, instead of requiring that H is given as a conjunction of affine linear constraints, we can also handle the case of polynomial constraints. The same holds true for the probabilities of choosing certain actions $p_{s_i, a_j}(x)$. While we have defined these as fractions of affine linear expressions, we could replace them with rational functions, which we chose to exclude for sake of readability.

Uninitialized and Restricted Initial Case. We remark that we can directly incorporate the uninitialized case in our algorithm. In particular, instead of requiring that $I(\mu_0)$ holds for the concretely given initial values, we can instead existentially quantify over the values of $\mu_0(s_i)$ and add the constraint that μ_0 is a distribution, i.e. $\mu_0(s_i) \in \Delta(S)$. This does not add universal quantification, thus we do not need to apply any quantifier elimination for these variables. This also subsumes and generalizes the ideas of [5], which observes that checking whether a fixpoint of the transition dynamics lies within H is sufficient. Choosing $I = \{\mu^*\}$ where μ^* is such a fixpoint satisfies all of our constraints. See [4, Sec. 6] for details.

Our algorithm is also able to handle the "intermediate" case, as follows. The uninitialized case leaves absolute freedom in the choice of initial distribution, while the initialized case concretely specifies one initial distribution. Here, we could as well impose *some* constraints on the initial distribution without fixing it completely, i.e. ask whether there exists an H-safe initial distribution μ_0 which satisfies a predicate Φ_{init}. If Φ_{init} is a conjunction of affine linear constraints, we can directly handle this query, too. Note that both initialized and uninitialized are special cases thereof.

Non-Inductive Initial Steps. Instead of requiring to synthesize an invariant which contains the initial distribution, we can explicitly write down the first k distributions and only then require an invariant and strategy to be found. More concretely, the set of distributions that can be achieved in a given step k while remaining in H can be explicitly computed, denote this set as Δ^k. For a different perspective, this describes the set of states reachable in $\mathcal{T}_\mathcal{M}$ within k steps and corresponds to "unrolling" the MDP for a fixed number of steps. This then goes hand in hand with the above "restricted initial case", where we ask whether there exists an H-safe distribution in Δ^k. We conjecture that this could simplify the search for distributional invariants for systems which have a lot of "transient" behaviour, as observed in searching for invariants for state reachability [11].

Fig. 3. Our Split toy example. The MDP comprises two disconnected parts. Probability mass flows from A to B and from C to D under all strategies.

7   Implementation and Evaluation

While the main focus of our contribution lies on the theory, we validate the applicability through an unoptimized prototype implementation. We implemented our approach in Python 3.10, using SymPy 1.11 [50] to handle and simplify symbolic expressions, and PySMT 0.9 [36] to abstract communication with constraint solvers. We use z3 4.8 [53] and mathsat 5.6 [26] as back-ends. Our experiments were executed on consumer hardware (AMD Ryzen 3600 CPU with 16 GB RAM).

Caveats. While the existential (non-linear) theory of the reals is known to be decidable, practical algorithms are less explored than, for example, SAT solving. In particular, runtimes are quite sensitive to minor changes in the input structure and initial randomization (many solvers apply randomized algorithms). We observed differences of several orders of magnitude (going from seconds to hours) simply due to restarting the computation (leading to different initial seeds). Similarly, by strengthening the antecedents of implications by known facts, we also observed significant improvements. Concretely, given that we have constraints of the form $I(\boldsymbol{x}) \implies H(\boldsymbol{x})$ and $I(\boldsymbol{x}) \implies \Phi(\boldsymbol{x})$, we observed that changing the second constraint to $I(\boldsymbol{x}) \wedge H(\boldsymbol{x}) \implies \Phi(\boldsymbol{x})$ would drastically improve the runtime even though the two are semantically equivalent.

This suggests that both improvements of our implementation as well as further work on constraint solvers are likely to have a significant impact on the runtime.

Models. Aside from our running example of Fig. 1, which we refer to as Running here, we consider two further toy examples.

The first model, called Chain, is a Markov chain defined as follows: We consider the states $S = \{s_1, \ldots, s_{10}\}$ and set $\delta(s_i) = \{s_{i+1} \mapsto 1\}$ for all $i < 10$ and $\delta(s_{10}) = \{s_9 \mapsto \frac{1}{2}, s_{10} \mapsto \frac{1}{2}\}$. The initial distribution is given as $\mu_0(s_i) = \frac{1}{10}$ for all $s_i \in SS$ and the safe set by $H = \{\mu(s_{10}) \geq \frac{1}{10}\}$. We are mainly interested in this model to investigate demonstrate applicability to "larger" systems.

The second model, called Split, is an MDP which actually comprises two independent subsystems. We depict the model in Fig. 3. The initial distribution is $\mu_0 = \{A \mapsto \frac{1}{2}, C \mapsto \frac{1}{2}\}$ and the safe set $H = \{\mu(A) + \mu(D) \geq \frac{1}{2}\}$. This aims to explore both disconnected models as well as a safe set which imposes a constraint on multiple states at once. In particular, observe that initially $\mu_0(D) = 0$ but $\mu_i(D)$ converges to 1 while $\mu_i(A)$ converges to 0, even if choosing action a_1. Thus, the invariant needs to identify the simultaneous flow from A to B and C to D.

Table 1. Overview of our results for the five considered models. From left to right, we list the name of the model, the runtime, and size of the invariant, followed by the number of variables, constraints, and total size of the query passed to the constraint solvers. For Running, we provided additional hints to the solver to achieve a more consistent runtime, indicated by the dagger symbol.

Model	Runtime	N_I	#Var.	#Constr.	Size.
Running	$3s^\dagger$	3	92	123	849
Chain	10s	2	69	82	666
Split	3s	3	60	69	571
PageRank	3s	2	44	52	536
Insulin-^{131}I	2s	2	44	52	476

Table 2. The invariants and strategies computed for our models. We omit the invariants for the two real-world scenarios since they are too large to fit.

Model	Computed Invariant and Strategy
Running	$\{A \geq \frac{1}{4}, B = \frac{1}{4}\}$ $\pi(\mu) = \{a_1 \mapsto \frac{1}{4 \cdot \mu(A)}, a_2 \mapsto \frac{4 \cdot \mu(A) - 1}{4 \cdot \mu(A)}\}$
Chain	$\{s_9 + s_{10} \geq \frac{1}{5}, s_{10} \geq \frac{1}{10}\}$ $\pi = \emptyset$ (Markov chain)
Split	$\{B \leq D, A + B \geq C + D, 3 \cdot (C + D) - (A + B) \geq 1\}$ $\pi = \{a \mapsto 1\}$

We additionally consider two examples from the literature, namely the PageRank example from [1, Fig. 3], based on [51], and Insulin-^{131}I, a pharmacokinetics system [1, Example 2], based on [17]. Both are Markov chains.

Results. We summarize our findings briefly in Table 1. We again underline that not too much attention should be put on runtimes, since they are very sensitive to minimal changes in the model. The evaluation is mainly intended to demonstrate that our methods are actually able to provide results. For completeness, we report the size of the invariant N_I and the size of the constraint problem in terms of number of variables, constraints, and operations inside these constraints. We also provide the invariants and strategy identified by our method in Table 2. Note that for Running we used AlgDist, while the other two examples are handled by AlgMemLess. For Running, we observed a significant dependence on the initialization of the solvers. Thus we added several "hints", i.e. known correct values for some variables. (To be precise, we set the value for eight of the 92 variables.)

Discussion. We remark two related points: Firstly, we observe that very often most of the involved auxiliary variables introduced by the quantifier elimination have a value of zero. Thus, a potential optimization is to explicitly set most such variables to zero, check whether the formula is satisfiable, and, if not, gradually remove these constraints either at random or guided by unsat-cores if available (i.e. clauses which are the "reason" for unsatisfiability). Moreover, we observed significant differences between the solvers: While z3 seems to be much quicker to identify unsatisfiability, mathsat usually is better at finding satisfying assignments. Hence, using both solvers in tandem seems to be very beneficial.

8 Conclusion

We developed a framework for defining certificates for safety objectives in MDPs as distributional inductive invariants. Using this, we came up with two algorithms that synthesize linear/affine invariants and corresponding memoryless/general strategies for safety in MDPs. To the best of our knowledge this is the first time the template-based invariant approach, already known to be successful for programs, has been applied to synthesis strategies in MDPs for distributional safety properties. Our experimental results show that affine invariants are sufficient for many interesting examples. However, the second approach can be lifted to synthesize polynomial invariants, and hence potentially, a large set of MDPs. Exploring this could be a future line of work. It would also be interesting to explore how one can automate distributional invariant synthesis if the safe set H is specified in terms of both strict and non-strict inequalities. Finally, in terms of applicability, we would like to apply this approach to solve more benchmarks and problems, e.g., to synthesize risk-aware strategies for MDPs [46,49].

References

1. Agrawal, M., Akshay, S., Genest, B., Thiagarajan, P.S.: Approximate verification of the symbolic dynamics of Markov chains. J. ACM **62**(1), 2:1-2:34 (2015). https://doi.org/10.1145/2629417
2. Agrawal, S., Chatterjee, K., Novotný, P.: Lexicographic ranking supermartingales: an efficient approach to termination of probabilistic programs. Proc. ACM Program. Lang. **2**(POPL), 34:1–34:32 (2018). https://doi.org/10.1145/3158122
3. Akshay, S., Antonopoulos, T., Ouaknine, J., Worrell, J.: Reachability problems for Markov chains. Inf. Process. Lett. **115**(2), 155–158 (2015). https://doi.org/10.1016/j.ipl.2014.08.013
4. Akshay, S., Chatterjee, K., Meggendorfer, T., Đorđe Žikelić: MDPs as distribution transformers: affine invariant synthesis for safety objectives (2023). https://arxiv.org/abs/2305.16796
5. Akshay, S., Genest, B., Vyas, N.: Distribution-based objectives for markov decision processes. In: Dawar, A., Grädel, E. (eds.) Proceedings of the 33rd Annual ACM/IEEE Symposium on Logic in Computer Science, LICS 2018, Oxford, UK, July 09–12, 2018, pp. 36–45. ACM (2018). https://doi.org/10.1145/3209108.3209185
6. Alias, C., Darte, A., Feautrier, P., Gonnord, L.: Multi-dimensional rankings, program termination, and complexity bounds of flowchart programs. In: Cousot, R., Martel, M. (eds.) SAS 2010. LNCS, vol. 6337, pp. 117–133. Springer, Heidelberg (2010). https://doi.org/10.1007/978-3-642-15769-1_8
7. Alur, R., et al.: Syntax-guided synthesis. In: Irlbeck, M., Peled, D.A., Pretschner, A. (eds.) Dependable Software Systems Engineering, NATO Science for Peace and Security Series, D: Information and Communication Security, vol. 40, pp. 1–25. IOS Press (2015). https://doi.org/10.3233/978-1-61499-495-4-1

8. Asadi, A., Chatterjee, K., Fu, H., Goharshady, A.K., Mahdavi, M.: Polynomial reachability witnesses via stellensätze. In: Freund, S.N., Yahav, E. (eds.) PLDI 2021: 42nd ACM SIGPLAN International Conference on Programming Language Design and Implementation, Virtual Event, Canada, June 20–25, 2021, pp. 772–787. ACM (2021). https://doi.org/10.1145/3453483.3454076
9. Baier, C., Katoen, J.: Principles of Model Checking. MIT Press, Cambridge (2008)
10. Batz, K., Chen, M., Junges, S., Kaminski, B.L., Katoen, J., Matheja, C.: Probabilistic program verification via inductive synthesis of inductive invariants. In: Sankaranarayanan, S., Sharygina, N. (eds.) TACAS 2023, Part II. LNCS, vol. 13994, pp. 410–429. Springer, Cham (2023). https://doi.org/10.1007/978-3-031-30820-8_25
11. Batz, K., Chen, M., Kaminski, B.L., Katoen, J.-P., Matheja, C., Schröer, P.: Latticed k-induction with an application to probabilistic programs. In: Silva, A., Leino, K.R.M. (eds.) CAV 2021. LNCS, vol. 12760, pp. 524–549. Springer, Cham (2021). https://doi.org/10.1007/978-3-030-81688-9_25
12. Beauquier, D., Rabinovich, A.M., Slissenko, A.: A logic of probability with decidable model checking. J. Log. Comput. 16(4), 461–487 (2006). https://doi.org/10.1093/logcom/exl004
13. Billingsley, P.: Probability and Measure. Wiley, New York (2008)
14. Bradley, A.R., Manna, Z., Sipma, H.B.: Linear ranking with reachability. In: Etessami, K., Rajamani, S.K. (eds.) CAV 2005. LNCS, vol. 3576, pp. 491–504. Springer, Heidelberg (2005). https://doi.org/10.1007/11513988_48
15. Canny, J.F.: Some algebraic and geometric computations in PSPACE. In: Simon, J. (ed.) Proceedings of the 20th Annual ACM Symposium on Theory of Computing, May 2–4, 1988, Chicago, Illinois, USA, pp. 460–467. ACM (1988). https://doi.org/10.1145/62212.62257
16. Carbonneaux, Q., Hoffmann, J., Shao, Z.: Compositional certified resource bounds. In: Grove, D., Blackburn, S.M. (eds.) Proceedings of the 36th ACM SIGPLAN Conference on Programming Language Design and Implementation, Portland, OR, USA, June 15–17, 2015, pp. 467–478. ACM (2015). https://doi.org/10.1145/2737924.2737955
17. Chadha, R., Korthikanti, V.A., Viswanathan, M., Agha, G., Kwon, Y.: Model checking MDPs with a unique compact invariant set of distributions. In: Eighth International Conference on Quantitative Evaluation of Systems, QEST 2011, Aachen, Germany, 5–8 September, 2011, pp. 121–130. IEEE Computer Society (2011). https://doi.org/10.1109/QEST.2011.22
18. Chakarov, A., Sankaranarayanan, S.: Probabilistic program analysis with martingales. In: Sharygina, N., Veith, H. (eds.) CAV 2013. LNCS, vol. 8044, pp. 511–526. Springer (2013). https://doi.org/10.1007/978-3-642-39799-8_34
19. Chatterjee, K., Fu, H., Goharshady, A.K.: Termination analysis of probabilistic programs through Positivstellensatz's. In: Chaudhuri, S., Farzan, A. (eds.) CAV 2016. LNCS, vol. 9779, pp. 3–22. Springer, Cham (2016). https://doi.org/10.1007/978-3-319-41528-4_1
20. Chatterjee, K., Fu, H., Goharshady, A.K., Goharshady, E.K.: Polynomial invariant generation for non-deterministic recursive programs. In: Donaldson, A.F., Torlak, E. (eds.) Proceedings of the 41st ACM SIGPLAN International Conference on Programming Language Design and Implementation, PLDI 2020, London, UK, June 15–20, 2020, pp. 672–687. ACM (2020). https://doi.org/10.1145/3385412.3385969

21. Chatterjee, K., Fu, H., Novotný, P., Hasheminezhad, R.: Algorithmic analysis of qualitative and quantitative termination problems for affine probabilistic programs. TOPLAS **40**(2), 7:1–7:45 (2018). https://doi.org/10.1145/3174800
22. Chatterjee, K., Goharshady, A.K., Meggendorfer, T., Zikelic, D.: Sound and complete certificates for quantitative termination analysis of probabilistic programs. In: Shoham, S., Vizel, Y. (eds.) CAV 2022, Part I. LNCS, vol. 13371, pp. 55–78. Springer, Cham (2022). https://doi.org/10.1007/978-3-031-13185-1_4
23. Chatterjee, K., Goharshady, E.K., Novotný, P., Žikelić, Đ.: Proving nontermination by program reversal. In: Freund, S.N., Yahav, E. (eds.) PLDI 2021: 42nd ACM SIGPLAN International Conference on Programming Language Design and Implementation, Virtual Event, Canada, June 20–25, 20211, pp. 1033–1048. ACM (2021). https://doi.org/10.1145/3453483.3454093
24. Chatterjee, K., Goharshady, E.K., Novotný, P., Zárevúcky, J., Žikelić, Đ: On lexicographic proof rules for probabilistic termination. In: Huisman, M., Păsăreanu, C., Zhan, N. (eds.) FM 2021. LNCS, vol. 13047, pp. 619–639. Springer, Cham (2021). https://doi.org/10.1007/978-3-030-90870-6_33
25. Chatterjee, K., Novotný, P., Žikelić, Đ.: Stochastic invariants for probabilistic termination. In: POPL, pp. 145–160 (2017). https://doi.org/10.1145/3009837.3009873
26. Cimatti, A., Griggio, A., Schaafsma, B.J., Sebastiani, R.: The MathSAT5 SMT solver. In: Piterman, N., Smolka, S.A. (eds.) TACAS 2013. LNCS, vol. 7795, pp. 93–107. Springer, Heidelberg (2013). https://doi.org/10.1007/978-3-642-36742-7_7
27. Colón, M.A., Sankaranarayanan, S., Sipma, H.B.: Linear invariant generation using non-linear constraint solving. In: Hunt, W.A., Somenzi, F. (eds.) CAV 2003. LNCS, vol. 2725, pp. 420–432. Springer, Heidelberg (2003). https://doi.org/10.1007/978-3-540-45069-6_39
28. Colóon, M.A., Sipma, H.B.: Synthesis of linear ranking functions. In: Margaria, T., Yi, W. (eds.) TACAS 2001. LNCS, vol. 2031, pp. 67–81. Springer, Heidelberg (2001). https://doi.org/10.1007/3-540-45319-9_6
29. Cousot, P., Cousot, R.: Abstract interpretation: A unified lattice model for static analysis of programs by construction or approximation of fixpoints. In: Graham, R.M., Harrison, M.A., Sethi, R. (eds.) Conference Record of the Fourth ACM Symposium on Principles of Programming Languages, Los Angeles, California, USA, January 1977, pp. 238–252. ACM (1977). https://doi.org/10.1145/512950.512973
30. Cousot, P., Cousot, R., Feret, J., Mauborgne, L., Miné, A., Monniaux, D., Rival, X.: The ASTREÉ analyzer. In: Sagiv, M. (ed.) ESOP 2005. LNCS, vol. 3444, pp. 21–30. Springer, Heidelberg (2005). https://doi.org/10.1007/978-3-540-31987-0_3
31. Farkas, J.: Theorie der einfachen ungleichungen. Journal für die reine und angewandte Mathematik (Crelles Journal) **1902**(124), 1–27 (1902)
32. Farzan, A., Kincaid, Z.: Compositional recurrence analysis. In: Kaivola, R., Wahl, T. (eds.) Formal Methods in Computer-Aided Design, FMCAD 2015, Austin, Texas, USA, September 27–30, 2015, pp. 57–64. IEEE (2015)
33. Feautrier, P., Gonnord, L.: Accelerated invariant generation for C programs with aspic and c2fsm. In: Delmas, D., Rival, X. (eds.) Proceedings of the Tools for Automatic Program AnalysiS, TAPAS@SAS 2010, Perpignan, France, September 17, 2010. Electronic Notes in Theoretical Computer Science, vol. 267, pp. 3–13. Elsevier (2010). https://doi.org/10.1016/j.entcs.2010.09.014

34. Garg, P., Löding, C., Madhusudan, P., Neider, D.: ICE: a robust framework for learning invariants. In: Biere, A., Bloem, R. (eds.) CAV 2014. LNCS, vol. 8559, pp. 69–87. Springer, Cham (2014). https://doi.org/10.1007/978-3-319-08867-9_5

35. Garg, P., Neider, D., Madhusudan, P., Roth, D.: Learning invariants using decision trees and implication counterexamples. In: Bodík, R., Majumdar, R. (eds.) Proceedings of the 43rd Annual ACM SIGPLAN-SIGACT Symposium on Principles of Programming Languages, POPL 2016, St. Petersburg, FL, USA, January 20–22, 2016, pp. 499–512. ACM (2016). https://doi.org/10.1145/2837614.2837664

36. Gario, M., Micheli, A.: Pysmt: a solver-agnostic library for fast prototyping of SMT-based algorithms. In: SMT Workshop, vol. 2015 (2015)

37. Gärtner, B., Matousek, J.: Understanding and using linear programming. Universitext, Springer, Heidelberg (2007). https://doi.org/10.1007/978-3-540-30717-4

38. Handelman, D.: Representing polynomials by positive linear functions on compact convex Polyhedra. Pacific J. Math. $132(1)$, 35–62 (1988)

39. Hoffmann, J., Aehlig, K., Hofmann, M.: Multivariate amortized resource analysis. ACM Trans. Program. Lang. Syst. $34(3)$, 14:1–14:62 (2012). https://doi.org/10.1145/2362389.2362393

40. Kaminski, B.L., Katoen, J., Matheja, C., Olmedo, F.: Weakest precondition reasoning for expected runtimes of randomized algorithms. J. ACM 65(5), 30:1–30:68 (2018). https://doi.org/10.1145/3208102

41. Karimov, T., Kelmendi, E., Ouaknine, J., Worrell, J.: What's decidable about discrete linear dynamical systems? In: Raskin, J., Chatterjee, K., Doyen, L., Majumdar, R. (eds.) Principles of Systems Design - Essays Dedicated to Thomas A. Henzinger on the Occasion of His 60th Birthday. Lecture Notes in Computer Science, vol. 13660, pp. 21–38. Springer (2022). https://doi.org/10.1007/978-3-031-22337-2_2

42. Kincaid, Z., Breck, J., Boroujeni, A.F., Reps, T.W.: Compositional recurrence analysis revisited. In: Cohen, A., Vechev, M.T. (eds.) Proceedings of the 38th ACM SIGPLAN Conference on Programming Language Design and Implementation, PLDI 2017, Barcelona, Spain, June 18–23, 2017, pp. 248–262. ACM (2017). https://doi.org/10.1145/3062341.3062373

43. Kincaid, Z., Cyphert, J., Breck, J., Reps, T.W.: Non-linear reasoning for invariant synthesis. Proc. ACM Program. Lang. 2(POPL), 54:1–54:33 (2018). https://doi.org/10.1145/3158142

44. Korthikanti, V.A., Viswanathan, M., Agha, G., Kwon, Y.: Reasoning about MDPs as transformers of probability distributions. In: QEST 2010, Seventh International Conference on the Quantitative Evaluation of Systems, Williamsburg, Virginia, USA, 15–18 September 2010, pp. 199–208. IEEE Computer Society (2010). https://doi.org/10.1109/QEST.2010.35

45. Kozen, D.: A probabilistic PDL. In: Johnson, D.S., et al. (eds.) Proceedings of the 15th Annual ACM Symposium on Theory of Computing, 25–27 April, 1983, Boston, Massachusetts, USA, pp. 291–297. ACM (1983). https://doi.org/10.1145/800061.808758

46. Kretínský, J., Meggendorfer, T.: Conditional value-at-risk for reachability and mean payoff in Markov decision processes. In: Dawar, A., Grädel, E. (eds.) Proceedings of the 33rd Annual ACM/IEEE Symposium on Logic in Computer Science, LICS 2018, Oxford, UK, July 09–12, 2018, pp. 609–618. ACM (2018). https://doi.org/10.1145/3209108.3209176

47. Kwon, Y., Agha, G.A.: Verifying the evolution of probability distributions governed by a DTMC. IEEE Trans. Software Eng. **37**(1), 126–141 (2011). https://doi.org/10.1109/TSE.2010.80
48. McIver, A., Morgan, C.: Abstraction, Refinement and Proof for Probabilistic Systems. Monographs in Computer Science, Springer, Cham (2005). https://doi.org/10.1007/b138392
49. Meggendorfer, T.: Risk-aware stochastic shortest path. In: Thirty-Sixth AAAI Conference on Artificial Intelligence, AAAI 2022, Thirty-Fourth Conference on Innovative Applications of Artificial Intelligence, IAAI 2022, The Twelveth Symposium on Educational Advances in Artificial Intelligence, EAAI 2022 Virtual Event, February 22 - March 1, 2022, pp. 9858–9867. AAAI Press (2022). https://ojs.aaai.org/index.php/AAAI/article/view/21222
50. Meurer, A., et al.: Sympy: symbolic computing in python. PeerJ Comput. Sci. **3**, e103 (2017). https://doi.org/10.7717/peerj-cs.103
51. Mieghem, P.V.: Performance Analysis of Communications Networks and Systems. Cambridge University Press, Cambridge (2006)
52. Morgan, C., McIver, A., Seidel, K.: Probabilistic predicate transformers. ACM Trans. Program. Lang. Syst. **18**(3), 325–353 (1996). https://doi.org/10.1145/229542.229547
53. de Moura, L., Bjørner, N.: Z3: an efficient SMT solver. In: Ramakrishnan, C.R., Rehof, J. (eds.) TACAS 2008. LNCS, vol. 4963, pp. 337–340. Springer, Heidelberg (2008). https://doi.org/10.1007/978-3-540-78800-3_24
54. Ouaknine, J., Worrell, J.: Decision problems for linear recurrence sequences. In: Finkel, A., Leroux, J., Potapov, I. (eds.) RP 2012. LNCS, vol. 7550, pp. 21–28. Springer, Heidelberg (2012). https://doi.org/10.1007/978-3-642-33512-9_3
55. Ouaknine, J., Worrell, J.: Positivity problems for low-order linear recurrence sequences. In: Chekuri, C. (ed.) Proceedings of the Twenty-Fifth Annual ACM-SIAM Symposium on Discrete Algorithms, SODA 2014, Portland, Oregon, USA, January 5–7, 2014, pp. 366–379. SIAM (2014). https://doi.org/10.1137/1.9781611973402.27
56. Ouaknine, J., Worrell, J.: On linear recurrence sequences and loop termination. ACM SIGLOG News **2**(2), 4–13 (2015). https://doi.org/10.1145/2766189.2766191
57. Podelski, A., Rybalchenko, A.: A complete method for the synthesis of linear ranking functions. In: Steffen, B., Levi, G. (eds.) VMCAI 2004. LNCS, vol. 2937, pp. 239–251. Springer, Heidelberg (2004). https://doi.org/10.1007/978-3-540-24622-0_20
58. Puterman, M.L.: Markov Decision Processes: Discrete Stochastic Dynamic Programming. Wiley Series in Probability and Statistics, Wiley (1994). https://doi.org/10.1002/9780470316887
59. Putinar, M.: Positive polynomials on compact semi-algebraic sets. Indiana University Math. J. **42**(3), 969–984 (1993)
60. Rodríguez-Carbonell, E., Kapur, D.: Automatic generation of polynomial invariants of bounded degree using abstract interpretation. Sci. Comput. Program. **64**(1), 54–75 (2007). https://doi.org/10.1016/j.scico.2006.03.003
61. Si, X., Dai, H., Raghothaman, M., Naik, M., Song, L.: Learning loop invariants for program verification. In: Bengio, S., Wallach, H.M., Larochelle, H., Grauman, K., Cesa-Bianchi, N., Garnett, R. (eds.) Advances in Neural Information Processing Systems 31: Annual Conference on Neural Information Processing Systems 2018, NeurIPS 2018(December), pp. 3–8, 2018. Montréal, Canada, pp. 7762–7773 (2018). https://proceedings.neurips.cc/paper/2018/hash/65b1e92c585fd4c2159d5f33b5030ff2-Abstract.html

62. Takisaka, T., Oyabu, Y., Urabe, N., Hasuo, I.: Ranking and repulsing supermartingales for reachability in randomized programs. ACM Trans. Program. Lang. Syst. **43**(2), 5:1-5:46 (2021). https://doi.org/10.1145/3450967

63. Wang, P., Fu, H., Goharshady, A.K., Chatterjee, K., Qin, X., Shi, W.: Cost analysis of nondeterministic probabilistic programs. In: McKinley, K.S., Fisher, K. (eds.) Proceedings of the 40th ACM SIGPLAN Conference on Programming Language Design and Implementation, PLDI 2019, Phoenix, AZ, USA, June 22–26, 2019, pp. 204–220. ACM (2019). https://doi.org/10.1145/3314221.3314581

64. Zikelic, D., Chang, B.E., Bolignano, P., Raimondi, F.: Differential cost analysis with simultaneous potentials and anti-potentials. In: Jhala, R., Dillig, I. (eds.) 43rd ACM SIGPLAN International Conference on Programming Language Design and Implementation, PLDI 2022, San Diego, CA, USA, 13–17 June 2022, pp. 442–457. ACM (2022). https://doi.org/10.1145/3519939.3523435

Search and Explore: Symbiotic Policy Synthesis in POMDPs

Roman Andriushchenko[1] ![ORCID], Alexander Bork[2] ![ORCID], Milan Češka[1]([✉]) ![ORCID], Sebastian Junges[3] ![ORCID], Joost-Pieter Katoen[2] ![ORCID], and Filip Macák[1] ![ORCID]

[1] Brno University of Technology, Brno, Czech Republic
ceskam@fit.vutbr.cz
[2] RWTH Aachen University, Aachen, Germany
[3] Radboud University, Nijmegen, The Netherlands

Abstract. This paper marries two state-of-the-art controller synthesis methods for partially observable Markov decision processes (POMDPs), a prominent model in sequential decision making under uncertainty. A central issue is to find a POMDP controller—that solely decides based on the observations seen so far—to achieve a total expected reward objective. As finding optimal controllers is undecidable, we concentrate on synthesising good finite-state controllers (FSCs). We do so by tightly integrating two modern, orthogonal methods for POMDP controller synthesis: a belief-based and an inductive approach. The former method obtains an FSC from a finite fragment of the so-called belief MDP, an MDP that keeps track of the probabilities of equally observable POMDP states. The latter is an inductive search technique over a set of FSCs, e.g., controllers with a fixed memory size. The key result of this paper is a symbiotic anytime algorithm that tightly integrates both approaches such that each profits from the controllers constructed by the other. Experimental results indicate a substantial improvement in the value of the controllers while significantly reducing the synthesis time and memory footprint.

1 Introduction

A formidable synthesis challenge is to find a decision-making policy that satisfies temporal constraints even in the presence of stochastic noise. *Markov decision processes (MDPs)* [26] are a prominent model to reason about such policies under stochastic uncertainty. The underlying decision problems are efficiently solvable and probabilistic model checkers such as PRISM [22] and STORM [13] are well-equipped to synthesise policies that provably (and optimally) satisfy a given specification. However, a major shortcoming of MDPs is the assumption that the policy can depend on the precise state of a system. This assumption is unrealistic whenever the state of the system is only observable via sensors. *Partially*

This work has been supported by the Czech Science Foundation grant GA23-06963S (VESCAA), the ERC AdG Grant 787914 (FRAPPANT) and the DFG RTG 2236/2 (UnRAVeL).

C. Enea and A. Lal (Eds.): CAV 2023, LNCS 13966, pp. 113–135, 2023.
https://doi.org/10.1007/978-3-031-37709-9_6

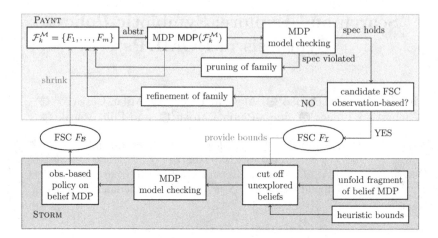

Fig. 1. Schematic depiction of the symbiotic approach

observable MDPs (POMDPs) overcome this shortcoming, but policy synthesis for POMDPs and specifications such as *the probability to reach the exit is larger than 50%* requires solving undecidable problems [23]. Nevertheless, in recent years, a variety of approaches have been successfully applied to a variety of challenging benchmarks, but the approaches also fail somewhat spectacularly on seemingly tiny problem instances. From a user perspective, it is hard to pick the right approach without detailed knowledge of the underlying methods. This paper sets out to develop a framework in which conceptually orthogonal approaches symbiotically alleviate each other's weaknesses and find policies that maximise, e.g., the expected reward before a target is reached. We show empirically that the combined approach can find compact policies achieving a significantly higher reward than the policies that either individual approach constructs.

Belief Exploration. Several approaches for solving POMDPs use the notion of *beliefs* [27]. The key idea is that each sequence of observations and actions induces a belief—a distribution over POMDP states that reflects the probability to be in a state conditioned on the observations. POMDP policies can decide optimally solely based on the belief. The evolution of beliefs can be captured by a fully observable, yet possibly infinite *belief MDP*. A practical approach (see the lower part of Fig. 1) is to unfold a finite fragment of this belief MDP and make its frontier absorbing. This finite fragment can be analysed with off-the-shelf MDP model checkers. Its accuracy can be improved by using an arbitrary but fixed cut-off policy from the frontier onwards. Crucially, the probability to reach the target under such a policy can be efficiently pre-computed for all beliefs. This paper considers the belief exploration method from [8] realised in STORM [13].

Policy Search. An orthogonal approach searches a (finite) space of policies [14, 24] and evaluates these policies by verifying the induced Markov chain. To ensure scalability, sets of policies must be efficiently analysed. However, policy spaces explode whenever they require memory. The open challenge is to adequately define the space of policies to search in. In this paper, we consider the policy-search method from [5] as implemented in PAYNT [6] that explores spaces of finite-state controllers (FSCs), represented as deterministic Mealy machines [2], using a combination of abstraction-refinement, counterexamples (to prune sets of policies), and increasing a controller's memory, see the upper part of Fig. 1.

Our Symbiotic Approach. In essence, our idea relies on the fact that a policy found via one approach can boost the other approach. The key observation is that such a policy is beneficial even when it is sub-optimal in terms of the objective at hand. Figure 1 sketches the symbiotic approach. The FSCs F_I obtained by policy search are used to guide the partial belief MDP to the target. Vice versa, the FSCs F_B obtained from belief exploration are used to shrinken the set of policies and to steer the abstraction. Our experimental evaluation, using a large set of POMDP benchmarks, reveals that (a) belief exploration can yield better FSCs (sometimes also faster) using FSCs F_I from PAYNT—even if the latter FSCs are far from optimal, (b) policy search can find much better FSCs when using FSCs from belief exploration, and (c) the FSCs from the symbiotic approach are superior in value to the ones obtained by the standalone approaches.

Beyond Exploration and Policy Search. In this work, we focus on two powerful orthogonal methods from the set of belief-based and search-based methods. Alternatives exist. Exploration can also be done using a fixed set of beliefs [25]. Prominently, HSVI [18] and SARSOP [20] are belief-based policy synthesis approaches typically used for discounted properties. They also support undiscounted properties, but represent policies with α-vectors. Bounded policy synthesis [29] uses a combination of belief-exploration and inductive synthesis over paths and addresses finite horizon reachability. α-vector policies lead to more complex analysis downstream: the resulting policies must track the belief and do floating-point computations to select actions. For policy search, prominent alternatives are to search for randomised controllers via gradient descent [17] or via convex optimization [1,12,19]. Alternatively, FSCs can be extracted via deep reinforcement learning [9]. However, randomised policies limit predictability, which hampers testing and explainability. The area of programmatic reinforcement learning [28] combines inductive synthesis ideas with RL. While our empirical evaluation is method-specific, the lessons carry over to integrating other methods.

Contributions. The key contribution of this paper is the symbiosis of belief exploration [8] and policy search [5]. Though this seems natural, various technical obstacles had to be addressed, e.g., obtaining F_B from the finite fragment of the belief MDP and the policies for its frontier and developing an interplay between the exploration and search phases that minimises the overhead. The benefits of the symbiotic algorithm are manifold, as we show by a thorough empirical evaluation. It can solve POMDPs that cannot be tackled with either of the two approaches alone. It outputs FSCs that are superior in value (with relative improvements of up to 40%) as well as FSCs that are more succinct (with reduction of a factor of up to two orders of magnitude) with only a small penalty in their values. Additionally, the integration reduces the memory footprint compared to belief exploration by a factor of 4. In conclusion, the proposed symbiosis offers a powerful push-button, anytime synthesis algorithm producing, in the given time, superior and/or more succinct FSCs compared to the state-of-the-art methods.

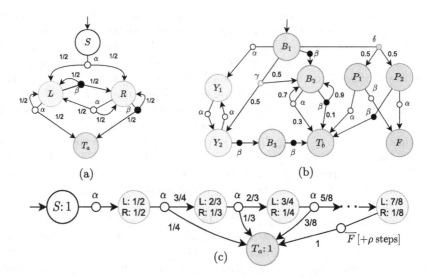

Fig. 2. (a) and (b) contain two POMDPs. Colours encode observations. Unlabelled transitions have probability 1. Omitted actions (e.g. γ, δ in state B_2) execute a self-loop. (c) Markov chain induced by the minimising policy σ_B in the finite abstraction $\overline{\mathcal{M}_a^B}$ of the POMDP from Fig. 2a. In the rightmost state, policy $\overline{F}$ is applied (cut-off), allowing to reach the target in ρ steps. (Color figure online)

2   Motivating Examples

We give a sample POMDP that is hard for the belief exploration, a POMDP that challenges the policy search approach, and indicate why a symbiotic approach overcomes this. A third sample POMDP is shown to be unsolvable by either approach alone but can be treated by the symbiotic one.

A Challenging POMDP for Belief-Based Exploration. Consider POMDP $\mathcal{M}_a$ in Fig. 2a. The objective is to minimise the expected number of steps to the target T_a. An optimal policy is to always take action α yielding 4 expected steps. An FSC realising this policy can be found by a policy search under 1s.

Belief MDPs. States in the *belief MDP* $\mathcal{M}_a^B$ are *beliefs*, probability distributions over POMDP states with equal observations. The initial belief is $\{S \mapsto 1\}$. By taking action α, 'yellow' is observed and the belief becomes $\{L \mapsto \frac{1}{2}, R \mapsto \frac{1}{2}\}$.

Closer inspection shows that the set of reachable beliefs is infinite rendering $\mathcal{M}_a^{\mathcal{B}}$ to be infinite. Belief exploration constructs a finite fragment $\overline{\mathcal{M}_a^{\mathcal{B}}}$ by exploring $\mathcal{M}_a^{\mathcal{B}}$ up to some depth while *cutting off* the frontier states. From cut-off states, a shortcut is taken directly to the target. These shortcuts are heuristic over-approximations of the true number of expected steps from the cut-off state to the target. The finite MDP $\overline{\mathcal{M}_a^{\mathcal{B}}}$ can be analysed using off-the-shelf tools yielding the minimising policy $\sigma_{\mathcal{B}}$ assigning to each belief state the optimal action.

Admissible Heuristics. A simple way to over-approximate the minimal number of the expected number of steps to the target is to use an arbitrary controller $\overline{F}$ and use the expected number of steps under $\overline{F}$. The latter is cheap if $\overline{F}$ is compact, as detailed in Sect. 4.2. Figure 2c shows a Markov chain induced by $\sigma_{\mathcal{B}}$ in $\overline{\mathcal{M}_a^{\mathcal{B}}}$, where the belief $\{L \mapsto \frac{7}{8}, R \mapsto \frac{1}{8}\}$ is cut off using $\overline{F}$. The belief exploration in STORM [8] unfolds 1000 states of $\mathcal{M}_a^{\mathcal{B}}$ and finds controller $\overline{F}$ that uniformly randomises over all actions in the rightmost state. The resulting sub-optimal controller $F_{\mathcal{B}}$ reaches the target in ≈ 4.1 steps. Exploring only a few states suffices when replacing $\overline{F}$ by a (not necessarily optimal) FSC provided by a policy search.

A Challenging POMDP for Policy Search. Consider POMDP $\mathcal{M}_b$ in Fig. 2b. The objective is to minimise the expected number of steps to T_b. Its 9-state belief MDP $\mathcal{M}_b^{\mathcal{B}}$ is trivial for the belief-based method. Its optimal controller $\sigma_{\mathcal{B}}$ first picks action γ; on observing 'yellow' it plays β twice, otherwise it always picks α. This is realised by an FSC with 3 memory states. The inductive policy search in PAYNT [5] explores families of FSCs of increasing complexity, i.e., of increasing memory size. It finds the optimal FSC after consulting about 20 billion candidate policies. This requires 545 model-checking queries; the optimal one is found after 105 queries while the remaining queries prove that no better 3-state FSC exists.

Reference Policies. The policy search is guided by a reference policy, in this case the fully observable MDP policy that picks (senseless) action δ in B_1 first. Using policy $\sigma_{\mathcal{B}}$—obtained by the belief method—instead, δ is never taken. As $\sigma_{\mathcal{B}}$ picks in each 'blue' state a different action, mimicking this requires at least three memory states. Using $\sigma_{\mathcal{B}}$ reduces the total number of required model-checking queries by a factor of ten; the optimal 3-state FSC is found after 23 queries.

The Potential of Symbiosis. To further exemplify the limitation of the two approaches and the potential of their symbiosis, we consider a synthetic POMDP, called Lanes+, combining a Lane model with larger variants of the POMDPs in Fig. 2; see Table 2 on page 14 for the model statistics and Appendix C of [3] for the model description. We consider minimisation of the expected number of steps and a 15-min timeout. The belief-based approach by STORM yields the value 18870. The policy search method by PAYNT finds an FSC with 2 memory states achieving the value 8223. This sub-optimal FSC significantly improves the belief MDP approximation and enables STORM to find an FSC with value 6471. The symbiotic synthesis loop finds the optimal FSC with value 4805.

3   Preliminaries and Problem Statement

A (discrete) *distribution* over a countable set A is a function $\mu \colon A \to [0,1]$ s.t. $\sum_a \mu(a) = 1$. The set $\mathrm{supp}(\mu) := \{a \in A \mid \mu(a) > 0\}$ is the *support* of μ. The set $Distr(A)$ contains all distributions over A. We use Iverson bracket notation, where $[x] = 1$ if the Boolean expression x evaluates to true and $[x] = 0$ otherwise.

Definition 1 (MDP). *A* Markov decision process (MDP) *is a tuple* $M = (S, s_0, Act, \mathcal{P})$ *with a countable set* S *of states, an initial state* $s_0 \in S$, *a finite set* Act *of actions, and a partial transition function* $\mathcal{P} \colon S \times Act \nrightarrow Distr(S)$. $Act(s) := \{\alpha \in Act \mid \mathcal{P}(s, \alpha) \neq \bot\}$ *denotes the set of actions available in state* $s \in S$. *An MDP with* $|Act(s)| = 1$ *for each* $s \in S$ *is a* Markov chain (MC).

Unless stated otherwise, we assume $Act(s) = Act$ for each $s \in S$ for conciseness. We denote $\mathcal{P}(s, \alpha, s') := \mathcal{P}(s, \alpha)(s')$. A (finite) *path* of an MDP M is a sequence $\pi = s_0 \alpha_0 s_1 \alpha_1 \ldots s_n$ where $\mathcal{P}(s_i, \alpha_i, s_{i+1}) > 0$ for $0 \leq i < n$. We use $last(\pi)$ to denote the last state of path π. Let $Paths^M$ denote the set of all finite paths of M. State s is absorbing if $\mathrm{supp}(\mathcal{P}(s, \alpha)) = \{s\}$ for all $\alpha \in Act$.

Definition 2 (POMDP). *A* partially observable MDP (POMDP) *is a tuple* $\mathcal{M} = (M, Z, O)$, *where* M *is the underlying MDP,* Z *is a finite set of observations and* $O \colon S \to Z$ *is a (deterministic) observation function.*

For POMDP $\mathcal{M}$ with underlying MDP M, an *observation trace* of path $\pi = s_0 \alpha_0 s_1 \alpha_1 \ldots s_n$ is a sequence $O(\pi) := O(s_0) \alpha_0 O(s_1) \alpha_1 \ldots O(s_n)$. Every MDP can be interpreted as a POMDP with $Z = S$ and $O(s) = s$ for all $s \in S$.

A (deterministic) *policy* is a function $\sigma \colon Paths^M \to Act$. Policy σ is *memoryless* if $last(\pi) = last(\pi') \implies \sigma(\pi) = \sigma(\pi')$ for all $\pi, \pi' \in Paths^M$. A memoryless policy σ maps a state $s \in S$ to action $\sigma(s)$. Policy σ is *observation-based* if $O(\pi) = O(\pi') \implies \sigma(\pi) = \sigma(\pi')$ for all $\pi, \pi' \in Paths^M$. For POMDPs, we always consider observation-based policies. We denote by Σ_{obs} the set of all observation-based policies. A policy $\sigma \in \Sigma_{obs}$ induces the MC $\mathcal{M}^\sigma$.

We consider indefinite-horizon reachability or expected total reward properties. Formally, let $M = (S, s_0, Act, \mathcal{P})$ be an MC, and let $T \subseteq S$ be a set of *target states*. $\mathbb{P}^M[s \models \Diamond T]$ denotes the probability of reaching T from state $s \in S$. We use $\mathbb{P}^M[\Diamond T]$ to denote $\mathbb{P}^M[s_0 \models \Diamond T]$ and omit the superscript if the MC is clear from context. Now assume POMDP $\mathcal{M}$ with underlying MDP $M = (S, s_0, Act, \mathcal{P})$, and a set $T \subseteq S$ of absorbing target states. Without loss of generality, we assume that the target states are associated with the unique observation $z^T \in Z$, i.e. $s \in T$ iff $O(s) = z^T$. For a POMDP $\mathcal{M}$ and $T \subseteq S$, the *maximal reachability probability* of T for state $s \in S$ in $\mathcal{M}$ is $\mathbb{P}^{\mathcal{M}}_{\max}[s \models \Diamond T] := \sup_{\sigma \in \Sigma_{obs}} \mathbb{P}^{\mathcal{M}^\sigma}[s \models \Diamond T]$. The minimal reachability probability $\mathbb{P}^{\mathcal{M}}_{\min}[s \models \Diamond T]$ is defined analogously.

Finite-state controllers are automata that compactly encode policies.

Definition 3 (FSC).   *A* finite-state controller (FSC) *is a tuple* $F = (N, n_0, \gamma, \delta)$, *with a finite set* N *of* nodes, *the* initial node $n_0 \in N$, *the* action function $\gamma \colon N \times Z \to Act$ *and the* update function $\delta \colon N \times Z \times Z \to N$.

A k-*FSC* is an FSC with $|N| = k$. If $k=1$, the FSC encodes a memoryless policy. We use $\mathcal{F}^{\mathcal{M}}$ ($\mathcal{F}_k^{\mathcal{M}}$) to denote the family of all (k-)FSCs for POMDP $\mathcal{M}$. For a POMDP in state s, an agent receives observation $z = O(s)$. An agent following an FSC F executes action $\alpha = \gamma(n, z)$ associated with the current node n and the current (prior) observation z. The POMDP state is updated accordingly to some s' with $\mathcal{P}(s, \alpha, s') > 0$. Based on the next (posterior) observation $z' = O(s')$, the FSC evolves to node $n' = \delta(n, z, z')$. The *induced MC* for FSC F is $\mathcal{M}^F = (S \times N, (s_0, n_0), \{\alpha\}, \mathcal{P}^F)$, where for all $(s, n), (s', n') \in S \times N$ we have

$$\mathcal{P}^F\left((s, n), \alpha, (s', n')\right) = [n' = \delta\left(n, O(s), O(s')\right)] \cdot \mathcal{P}(s, \gamma(n, O(s)), s').$$

We emphasise that for MDPs with infinite state space and POMDPs, an FSC realising the maximal reachability probability generally does not exist. For FSC $F \in \mathcal{F}^{\mathcal{M}}$ with the set N of memory nodes, let $\mathbb{P}^{\mathcal{M}^F}[(s, n) \models \Diamond T] := \mathbb{P}^{\mathcal{M}^F}[(s, n) \models \Diamond(T \times N)]$ denote the probability of reaching target states T from state $(s, n) \in S \times N$. Analogously, $\mathbb{P}^{\mathcal{M}^F}[\Diamond T] := \mathbb{P}^{\mathcal{M}^F}[\Diamond(T \times N)]$ denotes the probability of reaching target states T in the MC $\mathcal{M}^F$ induced on $\mathcal{M}$ by F.

Problem Statement. The classical synthesis problem [23] for POMDPs asks: given POMDP $\mathcal{M}$, a set T of targets, and a threshold λ, find an FSC F such that $\mathbb{P}^{\mathcal{M}^F}[\Diamond T] \geq \lambda$, if one exists. We take a more practical stance and aim instead to optimise the value $\mathbb{P}^{\mathcal{M}^F}[\Diamond T]$ in an anytime fashion: the faster we can find FSCs with a high value, the better.

Remark 1. Variants of the maximising synthesis problem for the expected total reward and minimisation are defined analogously. For conciseness, in this paper, we always assume that we want to maximise the value.

In addition to the value of the FSC F, another key characteristic of the controller is its *size*, which we treat as a secondary objective and discuss in detail in Sect. 6.

4   FSCs for and from Belief Exploration

We consider *belief exploration* as described in [8]. A schematic overview is given in the lower part of Fig. 1. We recap the key concepts of belief exploration. This section explains two contributions: we discuss how arbitrary FSCs are included and present an approach to export the associated POMDP policies as FSCs.

4.1   Belief Exploration with Explicit FSC Construction

Finite-state controllers for a POMDP can be obtained by analysing the (fully observable) *belief MDP* [27]. The state space of this MDP consists of *beliefs*:

probability distributions over states of the POMDP $\mathcal{M}$ having the same observation. Let $S_z := \{s \in S \mid O(s) = z\}$ denote the set of all states of $\mathcal{M}$ with observation $z \in Z$. Let the set of all beliefs $\mathcal{B}_{\mathcal{M}} := \bigcup_{z \in Z} Distr(S_z)$ and denote for $b \in \mathcal{B}_{\mathcal{M}}$ by $O(b) \in Z$ the unique observation $O(s)$ of any $s \in \mathrm{supp}(b)$.

In a belief b, taking action α yields an updated belief as follows: let $\mathcal{P}(b, \alpha, z') := \sum_{s \in S_{O(b)}} b(s) \cdot \sum_{s' \in S_{z'}} \mathcal{P}(s, \alpha, s')$ denote the probability of observing $z' \in Z$ upon taking action $\alpha \in Act$ in belief $b \in \mathcal{B}_{\mathcal{M}}$. If $\mathcal{P}(b, \alpha, z') > 0$, the corresponding successor belief $b' = [\![b|\alpha, z']\!]$ with $O(b') = z'$ is defined component-wise as

$$[\![b|\alpha, z']\!](s') := \frac{\sum_{s \in S_{O(b)}} b(s) \cdot \mathcal{P}(s, \alpha, s')}{\mathcal{P}(b, \alpha, z')}$$

for all $s' \in S_{z'}$. Otherwise, $[\![b|\alpha, z']\!]$ is undefined.

Definition 4 (Belief MDP). *The* belief MDP *of POMDP $\mathcal{M}$ is the MDP $\mathcal{M}^{\mathcal{B}} = (\mathcal{B}_{\mathcal{M}}, b_0, Act, \mathcal{P}^{\mathcal{B}})$, with initial belief $b_0 := \{s_0 \mapsto 1\}$ and transition function $\mathcal{P}^{\mathcal{B}}(b, \alpha, b') := [b' = [\![b|\alpha, z']\!]] \cdot \mathcal{P}(b, \alpha, z')$ where $z' = O(b')$.*

The belief MDP captures the behaviour of its POMDP. It can be unfolded by starting in the initial belief and computing all successor beliefs.

Deriving FSCs from Finite Belief MDPs. Let $T^{\mathcal{B}} := \{b \in \mathcal{B}_{\mathcal{M}} \mid O(b) = z^T\}$ denote the set of *target beliefs*. If the reachable state space of the belief MDP $\mathcal{M}^{\mathcal{B}}$ is finite, e.g. because the POMDP is acyclic, standard model checking techniques can be applied to compute the memoryless policy $\sigma_{\mathcal{B}} \colon \mathcal{B}_{\mathcal{M}} \to Act$ that selects in each belief state $b \in \mathcal{B}_{\mathcal{M}}$ the action that maximises $\mathbb{P}\,[b \models \Diamond T^{\mathcal{B}}]$[1]. We can translate the deterministic, memoryless policy $\sigma_{\mathcal{B}}$ into the corresponding FSC $F_{\mathcal{B}} = (\mathcal{B}_{\mathcal{M}}, b_0, \gamma, \delta)$ with action function $\gamma(b, z) = \sigma_{\mathcal{B}}(b)$ and update function $\delta(b, z, z') = [\![b|\sigma_{\mathcal{B}}(b), z']\!]$ for all $z, z' \in Z$.[2]

Handling Large and Infinite Belief MDPs. In case the reachable state space of the belief MDP $\mathcal{M}^{\mathcal{B}}$ is infinite or too large for a complete unfolding, a finite approximation $\overline{\mathcal{M}^{\mathcal{B}}}$ is used instead [8]. Assuming $\mathcal{M}^{\mathcal{B}}$ is unfolded up to some depth, let $\mathcal{E} \subset \mathcal{B}_{\mathcal{M}}$ denote the set of explored beliefs and let $\mathcal{U} \subset \mathcal{B}_{\mathcal{M}} \backslash \mathcal{E}$ denote the *frontier*: the set of unexplored beliefs reachable from $\mathcal{E}$ in one step. To complete the finite abstraction, we require handling of the frontier beliefs. The idea is to use for each $b \in \mathcal{U}$ a *cut-off value* $\underline{V}(b)$: an under-approximation of the maximal reachability probability $\mathbb{P}_{\max}^{\mathcal{M}^{\mathcal{B}}}\,[b \models \Diamond T^{\mathcal{B}}]$ for b in the belief MDP. We explain how to compute cut-off values systematically given an FSC in Sect. 4.2.

Ultimately, we define a finite MDP $\overline{\mathcal{M}^{\mathcal{B}}} = (\mathcal{E} \cup \mathcal{U} \cup \{b_{\top}, b_{\bot}\}, b_0, Act, \overline{\mathcal{P}^{\mathcal{B}}})$ with the transition function: $\overline{\mathcal{P}^{\mathcal{B}}}(b, \alpha) := \mathcal{P}^{\mathcal{B}}(b, \alpha)$ for explored beliefs $b \in \mathcal{E}$ and all $\alpha \in Act$, and $\overline{\mathcal{P}^{\mathcal{B}}}(b, \alpha) := \{b_{\top} \mapsto \underline{V}(b), b_{\bot} \mapsto 1 - \underline{V}(b)\}$ for frontier beliefs $b \in \mathcal{U}$ and all $\alpha \in Act$, where $b_{\top}$ and $b_{\bot}$ are fresh sink states, i.e. $\overline{\mathcal{P}^{\mathcal{B}}}(b_{\top}, \alpha) := \{b_{\top} \mapsto 1\}$

---

[1] Memoryless policies suffice to maximise the value in a fully observable MDP [26].

[2] The assignments of missing combinations where $z \neq O(b)$ are irrelevant.

and $\overline{\mathcal{P}^{\mathcal{B}}}(b_\perp, \alpha) := \{b_\perp \mapsto 1\}$ for all $\alpha \in Act$. The reachable state space of $\overline{\mathcal{M}^{\mathcal{B}}}$ is finite, enabling its automated analysis; since our method to compute cut-off values emulates an FSC, a policy maximising $\mathbb{P}_{\max}^{\overline{\mathcal{M}^{\mathcal{B}}}}[\Diamond(T^{\mathcal{B}} \cup \{b_\top\})]$ induces an FSC for the original POMDP $\mathcal{M}$. We discuss how to obtain this FSC in Sect. 4.3.

4.2   Using FSCs for Cut-Off Values

A crucial aspect when applying the belief exploration with cut-offs is the choice of suitable cut-off values. The closer the cut-off value is to the actual optimum in a belief, the better the approximation we obtain. In particular, if the cut-off values coincide with the optimal value, cutting off the initial state is optimal. However, finding optimal values is as hard as solving the original POMDP. We consider *under-approximative value functions* induced by applying *any*[3] FSC to the POMDP and lifting the results to the belief MDP. The better the FSC, the better the cut-off value. We generalise belief exploration with cut-offs such that the approach supports arbitrary sets of FSCs with additional flexibility.

Let $F_{\mathcal{I}} \in \mathcal{F}^{\mathcal{M}}$ be an arbitrary, but fixed FSC for POMDP $\mathcal{M}$. Let $p_{s,n} := \mathbb{P}^{\mathcal{M}^{F_{\mathcal{I}}}}[(s,n) \models \Diamond T]$ for state $(s,n) \in S \times N$ in the corresponding induced MC. For fixed $n \in N$, $V(b,n) := \sum_{s \in S_{O(b)}} b(s) \cdot p_{s,n}$ denotes the cut-off value for belief b and memory node n. It corresponds to the probability of reaching a target state in $\mathcal{M}^{F_{\mathcal{I}}}$ when starting in memory node $n \in N$ and state $s \in S$ according to the probability distribution b. We define the overall cut-off value for b induced by F as $\underline{V}(b) := \max_{n \in N} V(b,n)$. It follows straightforwardly that $\underline{V}(b) \leq \mathbb{P}_{\max}^{\mathcal{M}^{\mathcal{B}}}[b \models \Diamond T^{\mathcal{B}}]$. As values $p_{s,n}$ only need to be computed once, computing $\underline{V}(b)$ for a given belief b is relatively simple. However, the complexity of the FSC-based cut-off approach depends on the size of the induced MC. Therefore, it is essential that the FSCs used to compute cut-off values are concise.

4.3   Extracting FSC from Belief Exploration

Model checking the finite approximation MDP $\overline{\mathcal{M}^{\mathcal{B}}}$ with cut-off values induced by an FSC $F_{\mathcal{I}}$ yields a maximising memoryless policy $\sigma_{\mathcal{B}}$. Our goal is to represent this policy as an FSC $F_{\mathcal{B}}$. We construct $F_{\mathcal{B}}$ by considering both $F_{\mathcal{I}}$ and the necessary memory nodes for each explored belief $b \in \mathcal{E}$. Concretely, for each explored belief, we introduce a corresponding memory node. In each such node, the action $\sigma_{\mathcal{B}}(b)$ is selected. For the memory update, we distinguish between two cases based on the next belief after executing $\sigma_{\mathcal{B}}(b)$ in $\overline{\mathcal{M}^{\mathcal{B}}}$. If for observation $z' \in Z$, the successor belief $b' = [\![b|\sigma_{\mathcal{B}}(b), z']\!] \in \mathcal{E}$, the memory is updated to the corresponding node. Otherwise, $b' \in \mathcal{U}$ holds, i.e., the successor is part of the frontier. The memory is then updated to the memory node n of FSC $F_{\mathcal{I}}$ that maximises the cut-off value $V(b', n)$. This corresponds to the notion that if the frontier is encountered, we switch from acting according to policy $\sigma_{\mathcal{B}}$ to following $F_{\mathcal{I}}$ (initialised in the correct memory node). This is formalised as:

---

[3] We remark that [8] considers memoryless FSCs only.

Definition 5 (Belief-based FSC with cut-offs). *Let* $F_{\mathcal{I}} = (N, n_0, \gamma_{\mathcal{I}}, \delta_{\mathcal{I}})$ *and* $\overline{\mathcal{M}^{\mathcal{B}}}$ *as before. The* belief-based FSC with cut-offs *is* $F_{\mathcal{B}} = (\mathcal{E} \cup N, b_0, \gamma, \delta)$ *with action function* $\gamma(b, z) = \sigma_{\mathcal{B}}(b)$ *for* $b \in \mathcal{E}$ *and* $\gamma(n, z) = \gamma_{\mathcal{I}}(n, z)$ *for* $n \in N$ *and arbitrary* $z \in Z$. *The update function* δ *is defined for all* $z, z' \in Z$ *by* $\delta(n, z, z') = \delta_{\mathcal{I}}(n, z, z')$ *if* $n \in N$, *and for* $b \in \mathcal{E}$ *with* $b' = [\![b | \sigma_{\mathcal{B}}(b), z']\!]$ *by:*

$$\delta(b, z, z') = b' \text{ if } b' \in \mathcal{E}, \text{ and } \delta(b, z, z') = \operatorname{argmax}_{n \in N} V(b', n) \text{ otherwise.}$$

5   Accelerated Inductive Synthesis

In this section, we consider inductive synthesis [5], an approach for finding controllers for POMDPs in a set of FSCs. We briefly recap the main idea, then first explain how to use a reference policy. Finally, we introduce and discuss a novel search space for the controllers that we consider in this paper in detail.

5.1   Inductive Synthesis with k-FSCs

In the scope of this paper, inductive synthesis [4] considers a finite family of FSCs $\mathcal{F}_k^{\mathcal{M}}$ of k-FSCs with memory nodes $N = \{n_0, \ldots, n_{k-1}\}$, and the family $\mathcal{M}^{\mathcal{F}_k^{\mathcal{M}}} := \{\mathcal{M}^F \mid F \in \mathcal{F}_k^{\mathcal{M}}\}$ of associated induced MCs. The states for each MC are tuples $(s, n) \in S \times N$. For conciseness, we only discuss the abstraction-refinement framework [10] within the inductive synthesis loop. The overall image is as in Fig. 1. Informally, the *MDP abstraction* of the family $\mathcal{M}^{\mathcal{F}_k^{\mathcal{M}}}$ of MCs is an MDP $\mathsf{MDP}(\mathcal{F}_k^{\mathcal{M}})$ with the set $S \times N$ of states such that, if some MC $M \in \mathcal{M}^{\mathcal{F}_k^{\mathcal{M}}}$ executes action α in state $(s, n) \in S \times N$, then this action (with the same effect) is also enabled in state (s, n) of $\mathsf{MDP}(\mathcal{F}_k^{\mathcal{M}})$. Essentially, $\mathsf{MDP}(\mathcal{F}_k^{\mathcal{M}})$ over-approximates the behaviour of all the MCs in the family $\mathcal{M}^{\mathcal{F}_k^{\mathcal{M}}}$: it simulates an arbitrary family member in every step, but it may switch between steps.[4]

Definition 6. *MDP abstraction for POMDP* $\mathcal{M}$ *and family* $\mathcal{F}_k^{\mathcal{M}} = \{F_1, \ldots, F_m\}$ *of* k-*FSCs is the MDP* $\mathsf{MDP}(\mathcal{F}_k^{\mathcal{M}}) := (S \times N, (s_0, n_0), \{1, \ldots, m\}, \mathcal{P}^{\mathcal{F}_k^{\mathcal{M}}})$ *with*

$$\mathcal{P}^{\mathcal{F}_k^{\mathcal{M}}}((s, n), i) = \mathcal{P}^{F_i}.$$

While this MDP has m actions, practically, many actions coincide. Below, we see how to utilise the structure of the FSCs. Here, we finish by observing that the MDP is a proper abstraction:

Lemma 1. *[10] For all* $F \in \mathcal{F}_k^{\mathcal{M}}$, $\mathbb{P}_{\min}^{MDP(\mathcal{F}_k^{\mathcal{M}})}[\lozenge T] \leq \mathbb{P}^{\mathcal{M}^F}[\lozenge T] \leq \mathbb{P}_{\max}^{MDP(\mathcal{F}_k^{\mathcal{M}})}[\lozenge T]$.

With that result, we can naturally start with the set of all k-FSCs and search through this family by selecting suitable subsets [10]. Since the number k of memory nodes necessary is not known in advance, one can iteratively explore the sequence $\mathcal{F}_1^{\mathcal{M}}, \mathcal{F}_2^{\mathcal{M}}, \ldots$ of families of FSCs of increasing complexity.

---

[4] The MDP is an game-based abstraction [21] of the all-in-one MC [11].

5.2   Using Reference Policies to Accelerate Inductive Synthesis

Consider the synthesis process of the optimal k-FSC $F \in \mathcal{F}_k^{\mathcal{M}}$ for POMDP $\mathcal{M}$. To accelerate the search for F within this family, we consider a reference policy, e.g., a policy $\sigma_\mathcal{B}$ extracted from an (approximation of the) belief MDP, and shrink the FSC family. For each observation $z \in Z$, we collect the set $Act[\sigma_\mathcal{B}](z) := \{\sigma_\mathcal{B}(b) \mid b \in \mathcal{B}_\mathcal{M}, O(b) = z\}$ of actions that were selected by $\sigma_\mathcal{B}$ in beliefs with observation z. The set $Act[\sigma_\mathcal{B}](z)$ contains the actions used by the reference policy when in observation z. We focus the search on these actions by constructing a subset of FSCs $\{ (N, n_0, \gamma, \delta) \in \mathcal{F}_k^{\mathcal{M}} \mid \forall n \in N, z \in Z. \gamma(n, z) \in Act[\sigma_\mathcal{B}](z)\}$.

Restricting the action selection may exclude the optimal k-FSC. It also does not guarantee that the optimal FSC in the restricted family achieves the same value as the reference policy $\sigma_\mathcal{B}$ as $\sigma_\mathcal{B}$ may have more memory nodes. We first search the restricted space of FSCs before searching the complete space. This also accelerates the search: The earlier a good policy is found, the easier it is to discard other candidates (because they are provably not optimal). Furthermore, in case the algorithm terminates earlier (notice the anytime aspect of our problem statement), we are more likely to have found a reasonable policy.

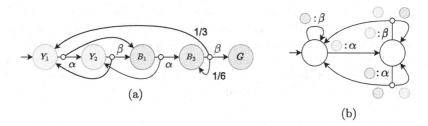

(a)

(b)

Fig. 3. (a) A POMDP where colours and capital letters encode observations; unlabelled transitions have probability $1/2$; omitted actions (e.g. action β in the initial state) are self-loops; the objective is to minimise the expected number of steps to reach state G. (b) The optimal posterior-aware 2-FSC. (Color figure online)

Additionally, we could use sets $Act[\sigma_\mathcal{B}]$ to determine with which k to search. If in some observation $z \in Z$ the belief policy $\sigma_\mathcal{B}$ uses $|Act[\sigma_\mathcal{B}](z)|$ distinct actions, then in order to enable the use of all of these actions, we require at least $k = \max_{z \in Z} |Act[\sigma_\mathcal{B}](z)|$ memory states. However, this may lead to families that are too large and thus we use a more refined view discussed below.

5.3   Inductive Synthesis with Adequate FSCs

In this section, we discuss the set of candidate FSCs in more detail. In particular, we take a more refined look at the families that we consider.

More Granular FSCs. We consider memory models [5] that describe per-observation how much memory may be used:

Definition 7 (μ-FSC). *A* memory model *for POMDP $\mathcal{M}$ is a function $\mu\colon Z \to \mathbb{N}$. Let $k = \max_{z \in Z} \mu(z)$. The k-FSC $F \in \mathcal{F}_k^{\mathcal{M}}$ with nodes $N = \{n_0, \ldots, n_{k-1}\}$ is a μ-FSC iff for all $z \in Z$ and for all $i > \mu(z)$ it holds: $\gamma(n_i, z) = \gamma(n_0, z)$ and $\delta(n_i, z, z') = \delta(n_0, z, z')$ for any $z' \in Z$.*

$\mathcal{F}_\mu^{\mathcal{M}}$ denotes the family of all μ-FSCs. Essentially, memory model μ dictates that for prior observation z only $\mu(z)$ memory nodes are utilised, while the rest behave exactly as the default memory node n_0. Using memory model μ with $\mu(z) < k$ for some observations $z \in Z$ greatly reduces the number of candidate controllers. For example, if $|S_z| = 1$ for some $z \in Z$, then upon reaching this state, the history becomes irrelevant. It is thus sufficient to set $\mu(z) = 1$ (for the specifications in this paper). It also significantly reduces the size of the abstraction, see Appendix A of [3].

Posterior-aware or Posterior-unaware. The technique outlined in [5] considers *posterior-unaware FSCs* [2]. An FSC with update function δ is posterior-unaware if the posterior observation is not taken into account when updating the memory node of the FSC, i.e. $\delta(n, z, z') = \delta(n, z, z'')$ for all $n \in N, z, z', z'' \in Z$. This restriction reduces the policy space and thus the MDP abstraction $\mathsf{MDP}(\mathcal{F}_k^{\mathcal{M}})$. On the other hand, general (posterior-aware) FSCs can utilise information about the next observation to make an informed decision about the next memory node. As a result, fewer memory nodes are needed to encode complex policies. Consider Fig. 3a which depicts a simple POMDP. First, notice that in yellow states Y_i we want to be able to execute two different actions, implying that we need at least

---

Algorithm 1: Anytime algorithm

    Input   : POMDP $\mathcal{M}$, set T of target states, timeout values $t, t_{\mathcal{I}}, t_{\mathcal{B}}$
    Output: Best FSCs $F_{\mathcal{I}}$ and $F_{\mathcal{B}}$ found so far

1   $F_{\mathcal{I}} \leftarrow \bot, \mathcal{F} \leftarrow \mathcal{F}_1^{\mathcal{M}}, k \leftarrow 0, \mu \leftarrow \{z \mapsto 1 \mid z \in Z\}, F_{\mathcal{B}} \leftarrow \bot, \sigma_{\mathcal{B}} \leftarrow \bot$
2   **while** *not timeout t* **do**
3 | **while** *not timeout $t_{\mathcal{I}}$* **do**
4 | | **if** $\mathcal{F} = \emptyset$ **then**
5 | | | $k \leftarrow k + 1$
6 | | | $\forall z \in Z\colon \mu(z) \leftarrow \max\{\mu(z), k\}$
7 | | | $\mathcal{F} \leftarrow \mathcal{F}_\mu^{\mathcal{M}}$
8 | | $\mathcal{F}, F_{\mathcal{I}} \leftarrow \mathsf{search}(\mathcal{F}, F_{\mathcal{I}}, Act[\sigma_{\mathcal{B}}]$ **if** $\mathbb{P}^{\mathcal{M}^{F_{\mathcal{I}}}}[\lozenge T] > \mathbb{P}^{\mathcal{M}^{F_{\mathcal{B}}}}[\lozenge T]$ **else** $\bot)$
9 | $\sigma_{\mathcal{B}}, F_{\mathcal{B}} \leftarrow \mathsf{explore}(t_{\mathcal{B}}, F_{\mathcal{I}})$
10 | **if** $\mathbb{P}^{\mathcal{M}^{F_{\mathcal{I}}}}[\lozenge T] \leq \mathbb{P}^{\mathcal{M}^{F_{\mathcal{B}}}}[\lozenge T]$ *and* $\exists z \in Z\colon \mu(z) < |Act[\sigma_{\mathcal{B}}](z)|$ **then**
11 | | $\forall z \in Z\colon \mu(z) \leftarrow |Act[\sigma_{\mathcal{B}}](z)|$
12 | | $\mathcal{F} \leftarrow \mathcal{F}_\mu^{\mathcal{M}}$
13 | **yield** $F_{\mathcal{I}}, F_{\mathcal{B}}$

---

two memory nodes to distinguish between the two states, and the same is true for the blue states B_i. Second, notice that in each state the visible action always leads to states having different observations, implying that the posterior observation z' is crucial for the optimal decision making. If z' is ignored, it is impossible to optimally update the memory node. Figure 3b depicts the optimal posterior-aware 2-FSC allowing to reach the target within 12 steps on expectation. The optimal posterior-unaware FSC has at least 4 memory nodes and the optimal posterior-unaware 2-FSC uses 14 steps.

MDP Abstraction. To efficiently and precisely create and analyse MDP abstractions, Definition 6 is overly simplified. In Appendix A of [3], we present the construction for general, posterior-aware FSCs including memory models.

6 Integrating Belief Exploration with Inductive Synthesis

We clarify the symbiotic approach from Fig. 1 and review FSC sizes.

Symbiosis by Closing the Loop. Section 4 shows the potential to improve belief exploration using FSCs, e.g., obtained from an inductive synthesis loop, whereas Sect. 5 shows the potential to improve inductive synthesis using policies from, e.g., belief exploration. A natural next step is to use improved inductive synthesis for belief exploration and improved belief exploration for inductive synthesis, i.e., to alternate between both techniques. This section briefly clarifies the symbiotic approach from Fig. 1 using Algorithm 1.

Table 1. Sizes of different types of FSCs.

FSC class	$size(\gamma)$	$size(\delta)$
k-FSC	$k \cdot |Z|$	$2 \cdot \sum_{n \in N} \sum_{z \in Z} |post(n, z)|$
μ-FSC	$\sum_{z \in Z} \mu(z)$	$2 \cdot \sum_{z \in Z} \sum_{i=0}^{\mu(z)-1} |post(n_i, z)|$
posterior-unaware μ-FSC	$\sum_{z \in Z} \mu(z)$	$\sum_{z \in Z} \mu(z)$
$F_\mathcal{B}$ using $F_\mathcal{I}$ for cut-offs	$size(\gamma_\mathcal{I}) + |\mathcal{E}|$	$size(\delta_\mathcal{I}) + 2 \cdot \sum_{b \in \mathcal{E}} |post(b, O(b))|$

We iterate until a global timeout t: in each iteration, we make both controllers available to the user as soon as they are computed (Algorithm 1, l. 13). We start in the inductive mode (l. 3-8), where we initially consider the 1-FSCs represented in $\mathcal{F}_\mu^\mathcal{M}$. Method search (l. 8) investigates $\mathcal{F}$ and outputs the new maximising FSC $F_\mathcal{I}$ (if it exists). If the timeout $t_\mathcal{I}$ interrupts the synthesis process, the method additionally returns yet unexplored parameter assignments. If $\mathcal{F}$ is fully explored within the timeout $t_\mathcal{I}$ (l. 4), we increase k and repeat the process. After the timeout $t_\mathcal{I}$, we run belief exploration explore for $t_\mathcal{B}$ seconds, where we use $F_\mathcal{I}$ as backup controllers (l. 9). After the timeout $t_\mathcal{B}$ (exploration will continue from a stored configuration in the next belief phase), we use $F_\mathcal{I}$ to obtain cut-off values at unexplored states, compute the optimal policy $\sigma^{\mathcal{M}^{\mathcal{B}}}$ (see Sect. 4) and extract the FSC $F_{\mathcal{B}}$ which incorporates $F_{\mathcal{I}}$. Before we continue the search, we check whether the belief-based FSC is better and whether that FSC gives any reason to update the memory model (l. 10). If so, we update μ and reset the $\mathcal{F}$ (l. 11-12).

The Size of an FSC. We have considered several sub-classes of FSCs and wish to compare the sizes of these controllers. For FSC $F = (N, n_0, \gamma, \delta)$, we define its size $size(F) := size(\gamma) + size(\delta)$ as the memory required to encode functions γ and δ. Encoding $\gamma \colon N \times Z \to Act$ of a general k-FSC requires $size(\gamma) = \sum_{n \in N} \sum_{z \in Z} 1 = k \cdot |Z|$ memory. Encoding $\delta \colon N \times Z \times Z \to N$ requires $k \cdot |Z|^2$ memory. However, it is uncommon that in each state-memory pair (s, n) all posterior observations can be observed. We therefore encode $\delta(n, z, \cdot)$ as a sparse adjacency list, i.e., as a list of pairs $(z', \delta(n, z, z'))$. To define the size of such a list properly, consider the induced MC $\mathcal{M}^F = (S \times N, (s_0, n_0), \{\alpha\}, \mathcal{P}^F)$. Let $post(n, z) := \{O(s') \mid \exists s \in S_z \colon (s', \cdot) \in \mathrm{supp}(\mathcal{P}^F((s, n), \alpha))\}$ denote the set of posterior observations reachable when taking a transition in a state (s, n) of $\mathcal{M}^F$ with $O(s) = z$. Table 1 summarises the resulting sizes of FSCs of various sub-classes. The derivation is included in Appendix B of [3]. Table 4 on p. 18 shows that we typically find much smaller μ-FSCs ($F_{\mathcal{I}}$) than belief-based FSCs ($F_{\mathcal{B}}$).

7 Experiments

Our evaluation focuses on the following three questions:

Q1: *Do the FSCs from inductive synthesis raise the accuracy of the belief MDP?*
Q2: *Does exploiting the belief MDP boost the inductive synthesis of FSCs?*
Q3: *Is the symbiotic approach improving run time, controller's value and size?*

Table 2. Information about the benchmark POMDPs.

Model	$|S|$	$\sum Act$	$|Z|$	Spec.	Over-approx	Model	$|S|$	$\sum Act$	$|Z|$	Spec.	Over-approx.
4×3-95	22	82	9	$R_{\max}$	≤ 2.24	Drone-4-2	1226	2954	761	$P_{\max}$	≤ 0.98
4×5×2-95	79	310	7	$R_{\max}$	≤ 3.26	Drone-8-2	13k	32k	3195	$P_{\max}$	≤ 0.99
Hallway	61	301	23	$R_{\min}$	≥ 11.5	Lanes+	2741	5285	11	$R_{\min}$	≥ 4805
Milos-97	165	980	11	$R_{\max}$	≤ 80	Netw-3-8-20	17k	30k	2205	$R_{\min}$	≥ 4.31
Network	19	70	5	$R_{\max}$	≤ 359	Refuel-06	208	565	50	$P_{\max}$	≤ 0.78
Query-s3	108	320	6	$R_{\max}$	≤ 600	Refuel-20	6834	25k	174	$P_{\max}$	≤ 0.99
Tiger-95	14	50	7	$R_{\max}$	≤ 159	Rocks-12	6553	32k	1645	$R_{\min}$	≥ 17.8

Selected Benchmarks and Setup. Our baseline are the recent belief exploration technique [8] implemented in STORM [13] and the inductive (policy) synthesis method [5] implemented in PAYNT [6]. PAYNT uses STORM for parsing and model checking of MDPs, but not for solving POMDPs. Our symbiotic framework (Algorithm 1) has been implemented on top of PAYNT and STORM. In the following, we use STORM and PAYNT to refer to the implementation of belief exploration and inductive synthesis respectively, and SAYNT to refer to the symbiotic framework. The implementation of SAYNT and all benchmarks are publicly available[5]. Additionally, the implementation and the benchmarks in the form of an artifact are also available at https://doi.org/10.5281/zenodo. 7874513.

Setup. The experiments are run on a single core of a machine equipped with an Intel i5-12600KF @4.9GHz CPU and 64GB of RAM. PAYNT searches for posterior-unaware FSCs using abstraction-refinement, as suggested by [5]. By default, STORM applies the cut-offs as presented in Sect. 4.1. SAYNT uses the default settings for PAYNT and STORM while $t_I = 60s$ and $t_B = 10s$ were taken for Algorithm 1. Under Q3, we discuss the effect of changing these values.

Benchmarks. We evaluate the methods on a selection of models from [5,7,8] supplemented by larger variants of these models (Drone-8-2 and Refuel-20), by one model from [16] (Milos-97) and by the synthetic model (Lanes+) described in Appendix C of [3]. We excluded benchmarks for which PAYNT or STORM finds the (expected) optimal solution in a matter of seconds. The benchmarks were selected to illustrate advantages as well as drawbacks of all three synthesis approaches: belief exploration, inductive (policy) search, and the symbiotic technique. Table 2 lists for each POMDP the number $|S|$ of states, the total number $\sum Act := \sum_s |Act(s)|$ of actions, the number $|Z|$ of observations, the specification (either maximising or minimising a reachability probability P or expected reward R), and a known over-approximation on the optimal value computed using the technique from [7]. These over-approximations are solely used as rough estimates of the optimal values. Table 5 on p. 20 reports the quality of the resulting FSCs on a broader range of benchmarks and demonstrates the impact of the non-default settings.

Q1: FSCs provide better approximations of the belief MDP

In these experiments, PAYNT is used to obtain a sub-optimal F_I within 10s which is then used by STORM. Table 3 (left) lists the results. Our main finding is that *belief exploration can yield better FSCs (and sometimes faster) using FSCs from PAYNT*—even if the latter FSCs are far from optimal. For instance, STORM with provided F_I finds an FSC with value 0.97 for the Drone-4-2 benchmark within a total of 10s (1s+9s for obtaining F_I), compared to obtaining an FSC of value 0.95 in 56s on its own. A value improvement is also obtained if STORM runs longer. For the Network model, the value improves with 37% (short-term) and 47% (long-term) respectively, at the expense of investing 3s to find F_I. For the other models, the relative improvement ranges from 3% to 25%. A further value improvement can be achieved when using better FSCs F_I from PAYNT;

---

[5] https://github.com/randriu/synthesis.

see Q3. Sometimes, belief exploration does not profit from $F_{\mathcal{I}}$. For Hallway, the unexplored part of the belief MDP becomes insignificant rather quickly, and so does the impact of $F_{\mathcal{I}}$. Clipping [8], a computationally expensive extension of cut-offs, is beneficial only for Rocks-12, rendering $F_{\mathcal{I}}$ useless. Though even in this case, using $F_{\mathcal{I}}$ significantly improves Short STORM that did not have enough time to apply clipping.

Q2: Belief-based FSCs improve inductive synthesis

In this experiment, we run STORM for at most 1s, and use the result in PAYNT. Table 3 (right) lists the results. Our main finding is that *inductive synthesis can find much better FSCs—and sometimes much faster—when using FSCs from belief exploration.* For instance, for the $4 \times 5 \times 2$ benchmark, an FSC is obtained about six times faster while improving the value by 116%. On some larger models, PAYNT alone struggles to find any good $F_{\mathcal{I}}$ and using $F_{\mathcal{B}}$ boosts this; e.g., the value for the Refuel-20 model is raised by a factor 20 at almost no run time penalty. For the Tiger benchmark, a value improvement of 860% is achieved (albeit not as good as $F_{\mathcal{B}}$ itself) at the expense of doubling the run time. Thus: *even a shallow exploration of the belief MDP pays off in the inductive synthesis.* The inductive search typically profits even more when exploring the belief MDP further. This is demonstrated, e.g., in the Rocks-12 model: using the FSC $F_{\mathcal{B}}$ computed using clipping (see Table 3 (left)) enables PAYNT to find FSC $F_{\mathcal{I}}$ with the same (optimal) value 20 as $F_{\mathcal{B}}$ within 1s. Similarly, for the Milos-97 model, running STORM for 45s (producing a more precise $F_{\mathcal{B}}$) enables PAYNT to find an FSC $F_{\mathcal{I}}$ achieving a better value than controllers found by STORM or PAYNT alone within the timeout. (These results are not reported in the tables.) However, as opposed to Q1, where a better FSC $F_{\mathcal{I}}$ naturally improves the belief MDP, longer exploring the belief MDP does not always yield a better $F_{\mathcal{I}}$: a larger $\overline{\mathcal{M}^{\mathcal{B}}}$ with a better $F_{\mathcal{B}}$ may yield a larger memory model μ, thus inducing a significantly larger family where PAYNT struggles to identify good FSCs.

Q3: The practical benefits of the symbiotic approach

The goals of these experiments are to investigate whether the symbiotic approach improves the run time (can FSCs of a certain value be obtained faster?), the memory footprint (how is the total memory consumption affected?), the controller's value (can better FSCs be obtained with the same computational resources?) and the controller's size (are more compact FSCs obtained?).

Value of the Synthesised FSCs. Figure 4 plots the value of the FSCs produced by STORM, PAYNT, and SAYNT versus the computation time. Note that for maximal objectives, the aim is to obtain a high value (the first 4 plots) whereas for minimal objectives a lower value prevails. From the plots, it follows that *the FSCs from the symbiotic approach are superior in value to the ones obtained by the standalone approaches.* The relative improvement of the value of the resulting FSCs differs across individual models, similar to the trends in Q1 and Q2. When

Table 3. Left (Q1): Experimental results on how a (quite sub-optimal) FSC F_I computed by PAYNT within 10s impacts STORM. (For Drone-8-2, the largest model in our benchmark, we use 30s). The "PAYNT" column indicates the value of F_I and its run time. The "Short STORM" column runs storm for 1s and compares the value of FSC F_B found by STORM alone to STORM using F_I. The "Long STORM" column is analogous, but with a 300s timeout for STORM. In the last row, * indicates that clipping was used. **Right (Q2):** Experimental results on how an FSC F_B obtained by a shallow exploration of the belief MDP impacts the inductive synthesis by PAYNT. The "STORM" column reports the value of F_B computed within 1s. The "PAYNT" column compares the values of the FSCs F_I obtained by PAYNT itself to PAYNT using the FSCs F_B within a 300s timeout.

Model	PAYNT F_I	Short STORM	+F_I	Long STORM	+F_I
Drone-4-2	0.94	0.92	0.97	0.95	0.97
P_{max}	9s	1s	1s	56s	57s
Network	266.1	186.7	274.5	202.1	277.1
R_{max}	3s	<1s	<1s	26s	33s
Drone-8-2	0.9	0.6	0.96	0.68	0.97
P_{max}	28s	3s	3s	101s	103s
4x3-95	1.66	1.62	1.82	1.84	1.88
R_{max}	7s	<1s	<1s	60s	72s
Query-s3	425.2	417.4	430.0	419.6	432.0
R_{max}	7s	2s	2s	91s	94s
Milos-97	31.56	37.15	39.15	38.35	40.64
R_{max}	3s	<1s	<1s	42s	42s
Hallway	16.05	13.07	12.63	12.55	12.55
R_{min}	9s	1s	1s	160s	167s
Rocks-12	42	38	31.89	20*	20*
R_{min}	<1s	<1s	<1s	10s	10s

Model	STORM F_B	PAYNT	+F_B
4x5x2-95	2.08	0.94	2.03
R_{max}	<1s	258s	38s
Refuel-20	0.09	<0.01	0.19
P_{max}	1s	10s	11s
Tiger-95	50.38	2.99	28.73
R_{max}	<1s	14s	23s
4x3-95	1.62	1.75	1.84
R_{max}	<1s	14s	238s
Refuel-06	0.67	0.35	0.67
P_{max}	<1s	<1s	42s
Milos-97	37.15	31.56	39.29
R_{max}	<1s	3s	215s
Netw-3-8-20	11.93	11.07	10.95
R_{min}	1s	185s	271s
Rocks-12	38	42	38
R_{min}	<1s	<1s	<1s

comparing the best FSC found by STORM or PAYNT alone with the best FSC found by SAYNT, the improvement ranges from negligible (4 × 3-95) to around 3%-7% (Netw-3-8-20, Milos-97, Query-s3) and sometimes goes over 40% (Refuel-20, Lines+). We note that the distance to the (unknown) optimal values remains unclear. The FSC value never decreases but sometimes does also not increase, as indicated by Hallway and Rocks-12 (see also Q2). Our experiments (see Table 5) also indicate that the improvement over the baseline algorithms is typically more significant in the larger variants of the models. Furthermore, the plots in Fig. 4 also include the FSC value by the one-shot combination of STORM and PAYNT. We see that SAYNT *can improve the FSC value over the one-shot combination.* This is illustrated in, e.g., the 4 × 3-95 and Lanes+ benchmarks, see the 1st and 3rd plots in Fig. 4 (left).

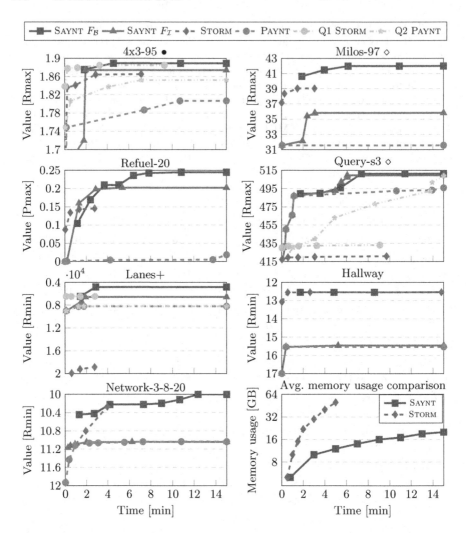

Fig. 4. Value of the generated FSCs over time. The last graph shows the average memory usage of STORM and SAYNT. The lines ending before the timeout indicate that the 64GB memory limit was hit. • indicates that PAYNT and SAYNT synthesised posterior-aware FSCs. ◇ indicates that SAYNT ran with $t_\mathcal{I}$ =90s. (Color figure online)

Total Synthesis Time. SAYNT initially needs some time for the first iteration (one inductive and one belief phase) in Algorithm 1 and thus during the beginning of the synthesis process, the standalone tools may provide FSCs of a certain value faster. *After the first iteration, however,* SAYNT *typically provides better FSCs in a shorter time.* For instance, for the Refuel-20 benchmark SAYNT swiftly overtakes STORM after the first iteration. The only exception is Rocks-12 (discussed before), where SAYNT with the default settings needs significantly more time than STORM to obtain an FSC of the same value.

Table 4. Trade-offs between the value and size in the resulting FSCs F_I and F_B found by SAYNT. Each cell reports value/size. The first three models have a minimising objective. $\diamond$ indicates that SAYNT ran with $t_I =$90s.

Models:	Lanes+	Hallway	Netw-3-8-20	Query-s3$\diamond$	Refuel-06	Drone-8-2	Refuel-20
F_B	4805/8.1k	12.55/2k	10/40k	511.32/7.7k	0.67/84	0.96/237k	0.24/1.5k
F_I	6591/34	15.46/86	11.04/4.8k	509.49/26	0.67/156	0.90/6.4k	0.2/362

Memory Footprint. Belief exploration typically has a large memory footprint: STORM quickly hits the 64GB memory limit on exploring the belief MDP. SAYNT *reduces the memory footprint of* STORM *alone by a factor 3 to 4*, see the bottom right plot of Fig. 4. The average memory footprint of running PAYNT standalone quickly stabilises around 700MB. The memory footprint of SAYNT is thus dominated by the restricted exploration of the belief MDP.

The Size of the Synthesised FSCs. For selected models, Table 4 shows the trade-offs between the value and size of the resulting FSCs F_I and F_B found by SAYNT. The experiments show that *the FSCs F_I provided by inductive synthesis are typically about one to two orders of magnitude smaller than the belief-based FSCs F_B with only a small penalty in their values.* There are models (e.g. Refuel-06) where a very small F_B, having even slightly smaller size than F_I, does exist. The integration mostly reduces the size of F_B due to the better approximation of the belief MDP by up to a factor of two. This reduction has a negligible effect on the size of F_I. This observation further strengthens the usefulness of SAYNT that jointly improves the value of F_I and F_B. Hence, SAYNT gives users a unique opportunity to run a single, time-efficient synthesis and select the FSC according to the trade-off between its value and size.

Customising the SAYNT *Setup.* In contrast to the standalone approaches as well as to the one-way integrations presented in Q1 and Q2, SAYNT *provides a single synthesis method that is efficient for a general class of models without tuning its parameters.* Naturally, adjusting the parameters to individual benchmarks can further improve the quality of the computed controllers: captions of Fig. 4 and Table 4 describe which non-default settings were used for selected models.

Additional Results

In Table 5, we compare values and sizes of FSCs synthesised by the particular methods on a broader range of benchmarks. We can see that FSCs F_I obtained by SAYNT achieve better values than the controllers computed by PAYNT; size-wise, these better FSCs of SAYNT are similar or only slightly bigger. Meanwhile, for FSCs F_B obtained by SAYNT, we sometimes observe a significant size reduction while still improving the value compared to the FSCs produced by STORM. Two models are notable: On Drone-8-2, SAYNT obtains 50% smaller F_B while having a 41% better value. On Network-3-8-20, the size of F_B is reduced by 40% while again providing better value.

Table 5. The quality and size of resulting FSCs provided by PAYNT, STORM, and SAYNT within the 15-min timeout. The run times indicate the time needed to find the best FSC. Non-default settings: $*$ marks experiments where clipping was enabled, $\bullet$ marks experiments where PAYNT synthesised posterior-aware FSCs, $\diamond$ marks experiments where integration parameter t_I was set to 90 s.

| Benchmark | | Model Size | | PAYNT | | STORM | | SAYNT | | | |
Model	Spec.	$S/\Sigma Act$	Z	F_I	Size	F_B	Size	F_B	Size	F_I	Size
4x3 95	R_{max}	22/82	9	1.81 764s	36	1.87 414s	999	1.89• 283s	968	1.87• 120s	126
								1.89 303s	869	1.79 678s	36
4x5x2 95	R_{max}	79/310	7	0.94 305s	26	2.08 3s	102	2.08 71s	102	2.03 378s	38
Drone 4-1	P_{max}	1226/3026	384	0.87 665s	768	0.84 110s	170k	0.89• 390s	169k	0.87• 453s	2.5k
								0.89 180s	176k	0.79 45s	922
Drone 4-2	P_{max}	1226/3026	761	0.95 900s	1.5k	0.95 110s	135k	0.97 194s	140k	0.94 1s	1.5k
Drone 8-2	P_{max}	13k/32k	3195	0.9 260s	6.4k	0.68 98s	280k	0.96 247s	140k	0.9 30s	6.4k
Hallway	R_{min}	61/301	23	15.54 26s	66	12.55 916s	1.9k	12.55 263s	1.8k	15.46 293s	86
Lanes+	R_{min}	2741/5289	11	8223 118s	42	18870 376s	8.1k	4805 173s	8.1k	6591 114s	34
Milos-97	R_{max}	165/980	11	31.56 4s	40	39.03 88s	823	41.99◇ 370s	692	35.82◇ 185s	40
								41.55 270s	290	35.41 114s	40
Network	R_{max}	19/70	5	280.33 38s	22	209.71 110s	2.4k	289.18• 395s	2k	287.23• 106s	54
								284.51 85s	1.8k	280.33 41s	22
Netw 2-8-20	R_{min}	4589/6973	1173	4.24 .914s	2.3k	3.21 11s	34k	3.2 71s	23k	4.19 211s	2.5k
Netw 3-8-20	R_{min}	17k/30k	2205	11.04 638s	4.4k	10.27 238s	64k	10 742s	38k	11.04 379s	4.8k
Query s3	R_{max}	108/320	6	502.3 931s	28	420.11 184s	12.9k	511.32◇ 566s	7.7k	509.49◇ 362s	26
								482.21 700s	7.7k	478.59 610s	28
Refuel 06	P_{max}	208/565	50	0.35 <1s	100	0.67 182s	343	0.67 178s	84	0.67 84s	156
Refuel 08	P_{max}	470/1431	66	0.32 253s	132	0.44 96s	534	0.45 186s	140	0.3 84s	142
Refuel 20	P_{max}	6834/24k	174	0.02 922s	348	0.15 468s	1.2k	0.24 386s	1.5k	0.2 173s	360
Rocks 12	R_{min}	6553/32k	1645	42 <1s	3.3k	20* 15s	115	20* 235s	115	20* 236s	3.3k
Tiger 95	R_{max}	14/50	7	7.93 547s	34	50.38 <1s	58	50.38 71s	58	31.61 513s	48

In the following, we further discuss the impact of non-default settings for selected benchmarks, as presented in Table 5. For instance, using posterior-aware FSCs generally significantly slows down the synthesis process, however, for Network and 4×3-95, it helps improve the value of the default posterior-unaware FSCs by 2% and 4%, respectively. For the former model, a better $F_{\mathcal{I}}$ also improves $F_{\mathcal{B}}$ by about a similar value. In some cases, e.g. for Query-s3, it is beneficial to increase the parameter $t_{\mathcal{I}}$, giving PAYNT enough time to search for a good FSC $F_{\mathcal{I}}$ (the relative improvement is 6%), which also improves the value of the resulting FSC $F_{\mathcal{B}}$ by about a similar value. Tuning $t_{\mathcal{I}}$ and $t_{\mathcal{B}}$ can also have an impact on the value-size trade-off, as seen in the Milos-97 model, where setting longer timeout $t_{\mathcal{I}}$ results in finding a 2% better $F_{\mathcal{B}}$ with 130% size increase. A detailed analysis of the experimental results suggests that usually, it is more beneficial to invest time into searching for good $F_{\mathcal{I}}$ that is used to compute better cut-off values, rather than into deeper exploration of belief MDP. However, the timeouts still need to allow for multiple subsequent iterations of the algorithm in order to utilise the full potential of the symbiosis.

8   Conclusion and Future Work

We proposed SAYNT, a symbiotic integration of the two main approaches for controller synthesis in POMDPs. Using a wide class of models, we demonstrated that SAYNT substantially improves the value of the resulting controllers and provides an any-time, push-button synthesis algorithm allowing users to select the controller based on the trade-off between its value and size, and the synthesis time.

In future work, we plan to explore if the inductive policy synthesis can also be successfully combined with point-based approximation methods, such as SAR-SOP, and on discounted reward properties. A preliminary comparison on discounting properties provides two interesting observations: 1) For models with large reachable belief space and discount factors (very) close to one, SARSOP typically fails to update its initial *alpha-vectors* and thus produces low-quality controllers. In these cases, SAYNT outperforms SARSOP. 2) For common discount factors, SARSOP beats SAYNT on the majority of benchmarks. This is not surprising, as the MDP engine underlying SAYNT does not natively support discounting and instead computes a much harder fixed point. See [15], for a recent discussion on the differences between discounting and not discounting.

References

1. Amato, C., Bernstein, D.S., Zilberstein, S.: Optimizing fixed-size stochastic controllers for POMDPs and decentralized POMDPs. Auton. Agent. Multi-Agent Syst. **21**(3), 293–320 (2010)
2. Amato, C., Bonet, B., Zilberstein, S.: Finite-state controllers based on Mealy machines for centralized and decentralized POMDPs. In: AAAI, pp. 1052–1058. AAAI Press (2010)
3. Andriushchenko, R., Bork, A., Češka, M., Junges, S., Katoen, J.P., Macák, F.: Search and explore: symbiotic policy synthesis in POMDPs. arXiv preprint arXiv:2305.14149 (2023)

4. Andriushchenko, R., Češka, M., Junges, S., Katoen, J.-P.: Inductive synthesis for probabilistic programs reaches new horizons. In: TACAS 2021. LNCS, vol. 12651, pp. 191–209. Springer, Cham (2021). https://doi.org/10.1007/978-3-030-72016-2_11

5. Andriushchenko, R., Češka, M., Junges, S., Katoen, J.P.: Inductive synthesis of finite-state controllers for POMDPs. In: UAI, vol. 180, pp. 85–95. PMRL (2022)

6. Andriushchenko, R., Češka, M., Junges, S., Katoen, J.-P., Stupinský, Š: PAYNT: a tool for inductive synthesis of probabilistic programs. In: Silva, A., Leino, K.R.M. (eds.) CAV 2021. LNCS, vol. 12759, pp. 856–869. Springer, Cham (2021). https://doi.org/10.1007/978-3-030-81685-8_40

7. Bork, A., Junges, S., Katoen, J.-P., Quatmann, T.: Verification of indefinite-horizon POMDPs. In: Hung, D.V., Sokolsky, O. (eds.) ATVA 2020. LNCS, vol. 12302, pp. 288–304. Springer, Cham (2020). https://doi.org/10.1007/978-3-030-59152-6_16

8. Bork, A., Katoen, J.-P., Quatmann, T.: Under-approximating expected total rewards in POMDPs. In: TACAS 2022. LNCS, vol. 13244, pp. 22–40. Springer, Cham (2022). https://doi.org/10.1007/978-3-030-99527-0_2

9. Carr, S., Jansen, N., Topcu, U.: Task-aware verifiable RNN-based policies for partially observable Markov decision processes. J. Artif. Intell. Res. **72**, 819–847 (2021)

10. Češka, M., Jansen, N., Junges, S., Katoen, J.-P.: Shepherding hordes of Markov chains. In: Vojnar, T., Zhang, L. (eds.) TACAS 2019. LNCS, vol. 11428, pp. 172–190. Springer, Cham (2019). https://doi.org/10.1007/978-3-030-17465-1_10

11. Chrszon, P., Dubslaff, C., Klüppelholz, S., Baier, C.: ProFeat: feature-oriented engineering for family-based probabilistic model checking. Formal Aspects Comput. **30**(1), 45–75 (2018)

12. Cubuktepe, M., Jansen, N., Junges, S., Marandi, A., Suilen, M., Topcu, U.: Robust finite-state controllers for uncertain POMDPs. In: AAAI, pp. 11792–11800. AAAI Press (2021)

13. Dehnert, C., Junges, S., Katoen, J.-P., Volk, M.: A storm is coming: a modern probabilistic model checker. In: Majumdar, R., Kunčak, V. (eds.) CAV 2017. LNCS, vol. 10427, pp. 592–600. Springer, Cham (2017). https://doi.org/10.1007/978-3-319-63390-9_31

14. Hansen, E.A.: Solving POMDPs by searching in policy space. In: UAI, pp. 211–219. Morgan Kaufmann (1998)

15. Hartmanns, A., Junges, S., Quatmann, T., Weininger, M.: A practitioner's guide to MDP model checking algorithms. In: Sankaranarayanan, S., Sharygina, N. (eds.) Tools and Algorithms for the Construction and Analysis of Systems. TACAS 2023. Lecture Notes in Computer Science, vol. 13993, pp. 469–488. Springer, Cham (2023). https://doi.org/10.1007/978-3-031-30823-9_24

16. Hauskrecht, M.: Incremental methods for computing bounds in partially observable Markov decision processes. In: AAAI/IAAI, pp. 734–739 (1997)

17. Heck, L., Spel, J., Junges, S., Moerman, J., Katoen, J.-P.: Gradient-descent for randomized controllers under partial observability. In: Finkbeiner, B., Wies, T. (eds.) VMCAI 2022. LNCS, vol. 13182, pp. 127–150. Springer, Cham (2022). https://doi.org/10.1007/978-3-030-94583-1_7

18. Horak, K., Bosansky, B., Chatterjee, K.: Goal-HSVI: heuristic search value iteration for Goal POMDPs. In: IJCAI, pp. 4764–4770. AAAI Press (2018)

19. Junges, S., et al.: Finite-state controllers of POMDPs via parameter synthesis. In: UAI, pp. 519–529 (2018)

20. Kurniawati, H., Hsu, D., Lee, W.S.: SARSOP: efficient point-based POMDP planning by approximating optimally reachable belief spaces. In: Robotics: Science and Systems. MIT Press (2008)

21. Kwiatkowska, M.Z., Norman, G., Parker, D.: Game-based abstraction for Markov decision processes. In: QEST, pp. 157–166. IEEE Computer Society (2006)
22. Kwiatkowska, M., Norman, G., Parker, D.: PRISM 4.0: verification of probabilistic real-time systems. In: Gopalakrishnan, G., Qadeer, S. (eds.) CAV 2011. LNCS, vol. 6806, pp. 585–591. Springer, Heidelberg (2011). https://doi.org/10.1007/978-3-642-22110-1_47
23. Madani, O., Hanks, S., Condon, A.: On the undecidability of probabilistic planning and related stochastic optimization problems. Artif. Intell. **147**(1), 5–34 (2003)
24. Meuleau, N., Kim, K., Kaelbling, L.P., Cassandra, A.R.: Solving POMDPs by searching the space of finite policies. In: UAI, pp. 417–426. Morgan Kaufmann (1999)
25. Norman, G., Parker, D., Zou, X.: Verification and control of partially observable probabilistic systems. Real-Time Syst. **53**(3), 354–402 (2017). https://doi.org/10.1007/s11241-017-9269-4
26. Puterman, M.L.: Markov decision processes: discrete stochastic dynamic programming. John Wiley & Sons (1994)
27. Smallwood, R.D., Sondik, E.J.: The optimal control of partially observable Markov processes over a finite horizon. Oper. Res. **21**(5), 1071–1088 (1973)
28. Verma, A., Murali, V., Singh, R., Kohli, P., Chaudhuri, S.: Programmatically interpretable reinforcement learning. In: ICML, vol. 80, pp. 5052–5061. PMLR (2018)
29. Wang, Y., Chaudhuri, S., Kavraki, L.E.: Bounded policy synthesis for pomdps with safe-reachability objectives. In: AAMAS, pp. 238–246. International Foundation for Autonomous Agents and Multiagent Systems Richland, SC, USA/ACM (2018)

Security and Quantum Systems

AutoQ: An Automata-Based Quantum Circuit Verifier

Yu-Fang Chen[1]($\boxtimes$) iD, Kai-Min Chung[1] iD, Ondřej Lengál[2]($\boxtimes$) iD,
Jyun-Ao Lin[1] iD, and Wei-Lun Tsai[1]($\boxtimes$) iD

[1] Institute of Information Science, Academia Sinica,
Taipei, Taiwan
yfc@iis.sinica.edu.tw, alan23273850@gmail.com
[2] Faculty of Information Technology, Brno University
of Technology, Brno, Czech Republic
lengal@fit.vutbr.cz

Abstract. We present a specification language and a fully automated tool named AutoQ for verifying quantum circuits symbolically. The tool implements the automata-based algorithm from [14] and extends it with the capabilities for symbolic reasoning. The extension allows to specify *relational* properties, i.e., relationships between states before and after executing a circuit. We present a number of use cases where we used AutoQ to fully automatically verify crucial properties of several quantum circuits, which have, to the best of our knowledge, so far been proved only with human help.

1 Introduction

Recently, quantum computing has received much attention, driven by several technological breakthroughs [7] and increasing investments. Prototype quantum computers are already available. The opportunities for the general public—particularly students, researchers, and technology enthusiasts—to access quantum computing devices are rapidly increasing, e.g., through cloud services such as Amazon Braket [1] or IBM Quantum [2]. Due to the complexity and probabilistic nature of quantum computing, the chance of errors in quantum programs is much higher than that of traditional programs, and conventional means for correctness assurance, such as testing, are much less applicable in the quantum world. Quantum programmers need better tools to help them write correct programs. Therefore, researchers anticipate that formal verification will play a crucial role in quantum software quality assurance and have, in recent years, invested significant effort in this direction [5,11,21,41–43,45,46]. Nevertheless, practical tools for automated quantum program/circuit verification are still missing.

This paper introduces AutoQ[1], a fully automated tool for quantum circuit verification based on the approach proposed in [14]. In particular, AutoQ checks the validity of a Hoare-style specification {Pre} C {Post}, where C is a quantum circuit (a sequence of quantum gates) in the OpenQASM format [17] and the

---

[1] Available at https://github.com/alan23273850/AutoQ.

© The Author(s) 2023
C. Enea and A. Lal (Eds.): CAV 2023, LNCS 13966, pp. 139–153, 2023.
https://doi.org/10.1007/978-3-031-37709-9_7

precondition `Pre` and postcondition `Post` represent sets of (pure) quantum states. The check is done by executing the circuit with all quantum states satisfying `Pre` (using a symbolic representation) and testing that all resulting quantum states are in the set denoted by `Post`.

AUTOQ combines two main techniques to efficiently and effectively represent and reason about (potentially infinite) sets of quantum states:

1. As in [14], we use *tree automata* (TAs), finite-state automata accepting languages of trees, to efficiently represent *sets* of quantum states: Each quantum state over n qubits can be seen as a binary decision tree over n variables such that, e.g., in a 3-qubit circuit with qubits $|x_1 x_2 x_3\rangle$, if the computational basis state $|010\rangle$ in a quantum state has the probability amplitude $\frac{1}{4}$, then there will be a branch $x_1 \xrightarrow{0} x_2 \xrightarrow{1} x_3 \xrightarrow{0} \frac{1}{4}$ in the corresponding tree. The use of TA-based representation of a set of quantum states has several advantages: (a) It is *concise*: e.g., in order to represent the set of all 2^n basis states of an n-qubit quantum circuit, we suffice with a TA with $\mathcal{O}(n)$ states and transitions. (b) It allows to *efficiently perform quantum gate operations* on the whole set of quantum states represented by a TA at once [14].

2. In this work, we further consider *symbolic quantum states*, represented by assigning symbolic values to computational basis states (and having an additional formula to relate these symbolic values). For instance, we can represent the set of all n-qubit quantum states where the computational basis $|0\ldots0\rangle$ has a strictly larger probability of measurement than all other basis states by a symbolic quantum state assigning $|0\ldots0\rangle \mapsto v_h$ and $|y_1\ldots y_n\rangle \mapsto v_\ell$ for all $y_1\ldots y_n \neq 0\ldots0$, together with the formula $|v_h|^2 > |v_\ell|^2 \wedge |v_h|^2 + (2^n-1)|v_\ell|^2 = 1$, where v_h and v_ℓ are symbolic variables ranging over complex numbers

By combining these two techniques, i.e., using TAs with symbolic variables in leaves, we can have a representation of all n-qubit quantum states where an arbitrary basis has a strictly larger amplitude than other basis states using $\mathcal{O}(n)$ states and transitions.

Using such a symbolic encoding is essential to allow us to describe *relational specifications*, e.g., it allows us to express properties like "the probability amplitude of the basis state $|000\rangle$ is increased after executing the circuit C" (for this, in the postcondition, we use TAs accepting trees with *predicates* in leaves, a subclass of symbolic tree automata of [36]). Such a property can then be verified by executing the quantum circuit *symbolically* in the spirit of symbolic execution [27] (i.e., such that the values of amplitudes are not complex numbers but, instead, *symbolic terms*) and checking whether all trees in the language of the resulting TA satisfy the desired property (using a modified antichain-based algorithm for testing TA language inclusion [4,10]). Combining TAs and symbolic variables as the language for quantum predicates allows full automation and can be used to express many crucial properties of quantum circuits, as we will demonstrate later. AUTOQ is the first tool implementing this approach.

Related Work. Our work belongs to the line of *Hoare-style verification* of quantum programs, which has been widely discussed in the past [22,29,35,40,44]. This family of approaches follows D'Hondt and Panangaden's suggestion of using various Hermitian operators as quantum predicates, resulting in a very powerful yet complete proof system [20]. However, specifying properties using Hermitian operators is often not intuitive and is inconvenient for automation due to their enormous matrix sizes. Therefore, often these approaches are implemented on top of proof assistants such as Coq [9] and Isabelle [37] and require significant manual work in proof search. The Qbricks [12] approach alleviates the difficulty of the proof search by combining state-of-the-art theorem provers with decision procedures building on top of the Why3 platform [24]. The approach, however, still requires a significant amount of human intervention.

Regarding other quantum program/circuit/protocol verification tools, *circuit equivalence checkers* [5,11,15,26,39] are often quite efficient but less flexible in specifying the desired property (only equivalence). They are particularly useful in *compiler validation*; notable tools include Qcec [11], and Feynman [5]. *Quantum model checking* supports a rich specification language (flavors of temporal logic [23,30,38]) and is more suitable for *verifying high-level protocols* due to the quite limited scalability [6]. One notable tool in this category is QPMC [23]. *Quantum abstract interpretation* [32,43] is particularly efficient in processing large-scale circuits, but it grossly over-approximates the state space (it cannot verify basic properties of, e.g., Grover's algorithm) and cannot conclude anything when verification fails. In contrast, AutoQ can be conveniently used for quantum program development and debugging since it automatically computes the exact set of reachable states[2]. The mentioned tools are fully automated but have different goals or address different parts of the software development cycle than AutoQ.

Contributions. AutoQ evolved from a simple prototype used for performance evaluation in [14] into a robust tool. In addition, we added the following major extensions:

1. We combined the TA specification with symbolic variables, allowing users to specify advanced relational properties of quantum circuits.
2. We developed a new entailment-checking algorithm for the symbolic TA specification based on the antichain algorithm for automata language inclusion testing.
3. We introduced a high-level language to simplify writing TA specifications.

These improvements are pushing the capabilities of AutoQ, and also of practical quantum circuit verification itself, much further.

Outline. In Sect. 2, we describe our approach to TA-based specification and verification of quantum circuits. In Sect. 3, we discuss the new entailment-checking algorithm for the symbolic TA representation. We discuss the architecture of AutoQ in Sect. 4 and demonstrate the use of the specification language and AutoQ for automated verification of several case studies in Sect. 5.

---

[2] A predecessor of the presented version of AutoQ has already caught a bug in Qcec, cf. [3].

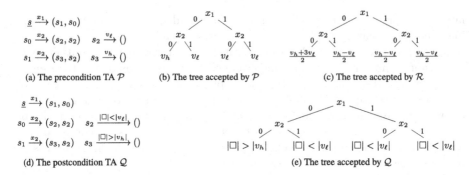

(a) The precondition TA $\mathcal{P}$ (b) The tree accepted by $\mathcal{P}$ (c) The tree accepted by $\mathcal{R}$

(d) The postcondition TA $\mathcal{Q}$ (e) The tree accepted by $\mathcal{Q}$

Fig. 1. Verification of a circuit C amplifying the amplitude of $|00\rangle$ w.r.t. the specification $\{\mathcal{P}, \varphi\}\, C\, \{\mathcal{Q}\}$ with $\varphi\colon |v_h + 3v_\ell| > |2v_h|$. $\mathcal{R}$ is the TA obtained by executing $\mathcal{P}$ on C.

2   Tree Automata-Based Verification of Quantum Circuits

We will begin with minimal formal definitions of the TA-based specification and demonstrate how to use them to verify quantum circuits in AUTOQ with examples. We assume a basic knowledge of quantum computation (see, e.g., the classical textbook [31]).

Let us fix a finite set of *quantum variables* $\mathbb{X} = \{x_1, \ldots, x_n\}$ with a linear ordering (we assume $x_1 < \ldots < x_n$) and a disjoint non-empty leaf alphabet Σ. We will, in particular, work with $\Sigma = \Sigma_t \uplus \Sigma_p$ where Σ_t is the alphabet of *terms* and Σ_p is the alphabet of *predicates* in a suitable first-order theory (discussed later).

We use $\{0,1\}^{\leq n}$ to denote $\bigcup_{0 \leq i \leq n} \{0,1\}^i$. A *(symbolic binary decision) tree* over $\mathbb{X}$ and Σ is a function $\tau\colon \{0,1\}^{\leq n} \to (\mathbb{X} \cup \Sigma)$ such that for all positions $p \in \{0,1\}^i$ with $i < n$, we have $\tau(p) = x_{i+1}$ and for all positions $p \in \{0,1\}^n$, we have $\tau(p) \in \Sigma$. An example of a tree τ can be found in Fig. 1b, where $\Sigma = \{v_h, v_\ell\}$, $\tau(\epsilon) = x_1$, $\tau(0) = \tau(1) = x_2$, $\tau(00) = v_h$, and $\tau(p) = v_\ell$ for $p \in \{0,1\}^2 \setminus \{00\}$.

A *(symbolic) tree automaton* (TA) is a tuple $\mathcal{A} = (S, \Delta, F)$ where S is a finite set of *states*, $\Delta \subseteq (S \times \mathbb{X} \times S \times S) \cup (S \times \Sigma)$ is a *transition relation*, and $F \subseteq S$ is the set of *root (final) states*. We denote transitions from Δ as $s \xrightarrow{x_i} (s_0, s_1)$ and $s \xrightarrow{a} ()$ respectively. An example of a TA with the set of root states $\{s\}$ can be found in Fig. 1a.

A *run* of $\mathcal{A}$ on τ is a function $\rho\colon \{0,1\}^{\leq n} \to S$ s.t. for all positions $p \in \{0,1\}^i$ with $i < n$, it holds that $\rho(p) \xrightarrow{\tau(p)} (\rho(p.0), \rho(p.1)) \in \Delta$ and for all positions $p \in \{0,1\}^n$, it holds that $\rho(p) \xrightarrow{\tau(p)} () \in \Delta$. The run ρ is *accepting* iff $\rho(\epsilon) \in F$ and the *language* of $\mathcal{A}$ is $\mathcal{L}(\mathcal{A}) = \{\tau \mid \mathcal{A} \text{ has an accepting run on } \tau\}$. Observe that the tree in Fig. 1b is in the language of the TA $\mathcal{P}$ in Fig. 1a with the run ρ such that $\rho(\epsilon) = s$, $\rho(0) = s_1$, $\rho(1) = s_0$, $\rho(00) = s_3$, and $\rho(p) = s_2$ for $p \in \{0,1\}^2 \setminus \{00\}$.

Now we are ready to demonstrate how to write specifications of quantum circuits with TAs using a running example. We assume that C is a 2-qubit circuit that amplifies the amplitude of the basis state $|00\rangle$ (under some constraint φ over input states) and reduces the amplitudes of other basis states. We first prepare the precondition of C, which consists of a pair $(\mathcal{P}, \varphi)$, where $\mathcal{P}$ is a TA with the root state s, a set of terms Σ_t as the leaf alphabet, and the set of transitions from Fig. 1a, and φ is a first-order constraint over the variables used in Σ_t. In Σ_t, we use two variables over complex numbers, v_ℓ and v_h, to denote the corresponding amplitude (*low* and *high*). The constraint φ states that $|v_h + 3v_\ell| > |2v_h|$ (required by this circuit C, cf. Sect. 5.4). Recall that the TA $\mathcal{P}$ from Fig. 1a accepts the tree from Fig. 1b, which in turn represents the quantum state

$$s = v_h \,|00\rangle + v_\ell \,|01\rangle + v_\ell \,|10\rangle + v_\ell \,|11\rangle. \tag{1}$$

AutoQ will execute the gates in C to transform the TA $\mathcal{P}$ to another TA $\mathcal{R}$ capturing the effect of executing C over all quantum states encoded in $\mathcal{P}$. The algorithm for gate operations is almost the same as the one in [14], except that now the update of leaf symbols works symbolically (similarly to symbolic execution [27]: each leaf symbol is a term over v_h and v_ℓ and quantum gates change the terms by accumulating the operations that would be performed on them, potentially simplifying them). In this example, the TA $\mathcal{R}$ will accept only one tree representing the quantum state

$$s' = \left(\tfrac{v_h + 3v_\ell}{2}\right)|00\rangle + \left(\tfrac{v_h - v_\ell}{2}\right)|01\rangle + \left(\tfrac{v_h - v_\ell}{2}\right)|10\rangle + \left(\tfrac{v_h - v_\ell}{2}\right)|11\rangle, \tag{2}$$

Observe that under the precondition $\varphi = |v_h + 3v_\ell| > |2v_h|$, the probability of $|00\rangle$ is indeed increased ($|\tfrac{v_h + 3v_\ell}{2}|^2 > |v_h|^2$). The tree representation of s' can be found in Fig. 1c. The TA $\mathcal{Q}$ of the postcondition can be found in Fig. 1a. The leaf alphabet of $\mathcal{Q}$ is the set of predicates $\Sigma_p = \{|\square| > |v_h|, |\square| < |v_\ell|\}$ where $\square$ denotes a free variable. Observe that $\mathcal{Q}$ accepts the tree from Fig. 1e.

2.1 High-Level Specification Language

In AutoQ, we provide a simple specification language that can be automatically translated to TAs. The language allows users to focus on the properties they want to express without the need to specify details of the TA structure. Our language is particularly suitable for describing sets of states with one high probability branch and other branches with uniformly low or zero probability, a very common pattern of quantum circuit's correctness properties. For example, in the language, we can use $(|00\rangle\colon v_h, |*\rangle\colon v_\ell)$, where "$|*\rangle$" denotes "other basis states," to define the tree language of the TA in Fig. 1a, which accepts a single tree representing the quantum state $v_h\,|00\rangle + v_\ell\,|01\rangle + v_\ell\,|10\rangle + v_\ell\,|11\rangle$ from Fig. 1b. Similarly, we can use $(|00\rangle\colon |\square| > |v_h|, |*\rangle\colon |\square| < |v_\ell|)$ to represent the language of the TA in Fig. 1d. The set of all 2-qubit basis states $\{|i\rangle \mid i \in \{0,1\}^2\}$ is expressed as $\exists i \in \{0,1\}^2\colon (|i\rangle\colon 1, |*\rangle\colon 0)$ (we can see it as a predicate that is satisfied by the described quantum states). We also allow the *tensor product* $\otimes$ operator, which multiplies the amplitude of the product basis states. For example, $(|00\rangle\colon 1, |*\rangle\colon 0) \otimes (|00\rangle\colon v_h, |*\rangle\colon v_\ell) \otimes (|00\rangle\colon 1, |*\rangle\colon 0)$ represents the (singleton) set of states compactly $\{v_h\,|000000\rangle + \sum_{j \in \{01,11,10\}} v_\ell\,|00j00\rangle\}$.

A more challenging example is to represent the set of states

$$\left\{ v_h \left| ii000 \right\rangle + \sum_{j \in \{0,1\}^3 \wedge j \neq i} v_\ell \left| ij000 \right\rangle \;\middle|\; i \in \{0,1\}^3 \right\}. \tag{3}$$

Such a set can be described with the help of the $\otimes$ and $\exists$ operators as follows:

$$\exists i \in \{0,1\}^3 : (|i\rangle\colon 1, |*\rangle\colon 0) \otimes (|i\rangle\colon v_h, |*\rangle\colon v_\ell) \otimes (|000\rangle\colon 1, |*\rangle\colon 0). \tag{4}$$

Below is the grammar of specification *spec*:

$$spec ::= state \mid \exists i \in \{0,1\}^n : state \mid spec, state$$
$$state ::= (|c_1\rangle\colon t, \ldots, |c_k\rangle\colon t, |*\rangle\colon t) \mid (|i\rangle\colon t, |*\rangle\colon t) \mid state \otimes state$$
$$t \in \Sigma, \; n \in \mathbb{N}, \text{ and } c_1, \ldots, c_k \in \{0,1\}^n$$

A *spec* is ill-formed when a free variable i appears in *state*, if some basis is repeated in the rule $(|c_1\rangle\colon t, \ldots, |c_k\rangle\colon t, |*\rangle\colon t)$, or if the previous rule contains two bases of different lengths. If all basis states of the given length are specified in $(|c_1\rangle\colon t, \ldots, |c_k\rangle\colon t, |*\rangle\colon t)$, the $|*\rangle\colon t$ part is not required any more. The specification is then converted into a TA using a straightforward algorithm; in the following we often confuse a TA and its specification.

2.2   Complex Number Representation

In a (pure) quantum state, the amplitude of a basis computational state is a *complex number*, and the corresponding probability is the square of the absolute value of the amplitude. For verification, we need an exact representation of complex numbers that can be used in computers. In AUTOQ, we use a subset of complex numbers that can be expressed by the following algebraic encoding (cf. [14,34,46]):

$$\left(\frac{1}{\sqrt{2}} \right)^k (a + b\omega + c\omega^2 + d\omega^3), \tag{5}$$

where $a, b, c, d \in \mathbb{Z}$, $k \in \mathbb{N}$, and $\omega = e^{\frac{i\pi}{4}} = \cos 45° + i \sin 45° = \frac{\sqrt{2}}{2} + i\frac{\sqrt{2}}{2}$, the unit vector that makes an angle of $45°$ with the positive real axis in the complex plane. A complex number is then represented by a quadruple (a, b, c, d) of integers and a normalization factor k. Although the considered set of complex numbers is only a small subset of all complex numbers (it is countable, while the set of all complex numbers is uncountable), the subset is sufficient to describe various standard quantum gates. Currently, AUTOQ supports the set of quantum gates X, H, Y, Z, S, T, Rx($\frac{\pi}{2}$), Ry($\frac{\pi}{2}$), CNOT, CZ, Toffoli (cf. the list in [14]), which already includes a set of universal quantum gates. From the Solovay-Kitaev theorem [18], gates performing rotations of $\frac{\pi}{2^n}$, used, e.g., in Shor's algorithm [33] and *quantum Fourier transform* (QFT) [16], can be approximated with an error rate ϵ by $\mathcal{O}(\log^{3.97}(\frac{1}{\epsilon}))$-many H, CNOT, and T gates. The algebraic representation is also sufficient to represent all reachable states in OPENQASM circuits with the set of supported gates, where the initial basis state is $|0 \ldots 0\rangle$.

AutoQ operates on the introduced representation of complex numbers. More precisely, for a specification $\{\mathcal{P}, \varphi\}\ C\ \{\mathcal{Q}\}$, the leaf symbols of $\mathcal{P}$ are quadruples of integer terms (a, b, c, d). We assume that all leaf symbols of $\mathcal{P}$ share a common normalization factor k, so we do not store the value of k explicitly since it can be inferred from the fact that the probability sum over all basis states is one. Instead, we remember a constant natural number value k_c, the difference of the k value between $\mathcal{P}$ and $\mathcal{R}$, and use it to normalize the amplitudes. Recall that $\mathcal{R}$ is the TA accepting all states after executing C from some states accepted by $\mathcal{P}$. The initial value of k_c is zero, and each application of H, Rx($\frac{\pi}{2}$), or Ry($\frac{\pi}{2}$) gates will increase it by one (cf. [14]). We normalize all quadruple leaf symbols (a, b, c, d) of $\mathcal{R}$ by multiplying them with $\left(\frac{1}{\sqrt{2}}\right)^{k_c}$ once $\mathcal{R}$ is computed.

Next, we show how to compose a specification of our running example from Fig. 1 using the algebraic representation. The specification can now be written as

$\mathcal{P}$: $(|00\rangle$: $(v_h^a, v_h^b, v_h^c, v_h^d), |*\rangle$: $(v_\ell^a, v_\ell^b, v_\ell^c, v_\ell^d))$

$\mathcal{Q}$: $(|00\rangle$: $|(\square_1, \square_2, \square_3, \square_4)|^2 > |(v_h^a, v_h^b, v_h^c, v_h^d)|^2, |*\rangle$: $|(\square_1, \square_2, \square_3, \square_4)|^2 < |(v_\ell^a, v_\ell^b, v_\ell^c, v_\ell^d)|^2)$,

where $|(a, b, c, d)|^2 = |a + b\omega + c\omega^2 + d\omega^3|^2$

$$= \left| a + b(\tfrac{\sqrt{2}}{2} + \tfrac{\sqrt{2}}{2}i) + ci + d(-\tfrac{\sqrt{2}}{2} + \tfrac{\sqrt{2}}{2}i) \right|^2$$

$$= (a + b\tfrac{\sqrt{2}}{2} - d\tfrac{\sqrt{2}}{2})^2 + (b\tfrac{\sqrt{2}}{2} - c + d\tfrac{\sqrt{2}}{2})^2$$

2.3   Precise Semantics of the Specification

As mentioned above, for verifying $\{\mathcal{P}, \varphi\}\ C\ \{\mathcal{Q}\}$, we start with a TA $\mathcal{P}$ representing the set of all quantum states satisfying the precondition and compute a TA $\mathcal{R}$ representing the set of states reachable after executing the circuit C. Then, we test whether $\mathcal{R}$ entails $\mathcal{Q}$ (w.r.t. φ), i.e., whether all reachable states satisfy the postcondition.

Formally, we say that a tree τ_1 is *entailed* by a tree τ_2 w.r.t. a first-order formula φ, denoted as $\tau_1 \models_\varphi \tau_2$, if for all positions $p \in \{0, 1\}^n$ it holds that either (i) $\tau_1(p) = \tau_2(p)$ or (ii) $\tau_1(p) = (t_1, \ldots, t_k) \in \Sigma_t$, $\tau_2(p) = \psi \in \Sigma_p$, and $\varphi \Rightarrow \psi[t_1/\square_1] \ldots [t_k/\square_k]$. We lift the entailment to TAs: $\mathcal{A}_1 \models_\varphi \mathcal{A}_2$ iff for all trees $\tau_1 \in \mathcal{L}(\mathcal{A}_1)$ there exists a tree $\tau_2 \in \mathcal{L}(\mathcal{A}_2)$ s.t. $\tau_1 \models_\varphi \tau_2$.[3]

3   Entailment Checking

We will now describe how we perform the entailment check $\mathcal{R} \models_\varphi \mathcal{Q}$. Since we operate with trees and tree automata over symbolic values, we cannot establish entailment by running a classical TA language inclusion test based on complementing the automaton $\mathcal{Q}$ first. Instead, our algorithm for testing the entailment $\mathcal{R} \models_\varphi \mathcal{Q}$ is based on an on-the-fly TA inclusion checking algorithm [4,10],

---

[3]   We never have a predicate from Σ_p on the left-hand side of the entailment test, so we do not need to test implication between predicates, which would be needed for a complete procedure.

Algorithm 1: Checking $\mathcal{R} \models_\varphi \mathcal{Q}$

Input: A TA $\mathcal{R} = (S_r, \Delta_r, F_r)$, a TA $\mathcal{Q} = (S_q, \Delta_q, F_q)$, a formula φ

Output: *true* if $\mathcal{R} \models_\varphi \mathcal{Q}$, *false* otherwise

1 $Processed \leftarrow \emptyset$;

2 $Worklist \leftarrow Min\{(s_r, U_q) \mid s_r \xrightarrow{t_r} () \in \Delta_r,$

3        $U_q = \{u_q \in Q_q \mid u_q \xrightarrow{t_r} () \vee \exists u_q \xrightarrow{p_q} () \in \Delta_q : \varphi \Rightarrow p_q[t_r/\square]\}\}$;

4 **while** $Worklist \neq \emptyset$ **do**

5 $\quad$ $(s_r, U_q) \leftarrow Worklist.pop()$;

6 $\quad$ **if** $s_r \in F_r \wedge U_q \cap F_q = \emptyset$ **then return** *false* ;

7 $\quad$ $Processed \leftarrow Min(Processed \cup \{(s_r, U_q)\})$;

8 $\quad$ $tmp \leftarrow (\{(s_r, U_q)\} \times Processed) \cup (Processed \times \{(s_r, U_q)\})$;

9 $\quad$ **foreach** $((s_r^1, U_q^1), (s_r^2, U_q^2)) \in tmp, \alpha \in \mathbb{X}$ **do**

10 $\quad\quad$ $H_r \leftarrow \{s_r' \in Q_r \mid s_r' \xrightarrow{\alpha} (s_r^1, s_r^2) \in \Delta_r\}$;

11 $\quad\quad$ $U_q' \leftarrow \{s_q \in Q_q \mid \exists s_q^1 \in U_q^1, \exists s_q^2 \in U_q^2 : s_q \xrightarrow{\alpha} (s_q^1, s_q^2) \in \Delta_q\}$;

12 $\quad\quad$ **foreach** $s_r' \in H_r$ *s.t.* $(s_r', U_q') \notin \lceil Processed \cup Worklist \rceil$ **do**

13 $\quad\quad\quad$ $\mid$ $Worklist \leftarrow Min(Worklist \cup \{(s_r', U_q')\})$;

14 **return** *true*;

---

which avoids complementation. The on-the-fly inclusion-checking algorithm can be seen as an optimization of the classical construction, which would establish $\mathcal{L}(\mathcal{R}) \cap \overline{\mathcal{L}(\mathcal{Q})} \stackrel{?}{=} \emptyset$ by first computing the complement $\mathcal{Q}^\complement$ of $\mathcal{Q}$ (using a bottom-up TA determinization), followed by computing the intersection $\mathcal{A}_\cap$ of $\mathcal{Q}^\complement$ and $\mathcal{R}$, and, finally, checking language emptiness of $\mathcal{A}_\cap$. In particular, the on-the-fly inclusion checking algorithm can be seen as doing all the operations at once. Furthermore, the algorithms in [4,10] also make use of the so-called *antichains* and TA *simulation* to prune the explored state space.

Our modification of the inclusion algorithm to test TA entailment, given in Algorithm 1, mainly differs from [4,10] in the way initial sets of state pairs are computed on Line 3. In particular, we match a state s_r that can perform a leaf transition over t_r in $\mathcal{R}$ with the set U_q of all states in $\mathcal{Q}$ that can perform a leaf transition either over t_r or over a predicate p_q such that $\varphi \Rightarrow p_q[t_r/\square]$ (we use $p_q[t_r/\square]$ for a tuple t_r to denote the substitution of the tuple's components into the corresponding free variables of p_q).

After that, the algorithms perform a simultaneous bottom-up traversal through $\mathcal{R}$ (represented by states s_r) and the determinized version of $\mathcal{Q}$ (represented by sets of states U_q). For each such pair (s_r, U_q), the algorithm first checks whether s_r is a root state and U_q does not contain any root state (cf. Line 6; this would mean that $\mathcal{R}$ accepts some tree that is not accepted by $\mathcal{Q}$). If this does not hold, then the algorithm tries to find all already processed pairs that can make a transition with (s_r, U_q) (cf. Line 8) and continue from all such pairs. Each bottom-up successor (s_r', U_q') is then added to *Worklist* in the case it has not been seen previously (cf. Line 13).

The algorithm uses the function *Min* (cf. Lines 3, 7, and 13) to minimize the sets *Worklist* and *Processed* w.r.t. a subsumption relation, and the downward closure for $\lceil Processed \cup Worklist \rceil$ on Line 12 to prune the explored state space. Due to lack of space, we refer to the works [4,10] for more details about these optimizations.

4   Architecture

We illustrate the architecture of AutoQ in Fig. 2. The tool is written in C++ and uses the following external tools: the TA library Vata [28] for efficient testing of TA inclusion (when the postcondition uses only the term alphabet Σ_t) and the SMT solver Z3 for entailment checking of leaf symbols in

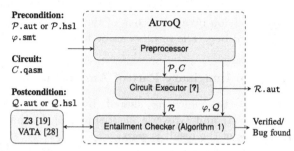

Fig. 2. The architecture of AutoQ. The input verification problem is $\{\mathcal{P}, \varphi\}\ C\ \{\mathcal{Q}\}$.

Algorithm 1. We allow any theory solver supported by Z3. In our experiment, we use QF_NIRA. AutoQ takes as an input a quantum circuit in the OpenQASM format accompanied with the specification written as tree automata (.aut files) or the high-level specification language (.hsl files) introduced in Sect. 2.1.

Preprocessor reads the input files (.aut, .smt, .qasm, and .hsl files), translates specifications in the .hsl files into tree automata, and stores them using AutoQ's internal data structures. *Circuit Executor* then reads the circuit C and the TA $\mathcal{P}$ and generates another TA $\mathcal{R}$ obtained as the result after executing C from states in $\mathcal{P}$, using the approach of [14] with the symbolic extension discussed in Sect. 2. AutoQ can also output the TA $\mathcal{R}$ for further analysis. Finally, *Entailment Checker* checks whether $\mathcal{R} \models_\varphi \mathcal{Q}$ and reports "verified" when the entailment holds and "bug found" otherwise.

5   Use Cases

In this section, we describe several use cases of quantum algorithms and their important properties that we were able to verify using AutoQ fully automatically. We focus on the use of symbolic TA in this set of experiments and refer the readers to [14] for other experimental results. A selection of the obtained results is given in Table 1. An artifact that allows reproduction of the results is available as [13].

5.1   Hadamard Square is Identity

Our first use case shows that the single qubit gate C that runs two consecutive H gates has the same effect as an identity matrix. We use the specification

$\{\mathcal{P}, \varphi\} \, C \, \{\mathcal{Q}\}$ with

$\mathcal{P}$: $(|0\rangle: (v_a, v_b, v_c, v_d), |1\rangle: (v'_a, v'_b, v'_c, v'_d))$, φ: $true$,

$\mathcal{Q}$: $(|0\rangle: (\Box_a, \Box_b, \Box_c, \Box_d) = (v_a, v_b, v_c, v_d), |1\rangle: (\Box_a, \Box_b, \Box_c, \Box_d) = (v'_a, v'_b, v'_c, v'_d))$.

In this simple example, the precondition $\mathcal{P}$ encodes an infinite number of quantum states, which is not expressible using the technique in [14]. We also included a buggy version by altering one of the H gates, and AUTOQ managed to detect the injected bug. The results can be found in rows H^2 in Table 1.

5.2   Zero Imaginary Part of Amplitudes

One property, which is shared by multiple algorithms, e.g., Bernstein-Vazirani's [8] and Grover's algorithm [25], is that the imaginary part of all amplitudes of the result is zero.

Let us focus on Bernstein-Vazirani's algorithm [8], which finds a secret bit-string s from an oracle using a single query. The algorithm begins with the quantum state $|0^n\rangle$, where n is the length of s, and ends with the quantum state $|s\rangle$. The amplitudes of all basis states are either zero or one, the imaginary part of the amplitudes is, therefore, always zero. For a three-qubit circuit C implementing the algorithm, we can therefore use the specification: $\{\mathcal{P}, \varphi\} \, C \, \{\mathcal{Q}\}$ with

$$\mathcal{P}: (|000\rangle: (1,0,0,0), |*\rangle: (0,0,0,0)), \qquad \varphi: true, \qquad \mathcal{Q}: (|*\rangle: \psi_{\text{Im}}),$$

where $\psi_{\text{Im}} \equiv (\Box_b = -\Box_d \wedge \Box_c = 0)$ (it will also be used later). In the definition of $\mathcal{P}$, recall that we use the integer-quadruple representation of complex numbers (cf. Eq. (5)). In the postcondition $\mathcal{Q}$, the free variables $\Box_a, \Box_b, \Box_c, \Box_d$ are to be substituted by the corresponding terms in the obtained integer term quadruple (a, b, c, d) in the entailment check. Note that (a, b, c, d) represents the complex number $(a + b\frac{\sqrt{2}}{2} - d\frac{\sqrt{2}}{2}) + i(b\frac{\sqrt{2}}{2} - c + d\frac{\sqrt{2}}{2})$ (obtained from Eq. (5)). Because a, b, c, d are all integers, for the imaginary part to be zero, it must hold that $c = 0$ and $b = -d$.

When we run C from $\mathcal{P}$, we obtain a TA $\mathcal{R}$ encoding $(|010\rangle: (1,0,0,0), |*\rangle: (0,0,0,0))$ and the entailment $\mathcal{R} \models_\varphi \mathcal{Q}$ holds. See the rows $BV(n)$ in Table 1 for the results of verifying the algorithm for circuits with secrets of size n. As in the previous example, we also included a buggy version to demonstrate AUTOQ's bug-finding capability. We can see that AUTOQ could verify the algorithm for secrets of a quite large size.

5.3   Probability of Measuring the Correct Answer

Grover's algorithm [25] assumes a Boolean function f over n bits with only one satisfying assignment s and an oracle that evaluates f for a given input. The algorithm finds s with a high probability, say > 0.9, using only $\mathcal{O}(\sqrt{2^n})$ oracle queries. The algorithm works iteratively, where each *Grover iteration* queries the oracle once and amplifies the amplitude of $|s\rangle$. First, let C be a 6-qubit circuit

Table 1. Results of verifying our use cases with AutoQ. The maximum peak memory consumption was 52 MiB for Grover$_{\text{All}}$(9). In most cases, the time of entailment was negligible, with the exception of Grover$_{\text{All}}$ circuits. For instance, Grover$_{\text{All}}$(8) takes 2 m18 s for entailment checking (70% of the total time) and Grover$_{\text{All}}$(9) takes 21 m36 s for entailment checking (85% of the total time).

circuit	qubits	gates	property	result	time	circuit	qubits	gates	property	result	time
H^2	1	2	H^2 = I	OK	0.22s	Grover$_{\text{Single}}$(3)	6	54	P(Correct) > 0.9	OK	0.34s
H^2 (bug)	1	2	H^2 = I	Bug	0.17s	Grover$_{\text{Single}}$(16)	32	28,159	P(Correct) > 0.9	OK	2m21s
BV(2)	2	6	ψ_{Im}	OK	0.11s	Grover$_{\text{Single}}$(18)	36	63,537	P(Correct) > 0.9	OK	6m37s
BV(2) (bug)	2	6	ψ_{Im}	Bug	0.15s	Grover$_{\text{Single}}$(20)	40	141,527	P(Correct) > 0.9	OK	19m57s
BV(100)	100	251	ψ_{Im}	OK	10.90s	Grover$_{\text{Iter}}$(2)	3	13	P(Correct) Increased	OK	0.40s
BV(1,000)	1,000	2,500	ψ_{Im}	OK	198m28s	Grover$_{\text{Iter}}$(18)	36	157	P(Correct) Increased	OK	1.95s
Grover$_{\text{All}}$(3)	9	64	P(Correct) > 0.9	OK	0.40s	Grover$_{\text{Iter}}$(50)	100	445	P(Correct) Increased	OK	47.76s
Grover$_{\text{All}}$(8)	24	939	P(Correct) > 0.9	OK	3m18s	Grover$_{\text{Iter}}$(75)	150	671	P(Correct) Increased	OK	3m29s
Grover$_{\text{All}}$(9)	27	1,492	P(Correct) > 0.9	OK	25m16s	Grover$_{\text{Iter}}$(100)	200	895	P(Correct) Increased	OK	10m53s

implementing Grover's search with the satisfying assignment $s = 010$, where the first three qubits of C are the work tape, and the following three are the ancillae. We use the following specification:

$$\mathcal{P}: (|000000\rangle: \vec{1}, |*\rangle: \vec{0}) \text{ where } \vec{1} = (1,0,0,0) \text{ and } \vec{0} = (0,0,0,0), \qquad \varphi: \text{true},$$

$$\mathcal{Q}: (|010\rangle: |\Box_a|^2 > 0.9 \wedge \psi_{\text{Im}}, |*\rangle: |\Box_a|^2 < 0.1 \wedge \psi_{\text{Im}}) \otimes (|000\rangle: \vec{1}, |*\rangle: \vec{0}).$$

Note that the postcondition $\mathcal{Q}$ also checks that all amplitudes in the result of the algorithm have a zero imaginary part (using ψ_{Im}). See rows Grover$_{\text{Single}}$(n) in Table 1 for the results on circuits for n-bit functions f and a single oracle.

Next, we also show the correctness of Grover's algorithm w.r.t. all possible 3-qubit oracles. Let C' be a 9-qubit circuit implementing the algorithm, where the first three qubits are used for oracle generation, and the following six are the work tape and ancillae, similarly to Grover$_{\text{Single}}$. Our specification is now

$$\mathcal{P}: \exists i \in \{0,1\}^3: (|i000000\rangle: \vec{1}, |*\rangle: \vec{0}), \qquad \varphi: \text{true},$$

$$\mathcal{Q}: \exists i \in \{0,1\}^3: (|i\rangle: \vec{1}, |*\rangle: 0) \otimes (|i\rangle: |\Box_a|^2 > 0.9 \wedge \psi_{\text{Im}}, |*\rangle: |\Box_a|^2 < 0.1 \wedge \psi_{\text{Im}})$$
$$\otimes (|000\rangle: \vec{1}, |*\rangle: \vec{0}).$$

Note that in the postcondition, we use i to relate the oracle value and the value on the work tape. The results are in rows Grover$_{\text{All}}$(n) in Table 1.

5.4   Increasing Amplitude of the Correct Answer

Above, we show that we are able to automatically verify moderate-sized circuits for Grover's algorithm for the values of n up to 9 (for Grover$_{\text{All}}$) and 20 (for Grover$_{\text{Single}}$), which is quite large, but have difficulties going beyond that. The size of the circuit is $\mathcal{O}(\sqrt{2^n})$, which is quite large. Therefore, we also verify the algorithm w.r.t. a weaker property, which is, that in one iteration, the amplitude of the correct answer will increase.

Consider a function f over 2 bits with 01 being the only satisfying assignment and let C be a 4-qubit circuit encoding one Grover iteration, with two qubits as the work tape and two ancilla qubits. From Grover's correctness proof [25], we can derive that when $v_\ell > 0 \land v_h > 0 \land (2^n - 1)v_\ell > v_h$, a correct implementation will increase the probability of $|01\rangle$ and reduce others. We specify the verification problem as follows:

$$\mathcal{P}: (|01\rangle: (v_h, 0, 0, 0), |*\rangle: (v_\ell, 0, 0, 0)) \otimes (|00\rangle: \vec{1}, |*\rangle: \vec{0}),$$

$$\varphi: v_\ell > 0 \land v_h > 0 \land (2^2 - 1)v_\ell > v_h,$$

$$\mathcal{Q}: (|01\rangle: |\square_a| > |v_h| \land \psi_{\text{Im}}, |*\rangle: |\square_a| < |v_\ell| \land \psi_{\text{Im}}) \otimes (|00\rangle: \vec{1}, |*\rangle: \vec{0}).$$

The results can be found in rows $\text{Grover}_{\text{Iter}}(n)$ in Table 1. We can see that verification of one Grover iteration w.r.t. the weaker (but still quite useful) property scales much better than verification of full Grover's circuits, scaling to sizes of $n \geq 100$.

6   Conclusion

We presented a specification language for specifying useful properties of quantum circuits and a tool AUTOQ that can establish the correctness of the specification using an approach combining the technique from [14] with symbolic execution. Using the tool, we were able to fully automatically verify several important properties of a selection of quantum circuits. To the best of our knowledge, for some of the properties, we are the first ones that could verify them fully automatically.

Acknowledgements. We thank the reviewers for their useful remarks that helped us improve the quality of the paper. This work was supported by the Czech Ministry of Education, Youth and Sports project LL1908 of the ERC.CZ programme, the Czech Science Foundation project GA23-07565S, the FIT BUT internal project FIT-S-23-8151, and the NSTC QC project under Grant no. NSTC 111-2119-M-001-004- and 112-2119-M-001-006-.

References

1. Aws braket. https://aws.amazon.com/braket/
2. IBM quantum. https://quantum-computing.ibm.com
3. The QCEC repository: Issue #200 (ZX-Checker produces invalid result) (2022). https://github.com/cda-tum/qcec/issues/200
4. Abdulla, P.A., Chen, Y.-F., Holík, L., Mayr, R., Vojnar, T.: When simulation meets antichains. In: Esparza, J., Majumdar, R. (eds.) TACAS 2010. LNCS, vol. 6015, pp. 158–174. Springer, Heidelberg (2010). https://doi.org/10.1007/978-3-642-12002-2_14
5. Amy, M.: Towards large-scale functional verification of universal quantum circuits. In: Quantum Physics and Logic (2018)
6. Anticoli, L., Piazza, C., Taglialegne, L., Zuliani, P.: Towards quantum programs verification: from quipper circuits to QPMC. In: Devitt, S., Lanese, I. (eds.) RC 2016. LNCS, vol. 9720, pp. 213–219. Springer, Cham (2016). https://doi.org/10.1007/978-3-319-40578-0_16

7. Arute, F., et al.: Quantum supremacy using a programmable superconducting processor. Nature **574**(7779), 505–510 (2019). https://doi.org/10.1038/s41586-019-1666-5, number: 7779 Publisher: Nature Publishing Group
8. Bernstein, E., Vazirani, U.V.: Quantum complexity theory. In: Kosaraju, S.R., Johnson, D.S., Aggarwal, A. (eds.) Proceedings of the Twenty-Fifth Annual ACM Symposium on Theory of Computing, May 16–18, 1993, San Diego, CA, USA, pp. 11–20. ACM (1993). https://doi.org/10.1145/167088.167097
9. Bertot, Y., Castéran, P.: Interactive theorem proving and program development: Coq'Art: the calculus of inductive constructions. Springer Science & Business Media (2013)
10. Bouajjani, A., Habermehl, P., Holík, L., Touili, T., Vojnar, T.: Antichain-based universality and inclusion testing over nondeterministic finite tree automata. In: Ibarra, O.H., Ravikumar, B. (eds.) CIAA 2008. LNCS, vol. 5148, pp. 57–67. Springer, Heidelberg (2008). https://doi.org/10.1007/978-3-540-70844-5_7
11. Burgholzer, L., Wille, R.: Advanced equivalence checking for quantum circuits. IEEE Trans. Comput. Aided Des. Integr. Circuits Syst. **40**(9), 1810–1824 (2020)
12. Chareton, C., Bardin, S., Bobot, F., Perrelle, V., Valiron, B.: An automated deductive verification framework for circuit-building quantum programs. In: ESOP 2021. LNCS, vol. 12648, pp. 148–177. Springer, Cham (2021). https://doi.org/10.1007/978-3-030-72019-3_6
13. Chen, Y., Chung, K., Lengál, O., Lin, J., Tsai, W.: AutoQ: an automata-based quantum circuit verifier (May 2023). https://doi.org/10.5281/zenodo.7966542
14. Chen, Y., Chung, K., Lengál, O., Lin, J., Tsai, W., Yen, D.: An automata-based framework for verification and bug hunting in quantum circuits. In: 44th ACM SIGPLAN Conference on Programming Language Design and Implementation–PLDI'23. ACM (2023)
15. Coecke, B., Duncan, R.: Interacting quantum observables: categorical algebra and diagrammatics. New J. Phys. **13**(4), 043016 (2011). https://doi.org/10.1088/1367-2630/13/4/043016
16. Coppersmith, D.: An approximate Fourier transform useful in quantum factoring (2002). https://doi.org/10.48550/arxiv.quant-ph/0201067
17. Cross, A.W., Bishop, L.S., Smolin, J.A., Gambetta, J.M.: Open quantum assembly language. arXiv preprint arXiv:1707.03429 (2017)
18. Dawson, C.M., Nielsen, M.A.: The Solovay-Kitaev algorithm. arXiv preprint quant-ph/0505030 (2005)
19. de Moura, L., Bjørner, N.: Z3: an efficient SMT solver. In: Ramakrishnan, C.R., Rehof, J. (eds.) TACAS 2008. LNCS, vol. 4963, pp. 337–340. Springer, Heidelberg (2008). https://doi.org/10.1007/978-3-540-78800-3_24
20. D'Hondt, E., Panangaden, P.: Quantum weakest preconditions. Math. Struct. Comput. Sci. **16**(3), 429–451 (2006)
21. Feng, Y., Hahn, E.M., Turrini, A., Zhang, L.: QPMC: a model checker for quantum programs and protocols. In: Bjørner, N., de Boer, F. (eds.) FM 2015. LNCS, vol. 9109, pp. 265–272. Springer, Cham (2015). https://doi.org/10.1007/978-3-319-19249-9_17
22. Feng, Y., Ying, M.: Quantum Hoare logic with classical variables. ACM Trans. Quantum Comput. **2**(4), 1–43 (2021)
23. Feng, Y., Yu, N., Ying, M.: Model checking quantum Markov chains. J. Comput. Syst. Sci. **79**(7), 1181–1198 (2013). https://doi.org/10.1016/j.jcss.2013.04.002
24. Filliâtre, J.-C., Paskevich, A.: Why3 — where programs meet provers. In: Felleisen, M., Gardner, P. (eds.) ESOP 2013. LNCS, vol. 7792, pp. 125–128. Springer, Heidelberg (2013). https://doi.org/10.1007/978-3-642-37036-6_8

25. Grover, L.K.: A fast quantum mechanical algorithm for database search. In: Miller, G.L. (ed.) Proceedings of the Twenty-Eighth Annual ACM Symposium on the Theory of Computing, Philadelphia, Pennsylvania, USA, May 22–24, 1996, pp. 212–219. ACM (1996). https://doi.org/10.1145/237814.237866

26. Hietala, K., Rand, R., Hung, S.H., Wu, X., Hicks, M.: Verified optimization in a quantum intermediate representation. arXiv preprint arXiv:1904.06319 (2019)

27. King, J.C.: Symbolic execution and program testing. Commun. ACM **19**(7), 385–394 (1976). https://doi.org/10.1145/360248.360252

28. Lengál, O., Šimáček, J., Vojnar, T.: VATA: a library for efficient manipulation of non-deterministic tree automata. In: Flanagan, C., König, B. (eds.) TACAS 2012. LNCS, vol. 7214, pp. 79–94. Springer, Heidelberg (2012). https://doi.org/10.1007/978-3-642-28756-5_7

29. Liu, J., Zhan, B., Wang, S., Ying, S., Liu, T., Li, Y., Ying, M., Zhan, N.: Formal verification of quantum algorithms using quantum hoare logic. In: Dillig, I., Tasiran, S. (eds.) CAV 2019. LNCS, vol. 11562, pp. 187–207. Springer, Cham (2019). https://doi.org/10.1007/978-3-030-25543-5_12

30. Mateus, P., Ramos, J., Sernadas, A., Sernadas, C.: Temporal Logics for Reasoning about Quantum Systems, pp. 389–413. Cambridge University Press (2009). https://doi.org/10.1017/CBO9781139193313.011

31. Nielsen, M.A., Chuang, I.L.: Quantum Computation and Quantum Information: 10th Anniversary Edition, 10th edn. Cambridge University Press, USA (2011)

32. Perdrix, S.: Quantum entanglement analysis based on abstract interpretation. In: International Static Analysis Symposium, pp. 270–282. Springer (2008)

33. Shor, P.W.: Algorithms for quantum computation: Discrete logarithms and factoring. In: 35th Annual Symposium on Foundations of Computer Science, Santa Fe, New Mexico, USA, 20–22 November 1994. pp. 124–134. IEEE Computer Society (1994). https://doi.org/10.1109/SFCS.1994.365700

34. Tsai, Y., Jiang, J.R., Jhang, C.: Bit-slicing the Hilbert space: Scaling up accurate quantum circuit simulation. In: 58th ACM/IEEE Design Automation Conference, DAC 2021, San Francisco, CA, USA, December 5–9, 2021, pp. 439–444. IEEE (2021). https://doi.org/10.1109/DAC18074.2021.9586191

35. Unruh, D.: Quantum Hoare logic with ghost variables. In: 2019 34th Annual ACM/IEEE Symposium on Logic in Computer Science (LICS), pp. 1–13. IEEE (2019)

36. Veanes, M., Bjørner, N.S.: Symbolic tree automata. Inf. Process. Lett. **115**(3), 418–424 (2015). https://doi.org/10.1016/j.ipl.2014.11.005

37. Wenzel, M., Paulson, L.C., Nipkow, T.: The isabelle framework. In: Mohamed, O.A., Muñoz, C., Tahar, S. (eds.) TPHOLs 2008. LNCS, vol. 5170, pp. 33–38. Springer, Heidelberg (2008). https://doi.org/10.1007/978-3-540-71067-7_7

38. Xu, M., Fu, J., Mei, J., Deng, Y.: Model checking QCTL plus on quantum Markov chains. Theor. Comput. Sci. **913**, 43–72 (2022). https://doi.org/10.1016/j.tcs.2022.01.044

39. Xu, M., et al.: Quartz: superoptimization of quantum circuits. In: Proceedings of the 43rd ACM SIGPLAN International Conference on Programming Language Design and Implementation, pp. 625–640 (2022)

40. Ying, M.: Floyd-Hoare logic for quantum programs. ACM Trans. Programm. Lang. Syst. (TOPLAS) **33**(6), 1–49 (2012)

41. Ying, M.: Model checking for verification of quantum circuits. In: International Symposium on Formal Methods, pp. 23–39. Springer (2021)

42. Ying, M., Feng, Y.: Model Checking Quantum Systems: Principles and Algorithms. Cambridge University Press (2021)

43. Yu, N., Palsberg, J.: Quantum abstract interpretation. In: Proceedings of the 42nd ACM SIGPLAN International Conference on Programming Language Design and Implementation, pp. 542–558 (2021)
44. Zhou, L., Yu, N., Ying, M.: An applied quantum Hoare logic. In: Proceedings of the 40th ACM SIGPLAN Conference on Programming Language Design and Implementation, pp. 1149–1162 (2019)
45. Zulehner, A., Hillmich, S., Wille, R.: How to efficiently handle complex values? implementing decision diagrams for quantum computing. In: Pan, D.Z. (ed.) Proceedings of the International Conference on Computer-Aided Design, ICCAD 2019, Westminster, CO, USA, November 4–7, 2019. pp. 1–7. ACM (2019). https://doi.org/10.1109/ICCAD45719.2019.8942057
46. Zulehner, A., Wille, R.: Advanced simulation of quantum computations. IEEE Trans. Comput. Aided Des. Integr. Circuits Syst. **38**(5), 848–859 (2019). https://doi.org/10.1109/TCAD.2018.2834427

Bounded Verification
for Finite-Field-Blasting

In a Compiler for Zero Knowledge Proofs

Alex Ozdemir[1]([⊠]), Riad S. Wahby[2], Fraser Brown[2], and Clark Barrett[1]

[1] Stanford University, Stanford, USA
aozdemir@cs.stanford.edu
[2] Carnegie Mellon University,
Pittsburgh, USA

Abstract. Zero Knowledge Proofs (ZKPs) are cryptographic protocols by which a prover convinces a verifier of the truth of a statement without revealing any other information. Typically, statements are expressed in a high-level language and then compiled to a low-level representation on which the ZKP operates. Thus, *a bug in a ZKP compiler can compromise the statement that the ZK proof is supposed to establish*. This paper takes a step towards ZKP compiler correctness by partially verifying a *field-blasting* compiler pass, a pass that translates Boolean and bit-vector logic into equivalent operations in a finite field. First, we define correctness for field-blasters and ZKP compilers more generally. Next, we describe the specific field-blaster using a set of encoding rules and define verification conditions for individual rules. Finally, we connect the rules and the correctness definition by showing that if our verification conditions hold, the field-blaster is correct. We have implemented our approach in the CirC ZKP compiler and have proved bounded versions of the corresponding verification conditions. We show that our partially verified field-blaster does not hurt the performance of the compiler or its output; we also report on four bugs uncovered during verification.

1 Introduction

Zero-Knowledge Proofs (ZKPs) are powerful tools for building privacy-pre-serving systems. They allow one entity, the *prover* $\mathcal{P}$, to convince another, the *verifier* $\mathcal{V}$, that some secret data satisfies a public property, *without revealing anything else about the data*. ZKPs underlie a large (and growing!) set of critical applications, from billion-dollar private cryptocurrencies, like Zcash [24,53] and Monero [2], to research into auditable sealed court orders [20], private gun registries [26], privacy-preserving middleboxes [23], and zero-knowledge proofs of exploitability [11]. This breadth of applications is possible because of the generality of ZKPs. In general, $\mathcal{P}$ knows a secret *witness* w, whereas $\mathcal{V}$ knows a *property* ϕ and a public *instance* x. $\mathcal{P}$ must show that $\phi(x, w) = \top$. Typically, x and w are vectors of variables in a finite field $\mathbb{F}$, and ϕ can be any system of equations over the variables, using operations $+$ and $\times$. Because ϕ itself is an

C. Enea and A. Lal (Eds.): CAV 2023, LNCS 13966, pp. 154–175, 2023.
https://doi.org/10.1007/978-3-031-37709-9_8

input to $\mathcal{P}$ and $\mathcal{V}$, and because of the expressivity of field equations, a single implementation of $\mathcal{P}$ and $\mathcal{V}$ can serve many different purposes.

Humans find it difficult to express themselves directly with field equations, so they use *ZKP compilers*. A ZKP compiler converts a high-level predicate ϕ' into an equivalent system of field equations ϕ. In other words, a ZKP compiler *generalizes* a ZKP: by compiling ϕ' to ϕ and then using a ZKP for ϕ, one obtains a ZKP for ϕ'. There are many industrial [3,5,6,14,21,45,55,66] and academic [4,18,28,29,46,48,50,54,63] ZKP compilers.

The correctness of a ZKP compiler is critical for security— a bug in the compiler could admit proofs of false statements— but verification is challenging for three reasons. First, the definition of correctness for a ZKP compiler is non-trivial; we discuss later in this section. Second, ZKP compilers span multiple domains. The high-level predicate ϕ' is typically expressed in a language with common types such as Booleans and fixed-width integers, while the output ϕ is over a large, prime-order field. Thus, any compiler correctness definition must span these domains. Third, ZKP compilers are evolving and performance-critical; verification must not inhibit future changes or degrade compiler performance.

In this work, we develop tools for automatically verifying the *field-blaster* of a ZKP compiler. A ZKP compiler's field-blaster is the pass that converts from a formula over Booleans, fixed-width integers, and finite-field elements, to a system of field equations; as a transformation from bit-like types to field equations, the field-blaster exemplifies the challenge of cross-domain verification.

Our paper makes three contributions. First, we formulate a precise correctness definition for a ZKP compiler. Our definition ensures that a correct compiler preserves the completeness and soundness of the underlying ZK proof system.[1] More specifically, given a ZK proof system where statements are specified in a low-level language L, and a compiler from a high-level language H to L, if the compiler is correct by our definition, it extends the ZK proof system's soundness and completeness properties to statements in H. Further, our definition is preserved under sequential composition, so proving the correctness of each compiler pass individually suffices to prove correctness of the compiler itself.

Second, we give an architecture for a verifiable field-blaster. In our architecture, a field-blaster is a set of "encoding rules." We give verification conditions (VCs) for these rules, and we show that if the VCs hold, then the field-blaster is correct. Our approach supports *automated* verification because (bounded versions of) the VCs can be checked automatically. This reduces both the up-front cost of verification and its maintenance cost.

Third, we do a case study. Using our architecture, we implement a new field-blaster for CirC [46] ("SIR-see"), an infrastructure used by state-of-the-art ZKP compilers. We verify bounded versions of our field-blaster's VCs using SMT-based finite-field reasoning [47], and show that our field blaster does not compromise CirC's performance. We also report on four bugs that our verification effort uncovered, including a soundness bug that allowed the prover to "lie" about the results of certain bit-vector comparisons. We note that the utility of

---

[1] Roughly speaking, a ZK proof system is complete if it is possible to prove every true statement, and is sound if it is infeasible to prove false ones.

our techniques is not limited to CirC: most ZKP compilers include something like the field-blaster we describe here.

In the next sections, we discuss related work (Sect. 1.1), give background on ZKPs and CirC (Sect. 2), present a field-blasting example (Sect. 3), describe our architecture (Sect. 4), give our verification conditions (Sect. 5), and present the case study (Sect. 6).

1.1 Related Work

Verified Compilers. There is a rich body of work on verifying the correctness of traditional compilers. We focus on compilation for ZKPs; this requires different correctness definitions that relate bit-like types to prime field elements. In the next paragraphs, we discuss more fine-grained differences.

Compiler verification efforts fall into two broad categories: *automated*—verification leveraging automated reasoning solvers—and *foundational*—manual verification using proof assistants (e.g., Coq [8] or Isabelle [44]). CompCert [36], for example, is a Coq-verified C compiler with verified optimization passes (e.g., [40]). Closest to our work is backend verification, which proves correct the translation from an intermediate representation to machine code. CompCert's lowering [37] is verified, as is CakeML's [31] lowering to different ISAs [19,57]. While such foundational verification offers strong guarantees, it imposes a heavy proof burden; creating CompCert, for example, took an expert team eight years [56], and any updates to compiler code require updates to proofs.

Automated verification, in contrast, does not require writing and maintaining manual proofs.[2] Cobalt [34], Rhodium [35], and PEC [32] are domain-specific languages (DSLs) for writing automatically-verified compiler optimizations and analyses. Most closely related to our work is Alive [39], a DSL for expressing verified peephole optimizations, local rewrites that transform snippets of LLVM IR [1] to better-performing ones. Alive addresses transformations over fixed types (while we address lowering to finite field equations) and formulates correctness in the presence of undefined behavior (while we formulate correctness for ZKPs). Beyond Alive, Alive2 [38] provides translation validation [41,51] for LLVM [33], and VeRA [10] verifies range analysis in the Firefox JavaScript engine.

There is also work on verified compilation for domains more closely related to ZKPs. The Porcupine [15] compiler automatically synthesizes representations for fully-homomorphic encryption [62], and Gillar [58] proves that optimization passes in the Qiskit [60] quantum compiler are semantics-preserving. While these works compile from high-level languages to circuit representations, the correctness definitions for their domains do not apply to ZKP compilers.

Verified Compilation to Cryptographic Proofs. Prior works on verified compilation for ZKPs (or similar) take the foundational approach (with attendant proof maintenance burdens), and they do not formulate a satisfactory definition of compiler correctness. PinocchioQ [18] builds on CompCert [36]. The

---

[2] Automated verification generally leverages solvers. This is a particularly appealing approach in our setting, since CirC (our compiler infrastructure of interest) already supports compilation to SMT formulas.

authors formulate a correctness definition that preserves the *existential sound-ness* of a ZKP but does not consider completeness, knowledge soundness, or zero-knowledge (see Sect. 2.2). Leo [14] is a ZKP compiler that produces (partial) ACL2 [27] proofs of correct compilation; work to emit proofs from its field-blaster is ongoing.

Recent work defines security for *reductions of knowledge* [30]. These let $\mathcal{P}$ convince $\mathcal{V}$ that it knows a witness for an instance of relation $\mathcal{R}_1$ by proving it knows a witness for an instance of an easier-to-prove relation $\mathcal{R}_2$. Unlike ZKP compilers, $\mathcal{P}$ and $\mathcal{V}$ *interact* to derive $\mathcal{R}_2$ using $\mathcal{V}$'s randomness (e.g., proving that two polynomials are nonzero w.h.p. by proving that a random linear combination of them is), whereas ZKP compilers run ahead of time and non-interactively.

Further afield, Ecne [65] is a tool that attempts to verify that the input to a ZKP encodes a *deterministic* computation. It does not consider any notion of a specification of the intended behavior. A different work [25] attempts to automatically verify that a "widget" given to a ZKP meets some specification. They consider widgets that could be constructed manually or with a compiler. Our focus is on verifying a compiler pass.

2   Background

2.1   Logic

We assume usual terminology for many-sorted first-order logic with equality ([17] gives a complete presentation). We assume every signature includes the sort Bool, constants True and False of sort Bool, and symbol family $\approx_\sigma$ (abbreviated $\approx$) with sort $\sigma \times \sigma \to$ Bool for each sort σ. We also assume a family of conditionals: symbols ite_σ ("if-then-else", abbreviated ite) of sort Bool $\times \sigma \times \sigma \to \sigma$.

A *theory* is a pair $\mathcal{T} = (\Sigma, \mathbf{I})$, where Σ is a signature and $\mathbf{I}$ is a class of Σ-interpretations. A Σ-*formula* is a term of sort Bool. A Σ-formula ϕ is *satisfiable* (resp., *unsatisfiable*) in $\mathcal{T}$ if it is satisfied by some (resp., no) interpretation in $\mathbf{I}$. We focus on two theories. The first is $\mathcal{T}_{BV}$, the SMT-LIB theory of bit-vectors [52,61], with signature Σ_{BV} including a bit-vector sort $\mathsf{BV}_{[n]}$ for each $n > 0$ with bit-vector constants $c_{[n]}$ of sort $\mathsf{BV}_{[n]}$ for each $c \in [0, 2^n - 1]$, and operators including & and | (bitwise and, or) and $+_{[n]}$ (addition modulo 2^n). We write $t[i]$ to refer to the ith bit of bit-vector t, where $t[0]$ is the least-significant bit. The other theory is $\mathcal{T}_{F_p}$, which is the theory corresponding to the finite field of order p, for some prime p [47]. This theory has signature Σ_{F_p} containing the sort FF_p, constant symbols $0, \ldots, p - 1$, and operators $+$ and $\times$.

In this paper, we assume all interpretations interpret sorts and symbols in the same way. We write dom(v) for the set interpreting the sort of a variable v. We assume that Bool, True, and False are interpreted as $\{\top, \bot\}$, $\top$, and $\bot$, respectively; Σ_{BV}-interpretations follow the SMT-LIB standard; and Σ_{F_p}-interpretations interpret symbols as the corresponding elements and operations in $\mathbb{F}_p$, a finite field of order p (for concreteness, this could be the integers modulo p). Note that only the values of variables can vary between two interpretations.

For a signature Σ, let t be a Σ-term of sort σ, with free variables $x_1, \ldots, x_n$, respectively of sort $\sigma_1, \ldots, \sigma_n$. We define the function $\hat{t} :$ dom(x_1) $\times \cdots \times$

$$\begin{array}{ccc}
 & \text{pk} \quad \text{Setup}(\phi) \quad \text{vk} & \\
\mathcal{P}(\phi, x, w) & \xleftarrow{\quad\quad} \quad \pi \quad \xrightarrow{\quad\quad} & \mathcal{V}(\phi, x) \\
\hline
\text{Prove}(\text{pk}, x, w) & \xrightarrow{\hspace{4cm}} & \text{Verify}(\text{vk}, x, \pi)
\end{array}$$

Fig. 1. The information flow for a zero-knowledge proof.

$\text{dom}(x_n) \to \text{dom}(t)$ as follows. Let $\mathbf{x} \in \text{dom}(x_1) \times \cdots \times \text{dom}(x_n)$. Let $\mathcal{M}$ be an interpretation that interprets each x_i as x_i. Then $\hat{t}(\mathbf{x}) = t^{\mathcal{M}}$ (i.e., the interpretation of t in $\mathcal{M}$). For example, the term $t = a \wedge \neg a$ defines $\hat{t} : \text{Bool} \to \text{Bool} = \lambda x. \bot$. In the following, we follow the convention used above in using the standard font (e.g., x) for logical variables and a sans serif font (e.g., x) to denote meta-variables standing for values (i.e., elements of $\sigma^{\mathcal{M}}$ for some σ and $\mathcal{M}$). Also, abusing notation, we'll conflate single variables (of both kinds) with vectors of variables when the distinction doesn't matter. Note that a formula ϕ is *satisfiable* if there exist values x such that $\hat{\phi}(\mathsf{x}) = \top$. It is *valid* if for all values x, $\hat{\phi}(\mathsf{x}) = \top$.

For terms s, t and variable x, $t[x \mapsto s]$ denotes t with all occurrences of x replaced with s. For a sequence of variable-term pairs, $S = (x_1 \mapsto s_1, \ldots, x_n \mapsto s_n)$, $t[S]$ is defined to be $t[x_1 \mapsto s_1] \cdots [x_n \mapsto s_n]$.

2.2 Zero Knowledge Proofs

As mentioned above, Zero-knowledge proofs (ZKPs) make it possible to prove that some secret data satisfies a public property—without revealing the data itself. See [59] for a full presentation; we give a brief overview here, and then describe how general-purpose ZKPs are used.

Overview and Definitions. In a cryptographic proof system, there are two parties: a *verifier* $\mathcal{V}$ and a *prover* $\mathcal{P}$. $\mathcal{V}$ knows a public *instance* x and asks $\mathcal{P}$ to show that it has knowledge of a secret *witness* w satisfying a public *predicate* $\phi(x, w)$ from a predicate class Φ (a set of formulas) (i.e., $\hat{\phi}(\mathsf{x}, \mathsf{w}) = \top$). Figure 1 illustrates the workflow. First, a trusted party runs an efficient (i.e., polytime in an implicit security parameter λ) algorithm $\text{Setup}(\phi)$ which produces a *proving key* pk and a *verifying key* vk. Then, $\mathcal{P}$ runs an efficient algorithm $\text{Prove}(\text{pk}, x, w) \to \pi$ and sends the resulting *proof* π to $\mathcal{V}$. Finally, $\mathcal{V}$ runs an efficient verification algorithm $\text{Verify}(\text{vk}, x, \pi) \to \{\top, \bot\}$ that accepts or rejects the proof. A zero-knowledge argument of knowledge for class Φ is a tuple $\Pi = (\text{Setup}, \text{Prove}, \text{Verify})$ with three informal properties for every $\phi \in \Phi$ and every $\mathsf{x} \in \text{dom}(x), \mathsf{w} \in \text{dom}(w)$:

- *perfect completeness*: if $\hat{\phi}(\mathsf{x}, \mathsf{w})$ holds, then $\text{Verify}(\text{vk}, x, \pi)$ holds;
- *computational knowledge soundness* [9]: an efficient adversary that does not know w cannot produce a π such that $\text{Verify}(\text{vk}, x, \pi)$ holds; and
- *zero-knowledge* [22]: π reveals nothing about w, other than its existence.

Technically, the system is an "argument" rather than a "proof" because soundness only holds against efficient adversaries. Also note that knowledge soundness requires that an entity must "know" a valid w' to produce a proof; it is not enough for a valid w' to simply exist. We give more precise definitions in Appendix A.

Representations for ZKPs. As mentioned above, ZKP applications are manifold (Sect. 1)—from cryptocurrencies to private registries. This breadth of applications is possible because ZKPs support a broad class of predicates. Most commonly, these predicates are expressed as *rank-1 constraint systems* (R1CSs). Recall that $\mathbb{F}_p$ is a prime-order finite field (also called a *prime field*). We will drop the subscript p when it is not important. In an R1CS, x and w are vectors of elements in $\mathbb{F}$; let $z \in \mathbb{F}^m$ be their concatenation. The function $\hat{\phi}$ can be defined by three matrices $A, B, C \in \mathbb{F}^{n \times m}$; $\hat{\phi}(x, w)$ holds when $Az \circ Bz = Cz$, where $\circ$ is the element-wise product. Thus, ϕ can be viewed as n conjoined *constraints*, where each constraint i is of the form $(\sum_j a_{ij} z_j) \times (\sum_j b_{ij} z_j) \approx (\sum_j c_{ij} z_j)$ (where the a_{ij}, b_{ij} and c_{ij} are constant symbols from Σ_{F_p}, and the z_j are a vector of variables of sort FF_p). That is, each constraint enforces a single non-linear multiplication.

2.3   Compilation Targeting Zero Knowledge Proofs

To write a ZKP about a high-level predicate ϕ, that predicate is first compiled to an R1CS. A *ZKP compiler* from class Φ (a set of Σ-formulas) to class Φ' (a set of Σ'-formulas) is an efficient algorithm $\mathsf{Compile}(\phi \in \Phi) \to (\phi' \in \Phi', \mathsf{Ext}_x, \mathsf{Ext}_w)$. Given a predicate $\phi(x, w)$, it returns a predicate $\phi'(x', w')$ as well as two efficient and deterministic algorithms, instance and witness *extenders*: $\mathsf{Ext}_x : \mathrm{dom}(x) \to \mathrm{dom}(x')$ and $\mathsf{Ext}_w : \mathrm{dom}(x) \times \mathrm{dom}(w) \to \mathrm{dom}(w')$.[3] For example, CirC [46] can compile a Boolean-returning C function (in a subset of C) to an R1CS.

At a high-level, ϕ and ϕ' should be "equisatisfiable", with Ext_x and Ext_w mapping satisfying values for ϕ to satisfying values for ϕ'. That is, for all x $\in$ $\mathrm{dom}(x)$ and w $\in$ $\mathrm{dom}(w)$ such that $\hat{\phi}(x, w) = \top$, if x$' = \mathsf{Ext}_x(x)$ and w$' = \mathsf{Ext}_w(x, w)$, then $\hat{\phi}'(x', w') = \top$. Furthermore, for any x, it should be impossible to (efficiently) find w$'$ satisfying $\hat{\phi}'(\mathsf{Ext}_x(x), w') = \top$ without knowing a w satisfying $\hat{\phi}(x, w) = \top$. In Sect. 5.1, we precisely define correctness for a predicate compiler.

One can build a ZKP for class Φ from a compiler from Φ to Φ' and a ZKP for Φ'. Essentially, one runs the compiler to get a predicate $\phi' \in \Phi'$, as well as Ext_x and Ext_w. Then, one writes a ZKP to show that $\hat{\phi}'(\mathsf{Ext}_x(x), \mathsf{Ext}_w(x, w)) = \top$. In Appendix A, we give this construction in full and prove it is secure.

Optimization. The primary challenge when using ZKPs is cost: typically, Prove is at least three orders of magnitude slower than checking ϕ directly [64]. Since Prove's cost scales with n (the constraint count), it is *critical* for the compiler to minimize n. The space of optimizations is large and complex, for two reasons. First, the compiler can introduce fresh variables. Second, only equisatisfiability—not logical equivalence—is needed. Compilers in this space exploit equisatisfiability heavily to efficiently represent high-level constructs (e.g., Booleans, bit-vectors, arrays, ...) as an R1CS.

---

[3] For technical reasons, the runtime of Ext_x and the size of its description must be $\mathsf{poly}(\lambda, |x|)$—not just $\mathsf{poly}(\lambda)$ (Appendix A). .

$$\text{pgm} \xrightarrow{(1)} \boxed{\text{front-end}} \mapsto \text{IR} \rightarrow \cdots \rightarrow \text{IR}[\Sigma_{BV} \cup \Sigma_F] \xrightarrow{(3)} \boxed{\text{lowering}} \mapsto \text{R1CS}$$

$$\boxed{\text{field-blasting}} \mapsto \text{IR}[\Sigma_F] \rightarrow \boxed{\text{flattening}}$$

Fig. 2. The architecture of CirC

As a (simple!) example, consider the Boolean computation $a \approx c_1 \vee \cdots \vee c_k$. Assume that $c'_1, \ldots, c'_k$ are variables of sort FF and that we add constraints $c'_i(1 - c'_i) \approx 0$ to ensure that c'_i has to be 0 or 1 for each i. Assume further that $(c'_i \approx 1)$ encodes c_i for each i. How can one additionally ensure that a' (also of sort FF) is also forced to be equal to 0 or 1 and that $(a' \approx 1)$ is a correct encoding of a? Given that there are $k - 1$ ORs, natural approaches use $\Theta(k)$ constraints. One clever approach is to introduce variable x' and enforce constraints $x'(\sum_i c'_i) \approx a'$ and $(1 - a')(\sum_i c'_i) \approx 0$. In any interpretation where any c_i is true, the corresponding interpretation for a' must be 1 to satisfy the second constraint; setting x' to the sum's inverse satisfies the first. If all c_i are false, the first constraint ensures a' is 0. This technique assumes the sum does not overflow; since ZKP fields are typically large (e.g., with p on the order of 2^{255}), this is usually a safe assumption.

CirC. CirC [46] is an infrastructure for building compilers from high-level languages (e.g., a C subset), to R1CSs. It has been used in research projects [4,12], and in industrial R&D. Figure 2 shows the structure of an R1CS compiler built with CirC. First, the front-end of the compiler converts the source program into CirC-IR. CirC-IR is a term IR based on SMT-LIB that includes: Booleans, bit-vectors, fixed-size arrays, tuples, and prime fields.[4] Second, the compiler optimizes and simplifies the IR so that the only remaining sorts are Booleans, bit-vectors, and the target prime field. Third, the compiler lowers the simplified IR to an R1CS predicate over the target field. For ZKPs built with CirC, *the completeness, soundness, and zero-knowledge of the end-to-end system depend on the correctness of CirC itself.*

3   Overview and Example

To start, we view CirC's lowering pass as two passes (Fig. 2). The first pass, "(finite-)field-blasting," converts a many-sorted IR (representable as a $(\Sigma_{BV} \cup \Sigma_F)$-formula) to a conjunction of field equations (Σ_F-equations). The second pass, "flattening," converts this conjunction of field equations to an R1CS.

Our focus is on verifying the first pass. We begin with a worked example of how to field-blast a small snippet of CirC-IR (Sect. 3.1). This example will illustrate four key ideas (Sect. 3.2) that inspire our field-blaster's architecture.

---

[4] We list all CirC-IR operators for Booleans, bit-vectors, and prime fields in Appendix C. Almost all are from SMT-LIB.

Table 1. New variables and assertions when compiling the example ϕ.

clause	term from ϕ	assertions	new variables	notes
1	x_0		x_0'	
	w_0	$w_0'(w_0' - 1) \approx 0$	w_0'	
	$x_0 \oplus w_0$	$1 \approx 1 - w_0' - x_0' + 2w_0'x_0'$		
2	x_1		$x_{1,u}'$	
	w_1	$w_{1,i}'(w_{1,i}' - 1) \approx 0$	$w_{1,i}'$	$i \in [0,3]$
	$x_1 +_{[4]} w_1$	$s' \approx x_{1,u}' + \sum_{i=0}^{3} 2^i w_{1,i}'$	s'	
		$s_i'(s_i' - 1) \approx 0$	s_i'	$i \in [0,4]$
		$s' \approx \sum_{i=0}^{4} 2^i s_i'$		
	$x_1 +_{[4]} w_1 \approx w_1$	$s_i' \approx w_{1,i}'$		$i \in [0,3]$
3	x_2		$x_{2,u}'$	
	x_2 (bits)	$x_{2,i}'(x_{2,i}' - 1) \approx 0$	$x_{2,i}'$	$i \in [0,3]$
		$x_{2,u}' \approx \sum_{i=0}^{3} 2^i x_{2,i}'$		
	$x_2 \,\&\, w_1 \approx x_2$	$x_{2,i}' w_{1,i}' \approx x_{2,i}'$		$i \in [0,3]$
4	x_3, w_2		x_3', w_2'	
	$x_3 \approx w_2 \times w_2$	$x_3' \approx w_2' \times w_2'$		

3.1   An Example of Field-Blasting

We start with an example CirC-IR predicate expressed as a $(\Sigma_{BV} \cup \Sigma_F)$-formula:

$$\phi \triangleq (x_0 \oplus w_0) \wedge (w_1 +_{[4]} x_1 \approx w_1) \wedge (x_2 \,\&\, w_1 \approx x_2) \wedge (x_3 \approx w_2 \times w_2) \quad (1)$$

The predicate includes: the XOR of two Booleans ("$\oplus$"), a bit-vector sum, a bit-vector AND, and a field product. x_0 and w_0 are of sort `Bool`, x_1, x_2, and w_1 are of sort $\mathsf{BV}_{[4]}$, and x_3 and w_2 are of sort FF_p. We'll assume that $p \gg 2^4$. Table 1 summarizes the new variables and assertions we create during field-blasting; we describe the origin of each assertion and new variable in the next paragraphs.

Lowering Clause One (Booleans). We begin with the Boolean term $(x_0 \oplus w_0)$. We will use 1 and 0 to represent $\top$ and $\bot$. We introduce variables x_0' and w_0' of sort FF_p to represent x_0 and w_0 respectively. To ensure that w_0' is 0 or 1, we assert: $w_0'(w_0' - 1) \approx 0$.[5] $x_0 \oplus w_0$ is then represented by the expression $1 - x_0' - w_0' + 2x_0'w_0'$. Setting this equal to 1 enforces that $x_0 \oplus w_0$ must be true. These new assertions and fresh variables are reflected in the first three rows of the table.

Lowering Clause Two and Three (Bit-vectors). Before describing how to bit-blast the second and third clauses in ϕ, we discuss bit-vector representations in

---

[5] Later (Sect. 5), we will see that "well-formedness" constraints like this are unnecessary for instance variables, such as x_0. .

general. A bit-vector t can be viewed as a sequence of b bits or as a non-negative integer less than 2^b. These two views suggest two natural representations in a prime-order field: first, as one field element t'_u, whose unsigned value agrees with t (assuming the field's size is at least 2^b); second, as b elements $t'_0, \ldots, t'_{b-1}$, that encode the bits of t as 0 or 1 (in our encoding, t'_0 is the least-significant bit and t'_{b-1} is the most-significant bit). The first representation is simple, but with it, some field values (e.g., 2^b) don't corresponding to any possible bit-vector. With the second approach, by including equations $t'_i(t'_i-1) \approx 0$ in our system, we ensure that any satisfying assignment corresponds to a valid bit-vector. However, the extra b equations increase the size of our compiler's output.

We represent ϕ's w_1 bit-wise: as $w'_{1,0}, \ldots, w'_{1,3}$, and we represent the instance variable x_1 as $x'_{1,u}$.[6] For the constraint $w_1 +_{[4]} x_1 \approx w_1$, we compute the sum in the field and bit-decompose the result to handle overflow. First, we introduce new variable s' and set it equal to $x'_{1,u} + \sum_{i=0}^{3} 2^i w'_{1,i}$. Then, we bit-decompose s', requiring $s' \approx \sum_{i=0}^{4} 2^i s'_i$, and $s'_i(s'_i - 1) \approx 0$ for $i \in [0,4]$. Finally, we assert $s'_i \approx w'_{1,i}$ for $i \in [0,3]$. This forces the lowest 4 bits of the sum to be equal to w_1.

The constraint $x_2 \,\&\, w_1 \approx x_2$ is more challenging. Since x_2 is an instance variable, we initially encode it as $x'_{2,u}$. Then, we consider the bit-wise AND. There is no obvious way to encode a bit-wise operation, other than bit-by-bit. So, we convert $x'_{2,u}$ to a bit-wise representation: We introduce witness variables $x'_{2,0}, \ldots, x'_{2,3}$ and equations $x'_{2,i}(x'_{2,i} - 1) \approx 0$ as well as equation $x'_{2,u} \approx \sum_{i=0}^{3} 2^i x'_{2,i}$. Then, for each i we require $x'_{2,i} w'_{1,i} \approx x'_{2,i}$.

Lowering the Final Clause (Field Elements). Finally, we consider the field equation $x_2 \approx w_2 \times w_2$. Our target is also field equations, so lowering this is straightforward. We simply introduce primed variables and copy the equation.

3.2   Key Ideas

This example highlights four ideas that guide the design of our field-blaster:

1. *fresh variables and assertions*: Field-blasting uses two primitive operations: creating new variables in ϕ' (e.g., w'_0 to represent w_0) and adding new assertions to ϕ' (e.g., $w'_0(w'_0 - 1) \approx 0$).
2. *encodings*: For a term t in ϕ, we construct a field term (or collection of field terms) in ϕ' that represent the value of t. For example, the Boolean w_0 is represented as the field element w'_0 that is 0 or 1.
3. *operator rules*: if t is an operator applied to some arguments, we can encode t given encodings of the arguments. For example, if t is $x_0 \oplus w_0$, and x_0 is encoded as x'_0 and w_0 as w'_0, then t can be encoded as $1 - x'_0 - w'_0 + 2x'_0 w'_0$.
4. *conversions*: Some sorts can be represented by encodings of different kinds. If a term has multiple possible encodings, the compiler may need to convert between them to apply some operator rule. For example, we converted x_2 from an unsigned encoding to a bit-wise encoding before handling an AND.

---

[6] We represent w_1 bit-wise so that we can ensure the representation is well-formed with constraints $w'_{1,i}(w'_{1,i} - 1) \approx 0$. As previously noted, such well-formedness constraints are not needed for an instance variable like x_1. (See footnote 5).

Table 2. Encodings for each term sort. Only bit-vectors have two encoding kinds.

Variant Contents			Semantics
encoded_term	kind	terms	Validity Condition
t: Bool	bit	f	$f \approx ite(t, 1, 0)$
t: $BV_{[b]}$	uint	f	$f \approx \sum_i ite(t[i] \approx 1_{[1]}, 2^i, 0)$
t: $BV_{[b]}$	bits	$f_0, \ldots, f_{b-1}$	$\bigwedge_i f_i \approx ite(t[i] \approx 1_{[1]}, 1, 0)$
t: FF	field	f	$t \approx f$

4   Architecture

In this section, we present our field-blaster architecture. To compile a predicate ϕ to a system of field equations ϕ', our architecture processes each term t in ϕ using a post-order traversal. Informally, it represents each t as an "encoding" in ϕ': a term (or collection of terms) over variables in ϕ'. Each encoding is produced by a small algorithm called an "encoding rule".

Below, we define the type of encodings Enc (Sect. 4.1), the five different types of encoding rules (Sect. 4.2), and a calculus that iteratively applies these rules to compile all of ϕ (Sect. 4.3).

4.1   Encodings

Table 2 presents our tagged union type Enc of possible term encodings. Each variant comprises the term being encoded, its tag (the *encoding kind*), and a sequence of field terms. The encoding kinds are bit (a Boolean as $0/1$), uint (a bit-vector as an unsigned integer), bits (a bit-vector as a sequence of bits), and field (a field term trivially represented as a field term). Each encoding has an intended semantics: a condition under which the encoding is considered valid. For instance, a bit encoding of Boolean t is valid if the field term f is equal to $ite(t, 1, 0)$.

4.2   Encoding Rules

An encoding rule is an algorithm that takes and/or returns encodings, in order to represent some part of the input predicate as field terms and equations.

Primitive Operations. A rule can perform two primitive operations: creating new variables and emitting assertions. In our pseudocode, the primitive function $\mathsf{fresh}(\mathsf{name}, t, \mathsf{isInst}) \rightarrow x'$ creates a fresh variable. Argument isInst is a Boolean indicating whether x' is an instance variable (as opposed to a witness). Argument t is a field term (over variables from ϕ and previously defined primed variables) that expresses how to compute a value for x'. For example, to create a field variable w' that represents Boolean witness variable w, a rule can call $\mathsf{fresh}(w', ite(w, 1, 0), \bot)$. The compiler uses t to help create the Ext_x and Ext_w algorithms. A rule asserts a formula t' (over primed variables) by calling $\mathsf{assert}(t')$.

fn variable(t, isInst) → Enc :
  if isInst:
    $t' \leftarrow$ fresh(name(t) $\|$ 'u',
        $\sum_i ite(t[i] \approx 1_{[1]}, 2^i, 0), \top)$
    return t, uint, t'
  else:
    for i in $[0, \text{size}(\text{sort}(t)) - 1]$:
      $t'_i \leftarrow$ fresh(name(t) $\| i$,
        $ite(t[i] \approx 1_{[1]}, 1, 0), \bot)$
      assert($t'_i(t'_i - 1) = 0$)
    return t, bits, $t'_0, \ldots, t'_{\text{size}(\text{sort}(t))-1}$

fn const(t) → Enc :
  for i in $[0, \text{size}(\text{sort}(t)) - 1]$:
    $t'_i \leftarrow ite(t[i] \approx 1_{[1]}, 1, 0)$
  return t, bits, $t'_0, \ldots, t'_{\text{size}(\text{sort}(t))-1}$

fn assertEq(e : Enc, e' : Enc) :
  if kind(e) = bits:
    for i in $[0, \text{size}(\text{terms}(e)) - 1]$:
      assert(terms(e)$[i] \approx$ terms(e')$[i]$)
  elif kind(e) = uint:
    assert(terms(e)$[0] \approx$ terms(e')$[0]$)

fn convert(e : Enc, kind$'$: Kind) → Enc :
  $t \leftarrow$ encoded_term(e)
  if kind(e) = bits and kind$'$ = uint:
    return t, uint, $\sum_i 2^i \text{terms}(e)[i]$
  elif kind(e) = uint and kind$'$ = bits:
    $e' \leftarrow$ variable($t, \bot$)
    assert(terms(e)$[0] \approx \sum_i 2^i \text{terms}(e')[i]$)
    return e'

Fig. 3. Pseudocode for some bit-vector rules: variable uses a uint encoding for instances and bit-splits witnesses to ensure they're well-formed, const bit-splits the constant it's given, assertEq asserts unsigned or bit-wise equality, and convert either does a bit-sum or bit-split.

Rule Types. There are five types of rules: (1) Variable rules variable(t, isInst) → e take a variable t and its instance/witness status and return an encoding of that variable made up of fresh variables. (2) Constant rules const(t) → e take a constant term t and produce an encoding of t comprising terms that depend only on t. Since t is a constant, the terms in e can be evaluated to field constants (see the calculus in Sect. 4.3).[7] The const rule cannot call fresh or assert. (3) Equality rules assertEq(e, e') take two encodings of the same kind and emit assertions that equate the underlying terms. (4) Conversion rules convert(e, kind$'$) → e' take an encoding and convert it to an encoding of a different kind. Conversions are only non-trivial for bit-vectors, which have two encoding kinds: uint and bits. (5) Operator rules apply to terms t of form $o(t_1, \ldots, t_n)$. Each operator rule takes t, o, and encodings of the child terms t_i and returns an encoding of t. Some operator rules require specific kinds of encodings; before using such an operator rule, our calculus (Sect. 4.3) calls the convert rule to ensure the input encodings are the correct kind. Figure 3 gives pseudocode for the first four rule types, as applied to bit-vectors. Figure 4 gives pseudocode for two bit-vector operator encoding rules. A field blaster uses many operator rules: in our case study (Sect. 6) there are 46.

---

[7] Having const(t) return terms that depend on t (rather than directly returning constants) is useful for constructing verification conditions for const.

```
fn bvZeroExt(t, o : Op, e : Enc) :
    if kind(e) = bits:
        w ← size(terms(e))
        for i in [0, w − 1]:
            t′ᵢ ← terms(e)[i]
        for i in [0, o.newBits − 1]:
            t′_{w+i} ← 0
        return t, bits, t′₀, . . . , t′_{w+o.newBits−1}
    else:
        return t, kind(e), terms(e)
```

```
fn bvMulUint(t, o : Op, e⃗ : [Enc]) :
    w ← size(sort(encoded_term(e[0])))
    W ← size(e⃗) × w
    assume W < ⌊log₂ p⌋
    s′ ← ∏ᵢ terms(eᵢ)[0]
    b ← ff2bv(W, s′)
    for i in [0, W − 1]:
        t′ᵢ ← fresh(i, ite(b[i], 1, 0), ⊥)
        assert(t′ᵢ(t′ᵢ − 1) ≈ 0)
    assert(s′ ≈ ∑_{i=0}^{W−1} 2ⁱt′ᵢ)
    return t, bits, t′₀, . . . , t′_{w−1}
```

Fig. 4. Pseudocode for some bit-vector operator rules. bvZeroExt zero-extends a bit-vector; for bit-wise encodings, it adds zero bits, and for unsigned encodings, it simply copies the original encoding. bvMulUint multiplies bit-vectors, all assumed to be unsigned encodings. We show only the case where the multiplication cannot overflow in the field: in this case the rule performs the multiplication in the field, and bit-splits the result to implement reduction modulo 2^b. The rules use ff2bv, which converts from a field element to a bit-vector (discussed in Sect. 6.1).

4.3 Calculus

We now give a non-deterministic calculus describing how our field-blaster applies rules to compile a predicate $\phi(x, w)$ into a system of field equations.

A calculus state is a tuple of three items: (E, A, F). The *encoding store* E is a (multi-)map from terms to sets of encodings. The *assertions formula* A is a conjunction of all field equations asserted via assert. The *fresh variable definitions sequence* F is a sequence consisting of pairs, where each pair (v, t) matches a single call to fresh($v, t, \ldots$).

Figure 5 shows the transitions of our calculus. We denote the result of a rule as $A', F', e' \leftarrow r(\ldots)$, where A' is a formula capturing any new assertions, F' is a sequence of pairs capturing any new variable definitions, and e' is the rule's return value. We may omit one or more results if they are always absent for a particular rule. For encoding store E, $E \cup (t \mapsto e)$ denotes the store with e added to t's encoding set.

There are five kinds of transitions. The Const transition adds an encoding for a constant term. The const rule returns an encoding e whose terms depend on the constant c; e' is a new encoding identical to e, except that each of its terms has been evaluated to obtain a field constant. The Var transition adds an encoding for a variable term. The Conv transition takes a term that is already encoded and re-encodes it with a new encoding kind. The kinds operator returns all legal values of kind for encodings of a given sort. The Op_r transition applies operator rule r. This transition is only possible if r's operator kind agrees with o, and if its input encoding kinds agree with $e⃗$. The Finish transition applies when ϕ has been encoded. It uses const and assertEq to build assertions that hold when $\phi = \top$. Rather than producing a new calculus state, it returns the outputs of the calculus: the assertions and the variable definitions.

$$\frac{\text{constant term } c \qquad e \leftarrow \text{const}(c) \qquad e' \leftarrow \text{map(eval}, e)}{E := E \cup (c \mapsto e')} \text{ Const}$$

$$\frac{\text{variable term } v \qquad A', F', e \leftarrow \text{variable}(v, \text{isInst}(v))}{E := E \cup (v \mapsto e), \quad A := A \wedge A', \quad F := F \parallel F'} \text{ Var}$$

$$\frac{(t \mapsto e) \in E \qquad \text{kind} \in \text{kinds}(\text{sort}(t)) \qquad A', F', e' \leftarrow \text{convert}(e, \text{kind})}{E := E \cup (t \mapsto e'), \quad A := A \wedge A', \quad F := F \parallel F'} \text{ Conv}$$

$$\frac{(t_i \mapsto e_i) \in E \qquad t = o(\vec{t}) \qquad A', F', e' \leftarrow r(t, o, \vec{e})}{E := E \cup (t \mapsto e'), \quad A := A \wedge A', \quad F := F \parallel F'} \text{ Op}_r$$

$$\frac{(\phi \mapsto e) \in E \qquad e_\top \leftarrow \text{const}(\top) \qquad A', F' \leftarrow \text{assertEq}(e, e_\top)}{\text{return } (A \wedge A', \quad F \parallel F')} \text{ Finish}$$

Fig. 5. The transition rules of our rewriting calculus.

To meet the requirements of the ZKP compiler, our calculus must return two extension function: Ext_x and Ext_w (Sect. 2.2). Both can be constructed from the fresh variable definitions F. One subtlety is that $\text{Ext}_x(x)$ (which assigns values to fresh instance variables) is a function of x only—it cannot depend on the witness variables of ϕ. We ensure this by allowing fresh instance variables to only be created by the variable rule, and only when it is called with $\text{isInst} = \top$.

Strategy. Our calculus is non-deterministic: multiple transitions are possible in some situations; for example, some conversion is almost always applicable. The strategy that decides which transition to apply affects field blaster performance (Appendix D) but *not* correctness.

5   Verification Conditions

In this section, we first define correctness for a ZKP compiler (Sect. 5.1). Then, we give verification conditions (VCs) for each type of encoding rule (Sect. 5.2). Finally, we show that if these VCs hold, our calculus is a correct ZKP compiler (Sect. 5.3).

5.1   Correctness Definition

Definition 1 (Correctness). *A ZKP compiler* $\text{Compile}(\phi) \to (\phi', \text{Ext}_x, \text{Ext}_w)$ *is **correct** if it is demonstrably complete and demonstrably sound.*

- *demonstrable completeness: For all* $x \in \text{dom}(x), w \in \text{dom}(w)$ *such that* $\hat{\phi}(x, w) = \top$,

$$\hat{\phi}'(\text{Ext}_x(x), \text{Ext}_w(x, w)) = \top$$

- *demonstrable soundness*: There exists an efficient algorithm $\mathsf{Inv}(\mathsf{x}', \mathsf{w}') \to \mathsf{w}$ such that for all $\mathsf{x} \in \mathsf{dom}(x), \mathsf{w}' \in \mathsf{dom}(w')$ such that $\hat{\phi}'(\mathsf{Ext}_x(\mathsf{x}), \mathsf{w}') = \top$,

$$\hat{\phi}(\mathsf{x}, \mathsf{Inv}(\mathsf{Ext}_x(\mathsf{x}), \mathsf{w}')) = \top$$

Demonstrable completeness (respectively, soundness) requires the existence of a witness for ϕ' (resp., ϕ) when a witness exists for ϕ (resp., ϕ'); this existence is *demonstrated* by an efficient algorithm Ext_w (resp., Inv) that computes the witness.

Correct ZKP compilers are important for two reasons. First, since sequential composition preserves correctness, one can prove a multi-pass compiler is correct pass-by-pass. Second, a correct ZKP compiler from Φ to Φ' can be used to generalize a ZKP for Φ' to one for Φ. We prove both properties in Appendix A.

Theorem 1 (Compiler Composition). *If* Compile$'$ *and* Compile$''$ *are correct, then the compiler* Compose(Compile$'$, Compile$''$) *(Appendix A) is correct.*

Theorem 2 (ZKP Generalization). *(informal) Given a correct ZKP compiler* Compile *from Φ to Φ' and a ZKP for Φ', we can construct a ZKP for Φ.*

5.2   Rule VCs

Recall (Sect. 4) that our language manipulates encodings through five types of encoding rules. We give verification conditions for each type of rule. Intuitively, these capture the correctness of each rule in isolation. Next, we'll show that they imply the correctness of a ZKP compiler that follows our calculus.

Our VCs quantify over valid encodings. That is, they have the form: "for any valid encoding e of term t, ..." We can quantify over an encoding e by making each $t_i \in \mathsf{terms}(e)$ a fresh variable, and quantifying over the t_i. Encoding validity is captured by a predicate $valid(e, t)$, which is defined to be the validity condition in Table 2. Each VC containing encoding variables e implicitly represents a conjunction of instances of that VC, one for each possible tuple of kinds of e, which is fixed for each instance. If a VC contains $valid(e, t)$, the sort of t is constrained to be *compatible* with $\mathsf{kind}(e)$. For a kind and a sort to be compatible, they must occur in the same row of Table 2. We define the equality predicate $equal(e, e')$ as $\bigwedge_i \mathsf{terms}(e)[i] \approx \mathsf{terms}(e')[i]$.

Encoding Uniqueness. First, we require the uniqueness of valid encodings, for any fixed encoding kind. Table 3 shows the VCs that ensure this. Each row is a formula that must be valid, for all compatible encodings and terms. The first two rows ensure that there is a bijection from terms to their valid encodings (in the first row, we consider only instances for which $\mathsf{kind}(e) = \mathsf{kind}(e')$). The function $fromTerm(t, \mathsf{kind}) \to e$ maps a term and an encoding kind to a valid encoding of that kind, and the function $toTerm(e) \to t$ maps a valid encoding to its encoded term. The third and fourth rows ensure that $fromTerm$ and $toTerm$ are correctly defined. We will use $toTerm$ in our proof of calculus soundness (Appendix B) and we will use $fromTerm$ to optimize VCs for faster verification (Sect. 6.1).

Table 3. VCs related to encoding uniqueness.

Property	Condition
valid encoding uniqueness	$(valid(e,t) \wedge valid(e',t)) \rightarrow equal(e,e')$
valid encoding uniqueness	$(valid(e,t) \wedge valid(e,t')) \rightarrow t \approx t'$
fromTerm correctness	$valid(fromTerm(t,\mathsf{kind}),t)$
toTerm correctness	$valid(e,toTerm(e))$

Table 4. VCs for encoding rules.

Rule	Property	Condition
Operator	Sound	$(A \wedge \bigwedge_i valid(e_i,t_i)) \rightarrow valid(e',o(\mathbf{t}))$
$e' \leftarrow r_o(e)$	Complete	$((\bigwedge_i valid(e_i,t_i)) \rightarrow (A \wedge valid(e',o(\mathbf{t})))) \; [F]$
Equality	Sound	$(A \wedge \bigwedge_i valid(e_i,t_i)) \rightarrow (t_1 \approx t_2)$
$r_=(e_1,e_2)$	Complete	$(((t_1 \approx t_2) \wedge \bigwedge_i valid(e_i,t_i)) \rightarrow A) \; [F]$
Conversion	Sound	$(A \wedge valid(e,t)) \rightarrow valid(e',t)$
$e' \leftarrow r_\rightarrow(e)$	Complete	$((valid(e,t)) \rightarrow (A \wedge valid(e',t))) \; [F]$
Variable	Sound $(t \in w)$	$A \rightarrow \exists t'. \; valid(e',t')$
	Sound $(t \in x)$	$(A \rightarrow valid(e',t))[F_x]$
$e' \leftarrow r_v(t)$	Complete	$(A \wedge valid(e',t))[F]$
Constant	—	$valid(e,t)$
$e \leftarrow r_c(t)$		

For an example of the *valid*, *fromTerm*, and *toTerm* functions, consider a Boolean b encoded as an encoding e with kind bit and whose terms consist of a single field element f. Validity is defined as $valid(e,b) = f \approx ite(b,1,0)$, $toTerm(f)$ is defined as $f \approx 1$, and $fromTerm(b,\mathsf{bit})$ is $(b,\mathsf{bit},ite(b,1,0))$.

VCs for Encoding Rules. Table 4 shows our VCs for the rules of Fig. 5. For each rule application, A and F denote, respectively, the assertions and the variable declarations generated when that rule is applied. We explain some of the VCs in detail.

First, consider a rule r_o for operator o applied to inputs $t_1, \ldots, t_k$. The rule takes input encodings $e_1, \ldots, e_k$ and returns an output e'. It is sound if the validity of its inputs and its assertions imply the validity of its output. It is complete if the validity of its inputs implies its assertions and the validity of its output, after substituting fresh variable definitions.

Second, consider a variable rule. Its input is a variable term t, and it returns e', a putative encoding thereof. Note that e' does not actually contain t, though the substitutions in F may bind the fresh variables of e' to functions of t. For the rule to be sound when t is a witness variable $(t \in w)$, the assertions must imply that e' is valid for *some* term t'. For the rule to be sound when t is an instance variable $(t \in x)$, the assertions must imply that e' is valid for t, when the instance variables in e' are replaced with their definition (F_x denotes F, restricted to its declarations of instance variables).[8] For the variable rule to be complete (for an instance or a witness), the assertions and the validity of e' for t must follow from F.

Third, consider a constant rule. Its input is a constant term t, and it returns an encoding e. Recall that the terms of e are always evaluated, yielding e' which only contains constant terms. Thus, correctness depends only on the fact that e is always a valid encoding of the input t. This can be captured with a single VC.

5.3 A Correct Field-Blasting Calculus

Given rules that satisfy these verification conditions, we show that the calculus of Sect. 4.3 is a correct ZKP compiler. The proof is in Appendix B.

Theorem 3 (Correctness). *With rules that satisfy the conditions of Sect. 5.2, the calculus of Sect. 4.3 is demonstrably complete and sound (Def. 1).*

6 Case Study: A Verifiable Field-Blaster for CirC

We implemented and partially verified a field-blaster for CirC [46]. Our implementation is based on a refactoring of CirC's original field blaster to conform to our encoding rules (Sect. 4.2) and consists of ≈850 lines of code (LOC).[9] As described below, **we have (partially) verified our encoding rules**, but trust our calculus (Sect. 4.3, ≈150 LOC) and our flattening implementations (Fig. 2, ≈160 LOC).

While porting rules, **we found 4 bugs in CirC's original field-blaster** (see Appendix G), including a severe soundness bug. Given a ZKP compiled with CirC, the bug allowed a prover to incorrectly compare bit-vectors. The prover, for example, could claim that the unsigned value of 0010 is greater than *or less than* that of 0001. A patch to fix all 4 bugs (in the original field blaster) has been upstreamed, and we are in the process of upstreaming our new field blaster implementation into CirC.

6.1 Verification Evaluation

Our implementation constructs the VCs from Sect. 5.2 and emits them as SMT-LIB (extended with a theory of finite fields [47]). We verify them with cvc5, because it can solve formulas over bit-vectors and prime fields [47]. The verification is partial in that it is bounded in two ways. We set $b \in \mathbb{N}$ to be the maximum bit-width of any bit-vector and $a \in \mathbb{N}$ to be the maximum number of arguments to any n-ary operator. In our evaluation, we used $a = 4$ and $b = 4$. These bounds are small, but they were sufficient to find the bugs mentioned above.

---

[8] The different soundness conditions for instance and witness variables play a key role in the proof of Theorem 3. Essentially: since the condition for instances replaces variables with their definitions, the validity of the encodings of instance variables need not be explicitly enforced in A. This is why some constraints could be omitted in our field-blasting example.(See footnote 5).

[9] Our implementation is in Rust, as is CirC.

Optimizing Completeness VCs. Generally, cvc5 verifies soundness VCs more quickly than completeness VCs. This is surprising at first glance. To see why, consider the soundness (S) and completeness (C) conditions for a conversion rule from e to e' that generates assertions A and definitions F:

$$S \triangleq (A \wedge \mathit{valid}(e, t)) \to \mathit{valid}(e', t) \qquad C \triangleq (\mathit{valid}(e, t) \to (A \wedge \mathit{valid}(e', t)))[F]$$

In both, t is a variable, e contains variables, and there are variables in e' and A that are defined by F. In C, though, some variables are replaced by their definitions in F—which makes the number of variables (and thus the search space)—seem smaller for C than S. Yet, cvc5 is slower on C.

The problem is that, while the field operations in A are standard (e.g., $+$, $\times$, and $=$), the definitions in F use a CirC-IR operator that (once embedded into SMT-LIB) is hard for cvc5 to reason about. That operator, (ff2bv b), takes a prime field element x and returns a bit-vector v. If x's integer representative is less than 2^b, then v's unsigned value is equal to x; otherwise, v is zero.

The ff2bv operator is trivial to evaluate but hard to embed. cvc5's SMT-LIB extension for prime fields only supports $+$, $\times$ and $=$, so no operator can directly relate x to v. Instead, we encode the relationship through b Booleans that represent the bits of v. To test whether $x < 2^b$, we use the polynomial $f(x) = \prod_{i=0}^{2^b-1}(x-i)$, which is zero only on $[0, 2^b - 1]$. The bit-splitting essentially forces cvc5 to guess v's value; further, f's high degree slows down the Gröbner basis computations that form the foundation of cvc5's field solver.

To optimize verification of the completeness VCs, we reason about CirC-IR directly. First, we use the uniqueness of valid encodings and the *fromTerm* function. Since the VC assumes $\mathit{valid}(e, t)$, we know e is equal to $\mathit{fromTerm}(t, \mathsf{kind}(e))$. We use this equality to eliminate e from the completeness VC, leaving:

$$(A \wedge \mathit{valid}(e', t))[F][e \mapsto \mathit{fromTerm}(t, \mathsf{kind}(e))]$$

Since F defines all variables in A and e', the only variable after substitution is t. So, when t is a Boolean or small bit-vector, an exhaustive search is very effective;[10] we implemented such a solver in 56 LOC, using CirC's IR as a library.

For soundness VCs, this approach is less effective. The *fromTerm* substitution still applies, but if F introduces fresh field variables, they are not eliminated and thus, the final formula contains field variables, so exhaustion is infeasible.

Verification Results. We ran our VC verification on machines with Intel Xeon E5-2637 v4 CPUs.[11] Each attempt is limited to one physical core, 8GB memory, and 30 min. Figure 6 shows the number of VCs verified by cvc5 and our exhaustive solver. As expected, the exhaustive solver is effective on completeness VCs for Boolean and bit-vector rules, but ineffective on soundness VCs for rules that introduce fresh field variables. There are four VCs that neither solver verifies

---

[10] So long as the exhaustive solver reasons directly about all CirC-IR operators.

[11] We omit the completeness VCs for ff2bv. See Appendix C.

Type	Prop.	VCs	Verified			Unver.
			cvc5	exhaust	either	
const	—	6	6	5	6	0
conv	C	8	8	8	8	0
conv	S	8	8	4	8	0
eq	C	10	10	9	10	0
eq	S	10	10	9	10	0
op	C	259	247	247	259	0
op	S	263	259	126	259	4
uniq	—	40	40	0	40	0
var	C	12	12	10	12	0
var	S	6	6	0	6	0

Fig. 6. VCs verified by different solvers. 'uniq' denotes the VCs of Table 3; others are from Table 4. 'C' denotes completeness; 'S': soundness.

Metric	Unverified	Verified
Time (s)	27.27	25.05
Mem. (GB)	6.56	6.42
Constraints	559445	559445

Fig. 7. The performance of CirC with the verified and unverified field-blaster. Metrics are summed over the 61 functions in the Z# standard library.

within 30 min: bvadd with ($b = 4$, $a = 4$), and bvmul with ($b = 3$, $a = 4$) and ($b = 4$, $a \geq 3$). Most other VCs verify instantly. In Appendix E, we analyze how VC verification time depends on a and b.

6.2 Performance and Output Quality Evaluation

We compare CirC with our field-baster ("Verified") against CirC with its original field-blaster ("Unverified")[12] on three metrics: compiler runtime, memory usage, and the final R1CS constraint count. Our benchmark set is the standard library for CirC's Z# input language (which extends ZoKrates [16,68] v0.6.2). Our testbed runs Linux with 32GB memory and an AMD Ryzen 2700.

There is no difference in constraints, but the verified field-blaster slightly improves compiler performance: –8% time and –2% memory (Fig. 7). We think that the small improvement is unrelated to the fact that the new field blaster is verified. In Appendix E, we discuss compiler performance further.

7 Discussion

In this work, we present the first automatically verifiable field-blaster. We view the field-blaster as a set of rules; if some (automatically verifiable) conditions hold for each rule, then the field-blaster is correct. We implemented a performant and partially verified field-blaster for CirC, finding 4 bugs along the way.

Our approach has limitations. First, we require the field-blaster to be written as a set of encoding rules. Second, we only verify our rules for bit-vectors of bounded size and operators of bounded arity. Third, we assume that each rule is a pure function: for example, it doesn't return different results depending on

---

[12] After fixing the bugs we found. See Sect. 6.

the time. Future work might avoid the last two limitations through bit-width-independent reasoning [42,43,67] and a DSL (and compiler) for encoding rules. It would also be interesting to extend our approach to: a ZKP with a non-prime field [7,13], a compiler IR with partial or non-deterministic semantics, or a compiler with correctness that depends on computational assumptions.

Acknowledgements. We appreciate the help and guidance of Andres Nötzli, Dan Boneh, and Evan Laufer.

This material is in part based upon work supported by the DARPA SIEVE program and the Simons foundation. Any opinions, findings, and conclusions or recommendations expressed in this report are those of the author(s) and do not necessarily reflect the views of DARPA. It is also funded in part by NSF grant number 2110397 and the Stanford Center for Automated Reasoning.

A   Zero-Knowledge Proofs and Compilers

This appendix is available in the full version of the paper [49].

B   Compiler Correctness Proofs

This appendix is available in the full version of the paper [49].

C   CirC-IR

This appendix is available in the full version of the paper [49].

D   Optimizations to the CirC Field-Blaster

This appendix is available in the full version of the paper [49].

E   Verified Field-Blaster Performance Details

This appendix is available in the full version of the paper [49].

F   Verifier Performance Details

This appendix is available in the full version of the paper [49].

G   Bugs Found in the CirC Field Blaster

This appendix is available in the full version of the paper [49].

References

1. LLVM language reference manual. https://llvm.org/docs/LangRef.html
2. Monero technical specs. https://monerodocs.org/technical-specs/ (2022)
3. Airscript. https://github.com/0xPolygonMiden/air-script
4. Angel, S., Blumberg, A.J., Ioannidis, E., Woods, J.: Efficient representation of numerical optimization problems for SNARKs. In: USENIX Security (2022)
5. Bellés-Muñoz, M., Isabel, M., Muñoz-Tapia, J.L., Rubio, A., Baylina, J.: Circom: a circuit description language for building zero-knowledge applications. IEEE Transactions on Dependable and Secure Computing (2022)
6. Bellman. https://github.com/zkcrypto/bellman
7. Ben-Sasson, E., Bentov, I., Horesh, Y., Riabzev, M.: Scalable zero knowledge with no trusted setup. In: CRYPTO (2019)
8. Bertot, Y., Castéran, P.: Interactive theorem proving and program development: Coq'Art: the calculus of inductive constructions. Springer, Heidelberg (2013). https://doi.org/10.1007/978-3-662-07964-5
9. Blum, M., Feldman, P., Micali, S.: Non-interactive zero-knowledge and its applications. In: STOC (1988)
10. Brown, F., Renner, J., Nötzli, A., Lerner, S., Shacham, H., Stefan, D.: Towards a verified range analysis for JavaScript JITs. In: PLDI (2020)
11. Campanelli, M., Gennaro, R., Goldfeder, S., Nizzardo, L.: Zero-knowledge contingent payments revisited: attacks and payments for services. In: CCS (2017)
12. Chen, E., Zhu, J., Ozdemir, A., Wahby, R.S., Brown, F., Zheng, W.: Silph: a framework for scalable and accurate generation of hybrid MPC protocols (2023)
13. Chiesa, A., Hu, Y., Maller, M., Mishra, P., Vesely, N., Ward, N.: Marlin: preprocessing zkSNARKs with universal and updatable SRS. In: EUROCRYPT (2020)
14. Chin, C., Wu, H., Chu, R., Coglio, A., McCarthy, E., Smith, E.: Leo: a programming language for formally verified, zero-knowledge applications (2021). https://ia.cr/2021/651
15. Cowan, M., Dangwal, D., Alaghi, A., Trippel, C., Lee, V.T., Reagen, B.: Porcupine: a synthesizing compiler for vectorized homomorphic encryption. In: PLDI (2021)
16. Eberhardt, J., Tai, S.: ZoKrates–scalable privacy-preserving off-chain computations. In: IEEE Blockchain (2018)
17. Enderton, H.B.: A mathematical introduction to logic. Elsevier (2001)
18. Fournet, C., Keller, C., Laporte, V.: A certified compiler for verifiable computing. In: CSF (2016)
19. Fox, A., Myreen, M.O., Tan, Y.K., Kumar, R.: Verified compilation of CakeML to multiple machine-code targets. In: CPP (2017)
20. Frankle, J., Park, S., Shaar, D., Goldwasser, S., Weitzner, D.: Practical accountability of secret processes. In: USENIX Security (2018)
21. Goldberg, L., Papini, S., Riabzev, M.: Cairo - a Turing-complete STARK-friendly CPU architecture (2021). https://ia.cr/2021/0163
22. Goldwasser, S., Micali, S., Rackoff, C.: The knowledge complexity of interactive proof-systems. In: STOC (1985)
23. Grubbs, P., Arun, A., Zhang, Y., Bonneau, J., Walfish, M.: Zero-knowledge middleboxes. In: USENIX Security (2022)
24. Hopwood, D., Bowe, S., Hornby, T., Wilcox, N.: Zcash protocol specification. https://raw.githubusercontent.com/zcash/zips/master/protocol/protocol.pdf (2016)

25. Jiang, K., Chait-Roth, D., DeStefano, Z., Walfish, M., Wies, T.: Less is more: refinement proofs for probabilistic proofs. IEEE S&P (2023)
26. Kamara, S., Moataz, T., Park, A., Qin, L.: A decentralized and encrypted national gun registry. In: IEEE S&P (2021)
27. Kaufmann, M., Manolios, P., Moore, J.S.: Computer-aided reasoning: ACL2 case studies, vol. 4. Springer, NY (2013). https://doi.org/10.1007/978-1-4757-3188-0
28. Kosba, A., Papadopoulos, D., Papamanthou, C., Song, D.: MIRAGE: succinct arguments for randomized algorithms with applications to universal zk-SNARKs. In: USENIX Security (2020)
29. Kosba, A., Papamanthou, C., Shi, E.: xJsnark: A framework for efficient verifiable computation. In: IEEE S&P (2018)
30. Kothapalli, A., Parno, B.: Algebraic reductions of knowledge (2022). https://ia.cr/2022/009
31. Kumar, R., Myreen, M.O., Norrish, M., Owens, S.: CakeML: A verified implementation of ML. In: POPL (2014)
32. Kundu, S., Tatlock, Z., Lerner, S.: Proving optimizations correct using parameterized program equivalence. In: PLDI (2009)
33. Lattner, C., Adve, V.: LLVM: a compilation framework for lifelong program analysis & transformation. In: CGO (2004)
34. Lerner, S., Millstein, T., Chambers, C.: Automatically proving the correctness of compiler optimizations. In: PLDI (2003)
35. Lerner, S., Millstein, T., Rice, E., Chambers, C.: Automated soundness proofs for dataflow analyses and transformations via local rules. In: POPL (2005)
36. Leroy, X.: Formal verification of a realistic compiler. Commun. ACM **52**(7), 107–115 (2009)
37. Leroy, X.: A formally verified compiler back-end. J. Autom. Reason. **43**(4), 363–446 (2009)
38. Lopes, N.P., Lee, J., Hur, C.K., Liu, Z., Regehr, J.: Alive2: bounded translation validation for LLVM. In: PLDI (2021)
39. Lopes, N.P., Menendez, D., Nagarakatte, S., Regehr, J.: Provably correct peephole optimizations with Alive. In: PLDI (2015)
40. Mullen, E., Zuniga, D., Tatlock, Z., Grossman, D.: Verified peephole optimizations for CompCert. In: PLDI (2016)
41. Necula, G.C.: Translation validation for an optimizing compiler. In: PLDI (2000)
42. Niemetz, A., Preiner, M., Reynolds, A., Zohar, Y., Barrett, C., Tinelli, C.: Towards bit-width-independent proofs in SMT solvers. In: CADE (2019)
43. Niemetz, A., Preiner, M., Reynolds, A., Zohar, Y., Barrett, C., Tinelli, C.: Towards satisfiability modulo parametric bit-vectors. J. Autom. Reason. **65**(7), 1001–1025 (2021)
44. Nipkow, T., Wenzel, M., Paulson, L.C.: Isabelle/HOL: a proof assistant for higher-order logic. Springer, Heidelberg (2002). https://doi.org/10.1007/3-540-45949-9
45. Noir. https://noir-lang.github.io/book/index.html
46. Ozdemir, A., Brown, F., Wahby, R.S.: CirC: Compiler infrastructure for proof systems, software verification, and more. In: IEEE S&P (2022)
47. Ozdemir, A., Kremer, G., Tinelli, C., Barrett, C.: Satisfiability modulo finite fields. In: submission (2022). https://ia.cr/2023/091
48. Ozdemir, A., Wahby, R., Whitehat, B., Boneh, D.: Scaling verifiable computation using efficient set accumulators. In: USENIX Security (2020)
49. Ozdemir, A., Wahby, R.S., Brown, F., Barrett, C.: Bounded verification for finite-field-blasting. Cryptology ePrint Archive (2023) (Full version)

50. Parno, B., Howell, J., Gentry, C., Raykova, M.: Pinocchio: nearly practical verifiable computation. Commun. ACM **59**(2), 103–112 (2016)
51. Pnueli, A., Siegel, M., Singerman, E.: Translation validation. In: TACAS (1998)
52. Ranise, S., Tinelli, C., Barrett, C.: SMT fixed size bit-vectors theory. https://smtlib.cs.uiowa.edu/theories-FixedSizeBitVectors.shtml (2017)
53. Sasson, E.B., Chiesa, A., Garman, C., Green, M., Miers, I., Tromer, E., Virza, M.: Zerocash: decentralized anonymous payments from Bitcoin. In: IEEE S&P (2014)
54. Setty, S., Braun, B., Vu, V., Blumberg, A.J., Parno, B., Walfish, M.: Resolving the conflict between generality and plausibility in verified computation. In: EuroSys (2013)
55. Snarky. https://github.com/o1-labs/snarky
56. Stewart, G., Beringer, L., Cuellar, S., Appel, A.W.: Compositional CompCert. In: POPL (2015)
57. Tan, Y.K., Myreen, M.O., Kumar, R., Fox, A., Owens, S., Norrish, M.: The verified CakeML compiler backend. J. Funct. Programm. **29**, E2 (2019)
58. Tao, R., et al.: Giallar: push-button verification for the Qiskit quantum compiler. In: PLDI (2022)
59. Thaler, J.: Proofs, Arguments, and Zero-Knowledge. Manuscript (2022)
60. The Qiskit authors and maintainers: Qiskit: an open-source framework for quantum computing (2021). https://doi.org/10.5281/zenodo.2573505. The Qiskit maintainers request that the full list of Qiskit contributors be included in any citation. Regretfully, we cannot comply, as the list is two pages long
61. Tinelli, C.: SMT core theory. https://smtlib.cs.uiowa.edu/theories-Core.shtml (2015)
62. Viand, A., Jattke, P., Hithnawi, A.: SoK: fully homomorphic encryption compilers. In: IEEE S&P (2021)
63. Wahby, R.S., Setty, S., Howald, M., Ren, Z., Blumberg, A.J., Walfish, M.: Efficient RAM and control flow in verifiable outsourced computation. In: NDSS (2015)
64. Walfish, M., Blumberg, A.J.: Verifying computations without reexecuting them. Commun. ACM **58**(2), 74–84 (2015)
65. Wang, F.: Ecne: automated verification of ZK circuits (2022). https://0xparc.org/blog/ecne
66. Zinc. https://zinc.matterlabs.dev/
67. Zohar, Y., et al.: Bit-precise reasoning via Int-blasting. In: CADE (2022)
68. ZoKrates. https://zokrates.github.io/

Formally Verified EVM Block-Optimizations

Elvira Albert[1], Samir Genaim[1], Daniel Kirchner[2,3],
and Enrique Martin-Martin[1](✉)

[1] Complutense University of Madrid, Madrid, Spain
{elvira,samir.genaim}@fdi.ucm.es, emartinm@ucm.es
[2] Ethereum Foundation, Zug, Switzerland
daniel.kirchner@ethereum.org
[3] University of Bamberg, Bamberg, Germany

Abstract. The efficiency and the security of *smart contracts* are their two fundamental properties, but might come at odds: the use of optimizers to enhance efficiency may introduce bugs and compromise security. Our focus is on **EVM** (Ethereum Virtual Machine) *block-optimizations*, which enhance the efficiency of jump-free blocks of opcodes by eliminating, reordering and even changing the original opcodes. We reconcile efficiency and security by providing the verification technology to formally prove the correctness of **EVM** block-optimizations on smart contracts using the Coq proof assistant. This amounts to the challenging problem of proving semantic equivalence of two blocks of **EVM** instructions, which is realized by means of three novel Coq components: a symbolic execution engine which can execute an **EVM** block and produce a symbolic state; a number of simplification lemmas which transform a symbolic state into an equivalent one; and a checker of symbolic states to compare the symbolic states produced for the two **EVM** blocks under comparison.

Artifact: https://doi.org/10.5281/zenodo.7863483

Keywords: Coq · Ethereum Virtual Machine · Smart Contracts · Optimization · Theorem Proving

1 Introduction

In many contexts, security requirements are critical and formal verification today plays an essential role to verify/certify these requirements. One of such contexts is the blockchain, in which software bugs on *smart contracts* have already caused several high profile attacks (e.g., [14–17,30,37]). There is hence huge interest and investment in guaranteeing their correctness, e.g., Certora [1], Veridise [2], apriorit [3], Consensys [4], Dedaub [5] are companies that offer smart contract audits using formal methods' technology. In this context, efficiency is of high relevance as well, as deploying and executing smart contracts has a cost (in the corresponding cryptocurrency). Hence, optimization tools for smart contracts have

This work was funded partially by the Ethereum Foundation under Grant ID FY22-0698 and the Spanish MCI, AEI and FEDER (EU) project PID2021-122830OB-C41.

C. Enea and A. Lal (Eds.): CAV 2023, LNCS 13966, pp. 176–189, 2023.
https://doi.org/10.1007/978-3-031-37709-9_9

emerged in the last few years (e.g., ebso [29], SYRUP [12], GASOL [11], the solc optimizer [9]). Unfortunately, there is a dichotomy of efficiency and correctness: as optimizers can be rather complex tools (not formally verified), they might introduce bugs and potential users might be reluctant of optimizing their code. This has a number of disruptive consequences: owners will pay more to deploy (non-optimized) smart contracts; clients will pay more to run transactions every time they are executed; the blockchain will accept less transactions as they are more costly. Rather than accepting such a dichotomy, our work tries to overturn it by developing a fully automated formal verification tool for proving the correctness of the optimized code.

The general problem addressed by the paper is formally verifying semantic equivalence of two bytecode programs, an initial code I and an optimization of it O –what is considered a great challenge in formal verification. For our purpose, we will narrow down the problem by (1) considering fragments of code that are *jump-free* (i.e., they do not have loops nor branching), and by (2) considering only stack EVM operations (memory/storage opcodes and other blockchain-specific opcodes are not considered). These assumptions are realistic as working on jump-free blocks still allows proving correctness for optimizers that work at the level of the blocks of the CFG (e.g., super-optimizers [11,12,29] and many rule-based optimizations performed by the Solidity compiler [9]). Considering only stack optimizations, and leaving out memory and storage simplifications and blockchain-specific bytecodes, does not restrict the considered programs, as we work at the smaller block partitions induced by the not handled operations found in the block (splitting into the block before and after). Even in our narrowed setting, the problem is challenging as block-optimizations can include any elimination, reorder and even change of the original bytecodes.

Consider the next block I, taken from a real smart contract [8]. The GASOL optimizer [11], relying on the commutativity of OR and AND, optimizes it to O:

```
I: PUSH2 0x100 PUSH1 0x1 PUSH1 0xa8 SHL SUB NOT SWAP1 SWAP2 AND PUSH1 0x8 SWAP2 SWAP1
   SWAP2 SHL PUSH2 0x100 PUSH1 0x1 PUSH1 0xa8 SHL SUB AND OR PUSH1 0x5
O: PUSH2 0x100 PUSH1 0x1 PUSH1 0xa8 SHL SUB DUP1 NOT SWAP2 PUSH1 0x8 SHL AND
   SWAP2 AND OR PUSH1 0x5
```

This saves 11 bytes because (1) the expression SUB(SHL(168,1),256) –that corresponds to "PUSH2 0x100 PUSH1 0x1 PUSH1 0xa8 SHL SUB" – is computed twice; but it can be duplicated if the stack operations are properly made saving 8 bytes; and (2) two SWAPs are needed instead of 5, saving 3 more bytes.

This paper proposes a technique, and a corresponding tool, to automatically verify the correctness of EVM block-optimizations (as those above) on smart contracts using the Coq proof assistant. This amounts to the challenging problem of proving semantic equivalence of two blocks of EVM instructions, which is realized by means of three main components which constitute our main contributions (all formalized and proven correct in Coq): (1) a symbolic interpreter in Coq to symbolically execute the EVM blocks I and O and produce resulting symbolic states S_I and S_O, (2) a series of simplification rules, which transform S_I and S_O into equivalent ones S'_I and S'_0, (3) a checker of symbolic states in Coq to decide if two symbolic states S'_I and S'_0 are semantically equivalent.

2 Background

The Ethereum VM (EVM) [38] is a stack-based VM with a word size of 256-bits that is used to run the smart contracts on the Ethereum blockchain. The EVM has the following categories of bytecodes: *(1)* Stack operations; *(2)* Arithmetic operations; *(3)* Comparison and bitwise logic operations; *(4)* Memory and storage manipulation; *(5)* Control flow operations; *(6)* Blockchain-specific opcodes, e.g., block and transaction environment information, compute hash, calls, etc. The first three types of opcodes are handled within our verifier, and handling optimizations on opcodes of types 4-6 is discussed in Sect. 6.

The focus of our work is on optimizers that perform optimizations only at the level of the blocks of the CFG (i.e., intra-block optimizations). A well-known example is the technique called *super-optimization* [26] which, given a loop-free sequence of instructions searches for the optimal sequence of instructions that is semantically equivalent to the original one and has optimal cost (for the considered criteria). This technique dates back to 1987 and has had a revival [25,31] thanks to the availability of SMT solvers that are able to do the search efficiently. We distinguish two types of possible intra-block optimizations: *(i)* Rule-based optimizations which consist in applying arithmetic/bitwise simplifications like ADD(X,0)=X or NOT(NOT(X))=X (see a complete list of these rules in App. A in [10]); and *(ii)* Stack-data optimizations which consist in searching for alternative stack operations that lead to an output stack with exactly the same data.

Example 1 (Intra-block optimizations). The rule-based optimization *(i)* X+0 → X simplifies the block "PUSH1 0x5, PUSH1 0x0, ADD" to "PUSH1 0x5". On the other hand, stack-data optimizations *(ii)* can optimize to "ADD, DUP1" the block "DUP2, DUP2, ADD, SWAP2, ADD", as duplicating the operands and repeating the ADD operation is the same as duplicating the result. Unlike rule-based optimization, stack-data optimizations cannot be expressed as simple patterns that can be easily recognized.

The first type of optimizations are applied by the optimizer integrated in the Solidity compiler [9] as rule transformations, and they are also applied by EVM optimizers in different ways. ebso [29] encodes the semantics of arithmetic and bitwise operations in the SMT encoding so that the SMT solver searches for these optimizations together with those of type (ii). Instead, SYRUP [12] and GASOL [11] apply rule-based optimizations in a pre-phase and leave to the SMT solver only the search for the second type of optimizations. This classification of optimizations is also relevant for our approach as (i) will require integrating and proving all simplification rules correct (Sect. 4.2), while (ii) are implicit within the symbolic execution (Sect. 4.1). A block of EVM code that has been subject to optimizations of the two types above is in principle "provable" using our tool.

There is not much work yet on formalizing the EVM semantics in Coq. One of the most developed approaches is [22], which is a definition of the EVM semantics in the Lem [28] language that can be exported to interactive theorem provers like Isabelle/HOL or Coq. According to the comparison in [21], this implementation of EVM "is executable and passes all of the VM tests except for those dealing with more complicated intercontract execution". However, we have decided not to use it for our checker due to three reasons: *(a)* the generated Coq code from Lem definitions is not "necessarily idiomatic" and thus it would generate a very complex EVM formalization in Coq that would make theorems harder to state and prove; *(b)* the author of the Lem definition states that "the Coq version of the EVM definition is highly experimental"; and *(c)* it is not kept up-to-date.

The other most developed implementation of the EVM semantics in Coq that we have found is [23]. It supports all the basic EVM bytecodes we consider in our checker, and looked promising as our departing point. The implementation uses *Bedrock Bit Vectors (bbv)* [7] for representing the EVM 256-bit values, as we use as well. It is not a full formalization of the EVM because it does not support calling or creation of smart contracts, but provides a function that simulates consequent application of opcodes to the given execution state, call info and Ethereum state mocks. The latter two pieces of information would add complexity and are not needed for our purpose. Therefore, we decided to develop our own EVM formalization in Coq (presented in Sect. 3) which builds upon some ideas of [23], but introduces only the minimal elements we need to handle the instructions supported by the checker. This way the proofs will be simpler and conciser.

3   EVM Semantics in Coq

Our EVM formalization is a concrete interpreter that executes a block of EVM instructions. For representing EVM words we use EVMWord that stands for the type "word 256" of the bbv library [7]. For representing instructions we use:

```
Inductive stack_op_instr :=          Inductive instr :=
  | ADD                                | PUSH (size: nat) (w: EVMWord)
  | MUL                                | POP
  | SUB                                | DUP (pos: nat)
  | DIV                                | SWAP (pos: nat)
  | NOT.                               | StackInstr (label: stack_op_instr).
```

Type stack_oper_instr defines instructions that operate only on the stack, i.e., each pops a fixed number of elements and pushes a single value back (see App. B in [10] for the full list). Type instr encapsulates this category together with the stack manipulation instruction (PUSH, etc.). The type block stands for "list instr".

To keep the framework general, and simplify the proofs, the actual implementation of instructions from stack_op_instr are provided to the interpreter as input. For this, we use a map that associates instructions to implementations:

```
Inductive stack_operation :=
  | StackOp (comm: bool) (n : nat) (f : list EVMWord → option EVMWord).
```

```
Definition stack_op_map := map stack_oper_instr stack_operation.
```

The type `stack_operation` defines an implementation for a given operation: `comm` indicates if the operation is commutative; `n` is the number of stack elements to be removed and passed to the operation; and `f` is the actual implementation. The type `stack_op_map` maps keys of type `stack_oper_instr` to values of type `stack_operation`. Suppose `evm_add` and `evm_mul` are implementations of `ADD` and `MUL` (see App. C in [10]), the actual stack operations map is constructed as:

```
Definition evm_stack_opm : stack_op_map :=
  ADD |→i StackOp true 2 evm_add; MUL |→i StackOp true 2 evm_mul; ...
```

In addition, we require the operations in the map to be valid with respect to the properties that they claim to satisfy (e.g., commutativity), and that when applied to the right number of arguments they should succeed (i.e., do not return `None`). We refer to this property as `valid_stack_op_map`.

An execution state (or simply state) includes only a stack (currently we support only stack operations) which is as a list of `EVMWord`, and the interpreter is a function that takes a block, an initial state, and a stack operations map, and iteratively executes each of the block's instructions:

```
Definition stack := list EVMWord.
Inductive state :=
  | ExState (stk: stack).
Fixpoint concr_int (p: block) (st: state) (ops: stack_op_map): option state := ...
```

The result can be either `Some st` or `None` in case of an error which are caused only due to stack overflow. In particular, we are currently not taking into account the amount of *gas* needed to execute the block. Our implementation follows the EVM semantics [38], considering the simplicity of the supported operations, the concrete interpreter is a minimal trusted computing base. In the future, we plan to test it using the EVM test suite.

4   Formal Verification of EVM-Optimizations in Coq

Two jump-free blocks `p1` and `p2` are equivalent *wrt.* to an initial stack size `k`, if for any initial stack of size `k`, the executions of `p1` and `p2` succeed and lead to the same state. Formally:

```
Definition sem_eq_blocks: (p1 p2: block) (k: nat) (ops: stack_op_map) : Prop :=
  ∀ (in_st: state) (in_stk: stack),
    get_stack in_st = in_stk → length in_stk = k →
      ∃ (out_st : state), concr_int p1 in_st ops = Some out_st ∧
                          concr_int p2 in_st ops = Some out_st
```

Note that when `concr_int` returns `None` for both `p1` and `p2`, they are not considered equivalent because in the general case they can fail due to different reasons. Note also that EVM operations are deterministic, so if `concr_int` evaluates to a sucessful final state `out_st` it will be unique.

An EVM block equivalence checker is a function that takes two blocks, the size of the initial stack, and returns `true`/`false`. Providing the size `k` of the initial stack is not a limitation of the checker, as this information is statically known in advance. Note that the maximum stack size in EVM is bounded by 1024, and that if the execution (of one or both blocks) *wrt.* to this concrete initial stack size leads to under/over stack overflow they cannot be reported equivalent. The soundness of the equivalence checker is stated as follows:

```
Definition eq_block_chkr_snd (chkr : block → block → nat → bool) : Prop :=
  ∀ (p1 p2: block) (k: nat),
    chkr p1 p2 k = true → sem_equiv_blocks p1 p2 k evm_stack_opm
```

Given two blocks p_1 and p_2, checking their equivalence (in Coq) has the following components: *(i) Symbolic Execution (Sect.* 4.1*):* it is based on an interpreter that symbolically executes a block, *wrt.* an initial symbolic stack of size k, and generates a final symbolic stack. It is applied on both p_1 and p_2 to generate their corresponding symbolic output states S_1 and S_2. *(ii) Rule optimizations (Sect.* 4.2*):* it is based on simplification rules that are often applied by program optimizers, which rewrite symbolic states to equivalent "simpler" ones. This step simplifies S_1 and S_2 to S'_1 and S'_2. *(iii) Equivalence Checker (Sect.* 4.3*):* it receives the simplified symbolic states, and determines if they are equivalent for any concrete instantiation of the symbolic input stack. It takes into account, for example, the fact that some stack operations are commutative.

4.1 EVM Symbolic Execution in Coq

Symbolic execution takes an initial symbolic state (i.e., stack) $[s_0, \dots, s_k]$, a block, and a map of stack operations, and generates a final symbolic state (i.e., stack) with symbolic expressions, e.g., $[5+s_0, s_1, s_2]$, representing the corresponding computations. In order to incorporate rule-based optimizations in a simple and efficient way, we want to avoid compound expressions such as $5 + (s_0 * s_1)$, and instead use temporal fresh variables together with a corresponding map that assigns them to simpler expressions. E.g, the stack $[5 + (s_0 * s_1), s_2]$ would be represented as a tuple $([e_1, s_2], \{e_1 \mapsto 5 + e_0, e_0 \mapsto s_0 * s_1\})$ where e_i are fresh variables. To achieve this, we define the *symbolic stack* as a list of elements that can be numeric constant values, initial stack variables or fresh variables:

```
Inductive sstack_val : Type :=
  | Val (val: EVMWord) | InStackVar (var: nat) | FreshVar (var: nat).
Definition sstack := list sstack_val.
```

and the map that assigns meaning to fresh variables is a list that maps each fresh variable to a `sstack_val`, or to a compound expression:

```
Inductive smap_val : Type :=
  | SymBasicVal (val: sstack_val)
  | SymOp (opcode : stack_op_instr) (args : list sstack_val).
Definition smap  := list (nat*smap_val).
```

Finally, a symbolic state is defined as a `SymState` term where k is the size of the initial stack, `maxid` is the maximum id used for fresh variables (kept for efficiency), `sstk` is a symbolic stack, and `m` is the map of fresh variables.

```
Inductive sstate : Type := | SymState (k maxid: nat) (sstk: sstack) (m: smap).
```

Example 2 (Symbolic execution). Given $p_1 \equiv$ "PUSH1 0x5 SWAP2 MUL ADD" and $p_2 \equiv$ "PUSH1 0x0 ADD MUL PUSH1 0x5 ADD", symbolically executing them with k=3 we obtain the symbolic states represented by sst1 $\equiv ([e'_1, s_2], \{e'_1 \mapsto e'_0 + 5, e'_0 \mapsto s_1 * s_0\})$ and sst2 $\equiv ([e_2, s_2], \{e_2 \mapsto 5 + e_1, e_1 \mapsto e_0 * s_1, e_0 \mapsto 0 + s_0\})$.

Note that we impose some requirements on symbolic states to be valid. E.g., for any element $i \mapsto v$ of the fresh variables map, all fresh variables that appear in v have smaller indices than i. We refer to these requirements as valid_sstate.

Given a symbolic (final) state and a concrete initial state, we can convert the symbolic state into a concrete one by replacing each s_i by its corresponding value, and evaluating the corresponding expressions (following their definition in the stack operations map). We have a function to perform this evaluation that takes the stack operations map as input:

```
Definition eval_sstate (in_st: state) (sst: sstate) (ops : stack_op_map)
  : option state := ...
```

Our symbolic execution engine is a function that takes the size of the initial stack, a block, a map of stack operations, and generates a symbolic final state:

```
Definition sym_exec (p: block) (k: nat) (ops: stack_op_map) : option sstate := ...
```

Note that we do not pass an initial symbolic state, but rather we construct it inside using k. Also, the result can be None in case of failure (the causes are the same as those of conc_interpreter).

Soundness of sym_exec means that whenever it generates a symbolic state as a result, then the concrete execution from any stack of size k will succeed and produce a final state that agrees with the generated symbolic state:

```
Theorem sym_exec_snd:
  ∀ (p: block) (k: nat) (ops: stack_op_map) (sst: sstate),
      valid_stack_op_map ops →
      sym_exec p k ops = Some sst →
      valid_sstate sst ∧
      ∀ (in_st : state) (in_stk : stack),
        get_stack in_st = in_stk →
        length in_stk = k →
          ∃ (out_st : state),
            concr_int p in_st ops = Some out_st ∧
            eval_sstate in_st sst ops = Some out_st
```

4.2   Simplification Rules

To capture equivalence of programs that have been optimized according to "rule simplifications" (type (i) in Sect. 2) we need to include the same type of simplifications (see App. A in [10]) in our framework. Without this, we will capture EVM-blocks equivalence only for "data-stack equivalence optimizations" (type (ii) in Sect. 2).

An *optimization function* takes as input a symbolic state, and tries to simplify it to an equivalent state. E.g, if a symbolic state includes $e_i \mapsto s_3 + 0$, we can replace it by $e_i \mapsto s_3$. The following is the type used for optimization functions:

```
Definition optim := sstate → sstate*bool.
```

Optimization functions never fail, i.e., in the worst case they return the same symbolic state. This is why the returned value includes a Boolean to indicate if any optimization has been applied, which is useful when composing optimizations later. The soundness of an optimization function can be stated as follows:

```
Definition optim_snd (opt: optim) : Prop :=
  forall (sst: sstate) (sst': sstate) (b: bool),
    valid_sstate sst → opt sst = (sst', b) →
    (valid_sstate sst' ∧
       forall (st st': state), eval_sstate st sst evm_stack_opm = Some st' →
                               eval_sstate st sst' evm_stack_opm = Some st').
```

We have implemented and proven correct the most-used simplification rules (see App. A in [10]). E.g., there is an optimization function `optimize_add_zero` that rewrites expressions of the form $E + 0$ or $0 + E$ to E, and its soundness theorem is:

```
Theorem optimize_add_zero_snd: optim_snd optimize_add_zero.
```

Example 3. Consider again the blocks of Example 2. Using `optimize_add_zero` we can rewrite sst2 to $\text{sst2}' \equiv ([e_2, s_2], \{e_2 \mapsto 5 + e_1, e_1 \mapsto e_0 * s_1, e_0 \mapsto s_0\})$, by replacing $e_0 \mapsto 0 + s_0$ by $e_0 \mapsto s_0$.

Note that the checker can be easily extended with new optimization functions, simply by providing a corresponding implementation and a soundness proof. Optimization functions can be combined to define *simplification strategies*, which are also functions of type `optim`. E.g., assuming that we have *basic* optimization functions $f_1,...,f_n$: *(1)* Apply $f_1,...,f_n$ iteratively such that in iteration i function f_i is applied as many times as it can be applied. *(2)* Apply each f_i once in some order and repeat the process as many times as it can be applied. *(3)* Use the simplifications that were used by the optimizer (it needs to pass these hints).

4.3   Stacks Equivalence Modulo Commutativity

We say that two symbolic stacks sst1 and sst2 are equivalent if for every possible initial concrete state st they evaluate to the same state. Formally:

```
Definition eq_sstate (sst1 sst2: sstate) (ops : stack_op_map) : Prop :=
  ∀ (st: state), eval_sstate st sst1 ops = eval_sstate st sst2 ops.
```

However, this notion of semantic equivalence is not computable in general, and thus we provide an effective procedure to determine such equivalence by checking that at every position of the stack both contain "similar" expressions:

```
Definition eq_sstate_chkr (sst1 sst2: sstate) (ops : stack_op_map) : bool := ...
```

To determine if two stack elements are similar, we follow their definition in the map if needed until we obtain a value that is not a fresh variable, and then either (1) both are equal constant values; (2) both are equal initial stack variables; or (3) both correspond to the same instruction and their arguments are (recursively) equivalent (taking into account the commutativity of operations). E.g., the stack elements (viewed as terms) $DIV(MUL(s_0,ADD(s_1,s_2)),0x16)$ and $DIV(MUL(ADD(s_2,s1),s_0),0x16)$ are considered equivalent because the operations ADD and MUL are commutative.

Example 4. `eq_sstate_chkr` fails to prove equivalence of `sst1` and `sst2` of Example 2, because, when comparing e_2 and e'_1, it will eventually check if $0+s_0$ and s_0 are equivalent. It fails because the comparison is rather "syntactic". However, it succeeds when comparing `sst1` and `sst2`' (Example 3), which is a simplification of `sst2`.

This procedure is an approximation of the semantic equivalence, and it can produce false negatives if two symbolic states are equivalent but are expressed with different syntactic constructions. However, it is sound:

```
Theorem eq_sstate_chkr_snd:
 ∀ (sst1 sst2: sstate) (ops : stack_op_map),
   valid_stack_op_map ops → valid_sstate sst1 → valid_sstate sst2 →
       eq_sstate_chkr sst1 sst2 ops = true → eq_sstate sst1 sst2 ops.
```

Note that we require the stack operations map to be valid in order to guarantee that the operations declared commutative in `ops` are indeed commutative. In order to reduce the number of false negatives, the simplification rules presented in Sect. 4.2 are very important to rewrite symbolic states into closer syntactic shapes that can be detected by `eq_sstate_chkr`.

Finally, given all the pieces developed above, we can now define the block equivalence checker as follows:

```
Definition evm_eq_block_chkr (opt: optim) (p1 p2: block) (k: nat) : bool :=
match sym_exec p1 k evm_stack_opm with
| None ⇒ false
| Some sst1 ⇒
    match sym_exec p2 k evm_stack_opm with
    | None ⇒ false
    | Some sst2 ⇒ let (sst2', _) := opt sst1 in
                  let (sst1', _) := opt sst2 in
                     eq_sstate_chkr sst1' sst2' evm_stack_opm
    end
end.
```

It symbolically executes `p1` and `p2`, simplifies the resulting symbolic states by applying optimization `opt`, and finally calls `eq_sstate_chkr` to check if the states are equivalent. Note that it is important to apply the optimization rules to both blocks, as the checker might apply optimization rules that were not applied by the external optimizer. This would lead to equivalent symbolic states with different shapes that will not be detected by the symbolic state equivalence checker.

Table 1. Summary of experiments using `GASOL`.

	SIMP	#blocks	CHKR Yes	CHKR Time	CHKR* Yes	CHKR* Time		SIMP	#blocks	CHKR Yes	CHKR Time	CHKR* Yes	CHKR* Time
GAS	×	36624	36624	2.60	36624	11.76	SIZE	×	35754	35754	2.57	35754	12.59
	✓	43228	27149	4.69	43109	14.09		✓	32192	31488	2.50	31798	12.17

The above checker is sound when `opt` is sound:

```
Theorem evm_eq_block_chkr_snd:
  ∀ (opt: optim), optim_snd opt → eq_block_chkr_snd (evm_eq_block_chkr opt)
```

5   Implementation and Experimental Evaluation

The different components of the tool have been implemented in Coq v8.15.2, together with complete proofs of all the theoretical results (more than 180 proofs in ~7000 lines of Coq code). The source code, executables and benchmarks can be found at https://github.com/costa-group/forves/tree/stack-only and the artifact at https://doi.org/10.5281/zenodo.7863483. The tool currently includes 15 simplification rules (see App. A in [10]). We have tried our implementation on the outcome of two optimization tools: (1) the standalone `GASOL` optimizer and, (2) the optimizer integrated within the official Solidity compiler `solc`. For (1), we have already fully automated the communication among the optimizer and checker and have been able to perform a thorough experimental evaluation. While in (2), the communication is more difficult to automate because the CFG of the original program can change after optimization, i.e., it can make cross-block optimization. Hence, in this case, we have needed human intervention to disable intra-block optimizations and obtain the blocks for the comparison (we plan to automate this usage in the future). For evaluating (2) we have used as benchmarks 1,280 blocks extracted from the smart contracts in the semantic test suite of the `solc` compiler [6], succeeding to prove equivalence on 1,045 out of them. We have checked that the fails are due to the use of optimization rules not yet implemented by us. As these blocks are obtained from the test suite of the official `solc` Solidity compiler, optimized using the `solc` optimizer, the good results on this set suggest the validity can be generalized to other optimizers. Now we describe in detail the experimental evaluation on (1) for which we have used as benchmarks 147,798 blocks belonging to 96 smart contracts (see App. D in [10]).

`GASOL` allows enabling/disabling the application of simplification rules and choosing an optimization criteria: GAS consumption or bytes SIZE (of the code) [11]; combining these parameters we obtain 4 different sets of pairs-of-blocks to be verified by our tool. From these blocks, we consider only those that were actually optimized by `GASOL`, i.e., the optimized version is syntactically different from the original one. In all the cases, the average size of blocks is 8 instructions. Table 1 summarizes our results, where each row corresponds to one setting out of the 4 mentioned above: *Column 1* includes the optimization criteria; *Column 2* indicates if rule simplifications were applied by GASOL; *Column 3* indicates how many pairs-of-blocks were checked; *Columns 4-7* report the results of applying 2 versions of the checker, namely CHKR corresponds to the checker that only compares symbolic states and CHKR^s corresponds to the checker that also applies all the implemented rule optimizations iteratively as much as they can be applied (see Sect. 4.2). For each we report the number of instances it proved equivalent and the total runtime in seconds. The experiments have been performed on a machine with an Intel i7-4790 at 3.60 GHz and 16GB of RAM.

For sets in which GASOL does not apply simplification rules (marked with ×), both CHKR and CHKR^s succeed to prove equivalence of all blocks. When simplifications are applied (marked with ✓), CHKR^s succeeds in 99% of the blocks while CHKR ranges from 63% for GAS to 99% for SIZE. This difference is due to the fact that GASOL requires the application of rules to optimize more blocks *wrt.* GAS ($\sim 37\%$ of the total) than *wrt.* SIZE ($\sim 1\%$). Moreover, all the blocks that CHKR^s cannot prove equivalent have been optimized by GASOL using rules which are not currently implemented in the checker, so we predict a success rate of 100% when all the rules in App. A in [10] are integrated. Regarding time, CHKR^s is 3–5 times slower than CHKR because of the overhead of applying rule optimizations, but it is still very efficient (all 147.798 instances are checked in 50.61 seconds). As a final comment, thanks to the checker we found a bug in the parsing component of GASOL, that treated the SGT bytecode as GT. The bug was directly reported to the GASOL developers and is already fixed [19].

6   Conclusions, Related and Future Work

Our work provides the first tool able to formally verify the equivalence of jump-free EVM blocks and has required the development of all components within the verification framework. The implementation is not tied to any specific tool and could be easily integrated within any optimization tool. Ongoing work focuses on handling memory and storage optimizations. This extension needs to support the execution of memory/storage operations at the level of the concrete interpreter, and design an efficient data structure to represent symbolic memory/storage. Full handling of blockchain-specific opcodes is straightforward, it only requires adding the corresponding implementations to the stack operations map evm_stack_opm. A more ambitious direction for future work is to handle cross-block optimizations.

There are two approaches to verify program optimizations, (1) verify the correctness of the optimizations and develop a *verified tool*, e.g., this is the case of optimizations within the CompCert certified compiler [24] and a good number of optimizations that have been formally verified in Coq [13,18,27,32,33], (2) or use a *translation validation* approach [20,34–36] in which rather than verifying the tool, each of the compiled/optimized programs are formally checked to be correct using a verified checker. We argue that translation validation [34] is the most appropriate approach for verifying EVM optimizations because: (i) EVM compilers (together with their built-in optimizers) are continuously evolving to adjust to modifications in the rather new blockchain programming languages, (ii) existing EVM optimizers use external components such as SMT solvers to search for the optimized code and verifying an SMT solver would require a daunting effort, (iii) we aim at generality of our tool rather than restricting ourselves to a specific optimizer and, as already explained, the design of our checker has been done having generality and extensibility in mind, so that new optimizations can be easily incorporated. Finally, it is worth mentioning the KEVM framework [21], which in principle could be the basis for verifying optimizations as well. However, we have chosen to develop it in Coq due to its maturity.

References

1. https://www.certora.com/
2. https://veridise.com/
3. https://www.apriorit.com/
4. https://consensys.net/
5. https://www.dedaub.com/
6. https://github.com/ethereum/solidity/tree/develop/test/libsolidity/ semanticTests/externalContracts
7. Bedrock Bit Vectors (bbv) (2018). https://github.com/mit-plv/bbv
8. PausableERC20 Contract (2020). https://etherscan.io/address/ 0x32E6C34Cd57087aBBD59B5A4AECC4cB495924356
9. The solc optimizer (2021). https://docs.soliditylang.org/en/v0.8.7/internals/ optimizer.html
10. Albert, E., Genaim, S., Kirchner, D., Martin-Martin, E.: Formally Verified EVM Block-Optimizations (Extended Version). https://costa.fdi.ucm.es/papers/costa/ AlbertGKMM23_extended.pdf
11. Albert, E., Gordillo, P., Hernández-Cerezo, A., Rubio, A.: A Max-SMT super-optimizer for EVM handling memory and storage. In: TACAS 2022. LNCS, vol. 13243, pp. 201–219. Springer, Cham (2022). https://doi.org/10.1007/978-3-030-99524-9_11
12. Albert, E., Gordillo, P., Rubio, A., Schett, M.A.: Synthesis of super-optimized smart contracts using max-SMT. In: Lahiri, S.K., Wang, C. (eds.) CAV 2020. LNCS, vol. 12224, pp. 177–200. Springer, Cham (2020). https://doi.org/10.1007/ 978-3-030-53288-8_10
13. Barrière, A., Blazy, S., Flückiger, O., Pichardie, D., Vitek, J.: Formally verified speculation and deoptimization in a JIT compiler. Proc. ACM Program. Lang. 5(POPL), 1–26 (2021). https://doi.org/10.1145/3434327
14. Bernardi, T., et al.: Preventing reentrancy bugs - another use case for formal verification (2020). https://www.certora.com/blog/reentrancy.html
15. Bizga, A.: A hackers' dream payday: Ledf.me and uniswap lose $25 million worth of cryptocurrency (2020). https://securityboulevard.com/2020/04/a-hackers-dream-payday-ledf-me-and-uniswap-lose-25-million-worth-of-cryptocurrency/. [Online; accessed 11-May-2020]
16. Buterin, V.: CRITICAL UPDATE Re: DAO vulnerability (2016). https://blog. ethereum.org/2016/06/17/critical-update-re-dao-vulnerability/. Accessed 2-July-2017

17. Daian, P.: Analysis of the DAO exploit (2016). http://hackingdistributed.com/2016/06/18/analysis-of-the-dao-exploit/

18. Demange, D., Pichardie, D., Stefanesco, L.: Verifying fast and sparse SSA-based optimizations in Coq. In: Franke, B. (ed.) CC 2015. LNCS, vol. 9031, pp. 233–252. Springer, Heidelberg (2015). https://doi.org/10.1007/978-3-662-46663-6_12

19. elexcere: SGT and GT order when parsing. https://github.com/costa-group/gasol-optimizer/commit/fd78e126c23f192ed6c54aea713b5c94d3c943f5

20. Gourdin, L., Boulmé, S.: Certifying assembly optimizations in Coq by symbolic execution with hash-consing, p. 2 (2021)

21. Hildenbrandt, E., et al.: KEVM: a complete formal semantics of the ethereum virtual machine. In: 31st IEEE Computer Security Foundations Symposium, CSF 2018, Oxford, United Kingdom, July 9–12, 2018, pp. 204–217. IEEE Computer Society (2018). https://doi.org/10.1109/CSF.2018.00022

22. Hirai, Y.: Defining the ethereum virtual machine for interactive theorem provers. In: Brenner, M., Rohloff, K., Bonneau, J., Miller, A., Ryan, P.Y.A., Teague, V., Bracciali, A., Sala, M., Pintore, F., Jakobsson, M. (eds.) FC 2017. LNCS, vol. 10323, pp. 520–535. Springer, Cham (2017). https://doi.org/10.1007/978-3-319-70278-0_33

23. ivan71kmayshan27: Coq formalisation of the Ethereum Virtual Machine (WIP) (2020). https://github.com/ivan71kmayshan27/coq-evm

24. Leroy, X.: Formal verification of a realistic compiler. Commun. ACM 52(7), 107–115 (2009). https://doi.org/10.1145/1538788.1538814

25. Lopes, N.P., Menendez, D., Nagarakatte, S., Regehr, J.: Practical verification of peephole optimizations with alive. Commun. ACM 61(2), 84–91 (2018). https://doi.org/10.1145/3166064

26. Massalin, H.: Superoptimizer - a look at the smallest program. In: Proceedings of the Second International Conference on Architectural Support for Programming Languages and Operating Systems (ASPLOS II), pp. 122–126 (1987). https://dl.acm.org/citation.cfm?id=36194

27. Monniaux, D., Six, C.: Simple, light, yet formally verified, global common subexpression elimination and loop-invariant code motion. In: Henkel, J., Liu, X. (eds.) LCTES '21: 22nd ACM SIGPLAN/SIGBED International Conference on Languages, Compilers, and Tools for Embedded Systems, Virtual Event, Canada, 22 June, 2021, pp. 85–96. ACM (2021). https://doi.org/10.1145/3461648.3463850

28. Mulligan, D.P., Owens, S., Gray, K.E., Ridge, T., Sewell, P.: Lem: reusable engineering of real-world semantics. ACM SIGPLAN Notices 49(9), 175–188 (2014)

29. Nagele, J., Schett, M.A.: Blockchain superoptimizer. In: Preproceedings of 29th International Symposium on Logic-based Program Synthesis and Transformation (LOPSTR 2019) (2019). https://arxiv.org/abs/2005.05912

30. Palmer, D.: Spankchain loses $40k in hack due to smart contract bug (2018). https://www.coindesk.com/spankchain-loses-40k-in-hack-due-to-smart-contract-bug. Accessed 11 May 2020

31. Sasnauskas, R., et al.: Souper: A Synthesizing Superoptimizer. arXiv:1711.04422 [cs], November 2017

32. Six, C., Boulmé, S., Monniaux, D.: Certified and efficient instruction scheduling: application to interlocked VLIW processors. Proc. ACM Program. Lang. 4(OOPSLA), 129:1–129:29 (2020). https://doi.org/10.1145/3428197

33. Six, C., Gourdin, L., Boulmé, S., Monniaux, D., Fasse, J., Nardino, N.: Formally verified superblock scheduling. In: Popescu, A., Zdancewic, S. (eds.) CPP '22: 11th ACM SIGPLAN International Conference on Certified Programs and Proofs, Philadelphia, PA, USA, January 17–18, 2022, pp. 40–54. ACM (2022). https://doi.org/10.1145/3497775.3503679

34. Tristan, J., Leroy, X.: Formal verification of translation validators: a case study on instruction scheduling optimizations. In: Necula, G.C., Wadler, P. (eds.) Proceedings of the 35th ACM SIGPLAN-SIGACT Symposium on Principles of Programming Languages, POPL 2008, San Francisco, California, USA, January 7–12, 2008, pp. 17–27. ACM (2008). https://doi.org/10.1145/1328438.1328444

35. Tristan, J., Leroy, X.: Verified validation of lazy code motion. In: Hind, M., Diwan, A. (eds.) Proceedings of the 2009 ACM SIGPLAN Conference on Programming Language Design and Implementation, PLDI 2009, Dublin, Ireland, June 15–21, 2009, pp. 316–326. ACM (2009). https://doi.org/10.1145/1542476.1542512

36. Tristan, J., Leroy, X.: A simple, verified validator for software pipelining. In: Hermenegildo, M.V., Palsberg, J. (eds.) Proceedings of the 37th ACM SIGPLAN-SIGACT Symposium on Principles of Programming Languages, POPL 2010, Madrid, Spain, January 17–23, 2010, pp. 83–92. ACM (2010). https://doi.org/10.1145/1706299.1706311

37. Turley, C.: imBTC uniswap pool drained for $300k in ETH (2020). https://defirate.com/imbtc-uniswap-hack/. Accessed 11 May 2020

38. Wood, G.: Ethereum: A secure decentralised generalised transaction ledger (Berlin version 8fea825 - 2022-08-22) (2022)

SR-SFLL: Structurally Robust Stripped Functionality Logic Locking

Gourav Takhar[✉][ID] and Subhajit Roy[ID]

Indian Institute of Technology Kanpur,
Kanpur, India
{tgourav,subhajit}@cse.iitk.ac.in

Abstract. Logic locking was designed to be a formidable barrier to IP piracy: given a logic design, logic locking modifies the logic design such that the circuit operates correctly only if operated with the "correct" *secret* key. However, strong attacks (like SAT-based attacks) soon exposed the weakness of this defense. *Stripped functionality logic locking* (SFLL) was recently proposed as a strong variant of logic locking. SFLL was designed to be resilient against SAT attacks, which was the bane of conventional logic locking techniques. However, all SFLL-protected designs share certain "circuit patterns" that expose them to new attacks that employ *structural analysis* of the locked circuits.

In this work, we propose a new methodology—*Structurally Robust SFLL* ($\mathcal{SR}$-SFLL)—that uses the power of modern satisfiability and synthesis engines to produce semantically equivalent circuits that are resilient against such structural attacks. On our benchmarks, $\mathcal{SR}$-SFLL was able to defend all circuit instances against both structural and SAT attacks, while all of them were broken when defended using SFLL. Further, we show that designing such defenses is challenging: we design a variant of our proposal, $\mathcal{SR}$-SFLL(0), that is also robust against existing structural attacks but succumbs to a new attack, SYNTAK (also proposed in this work). SYNTAK uses synthesis technology to compile $\mathcal{SR}$-SFLL(0) locked circuits into semantically equivalent variants that have structural vulnerabilities. $\mathcal{SR}$-SFLL, however, remains resilient to SYNTAK.

Keywords: Logic Locking · SFLL · Program Synthesis

1 Introduction

Semiconductor design houses often outsource the fabrication of the integrated circuits (IC) to third-party foundries [17]. This allows effective use of the fabrication equipment and facilities at the foundry, while the design houses can concentrate solely on the design. Though this separation of concerns provides attractive cost benefits, it also opens up certain threats: malicious agents at a foundry may now fabricate illegal copies of the ICs that can be sold in the gray market leading to serious loss in revenue for the design house.

Logic locking was proposed as an effective mechanism to combat such intellectual property (IP) threats. Logic locking modifies the original IC in a manner

© The Author(s) 2023
C. Enea and A. Lal (Eds.): CAV 2023, LNCS 13966, pp. 190–212, 2023.
https://doi.org/10.1007/978-3-031-37709-9_10

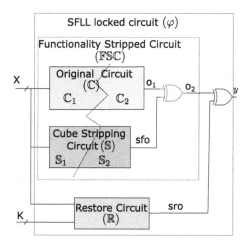

Fig. 1. SFLL-HD locked circuit (φ); $\mathbb{C}$ is the (unprotected) original circuit. (Color figure online)

that the circuit operates correctly only after it is activated with a *secret* key. This *secret* key is loaded into tamperproof memory by the design house post-fabrication. However, soon powerful attacks, especially those involving SAT solver [23,26,34], were invented to thwart this defense. Since then, more powerful defenses were proposed that were resistant to such SAT attacks. One such SAT-resilient attack that has gained a lot of popularity is Stripped Functionality Logic Locking (SFLL) [44].

SFLL operates by using the *secret* key to identify a set of inputs as *protected patterns*—the circuit is forced to produce incorrect results if the input matches any of these protected patterns. The *cube stripping circuit* (see Fig. 1) is responsible for matching the inputs to the protected patterns. An additional *restore circuit* is used to restore the correct functionality for the protected patterns. The circuit does not operate correctly with an incorrect key as the restore circuit, then, identifies a different set of patterns to be restored. Though quite potent against SAT attacks, attackers soon identified certain unique structural patterns in the design of SFLL that could be leveraged to build attacks via *structural analysis* [4,32,40].

In this work, we propose a scheme, *Structurally Robust Stripped Functionality Logic Locking* ($\mathcal{SR}$-SFLL), to defend against such structural analysis. $\mathcal{SR}$-SFLL uses efficient *synthesis* [33] machinery powered by modern SAT solvers to ensure that certain structural security constraints are met that ensures its resilience against the structural attacks.

$\mathcal{SR}$-SFLL operates as follows: (1) identify a "cut" of the original design $\mathbb{C}$ to break the design into two segments $\mathbb{C}_1$ and $\mathbb{C}_2$ (see Fig. 1), and (2) introduce a carefully synthesized perturbation unit $\mathbb{Q}$ between $\mathbb{C}_1$ and $\mathbb{C}_2$ (see Fig. 2b). As the perturbation unit does not have any specific structural signature and is hidden deep within the original design, our scheme is no more vulnerable to

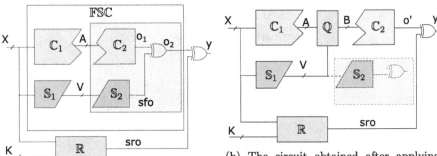

(a) SFLL locked circuit where the high-lighted part of the circuit is input for synthesis tool.

(b) The circuit obtained after applying $\mathcal{SR}$-SFLL. The highlighted circuit is the removed part of the original SFLL locked circuit.

Fig. 2. Transformation of SFLL locked circuit to $\mathcal{SR}$-SFLL locked circuit.

Table 1. Attack resilience of logic locking techniques: ✓ (resp. ✗) represents resilience (resp. vulnerability) to attacks.

Attack	Anti-SAT	SARLock	SFLL	$\mathcal{SR}$-SFLL(0)	$\mathcal{SR}$-SFLL
SAT [34]	✓	✓	✓	✓	✓
Removal [43]	✗	✗	✓	✓	✓
AppSAT [30]	✗	✗	✓	✓	✓
Structural [4,32,40]	✗	✗	✗	✓	✓
SYNTAK (this paper)	✗	✗	✗	✗	✓

attacks by structural analysis. Further, the location of the "cut" is unknown to the attacker and the perturbation unit misses any structural pattern, making it challenging to apply other attacks like removal attack [43].

We argue that designing such a defense scheme is non-trivial: we show a version ($\mathcal{SR}$-SFLL(0)) of $\mathcal{SR}$-SFLL that is also resistant to structural attacks. However, we could design a novel structural attack algorithm, SYN-TAK, that breaks $\mathcal{SR}$-SFLL(0): in our experiments, SYNTAK breaks 71.25% of $\mathcal{SR}$-SFLL(0) locked benchmark instances. Our attack algorithm, SYNTAK, is a novel attack that also uses synthesis machinery to compile an existing circuit to a semantically equivalent one that is amenable to structural analysis. However, $\mathcal{SR}$-SFLL is robust against SYNTAK.

Table 1 summarizes the resiliency of various logic locking techniques, with the attacks listed for the rows and the defenses in the columns. For a table cell (A, D), we use ✗ to show that attack A breaks defense D (in most cases); the mark ✓ shows that defense D is robust against attack A. The attack and defense techniques marked with a red background are proposed in this paper. As $\mathcal{SR}$-SFLL locked circuits remain semantically equivalent to the SFLL locked circuits, $\mathcal{SR}$-SFLL locked circuit provides the same security against the SAT-based [34], removal [43], and AppSAT [30] attacks.

We evaluated $\mathcal{SR}$-SFLL(0), $\mathcal{SR}$-SFLL, and SYNTAK on 80 benchmarks from the *ISCAS'85* and *MCNC* benchmark suites with different numbers of key inputs and cube stripping functionalities. Our experiments showed that circuits locked by $\mathcal{SR}$-SFLL are robust to structural attacks—none of the $\mathcal{SR}$-SFLL locked designs could be broken by existing structural attacks (like SFLLUnlock, FALL, and GNNUnlock), or by our SYNTAK (also proposed in this work). While the structural attacks failed to recover the structural patterns altogether, SYNTAK could not break the $\mathcal{SR}$-SFLL even over two days for circuits that were locked in less than an hour.

$\mathcal{SR}$-SFLL provides asymmetric advantage to the defender over the attacker on multiple counts: the secret key K used to lock the circuit, knowledge of the *secret cut* where $\mathbb{FSC}$ is partitioned, and a much harder synthesis problem (on attacks using SYNTAK).

We make the following contributions to this work:

– We propose, Structurally Robust Stripped Functionality Logic Locking ($\mathcal{SR}$-SFLL), a new defense against IP threats. In contrast, to SFLL, $\mathcal{SR}$-SFLL is not vulnerable to attacks via structural analysis;
– We propose a new attack, SYNTAK, and show its potency at breaking alternate structural attack resistant designs ($\mathcal{SR}$-SFLL(0)) that use similar ideas as $\mathcal{SR}$-SFLL but are not designed carefully. This shows the non-triviality of designing new defenses, and in particular, $\mathcal{SR}$-SFLL;
– We evaluate $\mathcal{SR}$-SFLL(0), and $\mathcal{SR}$-SFLL on circuits from two benchmark suites against existing structural attacks as well as SYNTAK. Our experimental results show that $\mathcal{SR}$-SFLL is not vulnerable to structural analysis or SYNTAK and the overheads of the technique are low (about 0.18% on average over SFLL).

2   Background

2.1   Stripped Functionality Logic Locking (SFLL)

Figure 1 shows a stripped functionality logic locked circuit, φ. The original circuit ($\mathbb{C}$) takes a set of input bits, X, and produces an output bit, o_1. The SFLL locked design, φ, consumes input bits, X, and a *secret key* (bits) K to output y.

The core idea of SFLL is to create a *functionality stripped circuit* ($\mathbb{FSC}$) that would produce incorrect output for certain *protected patterns*. The *cube stripping circuit* ($\mathbb{S}$) recognizes the protected patterns, and makes the signal sfo high if any of them is encountered; an XOR gate flips the output of the original circuit (o_1) for these protected patterns (i.e. when sfo is high). Hence, o_2 is the correct output for inputs not in the protected patterns, but the complement of it for the protected patterns.

The correct functionality is re-established using the *restore circuit* ($\mathbb{R}$). The restore circuit accepts (secret) key bits K along with the input X to produce the signal sro; if the correct key K is supplied, sro is high if and only if the input is amongst the protected bits. The cube stripping circuit ($\mathbb{S}$) is functionally equivalent to $\mathbb{R}$ but uses a hardcoded key value. Hence, the restore unit restores the correct output for the protected inputs (via an XOR of o_2 and sro). Hence, the locked circuit now works correctly if the correct key is applied (i.e. the key K supplied to $\mathbb{R}$ matches the hardcoded key in $\mathbb{S}$).

While many possible choices exist for a function that identifies protected patterns of inputs based on a key, the *hamming distance* was found to be an interesting choice [44]. The corresponding variant of SFLL, known as SFLL-HD, identifies an input (X) as a protected pattern if it has a certain hamming distance (h) from the key (K).

2.2   SFLL Attacks

SFLL is robust to all known attacks on (conventional) logic locking [4]. However, subsequently, many structural attacks were proposed that break SFLL. These attacks use one or more of the structural properties exhibited by SFLL implementations [4, 40]:

1. As the sfo signal is required to invert the signal from the original circuit $\mathbb{C}$ (for protected patterns), which, then, has to be reverted by the restore circuit, the sfo signal has to be on the boundary of FSC and the restore unit;
2. sfo does not depend on the key inputs;
3. sfo has *low activity*, i.e. it is 0 most of the time;
4. $\mathbb{S}$ and $\mathbb{R}$ can be removed from the circuit to restore the functionality of the original circuit.

All the following attacks assume that they know the hamming distance (h) used to lock the circuit.

SFLLUnlock. SFLLUnlock [40] uses the first and the second structural properties (see above) to identify a few signals that may be sfo (referred to as *candidate* signals). Next, for each of the candidates, the attack uses the following technique: it uses SAT solver to extract an input such that the candidate signal is 1; if the candidate signal is indeed sfo, this input must be a protected pattern (which has a hamming distance of h with the correct key). Then, it attempts to identify the correct key as follows:

- use a sequence of bit-flips to identify the bits that are different than the correct key using the properties of hamming distance;
- set up a system of equations to find the unknown key that must have a hamming distance of h from the inferred protected patterns.

The inferred key is, finally, validated using a working circuit as an oracle.

Functional Analysis Attacks on Logic Locking (FALL). The first step of FALL [32] is to identify a set of candidate signals that may be the output of the cube stripping circuit i.e. sfo. FALL achieves this by exploiting the first and second vulnerabilities of SFLL. To finalize if a signal is sfo (among these candidate signals), FALL derives a set of lemmas that exploit the functional properties of hamming distance. FALL proposes three algorithms based on these lemmas for a specific range of hamming distance values. For example, the AnalyzeUnateness algorithm is only applicable when $h = 0$, Hamming2D is applicable when $h \leq |K|/4$, and SlidingWindow is for larger hamming distances.

GNNUnlock. GNNUnlock [4] automates the removal of cube stripping circuit and restore circuit from the locked circuit to obtain the original circuit. For their analysis, the circuit is transformed into a graph representation where the nodes of the graph represent the gates, and the edges represent the wires. Each node in the graph is associated with a feature vector that contains information that describes its characteristics (in-degree, out-degree, type of gate of the node, whether the node is connected to key input (K), circuit input (X), or circuit output (Y), type of gates appearing in the neighborhood on the node, etc.).

GNNUnlock uses graph neural networks [45] to train over the nodes of the graph to classify the nodes belonging to the original circuit $(\mathbb{C})$, cube stripping circuit $(\mathbb{S})$, or restore circuit $(\mathbb{R})$. The final step is to remove the nodes classified as part of $\mathbb{S}$ and $\mathbb{R}$ from the locked circuit obtaining the original circuit $\mathbb{C}$.

2.3   Analysis of the Structural Attacks on SFLL

FALL and SFLLUnlock are dependent on finding the output of cube stripping circuit sfo. Hence, hiding/removing sfo from the locked circuit will ensure robustness against such attacks. GNNUnlock works by removing the cube stripping circuit and restore circuit from the SFLL locked circuit. Hence, removing/hiding a part or whole of the cube stripping circuit from the locked design makes the locked design robust to such attacks.

3   Overview

3.1   Preliminaries

Attack Model. We assume that the attacker has access to a functional circuit (which can be used as an *oracle*) and knows the hamming distance (h).

Graph Representation of Circuit. We work with the circuit in And Inverter Graph (AIG) format. An AIG consists of two inputs AND gates and NOT gates. We construct a graph G from the circuit in AIG format as follows: the gates in the circuit map to nodes in G. A wire (or signal) connecting gates map to edges on the graph. The input and output signals are marked as special nodes.

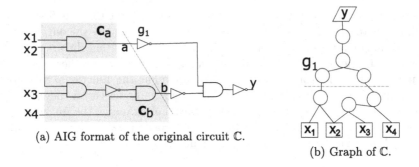

(a) AIG format of the original circuit $\mathbb{C}$.

(b) Graph of $\mathbb{C}$.

Fig. 3. An example of circuit $\mathbb{C}$ and its corresponding graph representation.

If not otherwise specified, we construct the graph of a circuit with the node representing the final output signal as the start node (we assume a single output bit in this paper for simplicity). Figure 3b shows the graph of the circuit in Fig. 3a.

The *distance* between two nodes (say g_1 and y in Fig. 3b) is the (minimum) number of edges in the path(s) from nodes g_1 to y (which is 3, in this case). We define the *depth*, d, of a node n as the maximum distance from the start node (y in Fig. 3b) of the graph to n.

We define a *cut* on graph G as a partitioning of nodes into two disjoint (connected) subsets such that the inputs and outputs belong to distinct partitions. A cut is defined by a *cut-set*, a selection of edges (which are said to *cross* a cut) such that its endpoints are in distinct partitions. We define the *depth of cut* as the maximum amongst the depths of the nodes in the subset containing the start node. In the rest of the paper, we refer to *cut on a circuit* to refer to the cut on the underlying graph. The dotted red lines show a cut at depth 3 in Fig. 3.

Notations. We show combinational circuits with n inputs X and m outputs Y as boolean functions $Y \leftrightarrow \mathbb{C}(X)$, where X is an n-bit vector $(x_1, x_2, \ldots, x_n)$, and Y is an m-bit vector $(y_1, y_2, \ldots, y_m)$. We also use the functional notation, $\mathbb{C}(X)$, to denote the output of the circuit $\mathbb{C}$, i.e. the signal Y. We use capital letters to denote bit-vectors and small letters to denote individual bits. We use $\oplus$ to denote the XOR gate and $\circ$ to denote function (or circuit) composition.

We use blackboard-bold capital letters for circuits (like $\mathbb{C}$). We use φ for complete SFLL locked designs and $\widehat{\varphi}$ for complete $\mathcal{SR}$-SFLL(0) or $\mathcal{SR}$-SFLL locked designs. We use subscripts to denote sub-parts of a circuit. For example, if we use $\mathbb{C}$ to denote the circuit shown in Fig. 3a, we use $\mathbb{C}_a$ and $\mathbb{C}_b$ to denote the subcircuits with outputs a (red block) and b (blue block).

3.2   Approach

Recall that the known structural attacks on SFLL exploit the structural characteristics of sfo (see Sect. 2.2). Our defense techniques attempt to synthesize

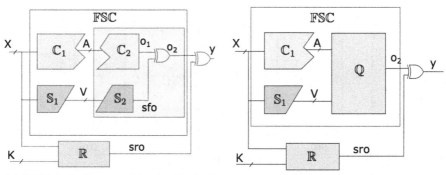

(a) SFLL locked circuit (blue highlighted part is input for synthesis).

(b) $\mathcal{SR}$-SFLL(0) locked circuit ($\mathbb{Q}$ is synthesized).

Fig. 4. Transformation of SFLL locked circuit to $\mathcal{SR}$-SFLL(0) locked circuit. (Color figure online)

a circuit that is semantically equivalent to the original circuit but misses these prominent structural characteristics that make structural attacks feasible.

$\mathcal{SR}$-SFLL(0). $\mathcal{SR}$-SFLL(0) identifies a cut on the FSC, through both the original circuit ($\mathbb{C}$) and the cube stripping circuit ($\mathbb{S}$), as shown by the red-dotted line in Fig. 1, separating the inputs (X) and the output (o_2) of the FSC. The cut-set is marked by the wires $\{A, V\}$ (as shown in Fig. 4a).

Next, it synthesizes a perturbation unit $\mathbb{Q}$ (as shown in Fig. 4b) such that it ensures the following conditions:

- $\mathbb{Q}$ is semantically equivalent to the removed circuit, i.e. $\mathbb{C}_2 \oplus \mathbb{S}_2$;
- No wire in $\mathbb{Q}$ is semantically equivalent to the output of $\mathbb{S}_2$ (i.e. sfo).

The first condition ensures *soundness*, that is the functioning of the new circuit is the same as that of the SFLL locked circuit. The second condition ensures *security* as sfo is not present in the new design, and hence, the new design misses all the structural characteristics (see Sect. 2.2) that made SFLL vulnerable to attacks.

SYNTAK. $\mathcal{SR}$-SFLL(0) is robust to existing attacks as reverse engineering using the sfo signal is not possible anymore. However, in contrast to existing attacks that attempt to reverse engineer an existing locked circuit, what if we synthesize an alternate, semantically equivalent circuit that has a structure amenable to reverse engineering? Our novel attack employs a similar strategy.

The attack attempts to recover an alternate locked design that exposes the XOR gate G_{xor} (as shown in Fig. 5b), in which case it becomes easy to identify the sfo signal—it must be one of i or j. SYNTAK, thus, side-steps the challenge of reverse engineering the $\mathcal{SR}$-SFLL(0) locked circuit with missing sfo by, instead, resynthesizing *another* locked circuit that has an easily identifiable sfo signal.

This algorithm proceeds as follows:

- cut the FSC of $\mathcal{SR}$-SFLL(0) locked circuit into FSC_1 and FSC_2;

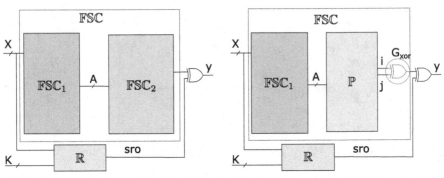

(a) FSC prtitioned into FSC_1 and FSC_2; FSC_2 is given to the synthesis tool.

(b) The circuit returned by SYNTAK. $\mathbb{P}$ is the synthesized circuit.

Fig. 5. SYNTAK on $\mathcal{SR}$-SFLL(0) locked circuit.

– synthesize a new circuit $\mathbb{P}_i \oplus \mathbb{P}_j$ that is semantic equivalent to FSC_2.

With sfo clearly identifiable, the existing SFLL attacks now become feasible.

However, this attack may only succeed if the identified cut is such that FSC_2 contains the whole of $\mathbb{Q}$. Hence, the attacker may have to "guess" different cuts (e.g. by progressively increasing the depth of the cut) till the attack succeeds. We say that the attack succeeds if any of the existing attacks are able to break the defense with the identified sfo signal in the resynthesized circuit.

The attack is made easier by the fact that it is not required to select a cut that *exactly* isolates $\mathbb{Q}$. The attack will still succeed even if some portion of $\mathbb{C}_1$ and $\mathbb{S}_1$ enters FSC_2 (see Fig. 7b). However, the synthesis of $\mathbb{P}_i \oplus \mathbb{P}_j$ becomes increasingly expensive with the increasing size of FSC_2.

Further, even with the "right" cut, not all synthesis candidates may yield a signal semantically equivalent to sfo. Hence, the attacker needs to correctly guess the cut as well as the correct synthesis candidate for a successful attack. However, our experiments demonstrate that even with these uncertainties, SYNTAK is able to break $\mathcal{SR}$-SFLL(0) in 71.25% of cases.

$\mathcal{SR}$-**SFLL.** The primary reason why SYNTAK breaks $\mathcal{SR}$-SFLL(0) is that we are able to synthesize a new circuit $\mathbb{P}_i \oplus \mathbb{P}_j$ such that there are two XOR gates at the *end of the circuit*. If instead, a new circuit that is synthesized introduces the functionality of $\mathbb{S}_2$ in the *middle* of $\mathbb{C}$, SYNTAK would not have been feasible.

Figure 2b shows our improved design for the SR-SFLL locked circuit. Instead of resynthesizing the circuits $\mathbb{C}_2$ and $\mathbb{S}_2$, we place a *perturbation unit* ($\mathbb{Q}$) in between $\mathbb{C}_1$ and $\mathbb{C}_2$. The perturbation unit is made to operate semantically equivalent to the original SFLL locked circuit. The shaded portion, consisting of $\mathbb{S}_2$ (that produces sfo) and one of the XOR gates, is eliminated from the design.

As the attacker is unaware of the location of the perturbation unit, and as the perturbation unit is *not at the end* of the circuit, the attacker's task gets more challenging: the attacker needs to synthesize a new circuit at the end of the

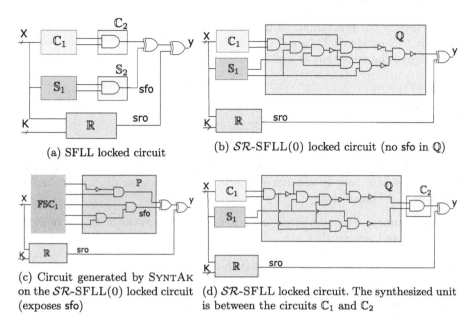

(a) SFLL locked circuit

(b) $\mathcal{SR}$-SFLL(0) locked circuit (no sfo in $\mathbb{Q}$)

(c) Circuit generated by SYNTAK on the $\mathcal{SR}$-SFLL(0) locked circuit (exposes sfo)

(d) $\mathcal{SR}$-SFLL locked circuit. The synthesized unit is between the circuits $\mathbb{C}_1$ and $\mathbb{C}_2$

Fig. 6. Illustration of SFLL, $\mathcal{SR}$-SFLL(0), and $\mathcal{SR}$-SFLL locked circuits along with SYNTAK on $\mathcal{SR}$-SFLL(0)

design with an XOR gate (that would provide access to sfo) that re-establishes the functionality of *both* $\mathbb{S}_2$ and $\mathbb{C}_2$. On the other hand, the defender only has to synthesize $\mathbb{Q}$ to re-establish the functionality of $\mathbb{S}_2$.

$\mathcal{SR}$-SFLL is scalable to large circuits. The scalability of $\mathcal{SR}$-SFLL depends on the depth of the cut, as the complexity of our synthesis problem only depends on the circuit that is subjected to (semantically equivalent) rewriting ($\mathbb{C}_2$ and $\mathbb{S}2$ in Fig. 2b). Hence, the size of the base circuit has no impact on the scalability of SR-SFLL.

Example. Figure 6a shows the SFLL locked version of a circuit. The $\mathcal{SR}$-SFLL(0) locked version is shown in Fig. 6b: we can see that the sfo signal (available in the SFLL locked circuit) is not available in the $\mathcal{SR}$-SFLL(0) locked circuit anymore; hence, it is robust to structural attacks. After applying SYNTAK (Fig. 6c), SYNTAK could recover the sfo signal in the synthesized circuit. Finally, Fig. 6d shows the $\mathcal{SR}$-SFLL locked circuit: it is structurally robust (does not include sfo) and does not succumb to SYNTAK.

$\mathcal{SR}$-SFLL provides a stronger asymmetric advantage versus $\mathcal{SR}$-SFLL(0): in $\mathcal{SR}$-SFLL(0), both the attack and the defense need to resynthesize the functionalities of $\mathbb{C}_2$ and $\mathbb{S}_2$ within $\mathbb{Q}$. This prevents the defense from taking deep cuts for $\mathbb{FSC}_2$ to keep the task of synthesizing $\mathbb{Q}$ feasible. Hence, $\mathcal{SR}$-SFLL(0) only holds the advantage of knowing the secret "cut". On the other hand, $\mathcal{SR}$-SFLL only needs to synthesize the functionalities of $\mathbb{S}_2$ while the attacker would need to resynthesize the functionalities of *both* $\mathbb{C}_2$ and $\mathbb{S}_2$ to recover sfo, making the synthesis task overly challenging. This gives $\mathcal{SR}$-SFLL a dual advantage of the knowledge of the secret cut as well as an asymmetric advantage in the synthesis task.

4 $\mathcal{SR}$-SFLL

4.1   Problem Statement

Given an SFLL locked circuit $\varphi(X, K)$ (where X is the input to the circuit and K is the key-bits used in the circuit), synthesize a structurally robust locked circuit $\widehat{\varphi}(X, K)$, such that:

(correctness) The altered circuit is semantically equivalent to the original SFLL locked circuit, that is,

$$\forall X. \, \forall K. \, \varphi(X, K) = \widehat{\varphi}(X, K) \tag{1}$$

(security) There does not exist any signal, z, in the altered circuit that is equivalent to sfo in φ; that is,

$$\forall z. \, \exists X. \varphi_{\mathsf{sfo}}(X) \neq \widehat{\varphi}_z(X) \tag{2}$$

The first condition ensures that functionality is preserved, that is, the synthesized circuit $\widehat{\varphi}$ preserves the properties of the input SFLL locked circuit φ. The second condition ensures that structural patterns that were available to attackers in SFLL, made available through the sfo signal, are not available in $\widehat{\varphi}$.

4.2   Intuition: $\mathcal{SR}$-SFLL

The current synthesis tools do not scale up to the above synthesis task for the whole locked circuit $\widehat{\varphi}$ (unless the locked circuit is very small). Hence, a straightforward implementation of the above equations is not feasible.

Instead, we construct the circuit $\widehat{\varphi}$ by synthesizing a "small" circuit $\mathbb{Q}$ that can be introduced *within* the original circuit $\mathbb{C}$, with $\mathbb{Q} \circ \mathbb{C}_2$ preserving the functionality of $\mathbb{S}_2 \oplus \mathbb{C}_2$.

We use the following (simplified) description to provide the necessary intuition. Let the functionality of the original circuit (i.e. $\mathbb{C}$) be denoted as $f(X)$, where X are the circuit inputs. Then, let the stripped functionality circuit (i.e. $\mathbb{S}$ in Fig. 1) be denoted as g, where g is a boolean function that returns true if and only if it detects the protected input patterns. The functionality of the circuit φ_{o_2} in Fig. 1 can then be represented as:

$$\varphi_{o_2} = (f \oplus g)(X) = \begin{cases} f(X) & \text{if } g(X) = 0 \\ \neg f(X) & \text{if } g(X) = 1 \end{cases} \tag{3}$$

We "cut" (or partition) f into two functions f_1 and f_2, such that $f = f_1 \circ f_2$. Then, we synthesize a perturbation unit ($\mathbb{Q}$), with functional definition h, such that:

Algorithm 1: $\mathcal{SR}$-SFLL

---

1 *Input* : $\mathbb{C}, \lambda$;
2 $\mathbb{S}, \mathbb{R} \leftarrow \text{SFLL}(\mathbb{C})$;
3 $\mathbb{C}_1, \mathbb{C}_2, \mathbb{S}_1, \mathbb{S}_2 \leftarrow \text{CUT}(\{\mathbb{C}, \mathbb{S}\}, \lambda)$;
4 $\mathbb{Q} \leftarrow \text{SYNTHESIZE}(\mathbb{C}_2, \mathbb{S}_2)$;
5 **if** $\mathbb{Q} == \perp$ **then**
6 $\quad$ | $\quad$ **return** $\perp$
7 **end**
8 $\hat{\varphi} \leftarrow \text{ASSEMBLE}(\mathbb{C}_1, \mathbb{C}_2, \mathbb{S}_1, \mathbb{R}, \mathbb{Q})$;
9 **return** $\hat{\varphi}(X, K)$;

$$(f_1 \circ h \circ f_2)(X) = \varphi_{o_2} = (f \oplus g)(X) = \begin{cases} f(X) & \text{if } g(X) = 0 \\ \neg f(X) & \text{if } g(X) = 1 \end{cases} \quad (4)$$

We use the definition of g (detector for protected patterns) as used in Eq. 3.

Now, we need to ensure the equivalence of $(f \oplus g)$, i.e. $(f_1 \circ (f_2 \oplus g))$, with that of $(f_1 \circ h \circ f_2)$. This can be ensured by simply checking for the equivalence of $(f_2 \oplus g)$ with that of $(h \circ f_2)$. If the selected f_2 is "small", the task of synthesizing h becomes feasible.

For simplicity, we do not assume the splitting of g in the above discussion, but our approach allows that.

4.3 Methodology: $\mathcal{SR}$-SFLL

Algorithm 1 takes the original circuit ($\mathbb{C}$), and a choice for the cut (λ). It first generates an SFLL locked circuit (Line 2), thereby generating the stripped functionality circuit ($\mathbb{S}(X)$), and the restore unit circuit ($\mathbb{R}(X, K)$).

Identify Cut. The circuit is "cut" (according to λ) to partition the original circuit $\mathbb{C}$ to segments $\mathbb{C}_1$ and $\mathbb{C}_2$ in Line 3. Similarly, the cube stripping circuit $\mathbb{S}$ is also partitioned into $\mathbb{S}_1$ and $\mathbb{S}_2$ in Line 3.

1. The edges at which the circuit is cut in the original circuit $\mathbb{C}(X)$ are the outputs for circuit $A \leftrightarrow \mathbb{C}_1(X)$ and the input for circuit $o_1 \leftrightarrow \mathbb{C}_2(A)$.
2. The edges at which the circuit is cut in the stripped functionality circuit $\mathbb{S}(X)$ are the output for $V \leftrightarrow \mathbb{S}_1(X)$ and the input for circuit $\mathsf{sfo} \leftrightarrow \mathbb{S}_2(V)$.

Synthesize Perturbation Unit Q. We introduce a perturbation unit $\mathbb{Q}$ between $\mathbb{C}_1$ and $\mathbb{C}_2$ such that this modified circuit (see Fig. 2b) satisfies the correctness and security properties (see Sect. 4.1).

Accordingly, we pose the synthesis conditions for $\mathbb{Q}$ as follows:

$$\forall A \ \forall V. \ (\mathbb{C}_2(A) \oplus \mathbb{S}_2(V)) = \mathbb{C}_2(\mathbb{Q}(A, V)) \quad (5)$$

$$\forall z \ \exists A \ \exists V. \ \mathbb{Q}_z(A, V) \neq \mathbb{S}_2(V) \quad (6)$$

Equation 5 imposes the soundness constraint that introducing $\mathbb{Q}$ should reinstall the functionality of $\mathbb{C}_2$. Equation 6 is the security constraint against structural attacks that ensures that none of the signals (z) in $\mathbb{Q}$ is equivalent to sfo.

Our algorithm is not complete, that is, our synthesis conditions are stronger than necessary: the signals A and V are universally quantified over all possibilities, while $\mathbb{Q}$ needs to satisfy these conditions only on the possible outputs from $\mathbb{C}_1$ and $\mathbb{S}_1$ respectively. Our formulation trades off completeness for scalability.

If Algorithm 1 fails to synthesize a locked circuit (i.e., the algorithm returns $\bot$), the algorithm is run again with a different choice for the cut (λ).

Theorem 1. *If Algorithm 1 succeeds (that is, does not return $\bot$), the returned locked circuit $\widehat{\varphi}(X, K)$ is both correct and secure.*

Proof. For the Algorithm 1 to succeed, the SYNTHESIZE function must succeed. SYNTHESIZE succeeds only if the synthesized $\mathbb{Q}$ satisfies Eq. 5 and Eq. 6.

- **Correctness.** As sfo is part of $\mathbb{S}_2$, from Eq. 5 and Fig. 2b, Eq. 1 holds whenever Eq. 5 holds.
- **Security.** From Eq. 6 and Fig. 2b, if Eqn 6 holds, so must Eq. 2.

$\mathcal{SR}$**-SFLL(0).** In case of $\mathcal{SR}$-SFLL(0), we only attempt to synthesize $\mathbb{Q}$ to replace the circuits $\mathbb{C}_2$ and $\mathbb{S}_2$ (Fig. 4b) instead of synthesizing a new circuit between $\mathbb{C}_1$ and $\mathbb{C}_2$. Hence, in this case, the synthesis condition reduces to:

$$\exists \mathbb{Q} \; \forall A \; \forall V. \; (\mathbb{C}_2(A) \oplus \mathbb{S}_2(V)) = \mathbb{Q}(A, V) \tag{7}$$

Circuit Optimization. The circuit may be subjected to optimizations (e.g. using *berkeley-abc* [1]); however, in that case, the security check (Eq. 2) needs to be repeated on the optimized circuit to ensure that the optimizations did not restore the sfo signal. In our experiments, we did perform optimizations on our circuits, and in no case did the security check fail post-optimization.

5   SYNTAK

Algorithm 2 accepts the locked circuit $\widehat{\varphi}$ to return the secret key, K_c. We use two hyperparameters on the number of attempts on creating cuts (ncuts) and enumerate synthesis candidates (nsynth).

At Line 3, the algorithm uses structural analysis to identify the functionality stripped circuit FSC and the restore unit $\mathbb{R}$. Identifying $\mathbb{R}$ is reasonably simple as it is the only part of the locked circuit that uses the key bits K. Hence, one can perform dependency analysis from the key bits to identify $\mathbb{R}$ (as also done in prior work [32, 40]).

Next, the algorithm enters a loop to guess a suitable cut (Line 5). If a new cut (different than the cuts obtained so far, accumulated in cuts (Line 9)) is found, it attempts to enumerate synthesis candidates. For every synthesis candidate $\mathbb{P}$ (Line 12), the algorithm assembles the complete circuit (Line 17) as per Fig. 5b.

Algorithm 2: SYNTAK

---

1 $Input : \widehat{\varphi}$, ncuts, nsynth;
2 cuts $\leftarrow \emptyset$;
3 $\mathbb{FSC}, \mathbb{R} \leftarrow$ STRUCTANALYSE($\widehat{\varphi}$);
4 **while** $|cuts| < ncuts$ **do**
5      $\mathbb{FSC}_1, \mathbb{FSC}_2 \leftarrow$ CUT($\mathbb{FSC}$, cuts);
6   **if** $\mathbb{FSC}_2 == \perp$ **then**
7 | **break**;
8   **end**
9   cuts $\leftarrow$ cuts $\cup \{\langle \mathbb{FSC}_1, \mathbb{FSC}_2 \rangle\}$;
10   synths $\leftarrow \emptyset$;
11   **while** $|synths| < nsynths$ **do**
12         $\mathbb{P} \leftarrow$ SYNTHESIZE($\mathbb{FSC}_2$, synths);
13   **if** $P == \perp$ **then**
14 | **break**;
15   **end**
16   synths $\leftarrow$ synths $\cup \{\mathbb{P}\}$;
17         $\varphi \leftarrow$ ASSEMBLE($\mathbb{FSC}_1, \mathbb{P}, \mathbb{R}$);
18         $K_c \leftarrow$ ATTACKWITHSFO($\varphi, \{i, k\}$);
19   **if** $K_c \neq \perp$ **then**
20 | **return** K_c;
21   **end**
22   **end**
23 **end**
24 **return** $\perp$;

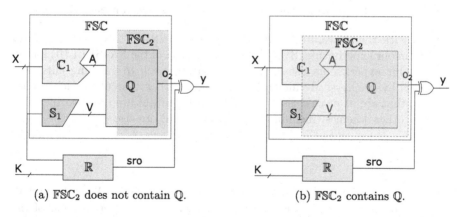

(a) $\mathbb{FSC}_2$ does not contain $\mathbb{Q}$.   (b) $\mathbb{FSC}_2$ contains $\mathbb{Q}$.

Fig. 7. SYNTAK will not succeed with (a) but may suceed with (b) (cuts shown by blue boxes). (Color figure online)

Then, it launches an existing structural attack (like FALL, SFLLUnlock) with the signals $\{i, j\}$ as potential candidates for the sfo signal (Line 18). If the existing attacks succeed, the respective key K_c is returned.

The SYNTHESIZE procedure synthesizes $(i, j) \leftrightarrow P(A)$, such that:

$$\forall A.\ \mathbb{FSC}_2(A) = (\mathbb{P}_i(A) \oplus \mathbb{P}_j(A)) \tag{8}$$

That is, it searches for a circuit $\mathbb{P}$ that is semantically equivalent to $\mathbb{FSC}$ such that it exposes the sfo signal. This imposition is due to the fact that a new XOR gate, G_{xor} (circled XOR gate in Fig. 5b), is forced on the output of $\mathbb{P}$; this is an attempt to make the new circuit resemble the SFLL circuit in Fig. 1, on which the existing structural attacks are potent.

However, the algorithm is not complete due to multiple factors:

- The choice of the cut is crucial; the attack only works if $\mathbb{FSC}_2$ is such that the perturbation unit of the locked circuit $\widehat{\varphi}$ is a part of $\mathbb{FSC}_2$. The attacker is thus invited to the challenging task of distinguishing $\mathbb{Q}$ (of $\mathcal{SR}$-SFLL(0)) in the locked circuit, $\widehat{\varphi}$. However, the attack is made a bit easier by the fact that it is not required to select a cut that *exactly* isolates $\mathbb{Q}$ (Fig. 7b). The attack will still succeed even if some portion of $\mathbb{C}_1$ and $\mathbb{S}_1$ enters $\mathbb{P}$. However, the synthesis phase of the attack gets expensive with the size of $\mathbb{FSC}_2$; thus, overly large $\mathbb{FSC}_2$ will not succeed either (will fail in SYNTHESIZE).
- Every synthesis candidate that satisfies Eq. 8 may not yield sfo: there may be multiple possible instantiations of $\mathbb{P}$, some, where none of i or j is sfo.
- The synthesis condition (Eq. 8) is overly strong: the synthesized candidate $\mathbb{P}$ is required to satisfy the condition for feasible values of A as emanating from $\mathbb{FSC}_1$ and that of sro from $\mathbb{R}$ (in fact, A and sro are correlated as both accept X). However, the synthesis condition forgoes this precondition for scalability and universally quantifies the condition on all possible values of A and sro.

Even with the above areas of incompleteness, SYNTAK is quite effective in practice: in our experiments, SYNTAK breaks 71.25% of the $\mathcal{SR}$-SFLL(0) locked circuits. Our experiments use an incremental approach to guessing cuts that select cuts by progressively increasing the depth (d) of the cut in each round; all nodes that are at most d distance far from the output are included in $\mathbb{FSC}_2$. However, other schemes (including randomized ones) are also possible.

6   Evaluation

Benchmarks and Setup. We have used 10 circuits from ISCAS'85 [2] and 10 circuits from MCNC [41]. Benchmarks were used for evaluation in most of the recent work, including SFLL [44], FALL [32], SFLLUnlock [40], and GNNUnlock [4]. Each of these designs was locked under four different configurations to produce SFLL-HD locked versions: 16 and 32 key-bits, each with hamming distances of 2 and 4 for 16 key-bits and 4 and 8 for 32 key-bits. So, overall, we perform our evaluations on a benchmark suite of 80 circuit instances.

ISCAS'85 benchmarks are available in bench and MCNC benchmarks are available in *blif* (Berkeley Logic Interchange Format) formats. We used *Berkeley-abc* to convert *blif* to the *bench* format for use by our framework.

Table 2. Summary of results on all our benchmarks: FL, SU, GU, and SA represent FALL, SFLLUnlock, GNNUnlock, and SYNTAK respectively. Under *Robustness*, each cell in the table shows the number of locked circuits successfully broken by the respective attack (smaller is better). Under *Overhd.*, we show the average (AVG) and the standard deviation (STD) of the percentage increase in the number of AND gates in the AIG w.r.t. the SFLL-HD locked design (smaller is better).

Bench.	SFLL-HD			$\mathcal{SR}$-SFLL(0)						$\mathcal{SR}$-SFLL					
	Robustness			Robustness				Overhd. %		Robustness				Overhd. %	
	FL	SU	GU	FL	SU	GU	SA	AVG	STD	FL	SU	GU	SA	AVG	STD
ISCAS	40	40	40	0	0	0	29	0.17	0.10	0	0	0	0	0.23	0.14
MCNC	40	40	40	0	0	0	28	0.10	0.03	0	0	0	0	0.12	0.05

We have used the popular SFLL-HD variant of SFLL where the cube stripping function is the hamming distance between the input and the key bits.

We use "cut" at depth 4 for selecting $\mathbb{C}_2$ both for $\mathcal{SR}$-SFLL(0) and for $\mathcal{SR}$-SFLL. For SYNTAK, we progressively increase the depth from one till the attack is successful; we use FALL and SFLLUnlock as the existing attacks on the circuit resynthesized using SYNTAK. We use a timeout of 1 h for $\mathcal{SR}$-SFLL(0) and $\mathcal{SR}$-SFLL timeout of 1 h; SYNTAK uses a time limit of 2 days.

We built our synthesis engine using *Berkeley-abc* [1] and the *Sketch* [33] synthesizer. Sketch, is primarily designed for program synthesis. It discharges Quantified Boolean formulas (QBF) at the backend to be solved using *Berkeley-abc* or Minisat [12]. We found Sketch to be quite an effective tool for our problem.

The rest of our framework is implemented in Python. We use open-source implementations of *SFLLUnlock* [40], *FALL* [32], and *GNNUnlock* [4] that were made available by the authors of these tools.

We conduct our experiments on a machine with 12-Core Intel(R) Xeon(R) Silver CPU E5-2620 CPU @ 2.00 GHz with 32 GB RAM.

Research Questions. Our experiments were designed to answer the following research questions:

1. How do the newly proposed $\mathcal{SR}$-SFLL(0) and $\mathcal{SR}$-SFLL compare with the state-of-the-art SFLL-HD on existing attacks (SAT and structural attacks)?
2. How do $\mathcal{SR}$-SFLL(0) and $\mathcal{SR}$-SFLL stand to the novel SYNTAK?
3. What is the overhead of $\mathcal{SR}$-SFLL w.r.t. SFLL-HD?

Both $\mathcal{SR}$-SFLL(0) and $\mathcal{SR}$-SFLL were able to defend against the existing attacks: SAT, FALL, SFLLUnlock, and GNNUnlock. However, 71.25% of the benchmarks locked using $\mathcal{SR}$-SFLL(0) were broken by SYNTAK, while no instance defended by $\mathcal{SR}$-SFLL could be broken by SYNTAK.

From the AIG of the circuits, we infer that $\mathcal{SR}$-SFLL uses 0.18% (on average) more AND gates than SFLL-HD locked circuits.

Table 3. Robustness and overhead of $\mathcal{SR}$-SFLL(0) and $\mathcal{SR}$-SFLL with respect to SFLL-HD locked circuits on a subset of our benchmarks. Benchmark names starting with "C" are part of ISCAS, rest are part of MCNC benchmarks. The mark ✗ indicates the attack is successful, ✓ indicates attack is not successful.

Bench.	Inst. (k,h)	SFLL-HD			$\mathcal{SR}$-SFLL(0)					$\mathcal{SR}$-SFLL				
		FALL	SFLLUnlock	GNNUnlock	FALL	SFLLUnlock	GNNUnlock	SynTak	Overhead %	FALL	SFLLUnlock	GNNUnlock	SynTak	Overhead %
C432	(16,2)	✗	✗	✗	✓	✓	✓	✗	0.26	✓	✓	✓	✓	0.26
i4	(32,4)	✗	✗	✗	✓	✓	✓	✓	0.12	✓	✓	✓	✓	0.18
C880	(32,8)	✗	✗	✗	✓	✓	✓	✗	0.11	✓	✓	✓	✓	0.11
apex2	(32,8)	✗	✗	✗	✓	✓	✓	✗	0.11	✓	✓	✓	✓	0.11
C499	(16,4)	✗	✗	✗	✓	✓	✓	✗	0.20	✓	✓	✓	✓	0.31
C1908	(32,8)	✗	✗	✗	✓	✓	✓	✓	0.11	✓	✓	✓	✓	0.21
C1355	(32,4)	✗	✗	✗	✓	✓	✓	✗	0.10	✓	✓	✓	✓	0.21
i9	(16,4)	✗	✗	✗	✓	✓	✓	✗	0.14	✓	✓	✓	✓	0.21
i7	(16,2)	✗	✗	✗	✓	✓	✓	✓	0.14	✓	✓	✓	✓	0.14
C2670	(16,2)	✗	✗	✗	✓	✓	✓	✗	0.31	✓	✓	✓	✓	0.31
C3540	(16,2)	✗	✗	✗	✓	✓	✓	✓	0.19	✓	✓	✓	✓	0.25
dalu	(32,4)	✗	✗	✗	✓	✓	✓	✓	0.11	✓	✓	✓	✓	0.11
frg2	(16,4)	✗	✗	✗	✓	✓	✓	✓	0.12	✓	✓	✓	✓	0.17
k2	(16,2)	✗	✗	✗	✓	✓	✓	✗	0.08	✓	✓	✓	✓	0.08
i8	(32,4)	✗	✗	✗	✓	✓	✓	✗	0.04	✓	✓	✓	✓	0.04
C5315	(32,8)	✗	✗	✗	✓	✓	✓	✗	0.06	✓	✓	✓	✓	0.12
seq	(32,8)	✗	✗	✗	✓	✓	✓	✓	0.05	✓	✓	✓	✓	0.05
C7552	(16,4)	✗	✗	✗	✓	✓	✓	✗	0.11	✓	✓	✓	✓	0.11
C6228	(32,4)	✗	✗	✗	✓	✓	✓	✓	0.08	✓	✓	✓	✓	0.16
des	(32,8)	✗	✗	✗	✓	✓	✓	✗	0.05	✓	✓	✓	✓	0.03

6.1 Robustness of $\mathcal{SR}$-SELL(0) and $\mathcal{SR}$-SELL on Existing Attacks

Table 2 provides a summary of the performance of SFLL-HD, $\mathcal{SR}$-SFLL(0), and $\mathcal{SR}$-SFLL against existing structural attacks (FALL, SFLLUnlock, and GNNUnlock) on a representative set of benchmarks: the table shows the number of instances where the respective attack break the defense. While the structural attacks (FALL, SFLLUnlock, and GNNUnlock) are able to break *all* of these instances for SFLL locked circuits, our structurally robust proposals ($\mathcal{SR}$-SFLL(0) and $\mathcal{SR}$-SFLL) are resilient against these attacks.

Table 3 shows the results on a representative subset of our benchmarks: ✗ represents the number of instances where the locked circuit gets broken by the respective attack, and ✓ represents the number of instances where the respective

Table 4. Overhead of $\mathcal{SR}$-SFLL(0) and $\mathcal{SR}$-SFLL vs SFLL. Overhead calculated over SFLL-HD locked circuits shown in Table 3. Benchmark names starting with "C" are part of ISCAS while the rest are part of MCNC benchmarks.

Benchmark	Inst. (k, h)	Original	SFLL-HD	$\mathcal{SR}$-SFLL(0) # gates	Overhead%	$\mathcal{SR}$-SFLL # gates	Overhead%
C432	(16, 2)	209	768	770	0.26	770	0.26
i4	(32, 4)	246	1673	1675	0.12	1676	0.18
C880	(32,8)	327	1754	1756	0.11	1756	0.11
C499	(16, 4)	400	957	959	0.20	960	0.31
C1908	(32, 8)	414	1842	1844	0.11	1846	0.11
apex2	(32, 8)	445	1873	1875	0.11	1875	0.11
C1355	(32, 4)	504	1931	1933	0.10	1935	0.21
C2670	(16, 2)	717	1277	1281	0.31	1281	0.31
i9	(16, 4)	889	1448	1450	0.14	1451	0.21
i7	(16, 2)	904	1463	1465	0.14	1465	0.14
C3540	(16, 2)	1038	1595	1598	0.19	1599	0.25
frg2	(16, 4)	1164	1727	1726	0.12	1727	0.17
dalu	(32, 4)	1371	2799	2802	0.11	2802	0.11
C5315	(32, 8)	1773	3201	3203	0.06	3205	0.12
k2	(16, 2)	1998	2558	2560	0.08	2560	0.08
C7552	(16, 4)	2074	2634	2637	0.11	2637	0.11
C6228	(32, 4)	2337	3765	3768	0.08	3771	0.16
seq	(32, 8)	2411	3837	3839	0.05	3839	0.05
i8	(32, 4)	3310	4737	4739	0.04	4739	0.04
des	(32, 8)	4123	5551	5554	0.05	5553	0.03

defense successfully defends against the attack. As the primary purpose for the design of SFLL was to be resilient against SAT attacks, it is not surprising that SAT attack times out on all instances of the SFLL locked designs. As $\mathcal{SR}$-SFLL(0) and $\mathcal{SR}$-SFLL are functionally equivalent to SFLL, they too are resilient to SAT attacks.

We also conducted experiments with impractically small key sizes of 5 key bits (with hamming distance 2). None of the structural analysis based attacks (FALL, SFLLUnlock, and GNNUnlock) could break either $\mathcal{SR}$-SFLL(0) or $\mathcal{SR}$-SFLL locked circuits even for these small key sizes.

6.2   Robustness of $\mathcal{SR}$-SELL(0) and $\mathcal{SR}$-SELL on SYNTAK

We apply SYNTAK on $\mathcal{SR}$-SFLL(0) and $\mathcal{SR}$-SFLL locked circuits to evaluate their robustness on this attack. We "guess" the cut for SYNTAK starting with a cut at a depth of 1; if the synthesis phase in SYNTAK or the subsequent structural attack (FALL and SFLLUnlock) fails, we reattempt the attack with the depth increased by one. We use a timeout of 2 days for SYNTAK.

On our novel SYNTAK attack, $\mathcal{SR}$-SFLL(0) succumbs on 71.25% of the cases, but $\mathcal{SR}$-SFLL successfully defends against this attack on all instances. Table 3 shows the performance of some representative benchmarks and Table 2 summarizes the overall results.

6.3   Overhead of $\mathcal{SR}$-SELL(0) and $\mathcal{SR}$-SELL

Table 4 shows the overhead (in terms of the number of AND gates in the AIG) for $\mathcal{SR}$-SFLL(0) and $\mathcal{SR}$-SFLL over that of SFLL on the benchmarks shown in Table 3. Table 2 provides a summary of the overheads over all our benchmarks.

$\mathcal{SR}$-SFLL(0) and has almost no additional overhead (average of about 0.14%) and $\mathcal{SR}$-SFLL also has a very low overhead (average of about 0.18%) over all our benchmarks. This is because while $\mathcal{SR}$-SFLL(0) essentially rewrites a part of the circuit, $\mathcal{SR}$-SFLL is required to insert additional machinery to substitute the functionality of $\mathbb{S}_2$ within $\mathbb{C}$.

7   Related Work

Initial logic locking schemes [7, 10, 11] introduced additional logic and new inputs to the circuit design in order to get the locked circuit. These locked circuits work correctly when the correct secret key is provided to the circuit by the designers post IC fabrication. These logic locking techniques are vulnerable to SAT based attacks [23, 26, 34]. To overcome the SAT based attacks Anti-SAT [39], and SARLock [42] were proposed. However, Anti-SAT was broken by SPS [43] attack. SARLock was broken by App-SAT [30] attack.

SFLL-HD [44] introduces a stripped functionality approach for logic locking which defend against the above-mentioned attacks. But this is also vulnerable to the FALL [32], SFLLUnlock [40], and GNNUnlock [4].

HOLL [35] exploits the power of program synthesis tools to generate the locked circuit by using a "secret" program (using programmable logic like EEPROM) as the key. As the attacker has to synthesize the "secret" program, HOLL becomes challenging to break. However, the requirement of having an embedded programming chip makes the approach both complicated and expensive; further, every invocation of the circuit requires the program in the slow EEPROM memory to be executed. Our approach, instead, builds on the popular SFLL technique and does not need embedded programmable chips.

Program synthesis has seen a significant growth in the recent years. Program synthesis algorithms have powered the synthesis of bit-vector programs [16], heap-manipulations [13, 24, 27], language parsers [21, 31], semantic actions in attribute grammars [18], abstract transformers [19], automata [5], invariants [6, 13, 20, 22], and even differentially private mechanisms [28]. Program synthesis has also been applied to synthesize bug corpora [29] as well as for debugging [8, 9], and repairing buggy programs like fixing incorrect heap manipulations [37, 38], or synthesize relevant fences and/or atomic sections in concurrent programs under relaxed memory models [36].

There exist boolean functional synthesis tools, like CADET [25], Manthan [14,15], and BFSS [3], that could have been used for our synthesis task. However, none of these tools allow us to control the "structure" of the synthesized formula. Hence, we built our synthesis engine using the *Sketch* synthesizer, which is designed for program synthesis.

8 Conclusions

$\mathcal{SR}$-SFLL provides security against structural analysis based attacks such as FALL, SFLLUnlock, and GNNUnlock. The core idea used by $\mathcal{SR}$-SFLL is to use modern synthesis engines to recover structural patterns that can be exploited by existing structural analysis based attacks.

$\mathcal{SR}$-SFLL provides an asymmetric advantage to the defender over the attacker on many counts:

- **secret key**: Similar to SFLL, $\mathcal{SR}$-SFLL uses a *secret key* to define a set of protected input patterns. The locked circuit behaves incorrectly when run with the wrong key;
- **secret cut**: The cut used to partition the SFLL locked circuit (where the synthesized component was inserted) is known to the defender but not to the attacker;
- **challenging synthesis task**: While the defender is required to synthesize a smaller circuit that only establishes the functionality of $\mathbb{S}_2$, the attacker is required to synthesize a much larger circuit that reestablishes the functionalities of both $\mathbb{C}_2$ and $\mathbb{S}_2$ (see Fig. 2b).

As the perturbation unit resides within the original circuit at a location unknown to the attacker and has no specific structural signature, structural analysis of the $\mathcal{SR}$-SFLL locked circuit becomes difficult. Also, as $\mathcal{SR}$-SFLL locked circuits are functionally equivalent to the respective SFLL locked circuits (see Eqn 1), $\mathcal{SR}$-SFLL retains all the theoretical robustness properties of SFLL.

Acknowledgements. We thank the anonymous reviewers for their valuable inputs. We are thankful to Google for supporting our research. We also thank Intel for their support via the Intel PhD Fellowship Program.

References

1. ABC: System for sequential logic synthesis and formal verification. https://github.com/berkeley-abc/abc. Accessed 2 Jan 2022
2. ISCAS'85 benchmarks. https://filebox.ece.vt.edu/~mhsiao/iscas85.html. Accessed 8 Jan 2022
3. Akshay, S., Chakraborty, S., Goel, S., Kulal, S., Shah, S.: What's hard about boolean functional synthesis? In: CAV, pp. 251–269. Springer (2018)
4. Alrahis, L., et al.: GNNUnlock: graph neural networks-based oracle-less unlocking scheme for provably secure logic locking. In: DATE, pp. 780–785. IEEE (2021)

5. Alur, R., D'Antoni, L., Gulwani, S., Kini, D., Viswanathan, M.: Automated grading of DFA constructions. In: IJCAI, pp. 1976–1982 (2013)
6. Bao, J., Trivedi, N., Pathak, D., Hsu, J., Roy, S.: Data-driven invariant learning for probabilistic programs. In: CAV, pp. 33–54. Springer (2022)
7. Baumgarten, A., Tyagi, A., Zambreno, J.: Preventing IC piracy using reconfigurable logic barriers. IEEE Des. Test Comput. **27**(1), 66–75 (2010)
8. Bavishi, R., Pandey, A., Roy, S.: Regression aware debugging for mobile applications. In: Mobile! 2016, pp. 21–22. ACM (2016)
9. Bavishi, R., Pandey, A., Roy, S.: To be precise: regression aware debugging. In: OOPSLA, pp. 897–915. ACM (2016)
10. Chakraborty, R.S., Bhunia, S.: Hardware protection and authentication through netlist level obfuscation. In: IEEE/ACM ICCAD, pp. 674–677. IEEE (2008)
11. Dupuis, S., Ba, P.S., Di Natale, G., Flottes, M.L., Rouzeyre, B.: A novel hardware logic encryption technique for thwarting illegal overproduction and hardware trojans. In: IEEE IOLTS, pp. 49–54. IEEE (2014)
12. Eén, N., Sörensson, N.: An extensible SAT-solver. In: Giunchiglia, E., Tacchella, A. (eds.) SAT 2003. LNCS, vol. 2919, pp. 502–518. Springer, Heidelberg (2004). https://doi.org/10.1007/978-3-540-24605-3_37
13. Garg, A., Roy, S.: Synthesizing heap manipulations via integer linear programming. In: Blazy, S., Jensen, T. (eds.) SAS 2015. LNCS, vol. 9291, pp. 109–127. Springer, Heidelberg (2015). https://doi.org/10.1007/978-3-662-48288-9_7
14. Golia, P., Roy, S., Meel, K.S.: Manthan: a data-driven approach for boolean function synthesis. In: Lahiri, S.K., Wang, C. (eds.) CAV 2020. LNCS, vol. 12225, pp. 611–633. Springer, Cham (2020). https://doi.org/10.1007/978-3-030-53291-8_31
15. Golia, P., Slivovsky, F., Roy, S., Meel, K.S.: Engineering an efficient boolean functional synthesis engine. In: IEEE/ACM ICCAD, pp. 1–9. IEEE (2021)
16. Gulwani, S., Jha, S., Tiwari, A., Venkatesan,R.: Synthesis of loop-free programs. In: PLDI, pp. 62–73. ACM (2011)
17. Hurtarte, J.S., Wolsheimer, E.A., Tafoya, L.M.: Understanding fabless ic technology. Newnes (2011)
18. Kalita, P.K., Kumar, M.J., Roy, S.: Synthesis of semantic actions in attribute grammars. In: IEEE FMCAD, pp. 304–314. IEEE (2022)
19. Kalita, P.K., Muduli, S.K., D'Antoni, L., Reps, T., Roy, S.: Synthesizing abstract transformers. PACMPL **6**(OOPSLA2), 1291–1319 (2022)
20. Lahiri, S., Roy, S.: Almost correct invariants: Synthesizing inductive invariants by fuzzing proofs. In: ISSTA, pp. 352–364. ACM (2022)
21. Leung, A., Sarracino, J., Lerner, S.: Interactive parser synthesis by example. In: PLDI, pp. 565–574. ACM (2015)
22. Padhi, S., Sharma, R., Millstein, T.D.: Data-driven precondition inference with learned features. In: PLDI, pp. 42–56. ACM (2016)
23. Plaza, S.M., Markov, I.L.: Solving the third-shift problem in ic piracy with test-aware logic locking. IEEE TCADICS **34**(6), 961–971 (2015)
24. Qiu, X., Solar-Lezama, A.: Natural synthesis of provably-correct data-structure manipulations. In: OOPSLA, pp. 1–28. ACM (2017)
25. Rabe, M.N., Tentrup, L., Rasmussen, C., Seshia, S.A.: Understanding and extending incremental determinization for 2QBF. In: Chockler, H., Weissenbacher, G. (eds.) CAV 2018. LNCS, vol. 10982, pp. 256–274. Springer, Cham (2018). https://doi.org/10.1007/978-3-319-96142-2_17
26. Rajendran, J., Pino, Y., Sinanoglu, O., Karri, R.: Security analysis of logic obfuscation. In: DAC, pp. 83–89 (2012)

27. Roy, S.: From concrete examples to heap manipulating programs. In: Logozzo, F., Fähndrich, M. (eds.) SAS 2013. LNCS, vol. 7935, pp. 126–149. Springer, Heidelberg (2013). https://doi.org/10.1007/978-3-642-38856-9_9

28. Roy, S., Hsu, J., Albarghouthi, A.: Learning differentially private mechanisms. In: S&P, pp. 852–865. IEEE (2021)

29. Roy, S., Pandey, A., Dolan-Gavitt, B., Hu, Y.: Bug synthesis: Challenging bug-finding tools with deep faults. In: ESEC/FSE, pp. 224–234. ACM (2018)

30. Shamsi, K., Li, M., Meade, T., Zhao, Z., Pan, D.Z., Jin, Y.: AppSAT: Approximately deobfuscating integrated circuits. In: HOST, pp. 95–100. IEEE (2017)

31. Singal, D., Agarwal, P., Jhunjhunwala, S., Roy, S.: Parse condition: symbolic encoding of LL(1) parsing. In: LPAR, pp. 637–655. EasyChair (2018)

32. Sirone, D., Subramanyan, P.: Functional analysis attacks on logic locking. IEEE TIFS **15**, 2514–2527 (2020)

33. Solar-Lezama, A.: Program sketching. Springer STTT **15**, 475–495 (2013)

34. Subramanyan, P., Ray, S., Malik, S.: Evaluating the security of logic encryption algorithms. In: HOST, pp. 137–143. IEEE (2015)

35. Takhar, G., Karri, R., Pilato, C., Roy, S.: HOLL: program synthesis for higher order logic locking. In: TACAS 2022. LNCS, vol. 13243, pp. 3–24. Springer, Cham (2022). https://doi.org/10.1007/978-3-030-99524-9_1

36. Verma, A., Kalita, P.K., Pandey, A., Roy, S.: Interactive debugging of concurrent programs under relaxed memory models. In: CGO, pp. 68–80. ACM (2020)

37. Verma, S., Roy, S.: Synergistic debug-repair of heap manipulations. In: ESEC/FSE, pp. 163–173. ACM (2017)

38. Verma, S., Roy, S.: Debug-localize-repair: a symbiotic construction for heap manipulations. Springer FMSD **58**(3), 399–439 (2021)

39. Xie, Y., Srivastava, A.: Anti-SAT: mitigating SAT attack on logic locking. IEEE TCADICS **38**(2), 199–207 (2018)

40. Yang, F., Tang, M., Sinanoglu, O.: Stripped functionality logic locking with hamming distance-based restore unit (SFLL-hd)-unlocked. IEEE TIFS **14**(10), 2778–2786 (2019)

41. Yang, S.: Logic synthesis and optimization benchmarks user guide: version 3.0. Microelectronics Center of North Carolina (MCNC) (1991)

42. Yasin, M., Mazumdar, B., Rajendran, J.J., Sinanoglu, O.: SARLock: SAT attack resistant logic locking. In: HOST, pp. 236–241. IEEE (2016)

43. Yasin, M., Mazumdar, B., Sinanoglu, O., Rajendran, J.: Security analysis of anti-sat. In: ASP-DAC, pp. 342–347. IEEE (2017)

44. Yasin, M., Sengupta, A., Nabeel, M.T., Ashraf, M., Rajendran, J., Sinanoglu, O.: Provably-secure logic locking: from theory to practice. In: ACM CCS, pp. 1601–1618 (2017)

45. Zeng, H., Zhou, H., Srivastava, A., Kannan, R., Prasanna, V.: GraphSAINT: graph sampling based inductive learning method. In: ICLR (2020)

Symbolic Quantum Simulation
with Quasimodo

Meghana Sistla[1]([⊠]), Swarat Chaudhuri[1], and Thomas Reps[2]

[1] The University of Texas at Austin, Austin, TX, USA
mesistla@utexas.edu, swarat@cs.utexas.edu
[2] University of Wisconsin-Madison, Madison, WI, USA
reps@cs.wisc.edu

Abstract. The simulation of quantum circuits on classical computers is an important problem in quantum computing. Such simulation requires representations of distributions over very large sets of basis vectors, and recent work has used symbolic data-structures such as Binary Decision Diagrams (BDDs) for this purpose. In this tool paper, we present QUASI-MODO, an extensible, open-source Python library for *symbolic simulation* of quantum circuits. QUASIMODO is specifically designed for easy extensibility to other backends. QUASIMODO allows simulations of quantum circuits, checking properties of the outputs of quantum circuits, and debugging quantum circuits. It also allows the user to choose from among several symbolic data-structures—both unweighted and weighted BDDs, and a recent structure called Context-Free-Language Ordered Binary Decision Diagrams (CFLOBDDs)—and can be easily extended to support other symbolic data-structures.

1 Introduction

Canonical, symbolic representations of Boolean functions—for example, Binary Decision Diagrams (BDDs) [5]—have a long history in automated system design and verification. More recently, such data-structures have found exciting new applications in *quantum simulation*. Quantum computers can theoretically solve certain problems much faster than traditional computers, but current quantum computers are error-prone and access to them is limited. The simulation of quantum algorithms on classical machines allows researchers to experiment with quantum algorithms even without access to reliable hardware.

Symbolic function representations are helpful in quantum simulation because a quantum system's state can be viewed as a distribution over an exponential-sized set of basis-vectors (each representing a "classical" state). Such a state, as well as transformations that quantum algorithms typically apply to them, can often be efficiently represented using a symbolic data-structure. Simulating an algorithm then amounts to performing a sequence of symbolic operations.

Currently, there are a small number of open-source software systems that support such *symbolic quantum simulation* [1,6,8,13,16]. However, the underly-

© The Author(s) 2023
C. Enea and A. Lal (Eds.): CAV 2023, LNCS 13966, pp. 213–225, 2023.
https://doi.org/10.1007/978-3-031-37709-9_11

ing symbolic data-structure can have an enormous effect on simulation performance. In this tool paper, we present QUASIMODO,[1] an extensible framework for symbolic quantum simulation. QUASIMODO is specifically designed for easy extensibility to other backends to make it possible to experiment with a variety of symbolic data-structures. QUASIMODO currently supports (i) BDDs [3,5,7], (ii) a weighted variant of BDDs [9,14], [19, Ch. 5], and (iii) Context-Free-Language Ordered Binary Decision Diagrams CFLOBDDs [11], a recent canonical representation of Boolean functions that has been shown to outperform BDDs in many quantum-simulation tasks. QUASIMODO also has a clean interface that formal-methods researchers can use to plug in new symbolic data-structures, which helps to lower the barrier to entry for formal-methods researchers interested in this area.

Users access QUASIMODO through a Python interface. They can define a quantum algorithm as a quantum circuit using 18 different kinds of quantum gates, such as Hadamard, CNOT, and Toffoli gates. They can simulate the algorithm using a symbolic data-structure of their own choosing. Users can sample outcomes from the probability distribution computed through simulation, and can query the simulator for the probability of a specific outcome of a quantum computation over a set of quantum bits (qubits). The system also allows for a form of correctness checking: users are allowed to ask for the set of *all* high-probability outcomes and to check that these satisfy a given assertion.

Along with QUASIMODO, we are releasing a suite of 7 established quantum algorithms encoded in the input language of QUASIMODO. We hope that these algorithms will serve as benchmarks for future research on symbolic simulation and verification of quantum algorithms.

Organization. Section 2 gives an overview of quantum simulation. Section 3 gives a user-level overview of QUASIMODO. Section 4 provides background on the symbolic data-structures available in QUASIMODO. Section 5 describes the programming model of QUASIMODO, and presents experimental results. Section 6 concludes.

2   Background on Quantum Simulation

Quantum algorithms on quantum computers can achieve polynomial to exponential speed-ups over classical algorithms on specific problems. However, because so far there are no practical scalable quantum computers, simulation of quantum circuits on classical computers can help in understanding how quantum algorithms work and scale. A simulation of a quantum-circuit computation [1,6,8,11,13,19] uses a representation qs of a quantum state and performs operations on qs that correspond to quantum-circuit operations (gate applications and measurements on qs).

Simulating a quantum circuit can have advantages compared to executing the circuit on a quantum computer. For instance, some quantum algorithms perform

---

[1] QUASIMODO is available at https://github.com/trishullab/Quasimodo.git.

```
1     import quasimodo #python package to import for Quasimodo
2     epsilon = 1e-8
3
4     # number of qubits in the quantum state
5     numQubits = 2 ** 12
6     # initialize the quantum state
7     qs = quasimodo.QuantumState("CFLOBDD", numQubits)
8     qs.h(0) # Apply Hadamard gate to Qubit 0
9     for i in range(1, numQubits):
10        qs.cx(0, i) # Apply CNOT Gate from Qubit 0 to Qubit i
11
12    qubit_mapping = {} # map from qubit number -> desired outcome
13    for i in range(0, numQubits):
14        qubit_mapping[i] = 1
15
16    # query probability of outcome as encoded in qubit mapping
17    prob = qs.prob(qubit_mapping)
18    if (abs(prob - 0.5)) < epsilon:
19        print ("Circuit is correct")
20    else
21        print ("Incorrect circuit")
```

Fig. 1. An example of a QUASIMODO program that performs a quantum-circuit computation in which the final quantum state is a GHZ state with 4,096 qubits. The program
verifies that a measurement of the final quantum state has a 50% chance of returning
the all-ones basis-state.

multiple iterations of a particular quantum operator Op (e.g., k iterations, where
$k = 2^j$). A simulation can operate on Op itself [19, Ch. 6], using j iterations of
repeated squaring to create matrices for $Op^2, Op^4, \ldots, Op^{2^j} = Op^k$. In contrast,
a physical device must apply Op sequentially, and thus performs $Op \ k = 2^j$
times.

Many quantum algorithms require multiple measurements on the final state.
After a measurement on a quantum computer, the quantum state collapses to
the measured state. Thus, every successive measurement requires re-running the
quantum circuit. However, with a simulation, the quantum state can be preserved
across measurements, and thus the quantum circuit need only be executed once.

3   Quasimodo's Programming and Analysis Interface

This section presents an overview of QUASIMODO from the perspective of a user
of the Python API. A user can define a quantum-circuit computation and check
the properties of the quantum state at various points in the computation. This
section also explains how QUASIMODO can be easily extended to include custom
representations of the quantum state.

Example. Figure 1 shows an example of a quantum-circuit computation written using the QUASIMODO API. To use the QUASIMODO library, one needs to

import the package, as shown in line 1. A user can then create a program that implements a quantum-circuit computation by

- Initializing the quantum state by making a call to `QuantumState` with an argument that selects the desired backend data-structure and the number of qubits in the quantum state. (See line 7.) The example in Fig. 1 uses CFLOBDD as the backend simulator, but other data-structures can be used by changing the backend parameter to BDD or WBDD. `QuantumState` sets the initial quantum state to the all-zeros basis-state.
- Applying single-qubit gates to the quantum state, such as Hadamard (h), Pauli-X (x), T-Gate (t), and others. The qubit to which they are to be applied is specified by passing the qubit number. (See line 8.)
- Applying multi-qubit gates to the quantum state, such as CNOT (cx), Toffoli (ccx), SWAP (swap), and others. The qubits to which they are to be applied is specified by passing the qubit numbers. (See line 10.)

Note that queries on the quantum state do not have to be made only at the end of the program; they can also be interspersed throughout the circuit-simulation computation.

QUASIMODO allows different backend data-structures to be used for representing quantum states. It comes with BDDs [3,5,7], a weighted variant of BDDs [9,14], [19, Ch. 5], and CFLOBDDs [11]. QUASIMODO also provides an interface for new backend data-structures to be incorporated by users. All three of the standard backends provide compressed representations of quantum states and quantum gates, although—as with all variants of decision diagrams—state representations may blow up as a sequence of gate operations are performed.

Quantum Simulation. Quantum simulation problems can be implemented using QUASIMODO by defining a quantum-circuit computation, and then invoking the API function `measure` to sample a basis-vector from the final quantum state. For instance, suppose that the final quantum state is $[0.5 \; 0 \; 0.5 \; 0.5 \; 0 \; 0 \; 0.5 \; 0]$. Then `measure` would return a string in the set $\{000, 010, 011, 110\}$ with probability 0.25 for each of the four strings.

Verification. As shown in line 17 of Fig. 1, QUASIMODO provides an API call to inquire about the probability of a specific outcome. The function `prob` takes as its argument a mapping from qubits to $\{0, 1\}$, which defines a basis-vector e of interest, and returns the probability that the state would be e if a measurement were carried out at that point. It can also be used to query the probability of a set of outcomes, using a mapping of just a subset S of the qubits, in which case `prob` returns the sum of all probabilities of obtaining a state that satisfies S. For example, if the quantum state computed by a 3-qubit circuit over $\langle q_0, q_1, q_2 \rangle$ is $[0.5 \; 0 \; 0.5 \; 0.5 \; 0 \; 0 \; 0.5 \; 0]$, the user can query the probability of states satisfying $q_1 = 1 \wedge q_2 = 0$ by calling `prob(1 : 1, 2 : 0)`, which would return 0.5 $(= Pr(q_0 = 0 \wedge q_1 = 1 \wedge q_2 = 0) + Pr(q_0 = 1 \wedge q_1 = 1 \wedge q_2 = 0) = (0.5)^2 + (0.5)^2)$.

Given a relational specification $R(x, y)$ and a quantum circuit $y = Q(x)$, this feature is useful for verifying properties of the form "$Pr[R(x, Q(x))] > \theta$," where θ is some desired probability threshold for the user's application.

Debugging Quantum Circuits. QUASIMODO additionally provides a feature to query the number of outcomes for a given probability. This feature is especially helpful for debugging large quantum circuits—large in-terms of qubit counts—when most outcomes have similar probabilities.

Consider the case of a quantum circuit whose final quantum state is intended to be $\frac{1}{\sqrt{6}} \begin{bmatrix} 1 & 1 & 1 & 0 & 1 & 1 & 1 & 0 \end{bmatrix}$. One can check if the final quantum state is the one intended by querying the number of outcomes that have probability $\frac{1}{6}$. If the returned value is 6, the user can then check if states 011 and 111 have probability 0 by calling `prob({0 : 0, 1 : 1, 2 : 1})` and `prob({0 : 1, 1 : 1, 2 : 1})`, respectively. The API function for querying the number of outcomes that have probability $p \pm \epsilon$ is `measurement_counts(p, ε)`. One can also query the number of outcomes that have probability $\geq p$ by invoking the function `tail_counts(p)`.

QUASIMODO's API provides the methods `get_state()` and `most_frequent()` to obtain the quantum state (as a pointer to the underlying data-structure) and the outcome with the highest probability, respectively.

3.1   Extending Quasimodo

The currently supported symbolic data-structures for representing quantum states and quantum gates are written in C++ with bindings for Python. All of the current representations implement an abstract C++ class that exposes (i) `QuantumState`, which returns a state object that represents a quantum state, (ii) eighteen quantum-gate operations, (iii) an operation for gate composition, (iv) an operation for applying a gate—either a primitive gate or the result of gate composition—to a quantum state, and (v) five query operations. Users can easily extend QUASIMODO to add a replacement backend by providing an operation to create a state object, as well as implementations of the seventeen gate operations and three query operations. Currently, the easiest path is to implement the custom representation in C++ as an implementation of the abstract C++ class used by QUASIMODO's standard backends.

4   The Internals of Quasimodo

In this section, we elaborate on the internals of QUASIMODO. Specifically, we briefly summarize the BDD, WBDD, and CFLOBDD data-structures that QUASIMODO currently supports, and illustrate how QUASIMODO performs symbolic simulation using these data-structures. For brevity, we illustrate the way QUASIMODO uses these data-structures using the example of the Hadamard gate, a commonly used quantum gate, defined by the matrix $H = \frac{1}{\sqrt{2}} \begin{bmatrix} 1 & 1 \\ 1 & -1 \end{bmatrix}$.

Binary Decision Diagrams (BDDs). QUASIMODO provides an option to use Binary Decision Diagrams (BDDs) [3,5,7] as the underlying data-structure. A BDD is a data-structure used to efficiently represent a function from Boolean variables to some space of values (Boolean or non-Boolean). The extension of

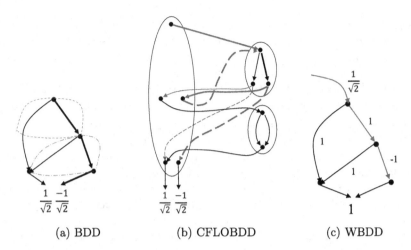

(a) BDD   (b) CFLOBDD   (c) WBDD

Fig. 2. Three representations of the Hadamard matrix $H = \frac{1}{\sqrt{2}} \begin{bmatrix} 1 & 1 \\ 1 & -1 \end{bmatrix}$. (a) A BDD, (b) a CFLOBDD, and (c) a WBDD. The variable ordering is $\langle x_0, y_0 \rangle$, where x_0 is the row decision variable and y_0 is the column decision variable.

BDDs to support a non-Boolean range is called Multi-Terminal BDDs (MTB-DDs) [7] or Algebraic DDs (ADDs) [3]. In this paper, we use "BDD" as a generic term for both BDDs proper and MTBDDs/ADDs. Each node in a BDD corresponds to a specific Boolean variable, and the node's outgoing edges represents a decision based on the variable's value (0 or 1). The leaves of the BDD represent the different outputs of the Boolean function. In the best case, BDDs provide an exponential compression in space compared to the size of the decision-tree representation of the function.[2] Figure 2(a) shows the BDD representation of the Hadamard matrix H with variable ordering $\langle x_0, y_0 \rangle$, where x_0 is the row decision variable and y_0 is the column decision variable.

We enhanced the CUDD library [12] by incorporating complex numbers at the leaf nodes and adding the ability to count paths.

Context-Free-Language Ordered Binary Decision Diagrams (CFLOBDDs). CFLOBDDs [11] are a binary decision diagram inspired by BDDs, but the two data-structures are based on different principles. A BDD is an acyclic finite-state machine (modulo ply-skipping), whereas a CFLOBDD is a particular kind of

---

[2] Technically, the BDD variant that, in the best case, is exponentially smaller than the corresponding decision tree, is called a *quasi-reduced BDD*. Quasi-reduced BDDs are BDDs in which variable ordering is respected, but don't-care nodes are *not* removed, and thus all paths from the root to a leaf have length n, where n is the number of variables. However, the size of a quasi-reduced BDD is at most a factor of $n+1$ larger than the size of the corresponding (reduced, ordered) BDD [15, Thm. 3.2.3]. Thus, although BDDs can give better-than-exponential compression compared to decision trees, at best, it is linear compression of exponential compression.

single-entry, multi-exit, non-recursive, hierarchical finite-state machine (HFSM) [2]. Whereas a BDD can be considered to be a special form of bounded-size, branching, but non-looping program, a CFLOBDD can be considered to be a bounded-size, branching, but non-looping program in which a certain form of *procedure call* is permitted.

CFLOBDDs can provide an exponential compression over BDDs and double-exponential compression over the decision-tree representation. The additional compression of CFLOBDDs can be roughly attributed to the following reasons:

- As with BDDs, one level of exponential compression comes from sharing in a directed-acyclic-graph (i.e., a complete binary tree is folded to a dag).
- In CFLOBDDs, there is a further level of exponential compression from reuse of "procedures": the same "procedure" can be called multiple times at different call sites.

Such "procedure calls" allow additional sharing of structure beyond what is possible in BDDs: a BDD can share sub-DAGs, whereas a procedure call in a CFLOBDD shares the "middle of a DAG". The CFLOBDD for Hadamard matrix H, shown in Fig. 2(b), illustrates this concept: the fork node (the node with a split) at the top right of Fig. 2(b) is shared twice—once during the red solid path (—) and again during the blue dashed path $(- \cdot -)$. The corresponding elements of the BDD for H are outlined in red and blue in Fig. 2(a). The cell entry $H[1][1]$, which corresponds to the assignment $\{x_0 \mapsto 1, y_0 \mapsto 1\}$, is shown in Fig. 2(a) (BDD) and Fig. 2(b) (CFLOBDD) as the paths highlighted in bold that lead to the value $\frac{-1}{\sqrt{2}}$.

Weighted Binary Decision Diagrams (WBDDs). A Weighted Binary Decision Diagram (WBDD) [9,14], [19, Ch. 5] is similar to a BDD, but each decision (edge) in the diagram is assigned a weight. To evaluate the represented function f on a given input a (i.e., a is an assignment in $\{0,1\}^n$), the path for a is followed; the value of $f(a)$ is the product of the weights encountered along the path. Consider how the WBDD in Fig. 2(c) represents Hadamard matrix H. The variable ordering used is $\langle x_0, y_0 \rangle$, where x_0 is the row decision variable and y_0 is the column decision variable. Consider the assignment $a = \{x_0 \mapsto 1, y_0 \mapsto 1\}$. This assignment corresponds to the path shown in red in Fig. 2(c). The WBDD has a weight $\frac{1}{\sqrt{2}}$ at the root, which is common to all paths. The weight corresponding to $\{x_0 \mapsto 1\}$ is 1 and $\{y_0 \mapsto 1\}$ is -1; consequently, a evaluates to $\frac{1}{\sqrt{2}} * 1 * -1 = \frac{-1}{\sqrt{2}}$, which is equal to the value in cell $H[1][1]$.

WBDDs have been used in a variety of applications, such as verification and quantum simulation [19]. In the case of quantum simulation, the weights on the edges of a WBDD are complex numbers. Additionally, the weight on the left-hand edge at every decision node is normalized to 1; this invariant ensures that WBDDs provide a canonical representation of Boolean functions. We use the MQT DD package [19] for backend WBDD support. As distributed, MQT DD supports at most 128 qubits; we modified it to support up to 2^{31} qubits.

Symbolic Simulation. A symbolic simulation of a quantum circuit-computation [11,13,19] uses a symbolic representation qs of a quantum state and performs operations on qs that correspond to quantum-circuit operations.

- A quantum state of n qubits is a vector of size $2^n \times 1$. Its entries are called *amplitudes*, and the vector represents the probability distribution given by the squares of the absolute values of the amplitudes. In QUASIMODO, CFLOBDDs, BDDs, and WBDDs are used to represent functions of the form $f : \{0,1\}^n \to \mathbb{C}$—i.e., f is a vector holding complex amplitudes.
- A quantum gate performs a linear transformation of a quantum state. Quantum-gate application is implemented by using a CFLOBDD, BDD, or WBDD to represent the matrix describing the quantum gate, and performing a matrix-vector multiplication ([11, Sect. 7.6–Sect. 7.7], [3]) of the gate matrix and the quantum state.
- For CFLOBDDs, BDDs, and WBDDs, operations like prob, measurement_counts, and tail_counts are implemented as exact operations—i.e., no sampling—via projection and path-counting operations ([11, Sect. 7.8], [5]). For CFLOBDDs and BDDs, QUASIMODO computes prob via an efficient path-counting operation [11, Sect. 7.8.1 and Sect. 10.1.2, respectively] to obtain the number of paths leading to each terminal value, and then projects the result onto the variables of interest (as specified by the user). QUASIMODO then returns the sum of the probabilities of the remaining paths. In the case of WBDDs as the backend, QUASIMODO computes the probability of every node ([19, Ch. 5]) instead of counting paths. To compute measurement_counts, QUASIMODO returns the number of paths that lead to the requested probability value within the provided threshold ϵ. On querying tail_counts, QUASIMODO returns the number of paths that lead to terminal values having probability prob $\geq$ p, where p is the requested probability.
- Once path-counts are computed, a measurement from the CFLOBDD, BDD, or WBDD symbolic representation of a quantum state is a data-structure traversal that can be carried out in time proportional to $\mathcal{O}(\max(\text{number of qubits in the circuit}, \text{size of argument CFLOBDD}))$

5   Experiments

In this section, we present some experimental results from using QUASIMODO on seven quantum benchmarks, Greenberger-Horne-Zeilinger state creation (GHZ), Bernstein-Vazirani algorithm (BV), Deutsch-Jozsa algorithm (DJ), Simon's algorithm, Grover's algorithm, Shor's algorithm ($2n + 3$ qubits circuit by [4]), and application of the Quantum Fourier Transform (QFT) to a basis state, for different numbers of qubits. Columns 2–4 of Table 1 show the time taken for running the benchmarks with CFLOBDDs, BDDs (CUDD 3.0.0 [12]), and WBDDs (MQT DD v2.1.0 [17]). For each benchmark and number of qubits, we created 50 random oracles and report the average time taken across the 50 runs. For each run of each benchmark, we performed a measurement at the end of the circuit computation and checked if the measured outcome is correct. We ran all of the experiments on AWS machines: t2.xlarge machines with 4 vCPUs, 16GB memory, and a stack size of 8192KB, running on an Ubuntu OS.

One sees that CFLOBDDs scale better than BDDs and WBDDs for the GHZ, BV, and DJ benchmarks as the number of qubits increases. BDDs perform better than CFLOBDDs and are comparable to WBDDs for Simon's algorithm, whereas WBDDs perform better than BDDs and CFLOBDDs for QFT, Grover's algorithm, and Shor's algorithm.

We noticed that the BDD implementation suffers from precision issues; i.e., if an algorithm with a large number of qubits contains too many Hadamard gates, it can lead to extremely low-probability values for each basis state, which are rounded to 0, which in turn causes leaves that really should hold different miniscule values to be coelesced unsoundly, leading to incorrect results. To overcome this issue, one needs to increase the floating-point precision of the floating-point package used to represent BDD leaf values. We increased the precision at 512 qubits (*) and again at 2048 qubits (**).

Part of these results are similar to the work reported in [11]; however, that paper did not use QUASIMODO. The results of the present paper were obtained using QUASIMODO, and we also report results for WBDDs, as well as BDDs and CFLOBDDs (both of which were used in [11]). The numbers given in Table 1 are slightly different from those given in [11] because these quantum circuits exclusively use gate operations that are applied in sequence to the initial quantum state. One can rewrite the quantum circuit to first compute various gate-gate operations (either Kronecker product or matrix-multiplication operations) and then apply the resultant gate to the initial quantum state. For example, consider a part of a circuit defined as follows:

```
for i in range(0, n):
    qc.cx(i, n)
```

Instead of applying CNOT (cx) sequentially for every i, one can construct a gate equivalent to $cx\_op = \Pi_{i=0}^{n-1} cx(i, n)$ and then apply cx_op to quantum state qc as follows:

```
cx_op = qc.create_cx(0, n)
for i in range(1, n):
    tmp = qc.create_cx(i, n)
    cx_op = qc.gate_gate_apply(cx_op, tmp)
qc.apply_gate(cx_op)
```

QUASIMODO supports such operations as Kronecker product and matrix product of two gate matrices. [11] uses such computations for both oracle construction and as part of the quantum algorithm. Table 2 shows the results on GHZ, BV, and DJ algorithms using the same circuit and oracle construction used in [11]. However, Simon's algorithm, Grover's algorithm, and Shor's algorithm in [11] use operations outside QUASIMODO's computational model, and

Table 1. Performance of CFLOBDDs, BDDs, WBDDs using QUASIMODO; and other simulators like MQT DDSim, Quimb, and Google Tensor Network (GTN)

Benchmark	#Qubits	CFLOBDD Time (sec)	BDD Time (sec)	WBDD Time (sec)	MQT DDSim Time (sec)	Quimb Time (sec)	GTN Time (sec)
GHZ	8	0.03	0.007	0.008	0.065	0.255	0.003
	16	0.03	0.008	0.011	0.068	0.368	0.010
	32	0.031	0.008	0.017	0.074	0.932	Memory Error
	64	0.032	0.012	0.03	0.087	3.16	
	128	0.035	0.026	0.06	0.116	12.1	
	256	0.041	0.1	0.134	Not Supported	Memory Error	
	512	0.053	0.552	0.35			
	1024	0.078	3.01	1.05			
	2048	0.13	18.8	3.59			
	4096	0.239	129.92	13.33			
BV	8	0.037	0.007	0.007	0.068	0.288	0.005
	16	0.045	0.009	0.009	0.072	0.461	0.017
	32	0.06	0.013	0.012	0.082	1.21	Memory Error
	64	0.095	0.033	0.019	0.105	4.64	
	128	0.17	0.116	0.036	Not Supported	20.72	
	256	0.33	0.42	0.082		Memory Error	
	512*	0.68	2.12	0.235			
	1024	1.43	10.65	0.753			
	2048**	3.1	Timeout (15 min.)	2.76			
	4096	6.78		10.77			
DJ	8	0.037	0.007	0.009	0.069	0.401	0.008
	16	0.045	0.01	0.012	0.075	0.873	0.034
	32	0.06	0.016	0.019	0.087	2.97	Memory Error
	64	0.092	0.042	0.036	0.115	8.63	
	128	0.16	0.17	0.082	Not Supported	43.53	
	256	0.3	0.72	0.235		Memory Error	
	512*	0.6	3.9	0.753			
	1024	1.22	20.92	2.76			
	2048**	2.55	Timeout (15 min.)	10.77			
	4096	5.55		43.94			
Simons Alg.	4	0.05	0.014	0.008	0.064	0.272	0.004
	8	0.076	0.043	0.015	0.101	0.653	0.02
	16	Timeout (15 min.)	9.8	8.89	1.267	2.56	Memory Error
	32		Timeout (15 min.)	Timeout (15 min.)	Timeout (15 min.)	17.34	
	64					267	
QFT	4	0.03	0.007	0.007	0.064	0.023	0.004
	8	0.04	0.043	0.009	0.068	0.035	0.012
	16	182.34	4.98	0.013	0.103	0.074	0.438
	32	Timeout (15 min.)	Timeout (15 min.)	0.027	0.154	0.231	Memory Error
	64			0.104	0.363	1.64	
	128			0.498	Not Supported	10.32	
	256			2.73		103.65	
	512			17.54		Timeout (15 min.)	
	1024			148.5			
Grovers Alg.	4	0.055	0.015	0.019	0.239	Memory Error	Memory Error
	8	1.62	6.55	0.013	0.145		
	16	Timeout (15 min.)	Timeout (15 min.)	0.369	2.45		
	32			Timeout (15 min.)	Timeout (15 min.)		
Shor's Alg. (15, 2)	4	Timeout (15 min.)	Timeout (15 min.)	0.034	2.83	Timeout (15 min.)	Timeout (15 min.)
Shor's Alg. (21, 2)	5	Timeout (15 min.)	Timeout (15 min.)	0.252	9.35	Timeout (15 min.)	Timeout (15 min.)
Shor's Alg. (39, 2)	5	Timeout (15 min.)	Timeout (15 min.)	0.766	21.94	Timeout (15 min.)	Timeout (15 min.)
Shor's Alg. (69, 4)	6	Timeout (15 min.)	Timeout (15 min.)	Timeout (15 min.)	204.08	Timeout (15 min.)	Timeout (15 min.)
Shor's Alg. (95, 8)	7	Timeout (15 min.)	Timeout (15 min.)	Timeout (15 min.)	192.05	Timeout (15 min.)	Timeout (15 min.)
Shor's Alg. (119, 2)	8	Timeout (15 min.)	Timeout (15 min.)	Timeout (15 min.)	206.62	Timeout (15 min.)	Timeout (15 min.)

the results on these benchmarks differ from [11]. (Note that the results reported in Table 2 do not include the time taken for the construction of the oracle.)

We also compared QUASIMODO with three other quantum-simulation tools: MQT DDSim [18], Quimb [8], and Google Tensor Network (GTN) [10]. MQT

Table 2. Performance of CFLOBDDs, BDDs, WBDDs using QUASIMODO on an alternate circuit implementation of GHZ, BV, DJ algorithms

Benchmark	#Qubits	CFLOBDD	BDD	WBDD
		Time (sec)	Time (sec)	Time (sec)
GHZ	8	0.03	0.008	0.009
	16	0.03	0.01	0.011
	32	0.034	0.035	0.017
	64	0.036	0.194	0.032
	128	0.04	1.47	Precision Issue
	256	0.05	11.77	
	512	0.07	Timeout (15 min.)	
	1024	0.11		
	2048	0.19		
	4096	0.36		
BV	8	0.001	0.001	0.001
	16	0.001	0.001	0.001
	32	0.002	0.006	0.001
	64	0.003	0.025	0.001
	128	0.005	0.089	Precision Issue
	256	0.009	0.46	
	512	0.015	Timeout (15 min.)	
	1024	0.027		
	2048	0.049		
	4096	0.086		
DJ	8	0.005	0.001	0.001
	16	0.005	0.002	0.001
	32	0.005	0.006	0.001
	64	0.006	0.025	0.001
	128	0.006	0.084	Precision Issue
	256	0.007	0.43	
	512	0.008	Timeout (15 min.)	
	1024	0.01		
	2048	0.013		
	4096	0.019		

DDSim is based on WBDDs (using MQT DD), whereas Quimb and GTN are based on tensor networks. Their performance is shown in columns 6–8 of Table 1. Note that MQT DDSim does not support more than 128 qubits.

6   Conclusion

In this paper, we presented QUASIMODO, an extensible, open-source framework for quantum simulation using symbolic data-structures. QUASIMODO supports CFLOBDDs and both unweighted and weighted BDDs as the underlying data-structures for representing quantum states and for performing quantum-circuit operations. QUASIMODO is implemented as a Python library. It provides an API to commonly used quantum gates and quantum operations, and also supports operations for (i) computing the probability of a measurement leading to a given set of states, (ii) obtaining a representation of the set of states that would be observed with a given probability, and (iii) measuring an outcome from a quantum state.

References

1. Aleksandrowicz, G., et al.: Qiskit: an open-source framework for quantum computing (2021). https://doi.org/10.5281/zenodo.2573505
2. Alur, R., Benedikt, M., Etessami, K., Godefroid, P., Reps, T., Yannakakis, M.: Analysis of recursive state machines. ACM Trans. Progr. Lang. Syst. **27**(4), 786–818 (2005)
3. Bahar, R.I., et al.: Algebraic decision diagrams and their applications. Formal Methods Syst. Des. **10**(2/3), 171–206 (1997). https://doi.org/10.1023/A:1008699807402
4. Beauregard, S.: Circuit for Shor's algorithm using 2n+3 qubits. arXiv preprint quant-ph/0205095 (2002)
5. Bryant, R.E.: Graph-based algorithms for Boolean function manipulation. IEEE Trans. Comp. **C-35**(6), 677–691 (1986)
6. Cirq Developers: Cirq (2022). https://doi.org/10.5281/zenodo.7465577. http://github.com/quantumlib/Cirq/graphs/contributors
7. Fujita, M., McGeer, P.C., Yang, J.C.: Multi-terminal binary decision diagrams: an efficient data structure for matrix representation. Formal Methods Syst. Des. **10**(2/3), 149–169 (1997). https://doi.org/10.1023/A:1008647823331
8. Gray, J.: quimb: a python library for quantum information and many-body calculations. J. Open Source Softw. **3**(29), 819 (2018). https://doi.org/10.21105/joss.00819
9. Niemann, P., Wille, R., Miller, D.M., Thornton, M.A., Drechsler, R.: QMDDs: efficient quantum function representation and manipulation. IEEE Trans. Comput. Aided Des. Integr. Circuits Syst. **35**(1), 86–99 (2016). https://doi.org/10.1109/TCAD.2015.2459034
10. Roberts, C., et al.: TensorNetwork: a library for physics and machine learning (2019)
11. Sistla, M., Chaudhuri, S., Reps, T.: CFLOBDDs: context-free-language ordered binary decision diagrams. arXiv:2211.06818 (2022)
12. Somenzi, F.: CUDD: CU decision diagram package-release 2.4.0. University of Colorado at Boulder (2012)
13. Tsai, Y.H., Jiang, J.H.R., Jhang, C.S.: Bit-slicing the Hilbert space: scaling up accurate quantum circuit simulation. In: Design Automation Conference (DAC), pp. 439–444 (2021). https://doi.org/10.1109/DAC18074.2021.9586191

14. Viamontes, G.F., Markov, I.L., Hayes, J.P.: High-performance QuIDD-based simulation of quantum circuits. In: 2004 Design, Automation and Test in Europe Conference and Exposition (DATE 2004), 16-20 February 2004, Paris, France, pp. 1354–1355. IEEE Computer Society (2004). https://doi.org/10.1109/DATE.2004.1269084

15. Wegener, I.: Branching programs and binary decision diagrams. SIAM Monographs on Disc. Math. and Appl., Society for Industrial and Applied Mathematics (2000)

16. Wille, R., Burgholzer, L., Artner, M.: Visualizing decision diagrams for quantum computing. In: Design, Automation and Test in Europe (2021)

17. Zulehner, A., Hillmich, S., Wille, R.: How to efficiently handle complex values? Implementing decision diagrams for quantum computing. International Conference on Computer Aided Design (ICCAD) (2019)

18. Zulehner, A., Wille, R.: Advanced simulation of quantum computations. Trans. CAD Integr. Circuit. Syst. **38**(5), 848–859 (2019). https://doi.org/10.1109/TCAD.2018.2834427

19. Zulehner, A., Wille, R.: Introducing Design Automation for Quantum Computing. Springer (2020). https://doi.org/10.1007/978-3-030-41753-6

Verifying the Verifier: eBPF Range Analysis Verification

Harishankar Vishwanathan$^{(\boxtimes)}$, Matan Shachnai, Srinivas Narayana, and Santosh Nagarakatte

Rutgers University, New Brunswick, USA
{harishankar.vishwanathan,m.shachnai,
srinivas.narayana,santosh.nagarakatte}@rutgers.edu

Abstract. This paper proposes an automated method to check the correctness of range analysis used in the Linux kernel's eBPF verifier. We provide the specification of soundness for range analysis performed by the eBPF verifier. We automatically generate verification conditions that encode the operation of the eBPF verifier directly from the Linux kernel's C source code and check it against our specification. When we discover instances where the eBPF verifier is unsound, we propose a method to generate an eBPF program that demonstrates the mismatch between the abstract and the concrete semantics. Our prototype automatically checks the soundness of 16 versions of the eBPF verifier in the Linux kernel versions ranging from 4.14 to 5.19. In this process, we have discovered new bugs in older versions and proved the soundness of range analysis in the latest version of the Linux kernel.

Keywords: Abstract interpretation · Program verification · Program synthesis · Kernel extensions · eBPF

1 Introduction

Extended Berkeley Packet Filter (eBPF) enables the Linux kernel to be extended with user-developed functionality. Historically, eBPF has its roots in a domain-specific language for efficient packet filtering [53], wherein a user can write a description of packets that must be captured by the network stack. In its modern form, eBPF is an in-kernel register-based virtual machine with a custom 64-bit RISC instruction set. eBPF programs can be Just-in-Time (JIT) compiled to the native processor hardware with access to a subset of kernel functions and memory. Programs written in eBPF are widely used in the industry, e.g. for load balancing [10], DDoS mitigation [38], and access control [12].

eBPF Verifier. A user should be able to attach expressive programs within the operating system, while ensuring that they are safe to run. For this purpose, Linux has a built-in eBPF verifier [11] which performs a static analysis of the eBPF program to check safety properties before allowing the program

---

H. Vishwanathan and M. Shachnai—Equal contribution.

ⓒ The Author(s) 2023
C. Enea and A. Lal (Eds.): CAV 2023, LNCS 13966, pp. 226–251, 2023.
https://doi.org/10.1007/978-3-031-37709-9_12

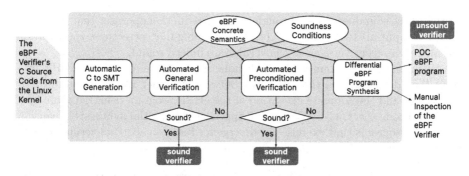

Fig. 1. Agni's methodology for automatically checking the correctness of the eBPF verifier on each commit. When we find the kernel to be unsound, we generate an eBPF program (i.e., a POC) highlighting the mismatch between abstract and concrete semantics. When we are not able to generate a POC, kernel requires a manual verification.

to be loaded. Given that the verifier is executed in a production kernel, any bug in the verifier creates a huge attack surface for exploits [50,51,62,66] and vulnerabilities [1–9,23–26,35,43–45].

Abstract Interpretation in the Kernel. The verifier, among other things, tracks the values of its variables which it subsequently uses to deem memory accesses to the kernel data structures to be safe. The eBPF static analyzer employs abstract interpretation [33] with multiple abstract domains to track the types, liveness, and values of program variables across all executions. It uses five abstract domains to track the values of variables (i.e., value tracking); four of them are variants of interval domains and the other is a bitwise domain named tnum [55,57,65,71]. The kernel implements abstract operators for each of these domains efficiently. Unlike traditional sound composition of sound operators typically done with abstract interpretation (i.e., modular reduced products) [31], the abstract operators are composed in a non-modular fashion. Specifically, the kernel mixes up the implementation of abstract operators in one domain with reduction operators that combine information across domains (Sect. 3, see Fig. 2(d)). Further, the Linux kernel does not provide any soundness guarantees for these operators. This makes the task of verification challenging because each abstract domain's correctness individually does not necessarily imply the correctness of their composition. To the best of our knowledge, there are no existing sound reduction operators for the abstract domains in the kernel.

This Paper. We propose an automated verification approach to check the soundness of the eBPF verifier for value tracking. To perform soundness checks on every kernel commit, we automatically generate a formula representing the actions of the abstract operator from the verifier's C code rather than manually writing them (Sect. 5). Figure 1 illustrates our workflow. We develop a general correctness specification to determine when a non-modular abstract operator that combines multiple domains is sound (Sect. 4.1). When we checked the validity of the formula generated from recent versions of the verifier with the correctness specification, we found that the verifier is unsound. We discovered that the verifier avoids manifesting these soundness bugs through a shared reduction operator that preconditions the input abstract values (Sect. 4.2). Refining our correctness specification revealed that recent versions of the verifier are indeed sound.

When our refined soundness check fails, we generate a concrete eBPF program that demonstrates the mismatch between abstract values maintained by the verifier and the concrete execution of the eBPF program using program synthesis methods (Sect. 4.3). We call our approach differential synthesis because it generates programs that exercise the divergence between abstract verifier semantics and concrete eBPF semantics in unsound kernels.

Prototype and Results. We have used our prototype, Agni [18,72]., to automatically check the soundness of 16 kernel versions starting from 4.14 to 5.19. In this process, we have discovered 27 previously unknown bugs, which have been subsequently fixed by unrelated patches. For each unsound verifier, we have generated an eBPF program with at most three instructions that shows the mismatch between the semantics in $\approx 97\%$ of the cases. The eBPF programs highlighting the mismatch are smaller than previously known ones. We have also shown that the newer versions of the kernel verifier are sound with respect to value tracking. The source code for our prototype is publicly available [18,72].

2   Background on Abstract Interpretation

Abstract interpretation is a form of static analysis that uses *abstract values* from an abstract domain to represent sets of values of program variables. For example, in the interval domain, the abstract value $[x, y]$, with $x, y \in \mathbb{Z}, x \le y$, tracks the set of concrete values $\{z \in \mathbb{Z} \mid x \le z \le y\}$. *Abstract operators* concisely represent the impact of the program's operations over its variables in the abstract domain.

Abstract Domains, Concretization, and Abstraction. Formally, concrete values form a partially ordered set (poset) with elements $\mathbb{C}$ and ordering relation $\sqsubseteq_{\mathbb{C}}$. The concrete poset is $\mathbb{C} \triangleq 2^{\mathbb{Z}}$ (i.e., power set of integers) with the ordering relationship $\sqsubseteq_{\mathbb{C}}$ being the subset relationship $\subseteq$. An abstract domain is also a poset, with a set of elements $\mathbb{A}$ and ordering relation $\sqsubseteq_{\mathbb{A}}$. A *concretization function* $\gamma \colon \mathbb{A} \to \mathbb{C}$, takes an abstract value $a \in \mathbb{A}$ and produces concrete values $c \in \mathbb{C}$. For example, the interval domain uses the abstract poset $\mathbb{A} \triangleq \mathbb{Z} \times \mathbb{Z}$ with the ordering relation $[x, y] \sqsubseteq_{\mathbb{A}} [a, b] \Leftrightarrow (a \le x) \land (b \ge y)$.

An *abstraction function* $\alpha \colon \mathbb{C} \to \mathbb{A}$, takes a concrete value $c \in \mathbb{C}$ and produces an abstract value $a \in \mathbb{A}$. For example, in the interval domain, abstracting the concrete value $\{1, 4, 6\}$ produces $\alpha(\{1, 4, 6\}) = [1, 6]$. Concretizing $[1, 6]$ yields $\gamma([1, 6]) = \{1, 2, 3, 4, 5, 6\}$. As seen in this example, the abstraction of a concrete value may over-approximate it to maintain concise representation in the abstract domain. A value $a \in \mathbb{A}$ is a *sound abstraction* of $c \in \mathbb{C}$ if $c \sqsubseteq_{\mathbb{C}} \gamma(a)$. For a sound abstraction a of c, the smaller the concrete value $\gamma(a)$, the higher the *precision* of the abstraction.

Abstract Operators. Intuitively, abstract operators capture the computation of concrete operators over program variables in the abstract domain. For example, in the range domain, the action of concrete unary negation $-_{\mathbb{C}}(\cdot)$ may be abstracted by $-_{\mathbb{A}}([x,y]) \triangleq [-y,-x]$. Consider a concrete operation $f\colon \mathbb{Z}_n \to \mathbb{Z}_n$ on a single program variable that is an n-bit value. We can lift f point-wise to any set $c \in \mathbb{C}$, where $f(c) \triangleq \{f(z) \mid z \in c\}$. An abstract operator $g\colon \mathbb{A} \to \mathbb{A}$ is a *sound abstraction* of f if $\forall a \in \mathbb{A} : f(\gamma(a)) \sqsubseteq_{\mathbb{C}} \gamma(g(a))$.

Galois Connection. Abstraction and concretization functions (α, γ) are said to form a Galois connection if: (1) α is monotonic (i.e. $x \sqsubseteq_{\mathbb{C}} y \implies \alpha(x) \sqsubseteq_{\mathbb{A}} \alpha(y)$), (2) γ is monotonic ($a \sqsubseteq_{\mathbb{A}} b \implies \gamma(a) \sqsubseteq_{\mathbb{C}} \gamma(b)$), (3) $\gamma \circ \alpha$ is extensive (i.e. $\forall c \in \mathbb{C} : c \sqsubseteq_{\mathbb{C}} \gamma(\alpha(c))$), and (4) $\alpha \circ \gamma$ is reductive (i.e. $\forall a \in \mathbb{A} : \alpha(\gamma(a)) \sqsubseteq_{\mathbb{A}} a$) [56].

The Galois connection is denoted as $(\mathbb{C}, \sqsubseteq_{\mathbb{C}}) \xleftrightarrow[\alpha]{\gamma} (\mathbb{A}, \sqsubseteq_{\mathbb{A}})$. The existence of a Galois connection enables reasoning about the soundness and the precision of any abstract operator. It is in principle possible to compute a sound and precise abstraction of any concrete operator f through the composition $\alpha \circ f \circ \gamma$. However, it is computationally expensive, due to the evaluation of the concretization γ.

Combining Multiple Abstract Domains Through Cartesian Product [31]. Suppose we are given two abstract domains (sets $\mathbb{A}_1, \mathbb{A}_2$) with sound abstraction functions $\alpha_{\mathbb{A}1}, \alpha_{\mathbb{A}2}$ and concretization functions $\gamma_{\mathbb{A}1}, \gamma_{\mathbb{A}2}$. The Cartesian product abstract domain uses the set $\mathbb{P} \triangleq \mathbb{A}_1 \times \mathbb{A}_2$, and the ordering relationship applied separately to each domain: $(a_1 \sqsubseteq_{\mathbb{A}1} b_1) \wedge (a_2 \sqsubseteq_{\mathbb{A}2} b_2) \implies (a_1, a_2) \sqsubseteq_{\mathbb{P}} (b_1, b_2)$. The concretization function intersects the results obtained from concretizing each element in its respective abstract domain: $\gamma_{\mathbb{P}}(a_1, a_2) \triangleq \gamma_{\mathbb{A}1}(a_1) \cap \gamma_{\mathbb{A}2}(a_2)$. For a concrete value $c \in \mathbb{C}$, the abstraction functions are applied domain-wise and combined: $\alpha_{\mathbb{P}}(c) \triangleq (\alpha_{\mathbb{A}1}(c), \alpha_{\mathbb{A}2}(c))$. The Cartesian product domain enjoys a Galois connection $(\mathbb{C}, \sqsubseteq_{\mathbb{C}}) \xleftrightarrow[\alpha_{\mathbb{P}}]{\gamma_{\mathbb{P}}} (\mathbb{P}, \sqsubseteq_{\mathbb{P}})$ building on the Galois connections of its component abstract domains.

For example, consider the interval domain $(\mathbb{A}_1, \sqsubseteq_{\mathbb{A}1}$ defined as above) and the parity domain $(\mathbb{A}_2 \triangleq \{\bot, odd, even, \top\}$ with ordering relationships $\bot \sqsubseteq_{\mathbb{A}2} odd, even \sqsubseteq_{\mathbb{A}2} \top)$. Suppose at some point the two interpretations produce abstract values $[3,5]$ and $even$ in the two domains. The concretization of the Cartesian product abstract value $([3,5], even)$ produces the set $\{4\}$, which is smaller than the concretizations of either abstract value $[3,5]$ or $even$ in their respective domains. However, since the abstraction functions are applied domain-wise, such information cannot be propagated to the abstract values themselves. For example, it is desirable to propagate information from the abstract value $even$ in $\mathbb{A}_2$ to reduce the interval to $[4,4]$ in $\mathbb{A}_1$.

Reduced Products. Intuitively, we wish to make an abstract value in one domain more precise using information available in an abstract value in a different domain. Suppose we are given an abstract value (a_1, a_2) from the Cartesian product domain. A *reduction operator* [34] attempts to find the smallest abstract value (a_1', a_2') such that its concretization is the same as that of (a_1, a_2), i.e. $\gamma_{\mathbb{A}1}(a_1) \cap \gamma_{\mathbb{A}2}(a_2)$. Formally, the reduction operator $\rho\colon \mathbb{P} \to \mathbb{P}$ is defined as the greatest lower bound of all abstract values whose concretization is larger than that of the given abstract value,

i.e. $\rho(a_1, a_2) \triangleq \bigsqcap_{\mathbb{P}} \{(a_1', a_2') \mid \gamma_{\mathbb{P}}(a_1, a_2) \sqsubseteq_{\mathbb{C}} \gamma_{\mathbb{P}}(a_1', a_2')\}$.

However, this definition is impractical to compute even on finite domains.

In general, more "relaxed" versions of reduction operators may be designed to improve precision with efficient computation. For example, Granger [40] introduces a set of reduction operators ρ_1, ρ_2 to reduce each abstract domain in turn, using information from the other, until a fixed point. The operator $\rho_1 \colon \mathbb{A}_1 \times \mathbb{A}_2 \to \mathbb{A}_1$ reduces the abstract value in domain $\mathbb{A}_1$, while $\rho_2 \colon \mathbb{A}_1 \times \mathbb{A}_2 \to \mathbb{A}_2$ reduces that in $\mathbb{A}_2$. The reduction using ρ_1 is sound if $\forall a_1 \in \mathbb{A}_1, a_2 \in \mathbb{A}_2 :$ $\gamma_{\mathbb{P}}(\rho_1(a_1, a_2), a_2) = \gamma_{\mathbb{P}}(a_1, a_2)$ (preserve concrete values in the intersection) and $\rho_1(a_1, a_2) \sqsubseteq_{\mathbb{A}1} a_1$ (improve precision). Similarly, reduction using ρ_2 is sound if $\forall a_1 \in \mathbb{A}_1, a_2 \in \mathbb{A}_2 : \gamma_{\mathbb{P}}(a_1, \rho_2(a_1, a_2)) = \gamma_{\mathbb{P}}(a_1, a_2)$ and $\rho_2(a_1, a_2) \sqsubseteq_{\mathbb{A}2} a_2$.

3   Abstract Interpretation in the Linux Kernel

The Linux kernel implements abstract interpretation to check the safety of eBPF programs loaded into the kernel. The kernel's algorithms are encoded into a component called the *eBPF verifier,* which is a part of the pre-compiled operating system image. The Linux kernel uses several abstract domains to track the type, liveness, and values of registers and memory locations used by eBPF programs. Among these, the abstract domains used by the kernel to track values are critical since they are used to guard statically against malicious programs that may access kernel memory. In Linux kernel v5.19 (latest as of this writing), these analyses constitute roughly 2100 lines of source code in the eBPF verifier. Implementing such analyses soundly in the kernel is challenging. This part of the verifier has been a source of several high-profile security vulnerabilities [1–9, 23–26, 35, 43–45] and exploits [50, 51, 62, 66].

The Linux kernel uses five abstract domains for value tracking, including intervals in unsigned 64-bit (u64), unsigned 32-bit (u32), signed 64-bit (s64), signed 32-bit (s32), and tri-state numbers (tnum [61, 71]). The kernel does not provide a formal specification of their abstraction or concretization functions, or proofs of soundness of the abstract operators. Below, we illustrate the abstract domains used in the Linux kernel with the unsigned 64-bit interval domain u64 and tristate numbers tnum.

The u64 Domain. The u64 abstract domain tracks an upper and lower bound of a 64-bit register interpreted as an unsigned 64-bit value. The eBPF verifier maintains the abstract u64 value as part of its static state for each register. Figure 2(a) provides a simplified C source code for abstract addition in the u64 domain. The operator takes two abstract values in1 and in2, with the two components of each abstract value denoted by the members u64_min and u64_max. The output abstract value is stored in out. Here, U64_MAX is the largest 64-bit non-negative integer. The first if condition detects if integer overflows may occur as a result of addition. If there is overflow, the analysis loses all precision, setting the 64-bit bounds of the result to the largest abstract value, [0, U64_MAX]. If there is no overflow (else clause), out is set to the component-wise sum of the bounds of in1 and in2, similar to unbounded bit-width interval arithmetic [32].

Formally, the abstract domain is $\mathbb{A}_{u64} \triangleq \{[x, y] \mid (x, y \in \mathbb{Z}_{64}^+) \wedge (x \leq_{u64} y)\}$, where $\mathbb{Z}_{64}^+$ is the set of 64-bit non-negative integers, and $\leq_{u64}$ represents a 64-bit unsigned comparison. The ordering relationship is $(x_1 \geq_{u64}$

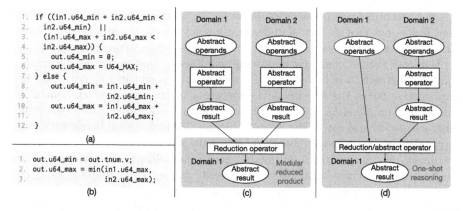

```
1.  if ((in1.u64_min + in2.u64_min <
2.      in2.u64_min) ||
3.      (in1.u64_max + in2.u64_max <
4.      in2.u64_max)) {
5.      out.u64_min = 0;
6.      out.u64_max = U64_MAX;
7.  } else {
8.      out.u64_min = in1.u64_min +
9.                   in2.u64_min;
10.     out.u64_max = in1.u64_max +
11.                  in2.u64_max;
12. }
```
(a)

```
1.  out.u64_min = out.tnum.v;
2.  out.u64_max = min(in1.u64_max,
3.                   in2.u64_max);
```
(b)

Fig. 2. Excerpts (simplified) from the kernel's implementation of the abstract operators for (a) addition (from the function `scalar_min_max_add` [14]), and (b) bitwise AND (from `scalar_min_max_and` [15]). (c) Example of reduced product abstract interpretation where one may use inductive assertions on abstract operators from each domain, along with the soundness of reduction operators, to reason about the correctness of the overall abstraction. The greyed boxes show modular reasoning about components within the boxes. (d) In the Linux kernel, it is challenging to reason modularly about the correctness of abstract operators in each domain independently from their pairwise reductions, since the implementation combines abstraction with reduction. Proving soundness requires one-shot reasoning about all operations together.

$x_2) \wedge (y_1 \leq_{u64} y_2) \Leftrightarrow [x_1, y_1] \sqsubseteq_{u64} [x_2, y_2]$. The *concretization function* is $\gamma_{u64}([x, y]) \triangleq \{z \mid (z \in \mathbb{Z}_{64}^+) \wedge (x \leq_{u64} z \leq_{u64} y)\}$. The *abstraction function* is $\alpha_{u64}(c) \triangleq [min_{u64}(c), max_{u64}(c)]$, where c is a member of the powerset of $\mathbb{Z}_{64}^+$, and $min_{u64}(\cdot)$ and $max_{u64}(\cdot)$ compute the minimum and maximum over a finite set c where each element of c is interpreted as a 64-bit unsigned value.

Tristate Numbers (`tnums`). This abstract domain in the Linux kernel tracks which bits of a variable are known to be 0, known to be 1, or unknown across executions of the program. This domain is similar to bitwise domains [55,57,65]. However, the kernel implements this abstract domain efficiently with a tuple of two unsigned integers (`v,m`). If `m` for a particular bit is 1, then the value of that bit is unknown. If `m` for a particular bit is 0, then value of that bit is equal to `v`'s value for the particular bit. More formally, the abstraction function (α_t) is written using two other functions defined as follows: $\alpha_\&(C) \triangleq \&\{c \mid c \in C\}$; and $\alpha_|(C) \triangleq |\{c \mid c \in C\}$. Then, $\alpha_t(C) \triangleq (\alpha_\&(C), \alpha_\&(C)^\wedge \alpha_|(C))$. The concretization function is written as: $\gamma_t(P) = \gamma_t((P.\mathsf{v}, P.\mathsf{m})) \triangleq \{c \in \mathbb{Z}_{64}^+ \mid c \& P.\mathsf{m} = P.\mathsf{v}\}$ [71].

Abstract Operators In The Linux Kernel and Challenges in Proving their Correctness. The Linux kernel implements an abstract operator in each abstract domain for each arithmetic and logic (ALU) instruction and each jump instruction in the eBPF instruction set.[1] The kernel verifier also provides

---

[1] The ALU instructions include 32 and 64-bit add, sub, mul, div, or, and, lsh, rsh, neg, mod, xor, arsh and the jump instructions include 32 and 64-bit ja, jeq, jgt, jge, jlt, jle, jset, jne, jsgt, jsge, jslt, jsle [13].

functions to propagate information between the abstractions (reductions). However, it does not provide formal underpinnings, e.g. Galois connections. The overall analysis appears to be a Reduced Product abstract interpretation (Sect. 2).

However, the key challenge in proving soundness is that the kernel's operators combine abstraction with reduction. Consider the excerpt in Fig. 2(b) from the implementation of the bitwise AND operation in the u64 abstract domain in the kernel, simplified for clarity. As before, in1 and in2 correspond to the input abstract values, and out to the output abstract value. The members with names tnum.* denote the components of the abstract tnum. Before the execution of these two lines, the tnum abstract output out.tnum.v has already been computed. In the first line, the lower bound of the u64 result, out.u64_min is updated using the output abstract value in a different domain (out.tnum.v). Hence, the operation overall is not (merely) an abstract operator in the u64 domain. In the second line, the output abstract state out.u64_max is updated using the abstract *inputs* in the u64 domain. Reduction operators consume abstract outputs, not inputs. Hence, the operation overall is not a reduction operator either.

These characteristics apply not just to the kernel's bitwise AND operation in the u64 domain. Figure 2(d) shows the structure of several of the kernel's abstract operators, compared against the typical structure of product domains and reduction operators (Fig. 2(c)). The kernel's algorithms combine abstraction with reduction, making it challenging to prove their soundness in a modular fashion. Instead, we must resort to a "one-shot" approach, which attempts to prove the soundness of the abstraction of an operator in one domain and the reductions across domains together. We call the kernel's abstract operators *abstraction/reduction operators* in the rest of this paper.

4   Automatic Verification of the Kernel's Algorithms

Given the non-modular structure of the kernel's abstract algorithms (Sect. 3), we cannot use traditional methods to prove their soundness, i.e. by showing the soundness of each domain and the reductions separately. Further, the kernel's algorithms have been evolving continuously with the inclusion of new features to the eBPF run-time environment. We want our methods to be applicable to every new update and commit to the Linux kernel.

Hence, our goal is to perform automatic verification using SMT solvers to prove the soundness of (or find bugs in) the C implementation of Linux's abstraction/reduction operators. We work with the input-output semantics of the kernel's abstraction/reduction operators in first-order logic extracted automatically from the kernel's C source code (details of the extraction deferred to Sect. 5).

Overview of Our Approach. We develop generic soundness specifications for the Linux kernel's abstraction/reduction operators, handling arithmetic, logic, and branching instructions (Sect. 4.1). We find that several kernel operators violate these soundness specifications. However, many of these violations flag latent bugs in the kernel's algorithms—bugs which are not necessarily manifested in concrete program executions. We observe that the kernel includes a shared "tail" of computation in all of its abstraction/reduction operators. We use this shared computation to refine our soundness specification by preconditioning the input abstract states (Sect. 4.2). This refinement enables proving the soundness of several of the kernel's operators. However, it still identifies many potential violations of soundness in the kernel. We present a method based on program synthesis to generate loop-free eBPF programs that manifest the bugs identified by the soundness specifications, automatically producing programs that have divergent concrete and abstract semantics. We call this method differential synthesis (Sect. 4.3).

Figure 1 illustrates our entire workflow. Starting from the Linux kernel source code, our techniques produce concrete eBPF programs that manifest soundness bugs in the kernel's algorithms. We have used this procedure to prove the soundness of multiple Linux kernel versions, discovered previously unknown soundness bugs (i.e. no CVEs assigned, to our knowledge), with validated proof-of-concept programs triggering those bugs.

4.1 Soundness Specification for Abstraction/Reduction Operators

We present verification conditions that are *sufficient* to assert the soundness of abstraction/reduction operators in the Linux kernel.

Preliminaries. Encoding Soundness for a Single Abstract Domain in SMT. We describe how to encode the soundness condition for an abstract operator of two operands as an SMT formula, since most eBPF instructions take two operands. Suppose $f: \mathbb{C} \times \mathbb{C} \to \mathbb{C}$ is a binary concrete operation (e.g. 64-bit addition) over the concrete domain (e.g. $\mathbb{C} \triangleq 2^{\mathbb{Z}_{64}^+}$). Suppose the operator $g: \mathbb{A} \times \mathbb{A} \to \mathbb{A}$ abstracts f. Operator g is sound (Sect. 2) if $\forall a_1, a_2 \in \mathbb{A} : f(\gamma(a_1), \gamma(a_2)) \sqsubseteq_{\mathbb{C}} \gamma(g(a_1, a_2))$.

We can check soundness with an SMT query as follows. Suppose we have SMT variables to denote a bitvector $x \in \mathbb{C}$ and an abstract value $a \in \mathbb{A}$. We can use the concretization function γ to represent the fact that x is included in the concretization of a. For example, for the u64 domain, we may use the formula $mem_{u64}(x, a) \triangleq (a.min \leq_{u64} x) \wedge (x \leq_{u64} a.max)$ to assert that $x \in \gamma(a)$.

The input-output relationship of abstract operator g is available as a first-order logic formula extracted from the kernel source code (Sect. 5). We represent the resulting formula as $a^o = abs_g(a_1^i, a_2^i)$, where a_1^i and a_2^i are input abstract values and a^o is the output abstract value.

The concrete semantics of the eBPF instruction set determines the input-output relationship of the concrete operation f. For example, the bpf_add64 instruction performs binary addition (with possibility of overflow) of two 64-bit registers, denoted by $+_{64}$. The action of this instruction is encoded through the formula $x^o = conc_f(x_1^i, x_2^i)$; for bpf_add64, $conc_f(x_1^i, x_2^i) \triangleq (x_1^i +_{64} x_2^i)$.

The concrete ordering relationship $\sqsubseteq_{\mathbb{C}}$ is just the subset operation $\subseteq$ between two sets. For two sets S_1, S_2, we can encode the relationship $S_1 \subseteq S_2$ by asserting that $\forall x : x \in S_1 \Rightarrow x \in S_2$. Putting all this together, we can check the soundness of a single abstract operator abs_g, by using an SMT solver to check the validity of the formula (i.e., by checking if the negation is unsatisfiable).

$$\forall x_1^i, \ x_2^i \in \mathbb{C}, \ a_1^i, a_2^i \in \mathbb{A} : mem_{\mathbb{A}}(x_1^i, a_1^i) \wedge mem_{\mathbb{A}}(x_2^i, a_2^i) \wedge$$
$$x^o = conc_f(x_1^i, x_2^i) \wedge a^o = abs_g(a_1^i, a_2^i) \Rightarrow mem_{\mathbb{A}}(x^o, a^o) \tag{1}$$

Generalizing Soundness To Abstraction/Reduction Operators Spanning Multiple Abstract Domains. For the abstraction/reduction operators in Linux (Sect. 3), we can no longer assert soundness for an abstract domain purely using abstract values from that domain. We show how to extend the reasoning to two abstract domains. Let us denote the two abstract domains by $\mathbb{A}_1$ and $\mathbb{A}_2$. An eBPF instruction has two inputs (x_1^i, x_2^i) and each input has the corresponding abstract value for each abstract domain. Suppose a_{11}^i and a_{12}^i correspond to abstract values for the first input from domains $\mathbb{A}_1$ and $\mathbb{A}_2$, respectively (similarly, a_{21}^i and a_{22}^i for the second input). Further, the concrete input x^i must be in the intersection of the concretizations of all its abstract values. Hence, the formula $mem_{\mathbb{A}_1}(x_1^i, a_{11}^i) \wedge mem_{\mathbb{A}_2}(x_1^i, a_{12}^i) \wedge mem_{\mathbb{A}_1}(x_2^i, a_{21}^i) \wedge mem_{\mathbb{A}_2}(x_2^i, a_{22}^i)$ must hold.

We denote the kernel's abstraction/reduction operation, extracted from C source code, as $\{a_1^o, a_2^o\} = abs_g(a_{11}^i, a_{12}^i, a_{21}^i, a_{22}^i)$. Note that the kernel's operation outputs a list of abstract values corresponding to each abstract domain (unlike Eq. 1). The concrete semantics dictates that $x^o = conc_f(x_1^i, x_2^i)$.

To establish the soundness of the abstraction/reduction operator, we ensure that the concrete output is included in the concretizations of the abstract outputs in each domain, i.e., $mem_{\mathbb{A}_1}(x^o, a_1^o) \wedge mem_{\mathbb{A}_2}(x^o, a_2^o)$. Putting it all together, we check the validity of the following SMT formula:

$$\forall x_1^i, \ x_2^i \in \mathbb{C}, \ a_{11}^i, \ a_{21}^i \subset \mathbb{A}_1, \ a_{12}^i, \ a_{22}^i \subset \mathbb{A}_2 :$$
$$mem_{\mathbb{A}_1}(x_1^i, a_{11}^i) \wedge mem_{\mathbb{A}_2}(x_1^i, a_{12}^i) \wedge mem_{\mathbb{A}_1}(x_2^i, a_{21}^i) \wedge mem_{\mathbb{A}_2}(x_2^i, a_{22}^i) \wedge$$
$$x^o = conc_f(x_1^i, x_2^i) \wedge \{a_1^o, a_2^o\} = abs_g(a_{11}^i, a_{12}^i, a_{21}^i, a_{22}^i)$$
$$\Rightarrow (mem_{\mathbb{A}_1}(x^o, a_1^o) \wedge mem_{\mathbb{A}_2}(x^o, a_2^o)) \qquad (2)$$

The kernel uses five abstract domains (Sect. 3). Extending from two domains to all five domains is straightforward. It involves the addition of membership queries for the inputs and the corresponding abstract values (i.e., mem predicate above). The encoding of each of the kernel's abstraction/reduction operators returns a list containing five abstract outputs (one for each domain). Finally, we check that the concrete output is included in the concretization of each abstract output.

Encoding Arithmetic and Logic (ALU) Instructions. Using the formulation above, we have encoded soundness specifications of abstraction/reduction operators for 16 eBPF ALU instructions, which include 32 and 64-bit add, sub, div, or, and, lsh, rsh, neg, mod, xor, arsh. Notably, we exclude the multiplication instruction mul, whose SMT formula involves a bitvector multiplication operation and a large unrolled loop, making it intractable in the bitvector theory.

Encoding Branch Instructions. We also encoded soundness specifications for conditional and unconditional branches (jeq, jlt, etc.) on both 64 and 32-bit register operands. These amount to 20 instructions, for a total of 36 instructions captured by our encodings. While the soundness of abstracting ALU instructions follows the general structure of Eq. 2, writing down the soundness conditions for branches is more involved. Branches do not concretely modify their input registers. However, the kernel learns new information in the abstract domains using the branch outcome (true vs. false). For example, in the u64 domain, consider two abstract registers $[1, 5], [3, 3]$. Jumping upon an = (equals) comparison shows that the first register can also be set to $[3, 3]$ in the true case. Indeed, each conditional jump instruction produces *four* abstract outputs (rather than the usual *one* output for ALU instructions), corresponding to updated abstract values for two registers across two branch outcomes.

We illustrate the encoding of the correctness condition for the jump instruction for a single abstract domain. Given two concrete operands x_1^i and x_2^i, the concrete interpretation for the jump instruction returns whether the condition is true or false. When $x^o = conc_f(x_1^i, x_2^i)$, x^o will be either true or false. The kernel's abstraction/reduction operator generates four output abstract values, $a_{1t}^o, a_{1f}^o, a_{2t}^o, a_{2f}^o$. There are two abstract outputs corresponding to each input. They reflect the updated abstract value for the true case (e.g., a_{1t}^o is the updated abstract value of the first input when the branch condition is true), and similarly for the false case. We represent the kernel's abstraction/reduction operator for branch instructions by the formula $\{a_{1t}^o, a_{1f}^o, a_{2t}^o, a_{2f}^o\} = abs_g(a_1^i, a_2^i)$.

Our correctness condition for jumps requires that the inputs are present in the concretizations of the corresponding abstract value in both the true and false branch outcomes. The formula below specifies this correctness condition.

$$\forall x_1^i, \ x_2^i \in \mathbb{C}, \ a_1^i, \ a_2^i \in \mathbb{A} : mem_\mathbb{A}(x_1^i, a_1^i) \wedge mem_\mathbb{A}(x_2^i, a_2^i) \wedge$$
$$x^o = conc_f(x_1^i, x_2^i) \wedge \{a_{1t}^o, a_{1f}^o, a_{2t}^o, a_{2f}^o\} = abs_g(a_1^i, a_2^i) \Rightarrow$$
$$((x^o \Rightarrow (mem_\mathbb{A}(x_1^i, a_{1t}^o) \wedge mem_\mathbb{A}(x_2^i, a_{2t}^o))) \wedge \qquad (3)$$
$$(\neg x^o \Rightarrow (mem_\mathbb{A}(x_1^i, a_{1f}^o) \wedge mem_\mathbb{A}(x_2^i, a_{2f}^o))))$$

The above correctness condition can be extended to multiple domains in a manner similar to Eq. 2. The kernel's implementation of the abstraction/reduction operator for a single jump instruction produces 20 output abstract values (2 inputs × 2 branch outcomes × 5 domains).

4.2 Refining Soundness Specification with Input Preconditioning

When we checked the soundness of the kernel's verifier using the soundness specifications in Sect. 4.1, we observed that many of the abstract operators are not sound. However, it is unclear whether these violations are latent unsound behaviors, or behaviors that could actually manifest with concrete eBPF programs. Specifically, the precondition in Eq. 2 is too general, including any combination of abstract values (across domains) as long as the intersection of their concretizations is non-empty. Indeed, the abstract operators in the Linux kernel are unsound if each instruction may start from any arbitrary abstract value across domains. However, these combinations of abstract values may never be encountered in any eBPF program. Our goal is to refine the soundness specifications from Sect. 4.1 to minimize reporting latent (but unmanifested) bugs.

Shared Suffix of Abstraction/Reduction Operator. Upon carefully analyzing the kernel's abstraction/reduction operators, we observed that the kernel performs certain common computations—a *shared suffix* of abstraction/reduction operations—right before producing each abstract output (Fig. 3(a)). As a concrete example, in kernel version 5.19, the function `reg_bounds_sync` is called at the end of each ALU operation [49], updating the signed domains using the unsigned domains, the u64 bounds from u32 bounds and tnums, besides other reductions [48].

Our key insight is that this shared suffix of abstraction/reduction has the effect of preconditioning the initial abstract values for any subsequent instruction, narrowing down the set of possible abstract values that a subsequent instruction may encounter as input. Further, all eBPF programs start executing from abstract values where each register in every domain is either $\top$ (any concrete value in the domain) or its concretization is a singleton (precisely known concrete value). We observe and show using an SMT solver that the shared suffix computation does not modify initial values.

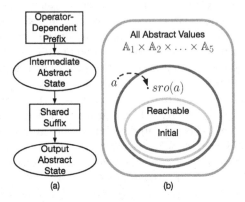

Fig. 3. (a) The structure of each abstraction/reduction operator in the kernel can be conceptualized as having a prefix that depends on the specific operator, generating an intermediate output, and a suffix that is shared across all the operators, resulting in the final abstract output. (b) We use a refined soundness specification that preconditions input abstract values a using the shared suffix $sro(.)$ of the reduction operators used in the Linux kernel.

Refined Soundness Specification by Preconditioning Input Abstract Values. We can leverage shared suffix operations to refine our soundness specification as follows. First, let $sro(a)$ denote the abstract outputs of computing the shared suffix of the abstraction/reduction over the abstract inputs $a \in \mathbb{A}_1 \times \mathbb{A}_2 \cdots \times \mathbb{A}_5$. The SMT formula encoding $sro(a)$ is extracted using our C to SMT encoder (Sect. 5). The main change from the specifications in Sect. 4.1 is that the shared suffix preconditions the input values to any abstract operator. Hence, for example, the soundness specification for two abstract domains from Eq. 2 is updated to use an input abstract value $sro(a)$ as shown below:

$$\forall x_1^i, \ x_2^i \in \mathbb{C}, \ a_{11}^i, \ a_{21}^i \in \mathbb{A}_1, \ a_{12}^i, \ a_{22}^i \in \mathbb{A}_2 :$$
$$(b_{11}^i, b_{12}^i) = sro(a_{11}^i, a_{12}^i) \wedge (b_{21}^i, b_{22}^i) = sro(a_{21}^i, a_{22}^i) \wedge$$
$$mem_{\mathbb{A}_1}(x_1^i, b_{11}^i) \wedge mem_{\mathbb{A}_2}(x_1^i, b_{12}^i) \wedge mem_{\mathbb{A}_1}(x_2^i, b_{21}^i) \wedge mem_{\mathbb{A}_2}(x_2^i, b_{22}^i) \wedge$$
$$x^o = conc_f(x_1^i, x_2^i) \wedge \{a_1^o, a_2^o\} = abs_g(b_{11}^i, b_{12}^i, b_{21}^i, b_{22}^i)$$
$$\Rightarrow (mem_{\mathbb{A}_1}(x^o, a_1^o) \wedge mem_{\mathbb{A}_2}(x^o, a_2^o)) \qquad (4)$$

It is straightforward to generalize to multiple domains. Refinement eliminated most of the latent violations reported from Sect. 4.1. We found that the latest kernel versions are sound with respect to value tracking.

4.3   Automatically Producing Programs Exercising Soundness Bugs

Even after refining the soundness specifications (Sect. 4.2), we still find a few violations of soundness. It is challenging to determine whether these violations are "real" (manifested in actual eBPF programs) or latent, since input abstract values preconditioned by sro still overapproximate the abstract values that may occur when analyzing actual eBPF programs (Fig. 3(b), Sect. 4.2).

We aim to automatically generate eBPF programs that manifest soundness bugs (uncovered by the techniques in Sect. 4.2) in an actual kernel verifier execution. Our problem is a form of *differential synthesis*: generating programs whose semantics diverge between the concrete execution and the abstract analysis. We propose a sound but incomplete approach to generate eBPF programs that demonstrate soundness violations. We enumerate loop-free programs up to a bounded length, using an SMT solver to identify concrete and abstract operands that manifest soundness violations.

Our approach is a combination of well-known existing techniques from enumerative [20,52,63] and deductive program synthesis [19,41,58,67]. However, unlike typical program synthesis problems which have a $\forall\exists$ formula structure (e.g. meet a specification on all inputs), our problem has a much more tractable $\exists$ structure, i.e. finding one concrete input and program to trigger a soundness violation. In this sense, it is more akin to property-directed reachability algorithms used in model checking [22,27].

Preliminaries. The eBPF run-time starts executing eBPF programs with all live registers holding values that are either precisely known at compile time (e.g. offsets into valid memory regions) or completely unknown (e.g. contents of packet memory). For an abstract value $a \in \mathbb{A}_1 \times \mathbb{A}_2 \cdots \times \mathbb{A}_5$, we say that $init(a)$ holds if a is either singleton (e.g. $\forall x \in \mathbb{Z}_{64}^+ : [x,x]$ in u64) or $\top$ in each domain $\mathbb{A}_i$. We refer to such abstract values as *initial abstract values*. It is straightforward to write down an SMT formula for $init(a)$ for the kernel's domains. We say an abstract value $b \in \mathbb{A}_1 \times \mathbb{A}_2 \cdots \times \mathbb{A}_5$ is *reachable* if there exists a sequence of eBPF instructions for which the abstract analysis can produce b for some register starting from input registers whose abstract values all satisfy $init(\cdot)$.

Overview. Given an abstract operator that violates the soundness specification in Sect. 4.2, our algorithm finds an eBPF instruction sequence that shows that the violating input abstract values are reachable. For a bounded program length k, we enumerate all sequences of eBPF concrete operators (i.e. arithmetic, logic, and branching instructions) of length $k - 1$, with the kth instruction being the violating concrete operator. This enumeration produces the "skeleton" of the program, filling out the opcodes, but leaving the operands as well as the data and control flow undetermined. For each skeleton, we discharge an SMT query that identifies the concrete and abstract operands for k instructions with well-formed data and control flow. The first instruction consumes eBPF initial abstract values. Starting from $k = 1$, if we cannot find an eBPF program of length k that manifests the violation, we increment k and try again until a timeout.

Single Instruction Programs $(k = 1)$. As the base case, we check whether initial abstract values along with suitable concrete values may already violate soundness (Sect. 4.2). For example, suppose our enumeration generated the 1-instruction program $v = \mathtt{bpf\_or}(t, u)$. For simplicity, below we work with just one abstract domain. Building on Eq. (1), we discharge the SMT formula:

$$t, u \in \mathbb{C}, \quad a_t, a_u \in \mathbb{A} :$$
$$init(a_t) \wedge init(a_u) \wedge mem_\mathbb{A}(t, a_t) \wedge mem_\mathbb{A}(u, a_u) \wedge$$
$$v = conc_{or}(t, u) \wedge a_v = abs_{or}(a_t, a_u) \wedge \neg(mem_\mathbb{A}(v, a_v)) \tag{5}$$

If the formula is satisfiable, the model provides the concrete operands t, u, with the result that $\mathtt{bpf\_or}(t, u)$ is an executable eBPF program manifesting the soundness violation. However, an unsound operator may fail to produce a model since the necessary abstract operands lie outside the initial abstract values.

Straight-line Programs, Length $k > 1$. Larger the length of the program k, larger the set of reachable input abstract values available to manifest a soundness violation at the kth instruction. We exhaustively enumerate all possible $(k - 1)$-long instruction sequences. To enable well-formed data flow between the k instructions, the inputs for each instruction are sourced either from the outputs of prior instructions or initial abstract values.

For example, consider a two-instruction program ($k = 2$) generated by the enumerator: $r = \mathtt{bpf\_and(p,q)}$; $v = \mathtt{bpf\_or(t,u)}$, We are looking for soundness violation in $\mathtt{bpf\_or}$. The variables p, q, r, t, u, v are concrete values, with corresponding abstract values $a_p, a_q, \cdots, a_v$. The abstract inputs of the first instruction $\mathtt{bpf\_and}$ are initial abstract values. The abstract inputs of the last instruction may be drawn from either a_p, a_q, a_r or the initial abstract values. We use the formula $assign(x, \{y_1, y_2, \cdots\})$ to denote that x is mapped to one of the variables $y_1, y_2, \cdots$ in both the concrete and abstract domains. We can write down $assign(x, \{y_1, y_2, \cdots\}) \triangleq (x = y_1 \wedge a_x = a_{y_1}) \vee (x = y_2 \wedge a_x = a_{y_2}) \vee \cdots$. We discharge the following SMT formula to a solver:

$$p, q, r, t, u, v \in \mathbb{C}, \quad a_p, a_q, a_r, a_t, a_u, a_v \in \mathbb{A} :$$
$$init(a_p) \wedge init(a_q) \wedge mem_\mathbb{A}(p, a_p) \wedge mem_\mathbb{A}(q, a_q) \wedge$$
$$r = conc_{and}(p, q) \wedge a_r = abs_{and}(a_p, a_q) \wedge mem_\mathbb{A}(r, a_r) \wedge$$
$$(init(a_t) \vee assign(t, \{p, q, r\})) \wedge (init(a_u) \vee assign(u, \{p, q, r\})) \wedge$$
$$mem_\mathbb{A}(t, a_t) \wedge mem_\mathbb{A}(u, a_u) \wedge$$
$$v = conc_{or}(t, u) \wedge a_v = abs_{or}(a_t, a_u) \wedge \neg(mem_\mathbb{A}(v, a_v)) \tag{6}$$

A model for the formula produces the concrete and abstract operands for the two instructions, leading to an executable bug-manifesting program. This approach is extensible to more instructions and more abstract domains.

Loop-free Programs. Incorporating branch instructions significantly broadens the set of input abstract values available to the kth instruction, improving the likelihood of finding a bug-manifesting program at a given length. We turn each branch into a single-instruction $\mathtt{ite}$ whose outputs are available for subsequent instructions. More concretely, (i) any of the $1 \cdots k - 1$ instructions may be $\mathtt{jump}$ instructions; (ii) the jump target of a branch instruction in the ith slot for both outcomes (i.e. true or false) points to the $i + 1^{th}$ slot, and (iii) the abstract outputs of the branch (e.g. from Eq. (3)) may be used as abstract inputs for subsequent instructions, similar to arithmetic and logic instructions.

As an example, suppose our enumerator produces r = bpf_jump_gt64(p,q,0); v = bpf_or(t,u). Here r is a concrete value which is either *true* or *false*. We use 0 as the jump target, always pointing branches to the next instruction. There are four abstract outputs from the jump: a_{pt}, a_{qt} for the true branch and a_{pf}, a_{qf} for the false branch (see Sect. 4.1). For convenience, we set the abstract value a_p^o (resp. a_q^o) to either a_{pt} or a_{pf} (resp. a_{qt} or a_{qf}) based on the branch outcome; and also assert that the corresponding final concrete values $p^o = p$ and $q^o = q$. Building on Eq. (3), we ask the SMT solver for a model of the formula:

$$p, q, t, u, v \in \mathbb{C}, \quad r \in \{true, false\}, \quad a_p, a_q, a_t, a_u, a_v \in \mathbb{A} :$$
$$init(a_p) \wedge init(a_q) \wedge mem_\mathbb{A}(p, a_p) \wedge mem_\mathbb{A}(q, a_q) \wedge$$
$$r = conc_{jump\_gt64}(p, q) \wedge \{a_{pt}, a_{pf}, a_{qt}, a_{qf}\} = abs_{jump\_gt64}(a_p, a_q) \wedge$$
$$(r \Rightarrow (mem_\mathbb{A}(p, a_{pt}) \wedge mem_\mathbb{A}(q, a_{qt}) \wedge a_p^o = a_{pt} \wedge a_q^o = a_{qt})) \wedge$$
$$(\neg r \Rightarrow (mem_\mathbb{A}(p, a_{pf}) \wedge mem_\mathbb{A}(q, a_{qf}) \wedge a_p^o = a_{pf} \wedge a_q^o = a_{qf})) \wedge$$
$$(init(a_t) \vee assign(t, \{p^o, q^o\})) \wedge (init(a_u) \vee assign(u, \{p^o, q^o\})) \wedge$$
$$mem_\mathbb{A}(t, a_t) \wedge mem_\mathbb{A}(u, a_u) \wedge$$
$$v = conc_{or}(t, u) \wedge a_v = abs_{or}(a_t, a_u) \wedge \neg(mem_\mathbb{A}(v, a_v)) \tag{7}$$

Validation of Manifested Soundness Violations. The programs generated by our approach for bugs with known CVEs were similar to the proof-of-concept implementations found in these CVEs. For previously unknown bugs, we logged the kernel verifier's state as it analyzes eBPF programs and also executed the eBPF program with the concrete operands produced by the SMT solver. We compared the parameters in the SMT solver's model and those from the kernel verifier and run-time result. This process entailed manually compiling and booting into each kernel version that we check, and running the generated programs. For the manifested bugs, we found exact agreement between the SMT model and the observed behaviors in all cases we checked.

5   C to Logic for Kernel's Abstract Operators

To prove the soundness of the kernel's abstract operators, we first have to extract the input-output semantics of the operators from the kernel's implementation in C into first-order logic. It is tedious and error-prone to manually write down the formulas for each version of the kernel. Further, the verifier's abstract semantics can change across versions. Hence, we automatically generate the first-order logic formula (in SMT-LIB format) directly from the verifier's C source code. Modeling C code in general is hard [42,46,64]. However, we observe that it is sufficient to handle a subset of C for the verifier's value-tracking routines.

Verifier's C Code for Value-tracking. The kernel uses two integers to represent abstract values for each of the five domains (Sect. 3). These 10 integers are encapsulated in a structure named bpf_reg_state (reg_st for short). The tnum domain is further encapsulated within reg_st in a struct called tnum. This static "register state" is maintained for each register in the eBPF program being analyzed. The kernel has a single top-level function called adjust_scalar_min_max_vals (adjust_scalar for short) that is called for each abstract operator corresponding to ALU instructions [16]. This function takes three arguments: opcode and two register states named dst and src that track the abstract value in the destination and source register of the eBPF instruction, respectively. Depending on the opcode, one of several switch-cases is executed, which leads to instruction-specific function calls that modify the abstract values in dst and src. None of the functions updating register state in the call-chain have recursion or loops. The kernel has a structured way of accessing the members of reg_st. We use these specific features to translate C code to logic. The structures of the corresponding functions for jumps (reg_set_min_max and descendants) are similar.

Preprocessing the Verifier's C Code. We use the LLVM compiler's [47] intermediate representation (IR) because it allows us to handle complex C code and provides a collection of tools to modify, optimize, and analyze the IR. Figure 4(a) shows an overview of our tool's pipeline. Consider the case where we want to generate the SMT-LIB file for the abstract operator corresponding to the 32-bit bitwise OR instruction (bpf_or32). After obtaining the verifier's code in IR (stage (1)), we proceed to apply our custom IR-transforming passes (stage (2)). First, we remove functions that are not relevant to our purpose because they do not modify register state. Next, we inline all the function calls that adjust_scalar makes. Inlining is possible because there are no recursive functions or loops in the call-graph. Next, we need to create a slice of the verifier that is only concerned with bpf_or32. We inject an LLVM instruction in the entry basic block of adjust_scalar which sets the opcode to bpf_or32. LLVM's optimizer removes all irrelevant code from this IR with constant propagation and dead-code elimination. Next, we adapt a transformation pass from Seahorn's [42] codebase, which allows us to lower memcpy instructions to a sequence of stores. The result is a single function in LLVM IR, which captures the action of the abstract operator given input abstract states (i.e., dst and src) for one instruction (bpf_or32).

The LLVMToSMT Pass. In step (3), we use the theory of bitvectors to generate the first-order logic formula for the function obtained from step (2). Since we encode everything with bitvectors, we need a memory model to capture memory accesses. We model memory as a set of two disjoint regions pointed to by dst and src. Given that the memory is only accessed via the structure reg_st's fields, we can further view memory as a set of named registers. This allows us to model the entire memory as a tree of bitvectors: the leaf nodes store bitvectors corresponding to the first-class members of reg_st (e.g. for u64_min), the non-leaf nodes store trees of aggregate types (e.g. for tnum). C struct member accesses in IR begin with a getelementptr (GEP) instruction, which calculates the pointer (address) of the struct's member. We use an indexing similar to that used by GEP to to identify the bitvector that corresponds to the accessed member.

Handling Straight Line Code and Branches. LLVM's IR is already in SSA form. Every IR instruction that produces a value defines a new temporary virtual

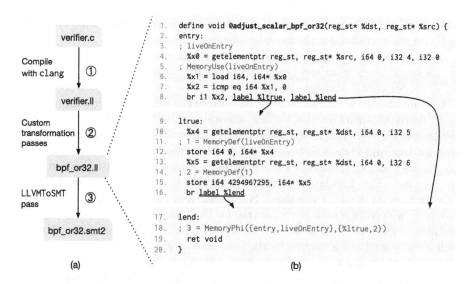

Fig. 4. (a) The pipeline for automatically generating an SMT-LIB file from the Linux kernel's `verifier.c`. Shown here is an instance of the pipeline for the `bpf_or32` instruction. (b) The LLVM IR presented as a CFG, overlaid with MemorySSA analysis in red, for a function `adjust_scalar_bpf_or32` that is representative of verifier code for `bpf_or32`. It takes as input two structs `dst` and `src` and modifies them.

register. We create a fresh bitvector variable when we encounter a temporary in the IR. Consider a simple addition instruction: `%y = add i64 %x, 3`. To encode the instruction, we create a formula that asserts an equality between a fresh bitvector BV_y and the existing one BV_x, based on the semantics of the instruction: $BV_y == BV_x + BV_{const3}$.

To handle branches, we precondition the SMT formula for each basic block with its path condition. As the IR we analyze does not contain loops, the control flow graph (CFG) is a directed acyclic graph. Hence, the path condition of each basic block is a disjunction of path conditions flowing through each incoming edge into the node corresponding to that block in the CFG. Phi nodes (ϕ's) in SSA merge the values flowing in from various paths. We use the `phi` instructions in IR to merge incoming values. We calculate an "edge condition" formula for each incoming edge to the `phi`. Then, we encode the `phi` instruction by appropriately setting the bitvector to the incoming values based on the edge condition.

Handling Memory Access Instructions. Our tool leverages LLVM's MemorySSA analysis [17] to handle `load`s and `store`s. The MemorySSA pass creates new versions of memory upon stores and branch merges, associates load instructions with specific versions, and provides a memory dependence graph between the memory versions. Figure 4 (b) shows an example CFG in IR overlaid with MemorySSA analysis (red). We maintain a one-to-one mapping between the different versions of memory presented by MemorySSA, and versions of our memory model consisting of bitvector-trees. `liveOnEntry` (line 3) is the memory version at the start of the function. The bitvectors in the corresponding bitvector-tree are the input operands for the kernel's abstract operators.

Every load instruction is annotated with a MemoryUse (e.g.. the load instruction on line 6 reads from the liveOnEntry memory version), and preceded by a GEP. Thus, we choose the appropriate bitvector-tree and index into it to obtain the appropriate bitvector (say BV_{src0}). We encode the load instruction as: (BV_{x1} == BV_{src0}). A store instruction (e.g. line 12, annotated using a MemoryDef) modifies an existing memory version (liveOnEntry) to create new version (1). We create a new bitvector-tree and map it to version 1. The bitvectors in this bitvector-tree are exactly the same as liveOnEntry's, except for the bitvector in the location that the store modifies. The latter bitvector is replaced with the bitvector mapped to the temporary used for the store. For a MemoryPhi node (e.g. line 18, creating version 3), we create a new bitvector-tree for the latest memory version (e.g. 3). Similar to regular phi nodes, we use the edge condition of the incoming edges to conditionally set each bitvector in the new bitvector-tree to the corresponding bitvector in the memory version propagated through that edge.

The bitvector-tree corresponding to the active memory version at the point of the (unique) ret instruction (e.g. 3 in the lend block) contains the output operands for the kernel's abstract operators.

6   Experimental Evaluation

Our prototype, Agni [18,72], automatically checks the soundness of the value tracking algorithms in various versions of the kernel eBPF verifier. It uses LLVM 12 [47] for the C to logic translation and the Z3 SMT solver [36] for checking formulas. The source code for our prototype is publicly available [18,72]. We evaluate Agni to determine the effectiveness in checking soundness of the kernel verifier and the ability to generate eBPF programs that manifest soundness violations (which we call proof-of-concepts, or POCs).

Checking Soundness Across Kernel Versions. We have automatically checked the soundness of all combinations of abstract operators and abstract domains for kernels between versions 4.14 and 5.19. Figure 5(a) provides a summary of our results. To keep the size of the table short, we only report kernel versions starting from 4.14 that are known to have a documented CVE or a bug that is distinct from one in a prior kernel version (4.14, 5.5, 5.7-rc1, 5.8, ...). We evaluated intermediate kernel versions that are not reported; our tool can support all kernel versions between 4.14 to 5.19 (the latest as of this writing).

We compare our generic soundness specification (Sect. 4.1, labeled *gen* in columns 2,4,6) and the refined one (Sect. 4.2, labeled *sro* in columns 3,5,7). A kernel with at least one potentially unsound domain or operator is considered unsound (columns 2 and 3). Operator+domain pairs that violated the soundness specification are reported in columns 4 and 5. Those operators that violated soundness in at least one domain are reported in columns 6 and 7.

All kernel versions including the latest ones are unsound with respect to the generic soundness specification (column 2). Even in one of the latest ver-

Kernel Version	Sound?		Num. of Violations		Num. of Unsound Operators		Kernel Version	Sound?		Num. of Violations		Num. of Unsound Operators	
	gen	sro	gen	sro	gen	sro		gen	sro	gen	sro	gen	sro
4.14	✗	✗	23	21	9	7	5.11	✗	✗	71	62	16	16
5.5	✗	✗	32	30	12	10	5.12	✗	✗	71	62	16	16
5.7-rc1	✗	✗	101	99	31	31	5.13	✗	✔	9	0	6	0
5.7	✗	✗	69	67	15	15	5.14	✗	✔	9	0	6	0
5.8	✗	✗	69	67	15	15	5.16	✗	✔	9	0	6	0
5.9	✗	✗	67	65	15	15	5.17	✗	✔	9	0	6	0
5.10	✗	✗	74	65	17	17	5.18	✗	✔	9	0	6	0
5.10-rc1	✗	✗	74	71	17	17	5.19	✗	✔	9	0	6	0

Kernel Version	Num. of Total Violations	All POCs Synth?	Program Length		
			1	2	3
4.14	21	✗	14	4	0
5.5	30	✗	0	20	2
5.7-rc1	99	✔	55	44	0
5.7	67	✔	39	28	0
5.8	67	✔	39	28	0
5.9	65	✔	39	26	0
5.10	65	✔	19	44	2
5.10-rc1	71	✔	39	32	0
5.11	62	✔	16	44	2
5.12	62	✔	16	44	2

(a)   (b)

Fig. 5. (a) Soundness violations detected with the generic soundness specification (Sect. 4.1, labeled *gen*) in comparison to the refined specification (Sect. 4.2, labeled *sro*). We show the number of violating operator+domain pairs (columns 4-5) and number of unsound operators (columns 6-7) (b) Number of generated POCs and their lengths for unsound operator+domains after *sro* checks.

sions of the kernel (v5.19), 6 operators corresponding to bpf_xor64, bpf_xor32, bpf_and64, bpf_or64, bpf_or32, and bpf_and32 are unsound according to the generic soundness specification (column 6, row of kernel version 5.19). Refining the soundness specification enables us to prove the soundness of all operators in kernels newer than 5.13 (column 3). However, even the latter reports violations for older kernels. Among those violations, 27 were previously unknown. A single wrong abstract operator can violate the soundness of many abstract domains (up to 5). The refined (*sro*) specification reduces the reported soundness violations by ≈ 6.8% in potentially unsound kernel versions and by 100% in sound ones.

We observed that the 64-bit jump instructions and 64-bit/32-bit bitwise instructions exhibited the largest number of soundness violations. The unsoundness persisted across multiple kernel versions (until eventually patched).

Generating POCs for Unsound kernels. We evaluate the ability of differential synthesis (Sect. 4.3) to generate eBPF programs that manifest soundness bugs. Figure 5(b) summarizes our results. Starting with operator+domain pairs from soundness violations uncovered by *sro* (column 2), we report whether all operator+domain violations were successfully manifested using POCs (column 3) and the lengths of the POCs successfully generated (columns 4,5,6). We produced a POC for ≈ 97% of soundness violations across kernel versions (validated as described in Sect. 4.3). The smallest POCs for many violations require multi-instruction programs. For example, none of the soundness violations in version 5.5 may be manifested with a single eBPF instruction. We generated a POC for all soundness violations for all but 2 versions of the kernel (for versions 4.14 and 5.5, we generated a POC for all but 3 and 8 violations respectively). The ability to manifest almost all of the reported *sro* violations speaks to the significance and precision of the refinement in the soundness specification. Our differential synthesis technique may enable developers to experiment with concrete eBPF programs to validate and debug unsound behaviors in the kernel verifier.

Some bugs in the eBPF verifier are well known security vulnerabilities and have known POCs [51,62]. We have generated a POC, of equal or lesser size, for all known CVEs in the kernel versions analyzed. For example, we have generated a POC for a well known bug with two instructions instead of four [62].

Time Taken to Verify kernels and Generate POCs. We conducted our experiments on the Cloudlab [37] testbed, using a machine with two 10-core Intel Skylake CPUs running at 2.20 GHz with 192 GB of memory. When using the generic soundness specifications, 90% of the abstract operators (eBPF instructions) were checked for soundness within ≈ 100 minutes. If deemed unsound, the refined specification was checked in ≈ 30 minutes for ≈ 90% of the unsound operators. On the extreme, verifying some operators, as well as finding a POC for some soundness violations, may take a long time (2000 min or more). We attribute this to the significant size of the SMT-LIB formulas that are generated. We were able to find POCs for 90% of the soundness violations in kernel versions 5.7-rc1 through 5.12 within a few hours.

7   Limitations and Caveats

The results in this paper must be interpreted with the following caveats.

Only Range Analysis is Considered. There are other static analyses in the kernel verifier beyond range analysis (Sect. 1). These include tracking register liveness for reading and writing, and detecting speculative execution vulnerabilities.

Coverage of eBPF Abstract Operators. We exclude verifying the soundness of the abstract operators corresponding to multiplication as they cause our SMT verifications to time out. This is primarily due to the presence of 64-bit bitvector multiplication in the SMT encoding of these operators. We have verified their soundness using 8-bit bitvectors. Our results on (un)soundness cover all other abstract arithmetic, logic, and branching operators (Sect. 4.1).

Trusted Computing Base. Our C to SMT translation (Sect. 5) and soundness proofs have software dependencies including the LLVM compiler infrastructure, the Z3 solver, and our translation passes, which together form our trusted computing base. We have unit tested our C-to-SMT translations extensively. We validated our synthesized POCs by manually executing them in Linux kernels running inside the QEMU emulator, replicating the soundness bugs. Despite our best efforts, it is possible that there are bugs in our software infrastructure.

Incompleteness of Differential Synthesis. The differential synthesis approach is incomplete (Sect. 4.3). If our refined verification condition (Eq. (4)) finds an operator unsound, and the synthesis is unable to produce a POC, there are two possibilities. First, there may be long programs which could manifest the unsound behavior. Our enumerative algorithm currently times out for programs of length ≥ 4. Second, it is possible that the bug cannot be manifested with any concrete eBPF program, and is reported due to overapproximation in the soundness specification.

8   Related Work

Closest Related Work. The two closely related prior works are: (1) a paper on tnum verification [71], and (2) a recent manuscript on verifying range analysis [21]. The tnum paper explores formal verification for a single abstract domain: tnums. The recent manuscript [21] also aims to prove the soundness of the eBPF verifier's value-tracking. In contrast, our work differs by (1) exposing the non-modular nature of the abstract operators in the kernel, and (2) proposing a method to reason about abstract operators for both arithmetic and branches, (3) automatically generating VCs from kernel source code, and (4) synthesizing eBPF programs that exercise the divergence of abstract and concrete semantics.

Safety of eBPF Programs And Static Analyzers. eBPF compilation and interpreter safety has been a site of recent endeavors [59,60,69,73,74]. PRE-VAIL [39] uses abstract interpretation using the zone abstract domain for checking safety outside the kernel. In contrast, we focus on proving the soundness of the in-kernel verifier.

Abstract Interpretation And Domain Refinement. Prior work on abstract interpretation [30,31,33] and value-tracking abstract domains [55,56,68] have indirectly influenced the eBPF verifier's design [61,71]. The idea of combining abstract domains to enhance the precision of abstract representations was first introduced by Cousot with the reduced product and disjunctive completion domain refinements [29,34] and further improved by others [70]. A systematic survey on product abstract operators is also available [28]. Specifically, we tailor our work to verify the abstract operators in the Linux kernel.

C to First-order Logic. Similar to our approach that generates first-order-logic formulas from C code, prior tools also generate verification conditions from C code [42,46,54,64]. A few of them, SMACK [64] and SeaHorn [42], use LLVM IR for this purpose. These tools support a rich subset of C. They typically model memory as a linear array of bytes, which is not ideal for modeling kernel source code. We explore a subset of C that is sufficient to handle kernel code and still generates queries using only the bitvector theory, which enables us to efficiently verify soundness for multiple versions of the kernel.

9   Conclusion

We present a fully automated method to verify the soundness of range analysis in the Linux kernel's eBPF verifier. We are able to check the soundness of multiple kernel versions automatically because we generate the verification conditions for the abstract operators directly from the kernel C code. We develop specifications for reasoning about soundness when multiple abstract domains are combined in a non-modular fashion in the kernel. Our refinement to this specification, capturing preconditioning in the kernel, proves the soundness of recent Linux kernels. We also successfully generate concrete eBPF programs that demonstrate the divergence between abstract and concrete semantics when soundness checks fail. Our next step is to push for incorporating this approach in the kernel development process, to help eliminate verifier bugs during code review.

Acknowledgement. This paper is based upon work supported in part by the National Science Foundation under FMITF-Track I Grant No. 2019302. We thank the CAV reviewers, and He Zhu for their valuable feedback. We also thank CloudLab for providing the research testbed for our experiments.

References

1. bpf: fix incorrect sign extension in check_alu_op(). Accessed 14 Jan 2020. https://github.com/torvalds/linux/commit/95a762e2c8c942780948091f8f2a4f32fce1ac6f
2. bpf, x32: Fix bug with ALU64 LSH, RSH, ARSH BPF_X shift by 0. Accessed 14 Apr 2021. https://github.com/torvalds/linux/commit/68a8357ec15bdce55266e9fba8b8b3b8143fa7d2
3. CVE-2017-16996 Mishandling of register truncation. Accessed 22 Jan 2023. https://nvd.nist.gov/vuln/detail/CVE-2017-16996
4. CVE-2017-17852 Mishandling of 32-bit ALU ops. Accessed 22 Jan 2023. https://nvd.nist.gov/vuln/detail/CVE-2017-17852
5. CVE-2017-17853 Mishandling of 32-bit ALU ops. Accessed 22 Jan 2023. https://nvd.nist.gov/vuln/detail/CVE-2017-17853
6. CVE-2017-17864 Mishandled comparison between pointer and unknown data types. Accessed 14 Jan 2020. https://nvd.nist.gov/vuln/detail/CVE-2017-17864
7. CVE-2018-18445 Mishandling of 32-bit RSH op. Accessed 22 Jan 2023. https://nvd.nist.gov/vuln/detail/CVE-2018-18445
8. CVE-2020-8835 Mishandling of bounds tracking for 32-bit JMPs. Accessed 22 Jan 2023. https://nvd.nist.gov/vuln/detail/CVE-2020-8835
9. CVE-2021-3490 The eBPF ALU32 bounds tracking for bitwise ops (AND, OR and XOR) in the Linux kernel did not properly update 32-bit bounds. Accessed 22 Jan 2023. CVE-2021-3490
10. Facebook's Katran load balancer: Kernel XDP program. Accessed 14 Jan 2020. https://github.com/facebookincubator/katran/blob/master/katran/lib/bpf/balancer_kern.c
11. Linux BPF verifier. Accessed 14 Jan 2020. https://github.com/torvalds/linux/blob/master/kernel/bpf/verifier.c
12. Netconf 2018 day 1. Accessed 19 Jan 2020. https://lwn.net/Articles/757201/
13. BPF instruction set. Accessed 14 Jan 2020. https://github.com/iovisor/bpf-docs/blob/master/eBPF.md (2017)
14. Linux verifier's abstract u64 addition (kernel v6.0). Accessed 08 Nov 2022. https://github.com/torvalds/linux/blob/v6.0/kernel/bpf/verifier.c#L8333 (2022)
15. Linux verifier's abstract u64 bitwise AND (kernel v6.0). Accessed 08 Nov 2022. https://github.com/torvalds/linux/blob/v6.0/kernel/bpf/verifier.c#L8513 (2022)
16. Linux verifier's top-level function for value-tracking in scalar for alu instructions (kernel v6.0): adjust_scalar_min_max_vals: Accessed 27 Jan 2023. https://github.com/torvalds/linux/blob/90aaef4e35c4a74b0f1593d06e39eda867ef13d3/kernel/bpf/verifier.c#L10524 (2023)

17. LLVM's MemorySSA. Accessed 27 Jan 2023. https://llvm.org/docs/MemorySSA. html (2023)

18. Verifying the Verifier: eBPF Range Analysis Verification (2023). https://doi.org/ 10.5281/zenodo.7931901

19. Alur, R., Singh, R., Fisman, D., Solar-Lezama, A.: Search-based program synthesis. Commun. ACM **61**(12), 84–93 (2018). https://doi.org/10.1145/3208071

20. Bansal, S., Aiken, A.: Automatic generation of peephole superoptimizers. SIGOPS Oper. Syst. Rev. **40**(5), 394–403 (2006). https://doi.org/10.1145/1168917.1168906

21. Bhat, S., Shacham, H.: Formal verification of the linux kernel eBPF verifier range analysis. Accessed 27 Jan 2023. https://sanjit-bhat.github.io/assets/pdf/ ebpf-verifier-range-analysis22.pdf (2022)

22. Biere, A., Cimatti, A., Clarke, E., Zhu, Y.: Symbolic model checking without BDDs. In: Cleaveland, W.R. (ed.) TACAS 1999. LNCS, vol. 1579, pp. 193–207. Springer, Heidelberg (1999). https://doi.org/10.1007/3-540-49059-0_14

23. Borkmann, D.: bpf: Fix scalar32_min_max_or bounds tracking. Accessed 6 Nov 2022. https://github.com/torvalds/linux/commit/ 5b9fbeb75b6a98955f628e205ac26689bcb1383e (2020)

24. Borkmann, D.: bpf: Undo incorrect __reg_bound_offset32 handling. Accessed 6 Nov 2022. https://git.kernel.org/pub/scm/linux/kernel/git/netdev/net-next.git/ commit/?id=f2d67fec0b43edce8c416101cdc52e71145b5fef (2020)

25. Borkmann, D.: bpf: Fix alu32 const subreg bound tracking on bitwise operations. Accessed 6 Nov 2022. https://git.kernel.org/pub/scm/linux/kernel/git/bpf/ bpf.git/commit/?id=049c4e13714ecbca567b4d5f6d563f05d431c80e (2021)

26. Borkmann, D.: bpf: Fix signed_sub, add32_overflows type handling. Accessed 6 Nov 2022. https://git.kernel.org/pub/scm/linux/kernel/git/torvalds/linux.git/ commit/?id=bc895e8b2a64e502fbba72748d59618272052a8b (2021)

27. Bradley, A.R.: SAT-based model checking without unrolling. In: Jhala, R., Schmidt, D. (eds.) VMCAI 2011. LNCS, vol. 6538, pp. 70–87. Springer, Heidelberg (2011). https://doi.org/10.1007/978-3-642-18275-4_7

28. Cortesi, A., Costantini, G., Ferrara, P.: A survey on product operators in abstract interpretation. Electr. Proceed. Theoret. Comput. Sci. **129**, 325–336 (2013). https://doi.org/10.4204/eptcs.129.19

29. Cousot, P., Cousot, R.: Higher-order abstract interpretation (and application to comportment analysis generalizing strictness, termination, projection and per analysis of functional languages). In: Proceedings of 1994 IEEE International Conference on Computer Languages (ICCL1994), pp. 95–112 (1994). https://doi.org/10. 1109/ICCL.1994.288389

30. Cousot, P.: Abstract interpretation based formal methods and future challenges. In: Wilhelm, R. (ed.) Informatics. LNCS, vol. 2000, pp. 138–156. Springer, Heidelberg (2001). https://doi.org/10.1007/3-540-44577-3_10

31. Cousot, P.: Lecture 13 notes: MIT 16.399, abstract interpretation. Accessed 16 Apr 2021. http://web.mit.edu/afs/athena.mit.edu/course/16/16.399/www/ lecture_13-abstraction1/Cousot_MIT_2005_Course_13_4-1.pdf (2005)

32. Cousot, P., Cousot, R.: Static determination of dynamic properties of programs. In: Proceedings of the 2nd International Symposium on Programming, Paris, France, pp. 106–130. Dunod (1976)

33. Cousot, P., Cousot, R.: Abstract interpretation: a unified lattice model for static analysis of programs by construction or approximation of fixpoints. In: Proceedings of the 4th ACM SIGACT-SIGPLAN Symposium on Principles of Programming Languages, pp. 238–252. POPL 1977, Association for Computing Machinery, New York, NY, USA (1977). https://doi.org/10.1145/512950.512973

34. Cousot, P., Cousot, R.: Systematic design of program analysis frameworks. In: Proceedings of the 6th ACM SIGACT-SIGPLAN Symposium on Principles of Programming Languages. p. 269–282. POPL 1979, Association for Computing Machinery, New York, NY, USA (1979). https://doi.org/10.1145/567752.567778

35. Cree, E.: bpf/verifier: fix bounds calculation on BPF_RSH. Accessed 6 Nov 2022. https://git.kernel.org/pub/scm/linux/kernel/git/torvalds/linux.git/commit/?id=4374f256ce8182019353c0c639bb8d0695b4c941 (2017)

36. de Moura, L., Bjørner, N.: Z3: an efficient SMT solver. In: Ramakrishnan, C.R., Rehof, J. (eds.) TACAS 2008. LNCS, vol. 4963, pp. 337–340. Springer, Heidelberg (2008). https://doi.org/10.1007/978-3-540-78800-3_24

37. Duplyakin, D., et al.: The design and operation of cloudLab. In: Proceedings of the 2019 USENIX Conference on Usenix Annual Technical Conference, pp. 1–14. USENIX ATC 2019, USENIX Association, USA (2019)

38. Fabre, A.: L4Drop: XDP DDoS mitigations. Accessed 19 Jan 2020. https://blog.cloudflare.com/l4drop-xdp-ebpf-based-ddos-mitigations/

39. Gershuni, E., et al.: Simple and precise static analysis of untrusted Linux Kernel extensions. In: Proceedings of the 40th ACM SIGPLAN Conference on Programming Language Design and Implementation, pp. 1069–1084. PLDI 2019, Association for Computing Machinery, New York, NY, USA (2019). https://doi.org/10.1145/3314221.3314590

40. Granger, P.: Improving the results of static analyses of programs by local decreasing iterations. In: Shyamasundar, R. (ed.) FSTTCS 1992. LNCS, vol. 652, pp. 68–79. Springer, Heidelberg (1992). https://doi.org/10.1007/3-540-56287-7_95

41. Gulwani, S., Jha, S., Tiwari, A., Venkatesan, R.: Synthesis of loop-free programs. SIGPLAN Not. **46**(6), 62–73 (2011). https://doi.org/10.1145/1993316.1993506

42. Gurfinkel, A., Kahsai, T., Komuravelli, A., Navas, J.A.: The SeaHorn verification framework. In: Kroening, D., Păsăreanu, C.S. (eds.) Computer Aided Verification, pp. 343–361. Springer International Publishing, Cham (2015)

43. Horn, J.: Arbitrary read+write via incorrect range tracking in ebpf. Accessed 19 Jan 2020. https://bugs.chromium.org/p/project-zero/issues/detail?id=1454

44. Horn, J.: BPF: fix 32-bit ALU op verification. Accessed 6 Nov 2022. https://git.kernel.org/pub/scm/linux/kernel/git/torvalds/linux.git/commit/?id=468f6eafa6c44cb2c5d8aad35e12f06c240a812a (2017)

45. Horn, J.: bpf: 32-bit RSH verification must truncate input before the ALU op. Accessed 6 Nov 2022. https://git.kernel.org/pub/scm/linux/kernel/git/torvalds/linux.git/commit/?id=b799207e1e1816b09e7a5920fbb2d5fcf6edd681 (2018)

46. Kroening, D., Tautschnig, M.: CBMC – C bounded model checker. In: Ábrahám, E., Havelund, K. (eds.) TACAS 2014. LNCS, vol. 8413, pp. 389–391. Springer, Heidelberg (2014). https://doi.org/10.1007/978-3-642-54862-8_26

47. Lattner, C., Adve, V.: Llvm: a compilation framework for lifelong program analysis & transformation. In: International symposium on code generation and optimization, 2004. CGO 2004, pp. 75–86. IEEE (2004). https://doi.org/10.1109/CGO.2004.1281665

48. Linux eBPF maintainers: bounds syncing for abstract registers. Accessed 31 Jan 2023. https://github.com/torvalds/linux/blob/v6.0/kernel/bpf/verifier.c#L1565 (2023)

49. Linux eBPF maintainers: using bounds syncing at end of alu operations. Accessed 31 Jan 2023. https://github.com/torvalds/linux/blob/v6.0/kernel/bpf/verifier.c#L9016 (2023)

50. Lucas Leong: ZDI-20-1440: An incorrect calculation bug in the Linux Kernel eBPF verifier. Accessed 22 Jan 2023. https://www.zerodayinitiative.com/blog/2021/1/18/zdi-20-1440-an-incorrect-calculation-bug-in-the-linux-kernel-ebpf-verifier
51. Manfred Paul: CVE-2020-8835: Linux kernel privilege escalation via improper eBPF program verification. Accessed 22 Jan 2023. https://www.zerodayinitiative.com/blog/2020/4/8/cve-2020-8835-linux-kernel-privilege-escalation-via-improper-ebpf-program-verification
52. Massalin, H.: Superoptimizer: A look at the smallest program. In: Proceedings of the Second International Conference on Architectual Support for Programming Languages and Operating Systems, pp. 122–126. ASPLOS II, Association for Computing Machinery, New York, NY, USA (1987). https://doi.org/10.1145/36206.36194
53. McCanne, S., Jacobson, V.: The BSD packet filter: a new architecture for user-level packet capture. In: USENIX Winter 1993 Conference (USENIX Winter 1993 Conference). USENIX Association, San Diego, CA (1993). https://www.usenix.org/conference/usenix-winter-1993-conference/bsd-packet-filter-new-architecture-user-level-packet
54. Merz, F., Falke, S., Sinz, C.: LLBMC: bounded model checking of C and C++ programs using a compiler IR. In: Joshi, R., Müller, P., Podelski, A. (eds.) VSTTE 2012. LNCS, vol. 7152, pp. 146–161. Springer, Heidelberg (2012). https://doi.org/10.1007/978-3-642-27705-4_12
55. Miné, A.: Abstract domains for bit-level machine integer and floating-point operations. In: WING2012 - 4th International Workshop on invariant Generation, p. 16. Manchester, United Kingdom (2012). https://hal.science/hal-00748094
56. Miné, A.: Tutorial on static inference of numeric invariants by abstract interpretation. Found. Trends® Programm. Lang. 4(3–4), 120–372 (2017). https://doi.org/10.1561/2500000034
57. Monniaux, D.: Verification of device drivers and intelligent controllers: a case study. In: Proceedings of the 7th ACM & IEEE international conference on Embedded software, pp. 30–36 (2007). https://doi.org/10.1145/1289927.1289937
58. Mukherjee, M., Kant, P., Liu, Z., Regehr, J.: Dataflow-based pruning for speeding up superoptimization. Proc. ACM Program. Lang. 4, 3428245 (OOPSLA) (2020). https://doi.org/10.1145/3428245
59. Nelson, L., Bornholt, J., Gu, R., Baumann, A., Torlak, E., Wang, X.: Scaling symbolic evaluation for automated verification of systems code with serval. In: Proceedings of the 27th ACM Symposium on Operating Systems Principles, pp. 225–242. SOSP 2019, Association for Computing Machinery, New York, NY, USA (2019). https://doi.org/10.1145/3341301.3359641
60. Nelson, L., Van Geffen, J., Torlak, E., Wang, X.: Specification and verification in the field: Applying formal methods to BPF just-in-time compilers in the Linux Kernel. In: Proceedings of the 14th USENIX Conference on Operating Systems Design and Implementation. OSDI2020, USENIX Association, USA (2020)
61. Onderka, J., Ratschan, S.: Fast three-valued abstract bit-vector arithmetic. In: Finkbeiner, B., Wies, T. (eds.) VMCAI 2022. LNCS, vol. 13182, pp. 242–262. Springer, Cham (2022). https://doi.org/10.1007/978-3-030-94583-1_12
62. Palmiotti, V.: Kernel pwning with eBPF: a love story. Accessed 31 August 2021. https://www.graplsecurity.com/post/kernel-pwning-with-ebpf-a-love-story
63. Phothilimthana, P.M., Thakur, A., Bodik, R., Dhurjati, D.: Scaling up superoptimization. In: Proceedings of the Twenty-First International Conference on Architectural Support for Programming Languages and Operating Systems, pp. 297–310. ASPLOS 2016, Association for Computing Machinery, New York, NY, USA (2016). https://doi.org/10.1145/2872362.2872387

64. Rakamarić, Z., Emmi, M.: SMACK: decoupling source language details from verifier implementations. In: Biere, A., Bloem, R. (eds.) CAV 2014. LNCS, vol. 8559, pp. 106–113. Springer, Cham (2014). https://doi.org/10.1007/978-3-319-08867-9_7

65. Regehr, J., Duongsaa, U.: Deriving abstract transfer functions for analyzing embedded software. In: Proceedings of the 2006 ACM SIGPLAN/SIGBED Conference on Language, Compilers, and Tool Support for Embedded Systems, pp. 34–43. LCTES 2006, Association for Computing Machinery, New York, NY, USA (2006). https://doi.org/10.1145/1134650.1134657

66. Rick Larabee: eBPF and Analysis of the get-rekt-linux-hardened.c Exploit for CVE-2017-16995. Accessed 22 Jan 2023. https://ricklarabee.blogspot.com/2018/07/ebpf-and-analysis-of-get-rekt-linux.html

67. Sasnauskas, R., Chen, Y., Collingbourne, P., Ketema, J., Taneja, J., Regehr, J.: Souper: a synthesizing superoptimizer. CoRR abs/1711.04422 (2017). https://doi.org/10.48550/arXiv.1711.04422

68. Singh, G., Püschel, M., Vechev, M.: Fast polyhedra abstract domain. In: Proceedings of the 44th ACM SIGPLAN Symposium on Principles of Programming Languages, pp. 46–59. POPL 2017, Association for Computing Machinery, New York, NY, USA (2017). https://doi.org/10.1145/3009837.3009885

69. Van Geffen, J., Nelson, L., Dillig, I., Wang, X., Torlak, E.: Synthesizing JIT compilers for in-Kernel DSLs. In: Lahiri, S.K., Wang, C. (eds.) CAV 2020. LNCS, vol. 12225, pp. 564–586. Springer, Cham (2020). https://doi.org/10.1007/978-3-030-53291-8_29

70. Venet, A.: Abstract cofibered domains: Application to the alias analysis of untyped programs. In: Cousot, R., Schmidt, D.A. (eds.) SAS 1996. LNCS, vol. 1145, pp. 366–382. Springer, Heidelberg (1996). https://doi.org/10.1007/3-540-61739-6_53

71. Vishwanathan, H., Shachnai, M., Narayana, S., Nagarakatte, S.: Sound, precise, and fast abstract interpretation with tristate numbers. In: Proceedings of the 20th IEEE/ACM International Symposium on Code Generation and Optimization, pp. 254–265. CGO 2022, IEEE Press (2022). https://doi.org/10.1109/CGO53902.2022.9741267

72. Vishwanathan, H., Shachnai, M., Narayana, S., Nagarakatte, S.: Agni: verifying the Verifier (eBPF Range Analysis Verification). Accessed 29 May 2023. https://github.com/bpfverif/ebpf-range-analysis-verification-cav23 (2023)

73. Wang, X., Lazar, D., Zeldovich, N., Chlipala, A., Tatlock, Z.: Jitk: a trustworthy in-Kernel interpreter infrastructure. In: Proceedings of the 11th USENIX Conference on Operating Systems Design and Implementation, pp. 33–47. OSDI2014, USENIX Association, USA (2014)

74. Xu, Q., Wong, M.D., Wagle, T., Narayana, S., Sivaraman, A.: Synthesizing safe and efficient kernel extensions for packet processing. In: Proceedings of the 2021 ACM SIGCOMM 2021 Conference, pp. 50–64. SIGCOMM 2021, Association for Computing Machinery, New York, NY, USA (2021). https://doi.org/10.1145/3452296.3472929

Software Verification

Automated Verification of Correctness for Masked Arithmetic Programs

Mingyang Liu[1], Fu Song[1,2,3(✉)], and Taolue Chen[4]

[1] ShanghaiTech University, Shanghai 201210, China
[2] Institute of Software, Chinese Academy of Sciences & University of Chinese Academy of Sciences, Beijing 100190, China
songfu@shanghaitech.edu.cn
[3] Automotive Software Innovation Center, Chongqing 400000, China
[4] Birkbeck, University of London, London WC1E 7HX, UK

Abstract. Masking is a widely-used effective countermeasure against power side-channel attacks for implementing cryptographic algorithms. Surprisingly, few formal verification techniques have addressed a fundamental question, i.e., whether the masked program and the original (unmasked) cryptographic algorithm are functional equivalent. In this paper, we study this problem for masked arithmetic programs over Galois fields of characteristic 2. We propose an automated approach based on term rewriting, aided by random testing and SMT solving. The overall approach is sound, and complete under certain conditions which do meet in practice. We implement the approach as a new tool FISCHER and carry out extensive experiments on various benchmarks. The results confirm the effectiveness, efficiency and scalability of our approach. Almost all the benchmarks can be proved for the first time by the term rewriting system solely. In particular, FISCHER detects a new flaw in a masked implementation published in EUROCRYPT 2017.

1 Introduction

Power side-channel attacks [42] can infer secrecy by statistically analyzing the power consumption during the execution of cryptographic programs. The victims include implementations of almost all major cryptographic algorithms, e.g., DES [41], AES [54], RSA [33], Elliptic curve cryptography [46,52] and post-quantum cryptography [56,59]. To mitigate the threat, cryptographic algorithms are often implemented via *masking* [37], which divides each secret value into $(d + 1)$ shares by randomization, where d is a given masking order. However, it is error-prone to implement secure and correct masked implementations for non-linear functions (e.g., finite-field multiplication, module addition and S-Box),

This work is supported by the National Natural Science Foundation of China (62072309), CAS Project for Young Scientists in Basic Research (YSBR-040), ISCAS New Cultivation Project (ISCAS-PYFX-202201), an oversea grant from the State Key Laboratory of Novel Software Technology, Nanjing University (KFKT2022A03), and Birkbeck BEI School Project (EFFECT).

C. Enea and A. Lal (Eds.): CAV 2023, LNCS 13966, pp. 255–280, 2023.
https://doi.org/10.1007/978-3-031-37709-9_13

which are prevalent in cryptography. Indeed, published implementations of AES S-Box that have been proved secure via paper-and-pencil [19,40,58] were later shown to be vulnerable to power side-channels when d is no less than 4 [24].

While numerous formal verification techniques have been proposed to prove resistance of masked cryptographic programs against power side-channel attacks (e.g., [7,13,26,29–32,64]), one fundamental question which is largely left open is the (functional) correctness of the masked cryptographic programs, i.e., whether a masked program and the original (unmasked) cryptographic algorithm are actually functional equivalent. It is conceivable to apply general-purpose program verifiers to masked cryptographic programs. Constraint-solving based approaches are available, for instance, Boogie [6] generates constraints via weakest precondition reasoning which then invokes SMT solvers; SeaHorn [36] and CPAChecker [12] adopt model checking by utilizing SMT or CHC solvers. More recent work (e.g., CryptoLine [28,45,53,62]) resorts to computer algebra, e.g., to reduce the problem to the ideal membership problem. The main challenge of applying these techniques to masked cryptographic programs lies in the presence of finite-field multiplication, affine transformations and bitwise exclusive-OR (XOR). For instance, finite-field multiplication is not natively supported by the current SMT or CHC solvers, and the increasing number of bitwise XOR operations causes the infamous state-explosion problem. Moreover, to the best of our knowledge, current computer algebra systems do not provide the full support required by verification of masked cryptographic programs.

Contributions. We propose a novel, term rewriting based approach to efficiently check whether a masked program and the original (unmasked) cryptographic algorithm (over Galois fields of characteristic 2) are functional equivalent. Namely, we provide a term rewriting system (TRS) which can handle affine transformations, bitwise XOR, and finite-field multiplication. The verification problem is reduced to checking whether a term can be rewritten to normal form 0. This approach is sound, i.e., once we obtain 0, we can claim functional equivalence. In case the TRS reduces to a normal form which is different from 0, most likely they are *not* functional equivalent, but a false positive is possible. We further resort to random testing and SMT solving by directly analyzing the obtained normal form. As a result, it turns out that the overall approach is complete if no uninterpreted functions are involved in the normal form.

We implement our approach as a new tool FISCHER (FunctionalIty of maSked CryptograpHic program verifiER), based on the LLVM framework [43]. We conduct extensive experiments on various masked cryptographic program benchmarks. The results show that our term rewriting system solely is able to prove almost all the benchmarks. FISCHER is also considerably more efficient than the general-purpose verifiers SMACK [55], SeaHorn, CPAChecker, and Symbiotic [22], cryptography-specific verifier CryptoLine, as well as a straightforward approach that directly reduces the verification task to SMT solving. For instance, our approach is able to handle masked implementations of finite-field multiplication with masking orders up to 100 in less than 153 s, while none of the compared approaches can handle masking order of 3 in 20 min.

In particular, for the first time we detect a flaw in a masked implementation of finite-field multiplication published in EUROCRYPT 2017 [8]. The flaw is tricky, as it only occurs for the masking order $d \equiv 1 \mod 4$.[1] This finding highlights the importance of the correctness verification of masked programs, which has been largely overlooked, but of which our work provides an effective solution.

Our main contributions can be summarized as follows.

- We propose a term rewriting system for automatically proving the functional correctness of masked cryptographic programs;
- We implement a tool FISCHER by synergistically integrating the term rewriting based approach, random testing and SMT solving;
- We conduct extensive experiments, confirming the effectiveness, efficiency, scalability and applicability of our approach.

Related Work. Program verification has been extensively studied for decades. Here we mainly focus on their application in cryptographic programs, for which some general-purpose program verifiers have been adopted. Early work [3] uses Boogie [6]. HACL* [65] uses F* [2] which verifies programs by a combination of SMT solving and interactive proof assistants. Vale [15] uses F* and Dafny [44] where Dafny harnesses Boogie for verification. Cryptol [61] checks equivalence between machine-readable cryptographic specifications and real-world implementations via SMT solving. As mentioned before, computer algebra systems (CAS) have also been used for verifying cryptographic programs and arithmetic circuits, by reducing to the ideal membership problem together with SAT/SMT solving. Typical work includes CryptoLine and AMulet [38,39]. However, as shown in Sect. 7.2, neither general-purpose verifiers (SMACK with Boogie and Corral, SeaHorn, CPAChecker and Symbiotic) nor the CAS-based verifier CryptoLine is sufficiently powerful to verify masked cryptographic programs. Interactive proof assistants (possibly coupled with SMT solvers) have also been used to verify unmasked cryptographic programs (e.g., [1,4,9,23,27,48,49]). Compared to them, our approach is highly automatic, which is more acceptable and easier to use for general software developers.

Outline. Section 2 recaps preliminaries. Section 3 presents a language on which the cryptographic program is formalized. Section 4 gives an example and an overview of our approach. Section 5 and Sect. 6 introduce the term rewriting system and verification algorithms. Section 7 reports experimental results. We conclude in Sect. 8. The source code of our tool and benchmarks are available at https://github.com/S3L-official/FISCHER.

2   Preliminaries

For two integers l, u with $l \leq u$, $[l, u]$ denotes the set of integers $\{l, l+1, \cdots, u\}$.

Galois Field. A *Galois field* $\mathbb{GF}(p^n)$ comprises polynomials $a_{n-1}X^{n-1} + \cdots + a_1 X^1 + a_0$ over $\mathbb{Z}_p = [0, p-1]$, where p is a prime number, n is a positive integer, and $a_i \in \mathbb{Z}_p$. (Here p is the *characteristic* of the field, and p^n

---

[1] This flaw has been confirmed by an author of [8].

is the *order* of the field.) Symmetric cryptography (e.g., DES [50], AES [25], SKINNY [10], PRESENT [14]) and bitsliced implementations of asymmetric cryptography (e.g., [17]) intensively uses $\mathbb{GF}(2^n)$. Throughout the paper, $\mathbb{F}$ denotes the Galois field $\mathbb{GF}(2^n)$ for a fixed n, and $\oplus$ and $\otimes$ denote the addition and multiplication on $\mathbb{F}$, respectively. Recall that $\mathbb{GF}(2^n)$ can be constructed from the quotient ring of the polynomial ring $\mathbb{GF}(2)[X]$ with respect to the ideal generated by an irreducible polynomial P of degree n. Hence, multiplication is the product of two polynomials modulo P in $\mathbb{GF}(2)[X]$ and addition is bitwise exclusive-OR (XOR) over the binary representation of polynomials. For example, AES uses $\mathbb{GF}(256) = \mathbb{GF}(2)[X]/(X^8 + X^4 + X^3 + X + 1)$. Here $n = 8$ and $P = X^8 + X^4 + X^3 + X + 1$.

Higher-Order Masking. To achieve order-d security against power side-channel attacks under certain leakage models, masking is usually used [37,60]. Essentially, masking partitions each secret value into (usually $d + 1$) shares so that knowing at most d shares cannot infer any information of the secret value, called *order-d masking*. In Boolean masking, a value $a \in \mathbb{F}$ is divided into shares $a_0, a_1, \ldots, a_d \in \mathbb{F}$ such that $a_0 \oplus a_1 \oplus \ldots \oplus a_d = a$. Typically, $a_1, \ldots, a_d$ are random values and $a_0 = a \oplus a_1 \oplus \ldots \oplus a_d$. The tuple $(a_0, a_1, \ldots, a_d)$, denoted by $\mathbf{a}$, is called an *encoding* of a. We write $\bigoplus_{i \in [0,d]} \mathbf{a}_i$ (or simply $\bigoplus \mathbf{a}$) for $a_0 \oplus a_1 \oplus \ldots \oplus a_d$. Additive masking can be defined similarly to Boolean masking, where $\oplus$ is replaced by the module arithmetic addition operator. In this work, we focus on Boolean masking as the XOR operation is more efficient to implement.

To implement a masked program, for each operation in the cryptographic algorithm, a corresponding operation on shares is required. As we will see later, when the operation is affine (i.e. the operation f satisfies $f(x \oplus y) = f(x) \oplus f(y) \oplus c$ for some constant c), the corresponding operation is simply to apply the original operation on each share a_i in the encoding $(a_0, a_1, \ldots, a_d)$. However, for non-affine operations (e.g., multiplication and addition), it is a very difficult task and error-prone [24]. Ishai et al. [37] proposed the first masked implementation of multiplication, but limited to the domain $\mathbb{GF}(2)$ *only*. The number of the required random values and operations is not optimal and is known to be vulnerable in the presence of glitches because the electric signals propagate at different speeds in the combinatorial paths of hardware circuits. Thus, various follow-up papers proposed ways to implement higher-order masking for the domain $\mathbb{GF}(2^n)$ and/or optimizing the computational complexity, e.g., [8,11,21,34,58], all of which are referred to as ISW scheme in this paper. In another research direction, new glitch-resistant Boolean masking schemes have been proposed, e.g., Hardware Private Circuits (HPC1 & HPC2) [20], Domain-oriented Masking (DOM) [35] and Consolidating Masking Schemes (CMS) [57]. In this work, we are interested in automatically proving the correctness of the masked programs.

3   The Core Language

In this section, we first present the core language MSL, given in Fig. 1, based on which the verification problem is formalized.

$\langle$expr$\rangle$ ::= $\langle$var$\rangle$ | $\langle$num$\rangle$ | $\langle$expr$\rangle\oplus\langle$expr$\rangle$ | $\langle$expr$\rangle\otimes\langle$expr$\rangle$ | $(\langle$expr$\rangle)$

$\langle$stmts$\rangle$ ::= $\langle$var$\rangle\leftarrow\langle$expr$\rangle$ | $\langle$var$\rangle\leftarrow$rand | $\langle$stmts$\rangle$ $\langle$stmts$\rangle$

$\quad\quad\quad\quad\langle$var$\rangle\leftarrow\langle$id$\rangle_{\text{proc}}(\langle$vars$\rangle)$ | $\langle$var$\rangle\leftarrow\langle$id$\rangle_{\text{affine}}(\langle$var$\rangle)$

$\langle$proc$\rangle$ ::= proc$\langle$id$\rangle$ input$\langle$ids$\rangle$ output$\langle$id$\rangle$ $\langle$stmts$\rangle_{\text{origin}}$ shares $\langle$num$\rangle$ $\langle$stmts$\rangle_{\text{masked}}$

$\langle$affine$\rangle$ ::= affine$\langle$id$\rangle$ [input$\langle$id$\rangle$ output$\langle$id$\rangle$ $\langle$stmts$\rangle$]

Fig. 1. Syntax of MSL in Backus-Naur form

A program $\mathcal{P}$ in MSL is given by a sequence of procedure definitions and affine transformation definitions/declarations. A procedure definition starts with the keyword proc, followed by a procedure name, a list of input parameters, an output and its body. The procedure body has two blocks of statements, separated by a special statement shares $d+1$, where d is the masking order. The first block $\langle$stmts$\rangle_{\text{origin}}$, called the *original block*, implements its original functionality on the input parameters without masking. The second block $\langle$stmts$\rangle_{\text{masked}}$, called the *masked block*, is a masked implementation of the original block over the input encodings $\mathbf{x}$ of the input parameters x. The input parameters and output x, declared using the keywords input and output respectively, are scalar variables in the original block, but are treated as the corresponding encodings (i.e., tuples) $\mathbf{x}$ in the masked block. For example, input x declares the scalar variable x as the input of the original block, while it implicitly declares an encoding $\mathbf{x} = (x_0, x_1, \ldots, x_d)$ as the input of the masked block with shares $d+1$.

We distinguish affine transformation definitions and declarations. The former starts with the keyword affine, followed by a name f, an input, an output and its body. It is expected that the affine property $\forall x, y \in \mathbb{F}.f(x \oplus y) = f(x) \oplus f(y) \oplus c$ holds for some affine constant $c \in \mathbb{F}$. (Note that the constant c is not explicitly provided in the program, but can be derived, cf. Sect. 6.2.) The transformation f is *linear* if its affine constant c is 0. In contrast, an affine transformation declaration f simply declares a transformation. As a result, it can only be used to declare a linear one (i.e., c must be 0), which is treated as an uninterpreted function. Note that non-linear affine transformation declarations can be achieved by declaring linear affine transformations and affine transformation definitions. Affine transformation here serves as an abstraction to capture complicated operations (e.g., shift, rotation and bitwise Boolean operations) and can accelerate verification by expressing operations as uninterpreted functions. In practice, a majority of cryptographic algorithms (in symmetric cryptography) can be represented by a composition of S-box, XOR and linear transformation only.

Masking an affine transformation can simply mask an input encoding in a share-wise way, namely, the masked version of the affine transformation $f(a)$ is

$$f(a_0 \oplus a_1 \oplus \ldots \oplus a_d) = \begin{cases} f(a_0) \oplus f(a_1) \oplus \ldots \oplus f(a_d), & \text{if } d \text{ is even;} \\ f(a_0) \oplus f(a_1) \oplus \ldots \oplus f(a_d) \oplus c, & \text{if } d \text{ is odd.} \end{cases}$$

This is default, so affine transformation definition only contains the original block but no masked block.

A statement is either an assignment or a function call. MSL features two types of assignments which are either of the form $x \leftarrow e$ defined as usual or of the form $r \leftarrow \text{rand}$ which assigns a uniformly sampled value from the domain $\mathbb{F}$ to the variable r. As a result, r should be read as a random variable. We assume that each random variable is defined only once. We note that the actual parameters and output are scalar if the procedure is invoked in an original block while they are the corresponding encodings if it is invoked in a masked block.

MSL is the core language of our tool. In practice, to be more user-friendly, our tool also accepts C programs with conditional branches and loops, both of which should be statically determinized (e.g., loops are bound and can be unrolled; the branching of conditionals can also be fixed after loop unrolling). Furthermore, we assume there is no recursion and dynamic memory allocation. These restrictions are sufficient for most symmetric cryptography and bitsliced implementations of public-key cryptography, which mostly have simple control graphs and memory aliases.

Problem Formalization. Fix a program $\mathcal{P}$ with all the procedures using order-d masking. We denote by $\mathcal{P}_o$ (resp. $\mathcal{P}_m$) the program $\mathcal{P}$ where all the masked (resp. original) blocks are omitted. For each procedure f, the procedures f_o and f_m are defined accordingly.

Definition 1. *Given a procedure f of $\mathcal{P}$ with m input parameters, f_m and f_o are functional equivalent, denoted by $f_m \cong f_o$, if the following statement holds:*

$$\forall a^1, \cdots, a^m, r_1, \cdots, r_h \in \mathbb{F}, \forall \mathbf{a}^1, \cdots, \mathbf{a}^m \in \mathbb{F}^{d+1}.$$
$$\left(\bigwedge_{i \in [1,m]} a^i = \bigoplus_{j \in [0,d]} \mathbf{a}_j^i \right) \rightarrow \left(f_o(a^1, \cdots, a^m) = \bigoplus_{i \in [0,d]} f_m(\mathbf{a}^1, \cdots, \mathbf{a}^m)_i \right)$$

where $r_1, \cdots, r_h$ are all the random variables used in f_m.

Note that although the procedure f_m is randomized (i.e., the output encoding $f_m(\mathbf{a}^1, \cdots, \mathbf{a}_i^m)$ is technically a random variable), for functional equivalence we consider a stronger notion, viz., to require that f_m and f_o are equivalent under any values in the support of the random variables $r_1, \cdots, r_h$. Thus, $r_1, \cdots, r_h$ are universally quantified in Definition 1.

The verification problem is to check if $f_m \cong f_o$ for a given procedure f where $\bigwedge_{i \in [1,m]} a^i = \bigoplus_{j \in [0,d]} \mathbf{a}_j^i$ and $f_o(a^1, \cdots, a^m) = \bigoplus_{i \in [0,d]} f_m(\mathbf{a}^1, \cdots, \mathbf{a}^m)_i$ are regarded as pre- and post-conditions, respectively. Thus, we assume the unmasked procedures themselves are correct (which can be verified by, e.g., CryptoLine). Our focus is on whether the masked counterparts are functional equivalent to them.

4   Overview of the Approach

In this section, we first present a motivating example given in Fig. 2, which computes the multiplicative inverse in $\mathbb{GF}(2^8)$ for the AES S-Box [58] using first-order

```
 1 affine exp2 input x output y
 2   y ← x ⊗ x
 3 affine exp4 input x output y
 4   y ← exp2(exp2(x))
 5 affine exp16 input x output y
 6   y ← exp4(exp4(x))
 7
 8 proc sec_mult input a b output c
 9   c ← a ⊗ b
10 shares 2
11   r₀ ← rand
12   r₁ ← r₀ ⊕ (a₀ ⊗ b₁) ⊕ (a₁ ⊗ b₀)
13   c₀ ← (a₀ ⊗ b₀) ⊕ r₀
14   c₁ ← (a₁ ⊗ b₁) ⊕ r₁
15
16 proc refresh_masks input x output y
17   y ← x
18 shares 2
19   r₀ ← rand
20   y₀ ← x₀ ⊕ r₀   y₁ ← x₁ ⊕ r₀
```

```
21 proc sec_exp254 input x output y
22   z ← exp2(x)
23   y ← z ⊗ x
24   w ← exp4(y)
25   y ← y ⊗ w
26   y ← exp16(y)
27   y ← y ⊗ w
28   y ← y ⊗ z
29 shares 2
30   z₀ ← exp2(x₀)
31   z₁ ← exp2(x₁)
32   z⃗ ← refresh_masks(z⃗)
33   y⃗ ← sec_mult(z⃗, x⃗)
34   w₀ ← exp4(y₀)
35   w₁ ← exp4(y₁)
36   w⃗ ← refresh_masks(w⃗)
37   y⃗ ← sec_mult(y⃗, w⃗)
38   y₀ ← exp16(y₀)
39   y₁ ← exp16(y₁)
40   y⃗ ← sec_mult(y⃗, w⃗)
41   y⃗ ← sec_mult(y⃗, z⃗)
```

Fig. 2. Motivating example, where $\mathbf{x}$ denotes (x_0, x_1).

Boolean masking. It consists of three affine transformation definitions and two procedure definitions. For a given input x, $\mathtt{exp2}(x)$ outputs x^2, $\mathtt{exp4}(x)$ outputs x^4 and $\mathtt{exp16}(x)$ outputs x^{16}. Obviously, these three affine transformations are indeed linear.

Procedure $\mathtt{sec\_mult}_o(a, b)$ outputs $a \otimes b$. Its masked version $\mathtt{sec\_mult}_m(\mathbf{a}, \mathbf{b})$ computes the encoding $\mathbf{c} = (c_0, c_1)$ over the encodings $\mathbf{a} = (a_0, a_1)$ and $\mathbf{b} = (b_0, b_1)$. Clearly, it is desired that $c_0 \oplus c_1 = a \otimes b$ if $a_0 \oplus a_1 = a$ and $b_0 \oplus b_1 = b$. Procedure $\mathtt{refresh\_masks}_o(x)$ is the identity function while its masked version $\mathtt{refresh\_masks}_m(\mathbf{x})$ re-masks the encoding $\mathbf{x}$ using a random variable r_0. Thus, it is desired that $y_0 \oplus y_1 = x$ if $x = x_0 \oplus x_1$. Procedure $\mathtt{sec\_exp254}_o(x)$ computes the multiplicative inverse x^{254} of x in $\mathbb{GF}(2^8)$. Its masked version $\mathtt{sec\_exp254}_m(\mathbf{x})$ computes the encoding $\mathbf{y} = (y_0, y_1)$ where $\mathtt{refresh\_masks}_m$ is invoked to avoid power side-channel leakage. Thus, it is desired that $y_0 \oplus y_1 = x^{254}$ if $x_0 \oplus x_1 = x$. In summary, it is required to prove $\mathtt{sec\_mult}_m \cong \mathtt{sec\_mult}_o$, $\mathtt{refresh\_masks}_m \cong \mathtt{refresh\_masks}_o$ and $\mathtt{sec\_exp254}_m \cong \mathtt{sec\_exp254}_o$.

4.1 Our Approach

An overview of FISCHER is shown in Fig. 3. The input program is expected to follow the syntax of MSL but in C language. Moreover, the pre-conditions and post-conditions of the verification problem are expressed by assume and assert statements in the masked procedure, respectively. Recall that the input program can contain conditional branches and loops when are statically determinized. Furthermore, affine transformations can use other common operations (e.g., shift, rotation and bitwise Boolean operations) besides the addition $\oplus$ and multiplication $\otimes$ on the underlying field $\mathbb{F}$. FISCHER leverages the LLVM framework to obtain the LLVM intermediate representation (IR) and call graph, where

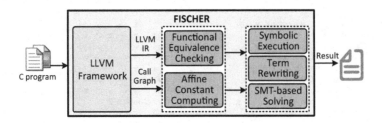

Fig. 3. Overview of FISCHER.

all the procedure calls are inlined. It then invokes *Affine Constant Computing* to iteratively compute the affine constants for affine transformations according to the call graph, and *Functional Equivalence Checking* to check functional equivalence, both of which rely on the underpinning engines, viz., *Symbolic Execution* (refer to symbolic computation without path constraint solving in this work), *Term Rewriting* and *SMT-based Solving*.

We apply intra-procedural symbolic execution to compute the symbolic outputs of the procedures and transformations, i.e., expressions in terms of inputs, random variables and affine transformations. The symbolic outputs are treated as terms based on which both the problems of functional equivalence checking and affine constant computing are solved by rewriting to their normal forms (i.e., sums of monomials w.r.t. a total order). The analysis result is often conclusive from normal forms. In case it is inconclusive, we iteratively inline affine transformations when their definitions are available until either the analysis result is conclusive or no more affine transformations can be inlined. If the analysis result is still inconclusive, to reduce false positives, we apply random testing and accurate (but computationally expansive) SMT solving to the normal forms instead of the original terms. We remark that the term rewriting system solely can prove almost all the benchmarks in our experiments.

Consider the motivating example. To find the constant $c \in \mathbb{F}$ of exp2 such that the property $\forall x, y \in \mathbb{F}.\mathtt{exp2}(x \oplus y) = \mathtt{exp2}(x) \oplus \mathtt{exp2}(y) \oplus c$ holds, by applying symbolic execution, $\mathtt{exp2}(x)$ is expressed as the term $x \otimes x$. Thus, the property is reformulated as $(x \oplus y) \otimes (x \oplus y) = (x \otimes x) \oplus (y \otimes y) \oplus c$, from which we can deduce that the desired affine constant c is equivalent to the term $((x \oplus y) \otimes (x \oplus y)) \oplus (x \otimes x) \oplus (y \otimes y)$. Our TRS will reduce the term as follows:

$$
\begin{aligned}
&\underline{((x \oplus y) \otimes (x \oplus y))} \oplus (x \otimes x) \oplus (y \otimes y) && \text{Distributive Law}\\
={}&\underline{(x \otimes (x \oplus y))} \oplus \underline{(y \otimes (x \oplus y))} \oplus (x \otimes x) \oplus (y \otimes y) && \text{Distributive Law}\\
={}&(x \otimes x) \oplus (x \otimes y) \oplus \underline{(y \otimes x)} \oplus (y \otimes y) \oplus (x \otimes x) \oplus (y \otimes y) && \text{Commutative Law}\\
={}&(x \otimes x) \oplus (x \otimes y) \oplus \underline{(x \otimes y)} \oplus (y \otimes y) \oplus \underline{(x \otimes x)} \oplus (y \otimes y) && \text{Commutative Law}\\
={}&\underline{(x \otimes x) \oplus (x \otimes x)} \oplus \underline{(x \otimes y) \oplus (x \otimes y)} \oplus \underline{(y \otimes y) \oplus (y \otimes y)} = 0 && \text{Zero Law of XOR}
\end{aligned}
$$

For the transformation $\mathtt{exp4}(x)$, by applying symbolic execution, it can be expressed as the term $\mathtt{exp2}(\mathtt{exp2}(x))$. To find the constant $c \in \mathbb{F}$ to satisfy $\forall x, y \in \mathbb{F}.\mathtt{exp4}(x \oplus y) = \mathtt{exp4}(x) \oplus \mathtt{exp4}(y) \oplus c$, we compute the term $\mathtt{exp2}(\mathtt{exp2}(x \oplus y)) \oplus \mathtt{exp2}(\mathtt{exp2}(x)) \oplus \mathtt{exp2}(\mathtt{exp2}(y))$. By applying our TRS, we have:

$$\text{exp2}(\text{exp2}(x \oplus y)) \oplus \text{exp2}(\text{exp2}(x)) \oplus \text{exp2}(\text{exp2}(y))$$
$$= \underline{\text{exp2}(\text{exp2}(x) \oplus \text{exp2}(y))} \oplus \text{exp2}(\text{exp2}(x)) \oplus \text{exp2}(\text{exp2}(y))$$
$$= \underline{\text{exp2}(\text{exp2}(x))} \oplus \text{exp2}(\text{exp2}(y)) \oplus \underline{\text{exp2}(\text{exp2}(x))} \oplus \text{exp2}(\text{exp2}(y))$$
$$= \text{exp2}(\text{exp2}(x)) \oplus \text{exp2}(\text{exp2}(x)) \oplus \underline{\text{exp2}(\text{exp2}(y)) \oplus \text{exp2}(\text{exp2}(y))} = 0$$

Clearly, the affine constant of exp4 is 0. Similarly, we can deduce that the affine constant of the transformation exp16 is 0 as well.

To prove $\text{sec\_mult}_o \cong \text{sec\_mult}_m$, by applying symbolic execution, we have that $\text{sec\_mult}_o(a, b) = a \otimes b$ and $\text{sec\_mult}_m(\mathbf{a}, \mathbf{b}) = \mathbf{c} = (c_0, c_1)$, where $c_0 = (a_0 \otimes b_0) \oplus r_0$ and $c_1 = (a_1 \otimes b_1) \oplus (r_0 \oplus (a_0 \otimes b_1) \oplus (a_1 \otimes b_0))$. Then, by Definition 1, it suffices to check

$$\forall a, b, a_0, a_1, b_0, b_1, r_0 \in \mathbb{F}. (a = a_0 \oplus a_1 \wedge b = b_0 \oplus b_1) \rightarrow$$
$$(a \otimes b = ((a_0 \otimes b_0) \oplus r_0) \oplus ((a_1 \otimes b_1) \oplus (r_0 \oplus (a_0 \otimes b_1) \oplus (a_1 \otimes b_0)))).$$

Thus, we check the term $((a_0 \oplus a_1) \otimes (b_0 \oplus b_1)) \oplus ((a_0 \otimes b_0) \oplus r_0) \oplus ((a_1 \otimes b_1) \oplus (r_0 \oplus (a_0 \otimes b_1) \oplus (a_1 \otimes b_0)))$ which is equivalent to 0 iff $\text{sec\_mult}_o \cong \text{sec\_mult}_m$. Our TRS is able to reduce the term to 0. Similarly, we represent the outputs of sec_exp254_o and sec_exp254_m as terms via symbolic execution, from which the statement $\text{sec\_exp254}_o \cong \text{sec\_exp254}_m$ is also encoded as a term, which can be reduced to 0 via our TRS without inlining any transformations.

5 Term Rewriting System

In this section, we first introduce some basic notations and then present our term rewriting system.

Definition 2. *Given a program $\mathcal{P}$ over $\mathbb{F}$, a signature $\Sigma_\mathcal{P}$ of $\mathcal{P}$ is a set of symbols $\mathbb{F} \cup \{\oplus, \otimes, f_1, \ldots, f_t\}$, where $s \in \mathbb{F}$ with arity 0 are all the constants in $\mathbb{F}$, $\oplus$ and $\otimes$ with arity 2 are addition and multiplication operators on $\mathbb{F}$, and $f_1, \cdots, f_t$ with arity 1 are affine transformations defined/declared in $\mathcal{P}$.*

For example, the signature of the motivating example is $\mathbb{F} \cup \{\oplus, \otimes, \text{exp2}, \text{exp4}, \text{exp16}\}$. When it is clear from the context, the subscript $\mathcal{P}$ is dropped from $\Sigma_\mathcal{P}$.

Definition 3. *Let V be a set of variables (assuming $\Sigma \cap V = \emptyset$), the set $T[\Sigma, V]$ of Σ-terms over V is inductively defined as follows:*

- $\mathbb{F} \subseteq T[\Sigma, V]$ *and* $V \subseteq T[\Sigma, V]$ *(i.e., every variable/constant is a Σ-term);*
- $\tau \oplus \tau' \in T[\Sigma, V]$ *and* $\tau \otimes \tau' \in T[\Sigma, V]$ *if* $\tau, \tau' \in T[\Sigma, V]$ *(i.e., application of addition and multiplication operators to Σ-terms yield Σ-terms);*
- $f_j(\tau) \in T[\Sigma, V]$ *if* $\tau \in T[\Sigma, V]$ *and* $j \in [1, t]$ *(i.e., application of affine transformations to Σ-terms yield Σ-terms).*

We denote by $T_{\backslash \oplus}(\Sigma, V)$ the set of Σ-terms that do not use the operator $\oplus$.

A Σ-term $\alpha \in T[\Sigma, V]$ is called a *factor* if $\tau \in \mathbb{F} \cup V$ or $\tau = f_i(\tau')$ for some $i \in [1, t]$ such that $\tau' \in T_{\backslash\oplus}(\Sigma, V)$. A *monomial* is a product $\alpha_1 \otimes \cdots \otimes \alpha_k$ of none-zero factors for $k \geq 1$. We denote by $M[\Sigma, V]$ the set of monomials. For instance, consider variables $x, y \in V$ and affine transformations $f_1, f_2 \in \Sigma$. All $f_1(f_2(x)) \otimes f_1(y)$, $f_1(2 \otimes f_2(4 \otimes x))$, $f_1(x \oplus y)$ and $f_1(f_2(x)) \oplus f_1(x)$ are Σ-terms, both $f_1(f_2(x)) \otimes f_1(y)$ and $f_1(2 \otimes f_2(4 \otimes x))$ are monomials, while neither $f_1(x \oplus y)$ nor $f_1(f_2(x)) \oplus f_1(x)$ is a monomial. For the sake of presentation, Σ-terms will be written as terms, and the operator $\otimes$ may be omitted, e.g., $\tau_1 \tau_2$ denotes $\tau_1 \otimes \tau_2$, and τ^2 denotes $\tau \otimes \tau$.

Definition 4. *A polynomial is a sum $\bigoplus_{i \in [1,t]} m_i$ of monomials $m_1 \ldots m_t \in M[\Sigma, V]$. We use $P[\Sigma, V]$ to denote the set of polynomials.*

To simplify and normalize polynomials, we impose a total order on monomials and their factors.

Definition 5. *Fix an arbitrary total order $\geq_s$ on $V \uplus \Sigma$.*

For two factors α and α', the factor order $\geq_l$ is defined such that $\alpha \geq_l \alpha'$ if one of the following conditions holds:

- *$\alpha, \alpha' \in \mathbb{F} \cup V$ and $\alpha \geq_s \alpha'$;*
- *$\alpha = f(\tau)$ and $\alpha' = f'(\tau')$ such that $f \geq_s f'$ or $(f - f'$ and $\tau \geq_p \tau')$;*
- *$\alpha = f(\tau)$ such that $f \geq_s \alpha'$ or $\alpha' = f(\tau)$ such that $\alpha \geq_s f$.*

Given a monomial $m = \alpha_1 \cdots \alpha_k$, we write $\mathsf{sort}_{\geq_l}(\alpha_1, \cdots, \alpha_k)$ for the monomial which includes $\alpha_1, \cdots, \alpha_k$ as factors, but sorts them in descending order.

Given two monomials $m = \alpha_1 \cdots \alpha_k$ and $m' = \alpha'_1 \cdots \alpha'_{k'}$, the monomial order $\geq_p$ is defined as the lexicographical order between $\mathsf{sort}_{\geq_l}(\alpha_1, \cdots, \alpha_k)$ and $\mathsf{sort}_{\geq_l}(\alpha'_1, \cdots, \alpha'_{k'})$.

Intuitively, the factor order $\geq_l$ follows the given order $\geq_s$ on $V \uplus \Sigma$, where the factor order between two factors with the same affine transformation f is determined by their parameters. We note that if $\mathsf{sort}_{\geq_l}(\alpha'_1, \cdots, \alpha'_{k'})$ is a prefix of $\mathsf{sort}_{\geq_l}(\alpha_1, \cdots, \alpha_k)$, we have: $\alpha_1 \cdots \alpha_k \geq_p \alpha'_1 \cdots \alpha'_{k'}$. Furthermore, if $\alpha_1 \cdots \alpha_k \geq_p \alpha'_1 \cdots \alpha'_{k'}$ and $\alpha'_1 \cdots \alpha'_{k'} \geq_p \alpha_1 \cdots \alpha_k$, then $\mathsf{sort}_{\geq_l}(\alpha'_1, \cdots, \alpha'_{k'}) = \mathsf{sort}_{\geq_l}(\alpha_1, \cdots, \alpha_k)$. We denote by $\alpha_1 \cdots \alpha_k >_p \alpha'_1 \cdots \alpha'_{k'}$ if $\alpha_1 \cdots \alpha_k \geq_p \alpha'_1 \cdots \alpha'_{k'}$ but $\mathsf{sort}_{\geq_l}(\alpha'_1, \cdots, \alpha'_{k'}) \neq \mathsf{sort}_{\geq_l}(\alpha_1, \cdots, \alpha_k)$.

Proposition 1. *The monomial order $\geq_p$ is a total order on monomials.*

Definition 6. *Given a program $\mathcal{P}$, we define the corresponding term rewriting system (TRS) $\mathcal{R}$ as a tuple $(\Sigma, V, \geq_s, \Delta)$, where Σ is a signature of $\mathcal{P}$, V is a set of variables of $\mathcal{P}$ (assuming $\Sigma \cap V = \emptyset$), $\geq_s$ is a total order on $V \uplus \Sigma$, and Δ is the set of term rewriting rules given below:*

$$R1 \frac{(m'_1, \cdots, m'_k) = \mathtt{sort}_{\geq_p}(m_1, \cdots, m_k) \neq (m_1, \cdots, m_k)}{m_1 \oplus \cdots \oplus m_k \mapsto m'_1 \oplus \cdots \oplus m'_k} \qquad R3 \frac{}{\tau \oplus \tau \mapsto 0} \qquad R5 \frac{}{0\tau \mapsto 0}$$

$$R2 \frac{(\alpha'_1, \cdots, \alpha'_k) = \mathtt{sort}_{\geq_l}(\alpha_1, \cdots, \alpha_k) \neq (\alpha_1, \cdots, \alpha_k)}{\alpha_1 \cdots \alpha_k \mapsto \alpha'_1 \cdots \alpha'_k} \qquad R4 \frac{}{\tau 0 \mapsto 0} \qquad R6 \frac{}{\tau \oplus 0 \mapsto \tau}$$

$$R7 \frac{}{0 \oplus \tau \mapsto \tau} \qquad R8 \frac{}{\tau 1 \mapsto \tau} \qquad R9 \frac{}{1\tau \mapsto \tau} \qquad R10 \frac{}{(\tau_1 \oplus \tau_2)\tau \mapsto (\tau_1\tau) \oplus (\tau_2\tau)}$$

$$R11 \frac{}{\tau(\tau_1 \oplus \tau_2) \mapsto (\tau\tau_1) \oplus (\tau\tau_2)} \qquad R12 \frac{}{f(\tau_1 \oplus \tau_2) \mapsto f(\tau_1) \oplus f(\tau_2) \oplus c} \qquad R13 \frac{}{f(0) \mapsto c}$$

where $m_1, m'_1, \cdots, m_k, m'_k \in M[\Sigma, V]$, $\alpha_1, \alpha_2, \alpha_3$ are factors, $\tau, \tau_1, \tau_2 \in T[\Sigma, V]$ are terms, $f \in \Sigma$ is an affine transformation with affine constant c.

Intuitively, rules R1 and R2 specify the commutativity of $\oplus$ and $\otimes$, respectively, by which monomials and factors are sorted according to the orders $\geq_p$ and $\geq_l$, respectively. Rule R3 specifies that $\oplus$ is essentially bitwise XOR. Rules R4 and R5 specify that 0 is the multiplicative zero. Rules R6 and R7 (resp. R8 and R9) specify that 0 (resp. 1) is additive (resp. multiplicative) identity. Rules R10 and R11 express the distributivity of $\otimes$ over $\oplus$. Rule R12 expresses the affine property of an affine transformation while rule R13 is an instance of rule R12 via rules R3 and R5.

Given a TRS $\mathcal{R} = (\Sigma, V, \geq_s, \Delta)$ for a given program $\mathcal{P}$, a term $\tau \in T[\Sigma, V]$ can be rewritten to a term τ', denoted by $\tau \Rightarrow \tau'$, if there is a rewriting rule $\tau_1 \mapsto \tau_2$ such that τ' is a term obtained from τ by replacing an occurrence of the sub-term τ_1 with the sub-term τ_2. A term is in a *normal form* if no rewriting rules can be applied. A TRS is *terminating* if all terms can be rewritten to a normal form after finitely many rewriting. We denote by $\tau \Rrightarrow \tau'$ with τ' being the normal form of τ.

We show that any TRS $\mathcal{R}$ associated with a program $\mathcal{P}$ is terminating, and that any term will be rewritten to a normal form that is a polynomial, independent of the way of applying rules.

Lemma 1. *For every normal form $\tau \in T[\Sigma, V]$ of the TRS $\mathcal{R}$, the term τ must be a polynomial $m_1 \oplus \cdots \oplus m_k$ such that (1) $\forall i \in [1, k-1]$, $m_i >_p m_{i+1}$, and (2) for every monomial $m_i = \alpha_1 \cdots \alpha_h$ and $\forall i \in [1, h-1]$, $\alpha_i \geq_l \alpha_{i+1}$.*

Proof. Consider a normal form $\tau \in T[\Sigma, V]$. If τ is not a polynomial, then there must exist some monomial m_i in which the addition operator $\oplus$ is used. This means that either rule R_{10} or R_{11} is applicable to the term τ which contradicts the fact that τ is normal form.

Suppose τ is the polynomial $m_1 \oplus \cdots \oplus m_k$.

- If there exists $i : 1 \leq i < k$ such that $m_i >_p m_{i+1}$ does not hold, then either $m_i = m_{i+1}$ or $m_{i+1} >_p m_i$. If $m_i = m_{i+1}$, then rule R3 is applicable to the term τ. If $m_{i+1} >_p m_i$, then rule R_1 is applicable to the term τ. Thus, for every $1 \leq i < k$, $m_i >_p m_{i+1}$.
- If there exist a monomial $m_i = \alpha_1 \cdots \alpha_h$ and $i : 1 \leq i < h$ such that $\alpha_i \geq_l \alpha_{i+1}$ does not hold, then $\alpha_{i+1} >_l \alpha_i$. This means that rule R2 is applicable to the term τ. Thus, for every monomial $m_i = \alpha_1 \cdots \alpha_h$ and every $i : 1 \leq i < h$, $\alpha_i \geq_l \alpha_{i+1}$. $\qquad\square$

Lemma 2. *The TRS $\mathcal{R} = (\Sigma, V, \geq_s, \Delta)$ of a given program $\mathcal{P}$ is terminating.*

Proof. Consider a term $\tau \in T[\Sigma, V]$. Let $\pi = \tau_1 \Rightarrow \tau_2 \Rightarrow \tau_3 \Rightarrow \cdots \Rightarrow \tau_i \Rightarrow \cdots$ be a reduction of the term τ by applying rewriting rules, i.e., $\tau = \tau_1$. We prove that the reduction π is finite by showing that all the rewriting rules can be applied finitely.

First, since rules R1 and R2 only sort the monomials and factors, respectively, while sorting always terminates using any classic sorting algorithm (e.g., quick sort algorithm), rules R1 and R2 can only be consecutively applied finitely for each term τ_i due to the premises $\mathtt{sort}_{\geq_p}(m_1, \cdots, m_k) \neq (m_1, \cdots, m_k)$ and $\mathtt{sort}_{\geq_l}(\alpha_1, \cdots, \alpha_k) \neq (\alpha_1, \cdots, \alpha_k)$ in rules R1 and R2, respectively.

Second, rules R10, R11 and R12 can only be applied finitely in the reduction π, as these rules always push the addition operator $\oplus$ toward the root of the syntax tree of the term τ_i when one of them is applied onto a term τ_i, while the other rules either eliminate or reorder the addition operator $\oplus$.

Algorithm 1: Term Normalization

---

1 **Function** TermNorm($\mathcal{R}$, τ, λ):
2   Rewrite τ by iteratively applying rules R3–R13 until no more update;
3      $\tau' \leftarrow \mathtt{sort}(\tau)$ by iteratively applying rule R2;
4      $\tau' \leftarrow \mathtt{sort}(\tau')$ by iteratively applying rule R1;
5   Rewrite τ' by iteratively applying rules R3, R6, R7 until no more update;
6   **return** τ'

Lastly, rules R3–9 and R13 can only be applied finitely in the reduction π, as these rules reduce the size of the term by 1 when one of them is applied onto a term τ_i while the rules R10–12 that increase the size of the term can only be applied finitely.

Hence, the reduction π is finite indicating that the TRS $\mathcal{R}$ is terminating. □

By Lemmas 1 and 2, any term $\tau \in T[\Sigma, V]$ can be rewritten to a normal form that must be a polynomial.

Theorem 1. *Let $\mathcal{R} = (\Sigma, V, \geq_s, \Delta)$ be the TRS of a program $\mathcal{P}$. For any term $\tau \in T[\Sigma, V]$, a polynomial $\tau' \in T[\Sigma, V]$ can be computed such that $\tau \Rightarrow \tau'$.*

Remark 1. Besides the termination of a TRS, confluence is another important property of a TRS, where a TRS is confluent if any given term $\tau \in T[\Sigma, V]$ can be rewritten to two distinct terms τ_1 and τ_2, then the terms τ_1 and τ_2 can be reduced to a common term. While we conjecture that the TRS $\mathcal{R}$ associated with the given program is indeed confluent which may be shown by its local confluence [51], we do not strive to prove its confluence, as it is irrelevant to the problem considered in the current work.

6 Algorithmic Verification

In this section, we first present an algorithm for computing normal forms, then show how to compute the affine constant for an affine transformation, and finally propose an algorithm for solving the verification problem.

6.1 Term Normalization Algorithm

We provide the function `TermNorm` (cf. Algorithm 1) which applies the rewriting rules in a particular order aiming for better efficiency. Fix a TRS $\mathcal{R} = (\Sigma, V, \geq_s, \Delta)$, a term $\tau \in T[\Sigma, V]$ and a mapping λ that provides required affine constants $\lambda(f)$. `TermNorm`$(\mathcal{R}, \tau, \lambda)$ returns a normal form τ' of τ, i.e., $\tau \Rrightarrow \tau'$.

Algorithm 2: Computing Affine Constants

---

1 **Function** AffConst$(\mathcal{P}, \mathcal{R}, G)$:
2   **foreach** *affine transformation f in a topological order of call graph G* **do**
3   **if** *f is only declared in $\mathcal{P}$* **then**
4             $\lambda(f) \leftarrow 0$;
5   **else**
6             $x \leftarrow$ input of f;
7             $\xi(x) \leftarrow$ symbolicExecution(f);
8             $\tau \leftarrow \xi(x)[x \mapsto x \oplus y] \oplus \xi(x) \oplus \xi(x)[x \mapsto y]$;
9   **while** True **do**
10                 $\tau \leftarrow$ TermNorm$(\mathcal{R}, \tau, \lambda)$;
11   **if** *τ is some constant c* **then**
12                     $\lambda(f) \leftarrow c$; **break**;
13   **else if** *g is defined in $\mathcal{P}$ but has not been inlined in τ* **then**
14   Inline g in τ; **continue**;
15   **else if** *τ does not contain any uninterpreted function* **then**
16                     $v_1, u_1, v_2, u_2 \leftarrow$ random values from $\mathbb{F}$ s.t. $v_1 \neq v_2 \vee u_1 \neq u_2$;
17   **if** $\tau[x \mapsto v_1, y \mapsto u_1] \neq \tau[x \mapsto v_2, y \mapsto u_2]$ **then**
18   Emit$(f$ is not affine$)$ and Abort;
19   **if** SMTSolver$(\forall x. \forall y. \tau = c)$=SAT **then**
20                   $\lambda(f) \leftarrow$ extract c from the model; **break**;
21   **else** Emit$(f$ may not be affine$)$ and Abort;
22   **return** λ;

`TermNorm` first applies rules R3–R13 to rewrite the term τ (line 2), resulting in a polynomial which does not have 0 as a factor or monomial (due to rules R4–R7), or 1 as a factor in a monomial unless the monomial itself is 1 (due to rules R_8 and R_9). Next, it recursively sorts all the factors and monomial involved in the polynomial from the innermost sub-terms (lines 3 and 4). Sorting factors and monomials will place the same monomials at adjacent positions. Finally, rules R3 and R6–R7 are further applied to simplify the polynomial (line 5), where consecutive syntactically equivalent monomials will be rewritten to 0 by rule R3, which may further enable rules R6–R7. Obviously, the final term τ' is a normal form of the input τ, although its size may be exponential in that of τ.

Lemma 3. *TermNorm*$(\mathcal{R}, \tau, \lambda)$ *returns a normal form* τ' *of* τ. $\qquad \square$

6.2   Computing Affine Constants

The function AffConst in Algorithm 2 computes the associated affine constant for an affine transformation f. It first sorts all affine transformations in a topological order based on the call graph G (lines 2–21). If f is *only* declared in $\mathcal{P}$, as mentioned previously, we assumed it is linear, thus 0 is assigned to $\lambda(f)$ (line 4). Otherwise, it extracts the input x of f and computes its output $\xi(x)$ via symbolic execution (line 7), where $\xi(x)$ is treated as $f(x)$. We remark that during symbolic execution, we adopt a lazy strategy for inlining invoked affine transformations in f to reduce the size of $\xi(x)$. Thus, $\xi(x)$ may contain affine transformations.

Recall that c is the affine constant of f iff $\forall x, y \in \mathbb{F}.f(x \oplus y) = f(x) \oplus f(y) \oplus c$ holds. Thus, we create the term $\tau = \xi(x)[x \mapsto x \oplus y] \oplus \xi(x) \oplus \xi(x)[x \mapsto y]$ (line 7), where $e[a \mapsto b]$ denotes the substitution of a with b in e. Obviously, the term τ is equivalent to some constant c iff c is the affine constant of f.

The while-loop (lines 9–21) evaluates τ. First, it rewrites τ to a normal form (line 10) by invoking TermNorm in Alg.1. If the normal form is some constant c, then c is the affine constant of f. Otherwise, AffConst repeatedly inlines each affine transformation g that is defined in P but has not been inlined in τ (lines 13 and 14) and rewrites the term τ to a normal form until either the normal form is some constant c or no affine transformation can be inlined. If the normal form is still not a constant, τ is evaluated using random input values. Clearly, if τ is evaluated to two distinct values (line 18), f is not affine. Otherwise, we check the satisfiability of the constraint $\forall x, y.\tau = c$ via an SMT solver in bitvector theory (line 19), where declared but undefined affine transformations are treated as uninterpreted functions provided with their affine properties. If $\forall x, y.\tau = c$ is satisfiable, we extract the affine constant c from its model (line 20). Otherwise, we emit an error and then abort (line 21), indicating that the affine constant of f cannot be computed. Since the satisfiability problem module bitvector theory is decidable, we can conclude that f is *not* affine if $\forall x.\forall y.\tau = c$ is unsatisfiable and no uninterpreted function is involved in τ.

Lemma 4. *Assume an affine transformation* f *in* $\mathcal{P}$. *If* AffConst$(\mathcal{P}, \mathcal{R}, G)$ *in Algorithm 2 returns a mapping* λ, *then* $\lambda(f)$ *is the affine constant of* f. $\qquad \square$

6.3   Verification Algorithm

The verification problem is solved by the function Verifier$(\mathcal{P})$ in Algorithm 3, which checks if $f_m \cong f_o$, for each procedure f defined in $\mathcal{P}$. It first preprocesses the given program $\mathcal{P}$ by inlining all the procedures, unrolling all the loops and eliminating all the branches (line 2). Then, it computes the corresponding TRS $\mathcal{R}$, call graph G and affine constants as the mapping λ, respectively (line 3). Next, it iteratively checks if $f_{\mathsf{m}} \cong f_{\mathsf{o}}$, for each procedure f defined in $\mathcal{P}$ (lines 4–23).

For each procedure f, it first extracts the inputs $a^1, \cdots, a^m$ of f_{o} that are scalar variables (line 5) and input encodings $\mathbf{a}^1, \cdots, \mathbf{a}^m$ of f_{m} that are vectors of variables (line 6). Then, it computes the output $\xi(a^1, \cdots, a^m)$ of f_{o} via symbolic execution, which yields an expression in terms of $a^1, \cdots, a^m$ and affine transformations (line 7). Similarly, it computes the output $\xi'(\mathbf{a}^1, \cdots, \mathbf{a}^m)$ of f_{m} via symbolic execution, i.e., a tuple of expressions in terms of the entries of the input encodings $\mathbf{a}^1, \cdots, \mathbf{a}^m$, random variables and affine transformations (line 8).

Recall that $f_{\mathsf{m}} \cong f_{\mathsf{o}}$ iff for all $a^1, \cdots, a^m, r_1, \cdots, r_h \in \mathbb{F}$ and for all $\mathbf{a}^1, \cdots, \mathbf{a}^m \in \mathbb{F}^{d+1}$, the following constraint holds (cf. Definition 1):

$$\left(\bigwedge\nolimits_{i \in [1,m]} a^i = \bigoplus\nolimits_{j \in [0,d]} \mathbf{a}^i_j \right) \rightarrow \left(f_{\mathsf{o}}(a^1, \cdots, a^m) = \bigoplus\nolimits_{i \in [0,d]} f_{\mathsf{m}}(\mathbf{a}^1, \cdots, \mathbf{a}^m_i) \right)$$

where $r_1, \cdots, r_h$ are all the random variables used in f_{m}. Thus, it creates the term $\tau = \xi(a^1, \cdots, a^m)[a^1 \mapsto \bigoplus \mathbf{a}^1, \cdots, a^m \mapsto \bigoplus \mathbf{a}^m] \oplus \bigoplus \xi'(\mathbf{a}^1, \cdots, \mathbf{a}^m)$ (line 9), where $a^i \mapsto \bigoplus \mathbf{a}^i$ is the substitution of a^i with the term $\bigoplus \mathbf{a}^i$ in the expression $\xi(a^1, \cdots, a^m)$. Obviously, τ is equivalent to 0 iff $f_{\mathsf{m}} \cong f_{\mathsf{o}}$.

Algorithm 3: Verification Algorithm

---

1 **Function** Verifier($\mathcal{P}$):
2   Inline all the procedures, unroll loops and eliminate branches in $\mathcal{P}$;
3      $\mathcal{R} \leftarrow$ buildTRS($\mathcal{P}$); $G \leftarrow$ buildCallGraph($\mathcal{P}$); $\lambda \leftarrow$ AffConst($\mathcal{P}, \mathcal{R}, G$);
4   **foreach** *procedure f defined in $\mathcal{P}$* **do**
5   Let $a^1, \cdots, a^m$ be the inputs of f_{o};
6   Let $\mathbf{a}^1, \cdots, \mathbf{a}^m$ be the input encodings of f_{m};
7          $\xi(a^1, \cdots, a^m) \leftarrow$ symbolicExecution(f_{o});
8          $\xi'(\mathbf{a}^1, \cdots, \mathbf{a}^m) \leftarrow$ symbolicExecution(f_{m});
9          $\tau \leftarrow \xi(a^1, \cdots, a^m)[a^1 \mapsto \bigoplus \mathbf{a}^1, \cdots, a^m \mapsto \bigoplus \mathbf{a}^m] \oplus \bigoplus \xi'(\mathbf{a}^1, \cdots, \mathbf{a}^m)$;
10   **while** True **do**
11              $\tau \leftarrow$ TermNorm($\mathcal{R}, \tau, \lambda$)
12   **if** τ *is some constant c* **then**
13   **if** $c = 0$ **then** Emit(f is correct); **break**;
14   **else** Emit(f is incorrect); **break**;
15   **else if** g *is defined in $\mathcal{P}$ but has not been inlined in τ* **then**
16   Inline g in τ; **continue**;
17   **else if** τ *does not contain any uninterpreted function* **then**
18                  $\mathbf{v}^1, \cdots, \mathbf{v}^m \leftarrow$ random values from $\mathbb{F}^{d+1}$;
19   **if** $\tau[\mathbf{a}^1 \mapsto \mathbf{v}^1, \cdots, \mathbf{a}^m \mapsto \mathbf{v}^m] \neq 0$ **then**
20   Emit(f is incorrect); **break**;
21   **if** SMTSolver($\tau \neq 0$)=UNSAT **then**
22   Emit(f is correct); **break**;
23   **else** Emit(f may be incorrect); **break**;

To check if τ is equivalent to 0, similar to computing affine constants in Algorithm 2, the algorithm repeatedly rewrites the term τ to a normal form by invoking `TermNorm` in Algorithm 1 until either the conclusion is drawn or no affine transformation can be inlined (lines 10–23). We declare that f is correct if the normal form is 0 (line 13) and incorrect if it is a non-zero constant (line 14). If the normal form is *not* a constant, we repeatedly inline affine transformation g defined in P which has not been inlined in τ and re-check the term τ.

If there is no definite answer after inlining all the affine transformations, τ is evaluated using random input values. f is *incorrect* if τ is non-zero (line 20). Otherwise, we check the satisfiability of the constraint $\tau \neq 0$ via an SMT solver in bitvector theory (line 21). If $\tau \neq 0$ is unsatisfiable, then f is *correct*. Otherwise we can conclude that f is *incorrect* if no uninterpreted function is involved in τ, but in other cases it is not conclusive.

Theorem 2. *Assume a procedure f in P. If $\mathtt{Verifier}(P)$ emits "f is correct", then $f_{\mathrm{m}} \cong f_o$; if $\mathtt{Verifier}(P)$ emits "f is incorrect" or "f may be incorrect" with no uninterpreted function involved in its final term τ, then $f_{\mathrm{m}} \ncong f_o$.* □

6.4   Implementation Remarks

To implement the algorithms, we use the total order $\geq_s$ on $V \uplus \Sigma$ where all the constants are smaller than the variables, which are in turn smaller than the affine transformations. The order of constants is the standard one on integers, and the order of variables (affine transformations) uses lexicographic order.

In terms of data structure, each term is primarily stored by a directed acyclic graph, allowing us to represent and rewrite common sub-terms in an optimised way. Once a (sub-)term becomes a polynomial during term rewriting, it is stored as a sorted nested list w.r.t. the monomial order $\geq_p$, where each monomial is also stored as a sorted list w.r.t. the factor order $\geq_l$. Moreover, the factor of the form α^k in a monomial is stored by a pair (α, k).

We also adopted two strategies: (i) By Fermat's little theorem [63], $x^{2^n - 1} = 1$ for any $x \in \mathbb{GF}(2^n)$. Hence each k in (α, k) can be simplified to $k \mod (2^n - 1)$. (ii) By rule R12, a term $f(\tau_1 \oplus \cdots \oplus \tau_k)$ can be directly rewritten to $f(\tau_1) \oplus \cdots \oplus (\tau_k)$ if k is odd, and $f(\tau_1) \oplus \cdots \oplus f(\tau_k) \oplus c$ if k is even, where c is the affine constant associated with the affine transformation f.

7   Evaluation

We implement our approach as a tool FISCHER for verifying masked programs in LLVM IR, based on the LLVM framework. We first evaluate FISCHER for computing affine constants (i.e., Algorithm 2), correctness verification, and scalability w.r.t. the masking order (i.e., Algorithm 3) on benchmarks using the ISW scheme. To show the generality of our approach, FISCHER is then used to verify benchmarks using glitch-resistant Boolean masking schemes and lattice-based public-key cryptography. All experiments are conducted on a machine with Linux kernel 5.10, Intel i7 10700 CPU (4.8 GHz, 8 cores, 16 threads) and 40 GB memory. Milliseconds (ms) and seconds (s) are used as the time units in our experiments.

7.1 Evaluation for Computing Affine Constants

To evaluate Algorithm 2, we compare with a pure SMT-based approach which directly checks $\exists c.\forall x, y \in \mathbb{F}.f(x \oplus y) = f(x) \oplus f(y) \oplus c$ using Z3 [47], CVC5 [5] and Boolector [18], by implementing $\oplus$ and $\otimes$ in bit-vector theory, where $\otimes$ is achieved via the Russian peasant method [16]. Technically, SMT solvers only deal with satisfiability, but they usually can eliminate the universal quantifiers in this case, as x, y are over a finite field. In particular, in our experiment, Z3 is configured with default (i.e. (check-sat)), simplify (i.e. (check-sat-using (then simplify smt))) and bit-blast (i.e. (check-sat-using (then bit-blast smt))), denoted by Z3-d, Z3-s and Z3-b, respectively. We focus on the following functions: $\exp i(x) = x^i$ for $i \in \{2, 4, 8, 16\}$; $\text{rotl}i(x)$ for $i \in \{1, 2, 3, 4\}$ that left rotates x by i bits; $\text{af}(x) = \text{rotl}1(x) \oplus \text{rotl}2(x) \oplus \text{rotl}3(x) \oplus \text{rotl}4(x) \oplus 99$ used in AES S-Box; $\text{L1}(x) = 7x^2 \oplus 14x^4 \oplus 7x^8$, $\text{L3}(x) = 7x \oplus 12x^2 \oplus 12x^4 \oplus 9x^8$, $\text{L5}(x) = 10x \oplus 9x^2$ and $\text{L7}(x) = 4x \oplus 13x^2 \oplus 13x^4 \oplus 14x^8$ used in PRESENT S-Box over $\mathbb{GF}(16) = \mathbb{GF}(2)[X]/(X^4 + X + 1)$ [14,19]; $\text{f1}(x) = x^3$, $\text{f2}(x) = x^2 \oplus x \oplus 1$, $\text{f3}(x) = x \oplus x^5$ and $\text{f4}(x) = \text{af}(\exp 2(x))$ over $\mathbb{GF}(2^8)$.

Table 1. Results of computing affine constants, where † means Algorithm 2 needs SMT solving, ‡ means affineness is disproved via testing, ✗ means nonaffineness, and Algorithm 2+B means Algorithm 2+Boolector.

Tool	exp2	exp4	exp8	exp16	rotl1	rotl2	rotl3	rotl4	af	L1	L3	L5	L7	f1	f2	f3	f4
Algorithm 2+Z3-d	3 ms	3 ms	3 ms	3 ms	18 ms†	18 ms†	18 ms†	18 ms†	21 ms†	3 ms	3 ms	3 ms	3 ms	3 ms‡	3 ms	3 ms‡	21 ms†
Algorithm 2+Z3-b	3 ms	3 ms	3 ms	3 ms	15 ms†	16 ms†	15 ms†	15 ms†	20 ms†	3 ms	3 ms	3 ms	3 ms	3 ms‡	3 ms	3 ms‡	20 ms†
Algorithm 2+B	3 ms	3 ms	3 ms	3 ms	8 ms†	8 ms†	8 ms†	8 ms†	13 ms†	3 ms	3 ms	3 ms	3 ms	3 ms‡	3 ms	3 ms‡	14 ms†
Z3-d	181 ms	333 ms	316 ms	521 ms	14 ms	14 ms	14 ms	14 ms	16 ms	113 ms	213 ms	73 ms	194 ms	33 ms	249 ms	38 ms	7.5 s
Z3-s	180 ms	373 ms	452 ms	528 ms	12 ms	12 ms	12 ms	12 ms	15 ms	158 ms	202 ms	194 ms	213 ms	28 ms	252 ms	35 ms	7.6 s
Z3-b	15 ms	16 ms	18 ms	20 ms	12 ms	12 ms	12 ms	12 ms	79 ms	45 ms	42 ms	21 ms	82 ms	17 ms	22 ms	24 ms	60 ms
Boolector	15 ms	18 ms	12 ms	17 ms	5 ms	5 ms	6 ms	5 ms	71 ms	25 ms	34 ms	27 ms	78 ms	14 ms	15 ms	17 ms	67 ms
CVC5	8.4 s	20.3 s	44.4 s	18.6 s	5 ms	5 ms	5 ms	5 ms	113 ms	158.4 s	263.4 s	43.7 s	214.9 s	92 ms	10.3 s	2.3 s	10.4 s
Result	0	0	0	0	0	0	0	0	99	0	0	0	0	✗	1	✗	99

The results are reported in Table 1, where the 2nd–8th rows show the execution time and the last row shows the affine constants if they exist otherwise ✗. We observe that Algorithm 2 significantly outperforms the SMT-based approach on most cases for all the SMT solvers, except for $\text{rotl}i$ and af (It is not surprising, as they use operations rather than $\oplus$ and $\otimes$, thus SMT solving is required). The term rewriting system is often able to compute affine constants *solely* (e.g., $\exp i$ and $\text{L}i$), and SMT solving is required *only* for computing the affine constants of $\text{rotl}i$. By comparing the results of Algorithm 2+Z3-b vs. Z3-b and Algorithm 2+B vs. Boolector on af, we observe that term rewriting is essential as checking normal form—instead of the original constraint—reduces the cost of SMT solving.

7.2 Evaluation for Correctness Verification

To evaluate Algorithm 3, we compare it with a pure SMT-based approach with SMT solvers Z3, CVC5 and Boolector. We also consider several promising general-purpose software verifiers SMACK (with Boogie and Corral engines), SeaHorn, CPAChecker and Symbiotic, and one cryptography-specific verifier CryptoLine (with SMT and CAS solvers), where the verification problem is expressed using assume and assert statements. Those verifiers are configured in two ways: (1) recommended ones in the manual/paper or used in the competition, and (2) by trials of different configurations and selecting the optimal one. Specifically:

- CryptoLine (commit 7e237a9). Both solvers SMT and CAS are used;
- SMACK v2.8.0. integer-encoding: bit-vector, verifier: corral/boogie (both used), solver: Z3/CVC4 (Z3 used), static-unroll: on, unroll: 99;
- SEAHORN v0.1.0 RC3 (commit e712712). pipeline: bpf, arch: m64, inline: on, track: mem, bmc: none/mono/path (mono used), crab: on/off (off used);
- CPAChecker v2.1.1. default.properties with cbmc: on/off (on used);
- Symbiotic v8.0.0. officially-provided SV-COMP configuration with exit-on-error: on.

The benchmark comprises five different masked programs sec_mult for finite-field multiplication over $\mathbb{GF}(2^8)$ by varying masking order $d = 0, 1, 2, 3$, where the $d = 0$ means the program is unmasked. We note that sec_mult in [8] is only available for masking order $d \geq 2$.

Table 2. Results on various sec_mult, where T.O. means time out (20 min), N/A means that UNKNOWN result, and ♮ means that verification result is incorrect.

Order d	Ref.	Algorithm 3	Z3 default	Z3 simplify	Z3 bit-blast	Boolector	CVC5	CryptoLine SMT	CryptoLine CAS	SMACK Boogie	SMACK Corral	SeaHorn	CPAChecker	Symbiotic
0	[58]	17 ms	29 ms	27 ms	42 ms	25 ms	29 ms	39 ms	N/A	29 s	66 s	132 ms	T.O	870 s
	[11]	20 ms	31 ms ms	31 ms	45 ms	28 ms	33 ms	35 ms	N/A	46 s	144 s	128 ms	T.O	899 s
	[34]	21 ms	33 ms	31 ms	46 ms	29 ms	33 ms	32 ms	N/A	23 s	43 s	127 ms	T.O	872 s
	[21]	18 ms	30 ms	28 ms	25 ms	26 ms	31 ms	32 ms	N/A	17 s	56 s	130 ms	T.O	876 s
1	[58]	18 ms	298 ms	299 ms	391 s	3.8 s	T.O	469 ms	N/A	T.O	T.O	13 s	T.O	T.O
	[11]	20 ms	299 ms	299 ms	1049 s	1.91049	T.O	582 ms	N/A	T.O	T.O	13 s	T.O	T.O
	[34]	24 ms	295 ms	295 ms	1199 s	1.8 s	T.O	951 ms	N/A	T.O	T.O	14 s	T.O	T.O
	[21]	20 ms	1180 s	921 s	T.O	7.7 s	T.O	21 s	N/A	T.O	T.O	T.O	T.O	T.O.
2	[58]	20 ms	4.1 s	4.2 s	T.O	T.O	T.O	T.O	N/A	T.O	T.O	T.O	T.O	T.O
	[11]	22 ms	4.2 s	4.4 s	T.O	T.O	T.O	T.O	N/A	T.O	T.O	T.O	T.O	T.O
	[8]	30 ms	4.2 s	4.1 s	T.O	T.O	T.O	T.O	N/A	T.O	26 s♮	T.O	T.O	T.O
	[34]	29 ms	4.2 s	4.2 s	T.O	T.O	T.O	T.O	N/A	T.O	T.O	T.O	T.O	T.O
	[21]	22 ms	T.O	T.O	T.O	T.O	T.O	T.O	N/A	T.O	T.O	T.O	T.O	T.O.
3	[58]	21 ms	T.O	T.O	T.O	T.O	T.O	T.O	N/A	T.O	T.O	T.O	T.O	T.O
	[11]	26 ms	T.O	T.O	T.O	T.O	T.O	T.O	N/A	T.O	T.O	T.O	T.O	T.O
	[8]	27 ms	T.O	T.O	T.O	T.O	T.O	T.O	N/A	T.O	1059 s♮	T.O	T.O	T.O
	[34]	29 ms	T.O	T.O	T.O	T.O	T.O	T.O	N/A	T.O	T.O	T.O	T.O	T.O
	[21]	24 ms	T.O	T.O	T.O	T.O	T.O	T.O	N/A	T.O	T.O	T.O	T.O	T.O

The results are shown in Table 2. We can observe that FISCHER is significantly more efficient than the others, and is able to prove all the cases using our term rewriting system *solely* (i.e., without random testing or SMT solving). With the increase of masking order d, almost all the other tools failed. Both CryptoLine (with the CAS solver) and CPAChecker fail to verify any of the cases due to the non-linear operations involved in sec_mult. SMACK with Corral engine produces two false positives (marked by ♮ in Table 2). These results suggest that dedicated verification approaches are required for proving the correctness of masked programs.

7.3   Scalability of FISCHER

To evaluate the scalability of FISCHER, we verify different versions of sec_mult and masked procedures sec_aes_sbox (resp. sec_present_sbox) of S-Boxes used in AES [58] (resp. PRESENT [19]) with varying masking order d. Since it is known that refresh_masks in [58] is vulnerable when $d \geq 4$ [24], a fixed version RefreshM [7] is used in all the S-Boxes (except that when sec_mult is taken from [8] its own version is used). We note that sec_present_sbox uses the affine transformations L1, L3, L5, L7, exp2 and exp4, while sec_aes_sbox uses the affine transformations af, exp2, exp4 and exp16.

The results are reported in Table 3. All those benchmarks are proved using our term rewriting system solely except for the three incorrect ones marked by ♮. FISCHER scales up to masking order of 100 or even 200 for sec_mult, which is remarkable. FISCHER also scales up to masking order of 30 or even 40 for sec_present_sbox. However, it is less scalable on sec_aes_sbox, as it computes the multiplicative inverse x^{254} on shares, and the size of the term encoding the equivalence problem explodes with the increase of the masking order. Furthermore, to better demonstrate the effectiveness of our term writing system in dealing with complicated procedures, we first use Algorithm 2 to derive affine constants on sec_aes_sbox with ISW [58] and then directly apply SMT solvers to solve the correctness constraints obtained at Line 9 of Algorithm 3. It takes about 1 s to obtain the result on the first-order masking, while fails to obtain the result within 20 min on the second-order masking.

Table 3. Results on sec_mult and S-Boxes, where T.O. means time out (20 min), and ♮ means that the program is *incorrect*.

Ref.	d																
	sec_mult						sec_present_sbox							sec_aes_sbox			
	5	10	20	50	100	200	1	2	5	10	20	30	40	1	2	4	5
ISW [58]	23 ms	33 ms	84 ms	1.0s	15s	545s	44 ms	51 ms	93 ms	535 ms	14s	118s	T.O.	87 ms	234 ms	25s	160s
ISW [11]	26 ms	44 ms	100 ms	712 ms	7.3s	212s	54 ms	63 ms	110 ms	673 ms	17s	163s	T.O.	108 ms	265 ms	23s	142s
ISW [8]	36 ms♮	49 ms	109 ms	601 ms	3.2s	18s	–	86 ms	142 ms♮	237 ms	841 ms	2.4s	5.3s	–	559 ms	9.7s	142s♮
ISW [34]	34 ms	50 ms	98 ms	518 ms	3.1s	19s	67 ms	91 ms	137 ms	700 ms	20s	173s	T.O.	140 ms	571 ms	63s	T.O.
ISW [21]	30 ms	109 ms	224 ms	5.0s	152s	T.O.	51 ms	61 ms	113 ms	354 ms	2.4s	9.7s	29s	133 ms	269 ms	13s	68s

Table 4. Results on `sec_mult` and S-Boxes for HPC, DOM and CMS.

Ref.	d															
	sec_mult						sec_present_sbox					sec_aes_sbox				
	0	1	2	3	4	5	1	2	3	4	5	1	2	3	4	5
HPC1 [20]	28 ms	30 ms	32 ms	35 ms	39 ms	42 ms	63 ms	72 ms	84 ms	98 ms	117 ms	104 ms	254 ms	1.8 s	13 s	67 s
HPC2 [20]	23 ms	25 ms	26 ms	28 ms	31 ms	33 ms	57 ms	66 ms	75 ms	92 ms	110 ms	92 ms	244 ms	1.9 s	13 s	65 s
DOM [35]	24 ms	24 ms	25 ms	26 ms	28 ms	29 ms	52 ms	60 ms	67 ms	77 ms	90 ms	80 ms	223 ms	1.8 s	12 s	66 s
CMS [57]	–	–	24 ms	–	–	–	–	53 ms	–	–	–	–	211 ms	–	–	–

A highlight of our findings is that FISCHER reports that `sec_mult` from [8] and the S-boxes based on this version are incorrect when $d = 5$. After a careful analysis, we found that indeed it is incorrect for any $d \equiv 1 \mod 4$ (i.e., 5, 9, 13, etc.). This is because [8] parallelizes the multiplication over the entire encodings (i.e., tuples of shares) while the parallelized computation depends on the value of $d \mod 4$. When the reminder is 1, the error occurs.

7.4   Evaluation for More Boolean Masking Schemes

To demonstrate the applicability of FISCHER on a wider range of Boolean masking schemes, we further consider glitch-resistant Boolean masking schemes: HPC1, HPC2 [20], DOM [35] and CMS [57]. We implement the finite-field multiplication `sec_mult` using those masking schemes, as well as masked versions of AES S-box and PRESENT S-box. We note that our implementation of DOM `sec_mult` is derived from [20], and we only implement the 2nd-order CMS `sec_mult` due to the difficulty of implementation. All other experimental settings are the same as in Sect. 7.3.

The results are shown in Table 4. Our term rewriting system *solely* is able to efficiently prove the correctness of finite-field multiplication `sec_mult`, masked versions of AES S-box and PRESENT S-box using the glitch-resistant Boolean masking schemes HPC1, HPC2, DOM and CMS. The verification cost of those benchmarks is similar to that of benchmarks using the ISW scheme, demonstrating the applicability of FISCHER for various Boolean masking schemes.

Table 5. Results on `sec_add`, `sec_add_modp` and `sec_a2b` [17], where T.O. means time out (20 min).

d	k																			
	sec_add							sec_add_modp						sec_a2b						
	2	3	4	6	8	12	16	2	3	4	6	8	12	2	3	4	6	8	12	16
1	34 ms	38 ms	42 ms	51 ms	61 ms	83 ms	109 ms	97 ms	248 ms	805 ms	7.5 s	44 s	623 s	41 ms	48 ms	55 ms	70 ms	87 ms	121 ms	156 ms
2	35 ms	40 ms	45 ms	55 ms	65 ms	91 ms	124 ms	111 ms	331 ms	1.1 s	11 s	67 s	936 s	58 ms	74 ms	93 ms	134 ms	199 ms	523 ms	1.5 s
3	36 ms	42 ms	47 ms	58 ms	71 ms	100 ms	139 ms	127 ms	417 ms	1.5 s	15 s	89 s	T.O.	73 ms	93 ms	118 ms	182 ms	293 ms	927 ms	3.0 s
4	38 ms	44 ms	50 ms	62 ms	76 ms	109 ms	155 ms	144 ms	506 ms	1.9 s	18 s	112 s	T.O.	93 ms	130 ms	190 ms	676 ms	3.3 s	49 s	366 s
5	39 ms	45 ms	51 ms	66 ms	81 ms	118 ms	168 ms	160 ms	586 ms	2.2 s	22 s	136 s	T.O.	109 ms	159 ms	256 ms	1.1 s	6.5 s	100 s	746 s

7.5 Evaluation for Arithmetic/Boolean Masking Conversions

To demonstrate a wider applicability of FISCHER other than masked implementations of symmetric cryptography, we further evaluate FISCHER on three key non-linear building blocks for bitsliced, masked implementations of lattice-based post-quantum key encapsulation mechanisms (KEMs [17]). Note that KEMs are a class of encryption techniques designed to secure symmetric cryptographic key material for transmission using asymmetric (public-key) cryptography. We implement the Boolean masked addition modulo 2^k (sec_add), Boolean masked addition modulo p (sec_add_modp) and the arithmetic-to-Boolean masking conversion modulo 2^k (sec_a2b) for various bit-width k and masking order d, where p is the largest prime number less than 2^k. Note that some bitwise operations (e.g., circular shift) are expressed by affine transformations, and the modulo addition is implemented by the simulation algorithm [17] in our implementations.

The results are reported in Table 5. FISCHER is able to efficiently prove the correctness of these functions with various masking orders (d) and bit-width (k), using the term rewriting system *solely*. With the increase of the bit-width k (resp. masking order d), the verification cost increases more quickly for sec_add_modp (resp. sec_a2b) than for sec_add. This is because sec_add_modp with bit-width k invokes sec_add three times, two of which have the bit-width $k + 1$, and the number of calls to sec_add in sec_a2b increases with the masking order d though using the same bit-width as sec_a2b. These results demonstrate the applicability of FISCHER for asymmetric cryptography.

8 Conclusion

We have proposed a term rewriting based approach to proving functional equivalence between masked cryptographic programs and their original unmasked algorithms over $\mathbb{GF}(2^n)$. Based on this approach, we have developed a tool FISCHER and carried out extensive experiments on various benchmarks. Our evaluation confirms the effectiveness, efficiency and applicability of our approach.

For future work, it would be interesting to further investigate the theoretical properties of the term rewriting system. Moreover, we believe the term rewriting approach extended with more operations may have a greater potential in verifying more general cryptographic programs, e.g., those from the standard software library such as OpenSSL.

References

1. Affeldt, R.: On construction of a library of formally verified low-level arithmetic functions. Innov. Syst. Softw. Eng. **9**(2), 59–77 (2013)
2. Ahman, D., et al.: Dijkstra monads for free. In: Proceedings of the 44th ACM SIGPLAN Symposium on Principles of Programming Languages, pp. 515–529 (2017)

3. Almeida, J.B., et al.: Jasmin: high-assurance and high-speed cryptography. In: Proceedings of the 2017 ACM SIGSAC Conference on Computer and Communications Security, pp. 1807–1823 (2017)
4. Appel, A.W.: Verification of a cryptographic primitive: SHA-256. ACM Trans. Program. Lang. Syst. **37**(2), 1–31 (2015)
5. Barbosa, H., et al.: cvc5: a versatile and industrial-strength SMT solver. In: Proceedings of the 28th International Conference on Tools and Algorithms for the Construction and Analysis of Systems, vol. 13243, pp. 415–442 (2022). v1.0.0 is used
6. Barnett, M., Chang, B.-Y.E., DeLine, R., Jacobs, B., Leino, K.R.M.: Boogie: a modular reusable verifier for object-oriented programs. In: de Boer, F.S., Bonsangue, M.M., Graf, S., de Roever, W.-P. (eds.) FMCO 2005. LNCS, vol. 4111, pp. 364–387. Springer, Heidelberg (2006). https://doi.org/10.1007/11804192_17
7. Barthe, G., et al.: Strong non-interference and type-directed higher-order masking. In: Proceedings of the 2016 ACM SIGSAC Conference on Computer and Communications Security, pp. 116–129 (2016)
8. Barthe, G., Dupressoir, F., Faust, S., Grégoire, B., Standaert, F.-X., Strub, P.-Y.: Parallel implementations of masking schemes and the bounded moment leakage model. In: Coron, J.-S., Nielsen, J.B. (eds.) EUROCRYPT 2017. LNCS, vol. 10210, pp. 535–566. Springer, Cham (2017). https://doi.org/10.1007/978-3-319-56620-7_19
9. Barthe, G., Dupressoir, F., Grégoire, B., Kunz, C., Schmidt, B., Strub, P.-Y.: EasyCrypt: a tutorial. In: Aldini, A., Lopez, J., Martinelli, F. (eds.) FOSAD 2012-2013. LNCS, vol. 8604, pp. 146–166. Springer, Cham (2014). https://doi.org/10.1007/978-3-319-10082-1_6
10. Beierle, C., et al.: The SKINNY family of block ciphers and its low-latency variant MANTIS. In: Robshaw, M., Katz, J. (eds.) CRYPTO 2016. LNCS, vol. 9815, pp. 123–153. Springer, Heidelberg (2016). https://doi.org/10.1007/978-3-662-53008-5_5
11. Belaïd, S., Benhamouda, F., Passelègue, A., Prouff, E., Thillard, A., Vergnaud, D.: Randomness complexity of private circuits for multiplication. In: Fischlin, M., Coron, J.-S. (eds.) EUROCRYPT 2016. LNCS, vol. 9666, pp. 616–648. Springer, Heidelberg (2016). https://doi.org/10.1007/978-3-662-49896-5_22
12. Beyer, D., Keremoglu, M.E.: CPACHECKER: a tool for configurable software verification. In: Gopalakrishnan, G., Qadeer, S. (eds.) CAV 2011. LNCS, vol. 6806, pp. 184–190. Springer, Heidelberg (2011). https://doi.org/10.1007/978-3-642-22110-1_16
13. Bloem, R., Gross, H., Iusupov, R., Könighofer, B., Mangard, S., Winter, J.: Formal verification of masked hardware implementations in the presence of glitches. In: Nielsen, J.B., Rijmen, V. (eds.) EUROCRYPT 2018. LNCS, vol. 10821, pp. 321–353. Springer, Cham (2018). https://doi.org/10.1007/978-3-319-78375-8_11
14. Bogdanov, A., et al.: PRESENT: an ultra-lightweight block cipher. In: Paillier, P., Verbauwhede, I. (eds.) CHES 2007. LNCS, vol. 4727, pp. 450–466. Springer, Heidelberg (2007). https://doi.org/10.1007/978-3-540-74735-2_31
15. Bond, B., et al.: Vale: verifying high-performance cryptographic assembly code. In: 26th USENIX security symposium, pp. 917–934 (2017)
16. Bowden, J.: The Russian peasant method of multiplication. Math. Teach. **5**(1), 4–8 (1912)
17. Bronchain, O., Cassiers, G.: Bitslicing arithmetic/Boolean masking conversions for fun and profit: with application to lattice-based KEMs. IACR Trans. Cryptograph. Hardw. Embed. Syst., 553–588 (2022)

18. Brummayer, R., Biere, A.: Boolector: an efficient SMT solver for bit-vectors and arrays. In: Kowalewski, S., Philippou, A. (eds.) TACAS 2009. LNCS, vol. 5505, pp. 174–177. Springer, Heidelberg (2009). https://doi.org/10.1007/978-3-642-00768-2_16

19. Carlet, C., Goubin, L., Prouff, E., Quisquater, M., Rivain, M.: Higher-order masking schemes for s-boxes. In: Canteaut, A. (ed.) FSE 2012. LNCS, vol. 7549, pp. 366–384. Springer, Heidelberg (2012). https://doi.org/10.1007/978-3-642-34047-5_21

20. Cassiers, G., Grégoire, B., Levi, I., Standaert, F.X.: Hardware private circuits: from trivial composition to full verification. IEEE Trans. Comput. **70**(10), 1677–1690 (2020)

21. Cassiers, G., Standaert, F.X.: Trivially and efficiently composing masked gadgets with probe isolating non-interference. IEEE Trans. Inf. Forensics Secur. **15**, 2542–2555 (2020)

22. Chalupa, M., Jašek, T., Novák, J., Řechtáčková, A., Šoková, V., Strejček, J.: Symbiotic 8: beyond symbolic execution. In: Groote, J.F., Larsen, K.G. (eds.) TACAS 2021. LNCS, vol. 12652, pp. 453–457. Springer, Cham (2021). https://doi.org/10.1007/978-3-030-72013-1_31

23. Chen, Y.F., et al.: Verifying curve25519 software. In: Proceedings of the 2014 ACM SIGSAC Conference on Computer and Communications Security, pp. 299–309 (2014)

24. Coron, J.-S., Prouff, E., Rivain, M., Roche, T.: Higher-order side channel security and mask refreshing. In: Moriai, S. (ed.) FSE 2013. LNCS, vol. 8424, pp. 410–424. Springer, Heidelberg (2014). https://doi.org/10.1007/978-3-662-43933-3_21

25. Daemen, J., Rijmen, V.: AES proposal: Rijndael (1999)

26. Eldib, H., Wang, C., Schaumont, P.: Formal verification of software countermeasures against side-channel attacks. ACM Trans. Softw. Eng. Methodol. **24**(2), 11 (2014)

27. Erbsen, A., Philipoom, J., Gross, J., Sloan, R., Chlipala, A.: Simple high-level code for cryptographic arithmetic - with proofs, without compromises. In: Proceedings of the 2019 IEEE Symposium on Security and Privacy, pp. 1202–1219 (2019)

28. Fu, Y., Liu, J., Shi, X., Tsai, M., Wang, B., Yang, B.: Signed cryptographic program verification with typed cryptoline. In: Proceedings of the 2019 ACM SIGSAC Conference on Computer and Communications Security, pp. 1591–1606 (2019)

29. Gao, P., Xie, H., Song, F., Chen, T.: A hybrid approach to formal verification of higher-order masked arithmetic programs. ACM Trans. Softw. Eng. Methodol. **30**(3), 1–42 (2021)

30. Gao, P., Xie, H., Sun, P., Zhang, J., Song, F., Chen, T.: Formal verification of masking countermeasures for arithmetic programs. IEEE Trans. Software Eng. **48**(3), 973–1000 (2022)

31. Gao, P., Xie, H., Zhang, J., Song, F., Chen, T.: Quantitative verification of masked arithmetic programs against side-channel attacks. In: Vojnar, T., Zhang, L. (eds.) TACAS 2019. LNCS, vol. 11427, pp. 155–173. Springer, Cham (2019). https://doi.org/10.1007/978-3-030-17462-0_9

32. Gao, P., Zhang, J., Song, F., Wang, C.: Verifying and quantifying side-channel resistance of masked software implementations. ACM Trans. Softw. Eng. Methodol. **28**(3), 1–32 (2019)

33. Goubin, L., Patarin, J.: DES and differential power analysis the "Duplication" method. In: Koç, Ç.K., Paar, C. (eds.) CHES 1999. LNCS, vol. 1717, pp. 158–172. Springer, Heidelberg (1999). https://doi.org/10.1007/3-540-48059-5_15

34. Gross, H., Mangard, S.: Reconciling $d + 1$ masking in hardware and software. In: Fischer, W., Homma, N. (eds.) CHES 2017. LNCS, vol. 10529, pp. 115–136. Springer, Cham (2017). https://doi.org/10.1007/978-3-319-66787-4_6

35. Groß, H., Mangard, S., Korak, T.: Domain-oriented masking: compact masked hardware implementations with arbitrary protection order. Cryptology ePrint Archive (2016)

36. Gurfinkel, A., Kahsai, T., Komuravelli, A., Navas, J.A.: The SeaHorn verification framework. In: Kroening, D., Păsăreanu, C.S. (eds.) CAV 2015. LNCS, vol. 9206, pp. 343–361. Springer, Cham (2015). https://doi.org/10.1007/978-3-319-21690-4_20

37. Ishai, Y., Sahai, A., Wagner, D.: Private circuits: securing hardware against probing attacks. In: Boneh, D. (ed.) CRYPTO 2003. LNCS, vol. 2729, pp. 463–481. Springer, Heidelberg (2003). https://doi.org/10.1007/978-3-540-45146-4_27

38. Kaufmann, D., Biere, A.: AMULET 2.0 for verifying multiplier circuits. In: TACAS 2021. LNCS, vol. 12652, pp. 357–364. Springer, Cham (2021). https://doi.org/10.1007/978-3-030-72013-1_19

39. Kaufmann, D., Biere, A., Kauers, M.: Verifying large multipliers by combining SAT and computer algebra. In: Proceedings of the 2019 Formal Methods in Computer Aided Design, pp. 28–36 (2019)

40. Kim, H.S., Hong, S., Lim, J.: A fast and provably secure higher-order masking of AES S-Box. In: Preneel, B., Takagi, T. (eds.) CHES 2011. LNCS, vol. 6917, pp. 95–107. Springer, Heidelberg (2011). https://doi.org/10.1007/978-3-642-23951-9_7

41. Kocher, P., Jaffe, J., Jun, B.: Differential power analysis. In: Wiener, M. (ed.) CRYPTO 1999. LNCS, vol. 1666, pp. 388–397. Springer, Heidelberg (1999). https://doi.org/10.1007/3-540-48405-1_25

42. Kocher, P.C.: Timing attacks on implementations of Diffie-Hellman, RSA, DSS, and other systems. In: Koblitz, N. (ed.) CRYPTO 1996. LNCS, vol. 1109, pp. 104–113. Springer, Heidelberg (1996). https://doi.org/10.1007/3-540-68697-5_9

43. Lattner, C., Adve, V.: LLVM: a compilation framework for lifelong program analysis & transformation. In: Proceedings of the 2nd IEEE/ACM International Symposium on Code Generation and Optimization, pp. 75–86 (2004)

44. Leino, K.R.M.: Dafny: an automatic program verifier for functional correctness. In: Clarke, E.M., Voronkov, A. (eds.) LPAR 2010. LNCS (LNAI), vol. 6355, pp. 348–370. Springer, Heidelberg (2010). https://doi.org/10.1007/978-3-642-17511-4_20

45. Liu, J., Shi, X., Tsai, M., Wang, B., Yang, B.: Verifying arithmetic in cryptographic C programs. In: Proceedings of the 34th IEEE/ACM International Conference on Automated Software Engineering, pp. 552–564 (2019)

46. Luo, C., Fei, Y., Kaeli, D.R.: Effective simple-power analysis attacks of elliptic curve cryptography on embedded systems. In: Proceedings of the International Conference on Computer-Aided Design, p. 115 (2018)

47. de Moura, L., Bjørner, N.: Z3: an efficient SMT solver. In: Ramakrishnan, C.R., Rehof, J. (eds.) TACAS 2008. LNCS, vol. 4963, pp. 337–340. Springer, Heidelberg (2008). https://doi.org/10.1007/978-3-540-78800-3_24

48. Myreen, M.O., Curello, G.: Proof pearl: a verified Bignum implementation in x86-64 machine code. In: Gonthier, G., Norrish, M. (eds.) CPP 2013. LNCS, vol. 8307, pp. 66–81. Springer, Cham (2013). https://doi.org/10.1007/978-3-319-03545-1_5

49. Myreen, M.O., Gordon, M.J.C.: Hoare logic for realistically modelled machine code. In: Grumberg, O., Huth, M. (eds.) TACAS 2007. LNCS, vol. 4424, pp. 568–582. Springer, Heidelberg (2007). https://doi.org/10.1007/978-3-540-71209-1_44

50. National Institute of Standards and Technology: Data encryption standard (DES). FIPS Publication, pp. 46–3, October 1999
51. Newman, M.H.A.: On theories with a combinatorial definition of equivalence. Annals Math., 223–243 (1942)
52. Örs, S.B., Oswald, E., Preneel, B.: Power-analysis attacks on an FPGA – first experimental results. In: Walter, C.D., Koç, Ç.K., Paar, C. (eds.) CHES 2003. LNCS, vol. 2779, pp. 35–50. Springer, Heidelberg (2003). https://doi.org/10.1007/978-3-540-45238-6_4
53. Polyakov, A., Tsai, M., Wang, B., Yang, B.: Verifying arithmetic assembly programs in cryptographic primitives (invited talk). In: Proceedings of the 29th International Conference on Concurrency Theory, pp. 1–16 (2018)
54. Prouff, E., Rivain, M., Bevan, R.: Statistical analysis of second order differential power analysis. IEEE Trans. Comput. 58(6), 799–811 (2009)
55. Rakamarić, Z., Emmi, M.: SMACK: decoupling source language details from verifier implementations. In: Biere, A., Bloem, R. (eds.) CAV 2014. LNCS, vol. 8559, pp. 106–113. Springer, Cham (2014). https://doi.org/10.1007/978-3-319-08867-9_7
56. Ravi, P., Roy, S.S., Chattopadhyay, A., Bhasin, S.: Generic side-channel attacks on CCA-secure lattice-based PKE and KEM schemes. IACR Cryptol. ePrint Arch. 2019, 948 (2019)
57. Reparaz, O., Bilgin, B., Nikova, S., Gierlichs, B., Verbauwhede, I.: Consolidating masking schemes. In: Gennaro, R., Robshaw, M. (eds.) CRYPTO 2015. LNCS, vol. 9215, pp. 764–783. Springer, Heidelberg (2015). https://doi.org/10.1007/978-3-662-47989-6_37
58. Rivain, M., Prouff, E.: Provably secure higher-order masking of AES. In: Mangard, S., Standaert, F.-X. (eds.) CHES 2010. LNCS, vol. 6225, pp. 413–427. Springer, Heidelberg (2010). https://doi.org/10.1007/978-3-642-15031-9_28
59. Schamberger, T., Renner, J., Sigl, G., Wachter-Zeh, A.: A power side-channel attack on the CCA2-secure HQC KEM. In: Liardet, P.-Y., Mentens, N. (eds.) CARDIS 2020. LNCS, vol. 12609, pp. 119–134. Springer, Cham (2021). https://doi.org/10.1007/978-3-030-68487-7_8
60. Shamir, A.: How to share a secret. Commun. ACM 22(11), 612–613 (1979)
61. Tomb, A.: Automated verification of real-world cryptographic implementations. IEEE Secur. Priv. 14(6), 26–33 (2016)
62. Tsai, M.H., Wang, B.Y., Yang, B.Y.: Certified verification of algebraic properties on low-level mathematical constructs in cryptographic programs. In: Proceedings of the 2017 ACM SIGSAC Conference on Computer and Communications Security, pp. 1973–1987 (2017)
63. Vinogradov, I.M.: Elements of Number Theory. Courier Dover Publications, New York (2016)
64. Zhang, J., Gao, P., Song, F., Wang, C.: SCInfer: refinement-based verification of software countermeasures against side-channel attacks. In: Chockler, H., Weissenbacher, G. (eds.) CAV 2018. LNCS, vol. 10982, pp. 157–177. Springer, Cham (2018). https://doi.org/10.1007/978-3-319-96142-2_12
65. Zinzindohoué, J.K., Bhargavan, K., Protzenko, J., Beurdouche, B.: HACL*: A verified modern cryptographic library. In: Proceedings of the 2017 ACM SIGSAC Conference on Computer and Communications Security, pp. 1789–1806 (2017)

Automatic Program Instrumentation
for Automatic Verification

Jesper Amilon[1]($\boxtimes$), Zafer Esen[2]($\boxtimes$), Dilian Gurov[1]($\boxtimes$),
Christian Lidström[1]($\boxtimes$), and Philipp Rümmer[2,3]($\boxtimes$)

[1] KTH Royal Institute of Technology, Stockholm, Sweden
{jamilon,dilian,clid}@kth.se
[2] Uppsala University, Uppsala, Sweden
{zafer.esen,philipp.ruemmer}@it.uu.se
[3] University of Regensburg, Regensburg, Germany

Abstract. In deductive verification and software model checking, dealing with certain specification language constructs can be problematic when the back-end solver is not sufficiently powerful or lacks the required theories. One way to deal with this is to transform, for verification purposes, the program to an equivalent one not using the problematic constructs, and to reason about its correctness instead. In this paper, we propose instrumentation as a unifying verification paradigm that subsumes various existing ad-hoc approaches, has a clear formal correctness criterion, can be applied automatically, and can transfer back witnesses and counterexamples. We illustrate our approach on the automated verification of programs that involve quantification and aggregation operations over arrays, such as the maximum value or sum of the elements in a given segment of the array, which are known to be difficult to reason about automatically. We implement our approach in the MONOCERA tool, which is tailored to the verification of programs with aggregation, and evaluate it on example programs, including SV-COMP programs.

1 Introduction

Overview. Program specifications are often written in expressive, high-level languages: for instance, in temporal logic [14], in first-order logic with quantifiers [28], in separation logic [40], or in specification languages that provide extended quantifiers for computing the sum or maximum value of array elements [7,33]. Specifications commonly also use a rich set of theories; for instance, specifications could be written using full Peano arithmetic, as opposed to bitvectors or linear arithmetic used in the program. Rich specification languages make it possible to express intended program behaviour in a succinct form, and as a result reduce the likelihood of mistakes being introduced in specifications.

There is a gap, however, between the languages used in specifications and the input languages of automatic verification tools. Software model checkers, in particular, usually require specifications to be expressed using program assertions

C. Enea and A. Lal (Eds.): CAV 2023, LNCS 13966, pp. 281–304, 2023.
https://doi.org/10.1007/978-3-031-37709-9_14

and Boolean program expressions, and do not directly support any of the more sophisticated language features mentioned. In fact, rich specification languages are challenging to handle in automatic verification, since satisfiability checks can become undecidable (i.e., it is no longer decidable whether assertion failures can occur on a program path), and techniques for inferring program invariants usually focus on simple specifications only.

To bridge this gap, it is common practice to *encode* high-level specifications in the low-level assertion languages understood by the tools. For instance, temporal properties can be translated to Büchi automata, and added to programs using ghost variables and assertions [14]; quantified properties can be replaced with non-determinism, ghost variables, or loops [13,37]; sets used to specify the absence of data-races can be represented using non-deterministically initialized variables [18]. By adding ghost variables and bespoke ghost code to programs [22], many specifications can be made effectively checkable.

The translation of specifications to assertions or ghost code is today largely designed, or even carried out, by hand. This is an error-prone process, and for complex specifications and programs it is very hard to ensure that the low-level encoding of a specification faithfully models the original high-level properties to be checked. Mistakes have been found even in industrial, very carefully developed specifications [39], and can result in assertions that are vacuously satisfied by any program. Naturally, the manual translation of specifications also tends to be an ad-hoc process that does not easily generalise to other specifications.

This paper proposes the first general framework to automate the translation of rich program specifications to simpler program assertions, using a process called *instrumentation.* Our approach models the semantics of specific complex operations using program-independent *instrumentation operators,* consisting of (manually designed) rewriting rules that define how the evaluation of the operator can be achieved using simpler program statements and ghost variables. The instrumentation approach is flexible enough to cover a wide range of different operators, including operators that are best handled by weaving their evaluation into the program to be analysed. While instrumentation operators are manually written, their application to programs can be performed in a fully automatic way by means of a search procedure. The soundness of an instrumentation operator is shown formally, once and for all, by providing an *instrumentation invariant* that ensures that the operator can never be used to show correctness of an incorrect program.

Additional instrumentation operator definitions, correctness proofs, and detailed evaluation results can be found in the accompanying extended report [4].

Motivating Example. We illustrate our approach on the computation of *triangular numbers* $s_N = (N^2 + N)/2$, see left-hand side of Fig. 1. For reasons of presentation, the program has been normalised by representing the square N*N using an auxiliary variable NN. While mathematically simple, verifying the postcondition s == (NN+N)/2 in the program turns out to be challenging even for state-of-the-art model checkers, as such tools are usually thrown off course by

```
1 // Triangular numbers          1 // Instrumented program
2 i = 0; /*A*/ s = 0; /*B*/      2 i=0; s=0; x_sq=0; x_shad=0;
3 assume(N>0);                    3 assume(N>0);
4 while(i < N) {                  4 while(i < N) {
5                                 5     // Begin-instrumentation
6                                 6     assert(i == x_shad);
7                                 7     x_sq   = x_sq + 2*i + 1;
8      i = i + 1; /*C*/           8     i      = i + 1;
9                                 9     x_shad = i;
10                                10     // End-instrumentation
11     s = s + i;                 11     s      = s + i;
12 }                              12 }
13                               13 // Begin-instrumentation
14                               14 assert(N == x_shad);
15 NN = N*N; /*D*/               15 NN = x_sq;
16                               16 // End-instrumentation
17 assert(s == (NN+N)/2);        17 assert(s == (NN+N)/2);
```

Fig. 1. Program computing triangular numbers, and its instrumented counterpart

the non-linear term N*N. Computing the value of NN by adding a loop in line 16 is not sufficient for most tools either, since the program in any case requires a non-linear invariant $0 <= i <= N$ && $2*s == i*i + i$ to be derived for the loop in lines 4–12.

The insight needed to elegantly verify the program is that the value $i*i$ can be tracked during the program execution using a ghost variable x_sq. For this, the program is instrumented to maintain the relationship x_sq == $i*i$: initially, i == x_sq == 0, and each time the value of i is modified, also the variable x_sq is updated accordingly. With the value x_sq == $i*i$ available, both the loop invariant and the post-condition turn into formulas over linear arithmetic, and program verification becomes largely straightforward. The challenge, of course, is to discover this program transformation automatically, and to guarantee the soundness of the process. For the example, the transformed program is shown on the right-hand side of Fig. 1, and discussed in the next paragraphs.

Our method splits the process of program instrumentation into two parts: (i) choosing an *instrumentation operator,* which is defined manually, designed to be program-independent, and induces a space of possible program transformations; and (ii) carrying out an automatic *application strategy* to find, among the possible program transformations, one that enables verification of a program.

An instrumentation operator for tracking squares is shown in Fig. 2, and consists of the declaration of two ghost variables (x_sq, x_shad) with initial value 0, respectively; four rules for rewriting program statements; and the instrumentation invariant witnessing correctness of the operator. The rewrite rules use formal variables x, y, which can represent arbitrary variables in the program (i, N, NN). An application of the operator to a program will declare the ghost variables in the form of global variables, and then rewrite some chosen set of program statements using the provided rules. Since the statements to be rewritten can

---

Ω_{square} **(Instrumentation operator)** ───────────────

  G_{square} **(Ghost variables)** ─────────────────

  `x_sq, x_shad : Int`

  $init(\texttt{x\_sq}) = 0,\ init(\texttt{x\_shad}) = 0$

  R_{square} **(Rewrite rules)** ──────────────────

$x = \alpha$	$\rightsquigarrow$ $x = \alpha;\ \texttt{x\_sq} = \alpha^2;\ \texttt{x\_shad} = x$	(R1)
$x = x + \alpha$	$\rightsquigarrow$ $\texttt{assert}(x == \texttt{x\_shad});$	(R2)
	$\texttt{x\_sq} = \texttt{x\_sq} + 2\alpha * x + \alpha^2;\ x = x + \alpha;\ \texttt{x\_shad} = x$	
$x = \alpha * x$	$\rightsquigarrow$ $\texttt{assert}(x == \texttt{x\_shad});$	(R3)
	$\texttt{x\_sq} = \alpha^2 * \texttt{x\_sq};\ x = \alpha * x;\ \texttt{x\_shad} = x$	
$y = x * x$	$\rightsquigarrow$ $\texttt{assert}(x == \texttt{x\_shad});\ y = \texttt{x\_sq}$	(R4)

  I_{square} **(Instrumentation invariant)** ──────────────

  $\texttt{x\_sq} = \texttt{x\_shad}^2$

Fig. 2. Definition of an instrumentation operator Ω_{square} for tracking squares

be chosen arbitrarily, and since moreover multiple rewrite rules might apply to some statements, rewriting can result in many different variants of a program. In the example, we rewrite the assignments C, D of the left-hand side program using rewrite rules (R2) and (R4), respectively, resulting in the instrumented and correct program on the right-hand side.

Instrumentation operators are designed to be *sound,* which means that rewriting a wrong selection of program statements might lead to an instrumented program that cannot be verified, i.e., in which assertions might fail, but instrumentation can never turn an incorrect source program into a correct instrumented program. This opens up the possibility to systematically search for the right program instrumentation. We propose a counterexample-guided algorithm for this purpose, which starts from some arbitrarily chosen instrumentation, checks whether the instrumented program can be verified, and otherwise attempts to fix the instrumentation using a refinement loop. As soon as a verifiable instrumented program has been found, the search can stop and the correctness of the original program has been shown.

The concept of instrumentation invariants is essential for guaranteeing soundness of an operator. Instrumentation invariants are formulas that can (only) refer to the ghost variables introduced by an instrumentation operator, and are formulated in such a way that they hold *in every reachable state of every instrumented program.* To maintain their invariants, instrumentation operators use shadow variables that duplicate the values of program variables. In the operator in Fig. 2, the purpose of the shadow variable `x_shad` is to reproduce the value of the program variable whose square is tracked (i). The rewriting rules introduce guards to detect incorrect instrumentation (the assertions in (R2), (R3), (R4)), which are particular cases in which some update of a relevant variable was missed and not correctly instrumented. The use of shadow variables and guards make instrumentation operators very flexible; in our example, note that instrumentation tracks the square of the value of i during the loop, but is also used later to simplify the expression N*N. This is possible because of the instrumentation invariant and because i == N holds after termination of the loop, which is verified through the assertion introduced in line 14.

Contributions and Outline. The operator shown in Fig. 2 is simple, and does not apply to all programs, but it can easily be generalised to other arithmetic operators and program statements. The framework presented in this paper provides the foundation for developing a (extendable) library of formally verified instrumentation operators. In the scope of this paper, we focus on two specification constructs that have been identified as particularly challenging in the literature: existential and universal *quantifiers* over arrays, and *aggregation* (or *extended quantifiers*), which includes computing the sum or maximum value of elements in an array. Our experiments on benchmarks taken from the SV-COMP [8] show that even relatively simple instrumentation operators can significantly extend the capabilities of a software model checker, and often make the automatic verification of otherwise hard specifications easy.

The contributions of the paper are: (i) a general *framework for program instrumentation*, which defines a space of program transformations that work by rewriting individual statements (Sect. 2); (ii) an application strategy *search algorithm* in this space, for a given program (Sect. 3); (iii) two *instantiations* of the framework—one for instrumentation operators to handle specifications with *quantifiers* (Sect. 4.1), and one for *extended quantifiers* (Sect. 4.2); (iv) machine-checked proofs of the correctness of the instrumentation operators for quantifiers $\forall$ and the extended quantifier \max; (v) a new *verification tool*, MONO-CERA, that is tailored to the verification of programs with aggregation; and (vi) an *evaluation* of our method and tool on a set of examples, including such from SV-COMP [8] (Sect. 5).

2   Instrumentation Framework

The next two sections formally introduce the instrumentation framework. Later, we instantiate the framework for quantification and aggregation over arrays. We split the instrumentation process into two parts:

1. An *instrumentation operator* that defines how to rewrite program statements with the purpose of eliminating language constructs that are difficult to reason about automatically, but leaves the choice of which occurrences of these statements to rewrite to the second part (this section).
2. An *application strategy* for the instrumentation operator, which can be implemented using heuristics or systematic search, among others. The strategy is responsible for selecting the right (if any) program instrumentation from the many possible ones, Sect. 3 is dedicated to the second part.

Table 1. Syntax of the core language.

$$
\begin{aligned}
\langle Type \rangle \ ::= \quad &\texttt{Int} \mid \texttt{Bool} \mid \texttt{Array} \ \langle Type \rangle \\
\langle Expr \rangle \ ::= \quad &\langle DecimalNumber \rangle \mid \texttt{true} \mid \texttt{false} \mid \langle Variable \rangle \\
\mid \quad &\langle Expr \rangle \ \texttt{==} \ \langle Expr \rangle \mid \langle Expr \rangle \ \texttt{<=} \ \langle Expr \rangle \mid \ \texttt{!}\langle Expr \rangle \mid \langle Expr \rangle \ \texttt{\&\&} \ \langle Expr \rangle \\
\mid \quad &\langle Expr \rangle \ \texttt{||} \ \langle Expr \rangle \mid \langle Expr \rangle \ \texttt{+} \ \langle Expr \rangle \mid \langle Expr \rangle \ \texttt{*} \ \langle Expr \rangle \\
\mid \quad &\texttt{select}(\langle Expr \rangle, \langle Expr \rangle) \mid \texttt{store}(\langle Expr \rangle, \langle Expr \rangle, \langle Expr \rangle) \\
\langle Prog \rangle \ ::= \quad &\texttt{skip} \mid \langle Variable \rangle \ \texttt{=} \ \langle Expr \rangle \mid \langle Prog \rangle \texttt{;} \ \langle Prog \rangle \mid \texttt{while} \ (\langle Expr \rangle) \ \langle Prog \rangle \\
\mid \quad &\texttt{assert}(\langle Expr \rangle) \mid \texttt{assume}(\langle Expr \rangle) \mid \texttt{if} \ (\langle Expr \rangle) \ \langle Prog \rangle \ \texttt{else} \ \langle Prog \rangle
\end{aligned}
$$

Even though instrumentation operators are non-deterministic, we shall guarantee their *soundness:* if the original program has a failing assertion, so will any instrumented program, regardless of the chosen application strategy; that is, instrumentation of an incorrect program will never yield a correct program.

We shall also guarantee a weak form of *completeness*, to the effect that if an assertion that has not been added to the program by the instrumentation fails in the instrumented program, then it will also fail in the original program. As a result, any counterexample (for such an assertion) produced when verifying the instrumented program can be transformed into a counterexample for the original program.

2.1   The Core Language

While our implementation works on programs represented as constrained Horn clauses [12], i.e., is language-agnostic, for readability purposes we present our approach in the setting of an imperative core programming language with datatypes for unbounded integers, Booleans, and arrays, and assert and assume statements. The language is deliberately kept simple, but is still close to standard C. The main exception is the semantics of arrays: they are defined here to be *functional* and therefore represent a value type. Arrays have integers as index type and are unbounded, and their signature and semantics are otherwise borrowed from the SMT-LIB theory of extensional arrays [6]:

- *Reading* the value of an array a at index i: select(a, i);
- *Updating* an array a at index i with a new value x: store(a, i, x).

The complete syntax of the core language is given in Table 1. Programs are written using a vocabulary $\mathcal{X}$ of typed program variables; the typing rules of the language are given in [4]. As syntactic sugar, we sometimes write a[i] instead of select(a, i), and a[i] = x instead of a = store(a, i, x).

We denote by D_σ the domain of a program type σ. The domain of an array type Array σ is the set of functions $f : \mathbb{Z} \to D_\sigma$.

Semantics. We assume the Flanagan-Saxe *extended execution model* of programs with assume and assert statements (see, e.g., [23]), in which executing an `assert` statement with an argument that evaluates to false *fails*, i.e., terminates abnormally. An `assume` statement with an argument that evaluates to false has the same semantics as a non-terminating loop. Partial correctness properties of programs are expressed using *Hoare triples* $\{Pre\}\ P\ \{Post\}$, which state that an execution of P, starting in a state satisfying *Pre*, never fails, and may only terminate in states that satisfy *Post*. As usual, a program P is considered *(partially) correct* if the Hoare triple $\{true\}\ P\ \{true\}$ holds.

The evaluation of program expressions is modelled using a function $[\![\cdot]\!]_s$ that maps program expressions t of type σ to their value $[\![t]\!]_s \in D_\sigma$ in the state s.

2.2   Instrumentation Operators

An instrumentation operator defines schemes to rewrite programs while preserving the meaning of the existing program assertions. Without loss of generality, we restrict program rewriting to assignment statements. Instrumentation can introduce *ghost state* by adding arbitrary fresh variables to the program. The main part of an instrumentation consists of *rewrite rules*, which are schematic rules $r = t \rightsquigarrow s$, where the meta-variable r ranges over program variables, t is an expression that can contain further meta-variables, and s is a schematic program in which the meta-variables from $r = t$ might occur. Any assignment that matches $r = t$ can be rewritten to s.

Definition 1 (Instrumentation Operator). *An* instrumentation operator *is a tuple* $\Omega = (G, R, I)$, *where:*

(i) $G = \langle (\mathbf{x}_1, init_1), \ldots, (\mathbf{x}_k, init_k) \rangle$ *is a tuple of pairs of ghost variables and their initial values;*

(ii) R *is a set of rewrite rules* $r = t \rightsquigarrow s$, *where* s *is a program operating on the ghost variables* $\mathbf{x}_1, \ldots, \mathbf{x}_k$ *(and containing meta-variables from* $r = t$*);*

(iii) I *is a formula over the ghost variables* $\mathbf{x}_1, \ldots, \mathbf{x}_k$, *called the* instrumentation invariant.

The rewrite rules R and the invariant I must adhere to the following constraints:

1. *The instrumentation invariant I is satisfied by the initial ghost values, i.e., it holds in the state* $\{\mathbf{x}_1 \mapsto init_1, \ldots, \mathbf{x}_k \mapsto init_k\}$.
2. *For all rewrites $r = t \rightsquigarrow s \in R$ the following hold:*
   (a) *s terminates (normally or abnormally) for pre-states satisfying I, assuming that all meta-variables are ordinary program variables.*
   (b) *s does not assign to variables other than r or the ghost variables* $\mathbf{x}_1, \ldots, \mathbf{x}_k$.
   (c) *s preserves the instrumentation invariant:* $\{I\}\ s'\ \{I\}$, *where s' is s with every* `assert`*(e) statement replaced by an* `assume`*(e) statement.*
   (d) *s preserves the semantics of the assignment $r = t$: the Hoare triple* $\{I\}\ \mathbf{z} = t;\ s'\ \{\mathbf{z} = r\}$, *where $\mathbf{z}$ is a fresh variable, holds.*

The conditions imposed in the definition ensure that all instrumentations are *correct*, in the sense that they are sound and weakly complete, as we show below. In particular, the instrumentation invariant guarantees that the rewrites of program statements are *semantics-preserving* w.r.t. the original program, and thus, the execution of any **assert** statement of the original program has the same effect before and after instrumentation. Observe that the conditions can themselves be deductively verified to hold for each concrete instrumentation operator, and that this check is *independent* of the programs to be instrumented, so that an instrumentation operator can be proven correct once and for all.

An instrumentation operator Ω does itself not define which occurrences of program statements are to be rewritten, but only how they are rewritten. Given a program P and the operator Ω, an instrumented program P' is derived by carrying out the following two steps: (i) variables $x_1, \ldots, x_k$ and the assignments $x_1 = init_1; \ldots; x_k = init_k$ are added at the beginning of the program, and (ii) some of the assignments in P, to which a rewriting rule $r = t \rightsquigarrow s$ in Ω is applicable, are replaced by s, substituting meta-variables with the actual terms occurring in the assignment. We denote by $\Omega(P)$ the set of all instrumented programs P' that can be derived in this way. An example of an instrumentation operator and its application was shown Fig. 1 and Fig. 2.

2.3   Instrumentation Correctness

Verification of an instrumented program produces one of two possible results: a *witness* if verification is successful, or a *counterexample* otherwise. A witness consists of the inductive invariants needed to verify the program, and is presented in the context of the programming language: it is translated back from the back-end theory used by the verification tool, and is a formula over the program variables and the ghost variables added during instrumentation. A counterexample is an execution trace leading to a failing assertion.

Definition 2 (Soundness). *An instrumentation operator Ω is called* sound *if for every program P and instrumented program $P' \in \Omega(P)$, whenever there is an execution of P where some **assert** statement fails, then there also is an execution of P' where some **assert** statement fails.*

Equivalently, existence of a witness for an instrumented program entails existence of a witness for the original program, in the form of a set of inductive invariants solely over the program variables. Notably, because of the semantics-preserving nature of the rewrites under the instrumentation invariant, a witness for the original program can be derived from one for the instrumented program. One such back-translation is to add the instrumentation invariant as a conjunct to the original witness, and to existentially quantify over the ghost variables.

Example. To illustrate the back-translation, we return to the instrumentation operator from Fig. 2 and the example program from Fig. 1. The witness produced by our verification tool in this case is the formula:

$$i = \mathtt{x\_shad} \land \mathtt{x\_sq} + \mathtt{x\_shad} = 2s \land \mathtt{N} \geq i \land \mathtt{N} \geq 1 \land 2s \geq i \land i \geq 0$$

After conjoining the instrumentation invariant x_sq = x_shad^2 and existentially quantifying over the involved ghost variables, we obtain an inductive invariant that is sufficient to verify the original program:

$$\exists x_{\text{sq}}, x_{\text{shad}}.\ (\texttt{i} = x_{\text{shad}} \land x_{\text{sq}} + x_{\text{shad}} = 2s\ \land$$
$$\texttt{N} \geq \texttt{i} \land \texttt{N} \geq \texttt{1} \land \texttt{2s} \geq \texttt{i} \land \texttt{i} \geq \texttt{0} \land x_{\text{sq}} = x_{\text{shad}}^2)$$

Definition 3 (Weak Completeness). *The operator Ω is called* weakly complete *if for every program P and instrumented program $P' \in \Omega(P)$, whenever an* assert *statement that has not been added to the program by the instrumentation fails in the instrumented program P', then it also fails in the original program P.*

Similarly to the back-translation of invariants, when verification fails, counterexamples for assertions of the original program, found during verification of the instrumented program, can be translated back to counterexamples for the original program. We thus obtain the following result.

Theorem 1 (Soundness and weak completeness). *Every instrumentation operator Ω is sound and weakly complete.*

Proof. Let $\Omega = (G, R, I)$ be an instrumentation operator. Since I is a formula over ghost variables only, which holds initially and is preserved by all rewrites, I is an invariant of the fully instrumented program. This entails that rewrites of assignments are semantics-preserving. Furthermore, since instrumentation code only assigns to ghost variables or to r (i.e., the left-hand side of the original statement), program variables have the same valuation in the instrumented program as in the original one. Furthermore, since all rewrites are terminating under I, the instrumented program will terminate if and only if the original program does.

In the case when verification succeeds, and a witness is produced, weak completeness follows vacuously. A witness consists of the inductive invariants sufficient to verify the instrumented program. Thus, they are also sufficient to verify the assertions existing in the original program, since assertions are not rewritten and all program variables have the same valuation in the original and the instrumented programs. Since a witness for the instrumented program can be back-translated to a witness for the original program, any failing assertion in the original program must also fail after instrumentation, and Ω is therefore sound.

In the case when verification fails, soundness follows vacuously, and if the failing assertion was added during instrumentation, also weak completeness follows. If the assertion existed in the original program, since such assertions are not rewritten, and since program variables have the same valuation in the instrumented program as in the original program, then any counterexample for the instrumented program is also a counterexample for the original program, when projected onto the program variables. $\qquad\square$

Input: Program P; statements S; instrumentation space R;
        oracle *IsCorrect*.
Result: Instrumentation $r \in R$ with *IsCorrect*(P_r); *Incorrect*; or
        Inconclusive.

```
1  begin
2  │   Cand ← R;
3  │   while Cand ≠ ∅ do
4  │   │   pick r ∈ Cand;
5  │   │   if IsCorrect(Pr) then
6  │   │   │   return r;
7  │   │   else
8  │   │   │   cex ← counterexample path for Pr;
9  │   │   │   if failing assertion in cex also exists in P then
   │   │   │   │   /* cex is also a counterexample for P        */
10 │   │   │   │   return Incorrect;
11 │   │   │   else
   │   │   │   │   /* instrumentation on cex may have been incorrect
   │   │   │   │      */
12 │   │   │   │   C' ← {p ∈ C | insr(p) occurs on cex};
13 │   │   │   │   Cand ← Cand \ {r' ∈ Cand | r(s) = r'(s) for all p ∈ C'};
14 │   │   │   end
15 │   │   end
16 │   end
17 │   return Inconclusive;
18 end
```

Algorithm 1: Counterexample-guided instrumentation search

3   Instrumentation Application Strategies

We will now define a counterexample-guided search procedure to discover applications of instrumentation operators that make it possible to verify a program.

For our algorithm, we assume that we are given an oracle *IsCorrect* that is able to check the correctness of programs after instrumentation. Such an oracle could be approximated, for instance, using a software model checker. The oracle is free to ignore the complex functions we are trying to eliminate by instrumentation; for instance, in Fig. 1, the oracle can over-approximate the term N*N by assuming that it can have any value. We further assume that C is the set of control points of a program P corresponding to the statements to which a given set of instrumentation operators can be applied. For each control point $p \in C$, let $Q(p)$ be the set of rewrite rules applicable to the statement at p, including also a distinguished value $\bot$ that expresses that p is not modified. For the program in Fig. 1, for instance, the choices could be defined by $Q(\text{A}) = Q(\text{B}) = \{(\text{R1}), \bot\}$, $Q(\text{C}) = \{(\text{R2}), \bot\}$, and $Q(\text{D}) = \{(\text{R4}), \bot\}$, referring to the rules in Fig. 2. Any function $r : C \to \bigcup_{p \in C} Q(p)$ with $r(p) \in Q(p)$

Table 2. Extension of the core language with quantified expressions.

$$\langle Expr \rangle ::= \quad (\lambda(\langle Variable \rangle, \langle Variable \rangle).\langle Expr \rangle) \ (\langle Expr \rangle, \ \langle Expr \rangle) \ |$$
$$\texttt{forall}(\langle Expr \rangle, \langle Expr \rangle, \langle Expr \rangle, \lambda(\langle Variable \rangle, \langle Variable \rangle).\langle Expr \rangle) \ |$$
$$\texttt{exists}(\langle Expr \rangle, \langle Expr \rangle, \langle Expr \rangle, \lambda(\langle Variable \rangle, \langle Variable \rangle).\langle Expr \rangle)$$

will then define one possible program instrumentation. We will denote the set of well-typed functions $C \rightarrow \bigcup_{p \in C} Q(p)$ by R, and the program obtained by rewriting P according to $r \in R$ by P_r. We further denote the control point in P_r corresponding to some $p \in C$ in P by $ins_r(p)$.

Algorithm 1 presents our algorithm to search for instrumentations that are sufficient to verify a program P. The algorithm maintains a set $Cand \subseteq R$ of remaining ways to instrument P, and in each loop considers one of the remaining elements $r \in Cand$ (line 4). If the oracle manages to verify P_r in line 5, due to soundness of instrumentation the correctness of P has been shown (line 6); if P_r is incorrect, there has to be a counterexample ending with a failing assertion (line 8). There are two possible causes of assertion failures: if the failing assertion in P_r already existed in P, then due to the weak completeness of instrumentation also P has to be incorrect (line 10). Otherwise, the program instrumentation has to be refined, and for this from $Cand$ we remove all instrumentations r' that agree with r regarding the instrumentation of the statements occurring in the counterexample (line 13).

Since R is finite, and at least one element of $Cand$ is eliminated in each iteration, the refinement loop terminates. The set $Cand$ can be exponentially big, however, and therefore should be represented symbolically (using BDDs, or using an SMT solver managing the set of blocking constraints from line 13).

We can observe soundness and completeness of the algorithm w.r.t. the considered instrumentation operators (proof in [4]):

Lemma 1 (Correctness of *Algorithm 1***).** *If Algorithm 1 returns an instrumentation $r \in R$, then P_r and P are correct. If Algorithm 1 returns Incorrect, then P is incorrect. If there is $r \in R$ such that P_r is correct, then Algorithm 1 will return r' such that $P_{r'}$ is correct.*

4 Instrumentation Operators for Arrays

4.1 Instrumentation Operators for Quantification over Arrays

To handle quantifiers in a programming setting, we extend the language defined in Table 1 by adding quantified expressions over arrays, as shown in Table 2. As seen, we also extend the language with a lambda expression over two variables. The rationale for this is that many quantified properties can be expressed as a binary predicate with the first argument corresponding to the value of an element and the second to the index. This allows us to express properties over both the value of an element and its index. For example, we can express that each element

```
1  Int N = nondet;
2  assume(N > 0);
3  Array Int a = const(0, N);
4  Int i = 0;
5  while(i < N) {
6      a = store(a, i, i);
7      i = i + 1;
8  }
9  Bool b = forall(a, 0, N, λ(i,x).(x == i));
10 assert(b);
```

Fig. 3. Example of program to be verified using a quantified assert statement.

should be equal to its index, as is done in the example program in Fig. 3. In the program, each element in the array is assigned the value corresponding to its index, after which it is asserted that this property indeed holds.

Using $P(x_0,i_0)$ as shorthand for $(\lambda(x,i).P)(x_0,i_0)$, the new expressions can be defined formally as:

$$[\![\texttt{forall(a, l, u, }\lambda(x,i).P)]\!]_s = \forall i \in [l,u). \; [\![P(a[i],i)]\!]_s$$
$$[\![\texttt{exists(a, l, u, }\lambda(x,i).P)]\!]_s = \exists i \in [l,u). \; [\![P(a[i],i)]\!]_s$$

Note that the types of x and a must be compatible and P be a Boolean-valued expression.

To handle programs such as the one in Fig. 3, we turn to the instrumentation framework outlined in Sect. 2.2, which we use here to define an instrumentation operator for universal quantification. The general idea is to instrument programs with a ghost variable, tracking if some predicate holds for all elements in an interval of the array, with shadow variables representing the tracked array, and the bounds of the interval. Naturally, an instrumentation operator for existential quantification can be defined in a similar fashion. For simplicity, we shall assume a *normal form* of programs, into which every program can be rewritten by introducing additional variables. In the normal form, store, select and forall can only occur in simple assignment statements. For example, stores are restricted to occur in statements of the form: a' = store(a, i, x).

Over such normalised programs, and for a universally quantified expression forall(a, l, u, $\lambda(x,i)(P)$), we define the instrumentation operator $\Omega_{\forall,P} = (G_{\forall,P}, R_{\forall,P}, I_{\forall,P})$ as shown in Fig. 4 over four ghost variables. The array over which quantification occurs is tracked by qu_ar and the variables qu_lo, qu_hi represent the bounds of the currently tracked interval. The result of the quantified expression is tracked by qu_P, whose value is *true* iff P holds for all elements in a in the interval [qu_lo, qu_hi). The rewrite rules for stores, selects and assignments of universally quantified expressions are then defined as follows. For stores, the first if-branch resets the tracking to the one element interval [i, i + 1) when accessing elements far outside of the currently tracked interval, or if we are tracking the empty interval (as is the case at initialisation). If an access occurs immediately adjacent to the currently tracked interval

```
Ωᵥ,ₚ (Instrumentation operator)

  Gᵥ,ₚ (Ghost variables)
  qu_ar : Array Int, qu_lo, qu_hi : Int, qu_P : Bool

  init(qu_ar) = [], init(qu_lo) = 0, init(qu_hi) = 0
  init(qu_P)  = true


  Rᵥ,ₚ (Rewrite rules)
  a' = store(a, i, x); ⤳
   1  a' = store(a, i, x);
   2  if (qu_lo == qu_hi || i < qu_lo - 1 || i > qu_hi ||
   3     (P(x, i) && !qu_P && qu_lo <= i && i < qu_hi)) {
   4     qu_lo = i;              // Reset, because either:
   5     qu_hi = i + 1;          // - tracking empty interval
   6     qu_P  = P(x, i);        // - storing far outside interval
   7  } else {                   // - possibly overwriting sole false
   8     assert(qu_ar == a);
   9     qu_P = qu_P && P(x, i);
  10     if (qu_lo - 1 == i) {
  11         qu_lo = i;          // Decrement lower bound by 1
  12     } else if (qu_hi == i) {
  13         qu_hi = i + 1;      // Increment upper bound by 1
  14     }
  15  }
  16  qu_ar = a';

  x = select(a, i); ⤳ similar to store

  b = forall(a, l, u,λx.P); ⤳
   1  if (u <= l) {
   2      b = true;
   3  } else {
   4      if (qu_P) {
   5          assert(qu_ar == a && l >= qu_lo && u <= qu_hi);
   6      } else {
   7          assert(qu_ar == a && l <= qu_lo && u >= qu_hi);
   8      }
   9      b = qu_P;
  10  }


  Iᵥ,ₚ (Instrumentation Invariant)
  qu_lo = qu_hi ∨
      (qu_lo < qu_hi ∧ qu_P = forall(qu_ar, qu_lo, qu_hi,λ(x, i).P))
```

Fig. 4. Definition of an instrumentation operator for universal quantification

(e.g., if $i = qu\_lo - 1$), then that element is added to the tracked interval, and the value of qu_P is updated to also account for the value of P at index i. If instead the access is within the tracked interval, then we either reset the interval (if qu_P is false) or keep the interval unchanged (if qu_P is true). Rewrites of selects are similar to stores, except tracking does not need to be reset when reading inside the tracked interval. For rewrites of quantified expressions, if the quantified interval is empty, b is assigned true. Otherwise, assertions check that the tracked interval matches the quantified interval before assigning t to qu_P. If qu_P is true, then it is sufficient that quantification occurs over a sub-interval of the tracked interval, and vice versa if qu_P is false.

The result of applying $\Omega_{\forall,P}$ to the program in Fig. 3 is shown in [4]. As exhibited by the experiments in Sect. 5, the resulting program is in many cases easier to verify by state-of-the-art verification tools. Note that the instrumentation operator defined is only one possibility among many. For example, one could track several ranges simultaneously over the array in question, or also track the index of some element in the array over which P holds, or make different choices on stores outside of the tracked interval.

The following lemma establishes correctness of the instrumentation operator. The proof can be found in [4].

Lemma 2 (Correctness of $\Omega_{\forall,P}$). $\Omega_{\forall,P}$ *is an instrumentation operator, i.e., it adheres to the constraints imposed in Definition 1.*

4.2   Instrumentation Operators for Aggregation over Arrays

We now turn to the verification of safety properties with *aggregation*. As examples of aggregation, we consider in particular the operators \sum and \max, calculating the sum and maximum value of an array, respectively. Aggregation is supported in the form of *extended quantifiers* in the specification languages JML [33] and ACSL [7], and is frequently needed for the specification of functional correctness properties. Although commonly used, most verification tools do not support aggregation, so that properties involving aggregation have to be manually rewritten using standard quantifiers, pure recursive functions, or ghost code involving loops. This reduction step is error-prone, and represents an additional complication for automatic verification approaches, but can be handled elegantly using the instrumentation framework. For generality, we formalise aggregation over arrays with the help of monoid homomorphisms.

Definition 4 (Monoid). *A monoid is a structure $(M, \circ, e)$ consisting of a nonempty set M, a binary associative operation $\circ$ on M, and a neutral element $e \in M$. A monoid is commutative if $\circ$ is commutative. A monoid is cancellative if $x \circ y = x \circ z$ implies $y = z$, and $y \circ x = z \circ x$ implies $y = z$, for all $x, y, z \in M$.*

For aggregation, we model finite intervals of arrays using the cancellative monoid $(D^*, \cdot, \epsilon)$ of finite sequences over some data domain D. The concatenation operator $\cdot$ is non-commutative.

Definition 5 (Monoid Homomorphism). *A monoid homomorphism is a function $h : M_1 \to M_2$ between monoids $(M_1, \circ_1, e_1)$ and $(M_2, \circ_2, e_2)$ with the properties $h(x \circ_1 y) = h(x) \circ_2 h(y)$ and $h(e_1) = e_2$.*

Ordinary quantifiers can be modelled as homomorphisms $D^* \to \mathbb{B}$, so that the instrumentation in this section strictly generalizes Sect. 4.1. A second classical example is the computation of the *maximum* (similarly, *minimum*) value in a sequence. For the domain of integers, the natural monoid to use is the algebra $(\mathbb{Z}_{-\infty}, \max, -\infty)$ of integers extended with $-\infty$,[1] and the homomorphism $h_{\max}$ is generated by mapping singleton sequences $\langle n \rangle$ to the value n. A

---

[1] For machine integers, $-\infty$ could be replaced with INT_MIN.

third example is the computation of the element *sum* of an integer sequence, corresponding to the monoid $(Z, +, 0)$ and the homomorphism h_{sum}. Similarly, the *number of occurrences* of some element can be computed. The considered monoid in the last two cases of aggregation is even cancellative.

Programming Language with Aggregation. We extend our core programming language with expressions $\texttt{aggregate}_{M,h}(\langle Expr \rangle, \langle Expr \rangle, \langle Expr \rangle)$, and use monoid homomorphisms to formalise them. Recall that we denote by D_σ the domain of a program type σ.

Definition 6. *Let* **Array** σ *be an array type, σ_M a program type, M a commutative monoid that is a subset of D_{σ_M}, and $h : D_\sigma^* \to M$ a monoid homomorphism. Let furthermore ar be an expression of type* **Array** σ, *and l and u integer expressions. Then,* $\texttt{aggregate}_{M,h}(ar, l, u)$ *is an expression of type σ_M, with semantics defined by:*

$$[\![\texttt{aggregate}_{M,h}(ar, l, u)]\!]_s = h(\langle [\![ar]\!]_s([\![l]\!]_s), [\![ar]\!]_s([\![l]\!]_s + 1), \ldots, [\![ar]\!]_s([\![u]\!]_s - 1) \rangle)$$

Intuitively, the expression $\texttt{aggregate}_{M,h}(ar, l, u)$ denotes the result of applying the homomorphism h to the slice $ar[l .. u - 1]$ of the array ar. As a convention, in case $u < l$ we assume that the result of $\texttt{aggregate}$ is $h(\langle \rangle)$. As with array accesses, we assume also that $\texttt{aggregate}$ only occurs in normalised statements of the form $\texttt{t} = \texttt{aggregate}_{M,h}(ar, l, u)$.

In our examples, we use derived operations as found in ACSL: \max as shorthand notation for $\texttt{aggregate}_{(\mathbb{Z}_{-\infty}, \max, -\infty), h_{\max}}$ [2], and \sum as short-hand notation for $\texttt{aggregate}_{(\mathbb{Z}, +, 0), h_{sum}}$.

An Instrumentation Operator for Maximum. For \max, an operator $\Omega_{max} = (G_{max}, R_{max}, I_{max})$ can be defined similarly to the operator $\Omega_{\forall, P}$ from Sect. 4.1, in that the maximum value in a particular interval of the array is tracked. One key difference is that an extra ghost variable $\texttt{ag\_max\_idx}$ is added to track an array index where the maximum value of the array interval is stored, in order to not have to reset tracking on every store inside of the tracked interval. A complete definition is proposed in [4].

An Instrumentation Operator for Sum. Cancellative aggregation is aggregation based on a cancellative monoid. Cancellative aggregation makes it possible to track aggregate values faithfully even when storing *inside* of the tracked interval, unlike \max and universal quantification. An example of a cancellative operator is the aggregate \sum .

The instrumentation operator $\Omega_{sum} = (G_{sum}, R_{sum}, I_{sum})$ is defined in Fig. 5. The instrumentation code tracks the sum of values in the interval, and

---

[2] With a slight abuse of the framework, we assume that $\mathbb{Z}_{-\infty}$ is represented by the program type Int, mapping $-\infty$ to some fixed integer number. More elegant solutions are not difficult to devise, but add unnecessary complexity.

Ω_{sum} **(Instrumentation operator)**

G_{sum} **(Ghost variables)**

ag_lo, ag_hi, ag_sum : Int, ag_ar : Array Int

init(ag_lo) = init(ag_hi) = init(ag_sum) = 0, init(ag_ar) = []

R_{sum} **(Rewrite rules)**

a' = store(a, i, x) ⤳

```
1   a' = store(a, i, x);
2   if (ag_lo == ag_hi || i < ag_lo - 1 || i > ag_hi) {
3       ag_lo     = i;          // Reset, because either:
4       ag_hi     = i + 1;      // - tracking empty interval
5       ag_sum    = x;          // - storing far outside interval
6   } else {
7       assert(ag_ar == a);
8       if (ag_lo <= i && i < ag_hi) {
9           // Subtract previous value from sum
10          ag_sum = ag_sum - select(ag_ar, i);
11      } else if (ag_lo - 1 == i) {
12          ag_lo = i;          // Decrease lower bound by 1
13      } else if (ag_hi == i) {
14          ag_hi = i + 1;      // Increase upper bound by 1
15      }
16      ag_sum = ag_sum + x;    // Add new value to sum
17  }
18  ag_ar = a';
```

x = select(a, i)   ⤳   code similar to rewrites of store

r = \sum(a, 1, u) ⤳

```
1   if (u <= 1) {
2       t = 0;
3   } else {
4       assert(ag_ar == a && 1 == ag_lo && u == ag_hi);
5       t = ag_sum;
6   }
```

I_{sum} **(Instrumentation invariant)**

ag_lo = ag_hi $\lor$ ag_sum = sum(ag_ar, ag_lo, ag_hi)

Fig. 5. Definition of an instrumentation operator Ω_{sum} for Sum

when increasing the bounds of the tracked interval, the new values are simply added to the tracked sum. Since \sum is cancellative, when storing inside of the tracked interval, the previous value at the index being written to is first subtracted from the sum, before adding the new value, ensuring that the correct aggregate value is computed. The following correctness result is proved in [4].

Lemma 3. (Correctness of Ω_{sum}). *Ω_{sum} is an instrumentation operator, i.e., it adheres to the constraints imposed in Definition 1.*

Deductive Verification of Instrumentation Operators. As stated in Sect. 2.2, instrumentation operators may be verified independently of the programs to be instrumented. The operators described in this paper, i.e. square, universal quantification, maximum, and sum, have been verified in the verification tool Frama-C [15]. The verified instrumentations are adaptations for the C language semantics and execution model. More specifically, the adapted operators assume C native arrays, rather than functional ones.

5   Evaluation

5.1   Implementation

To evaluate our instrumentation framework, we have implemented the instrumentation operators for quantifiers and aggregation over arrays. The implementation is done over constrained Horn clauses (CHCs), by adding the rewrite rules defined in Sect. 4 to ELDARICA [30], an open-source solver for CHCs. We also implemented the automatic application of the instrumentation operators, largely following Algorithm 1 but with a few minor changes due to the CHC setting. The CHC setting makes our implementation available to various CHC-based verification tools, for instance JAYHORN (Java) [32], KORN (C) [19], RUSTHORN (Rust) [36], SEAHORN (C/LLVM) [26] and TRICERA (C) [20].

In order to evaluate our approach at the level of C programs, we extended TRICERA, an open-source assertion-based model checker that translates C programs into a set of CHCs and relies on ELDARICA as back-end solver. TRICERA is extended to parse quantifiers and aggregation operators in its input C programs and to encode them as part of the translation into CHCs. We call the resulting toolchain MONOCERA. An artefact that includes MONOCERA and the benchmarks is available online [5].

To handle complicated access patterns, for instance a program processing an array from the beginning and end at the same time, the implementation can apply multiple instrumentation operators simultaneously; the number of operators is incremented when Algorithm 1 returns *Inconclusive*.

5.2   Experiments and Comparisons

To assess our implementation, we assembled a test suite and carried out experiments comparing MONOCERA with the state-of-the-art C model checkers CPA-CHECKER 2.1.1 [11], SEAHORN 10.0.0 [26] and TRICERA 0.2. It should be noted that deductive verification frameworks, such as Dafny and Frama-C, can handle, for example, the program in Fig. 3 if they are provided with a manually written loop invariant; however, since MONOCERA relies on automatic techniques for invariant inference, we only benchmark against tools using similar automatic techniques. We also excluded VERIABS [1], since its licence does not permit its use for scientific evaluation.

The tools were set up, as far as possible, with equivalent configurations; for instance, to use the SMT-LIB theory of arrays [6] in order to model C arrays, and a mathematical (as opposed to machine) semantics of integers. CPACHECKER was configured to use k-induction [10], which was the only configuration that worked in our tests using mathematical integers. SEAHORN was run using the default settings. All tests were run on a Linux machine with AMD Opteron 2220 SE @ 2.8 GHz and 6 GB RAM with a timeout of 300 s.

Table 3. Results for MonoCera (Mono), TriCera (Tri), SeaHorn (Sea), and CPAchecker (CPA). For MonoCera, also statistics are given for verification time (s), size of the instrumentation search space, and search iterations.

		Verification results				Ver. time			Inst. space		Inst. steps	
	#Tests	Mono	Tri	Sea	CPA	Min	Max	Avg	Max	Avg	Max	Avg
min	17	9	2	2	2	22	59	33	27	11	55	24
max	12	8	2	3	3	21	285	76	108	21	96	30
sum	26	16	3	3	3	26	245	78	2916	188	284	36
forall	96	30	1	0	2	14	236	91	59049	2446	334	59

Test Suite. The comparison includes a set of programs calculating properties related to the quantification and aggregation properties over arrays. The benchmarks and verification results are summarised in Table 3. The benchmark suite contains programs ranging between 16 to 117 LOC and is comprised of two parts: (i) 117 programs taken from the SV-COMP repository [9], and (ii) 26 programs crafted by the authors (min: 6, max: 8, sum: 9, forall: 3).

To construct the SV-COMP benchmark set for MonoCera we gathered all test files from the directories prefixed with `array` or `loop`, and singled out programs containing some assert statement that could be rewritten using a quantifier or an aggregation operator over a single array. For example, loops

```
for (int i = 0; i < N; i++) assert(a[i] <= 0);
```

can be rewritten using `forall` or `max` operators. We created a benchmark for each possible rewriting; for instance, in the case of `max`, by rewriting the loop into `assert(\max(a, 0, N) <= 0)` . The original benchmarks were used for the evaluation of the other tools, none of which supported (extended) quantifiers.

In (ii), we crafted 9 programs that make use of aggregation or quantifiers, and derived further benchmarks by considering different array sizes (10, 100 and unbounded size); one combination (unbounded array inside a struct) had to be excluded, as it is not valid C. In order to evaluate other tools on our crafted benchmarks, we reversed the process described for the SV-COMP benchmarks and translated the operators into corresponding loop constructs.

Results. In Table 3, we present the number of verified programs per instrumentation operator for each tool, as well as further statistics for MonoCera regarding verification times and instrumentation search space. The "Inst. space" column indicates the size of the instrumentation search space (i.e., number of instrumentations producible by applying the non-deterministic instrumentation operator). "Inst. steps" column indicates the number of attempted instrumentations, i.e., number of iterations in the while-loop in Algorithm 1. In our implementation, the check in Algorithm 1 line 5 can time out and cause the check to be repeated at a later time with a greater timeout, which can lead to more iterations than the size of the search space. In [4], we list results per benchmark for each tool.

For the SV-COMP benchmarks, CPACHECKER managed to verify 1 program, while SEAHORN and TRICERA could not verify any programs. MONOCERA verified in total 42 programs from SV-COMP. Regarding the crafted benchmarks, several tools could verify the examples with array size 10. However, when the array size was 100 or unbounded, only MONOCERA succeeded.

6 Related Work

It is common practice, in both model checking and deductive verification, to translate high-level specifications to low-level specifications prior to verification (e.g., [13,14,18,37]). Such translations often make use of ghost variables and ghost code, although relatively little systematic research has been done on the required properties of ghost code [22]. The addition of ghost variables to a program for tracking the value of complex expressions also has similarities with the concept of term abstraction in Horn solving [3]. To the best of our knowledge, we are presenting the first general framework for automatic program instrumentation.

A lot of research in *software model checking* considered the handling of standard quantifiers $\forall, \exists$ over arrays. In the setting of constrained Horn clauses, properties with universal quantifiers can sometimes be reduced to quantifier-free reasoning over non-linear Horn clauses [13,37]. Our approach follows the same philosophy of applying an up-front program transformation, but in a more general setting. Various direct approaches to infer quantified array invariants have been proposed as well: e.g., by extending the IC3 algorithm [27], syntax-guided synthesis [21], learning [24], by solving recurrence equations [29], backward reachability [3], or superposition [25]. To the best of our knowledge, such methods have not been extended to aggregation.

Deductive verification tools usually have rich support for quantified specifications, but rely on auxiliary assertions like loop invariants provided by the user, and on SMT solvers or automated theorem provers for quantifier reasoning. Although several deductive verification tools can parse extended quantifiers, few offer support for reasoning about them. Our work is closest to the method for handling comprehension operators in Spec# [35], which relies on code annotations provided by the user, but provides heuristics to automatically verify such annotations. The code instrumentation presented in this paper has similarity with the proof rules in Spec#; the main differences are that our method is based on an upfront program transformation, and that we aim at automatically finding required program invariants, as opposed to only verifying their correctness. The KeY tool provides proof rules similar to the ones in Spec# for some of the JML extended quantifiers [2]; those proof rules can be applied manually to verify human-written invariants. The Frama-C system [15] can parse ACSL extended quantifiers [7], but, to the best of our knowledge, none of the Frama-C plugins can automatically process such quantifiers. Other systems, e.g., Dafny [34], require users to manually define aggregation operators as recursive functions.

In the theory of *algebraic data-types*, several transformation-based approaches have been proposed to verify properties that involve recursive functions or catamorphisms [17,31]. Aggregation over arrays resembles the evaluation of recursive functions over data-types; a major difference is that data-types are more restricted with respect to accessing and updating data than arrays.

Array folds logic (AFL) [16] is a decidable logic in which properties on arrays beyond standard quantification can be expressed: for instance, counting the number of elements with some property. Similar properties can be expressed using automata on data words [41], or in variants of monadic second-order logic [38]. Such languages can be seen as alternative formalisms to aggregation or extended quantifiers; they do not cover, however, all kinds of aggregation we are interested in. Array sums cannot be expressed in AFL or data automata, for instance.

7   Conclusion

We have presented a framework for automatic and provably correct program instrumentation, allowing the automatic verification of programs containing certain expressive language constructs, which are not directly supported by the existing automatic verification tools. Our experiments with a prototypical implementation, in the tool MONOCERA, show that our method is able to automatically verify a significant number of benchmark programs involving quantification and aggregation over arrays that are beyond the scope of other tools.

There are still various other benchmarks that MONOCERA (as well as other tools) cannot verify. We believe that many of those benchmarks are in reach of our method, because of the generality of our approach. Ghost code is known to be a powerful specification mechanism; similarly, in our setting, more powerful instrumentation operators can be easily formulated for specific kinds of programs. In future work, we therefore plan to develop a library of instrumentation operators for different language constructs (including arithmetic operators), non-linear arithmetic, other types of structures with regular access patterns such as binary heaps, and general linked-data structures.

We also plan to refine our method for showing incorrectness of programs more efficiently, as the approach is currently applicable mainly for verifying correctness (experiments in [4]). Another line of work is the establishment of stronger completeness results than the weak completeness result presented here, for specific programming language fragments.

Acknowledgements. This work has been partially funded by the Swedish Vinnova FFI Programme under grant 2021-02519, the Swedish Research Council (VR) under grant 2018-04727, the Swedish Foundation for Strategic Research (SSF) under the project WebSec (Ref. RIT17-0011), and the Wallenberg project UPDATE. We are also grateful for the opportunity to discuss the research at the Dagstuhl Seminar 22451 on "Principles of Contract Languages."

References

1. Afzal, M., Chakraborty, S., Chauhan, A., Chimdyalwar, B., Darke, P., Gupta, A., Kumar, S., Babu M, C., Unadkat, D., Venkatesh, R.: VeriAbs: verification by abstraction and test generation (competition contribution). In: TACAS 2020. LNCS, vol. 12079, pp. 383–387. Springer, Cham (2020). https://doi.org/10.1007/978-3-030-45237-7_25

2. Ahrendt, W., Beckert, B., Bubel, R., Hähnle, R., Schmitt, P.H., Ulbrich, M. (eds.): Deductive Software Verification - The KeY Book - From Theory to Practice, Lecture Notes in Computer Science, vol. 10001. Springer (2016). https://doi.org/10.1007/978-3-319-49812-6

3. Alberti, F., Bruttomesso, R., Ghilardi, S., Ranise, S., Sharygina, N.: Lazy abstraction with interpolants for arrays. In: Bjørner, N., Voronkov, A. (eds.) LPAR 2012. LNCS, vol. 7180, pp. 46–61. Springer, Heidelberg (2012). https://doi.org/10.1007/978-3-642-28717-6_7

4. Amilon, J., Esen, Z., Gurov, D., Lidström, C., Rümmer, P.: Automatic program instrumentation for automatic verification (extended technical report). CoRR abs/2306.00004 (2023). https://doi.org/10.48550/arXiv.2306.00004

5. Amilon, J., Esen, Z., Gurov, D., Lidström, C., Rümmer, P.: Artifact for the CAV 2023 paper "Automatic Program Instrumentation for Automatic Verification", April 2023. https://doi.org/10.5281/zenodo.7875416

6. Barrett, C., Fontaine, P., Tinelli, C.: The SMT-LIB Standard: Version 2.6. Tech. rep., Department of Computer Science, The University of Iowa (2017), available at www.SMT-LIB.org

7. Baudin, P., Filliâtre, J.C., Marché, C., Monate, B., Moy, Y., Prevosto, V.: ACSL: ANSI/ISO C Specification Language. http://frama-c.com/acsl.html

8. Beyer, D.: Progress on software verification: SV-COMP 2022. In: TACAS 2022. LNCS, vol. 13244, pp. 375–402. Springer, Cham (2022). https://doi.org/10.1007/978-3-030-99527-0_20

9. Beyer, D.: SV-Benchmarks: Benchmark Set for Software Verification and Testing (SV-COMP 2022 and Test-Comp 2022), January 2022. https://doi.org/10.5281/zenodo.5831003

10. Beyer, D., Dangl, M., Wendler, P.: Boosting k-induction with continuously-refined invariants. In: Kroening, D., Păsăreanu, C.S. (eds.) CAV 2015. LNCS, vol. 9206, pp. 622–640. Springer, Cham (2015). https://doi.org/10.1007/978-3-319-21690-4_42

11. Beyer, D., Keremoglu, M.E.: CPACHECKER: a tool for configurable software verification. In: Gopalakrishnan, G., Qadeer, S. (eds.) CAV 2011. LNCS, vol. 6806, pp. 184–190. Springer, Heidelberg (2011). https://doi.org/10.1007/978-3-642-22110-1_16

12. Bjørner, N., Gurfinkel, A., McMillan, K., Rybalchenko, A.: Horn clause solvers for program verification. In: Beklemishev, L.D., Blass, A., Dershowitz, N., Finkbeiner, B., Schulte, W. (eds.) Fields of Logic and Computation II. LNCS, vol. 9300, pp. 24–51. Springer, Cham (2015). https://doi.org/10.1007/978-3-319-23534-9_2

13. Bjørner, N., McMillan, K., Rybalchenko, A.: On solving universally quantified horn clauses. In: Logozzo, F., Fähndrich, M. (eds.) SAS 2013. LNCS, vol. 7935, pp. 105–125. Springer, Heidelberg (2013). https://doi.org/10.1007/978-3-642-38856-9_8

14. Clarke, E.M., Henzinger, T.A., Veith, H., Bloem, R. (eds.): Handbook of Model Checking. Springer (2018). https://doi.org/10.1007/978-3-319-10575-8

15. Cuoq, P., Kirchner, F., Kosmatov, N., Prevosto, V., Signoles, J., Yakobowski, B.: Frama-C-A software analysis perspective. In: Eleftherakis, G., Hinchey, M., Hol-

combe, M. (eds.) SEFM 2012. LNCS, vol. 7504, pp. 233–247. Springer, Heidelberg (2012). https://doi.org/10.1007/978-3-642-33826-7_16

16. Daca, P., Henzinger, T.A., Kupriyanov, A.: Array folds logic. In: Chaudhuri, S., Farzan, A. (eds.) CAV 2016. LNCS, vol. 9780, pp. 230–248. Springer, Cham (2016). https://doi.org/10.1007/978-3-319-41540-6_13

17. De Angelis, E., Proietti, M., Fioravanti, F., Pettorossi, A.: Verifying catamorphism-based contracts using constrained Horn clauses. Theory Pract. Log. Program. **22**(4), 555–572 (2022). https://doi.org/10.1017/S1471068422000175'

18. Donaldson, A.F., Kroening, D., Rümmer, P.: Automatic analysis of scratch-pad memory code for heterogeneous multicore processors. In: Esparza, J., Majumdar, R. (eds.) TACAS 2010. LNCS, vol. 6015, pp. 280–295. Springer, Heidelberg (2010). https://doi.org/10.1007/978-3-642-12002-2_24

19. Ernst, G.: Korn - software verification with Horn clauses (competition contribution). In: Sankaranarayanan, S., Sharygina, N. (eds.) Tools and Algorithms for the Construction and Analysis of Systems - 29th International Conference, TACAS 2023, Held as Part of the European Joint Conferences on Theory and Practice of Software, ETAPS 2022, Paris, France, April 22–27, 2023, Proceedings, Part II. Lecture Notes in Computer Science, vol. 13994, pp. 559–564. Springer (2023). doi: https://doi.org/10.1007/978-3-031-30820-8_36

20. Esen, Z., Rümmer, P.: TriCera: Verifying C programs using the theory of heaps. In: 2022 Formal Methods in Computer Aided Design, FMCAD 2022, Trento, Italy, October 17 - October 21, 2022 (2022) (To appear)

21. Fedyukovich, G., Prabhu, S., Madhukar, K., Gupta, A.: Quantified invariants via syntax-guided synthesis. In: Dillig, I., Tasiran, S. (eds.) CAV 2019. LNCS, vol. 11561, pp. 259–277. Springer, Cham (2019). https://doi.org/10.1007/978-3-030-25540-4_14

22. Filliâtre, J., Gondelman, L., Paskevich, A.: The spirit of ghost code. Formal Methods Syst. Des. **48**(3), 152–174 (2016). https://doi.org/10.1007/s10703-016-0243-x

23. Flanagan, C., Saxe, J.B.: Avoiding exponential explosion: generating compact verification conditions. In: Hankin, C., Schmidt, D. (eds.) Proceedings of: Symposium on Principles of Programming Languages (POPL'01), pp. 193–205. ACM (2001). https://doi.org/10.1145/360204.360220

24. Garg, P., Löding, C., Madhusudan, P., Neider, D.: Learning universally quantified invariants of linear data structures. In: Sharygina, N., Veith, H. (eds.) CAV 2013. LNCS, vol. 8044, pp. 813–829. Springer, Heidelberg (2013). https://doi.org/10.1007/978-3-642-39799-8_57

25. Georgiou, P., Gleiss, B., Kovács, L.: Trace logic for inductive loop reasoning. In: 2020 Formal Methods in Computer Aided Design, FMCAD 2020, Haifa, Israel, September 21–24, 2020, pp. 255–263. IEEE (2020). https://doi.org/10.34727/2020/isbn.978-3-85448-042-6_33

26. Gurfinkel, A., Kahsai, T., Komuravelli, A., Navas, J.A.: The SeaHorn verification framework. In: Kroening, D., Păsăreanu, C.S. (eds.) CAV 2015. LNCS, vol. 9206, pp. 343–361. Springer, Cham (2015). https://doi.org/10.1007/978-3-319-21690-4_20

27. Gurfinkel, A., Shoham, S., Vizel, Y.: Quantifiers on demand. In: Lahiri, S.K., Wang, C. (eds.) ATVA 2018. LNCS, vol. 11138, pp. 248–266. Springer, Cham (2018). https://doi.org/10.1007/978-3-030-01090-4_15

28. Harrison, J.: Handbook of Practical Logic and Automated Reasoning. Cambridge University Press (2009)

29. Henzinger, T.A., Hottelier, T., Kovács, L., Rybalchenko, A.: Aligators for arrays (tool paper). In: Fermüller, C.G., Voronkov, A. (eds.) LPAR 2010. LNCS, vol. 6397, pp. 348–356. Springer, Heidelberg (2010). https://doi.org/10.1007/978-3-642-16242-8_25

30. Hojjat, H., Rümmer, P.: The ELDARICA Horn solver. In: FMCAD 2018. pp. 1–7 (2018). https://doi.org/10.23919/FMCAD.2018.8603013

31. K., H.G.V., Shoham, S., Gurfinkel, A.: Solving constrained Horn clauses modulo algebraic data types and recursive functions. Proc. ACM Program. Lang. 6(POPL), 1–29 (2022). https://doi.org/10.1145/3498722

32. Kahsai, T., Kersten, R., Rümmer, P., Schäf, M.: Quantified heap invariants for object-oriented programs. In: Eiter, T., Sands, D. (eds.) LPAR-21, 21st International Conference on Logic for Programming, Artificial Intelligence and Reasoning, Maun, Botswana, May 7–12, 2017. EPiC Series in Computing, vol. 46, pp. 368–384. EasyChair (2017). http://easychair.org/publications/paper/Pmh

33. Leavens, G.T., Baker, A.L., Ruby, C.: JML: A notation for detailed design. In: Kilov, H., Rumpe, B., Simmonds, I. (eds.) Behavioral Specifications of Businesses and Systems, The Kluwer International Series in Engineering and Computer Science, vol. 523, pp. 175–188. Springer (1999). https://doi.org/10.1007/978-1-4615-5229-1_12

34. Leino, K.R.M.: Dafny: an automatic program verifier for functional correctness. In: Clarke, E.M., Voronkov, A. (eds.) LPAR 2010. LNCS (LNAI), vol. 6355, pp. 348–370. Springer, Heidelberg (2010). https://doi.org/10.1007/978-3-642-17511-4_20

35. Leino, K.R.M., Monahan, R.: Reasoning about comprehensions with first-order SMT solvers. In: Shin, S.Y., Ossowski, S. (eds.) Proceedings of the 2009 ACM Symposium on Applied Computing (SAC), Honolulu, Hawaii, USA, March 9–12, 2009, pp. 615–622. ACM (2009). https://doi.org/10.1145/1529282.1529411

36. Matsushita, Y., Tsukada, T., Kobayashi, N.: RustHorn: CHC-based verification for Rust programs. ACM Trans. Program. Lang. Syst. 43(4), 15:1–15:54 (2021). 10.1145/3462205

37. Monniaux, D., Gonnord, L.: Cell morphing: from array programs to array-free horn clauses. In: Rival, X. (ed.) SAS 2016. LNCS, vol. 9837, pp. 361–382. Springer, Heidelberg (2016). https://doi.org/10.1007/978-3-662-53413-7_18

38. Neven, F., Schwentick, T., Vianu, V.: Finite state machines for strings over infinite alphabets. ACM Trans. Comput. Log. 5(3), 403–435 (2004). https://doi.org/10.1145/1013560.1013562

39. Priya, S., Zhou, X., Su, Y., Vizel, Y., Bao, Y., Gurfinkel, A.: Verifying verified code. In: Hou, Z., Ganesh, V. (eds.) ATVA 2021. LNCS, vol. 12971, pp. 187–202. Springer, Cham (2021). https://doi.org/10.1007/978-3-030-88885-5_13

40. Reynolds, J.C.: Separation logic: A logic for shared mutable data structures. In: 17th IEEE Symposium on Logic in Computer Science (LICS 2002), 22–25 July 2002, Copenhagen, Denmark, Proceedings, pp. 55–74. IEEE Computer Society (2002). https://doi.org/10.1109/LICS.2002.1029817

41. Segoufin, L.: Automata and logics for words and trees over an infinite alphabet. In: Ésik, Z. (ed.) CSL 2006. LNCS, vol. 4207, pp. 41–57. Springer, Heidelberg (2006). https://doi.org/10.1007/11874683_3

Boolean Abstractions for Realizability Modulo Theories

Andoni Rodríguez[1,2](✉) and César Sánchez[1]

[1] IMDEA Software Institute, Madrid, Spain
{andoni.rodriguez,cesar.sanchez}@imdea.org
[2] Universidad Politécnica de Madrid, Madrid, Spain

Abstract. In this paper, we address the problem of the (reactive) realizability of specifications of theories richer than Booleans, including arithmetic theories. Our approach transforms theory specifications into purely Boolean specifications by (1) substituting theory literals by Boolean variables, and (2) computing an additional Boolean requirement that captures the dependencies between the new variables imposed by the literals. The resulting specification can be passed to existing Boolean off-the-shelf realizability tools, and is realizable if and only if the original specification is realizable. The first contribution is a brute-force version of our method, which requires a number of SMT queries that is doubly exponential in the number of input literals. Then, we present a faster method that exploits a nested encoding of the search for the extra requirement and uses SAT solving for faster traversing the search space and uses SMT queries internally. Another contribution is a prototype in Z3-Python. Finally, we report an empirical evaluation using specifications inspired in real industrial cases. To the best of our knowledge, this is the first method that succeeds in non-Boolean LTL realizability.

1 Introduction

Reactive synthesis [30,31] is the problem of automatically producing a system that is guaranteed to model a given temporal specification, where the Boolean variables (i.e., atomic propositions) are split into variables controlled by the environment and variables controlled by the system. Realizability is the related decision problem of deciding whether such a system exists. These problems have been widely studied [17,21], specially in the domain of Linear Temporal Logic (LTL) [29]. Realizability corresponds to infinite games where players alternatively choose the valuations of the Boolean variables they control. The winning condition is extracted from the temporal specification and determines which player wins a given play. A system is realizable if and only if the system player

This work was funded in part by the Madrid Regional Gov. Project "S2018/TCS-4339 (BLOQUES-CM)", by PRODIGY Project (TED2021-132464B-I00) funded by MCIN/AEI/10.13039/501100011033/ and the European Union Next Generation EU/PRTR, and by a research grant from Nomadic Labs and the Tezos Foundation.

C. Enea and A. Lal (Eds.): CAV 2023, LNCS 13966, pp. 305–328, 2023.
https://doi.org/10.1007/978-3-031-37709-9_15

has a winning strategy, i.e., if there is a way to play such that the specification is satisfied in all plays played according to the strategy.

However, in practice, many real and industrial specifications use complex data beyond Boolean atomic propositions, which precludes the direct use of realizability tools. These specifications cannot be written in (propositional) LTL, but instead use literals from a richer domain. We use $LTL_{\mathcal{T}}$ for the extension of LTL where Boolean atomic propositions can be literals from a (multi-sorted) first-order theory $\mathcal{T}$. The $\mathcal{T}$ variables (i.e., non-Boolean) in the specification are again split into those controlled by the system and those controlled by the environment. The resulting realizability problem also corresponds to infinite games, but, in this case, players chose valuations from the domains of $\mathcal{T}$, which may be infinite. Therefore, arenas may be infinite and positions may have infinitely many successors. In this paper, we present a method that transforms a specification that uses data from a theory $\mathcal{T}$ into an equi-realizable Boolean specification. The resulting specification can then be processed by an off-the-shelf realizability tool.

The main element of our method is a novel *Boolean abstraction* method, which allows to transform $LTL_{\mathcal{T}}$ specifications into pure (Boolean) LTL specifications. The method first substitutes all $\mathcal{T}$ literals by fresh Boolean variables controlled by the system, and then extends the specification with an additional subformula that constrains the combination values of these variables. This method is described in Sect. 3. The main idea is that, after the environment selects values for its (data) variables, the system responds with values for the variables it controls, which induces a Boolean value for all the literals. The additional formula we compute captures the set of possible valuations of literals and the precise power of each player to produce each valuation.

Example 1. Consider the following specification $\varphi = \Box(R_0 \wedge R_1)$, where:

$$R_0 : (x < 2) \rightarrow \bigcirc(y > 1) \qquad\qquad R_1 : (x \geq 2) \rightarrow (y < x)$$

where x is a numeric variable that belongs to the environment and y to the system. In the game corresponding to this specification, each player has an infinite number of choices at each time step. For example, in $\mathcal{T}_{\mathbb{Z}}$ (the theory of integers), the environment player chooses an integer for x and the system responds with an integer for y. This induces a valuation of all literals in the formula, which in turn induces (also considering the valuations of the literals at other time instants, according to the temporal operators) a valuation of the full specification.

In this paper, we exploit that, from the point of view of the valuations of the literals, there are only *finitely many* cases and provide a systematic manner to compute these cases. This allows us to reduce a specification into a purely Boolean specification that is equi-realizable. This specification encodes the (finite) set of decisions of the environment, and the (finite) set of reactions of the system.   □

Example 1 suggests a naive algorithm to capture the powers of the environment and system to determine a combination of the valuations of the literals, by enumerating all these combinations and checking the validity of each potential reaction. Checking that a given combination is a possible reaction requires an $\exists^* \forall^*$ query (which can be delegated to an SMT solver for appropriate theories).

In this paper, we describe and prove correct a Boolean abstraction method based on this idea. Then, we propose a more efficient search method for the set of possible reactions using SAT solving to speed up the exploration of the set of reactions. The main idea of this faster method is to learn from an invalid reaction which other reactions are guaranteed to be invalid, and from a valid reaction which other reactions are not worth being explored. We encode these learnt sets as a incremental SAT formula that allows to prune the search space. The resulting method is much more efficient than brute-force enumeration because, in each iteration, the learning can prune an exponential number of cases. An important technical detail is that computing the set of cases to be pruned from the outcome of a given query can be described efficiently using a SAT solver.

In summary, our contributions are: (1) a proof that realizability is decidable for all LTL$_\mathcal{T}$ specifications for those theories $\mathcal{T}$ with a decidable $\exists^* \forall^*$ fragment; (2) a simple implementation of the resulting Boolean abstraction method; (3) a much faster method based on a nested-SAT implementation of the Boolean abstraction method that efficiently explores the search space of potential reactions; and (4) an empirical evaluation of these algorithms, where our early findings suggest that Boolean abstractions can be used with specifications containing different arithmetic theories, and also with industrial specifications. We used Z3 [10] both as an SMT solver and a SAT solver, and Strix [27] as the realizability checker. To the best of our knowledge, this is the first method that succeeds (and efficiently) in non-Boolean LTL realizability.

2 Preliminaries

We study realizability of LTL [26,29] specifications. The syntax of LTL is:

$$\varphi ::= T \mid a \mid \varphi \vee \varphi \mid \neg\varphi \mid \bigcirc \varphi \mid \varphi\, \mathcal{U}\, \varphi$$

where a ranges from an atomic set of proposition AP, $\vee$, $\wedge$ and $\neg$ are the usual Boolean disjunction, conjunction and negation, and $\bigcirc$ and $\mathcal{U}$ are the next and until temporal operators. The semantics of LTL associate traces $\sigma \in \Sigma^\omega$ with formulae as follows:

$$
\begin{array}{lll}
\sigma \models T & \text{always} & \\
\sigma \models a & \text{iff} & a \in \sigma(0) \\
\sigma \models \varphi_1 \vee \varphi_2 & \text{iff} & \sigma \models \varphi_1 \text{ or } \sigma \models \varphi_2 \\
\sigma \models \neg\varphi & \text{iff} & \sigma \not\models \varphi \\
\sigma \models \bigcirc\varphi & \text{iff} & \sigma^1 \models \varphi \\
\sigma \models \varphi_1\, \mathcal{U}\, \varphi_2 & \text{iff} & \text{for some } i \geq 0\ \ \sigma^i \models \varphi_2, \text{ and for all } 0 \leq j < i, \sigma^j \models \varphi_1
\end{array}
$$

We use common derived operators like $\vee$, $\mathcal{R}$, $\Diamond$ and $\Box$.

Reactive synthesis [4,5,14,28,33] is the problem of producing a system from an LTL specification, where the atomic propositions are split into propositions that are controlled by the environment and those that are controlled by the system. Synthesis corresponds to a turn-based game where, in each turn, the environment produces values of its variables (inputs) and the system responds with values of its variables (outputs). A play is an infinite sequence of turns. The system player wins a play according to an LTL formula φ if the trace of the play satisfies φ. A (memory-less) strategy of a player is a map from positions into a move for the player. A play is played according to a strategy if all the moves of the corresponding player are played according to the strategy. A strategy is winning for a player if all the possible plays played according to the strategy are winning.

Depending on the fragment of LTL used, the synthesis problem has different complexities. The method that we present in this paper generates a formula in the same temporal fragment as the original formula (e.g., starting from a safety formula another safety formula is generated). The generated formula is discharged into a solver capable to solve formulas in the right fragment. For simplicity in the presentation, we illustrate our method with safety formulae.

We use $\text{LTL}_{\mathcal{T}}$ as the extension of LTL where propositions are replaced by literals from a first-order theory $\mathcal{T}$. In realizability for $\text{LTL}_{\mathcal{T}}$, the variables that occur in the literals of a specification φ are split into those variables controlled by the environment (denoted by $\overline{v}_e$) and those controlled by the system ($\overline{v}_s$), where $\overline{v}_e \cap \overline{v}_s = \emptyset$. We use $\varphi(\overline{v}_e, \overline{v}_s)$ to remark that $\overline{v}_e \cup \overline{v}_s$ are the variables occurring in φ. The alphabet $\Sigma_{\mathcal{T}}$ is now a valuation of the variables in $\overline{v}_e \cup \overline{v}_s$. A trace is an infinite sequence of valuations, which induces an infinite sequence of Boolean values of the literals occurring in φ and, in turn, a valuation of the temporal formula.

Realizability for $\text{LTL}_{\mathcal{T}}$ corresponds to an infinite game with an infinite arena where positions may have infinitely many successors if the ranges of the variables controlled by the system and the environment are infinite. For instance, in Ex. 1 with $\mathcal{T} = \mathcal{T}_{\mathbb{Z}}$, valuation ranges over infinite values, and literal $(x \geq 2)$ can be satisfied with $x = 2$, $x = 3$, etc.

Arithmetic theories are a particular class of first-order theories. Even though our Boolean abstraction technique is applicable to any theory with a decidable $\exists^*\forall^*$ fragment, we illustrate our technique with arithmetic specifications. Concretely, we will consider $\mathcal{T}_{\mathbb{Z}}$ (i.e., linear integer arithmetic) and $\mathcal{T}_{\mathbb{R}}$ (i.e., non-linear real arithmetic). Both theories have a decidable $\exists^*\forall^*$ fragment. Note that the choice of the theory influences the realizability of a given formula.

Example 2. Consider Ex. 1. The formula $\varphi := R_0 \wedge R_1$ is not realizable for $\mathcal{T}_{\mathbb{Z}}$, since, if at a given instant t, the environment plays $x = 0$ (and hence $x < 2$ is true), then y must be greater than 1 at time $t+1$. Then, if at $t+1$ the environment plays $x = 2$ then $(x \geq 2)$ is true but there is no y such that both $(y > 1)$ and $(y < 2)$. However, for $\mathcal{T}_{\mathbb{R}}$, φ is realizable (consider the system strategy to always play $y = 1.5$).

The following slight modifications of Ex. 1 alters its realizability (R_1' substitutes R_1 by having the $\mathcal{T}$-predicate $y \leq x$ instead of $y < x$):

$$R_0 : (x < 2) \rightarrow \bigcirc(y > 1) \qquad\qquad R_1' : (x \geq 2) \rightarrow (y \leq x)$$

Now, $\varphi' = \Box(R_0 \wedge R_1')$ is realizable for both $\mathcal{T}_\mathbb{Z}$ and $\mathcal{T}_\mathbb{R}$, as the strategy of the system to always pick $y = 2$ is winning in both theories.   □

3   Boolean Abstraction

We solve the realizability problem modulo theories by transforming the specification into an equi-realizable Boolean specification. Given a specification φ with literals l_i, we get a new specification $\varphi[l_i \leftarrow s_i] \wedge \Box\varphi^{extra}$, where s_i are fresh Boolean variables and $\varphi^{extra} \in \text{LTL}_\mathbb{B}$ is a Boolean formula (without temporal operators). The additional sub-formula φ^{extra} uses the freshly introduced variables s_i controlled by the system, as well as additional Boolean variables controlled by the environment $\bar{e}$, and captures the precise combined power of the players to decide the valuations of the literals in the original formula. We call our approach *Booleanization* or *Boolean abstraction*. The approach is summarized in Fig. 1: given an LTL specification $\varphi_\mathcal{T}$, it is translated into a Boolean $\varphi_\mathbb{B}$ which can be analyzed with off-the-shelf realizability checkers. Note that $\mathcal{G}^\mathbb{B}$ and $\mathcal{G}^\mathcal{T}$ are the games constructed from specifications $\varphi_\mathbb{B}$ and $\varphi_\mathcal{T}$, respectively. Also, note that [20] shows that we can construct a game $\mathcal{G}$ from a specification φ and that φ is realizable if and only if $\mathcal{G}$ is winning for the system.

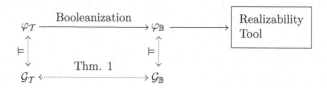

Fig. 1. The tool chain with the correctness argument.

The Booleanization procedure constructs an extra requirement φ^{extra} and conjoins $\Box\varphi^{extra}$ with the formula $\varphi[l_i \leftarrow s_i]$. In a nutshell, after the environment chooses a valuation of the variables it controls (including $\bar{e}$), the system responds with valuations of its variables (including s_i), which induces a Boolean value for all literals. Therefore, for each possible choice of the environment, the system has the power to choose a Boolean response among a specific collection of responses (a subset of all the possible combinations of Boolean valuations of the literals). Since the set of all possible responses is finite, so are the different cases. The extra requirement captures precisely the finite collection of choices of the environment and the resulting finite collection of responses of the system for each case.

3.1   Notation

In order to explain the construction of the extra requirement, we introduce some preliminary definitions. We will use Ex. 1 as the running example.

A literal is an atom or its negation, regardless of whether the atom is a Boolean variable or a predicate of a theory. Let $Lit(\varphi)$ be the collection of literals that appear in φ (or Lit, if the formula is clear from the context). For simplicity, we assume that all literals belong the same theory, but each theory can be Booleanized in turn, as each literal belongs to exactly one theory and we assume in this paper that literals from different theories do not share variables. We will use $\overline{x}$ as the environment controlled variables occurring in $Lit(\varphi)$ and $\overline{y}$ for the variables controlled by the system.

In Ex. 1, we first translate the literals in φ. Since $(x < 2)$ is equivalent to $\neg(x \geq 2)$, we use a single Boolean variable for both. The substitutions is:

$$(x < 2) \leftarrow s_0 \qquad (y > 1) \leftarrow s_1 \qquad (y < x) \leftarrow s_2$$
$$(x \geq 2) \leftarrow \neg s_0 \qquad (y \leq 1) \leftarrow \neg s_1 \qquad (y \geq x) \leftarrow \neg s_2$$

After the substitution we obtain $\varphi'' = \Box(R_0^{\mathbb{B}} \wedge R_1^{\mathbb{B}})$ where

$$R_0^{\mathbb{B}} : s_0 \rightarrow \bigcirc s_1 \qquad\qquad R_1^{\mathbb{B}} : \neg s_0 \rightarrow s_2$$

Note that φ'' may not be equi-realizable to φ, as we may be giving too much power to the system if s_0, s_1 and s_2 are chosen independently without restriction. Note that φ'' is realizable, for example by always choosing s_1 and s_2 to be true, but φ is not realizable in $LTL_{\mathcal{T}_{\mathbb{Z}}}$. This justifies the need of an extra sub-formula.

Definition 1 (Choice). *A choice $c \subseteq Lit(\varphi)$ is a subset of the literals of φ.*

The intended meaning of a choice is to capture what literals are true in the choice, while the rest (i.e., $Lit \setminus c$) are false. Once the environment picks values for $\overline{x}$, the system can realize some choice c by selecting $\overline{y}$ and making the literals in c true (and the rest false). However, for some values of $\overline{x}$, some choices may not be possible for the system for any $\overline{y}$. Given a choice c, we use $f(c(\overline{x}, \overline{y}))$ to denote the formula:

$$\bigwedge_{l \in c} l \wedge \bigwedge_{l \notin c} \neg l$$

which is a formula with variables $\overline{x}$ and $\overline{y}$ that captures logically the set of values of $\overline{x}$ and $\overline{y}$ that realize precisely choice c. We use $\mathcal{C}$ for the set of choices. Note that there are $|\mathcal{C}| = 2^{|Lit|}$ different choices. We call the elements of $\mathcal{C}$ choices because they may be at the disposal of the system to choose by picking the right values of its variables.

A given choice c can act as *potential* (meaning that the response is possible) or as *antipotential* (meaning that the response is not possible). A potential is a formula (that depends only on $\overline{x}$) that captures those values of $\overline{x}$ for which the system can respond and make precisely the literals in c true (and the rest of the literals false). The negation of the potential (i.e., an antipotential) captures precisely those values of $\overline{x}$ for which there are no values of $\overline{y}$ that lead to c.

Definition 2 (Potential and Antipotential). *Given a choice c, a potential is the following formula c^p and an antipotential is the following formula c^a:*

$$c^p(\overline{x}) = \exists \overline{y}.f(c(\overline{x}, \overline{y})) \qquad\qquad c^a(\overline{x}) = \forall \overline{y}.\neg f(c(\overline{x}, \overline{y}))$$

Example 3. We illustrate two choices for Ex. 1. Consider choices $c_0 = \{(x < 2), (y > 1), (y < x)\}$ and $c_1 = \{(x < 2), (y > 1)\}$. Choice c_0 corresponds to $f(c_0) = (x < 2) \wedge (y > 1) \wedge (y < x)$, that is, literals $(x < 2)$, $(y > 1)$ and $(y < x)$ are true. Choice c_1 corresponds to $f(c_1) = (x < 2) \wedge (y > 1) \wedge (y \geq x)$, that is, literals $(x < 2)$ and $(y > 1)$ being true and $(y < x)$ being false (i.e., $(y \geq x)$ being true). It is easy to see the meaning of c_2, c_3 etc. Then, the potential and antipotential formulae of e.g., choices c_0 and c_1 from Ex. 1 are as follows:

$$c_0^p = \exists y.(x < 2) \wedge (y > 1) \wedge (y < x) \qquad c_0^a = \forall y.\neg\big((x < 2) \wedge (y > 1) \wedge (y < x)\big)$$
$$c_1^p = \exists y.(x < 2) \wedge (y > 1) \wedge (y \geq x) \qquad c_1^a = \forall y.\neg\big((x < 2) \wedge (y > 1) \wedge (y \geq x)\big)$$

Note that potentials and antipotentials have $\overline{x}$ as the only free variables. □

Depending on the theory, the validity of potentials and antipotentials may be different. For instance, consider c_0^p and theories $\mathcal{T}_{\mathbb{Z}}$ and $\mathcal{T}_{\mathbb{R}}$:

- In $\mathcal{T}_{\mathbb{Z}}$: $\exists y.(x < 2) \wedge (y > 1) \wedge (y < x)$ is equivalent to *false*.
- In $\mathcal{T}_{\mathbb{R}}$: $\exists y.(x < 2) \wedge (y > 1) \wedge (y < x)$ is equivalent to $(x < 2)$.

These equivalences can be obtained using classic quantifier elimination procedures, e.g., with Cooper's algorithm [9] for $\mathcal{T}_{\mathbb{Z}}$ and Tarski's method [32] for $\mathcal{T}_{\mathbb{R}}$.

A reaction is a description of the specific choices that the system has the power to choose.

Definition 3 (Reaction). *Let P and A be a partition of $\mathcal{C}$ that is: $P \subseteq \mathcal{C}$, $A \subseteq \mathcal{C}$, $P \cap A = \emptyset$ and $P \cup A = \mathcal{C}$. The reaction $react_{(P,A)}$ is as follows:*

$$react_{(P,A)}(\overline{x}) \stackrel{def}{=} \bigwedge_{c \in P} c^p \wedge \bigwedge_{c \in A} c^a$$

The reaction $react_{(P,A)}$ is equivalent to:

$$react_{(P,A)}(\overline{x}) = \bigwedge_{c \in P} \big(\exists \overline{y}.f(c(\overline{x},\overline{y}))\big) \wedge \bigwedge_{c \in A} \big(\forall \overline{y}.\neg f(c(\overline{x},\overline{y}))\big).$$

There are $2^{2^{|Lit|}}$ different reactions.

A reaction r is called valid whenever there is a move of the environment for which r captures precisely the power of the system, that is exactly which choices the system can choose. Formally, a reaction is valid whenever $\exists \overline{x}.r(\overline{x})$ is a valid formula. We use $\mathcal{R}$ for the set of reactions and VR for the set of valid reactions. It is easy to see that, for all possible valuations of $\overline{x}$ the environment can pick, the system has a specific power to respond (among the finitely many cases). Therefore, the following formula is valid:

$$\varphi_{VR} = \forall \overline{x}. \bigvee_{r \in VR} r(\overline{x}).$$

Example 4. In Ex. 1, for theory $\mathcal{T}_{\mathbb{Z}}$, we find there are two valid reactions (using choices from Ex. 3):

$$r_1 : \exists x.c_0^a \wedge c_1^p \wedge c_2^p \wedge c_3^p \wedge c_4^a \wedge c_5^a \wedge c_6^a \wedge c_7^a$$
$$r_2 : \exists x.c_0^a \wedge c_1^a \wedge c_2^a \wedge c_3^a \wedge c_4^a \wedge c_5^p \wedge c_6^p \wedge c_7^a,$$

where reaction r_1 models the possible responses of the system after the environment picks a value for x with $(x < 2)$, whereas r_2 models the responses to $(x \geq 2)$. On the other hand, for $\mathcal{T}_{\mathbb{R}}$, there are three valid reactions:

$$r_1 : \exists x.c_0^a \wedge c_1^p \wedge c_2^p \wedge c_3^p \wedge c_4^a \wedge c_5^a \wedge c_6^a \wedge c_7^a$$
$$r_2 : \exists x.c_0^p \wedge c_1^p \wedge c_2^p \wedge c_3^a \wedge c_4^a \wedge c_5^a \wedge c_6^a \wedge c_7^a$$
$$r_3 : \exists x.c_0^a \wedge c_1^a \wedge c_2^a \wedge c_3^a \wedge c_4^p \wedge c_5^p \wedge c_6^p \wedge c_7^a$$

Note that there is one valid reaction more, since in $\mathcal{T}_{\mathbb{R}}$ there is one more case: $x \in (1, 2]$. Also, note that c_4 cannot be a potential in $\mathcal{T}_{\mathbb{Z}}$ (not even with a collaboration between environment and system), whereas it can in $\mathcal{T}_{\mathbb{R}}$.   □

3.2   The Boolean Abstraction Algorithm

Boolean abstraction is a method to compute $\varphi_{\mathbb{B}}$ from $\varphi_{\mathcal{T}}$. In this section we describe and prove correct a basic brute-force version of this method, and later in Sect. 4, we present faster algorithms. All Boolean abstraction algorithms that we present on this paper first compute the extra requirement, by visiting the set of reactions and computing a subset of the valid reactions that is sufficient to preserve realizability. The three main building blocks of our algorithms are (1) the stop criteria of the search for reactions; (2) how to obtain the next reaction to consider; and (3) how to modify the current set of valid reactions (by adding new valid reactions to it) and the set of remaining reactions (by pruning the search space). Finally, after the loop, the algorithm produces as φ^{extra} a conjunction of cases, one per valid reaction (P, A) in VR.

Algorithm 1: Brute-force

---
1 Input: $\varphi_{\mathcal{T}}$
2 $\varphi' \leftarrow \varphi_{\mathcal{T}}[l_i \leftarrow s_i]$ $VR \leftarrow \{\}$
3 $\mathcal{C} \leftarrow choices(literals(\varphi_{\mathcal{T}}))$
4 $\mathcal{R} \leftarrow 2^{\mathcal{C}}$
5 **for** $(P, A) \in \mathcal{R}$ **do**
6   **if** $\exists \overline{x}.react_{(P,A)}(\overline{x})$ **then**
7        $VR \leftarrow VR \cup \{(P, A)\}$

8 $\varphi^{extra} \leftarrow getExtra(VR)$
9 **return** $\varphi' \wedge \Box(A \rightarrow \varphi^{extra})$

We introduce a fresh variable $e_{(P,A)}$, controlled by the environment for each valid reaction (P, A), to capture that the environment plays values for $\overline{x}$ that correspond to the case where the system is left with the power to choose captured precisely by (P, A). Therefore, there is one additional environment Boolean variable per valid reaction (in practice we can enumerate the number of valid reactions and introduce only a logarithmic number of environment variables). Finally, the extra requirement uses P for each valid reaction (P, A) to encode the potential moves of the systems as a disjunction of the literals described by each choice in P. Each of these disjunction contains precisely the combinations of literals that are possible for the concrete case that (P, A) captures.

A brute-force algorithm that implements Boolean abstraction method by exhaustively searching all reactions is shown in Algorithm 1. The building blocks of this algorithm are:

(1) It stops when the remaining set of reactions is empty.
(2) It traverses the set $\mathcal{R}$ according to some predetermined order.
(3) To modify the set of valid reactions, if (P, A) is valid it adds (P, A) to the set VR (line 7). To modify the set of remaining reactions, it removes (P, A) from the search.

Finally, the extra sub-formula φ^{extra} is generated by $getExtra$ (line 8) defined as follows:

$$getExtra(VR) = \bigwedge_{(P,A)\in VR} (e_{(P,A)} \rightarrow \bigvee_{c\in P} (\bigwedge_{l_i\in c} s_i \wedge \bigwedge_{l_i\notin c} \neg s_i))$$

Note that there is an $\exists^*\forall^*$ validity query in the body of the loop (line 6) to check whether the candidate reaction is valid. This is why decidability of the $\exists^*\forall^*$ fragment is crucial because it captures the finite partitioning of the environment moves (which is existentially quantified) for which the system can react in certain ways (i.e., potentials, which are existentially quantified) by picking appropriate valuations but not in others (i.e., antipotentials, which are universally quantified). In essence, the brute-force algorithm iterates over all reactions, one at a time, checking whether each reaction is valid or not. In case the reaction (characterized by the set of potential choices[1]) is valid, it is added to VR.

Example 5. Consider again the specification in Ex. 1, with $\mathcal{T}_\mathbb{Z}$ as theory. Note that the valid reactions are r_1 and r_2, as shown in Ex. 4, where the potentials of r_1 are $\{c_1, c_2, c_3\}$ and the potentials of r_2 are $\{c_5, c_6\}$. Now, the creation of φ^{extra} requires two fresh variables d_0 and d_1 for the environment (they correspond to environment decisions $(x < 2)$ and $(x \geq 2)$, respectively), resulting into:

$$\varphi_{\mathcal{T}_\mathbb{Z}}^{extra} : \begin{pmatrix} d_0 \rightarrow \big((s_0 \wedge s_1 \wedge \neg s_2) \vee (s_0 \wedge \neg s_1 \wedge s_2) \vee (s_0 \wedge \neg s_1 \wedge \neg s_2)\big) \\ \wedge \\ d_1 \rightarrow \big((\neg s_0 \wedge s_1 \wedge \neg s_2) \vee (\neg s_0 \wedge \neg s_1 \wedge s_2)\big) \end{pmatrix}$$

For example $c_2 = \{s_0\}$ is a choice that appears as potential in valid reaction r_1, so it appears as a disjunct of d_0 as $(s_0 \wedge \neg s_1 \wedge \neg s_2)$. The resulting *Booleanized* specification $\varphi_\mathbb{B}$ is as follows:

$$\varphi_{\mathcal{T}_\mathbb{Z}}^\mathbb{B} = (\varphi'' \wedge \square(A_\mathbb{B} \rightarrow \varphi_{\mathcal{T}_\mathbb{Z}}^{extra}))$$

$\square$

---

[1] The potentials in a choice characterize the precise power of the system player, because the potentials correspond with what the system can respond.

Note that the Boolean encoding is extended with an assumption formula $A_{\mathbb{B}} = (d_0 \leftrightarrow \neg d_1) \wedge (d_0 \vee d_1)$ that restricts environment moves to guarantee that exactly one environment decision variable is picked. Also, note that a Boolean abstraction algorithm will output three (instead of two) decisions for the environment, but we acknowledge that one of them will never be played by it, since it gives strictly more power to the system. The complexity of this brute-force Booleanization algorithm is doubly exponential in the number of literals.

3.3   From Local Simulation to Equi-Realizability

The intuition about the correctness of the algorithm is that the extra requirement encodes precisely all reactions (i.e., collections of choices), for which there is a move of the environment that leaves the system with precisely that power to respond. As an observation, in the extra requirement, the set of potentials in valid reactions cannot be empty. This is stated in Lemma 1.

Lemma 1. *Let $C \in \mathcal{C}$ be such that $react_C \in VR$. Then $C \neq \emptyset$.*

Proof. Bear in mind $react_C \in VR$ is valid. Let $\bar{v}$ be such that $react_C[\bar{x} \leftarrow \bar{v}]$ is valid. Let $\bar{w}$ be an arbitrary valuation of $\bar{y}$ and let c be a choice and l a literal. Therefore:

$$\bigwedge_{l[\bar{x}\leftarrow\bar{v},\bar{y}\leftarrow\bar{w}] \text{ is true}} l \wedge \bigwedge_{l[\bar{x}\leftarrow\bar{v},\bar{y}\leftarrow\bar{w}] \text{ is false}} \neg l$$

It follows that $I[\bar{x} \leftarrow \bar{v}]\exists\bar{y}.c$, so $c \in C$.   □

Lemma 1 is crucial, because it ensures that once a Boolean abstraction algorithm is executed, for each fresh $\bar{e}$ variable in the extra requirement, at least one reaction with one or more potentials can be responded by the system.

Therefore, in each position in the realizability game, the system can respond to moves of the system leaving to precisely corresponding positions in the Boolean game. In turn, this leads to equi-realizability because each move can be simulated in the corresponding game. Concretely, it is easy to see that we can define a simulation between the positions of the games for φ_T and $\varphi_{\mathbb{B}}$ such that (1) each literal l_i and the corresponding variable s_i have the same truth value in related positions, (2) the extra requirement is always satisfied, and (3) moves of the system in each game from related positions in each game can be mimicked in the other game. This is captured by the following theorem:

Theorem 1. *System wins $\mathcal{G}^T$ if and only if System wins the game $\mathcal{G}^{\mathbb{B}}$. Therefore, φ_T is realizable if and only if $\varphi_{\mathbb{B}}$ is realizable.*

Proof. (Sketch). Since realizability games are memory-less determined, it is sufficient to consider only local strategies. Given a strategy $\rho_{\mathbb{B}}$ that is winning in $\mathcal{G}^{\mathbb{B}}$ we define a strategy ρ_T in $\mathcal{G}^T$ as follows. Assuming related positions, ρ_T

moves in $\mathcal{G}^{\mathcal{T}}$ to the successor that is related to the position where $\rho_{\mathbb{B}}$ moves in $\mathcal{G}^{\mathbb{B}}$. By (3) above, it follows that for every play played in $\mathcal{G}^{\mathbb{B}}$ according to $\rho_{\mathbb{B}}$ there is a play in $\mathcal{G}^{\mathcal{T}}$ played according to $\rho_{\mathcal{T}}$ that results in the same trace, and vice-versa: for every play played in $\mathcal{G}^{\mathcal{T}}$ according to $\rho_{\mathcal{T}}$ there is a play in $\mathcal{G}^{\mathbb{B}}$ played according to $\rho_{\mathbb{B}}$ that results in the same trace. Since $\rho_{\mathbb{B}}$ is winning, so is $\rho_{\mathcal{T}}$. The other direction follows similarly, because again $\rho_{\mathbb{B}}$ can be constructed from $\rho_{\mathcal{T}}$ not only guaranteeing the same valuation of literals and corresponding variables, but also that the extra requirement holds in the resulting position. $\square$

The following corollary of Thm. 1 follows immediately.

Theorem 2. *Let $\mathcal{T}$ be a theory with a decidable $\exists^*\forall^*$-fragment. Then, $\text{LTL}_{\mathcal{T}}$ realizability is decidable.*

4   Efficient Algorithms for Boolean Abstraction

4.1   Quasi-reactions

The basic algorithm presented in Sect. 3 exhaustively traverses the set of reactions, one at a time, checking whether each reaction is valid. Therefore, the body of the loop is visited $2^{|\mathcal{C}|}$ times. In practice, the running time of this basic algorithm quickly becomes unfeasible.

We now improve Alg. 1 by exploiting the observation that every SMT query for the validity of a reaction reveals information about the validity of other reactions. We will exploit this idea by learning uninteresting subsequent sets of reactions and pruning the search space. The faster algorithms that we present below encode the remaining search space using a SAT formula, whose models are further reactions to explore.

To implement the learning-and-pruning idea we first introduce the notion of quasi-reaction.

Definition 4 (Quasi-reaction). *A quasi-reaction is a pair (P, A) where $P \subseteq \mathcal{C}$, $A \subseteq \mathcal{C}$ and $P \cap A = \emptyset$.*

Quasi-reactions remove from reactions the constraint that $P \cup A = \mathcal{C}$. A quasi-reaction represents the set of reactions that would be obtained from choosing the remaining choices that are neither in P nor in A as either potential or antipotential. The set of quasi-reactions is:

$$\mathcal{Q} = \{(P, A) \mid P, A \subseteq \mathcal{C} \text{ and } P \cap A = \emptyset\}$$

Note that $\mathcal{R} = \{(P, A) \in \mathcal{Q} \mid P \cup A = \mathcal{C}\}$.

Example 6. Consider a case with four choices c_0, c_1, c_2 and c_3. The quasi-reaction $(\{c_0, c_2\}, \{c_1\})$ corresponds to the following formula:

$$\exists \overline{x}.\ (\exists \overline{y}.\ f(c_0(\overline{x}, \overline{y})) \wedge \forall \overline{y}.\ \neg f(c_1(\overline{x}, \overline{y})) \wedge \exists \overline{y}.\ f(c_2(\overline{x}, \overline{y})))$$

Note that nothing is stated in this quasi-reaction about c_3 (it neither acts as a potential nor as an antipotential). □

Consider the following order between quasi-reactions: $(P, A) \preceq (P', A')$ holds if and only if $P \subseteq P'$ and $A \subseteq A'$. It is easy to see that $\preceq$ is a partial order, that $(\emptyset, \emptyset)$ is the lowest element and that for every two elements (P, A) and (P', A') there is a greatest lower bound (namely $(P \cap P', A \cap A')$). Therefore $(P, A) \sqcap (P', A') \overset{\text{def}}{=} (P \cap P', A \cap A')$ is a meet operation (it is associative, commutative and idempotent). Note that $q \preceq q'$ if and only if $q \sqcap q' = q$. Formally:

Proposition 1. $(\mathcal{Q}, \sqcap)$ *is a lower semi-lattice.*

The quasi-reaction semi-lattice represents how *informative* a quasi-reaction is. Given a quasi-reaction (P, A), removing an element from either P or A results in a strictly less informative quasi-reaction. The lowest element $(\emptyset, \emptyset)$ contains the least information.

Given a quasi-reaction q, the set $\mathcal{Q}_q = \{q' \in \mathcal{Q} | q' \preceq q\}$ of the quasi-reactions below q form a full lattice with join $(P, Q) \sqcup (P', Q') \overset{\text{def}}{=} (P \cup P', Q \cup Q')$. This is well defined because P' and Q, and P and Q' are guaranteed to be disjoint.

Proposition 2. *For every* q, $(\mathcal{Q}_q, \sqcap, \sqcup)$ *is a lattice.*

As for reactions, quasi-reactions correspond to a formula in the theory as follows:

$$qreact_{(P,A)}(\overline{x}) = \bigwedge_{c \in P} (\exists \overline{y}.c(\overline{x}, \overline{y})) \wedge \bigwedge_{c \in A} (\forall \overline{y}.\neg c(\overline{x}, \overline{y}))$$

Again, given a quasi-reaction q, if $\exists \overline{x}.qreact_q(\overline{x})$ is valid we say that q is valid, otherwise we say that q is invalid. The following holds directly from the definition (and the fact that adding conjuncts makes a first-order formula "less satisfiable").

Proposition 3. *Let* q, q' *be two quasi-reactions with* $q \preceq q'$. *If* q *is invalid then* q' *is invalid. If* q' *is valid then* q *is valid.*

These results enable the following optimizations.

4.2 Quasi-reaction-based Optimizations

A Logic-Based Optimization. Consider that, during the search for valid reactions in the main loop, a reaction (P, A) is found to be invalid, that is

$react_{(P,A)}$ is unsatisfiable. If the algorithms explores the quasi-reactions below (P, A), finding $(P', A') \preceq (P, A)$ such that $qreact_{(P',A')}$, then by Prop. 3, every reaction (P'', A'') above (P', A') is guaranteed to be invalid. This allows to prune the search in the main loop by computing a more informative quasi-reaction q after an invalid reaction r is found, and skipping all reactions above q (and not only r). For example, if the reaction corresponding to $(\{c_0, c_2, c_3\}, \{c_1\})$ is found to be invalid, and by exploring quasi-reactions below it, we find that $(\{c_0\}, \{c_1\})$ is also invalid, then we can skip all reactions above $(\{c_0\}, \{c_1\})$. This includes for example $(\{c_0, c_2\}, \{c_1, c_3\})$ and $(\{c_0, c_3\}, \{c_1, c_2\})$. In general, the lower the invalid quasi-reaction in $\preceq$, the more reactions will be pruned. This optimization resembles a standard choosing of max/min elements in an anti-chain.

A Game-Based Optimization. Consider now two reactions $r = (P, A)$ and $r' = (P', A')$ such that $P \subseteq P'$ and assume that both are valid reactions. Since r' allows more choices to the system (because the potentials P determine these choices), the environment player will always prefer to play r than r'. Formally, if there is a winning strategy for the environment that chooses values for $\bar{x}$ (corresponding to a model of $react_r$), then choosing values for $\bar{x}'$ instead (corresponding to a model of $react_{r'}$) will also be winning.

Therefore, if a reaction r is found to be valid, we can prune the search for reactions r' that contain strictly more potentials, because even if r' is also valid, it will be less interesting for the environment player. For instance, if $(\{c_0, c_3\}, \{c_1, c_2\})$ is valid, then $(\{c_0, c_1, c_3\}, \{c_2\})$ and $(\{c_0, c_1, c_3, c_2\}, \{\})$ become uninteresting to be explored and can be pruned from the search.

4.3   A Single Model-Loop Algorithm (Algorithm 2)

We present now a faster algorithm that replaces the main loop of Algorithm 1 that performs exhaustive exploration with a SAT-based search procedure that prunes uninteresting reactions. In order to do so, we use a SAT formula ψ with one variable z_i per choice c_i, in a DPLL(T) fashion. An assignment $v : Vars(\psi) \to \mathbb{B}$ to these variables represents a reaction (P, A) where

$$P = \{c_i | v(z_i) = true\} \qquad A = \{c_j | v(z_j) = false\}$$

Similarly, a partial assignment $v : Vars(\psi) \rightharpoonup \mathbb{B}$ represents a quasi-reaction. The intended meaning of ψ is that its models encode the set of interesting reactions that remain to be explored. This formula is initialized with $\psi = true$ (note that $\neg(\bigwedge_{z_i} \neg z_i)$ is also a correct starting point because the reaction where all choices are antipotentials is invalid). Then, a SAT query is used to find a satisfying assignment for ψ, which corresponds to a (quasi-)reaction r whose validity is interesting to be explored. Algorithm 2 shows

---

Algorithm 2: Model-loop

---

10 Input: φ_T
11 $\varphi' \leftarrow \varphi_T[l_i \leftarrow s_i]$; $VR \leftarrow \{\}$
12 $C \leftarrow choices(literals(\varphi_T))$
13 $\mathcal{R} \leftarrow 2^C$; $\psi \leftarrow \top$
14 **while** $SAT(\psi)$ **do**
15     $m = model(\psi)$
16   **if** $\exists \overline{x}.\ (toTheory(m, C))$
    then
17        $P \leftarrow posVars(m)$
18        $\psi \leftarrow \psi \wedge \neg(\bigwedge_{p \in P} p)$
19        $VR \leftarrow VR \cup (e_t, P)$
20   **else**
21        $N \leftarrow negVars(m)$
22        $fh \leftarrow \bigwedge_{n \in N} n$
23   **if** $\exists \overline{x}.\ toTheory(fh, C)$
       then
24          $\psi \leftarrow \psi \wedge \neg m$
25   **else**
26          $\psi \leftarrow \psi \wedge \neg fh$
27 $\varphi^{extra} \leftarrow getExtra(VR)$
28 **return** $\varphi' \wedge \Box(A \to \varphi^{extra})$

---

the Model-loop algorithm. The three main building blocks of the model-loop algorithm are:

(1) Algorithm 2 stops when ψ is invalid (line 14).
(2) To explore a new reaction, Algorithm 2 obtains a satisfying assignment for ψ (line 15).
(3) Algorithm 2 checks the validity of the reaction (line 16) and enriches ψ o prune according to what can be learned, as follows:
  – If the reaction is invalid (as a result of the SMT query in line 16), then it checks the validity of quasi-reaction $q = (\emptyset, A)$ in line 23. If q is invalid, add the negation of q as a new conjunction of ψ (line 26). If q is valid, add the negation of the reaction (line 24). This prevents all SAT models that agree with one of these q, which correspond to reactions $q \preceq r'$, including r.
  – If the reaction is valid, then it is added to the set of valid reactions VR and the corresponding quasi-reaction that results from removing the antipotentials is added (negated) to ψ (line 18), preventing the exploration of uninteresting cases, according to the game-based optimization.

As for the notation in Algorithm 2 (also in Algorithm 3 and Algorithm 4), $model(\psi)$ in line 15 is a function that returns a satisfying assignment of the SAT formula ψ, $posVars(m)$ returns the positive variables of m (e.g., c_i, c_j etc.) and $negVars(m)$ returns the negative variables. Finally, $toTheory(m, C) = \bigwedge_{m_i} c_i^p \wedge \bigwedge_{\neg m_i} c_i^a$ (in lines 16 and 23) translates a Boolean formula into its corresponding formula in the given T theory. Note that unsatisfiable m can be minimized finding cores.

If r is invalid and $(\emptyset, A)$ is found also to be invalid, then exponentially many cases can be pruned. Similarly, if r is valid, also exponentially many cases can be pruned. The following result shows the correctness of Algorithm 2:

Theorem 3. *Algorithm 2 terminates and outputs a correct Boolean abstraction.*

Proof. (Sketch). Algorithm 2 terminates because, at each step in the loop, ψ removes at least one satisfying assignment and the total number is bounded by $2^{|C|}$. Also, the correctness of the generated formula is guaranteed because, for every valid reaction in Algorithm 1, either there is a valid reaction found in Algorithm 2 or a more promising reaction found in Algorithm 2. $\Box$

4.4 A Nested-SAT Algorithm (Algorithm 3)

We now present an improvement of Algorithm 2 that performs a more detailed search for a promising collection of invalid quasi-reactions under an invalid reaction r.

Algorithm 3: Nested-SAT

29 Input: φ_T
30 $\varphi' \leftarrow \varphi_T[l_i \leftarrow s_i]$; $VR \leftarrow \{\}$
31 $C \leftarrow choices(literals(\varphi_T))$
32 $\mathcal{R} \leftarrow 2^C$; $\psi \leftarrow \top$
33 **while** $SAT(\psi)$ **do**
34 $\quad$ $m = model(\psi)$
35 $\quad$ **if** $\exists \overline{x}.\ (toTheory(m, C))$
$\quad$ **then**
36 $\quad\quad$ $P \leftarrow posVars(m)$
37 $\quad\quad$ $\psi \leftarrow \psi \wedge \neg(\bigwedge_{p \in P} P)$
38 $\quad\quad$ $VR \leftarrow VR \cup (e_t, P)$
39 $\quad$ **else**
40 $\quad\quad$ $N \leftarrow negVars(m)$
41 $\quad\quad$ $\psi \leftarrow \psi \wedge \neg m$
42 $\quad\quad$ $I \leftarrow inner\_loop(m, C)$
43 $\quad\quad$ $\psi \leftarrow \psi \wedge \neg(\bigwedge_{i \in I} i)$

44 $\varphi^{extra} \leftarrow getExtra(VR)$
45 **return** $\varphi' \wedge \Box(A \rightarrow \varphi^{extra})$

Note that it is not necessary to find the precise collection of all the smallest quasi-reactions that are under an invalid reaction r, as long as at least one quasi-reaction under r is calculated (perhaps, r itself). Finding lower quasi-reactions allow to prune more, but its calculation is more costly, because more SMT queries need to be performed. The Nested-SAT algorithm (Algorithm 3) explores (using an inner SAT encoding) this trade-off between computing more exhaustively better invalid quasi-reactions and the cost of the search. The three main building blocks of the nested-SAT algorithm (see Algorithm 3) are:

(1) It stops when ψ is invalid (as in Algorithm 2), in line 33.
(2) To get the reaction, obtain a satisfying assignment m for ψ (as in Algorithm 2), in line 34.

(3) Check the validity of the corresponding reaction and prune ψ according to what can be learned as follows. If the reaction is valid, then we proceed as in Algorithm 2. If $r = (P, A)$ is invalid (as a result of the SMT query), then an inner SAT formula encodes whether a choice is masked (eliminated from P or A). Models of the inner SAT formula, therefore, correspond to quasi-reactions below r. If a quasi-reaction q found in the inner loop is invalid, the inner formula is additionally constrained and the set of invalid quasi-reactions is expanded. If a quasi-reaction q found is valid, then the inner SAT formula is pruned eliminating all quasi-reactions that are guaranteed to be valid. At the end of the inner loop, a (non-empty) collection of invalid quasi-reactions are added to ψ.

The inner loop, shown in Algorithm 4 (where VQ stands for *valid quasi-reactions*), explores a full lattice.

Algorithm 4: Inner loop

46 Input: m, C

47 $VQ \leftarrow \{\}$; $\beta \leftarrow \top$

48 **while** $SAT(\beta)$ **do**

49     $u = model(\beta)$

50   **if**
    $\exists \bar{x}.\ (toTheory\_inn(u, m, C))$
    then

51        $P \leftarrow posVars(u)$

52        $\beta \leftarrow \beta \wedge \neg(\bigwedge_{p \in P} p)$

53   **else**

54        $N \leftarrow negVars(u)$

55        $\beta \leftarrow \beta \wedge \neg(\bigwedge_{n \in N} n)$

56        $VQ \leftarrow VQ \cup u$

57 **return** VQ

Also, note that $\neg(\bigwedge_{z_i} \neg z_i)$ is, again, a correct starting point. Consider, for example, that the outer loop finds $(\{c_1, c_3\}, \{c_0, c_2\})$ to be invalid and that the inner loop produces assignment $w_0 \wedge w_1 \wedge w_2 \wedge \neg w_3$. This corresponds to c_3 being masked producing quasi-reaction $(\{c_1\}, \{c_0, c_2\})$. The pruning system is the following:

– If quasi-reaction q is valid then the inner SAT formula is pruned eliminating all inner models that agree with the model in the masked choices. In our example, we would prune all models that satisfy $\neg w_3$ if q is valid (because the resulting quasi-reactions will be inevitably valid).

– If quasi-reaction q is invalid, then we prune in the inner search all quasi-reactions that mask less than q, because these will be inevitably invalid. In our example, we would prune all models satisfying $\neg(w_0 \wedge w_1 \wedge w_2)$.

Note that $toTheory\_inn(u, m, C) = \bigwedge_{m_i \wedge u_j} c_i^p \wedge \bigwedge_{\neg m_i \wedge u_j} c_i^a$ is not the same function as the $toTheory()$ used in Algorithm 2 and Algorithm 3, since the inner loops needs both model m and mask u (which makes no sense to be negated) to translate a Boolean formula into a $\mathcal{T}$-formula. Also, note that there is again a trade-off in the inner loop because an exhaustive search is not necessary. Thus, in practice, we also used some basic heuristics: (1) entering the inner loop only when $(\emptyset, A)$ is invalid; (2) fixing a maximum number of inner model queries per outer model with the possibility to decrement this amount dynamically with a decay; and (3) reducing the number of times the inner loop is exercised (e.g., *enter the inner loop only if the number of invalid outer models so far is even*).

Example 7. We explore the results of Algorithm 3. A possible execution for 2 literals can be as follows:

1. Reaction $(\{c_0, c_3\}, \{c_1, c_2\})$ is obtained in line 34, which is declared invalid by the SMT solver in line 35. The inner loop called in line 42 produces $(\{c_0\}, \{c_1\})$, $(\{c_3\}, \{c_2\})$ and $(\{\}, \{c_1, c_2\})$ as three invalid quasi-reactions, and their negations are added to the SAT formula of the outer loop in line 43.

2. A second reaction $(\{c_0, c_1\}, \{c_3, c_4\})$ is obtained from the SAT solver in line 34, and now the SMT solver query is valid in line 35. Then, $\neg(c_0 \wedge c_1)$ is added to the outer SAT formula in line 37.

3. A third reaction $(\{c_2, c_3\}, \{c_0, c_1\})$ is obtained in line 33 , which is again valid in line 35. Similarly, $\neg(c_2 \wedge c_3)$ is added the outer SAT formula in line 37.

4. A fourth reaction ($\{c_1, c_2\}, \{c_0, c_3\}$) is obtained in line 33, which is now invalid (line 35). The inner loop called in line 42 generates the following cores: ($\{c_1\}, \{c_0\}$) and ($\{c_2\}, \{c_3\}$). The addition of the negation of these cores leads to an unsatisfiable outer SAT formula, and the algorithm terminates.

The execution in this example has performed 4 SAT+SMT queries in the outer loop, and 3+2 SAT+SMT queries in the inner loops. The brute-force Algorithm 1 would have performed 16 queries. Note that the difference between the exhaustive version and the optimisations soon increases exponentially when we consider specifications with more literals. $\square$

5 Empirical Evaluation

We perform an empirical evaluation on six specifications inspired by real industrial cases: *Lift* (*Li.*), *Train* (*Tr.*), *Connect* (*Con.*), *Cooker* (*Coo.*), *Usb* (*Usb*) and *Stage* (*St.*), and a synthetic example (*Syn.*) with versions from 2 to 7 literals. For the implementation, we used used Python 3.8.8 with Z3 4.11.

It is easy to see that "clusters" of literals that do not share variables can be Booleanized independently, so we split into clusters each of the examples. We report our results in Fig. 2. Each row contains the result for a cluster of an experiment (each one for the fastest heuristic). Each benchmark is split into clusters, where we show the number of variables (*vr.*) and literals (*lt.*) per cluster. We also show running times of each algorithm against each cluster; concretely, we test Algorithm 1 (*BF*), Algorithm 2 (*SAT*) and Algorithm 3 (*Doub.*). For Algorithm 2 and Algorithm3, we show the number of queries performed; in the case of Algorithm 3, we also show both outer and inner queries. Algorithm 1 and Algorithm 2 require no heuristics. For Algorithm 3, we report, left to right: maximum number of inner loops (*MxI.*), the modulo division criteria (*Md.*)[2], the number of queries after which we perform a decay of 1 in the maximum number of inner loops (*Dc.*), and if we apply the invalidity of ($\emptyset, A$) as a criteria to enter the inner loop (*A.*), where ✓ means that we do and × means the contrary. Also, $\perp$ means timeout (or *no data*).

The brute-force (BF) Algorithm 1 performs well with 3 or fewer literals, but the performance dramatically decreases with 4 literals. Algorithm 2 (single SAT) performs well up to 4 literals, and it can hardly handle cases with 6 or more literals. An exception is *Lift (1,7)* which is simpler since it has only one variable (and this implies that there is only one player). The performance improvement of SAT with respect to BF is due to the decreasing of queries. For example, *Train (3,6)* performs 13706 queries, whereas BF would need $2^{2^6} = 1.844 \cdot 10^{18}$ queries.

All examples are Booleanizable when using Algorithm 3 (two SAT loops), particularly when using a combination of concrete heuristics. For instance, in

---

[2] This means that the inner loop is entered if and only if the number of invalid models so far is divisible by *Md*, and we found *Md* values of 2, 3 and 20 to be interesting.

Bn. (nm.)	Cls. (vr, lt)	Time (s)			Queries (out+inn)		Heuristics (doub)				$\varphi^{\mathbb{B}}$	
		BF	SAT	Doub.	SAT	Doub.	MxI.	Md.	Dc.	A.	Val.	Tme.
Li.	(1, 7)	⊥	6740	**31.77**	30375	**72/1040**	40	2	0	✓	1	4.41
	(2, 4)	3911	**0.70**	0.91	**27**	25/20	10	2	0	×	16	
	(1, 3)	3.64	1.19	**0.52**	46	**10/20**	10	2	0	×	4	
	(1, 2)	0.23	**0.09**	0.14	4	**4/3**	3	3	0	×	3	
Tr.	(1, 3)	3.18	**0.04**	0.96	**16**	26/20	10	2	0	✓	5	5.13
	(2, 1)	0.05	**0.04**	**0.04**	**2**	**2/0**	1	1	0	✓	2	
	(1, 3)	3.10	1.64	**0.21**	74	**2/10**	10	2	0	✓	1	
	(1, 1)	**0.04**	0.06	0.11	**3**	3/2	1	1	0	✓	1	
	(3, 6)	⊥	1269	**112.5**	13706	**1170/4716**	100	20	40	×	15	
	(4, 5)	⊥	5251	**4144**	44177	**52623/12332**	100	20	40	×	24	
	(3, 5)	⊥	2044	**359.3**	31363	**9123/10158**	100	20	40	×	9	
	(4, 12)	⊥	⊥	**6571**	⊥	**2728/40920**	100	20	40	×	104	
Con.	(2, 2)	0.23	**0.09**	**0.09**	4	**4/0**	3	3	0	✓	4	4.37
Coo.	(3, 5)	⊥	1356	**2.81**	27883	**16/160**	20	2	0	✓	1	3.64
Usb.	(2, 3)	3.40	0.21	**0.17**	8	**8/0**	3	3	0	✓	8	3.93
	(3, 5)	⊥	**231.9**	364.4	5638	**5638/0**	20	2	0	✓	32	
St.	(8, 8)	⊥	**18.19**	18.20	256	**256/0**	40	2	0	✓	256	6.06
	(3, 6)	⊥	1311	**194.8**	14994	**1697/6536**	100	20	40	×	45	
Syn.	(2, 2)	0.21	0.24	**0.18**	11	**4/3**	3	3	0	✓	2	4.12
	(2, 3)	3.42	2.69	**1.24**	119	**14/40**	10	2	0	✓	3	4.11
	(2, 4)	2842	108.6	**16.51**	3982	**188/620**	10	2	0	✓	3	4.28
	(2, 5)	⊥	7151	**68.90**	44259	**380/2800**	20	2	0	✓	11	4.53
	(2, 6)	⊥	⊥	**402.2**	⊥	**4792/9941**	100	20	40	×	24	4.85
	(2, 7)	⊥	⊥	**3596**	⊥	**7344/139440**	40	2	0	✓	1	5.30
	(2, 7)	⊥	⊥	**3862**	⊥	**24311/40615**	200	20	40	×	45	5.99

Fig. 2. Empirical evaluation results of the different Boolean abstraction algorithms , where the best results are in **bold** and $\varphi_{\mathbb{B}}$ only refers to best times.

small cases (2 to 5 literals) it seems that heuristic-setups like $3/3/3/0/\checkmark$[3] are fast, whereas in bigger cases other setups like $40/2/0/\checkmark$ or $100/40/20/\times$ are faster. We conjecture that a non-zero decay is required to handle large inputs, since inner loop exploration becomes less useful after some time. However, adding a decay is not always faster than fixing a number of inner loops (see *Syn (2, 7)*), but it always yields better results in balancing the number of queries between the two nested SAT layers. Thus, since balancing the number of queries typically leads to faster execution times, we recommend to use decays. Note that we performed all the experiments reported in this section running all cases several times and computing averages, because Z3 exhibited a big volatility in the models it produces, which in turn influenced the running time of our algorithms. This significantly affects the precise reproducibility of the running times. For instance,

---

[3] This means: we only perform 3 inner loop queries per outer loop query (and there is no decay, i.e., *decay* = 0), we enter the inner loop once per 3 outer loops and we only enter the inner loop if $(\emptyset, A)$ is invalid.

Lits	Alg.	Performed queries (out+inn)	Out of	Needed queries ($\simeq$ %)
2	Alg 2	4	16	25
3	Alg 2	8	256	3.125
4	Alg 3	$83 + 380$	65536	0.709
5	Alg 3	$380 + 2800$	4294967296	$7.404 \cdot 10^{-5}$
6	Alg 3	$4792 + 9941$	$1.844 \cdot 10^{19}$	$1 \cdot 10^{-13}$
...	...	...	...	...
12	Alg 3	$2728 + 40920$	∞	0

Fig. 3. Best numbers of queries for Algorithm 2 and 3 relative to brute-force (Alg.1).

Lits	Heuristic setup	$T_{\mathbb{Z}}$ Time (s)	Queries (ou/in)	$T_{\mathbb{R}}$ Time (s)	Queries (ou/in)
3	10/2/0/✓	0.63	8/30	0.90	14/40
4	10/2/0/✓	16.14	308/500	11.19	125/560
5	20/2/0/✓	62.44	408/3220	88.55	357/3460
6	40/2/0/✓	678.71	2094/32760	722.64	1862/35840

Fig. 4. Comparison of $T_{\mathbb{Z}}$ and $T_{\mathbb{R}}$ for *Syn (2,3)* to *Syn (2,6)*.

for *Syn(2,5)* the worst case execution was almost three times worst than the average execution reported in Fig. 2. Studying this phenomena more closely is work in progress. Note that there are cases in which the number of queries of *SAT* and *Doub.* are the same (e.g., *Usb(3,5)*), which happened when the *A.* heuristic had the effect of making the search not to enter the inner loop.

In Fig. 2 we also analyzed the constructed $\varphi_{\mathbb{B}}$, measuring the number of valid reactions from which it is made (*Val.*) and the time (*Tme.*) that a realizability checker takes to verify whether $\varphi_{\mathbb{B}}$ (hence, φ_T) is realizable or not (expressed with dark and light gray colours, respectively). We used Strix [27] as the realizability checker. As we can see, there is a correspondence between the expected realizability in φ_T and the realizability result that Strix returns in $\varphi_{\mathbb{B}}$. Indeed, we can see all instances can be solved in less than 7 seconds, and the length of the Boolean formula (characterized by the number of valid reactions) hardly affects performance. This suggests that future work should be focused on reducing time necessary to produce Boolean abstraction to scale even further.

Also, note that Fig. 2 shows remarkable results as for ratios of queries required with respect to the (doubly exponential) brute-force algorithm: e.g., $4792 + 9941$ (outer + inner loops) out of the $1.844 \cdot 10^{19}$ queries that the brute-force algorithm would need, which is less than its $1 \cdot 10^{-13}$% (see Fig. 3 for more details). We also compared the performance and number of queries for two different theories $T_{\mathbb{Z}}$ and $T_{\mathbb{R}}$ for *Syn (2,3)* to *Syn (2,6)*. Note, again, that the realizability result may vary if a specification is interpreted in different theories, but this is not relevant for the experiment in Fig. 4, which suggests that time results are not dominated by the SMT solver; but, again, from the enclosing abstraction algorithms.

6   Related Work and Conclusions

Related Work. Constraint LTL [11] extends LTL with the possibility of expressing constraints between variables at bounded distance (of time). The theories considered are a restricted form of $T_{\mathbb{Z}}$ with only comparisons with additional restrictions to overcome undecidability. In comparison, we do not allow predicates to compare variables at different timesteps, but we prove decidability for all theories with an $\exists^*\forall^*$ decidable fragment. LTL modulo theories is studied in [12,19] for finite traces and they allow temporal operators within predicates, leading the logic to undecidability.

As for works closest to ours, [7] proposes numerical LTL synthesis using an interplay between an LTL synthesizer and a non-linear real arithmetic checker. However, [7] overapproximates the power of the system and hence it is not precise for realizability. Linear arithmetic games are studied in [13] introducing algorithms for synthesizing winning strategies for non-reactive specifications. Also, [22] considers infinite theories (like us), but it does not guarantee success or termination, whereas our Boolean abstraction is complete. They only consider safety, while our approach considers all LTL. The follow-up [23] has still similar limitations: only liveness properties that can be reduced to safety are accepted, and guarantees termination only for the unrealizability case. Similarly, [18] is incomplete, and requires a powerful solver for many quantifier alternations, which can be reduced to 1-alternation, but at the expense of the algorithm being no longer sound for the unrealizable case (e.g., depends on Z3 not answering "unknown"). As for [34], it (1) only considers safety/liveness GR(1) specifications, (2) is limited to the theory of fixed-size vectors and requires (3) quantifier elimination (4) and guidance. We only require $\exists^*\forall^*$-satisfiability (for Boolean abstraction) and we consider multiple infinite theories. The usual main difference is that Boolean abstraction generates a (Boolean) LTL specification so that existing tools can be used with any of their internal techniques and algorithms (bounded synthesis, for example) and will automatically benefit from further optimizations. Moreover, it preserves fragments like safety and GR(1) so specialized solvers can be used. On the contrary, all approaches above adapt one specific technique and implement it in a monolithic way.

Temporal Stream Logic (TSL) [16] extends LTL with complex data that can be related accross time, making use of a new *update* operator $[\![y \leftarrow fx]\!]$, to indicate that y receives the result of applying function f to variable x. TSL is later extended to theories in [15,25]. In all these works, realizability is undecidable. Also, in [8] reactive synthesis and syntax guided synthesis (SyGuS) [1] collaborate in the synthesis process, and generate executable code that guarantees reactive and data-level properties. It also suffers from undecidability: both due to the undecidability of TSL [16] and of SyGus [6]. In comparison, we cannot relate values accross time but we provide a decidable realizability procedure.

Comparing TSL with $\mathrm{LTL}_{\mathcal{T}}$, TSL is undecidable already for safety, the theory of equality and Presburger arithmetic. More precisely, TSL is only known to be decidable for three fragments (see Thm. 7 in [15]). TSL is (1) semi-decidable for the reachability fragment of TSL (i.e., the fragment of TSL that only permits the next operator and the eventually operator as temporal operators); (2) decidable for formulae consisting of only logical operators, predicates, updates, next operators, and at most one top-level eventually operator; and (3) semi-decidable for formulae with one cell (i.e., controllable outputs). All the specifications considered for empirical evaluation in Sect. 5 are not within the considered decidable or semi-decidable fragments. Also, TSL allows (finite) uninterpreted predicates, whereas we need to have predicates well defined within the semantics of theories of specifications for which we perform Boolean abstraction.

Conclusion. The main contribution of this paper is to show that $LTL_\mathcal{T}$ is decidable via a Boolean abstraction technique for all theories of data with a decidable $\exists^*\forall^*$ fragment. Our algorithms create, from a given $LTL_\mathcal{T}$ specification where atomic propositions are literals in such a theory, an equi-realizable specification with Boolean atomic propositions. We also have introduced efficient algorithms using SAT solvers for efficiently traversing the search space. A SAT formula encodes the space of reactions to be explore and our algorithms reduce this space by learning uninteresting areas from each reaction explores. The fastest algorithm uses a two layer SAT nested encoding, in a DPLL(T) fashion. This search yields dramatically more efficient running times and makes Boolean abstraction applicable to larger cases. We have performed an empirical evaluation of implementations of our algorithms. We found empirically that the best performances are obtained when there is a balance in the number of queries made by each layer of the SAT-search. To the best of our knowledge, this is the first method to propose a solution (and efficient) to realizability for general $\exists^*\forall^*$ decidable theories, which include, for instance, the theories of integers and reals.

Future work includes first how to improve scalability further. We plan to leverage quantifier elimination procedures [9] to produce candidates for the sets of valid reactions and then check (and correct) with faster algorithms. Also, optimizations based in quasi-reactions can be enhanced if state-of-the-art tools for satisfiability core search (e.g., [2,3,24]) are used. Another direction is to extend our realizability method into a synthesis procedure by synthesizing functions in $\mathcal{T}$ to produces witness values of variables controlled by the system given (1) environment and system moves in the Boolean game, and (2) environment values (consistent with the environment move). Finally, we plan to study how to extend $LTL_\mathcal{T}$ with controlled transfer of data accross time preserving decidability.

References

1. Alur, R., et al.: Syntax-guided synthesis. In: Proceedings of Formal Methods in Computer-Aided Design, (FMCAD) 2013, Portland, OR, USA, October 20–23, 2013, pp. 1–8. IEEE (2013)
2. Bendík, J., S. Meel, K.S.: Counting maximal satisfiable subsets. In: Proceedings of the 35th AAAI Conference on Artificial Intelligence, (AAAI'21), pp. 3651–3660. AAAI Press (2021)

3. Bendík, J., Meel, K.S.: Counting minimal unsatisfiable subsets. In: Silva, A., Leino, K.R.M. (eds.) CAV 2021. LNCS, vol. 12760, pp. 313–336. Springer, Cham (2021). https://doi.org/10.1007/978-3-030-81688-9_15
4. Bloem, R., Chockler, H., Ebrahimi, M., Strichman, O.: Vacuity in synthesis. Formal Meth. Syst. Des. **57**(3), 473–495 (2021). https://doi.org/10.1007/s10703-021-00381-5
5. Bloem, R., Jobstmann, B., Piterman, N., Pnueli, A., Sa'ar, Y.: Synthesis of reactive(1) designs. J. Comput. Syst. Sci. **78**(3), 911–938 (2012)
6. Caulfield, B., Rabe, M.N., Seshia, S.A., Tripakis, S.: What's decidable about syntax-guided synthesis? CoRR, abs/1510.08393 (2015)
7. Cheng, C.-H., Lee, E.A.: Numerical LTL synthesis for cyber-physical systems. CoRR, abs/1307.3722 (2013)
8. Choi, W., Finkbeiner, B., Piskac, R., Santolucito, M.: Can reactive synthesis and syntax-guided synthesis be friends? In: Proceedings of the 43rd ACM SIGPLAN Int'l Conference on Programming Language Design and Implementation (PLD'22), pp. 229–243. ACM (2022)
9. Cooper, D.W.: Theorem proving in arithmetic without multiplication. Mach. Intell. **7**(2), 91–100 (1972)
10. de Moura, L., Bjørner, N.: Z3: An Efficient SMT Solver. In: Ramakrishnan, C.R., Rehof, J. (eds.) TACAS 2008. LNCS, vol. 4963, pp. 337–340. Springer, Heidelberg (2008). https://doi.org/10.1007/978-3-540-78800-3_24
11. Demri, S., D'Souza, D.: An automata-theoretic approach to constraint LTL. Inf. Comput. **205**(3), 380–415 (2007)
12. Rachel Faran, R., Kupferman, O.: LTL with arithmetic and its applications in reasoning about hierarchical systems. In: Proceedings of the 22nd International Conference on Logic for Programming, Artificial Intelligence and Reasoning, (LPAR-22.), Awassa, Ethiopia, 16–21 November 2018, vol. 57 of EPiC Series in Computing, pp. 343–362. EasyChair (2018)
13. Farzan, A., Kincaid, Z.: Strategy synthesis for linear arithmetic games. Proc. ACM Program. Lang. **2**(POPL), 61:1–61:30 (2018)
14. Finkbeiner, B.: Synthesis of reactive systems. In: Esparza, J., Grumberg, O., Sickert, S., eds, Dependable Software Systems Engineering, vol. 45 of NATO Science for Peace and Security Series - D: Information and Communication Security, pp. 72–98. IOS Press (2016)
15. Finkbeiner, Bernd, Heim, Philippe, Passing, Noemi: Temporal Stream Logic modulo Theories. In: FoSSaCS 2022. LNCS, vol. 13242, pp. 325–346. Springer, Cham (2022). https://doi.org/10.1007/978-3-030-99253-8_17
16. Finkbeiner, B., Klein, F., Piskac, R., Santolucito, M.: Temporal Stream Logic: Synthesis Beyond the Bools. In: Dillig, I., Tasiran, S. (eds.) CAV 2019. LNCS, vol. 11561, pp. 609–629. Springer, Cham (2019). https://doi.org/10.1007/978-3-030-25540-4_35
17. Finkbeiner, B., Schewe, S.: Bounded synthesis. Int. J. Softw. Tools Technol. Transf. **15**(5–6), 519–539 (2013)
18. Gacek, A., Katis, A., Whalen, M.W., Backes, J., Cofer, D.: Towards Realizability Checking of Contracts Using Theories. In: Havelund, K., Holzmann, G., Joshi, R. (eds.) NFM 2015. LNCS, vol. 9058, pp. 173–187. Springer, Cham (2015). https://doi.org/10.1007/978-3-319-17524-9_13
19. Gianola, A., Gigante. N.: LTL modulo theories over finite traces: modeling, verification, open questions. In: Proceedings of the 4th Workshop on Artificial Intelligence and Formal Verification, Logic, Automata, and Synthesis, vol. 3311 of CEUR Workshop Proceedings, pp. 13–19, CEUR-WS.org (2022)

20. Grädel, E., Thomas, W., Wilke, T. (eds.): Automata Logics, and Infinite Games. LNCS, vol. 2500. Springer, Heidelberg (2002). https://doi.org/10.1007/3-540-36387-4

21. Jacobs, S.: The 4th reactive synthesis competition (SYNTCOMP 2017): Benchmarks, participants & results. In: Proceedings of the 6th Workshop on Synthesis (SYNT@CAV 2017), vol. 260 of EPTCS, pp. 116–143 (2017)

22. Katis, A., Fedyukovich, G., Gacek, A., Backes, J.D., Gurfinkel, A., Whalen. M.W.: Synthesis from assume-guarantee contracts using skolemized proofs of realizability. CoRR, abs/1610.05867 (2016)

23. Katis, A., Fedyukovich, G., Guo, H., Gacek, A., Backes, J., Gurfinkel, A., Whalen, M.W.: Validity-Guided Synthesis of Reactive Systems from Assume-Guarantee Contracts. In: Beyer, D., Huisman, M. (eds.) TACAS 2018. LNCS, vol. 10806, pp. 176–193. Springer, Cham (2018). https://doi.org/10.1007/978-3-319-89963-3_10

24. Liffiton, M.H., Previti, A., Malik, A., Marques-Silva, J.: Fast, flexible MUS enumeration. Constraints An Int. J. $21(2)$, 223–250 (2016)

25. Maderbacher, B., Bloem, R.:Reactive synthesis modulo theories using abstraction refinement. In: 22nd Formal Methods in Computer-Aided Design, (FMCAD'22), pp 315–324. IEEE (2022)

26. Manna, Z., Pnueli, A.: Temporal verification of reactive systems - safety. Springer, Springer New York, NY (1995). https://doi.org/10.1007/978-1-4612-422-2

27. Meyer, P.J., Sickert, S., Luttenberger, M.: Strix: Explicit Reactive Synthesis Strikes Back! In: Chockler, H., Weissenbacher, G. (eds.) CAV 2018. LNCS, vol. 10981, pp. 578–586. Springer, Cham (2018). https://doi.org/10.1007/978-3-319-96145-3_31

28. Piterman, N., Pnueli, A., Sa'ar, Y.: Synthesis of Reactive(1) Designs. In: Emerson, E.A., Namjoshi, K.S. (eds.) VMCAI 2006. LNCS, vol. 3855, pp. 364–380. Springer, Heidelberg (2005). https://doi.org/10.1007/11609773_24

29. Pnueli, A.: The temporal logic of programs. In: Proceedings of the 18th IEEE Symposium on Foundations of Computer Science (FOCS'77), pp. 46–67. IEEE CS Press (1977)

30. Pnueli, A., Rosner, R.: On the synthesis of a reactive module. In: Proceedings of the 16th Annual ACM Symposium on Principles of Programming Languages (POPL'89), pp. 179–190. ACM Press (1989)

31. Pnueli, A., Rosner, R.: On the synthesis of an asynchronous reactive module. In: Ausiello, G., Dezani-Ciancaglini, M., Della Rocca, S.R. (eds.) ICALP 1989. LNCS, vol. 372, pp. 652–671. Springer, Heidelberg (1989). https://doi.org/10.1007/BFb0035790

32. Tarski, A.: Theorem proving in arithmetic without multiplication. University of California Press (1951)

33. Thomas, W.: Church's Problem and a Tour through Automata Theory. In: Avron, A., Dershowitz, N., Rabinovich, A. (eds.) Pillars of Computer Science. LNCS, vol. 4800, pp. 635–655. Springer, Heidelberg (2008). https://doi.org/10.1007/978-3-540-78127-1_35

34. Walker, A., Ryzhyk, L.: Predicate abstraction for reactive synthesis. In Proceedings f the 14th Formal Methods in Computer-Aided Design, (FMCAD 2014), Lausanne, Switzerland, October 21–24, 2014, pp.19–226. IEEE (2014)

Certified Verification for Algebraic Abstraction

Ming-Hsien Tsai[4], Yu-Fu Fu[2], Jiaxiang Liu[5(⊠)], Xiaomu Shi[3], Bow-Yaw Wang[1], and Bo-Yin Yang[1]

[1] Academia Sinica, Taipei, Taiwan
{bywang,byyang}@iis.sinica.edu.tw
[2] Georgia Institute of Technology, Atlanta, USA
yufu@gatech.edu
[3] Institute of Software, Chinese Academy of Sciences, Beijing, China
xshi0811@gmail.com
[4] National Institute of Cyber Security, Taipei, Taiwan
mhtsai208@gmail.com
[5] Shenzhen University, Shenzhen, China
jiaxiang0924@gmail.com

Abstract. We present a certified algebraic abstraction technique for verifying bit-accurate non-linear integer computations. In algebraic abstraction, programs are lifted to polynomial equations in the abstract domain. Algebraic techniques are employed to analyze abstract polynomial programs; SMT QF_BV solvers are adopted for bit-accurate analysis of soundness conditions. We explain how to verify our abstraction algorithm and certify verification results. Our hybrid technique has verified non-linear computations in various security libraries such as BITCOIN and OPENSSL. We also report the certified verification of Number-Theoretic Transform programs from the post-quantum cryptosystem KYBER.

1 Introduction

Bit-accurate non-linear integer computations are infamously hard to verify. Conventional bit-accurate techniques such as bit blasting do not work well for non-linear computations. Approximation techniques through floating-point computation on the other hand are inaccurate. Non-linear integer computation nonetheless is essential to computer cryptography. Analyzing complex non-linear computation in cryptographic libraries is still one of the most challenging problems of the utmost importance today.

In this paper, we address the verification problem through algebraic abstraction. In algebraic abstraction, abstract programs are represented by polynomial equations. Non-linear computation about abstract polynomial programs is analyzed algebraically and hence more efficiently through techniques from commutative algebra. Algebraic abstraction however is unsound due to overflow in bounded integer computation. We characterize soundness conditions with queries using the Quantifier-Free Bit-Vector (QF_BV) logic from Satisfiability Modulo Theories (SMT) [2]. SMT solvers are then used to check soundness conditions before applying algebraic abstraction.

Our hybrid technique takes advantages of both algebraic and bit-accurate analyses. Non-linear algebraic properties are verified algebraically. Polynomials are computed

© The Author(s) 2023
C. Enea and A. Lal (Eds.): CAV 2023, LNCS 13966, pp. 329–349, 2023.
https://doi.org/10.1007/978-3-031-37709-9_16

and analyzed by algorithms from commutative algebra. Coefficients, variables and arithmetic functions are atomic in such algorithms. Our algebraic analysis is hence very efficient for non-linear computation. Soundness conditions, on the other hand, require bit-accurate analysis. Our technique applies SMT QF_BV solvers to check soundness conditions. By combining algebraic with bit-accurate analyses, algebraic abstraction successfully verifies non-linear computation in real-world cryptographic programs.

Cryptographic programs undoubtedly are widely deployed critical software. Errors in their verification need to be minimized. To this end, we use the proof assistant COQ [4] to verify the soundness theorem for algebraic abstraction. To ensure the correctness of external algebraic and bit-accurate analysis tools, results from external tools are certified in our technique as well. With verified abstraction and certified external results, verification of bit-accurate non-linear integer computation through algebraic abstraction is certified. We explain how to certify our hybrid verification technique.

We evaluate our certified technique with cryptographic programs from security libraries in BITCOIN [27], BORINGSSL [8,12], NSS [20], OPENSSL [23] and PQCRYPTO-SIDH [18]. These programs compute field and group operations in elliptic curve cryptography. We also verify Number-Theoretic Transform (NTT) programs from the post-quantum cryptosystem KYBER [6]. In lattice-based post-quantum cryptography, computation in polynomial rings is needed. NTT is a discrete variant of the Fast Fourier Transform used for polynomial multiplication in KYBER. Our certified algebraic abstraction technique verifies cryptographic programs from elliptic curve and post-quantum cryptography successfully. Our contributions are summarized as follows.

- We detail algebraic abstraction for checking non-linear modular equations with multiple moduli;
- We certify algebraic abstraction and its verification;
- We report certified verification results for 39 real-world cryptographic programs in elliptic curve and post-quantum cryptography.

Related Work. GFVERIF employs an ad hoc technique to verify non-linear computation in cryptographic programs with a computer algebra system [3]. CRYPTOLINE [9,24,29] is a tool designed for the specification and verification of cryptographic assembly codes. Its verification algorithm utilizes computer algebra systems in addition to SMT solvers. CRYPTOLINE is also leveraged to verify cryptographic C programs [9,17]. The optimized KYBER NTT program for avx2 is verified in [15], but the underlying verification algorithm is left unexplained. None of these works certified their verification results. Users had to trust these verification tools. BVCRYPTOLINE certifies algebraic abstraction but not soundness conditions [29]. It does not allow multiple moduli in modular equations either. Particularly, it cannot concisely specify NTT by the Chinese remainder theorem over polynomial rings. Compared with these works, our technique admits modular equations with multiple moduli in assumptions and assertions, and is fully certified. To explicate our advantages, consider the specification of multiplication in the field $\mathbb{Z}_{p434}/\langle x^2 + 1 \rangle$ where $p434$ is a prime number. An element in the field is of the form $u_0 + u_1 x$ where $x^2 + 1 = 0$. To specify $r_0 + r_1 x$ is the product of $u_0 + u_1 x$ and $v_0 + v_1 x$, one can write two modular equations with one modulo: $r_0 \equiv u_0 v_0 - u_1 v_1 \bmod [p434]$ and $r_1 \equiv u_0 v_1 + u_1 v_0 \bmod [p434]$. With multiple moduli, we write $r_0 + r_1 x \equiv (u_0 + u_1 x)(v_0 + v_1 x) \bmod [p434, x^2 + 1]$ succinctly. Our simple specifications are most useful for complicated fields such as $\mathbb{Z}_{p381}/\langle x^2 + 1, y^3 - x - 1, z^2 - y \rangle$. Each element of the complex field is of the form $\sum u_{i,j,k} x^i y^j z^k$ with $0 \leq i, k < 2$ and $0 \leq j < 3$. Twelve modular equations are needed previously. One modular equation with multiple moduli suffices to specify its field multiplication in this work. Furthermore, our technique is verified in CoQ. The correctness of our abstraction algorithm and soundness theorem are formally proven in CoQ. We also show how to certify results from external tools. In summary, the correctness of algebraic abstraction algorithm is verified and answers from external tools are certified. Verification results are therefore fully certified. We believe this is the best guarantee a model checker can offer. Our verified model checker is sufficiently practical to verify industrial cryptographic programs too!

Analysis of linear polynomial programs was discussed, for instance, in [21, 22]. The reduction from the root entailment problem to the ideal membership problem is discussed in [14]. In this work, the computer algebra system SINGULAR [13] is employed to compute standard bases of ideals and certificates. The certified SMT QF_BV solver COQQFBV [26] is adopted to certify soundness conditions.

The paper is organized as follows. Section 2 gives the needed backgrounds. It is followed by the syntax and semantics of the language TOYLANG. An implementation of the unsigned Montgomery reduction is given as a running example (Sect. 3). Section 4 presents algebraic abstraction and its verification algorithms. We briefly describe certified verification of algebraic abstraction in Sect. 5. Section 6 shows experimental results of real-world cryptographic programs. We conclude in Sect. 7.

2   Preliminaries

Let $\mathbb{N}$ and $\mathbb{Z}$ denote the set of non-negative and all integers respectively. Fix a set of variables $\overline{\mathbf{x}}$. We write $\mathbb{Z}[\overline{\mathbf{x}}]$ for the set of polynomials in variables $\overline{\mathbf{x}}$ with coefficients in $\mathbb{Z}$. A polynomial *equation* is of the form $e = e'$ with $e, e' \in \mathbb{Z}[\overline{\mathbf{x}}]$; a polynomial *modular equation* is of the form $e \equiv e' \bmod [f_0, f_1, \ldots, f_m]$ with $e, e', f_0, f_1, \ldots, f_m \in \mathbb{Z}[\overline{\mathbf{x}}]$. A *valuation* ρ of $\overline{\mathbf{x}}$ is a mapping from $\overline{\mathbf{x}}$ to $\mathbb{Z}$. Given a valuation ρ, a polynomial e *evaluates* to the integer $e[\rho]$ by replacing every variable x with $\rho(x)$. A valuation ρ is a *root* of the equation $e = e'$ if $(e - e')[\rho] = 0$. A valuation ρ is a *root* of the modular equation $e \equiv e' \bmod [f_0, f_1, \ldots, f_m]$ if $(e - e')[\rho] = z_0 f_0[\rho] + z_1 f_1[\rho] + \cdots + z_m f_m[\rho]$ for some $z_0, z_1, \ldots, z_m \in \mathbb{Z}$. A *(modular) equation* is an equation or a modular equation. A *system* of (modular) equations is a set of (modular) equations. A *root* of a system of (modular) equations is a common root of every (modular) equation in the system. Let Φ be a system of (modular) equations and ϕ a (modular) equation, roots of Φ *entail* roots of ϕ (written $\forall \overline{\mathbf{x}}. \Phi \implies \phi$) if all roots of Φ are also roots of ϕ. Given Φ and ϕ, the *root entailment* problem is to decide whether $\forall \overline{\mathbf{x}}. \Phi \implies \phi$.

An *ideal* in $\mathbb{Z}[\overline{\mathbf{x}}]$ generated by $f_0, f_1, \ldots, f_m \in \mathbb{Z}[\overline{\mathbf{x}}]$ is defined by $\langle f_0, f_1, \ldots, f_m \rangle = \{f_0 h_0 + f_1 h_1 + \cdots + f_m h_m | h_0, h_1, \ldots, h_m \in \mathbb{Z}[\overline{\mathbf{x}}]\}$. If $\langle f_0, f_1, \ldots, f_m \rangle$ and $\langle g_0, g_1, \ldots, g_n \rangle$ are ideals, define their *sum* $\langle f_0, f_1, \ldots, f_m \rangle + \langle g_0, g_1, \ldots, g_n \rangle = \langle f_0, f_1, \ldots, f_m, g_0, g_1, \ldots, g_n \rangle$. For instance, $\langle x \rangle = \{xf | f \in \mathbb{Z}[\overline{\mathbf{x}}]\}$ and $\langle 6 \rangle + \langle 10 \rangle = \langle 2 \rangle$. Given $f \in \mathbb{Z}[\overline{\mathbf{x}}]$ and an ideal I, the *ideal membership problem* is to decide whether $f \in I$.

A *bit-vector* is a bit sequence of a *width* w. A bit-vector denotes an integer between 0 and $2^w - 1$ inclusively using the most-significant-bit-first representation. The SMT QF_BV logic defines bit-vector functions. Assume bv_0 and bv_1 are bit-vectors of width w. The addition (*bvadd* bv_0 bv_1) and subtraction (*bvsub* bv_0 bv_1) functions return bit-vectors of width w representing the sum and difference respectively. The multiplication function (*bvmul* bv_0 bv_1) returns the least significant w bits of the product. The left shift function (*bvshl* bv_0 n) shifts bv_0 to the left by n bits; the logical right shift function (*bvlshr* bv_0 n) shifts bv_0 to the right by n bits. The zero extension function (*zero_extend* bv_0 n) appends n most significant 0's to bv_0. The extraction function (*bvextract* h l bv_0) extracts bits indexed h to l from bv_0 ($w > h \geq l \geq 0$). An SMT QF_BV *expression* is constructed from bit-vector values, variables, and functions. An SMT QF_BV *assertion* is of the form (*assert* $\bot$), (*assert* (= be be')), or (*assert* (*not* (= be be'))) with SMT QF_BV expressions be and be'. An SMT QF_BV *query* is a set of SMT QF_BV assertions. A *store* is a mapping from bit-vector variables to bit-vector values. An SMT QF_BV expression *evaluates* to a bit-vector value on a store. An SMT QF_BV assertion (*assert* (= be be')) is *satisfied* by a store if be and be' evaluate to the same bit-vector value on the store, and otherwise (*assert* (*not* (= be be'))) is satisfied. The SMT QF_BV assertion (*assert* $\bot$) is never satisfied. An SMT QF_BV query is *satisfiable* if all assertions are satisfied by a store.

3   TOYLANG

We consider a register transfer language called TOYLANG to illustrate algebraic abstraction. For clarity, many programming constructs are removed from TOYLANG. The language nevertheless is sufficiently expressive to implement Montgomery reduction [19], an indispensable algorithm found in real-world cryptographic programs.

3.1   Syntax and Semantics

The syntax of TOYLANG is shown in Fig. 1. For simplicity, we assume all numbers are unsigned and all variables are of widths 1 or w. Variables of width 1 are also called *bit* variables. An *atom* is a number or a variable.

$$
\begin{aligned}
\textit{Num } n &::= 0 \mid 1 \mid 2 \mid \cdots \quad \textit{Var } c, v ::= a \mid b \mid c \mid \cdots \quad \textit{Atom } a ::= \textit{Num} \mid \textit{Var} \\
\textit{Inst } s &::= \quad v \leftarrow \text{ADD } a_0\, a_1 \mid \quad v \leftarrow \text{ADC } a_0\, a_1\, d \mid \quad v \leftarrow \text{SUB } a_0\, a_1 \mid \\
& \quad\quad c : v \leftarrow \text{ADDS } a_0\, a_1 \mid c : v \leftarrow \text{ADCS } a_0\, a_1\, d \mid c : v \leftarrow \text{SUBS } a_0\, a_1 \mid \\
& \quad\quad v \leftarrow \text{MUL } a_0\, a_1 \mid \quad v \leftarrow \text{SHL } a_0\, n \mid \quad \text{ASSUME } q \mid \\
& \quad\quad v_H : v_L \leftarrow \text{MULL } a_0\, a_1 \mid \quad v \leftarrow \text{SHR } a_0\, n \mid \quad \boxed{\text{ASSERT } q} \\
\textit{Exp } e, f &::= n \mid v \mid e_0 + e_1 \mid e_0 - e_1 \mid e_0 \times e_1 \mid e_0^n \\
\textit{MEqn } q &::= e_0 = e_1 \mid e_0 \equiv e_1 \bmod [f_0, f_1, \ldots] \\
\textit{Program } P &::= \quad s \quad \mid \quad s\, P
\end{aligned}
$$

Fig. 1. TOYLANG – Syntax

TOYLANG supports several arithmetic instructions: addition (ADD), carrying addition (ADDS), addition-with-carry (ADC), carrying addition-with-carry (ADCS), subtraction (SUB), borrowing subtraction (SUBS), half- (MUL) and full-multiplication (MULL). Moreover, logical left shift (SHL) and logical right shift (SHR) instructions are allowed. In addition to assignments, (modular) equations can be specified in assumption (ASSUME) or assertion (ASSERT) instructions. A program is a sequence of instructions. We assume ASSERT instructions can only appear at the end of programs. They specify a (modular) equation to be verified and thus are emphasized with a framed box.

$$\frac{bv = bvadd \; [\![a_0]\!]_\sigma \; [\![a_1]\!]_\sigma}{(\!(\sigma, v \leftarrow ADD \; a_0 \; a_1, \sigma[v \mapsto bv]\!)\!)} \qquad \frac{bv = bvadd \; (bvadd \; [\![a_0]\!]_\sigma \; [\![a_1]\!]_\sigma) \; (zero\_extend \; [\![d]\!]_\sigma \; (w-1))}{(\!(\sigma, v \leftarrow ADC \; a_0 \; a_1 \; d, \sigma[v \mapsto bv]\!)\!)}$$

$$\frac{bvx = bvadd \; (zero\_extend \; [\![a_0]\!]_\sigma \; 1) \; (zero\_extend \; [\![a_1]\!]_\sigma \; 1)}{(\!(\sigma, c : v \leftarrow ADDS \; a_0 \; a_1, \sigma[c \mapsto bvextract \; w \; w \; bvx, v \mapsto bvextract \; (w-1) \; 0 \; bvx]\!)\!)}$$

$$\frac{bvx = bvadd \; (bvadd \; (zero\_extend \; [\![a_0]\!]_\sigma \; 1) \; (zero\_extend \; [\![a_1]\!]_\sigma \; 1)) \; (zero\_extend \; [\![d]\!]_\sigma \; w))}{(\!(\sigma, c : v \leftarrow ADCS \; a_0 \; a_1 \; d, \sigma[c \mapsto bvextract \; w \; w \; bvx, v \mapsto bvextract \; (w-1) \; 0 \; bvx]\!)\!)}$$

$$\frac{bv = bvsub \; [\![a_0]\!]_\sigma \; [\![a_1]\!]_\sigma}{(\!(\sigma, v \leftarrow SUB \; a_0 \; a_1, \sigma[v \mapsto bv]\!)\!)}$$

$$\frac{bvx = bvsub \; (zero\_extend \; [\![a_0]\!]_\sigma \; 1) \; (zero\_extend \; [\![a_1]\!]_\sigma \; 1)}{(\!(\sigma, c : v \leftarrow SUBS \; a_0 \; a_1, \sigma[c \mapsto bvextract \; w \; w \; bvx, v \mapsto bvextract \; (w-1) \; 0 \; bvx]\!)\!)}$$

$$\frac{bv = bvshl \; [\![a_0]\!]_\sigma \; n}{(\!(\sigma, v \leftarrow SHL \; a_0 \; n, \sigma[v \mapsto bv]\!)\!)} \quad \frac{bv = bvlshr \; [\![a_0]\!]_\sigma \; n}{(\!(\sigma, v \leftarrow SHR \; a_0 \; n, \sigma[v \mapsto bv]\!)\!)} \quad \frac{bv = bvmul \; [\![a_0]\!]_\sigma \; [\![a_1]\!]_\sigma}{(\!(\sigma, v \leftarrow MUL \; a_0 \; a_1, \sigma[v \mapsto bv]\!)\!)}$$

$$\frac{bv = bvmul \; (zero\_extend \; [\![a_0]\!]_\sigma \; w) \; (zero\_extend \; [\![a_1]\!]_\sigma \; w)}{(\!(\sigma, v_H : v_L \leftarrow MULL \; a_0 \; a_1, \sigma[v_H \mapsto bvextract \; (2w-1) \; w \; bv, v_L \mapsto bvextract \; (w-1) \; 0 \; bv]\!)\!)}$$

$$\frac{\sigma \models q}{(\!(\sigma, ASSUME \; q, \sigma)\!)} \quad \frac{\sigma \models q}{(\!(\sigma, \boxed{ASSERT \; q}, \sigma)\!)} \quad \frac{\sigma \not\models q}{(\!(\sigma, \boxed{ASSERT \; q}, fail)\!)} \quad \frac{(\!(\sigma, s, \sigma'')\!) \quad (\!(\sigma'', P, \sigma')\!)}{(\!(\sigma, s \; P, \sigma')\!)}$$

Fig. 2. TOYLANG – Semantics

Let σ be a store. We write $\sigma[v \mapsto bv]$ for the store obtained by mapping v to the bit-vector bv and other variables u to $\sigma(u)$. $[\![v]\!]_\sigma$ represents the bit-vector $\sigma(v)$ for any variable v; otherwise, $[\![n]\!]_\sigma$ is the bit-vector representing the number n of width w.

The semantics of TOYLANG is defined with SMT QF_BV bit-vector functions (Fig. 2). In the figure, $(\!(\sigma, s, \sigma')\!)$ denotes that the store σ' is obtained after executing the instruction s on the store σ. The addition instruction ADD corresponds to the bit-vector addition function. For the addition with carry instruction, the carry bit is extended with $w - 1$ zeros and added to the sum of the first two operands. The two carrying addition instructions compute the bit-vector sums of width $w + 1$. The most significant bit is stored in the output carry bit. Subtraction instructions are similar; their semantics are defined with the bit-vector subtraction function $bvsub$ instead. The semantics of SHL and SHR instructions are defined by corresponding bit-vector functions $bvshl$ and $bvlshr$

respectively. The semantics of half-multiplication instruction MUL uses the bit-vector multiplication function *bvmul*. For full-multiplication, both operands are extended to width $2w$ before computing their product.

$$\{\!|n|\!\}_\sigma = n \qquad\qquad \{\!|v|\!\}_\sigma = \mathsf{toZ}([\![v]\!]_\sigma)$$

$$\{\!|e_0 \pm e_1|\!\}_\sigma = \{\!|e_0|\!\}_\sigma \pm \{\!|e_1|\!\}_\sigma \qquad \{\!|e_0 \times e_1|\!\}_\sigma = \{\!|e_0|\!\}_\sigma \cdot \{\!|e_1|\!\}_\sigma$$

$$\frac{\{\!|e_0|\!\}_\sigma = \{\!|e_1|\!\}_\sigma}{\sigma \models e_0 = e_1} \qquad \frac{\{\!|e_0|\!\}_\sigma - \{\!|e_1|\!\}_\sigma \in \langle\{\!|f_0|\!\}_\sigma, \{\!|f_1|\!\}_\sigma, \ldots, \{\!|f_m|\!\}_\sigma\rangle}{\sigma \models e_0 \equiv e_1 \bmod [f_0, f_1, \ldots, f_m]}$$

Fig. 3. Semantics of (Modular) Equations

The ASSUME instruction filters computations by (modular) equations. Figure 3 defines when a store satisfies a (modular) equation. A number n denotes a non-negative integer. A variable denotes the integer $\mathsf{toZ}([\![v]\!]_\sigma)$ represented by the corresponding bit-vector $[\![v]\!]_\sigma$ in the store. Arithmetic operations denote corresponding integer operations. Particularly, the integer $\{\!|e|\!\}_\sigma$ is exact and not necessarily less than 2^w. Equality denotes integer equality. σ satisfies $e_0 \equiv e_1 \bmod [f_0, f_1, \ldots, f_m]$ if $\{\!|e_0|\!\}_\sigma - \{\!|e_1|\!\}_\sigma$ is in the ideal generated by $\{\!|f_0|\!\}_\sigma, \{\!|f_1|\!\}_\sigma, \ldots, \{\!|f_m|\!\}_\sigma$. The ASSERT instruction checks if the current store satisfies the given (modular) equation. The computation resumes if it *succeeds*. It is an error if the ASSERT instruction *fails*.

(* $R = 2^{64}, 0 \le T < R^2$ *)   (* $T = 2^{64}T_H + T_L$ *)

(* $N \cdot N' + 1 \equiv 0 \bmod R$ *)   ASSUME $N \times N' + 1 \equiv 0 \bmod [2^{64}]$

$m \leftarrow ((T \bmod R) \cdot N') \bmod R$ $m \qquad \leftarrow$ MUL T_L N'

$t \leftarrow (T + m \cdot N)/R$ $mN_H : mN_L \leftarrow$ MULL m N

$carry : t_L \quad \leftarrow$ ADDS T_L mN_L

$c : t_H \qquad \leftarrow$ ADCS T_H mN_H $carry$

ASSERT $t_L \equiv 0 \bmod [2^{64}]$

ASSUME $t_L = 0$

(* $t \cdot R \equiv T \bmod N$ *)   ASSERT $(c \times 2^{64} + t_H) \times 2^{64} \equiv T_H \times 2^{64} + T_L \bmod [N]$

(a) Algorithm   (b) TOYLANG code

Fig. 4. Simplified Montgomery Reduction

Montgomery reduction algorithm is widely used to compute remainders without division [19]. Figure 4a shows a simplified unsigned Montgomery reduction algorithm.[1] Suppose we want to compute the remainder of a number $0 \le T < R^2$ modulo N on 64-bit architectures with $R = 2^{64}$. Montgomery reduction algorithm needs another number N' with $NN' + 1 \equiv 0 \bmod R$ as an input. It first computes $m = ((T \bmod R)N') \bmod R$ and then $t = (T + mN)/R$. Observe that the remainder and quotient divided by

---

[1] The complete algorithm requires range analysis not discussed in this work.

$R = 2^{64}$ amount to bit masking and shifting respectively. Arithmetic division is never used. To prove $tR \equiv T \bmod N$, we first show $T + mN \equiv 0 \bmod R$. Observe $T + mN = T + (((T \bmod R)N') \bmod R)N \equiv T + TN'N \equiv T(1 + N'N) \equiv 0 \bmod R$. Therefore, $T + mN$ is a multiple of R and $t = (T + mN)/R$ is an integer. Hence $tR = T + mN \equiv T \bmod N$.

In the TOYLANG implementation (Fig. 4b), we represent T by two 64-bit variables T_H and T_L with $T = 2^{64}T_H + T_L$. Hence $T_L = T \bmod 2^{64}$. m is computed by the half-multiplication instruction MUL. The full-multiplication computes the product mN of m and N. The following two addition instructions compute the sum of T and the product mN. After adding T, the least significant 64 bits (t_L) should be zeros. We hence assert $t_L \equiv 0 \bmod [2^{64}]$. If the assertion succeeds, t_L is in fact 0 since it is a 64-bit variable. We thus assume $t_L = 0$. The last assertion checks that the result $2^{64}(2^{64}c + t_H)$ is indeed congruent to T modulo N.

4 Algebraic Abstraction

Algebraic abstraction is a technique to lift computation to an algebraic domain. In the abstract algebraic domain, program instructions are transformed to polynomial equations. Computation in turn is characterized by the roots of systems of polynomial equations. Algebraic abstraction hence allows us to apply algebraic tools from commutative algebra. The abstraction technique requires programs in the static single assignment form. We hence assume input programs are in the static single assignment form.

$$\lceil v \leftarrow \text{ADD } a_0\ a_1 \rceil = \{v = a_0 + a_1\} \qquad \lceil v \leftarrow \text{ADC } a_0\ a_1\ d \rceil = \{v = a_0 + a_1 + d\}$$
$$\lceil c : v \leftarrow \text{ADDS } a_0\ a_1 \rceil = \{c \cdot (c - 1) = 0, c \cdot 2^w + v = a_0 + a_1\}$$
$$\lceil c : v \leftarrow \text{ADCS } a_0\ a_1\ d \rceil = \{c \cdot (c - 1) = 0, c \cdot 2^w + v = a_0 + a_1 + d\}$$
$$\lceil v \leftarrow \text{SUB } a_0\ a_1 \rceil = \{v = a_0 - a_1\} \qquad \lceil v \leftarrow \text{MUL } a_0\ a_1 \rceil = \{v = a_0 \cdot a_1\}$$
$$\lceil c : v \leftarrow \text{SUBS } a_0\ a_1 \rceil = \{c \cdot (c - 1) = 0, v = a_0 - a_1 + c \cdot 2^w\}$$
$$\lceil v_H : v_L \leftarrow \text{MULL } a_0\ a_1 \rceil = \{v_H \cdot 2^w + v_L = a_0 \cdot a_1\}$$
$$\lceil v \leftarrow \text{SHL } a\ n \rceil = \{v = a \cdot 2^n\} \qquad \lceil v \leftarrow \text{SHR } a\ n \rceil = \{v \cdot 2^n = a\}$$
$$\lceil \text{ASSUME } q \rceil = \{q\} \qquad\qquad \lceil s\ P \rceil = \lceil s \rceil \cup \lceil P \rceil$$

Fig. 5. Algebraic Abstraction

Figure 5 lifts TOYLANG instructions to polynomial equations. Intuitively, we would like the semantics of each instruction characterized by roots of corresponding polynomial equations. For instance, $v \leftarrow \text{ADD } a_0\ a_1$ is lifted to $v = a_0 + a_1$. The ADC instruction is similar. The carrying addition instruction $c : v \leftarrow \text{ADDS } a_0\ a_1$ is lifted to two equations: $c \cdot (c - 1) = 0$ and $c \cdot 2^w + v = a_0 + a_1$. Since c is a carry, it must be 0 or 1, and hence a root of $c \cdot (c - 1) = 0$. The carrying addition-with-carry instruction ADCS is similar, as well as subtraction instructions SUB and SUBS.

The half-multiplication instruction $v \leftarrow \text{MUL } a_0\ a_1$ is lifted to $v = a_0 \cdot a_1$; the full-multiplication instruction $v_H : v_L \leftarrow \text{MULL } a_0\ a_1$ corresponds to $v_H \cdot 2^w + v_L = a_0 \cdot a_1$.

$$\text{ASSUME } N \times N' + 1 \equiv 0 \bmod [2^{64}] \qquad N \times N' + 1 \equiv 0 \bmod [2^{64}]$$

$$m \quad\leftarrow \text{MUL } T_L \; N' \qquad\qquad m = T_L \cdot N',$$

$$mN_H : mN_L \leftarrow \text{MULL } m \; N \qquad\qquad mN_H \cdot 2^{64} + mN_L = m \cdot N,$$

$$carry \cdot (carry - 1) = 0,$$

$$carry : t_L \quad\leftarrow \text{ADDS } T_L \; mN_L \qquad carry \cdot 2^{64} + t_L = T_L + mN_L,$$

$$c \cdot (c - 1) = 0,$$

$$c : t_H \quad\leftarrow \text{ADCS } T_H \; mN_H \; carry \qquad c \cdot 2^{64} + t_H = T_H + mN_H + carry,$$

$$\boxed{\text{ASSERT } t_L \equiv 0 \bmod [2^{64}]}$$

$$\text{ASSUME } t_L = 0 \qquad\qquad\qquad\qquad\qquad t_L = 0$$

$$\boxed{\text{ASSERT } (c \times 2^{64} + t_H) \times 2^{64} \equiv T_H \times 2^{64} + T_L \bmod [N]}$$

Fig. 6. Abstract Montgomery Reduction

The logical left shift instruction $v \leftarrow \text{SHL } a \; n$ corresponds to $v = a \cdot 2^n$; the logical right shift instruction $v \leftarrow \text{SHR } a \; n$ is lifted to $v \cdot 2^n = a$. The ASSUME q instruction is lifted to the (modular) equation q. All computations thus must satisfy q. A TOYLANG program is lifted to the system of (modular) equations from its instructions. The system of (modular) equations is called the *abstract polynomial program*. Figure 6 shows the abstract polynomial program for the Montgomery reduction program.

4.1 Soundness Conditions

Algebraic abstraction in Fig. 5 however is unsound. The TOYLANG semantics is defined over bounded integers of bit width w. Polynomial equations in algebraic abstraction are interpreted over integers. When overflow occurs in TOYLANG instructions, for instance, its computation is not captured by corresponding polynomial equations. Consider the instruction $v \leftarrow \text{ADD } 2^{w-1} \; 2^{w-1}$. By the TOYLANG semantics, v has the bit-vector value $bvadd \; [\![2^{w-1}]\!]_\sigma [\![2^{w-1}]\!]_\sigma = 0$ after execution. Clearly, 0 is not a root of the equation $v = 2^{w-1} + 2^{w-1}$. The abstraction is unsound.

In order to check soundness for algebraic abstraction, we define soundness conditions for TOYLANG instructions to ensure that all computations are captured by corresponding polynomial equations. Intuitively, we give an SMT QF_BV query for each instruction in a TOYLANG program such that the query is satisfiable if and only if the computation at the instruction can overflow.

To this end, we first use SMT QF_BV logic to characterize computations in TOY-LANG programs. Recall TOYLANG programs are in the static single assignment form. Figure 7 defines an SMT QF_BV query $\lfloor P \rceil$ for any TOYLANG program P. Except the ASSUME instruction, the figure follows the semantics of TOYLANG. For instance, $\lfloor v \leftarrow \text{ADC } a_0 \; a_1 \; d \rceil$ asserts v equal to the bit-vector sum of a_0 and a_1 with d extended by $w - 1$ zeros in the SMT QF_BV query. Others are similar. It is not hard to see that all computations of a TOYLANG program satisfy the corresponding SMT QF_BV query.

Lemma 1. *Let P be a TOYLANG program without ASSERT instructions and σ, σ' stores with $(\!|\sigma, P, \sigma'|\!)$. Then the SMT QF_BV query $\lfloor P \rceil$ is satisfied by the store σ'.*

$$\lfloor v \leftarrow \text{ADD } a_0 \ a_1 \rceil = \{(assert \ (= \ v \ (bvadd \ a_0 \ a_1)))\}$$

$$\lfloor v \leftarrow \text{ADC } a_0 \ a_1 \ d \rceil = \{(assert \ (= \ v \ (bvadd \ (bvadd \ a_0 \ a_1) \ (zero\_extend \ d \ (w - 1)))))\}$$

$$\lfloor c : v \leftarrow \text{ADDS } a_0 \ a_1 \rceil = \left\{ \begin{array}{l} (assert \ (= \ c \ (bvextract \ w \ w \ bvx))), \\ (assert \ (= \ v \ (bvextract \ (w - 1) \ 0 \ bvx))) \end{array} \right\}$$
$$\text{where } bvx \text{ is } (bvadd \ (zero\_extend \ a_0 \ 1) \ (zero\_extend \ a_1 \ 1))$$

$$\lfloor c : v \leftarrow \text{ADCS } a_0 \ a_1 \ d \rceil = \left\{ \begin{array}{l} (assert \ (= \ c \ (bvextract \ w \ w \ bvx))), \\ (assert \ (= \ v \ (bvextract \ (w - 1) \ 0 \ bvx))) \end{array} \right\}$$
$$\text{where } bvx \text{ is } (bvadd \ (bvadd \ (zero\_extend \ a_0 \ 1) \ (zero\_extend \ a_1 \ 1))$$
$$(zero\_extend \ d \ w))$$

$$\lfloor v \leftarrow \text{SUB } a_0 \ a_1 \rceil = \{(assert \ (= \ v \ (bvsub \ a_0 \ a_1)))\}$$

$$\lfloor c : v \leftarrow \text{SUBS } a_0 \ a_1 \rceil = \left\{ \begin{array}{l} (assert \ (= \ c \ (bvextract \ w \ w \ bvx))), \\ (assert \ (= \ v \ (bvextract \ (w - 1) \ 0 \ bvx))) \end{array} \right\}$$
$$\text{where } bvx \text{ is } (bvsub \ (zero\_extend \ a_0 \ 1) \ (zero\_extend \ a_1 \ 1))$$

$$\lfloor v \leftarrow \text{MUL } a_0 \ a_1 \rceil = \{(assert \ (= \ v \ (bvmul \ a_0 \ a_1)))\}$$

$$\lfloor v_H : v_L \leftarrow \text{MULL } a_0 \ a_1 \rceil = \left\{ \begin{array}{l} (assert \ (= \ v_H \ (bvextract \ (2w - 1) \ w \ bvx))), \\ (assert \ (= \ v_L \ (bvextract \ (w - 1) \ 0 \ bvx))) \end{array} \right\}$$
$$\text{where } bvx \text{ is } (bvmul \ (zero\_extend \ a_0 \ w) \ (zero\_extend \ a_1 \ w))$$

$$\lfloor v \leftarrow \text{SHL } a_0 \ n \rceil = \{(assert \ (= \ v \ (bvshl \ a_0 \ n)))\}$$

$$\lfloor v \leftarrow \text{SHR } a_0 \ n \rceil = \{(assert \ (= \ v \ (bvlshr \ a_0 \ n)))\}$$

$$\lfloor \text{ASSUME } q \rceil = \emptyset$$

$$\lfloor s \ P \rceil = \lfloor s \rceil \cup \lfloor P \rceil$$

Fig. 7. Soundness Conditions I

Our next task is to define SMT QF_BV queries for instructions such that their algebraic abstraction is unsound if and only if the corresponding SMT QF_BV query is satisfiable (Fig. 8). The instruction $v \leftarrow \text{ADD } a_0 \ a_1$ is lifted to $v = a_0 + a_1$. The abstraction is unsound when there is carry. That is, $(bvextract \ w \ w \ (bvadd \ (zero\_extend \ a_0 \ 1) \ (zero\_extend \ a_1 \ 1)))$ is 1. The instructions ADC and SUB are similar. Algebraic abstraction for the instructions ADDS, ADCS and SUBS is always sound. Their corresponding SMT QF_BV queries are not satisfiable ($assert \ \bot$). For the half-multiplication $v \leftarrow \text{MUL } a_0 \ a_1$, its abstraction $v = a_0 \cdot a_1$ is unsound when the most significant w bits of the product of a_0 and a_1 are not all zeros. The corresponding SMT QF_BV query is hence $(assert \ (not \ (= \ 0 \ (bvextract \ (2w - 1) \ w \ bvx))))$ where bvx is the bit-vector product of a_0 and a_1. The abstraction for full-multiplication instruction is never unsound. For the $v \leftarrow \text{SHL } a_0 \ n$ instruction, its algebraic abstraction is unsound if the most significant n bits of a_0 are not zeros. The algebraic abstraction of the $v \leftarrow \text{SHR } a_0 \ n$ instruction is unsound when the least significant n bits of a_0 are not zeros. Relevant bits are obtained by $bvextract$ respectively. The abstraction for ASSUME is always sound.

To check soundness of the algebraic abstraction $\lceil s \rceil$ for the instruction s in the TOYLANG program $P \ s$, we apply Lemma 1 to obtain a computation of P through $\lfloor P \rceil$ and check if $\lfloor s \rfloor$ for s is unsatisfiable. We say the soundness condition for the instruction s in the TOYLANG program $P \ s$ *holds* if $\lfloor P \ s \rfloor$ is unsatisfiable. In order to ensure the soundness of the abstract polynomial program $\lceil P \rceil$ for the TOYLANG program P, soundness conditions for all instructions in P must hold. That is, soundness conditions

$$\lfloor v \leftarrow \text{ADD } a_0 \, a_1 \rfloor = \{(assert \,(=\, 1 \,(bvextract \, w \, w \, bvx)))\}$$
$$\text{where } bvx \text{ is } (bvadd \,(zero\_extend \, a_0 \, 1) \,(zero\_extend \, a_1 \, 1))$$

$$\lfloor v \leftarrow \text{ADC } a_0 \, a_1 \, d \rfloor = \{(assert \,(=\, 1 \,(bvextract \, w \, w \, bvx)))\}$$
$$\text{where } bvx \text{ is } (bvadd \,(bvadd \,(zero\_extend \, a_0 \, 1) \,(zero\_extend \, a_1 \, 1))$$
$$(zero\_extend \, d \, w))$$

$$\lfloor c : v \leftarrow \text{ADDS } a_0 \, a_1 \rfloor = \{(assert \, \bot)\}$$

$$\lfloor c : v \leftarrow \text{ADCS } a_0 \, a_1 \, d \rfloor = \{(assert \, \bot)\}$$

$$\lfloor v \leftarrow \text{SUB } a_0 \, a_1 \rfloor = \{(assert \,(=\, 1 \,(bvextract \, w \, w \, bvx)))\}$$
$$\text{where } bvx \text{ is } (bvsub \,(zero\_extend \, a_0 \, 1) \,(zero\_extend \, a_1 \, 1))$$

$$\lfloor c : v \leftarrow \text{SUBS } a_0 \, a_1 \rfloor = \{(assert \, \bot)\}$$

$$\lfloor v \leftarrow \text{MUL } a_0 \, a_1 \rfloor = \{(assert \,(not \,(=\, 0 \,(bvextract \,(2w - 1) \, w \, bvx))))\}$$
$$\text{where } bvx \text{ is } (bvmul \,(zero\_extend \, a_0 \, w) \,(zero\_extend \, a_1 \, w))$$

$$\lfloor v_H : v_L \leftarrow \text{MULL } a_0 \, a_1 \rfloor = \{(assert \, \bot)\}$$

$$\lfloor v \leftarrow \text{SHL } a_0 \, n \rfloor = \{(assert \,(not \,(=\, 0 \,(bvextract \,(w - 1) \,(w - n) \, a_0))))\}$$

$$\lfloor v \leftarrow \text{SHR } a_0 \, n \rfloor = \{(assert \,(not \,(=\, 0 \,(bvextract \,(n - 1) \, 0 \, a_0))))\}$$

$$\lfloor \text{ASSUME } q \rfloor = \{(assert \, \bot)\}$$

$$\lfloor P \, s \rfloor = \lfloor P \rfloor \cup \lfloor s \rfloor$$

Fig. 8. Soundness Conditions II

for s in all prefixes P' s of P must hold. Define the valuation ρ_σ of the store σ by $\rho_\sigma(v) = \text{toZ}(\llbracket v \rrbracket_\sigma)$ for every $v \in \overline{\mathbf{x}}$. The next theorem gives the soundness condition.

Proposition 1 (Soundness). *Let P be a* TOYLANG *program without* ASSERT *instructions and σ, σ' stores with $(\!|\sigma, P, \sigma'|\!)$. $\rho_{\sigma'}$ is a root of the system of (modular) equations $\lceil P \rceil$ if soundness conditions for s in every prefix P' s of P hold.*

We say that the soundness condition for P *holds* if soundness conditions for s in all prefixes P' s of P hold. Let us take a closer look at the abstract Montgomery reduction program (Fig. 6). The half-multiplication instruction $m \leftarrow$ MUL $T_L \, N'$ is lifted to $m = T_L \cdot N'$. However, the soundness condition for the instruction requires the most significant 64 bits of the product to be zeros (Fig. 8). Since T_L is arbitrary, the soundness condition does not hold in general. To obtain a sound algebraic abstraction for Montgomery reduction, we modify the TOYLANG program slightly (Fig. 9).

In the revised program, the first full-multiplication instruction is used to compute the least significant 64 bits of the product of T_L and N' (marked by $\surd$). The most significant 64 bits of the product are stored in the variable dc (for *don't care*). Note that the soundness condition of the revised program holds trivially. The algebraic abstraction for the revised Montgomery reduction program is sound by Proposition 1.

4.2 Polynomial Program Verification

Let P be a TOYLANG program without ASSERT instructions. Our goal is to verify $\boxed{P \text{ ASSERT } \phi}$ with algebraic abstraction. Consider the system of (modular) equations $\Phi = \lceil P \rceil$. For any stores σ and σ' with $(\!|\sigma, P, \sigma'|\!)$, $\rho_{\sigma'}$ is a root of Φ if the soundness

$$\begin{array}{ll}
\text{ASSUME } N \times N' + 1 \equiv 0 \bmod [2^{64}] & N \times N' + 1 \equiv 0 \bmod [2^{64}] \\
\checkmark \quad dc : m \quad \leftarrow \text{MULL } T_L \ N' & dc \cdot 2^{64} + m = T_L \cdot N', \\
mN_H : mN_L \leftarrow \text{MULL } m \ N & mN_H \cdot 2^{64} + mN_L = m \cdot N, \\
& carry \cdot (carry - 1) = 0, \\
carry : t_L \quad \leftarrow \text{ADDS } T_L \ mN_L & carry \cdot 2^{64} + t_L = T_L + mN_L, \\
& c \cdot (c - 1) = 0, \\
c : t_H \quad \leftarrow \text{ADCS } T_H \ mN_H \ carry & c \cdot 2^{64} + t_H = T_H + mN_H + carry,
\end{array}$$

$$\boxed{\text{ASSERT } t_L \equiv 0 \bmod [2^{64}]}$$

$$\begin{array}{ll}
\text{ASSUME } t_L = 0 & t_L = 0
\end{array}$$

$$\boxed{\text{ASSERT } (c \times 2^{64} + t_H) \times 2^{64} \equiv T_H \times 2^{64} + T_L \bmod [N]}$$

Fig. 9. Abstract Montgomery Reduction (Revised)

condition for P holds by Proposition 1. To verify ASSERT ϕ on σ', we need to check if $\rho_{\sigma'}$ is also a root of the (modular) equation ϕ. That is, we want to show if $\forall \overline{x}.\Phi \implies \phi$.

Proposition 2. *Let P be a* TOYLANG *program without* ASSERT *instructions and ϕ a (modular) equation. Suppose the soundness condition for P holds. The assertion in* $\boxed{P \text{ ASSERT } \phi}$ *succeeds if* $\forall \overline{x}.\lceil P \rceil \implies \phi$.

We extend [14] to check the root entailment problem. Recall that Φ is a system of (modular) equations. We first simplify it to a system of equations. This is best seen by an example. Consider $\forall x \ y \ u \ v.x \equiv y \bmod [3u^2, u+v] \implies 0 = 0$. We have

$$\forall x \ y \ u \ v.x \equiv y \bmod [3u^2, u+v] \implies 0 = 0$$
$$\text{iff } \forall x \ y \ u \ v.[\exists k_0 \ k_1 (x - y = 3u^2 \cdot k_0 + (u+v) \cdot k_1)] \implies 0 = 0$$
$$\text{iff } \forall x \ y \ u \ v \ k_0 \ k_1.x - y = 3u^2 \cdot k_0 + (u+v) \cdot k_1 \implies 0 = 0.$$

Therefore, it suffices to consider the problem of checking $\forall \overline{x}.\Psi \implies \phi$ where Ψ is a system of equations and ϕ is a (modular) equation. We solve the simplified problem by constructing instances of the ideal membership problem.

Let $\Psi = \{e_0 = e'_0, e_1 = e'_1, \ldots, e_n = e'_n\}$. Consider the ideal $I = \langle e_0 - e'_0, e_1 - e'_1, \ldots, e_n - e'_n \rangle$ generated by the polynomial equations in Ψ. Suppose the polynomial $e - e' \in I$. We claim $\forall \overline{x}.\Psi \implies e = e'$. Indeed, $e - e' = (e_0 - e'_0) \cdot h_0 + (e_1 - e'_1) \cdot h_1 + \cdots + (e_n - e'_n) \cdot h_n$ for some $h_0, h_1, \ldots, h_n \in \mathbb{Z}[\overline{x}]$ since $e - e' \in I$. For any root ρ of Ψ, $(e_0 - e'_0)[\rho] = (e_1 - e'_1)[\rho] = \cdots = (e_n - e'_n)[\rho] = 0$. Hence $(e - e')[\rho] = ((e_0 - e'_0) \cdot h_0)[\rho] + ((e_1 - e'_1) \cdot h_1)[\rho] + \cdots + ((e_n - e'_n) \cdot h_n)[\rho] = 0$. ρ is also a root of $e - e' = 0$ and thus $\forall \overline{x}.\Psi \implies e = e'$.

Now suppose the polynomial $e - e' \in I + \langle f_0, f_1, \ldots, f_m \rangle$. We claim $\forall \overline{x}.\Psi \implies e \equiv e' \bmod [f_0, f_1, \ldots, f_m]$. Since $e - e' \in I + \langle f_0, f_1, \ldots, f_m \rangle$, $e - e' = (e_0 - e'_0) \cdot h_0 + (e_1 - e'_1) \cdot h_1 + \cdots + (e_n - e'_n) \cdot h_n + f_0 \cdot k_0 + f_1 \cdot k_1 + \cdots + f_m \cdot k_m$ for some $h_0, h_1, \ldots, h_n, k_0, k_1, \ldots, k_m \in \mathbb{Z}[\overline{x}]$. For any root ρ of Ψ, $(e - e')[\rho] = ((e_0 - e'_0) \cdot h_0)[\rho] + ((e_1 - e'_1) \cdot h_1)[\rho] + \cdots + ((e_n - e'_n) \cdot h_n)[\rho] + f_0 \cdot k_0[\rho] + f_1 \cdot k_1[\rho] + \cdots + f_m \cdot k_m[\rho] = 0 + f_0[\rho]k_0[\rho] + f_1[\rho]k_1[\rho] + \cdots + f_m[\rho]k_m[\rho]$. We again have $\forall \overline{x}.\Psi \implies e \equiv e' \bmod [f_0, f_1, \ldots, f_m]$ as required.

Our discussion is summarized as follows.

$$e = e' \rightsquigarrow \langle e - e' \rangle$$

$$e \equiv e' \bmod [f_0, f_1, \ldots, f_m] \rightsquigarrow \langle e - e' - f_0 \cdot k_0 - f_1 \cdot k_1 - \cdots - f_m \cdot k_m \rangle$$
$$k_0, k_1, \ldots, k_m : \text{fresh variables}$$

$$\frac{}{\emptyset \rightsquigarrow \langle 0 \rangle} \qquad \frac{\phi \rightsquigarrow I \quad \Phi \rightsquigarrow J}{\{\phi\} \cup \Phi \rightsquigarrow I + J}$$

Fig. 10. Polynomial Programs to Ideals

Proposition 3. *Let P be a* TOYLANG *program without* ASSERT *instructions and I the ideal with $\lceil P \rceil \rightsquigarrow I$ (Fig. 10). Then*

1. $\forall \overline{\mathbf{x}}.\lceil P \rceil \implies e = e'$ *if* $e - e' \in I$;
2. $\forall \overline{\mathbf{x}}.\lceil P \rceil \implies e \equiv e' \bmod [f_0, f_1, \ldots, f_m]$ *if* $e - e' \in I + \langle f_0, f_1, \ldots, f_m \rangle$.

In order to verify (modular) equations with algebraic abstraction, Proposition 1 is applied to ensure the soundness of abstraction. Proposition 3 then checks whether (modular) equations indeed are satisfied for abstract polynomial programs. The main theorem summarizes our theoretical developments.

Theorem 1. *Let P be a* TOYLANG *program without* ASSERT *instructions, σ, σ' stores with $(\! (\sigma, P, \sigma'\!))$ and I the ideal with $\lceil P \rceil \rightsquigarrow I$. If the soundness condition for P holds,*

1. *the assertion in* $\boxed{P \text{ ASSERT } e = e'}$ *succeeds provided* $e - e' \in I$;
2. *the assertion in* $\boxed{P \text{ ASSERT } e \equiv e' \bmod [f_0, f_1, \ldots, f_m]}$ *succeeds provided* $e - e' \in I + \langle f_0, f_1, \ldots, f_m \rangle$.

The ideal membership problem can be solved by computing Gröbner bases for ideals [7]. Many computer algebra systems compute Gröbner bases for ideals with simple commands. For instance, the **groebner** command in SINGULAR [13] computes a Gröbner basis for any ideal by a user-specified monomial ordering. The **reduce** command then checks if a polynomial belongs to the ideal via its Gröbner basis.

Recall the abstract polynomial program for revised Montgomery reduction in Fig. 9. Figure 11a shows the ideal for the abstract polynomial program before ASSUME $t_L = 0$. To verify the two ASSERT instructions, Figs. 11b and 11c show the instances of the ideal membership problem corresponding to the two assertions. Observe the ideal $\langle t_L \rangle$ corresponds to ASSUME $t_L = 0$ in Fig. 11c. Since the soundness condition for the abstract polynomial program holds trivially (Sect. 4.1), it remains to check the ideal membership problem. Both instances are verified immediately.

5   Certified Verification

In TOYLANG, we only highlight necessary instructions to verify unsigned Montgomery reduction. For real-world programs performing non-linear computation, more instructions are needed and the signed representation of bit-vectors is also used. In order to ver-

$$I = \left\langle \begin{array}{c} N \cdot N' + 1 - k_0 \cdot 2^{64}, dc \cdot 2^{64} + m - T_L \cdot N', mN_H \cdot 2^{64} + mN_L - m \cdot N, \\ carry \cdot (carry - 1), carry \cdot 2^{64} + t_L - (T_L + mN_L), c \cdot (c - 1), \\ c \cdot 2^{64} + t_H - (T_H + mN_H + carry) \end{array} \right\rangle$$

(a) Ideal I

$$t_L \in I + \langle 2^{64} \rangle$$

(b) $\boxed{\text{ASSERT } t_L \equiv 0 \bmod [2^{64}]}$

$$(c \cdot 2^{64} + t_H) \cdot 2^{64} - (T_H \cdot 2^{64} + T_L) \in I + \langle t_L \rangle + \langle N \rangle$$

(c) $\boxed{\text{ASSERT } (c \times 2^{64} + t_H) \times R \equiv T_H \times 2^{64} + T_L \bmod [N]}$

Fig. 11. Instances of Ideal Membership Problem

ify real-world cryptographic programs, we extend algebraic abstraction with these features found in CRYPTOLINE [9,29]. For such complicated languages, algebraic abstraction can be tedious to implement. Its verification algorithm moreover relies on complex algorithms from computer algebra systems and SMT QF_BV solvers. It is unclear whether these external tools function correctly on given instances. In order to improve the quality of verification results, we have verified algebraic abstraction with the proof assistant COQ, and certified results from external tools with COQ and a verified certificate checker. We briefly describe how to verify our algorithms and certify results from external tools. Please see the technical report [28] for details.

5.1 Verified Abstraction Algorithm

The proof assistant COQ with the SSREFLECT library [4,11] is used to verify our algebraic abstraction technique. We define the TOYLANG syntax as a COQ data type (Fig. 1). The COQ-NBITS theory [26] is adopted to formalize the semantics of TOYLANG (Fig. 2). The COQ binary integer theory Z is used to formalize the semantics of (modular) equations (Fig. 3). We formalize polynomial expressions with integral coefficients by the COQ polynomial expression theory PExpr Z.

To see how our algebraic abstraction algorithm is verified, consider Proposition 2. Let program be the COQ data type for TOYLANG programs and meqn the data type for (modular) equations. We define the predicate algsnd : program $\rightarrow$ Prop for the soundness condition for a given program (Figs. 7 and 8). Similarly, we define the function algabs : program $\rightarrow$ seq meqn for our algebraic abstraction algorithm where seq meqn is the COQ data type for sequences of meqn (Fig. 5). To write down the formal statement for Proposition 2, it remains to formalize the root entailment. Let exp and valuation be the data types for expressions and valuations respectively. Define the function eval_exp : exp $\rightarrow$ valuation $\rightarrow Z$ which evaluates an expression to an integer on a valuation; and eval_exps : seq exp $\rightarrow$ valuation $\rightarrow$ seq Z evaluates expressions to integers on a valuation. Consider the predicate eval_bexp : meqn $\rightarrow$ valuation $\rightarrow$ Prop defined by

$$\text{eval\_bexp } (e = e') \text{ rho} := \text{eval\_exp } e \text{ rho} = \text{eval\_exp } e' \text{ rho}$$
$$\text{eval\_bexp } (e = e' \text{ mod fs}) \text{ rho} := \exists ks, (\text{eval\_exp } e \text{ rho}) - (\text{eval\_exp } e' \text{ rho}) =$$
$$\text{zadds } (\text{zmuls ks } (\text{eval\_exps fs rho}))$$

where zadds zs := foldl Z.add 0 zs and zmuls xs ys := map2 Z.mul xs ys. The predicate eval_bexp (e = e') rho checks if the expressions e and e' evaluate to the same integer on the valuation rho; eval_bexp (e = e' mod fs) rho checks if the difference of eval_exp e rho and eval_exp e' rho is equal to a linear combination of the integers eval_exps fs rho. The predicate eval_bexp meq rho thus checks if rho is a root of the (modular) equation meq.

We are ready to formalize the root entailment. Consider the predicate entails (Phi : seq meqn) (psi : meqn) : Prop defined by

$$\forall \text{rho}, (\forall \text{phi, phi} \in \text{Phi} \rightarrow \text{eval\_bexp phi rho}) \rightarrow \text{eval\_bexp psi rho}.$$

That is, every common root of the system Phi is also a root of psi. The following proposition formalizes Proposition 2 and is proved in COQ.

Proposition 4. *Let P : program be without assert instructions and psi : meqn. If algsnd P and entails (algabs P) psi, then the assertion in* $\boxed{P \text{ assert psi}}$ *succeeds.*

To apply this proposition to a given program P and a (modular) equation psi, one needs to show algsnd P and entails (algabs P) psi in COQ. In principle, both predicates algsnd P and entails (algabs P) psi could be proved manually in COQ. However, it would be impractical even for programs of moderate sizes. To address this problem, we establish these predicates through certificates computed by external tools.

5.2 Verification through Certification

To show algsnd P for an arbitrary program P, we follow the certified verification technique developed in the SMT QF_BV solver COQQFBV [26]. More concretely, we specify our bit-blasting algorithm for soundness conditions in COQ (Figs. 7 and 8). The algorithm converts soundness conditions to Boolean formulae in the conjunctive normal form. We then formally verify that soundness conditions hold if and only if the corresponding Boolean formulae are unsatisfiable in COQ. The constructed Boolean formulae are sent to the SAT solver KISSAT [5]. For each Boolean formula, KISSAT checks its satisfiability with a certificate. We then use the verified certificate checker GRATCHK [16] to validate these certificates.

Our next goal is to show entails (algabs P) psi. More generally, we show entails Phi psi with arbitrary Phi : seq meqn and psi : meqn via the COQ polynomial ring theory and the computer algebra system SINGULAR [13]. To this end, we first formulate the root entailment of polynomial expressions in the COQ polynomial ring theory. Recall PExpr Z is the COQ data type for polynomial expressions with integral coefficients. Given integers, the function zpeval : PExpr Z $\rightarrow$ seq Z $\rightarrow$ Z evaluates a polynomial expression to an integer. We formalize the root entailment of polynomial expressions by the predicate zpentails (Pi : seq (PExpr Z)) (tau : PExpr Z):

$$\forall zs, (\forall \text{pi, pi} \in \text{Pi} \rightarrow \text{zpeval pi zs} = 0) \rightarrow \text{zpeval tau zs} = 0.$$

We proceed to connect the root entailment of (modular) equations to the root entailment of polynomial expressions. Let the functions zpexprs_of_exprs : seq expr → seq (PExpr Z) and zpexprs_of_meqns : seq meqn → seq (PExpr Z) convert expressions and (modular) equations to polynomial expressions respectively (Fig. 10). When the consequence of root entailment is a modular equation, recall that moduli in the consequence become ideal generators (Proposition 3). To extract moduli from consequences, define zpexpr_of_conseq : meqn → PExpr Z × seq (PExpr Z) by

$$\text{zpexpr\_of\_conseq } (e = e') := (e - e', [::])$$
$$\text{zpexpr\_of\_conseq } (e = e' \text{ mod } fs) := (e - e', \text{zpexprs\_of\_exprs } fs)$$

The following COQ lemma shows how to check the root entailment of (modular) equations through the root entailment of polynomial expressions:

Lemma 2. ∀ *(Phi : seq meqn) (psi : meqn), zpentails (Pi ++ zpexprs_of_meqns Phi) tau implies entails Phi psi where (tau, Pi) = zpexpr_of_conseq psi.*

Note that moduli in the consequence psi are added to the antecedents Phi.

Our last step is to show zpentails (Pi ++ zpexprs_of_meqns Phi) tau. Again, we establish the generalized form zpentails Pi tau for polynomial expressions Pi and a polynomial expression tau. We prove the predicate by showing that tau can be expressed as a combination of expressions in Pi. Consider the predicate validate_zpentails (Xi : seq (PExpr Z)) (Pi : seq (PExpr Z)) (tau : PExpr Z) defined by

$$\text{size Xi = size Pi } \wedge$$
$$\text{ZPeq (ZPnorm tau) (ZPnorm (foldl ZPadd 0 (map2 ZPmul Xi Pi))).}$$

The predicate validate_zpentails checks if the Xi and Pi are of the same size. It then normalizes the polynomials tau and foldl ZPadd 0 (map2 ZPmul Xi Pi) using ZPnorm. If normalized polynomials are equal (ZPeq), the predicate is true. In foldl ZPadd 0 (map2 ZPmul Xi Pi), ZPadd and ZPmul are the constructors for polynomial expression addition and multiplication respectively. The expression map2 ZPmul Xi Pi hence returns products of elements in Xi with corresponding elements in Pi. The expression foldl ZPadd 0 (map2 ZPmul Xi Pi) then computes the sum of these products. The predicate validate_zpentails Xi Pi tau therefore checks if tau is equal to a polynomial combination of expressions in Pi. In other words, tau belongs to the ideal generated by Pi. Using Lemma 2, we prove the following variant of Proposition 3 in COQ:

Proposition 5. ∀ *Phi psi Xi, validate_zpentails Xi (Pi ++ zpexprs_of_meqns Phi) tau implies entails Phi psi where (tau, Pi) = zpexpr_of_conseq psi.*

The main difference between Propositions 3 and 5 lies in certifiability. There are many ways to establish ideal membership. Proposition 5 asks for witnesses Xi to justify ideal membership explicitly. Most importantly, such Xi need not be constructed manually. They are in fact computed by external tools. Precisely, these polynomial expressions are computed by the `lift` command in the computer algebra system SINGULAR [13]. The `lift` command computes polynomial expressions representing tau in the ideal generated by Pi ++ zpexprs_of_meqns Phi. After SINGULAR computes these polynomial expressions, we convert them to polynomial expressions Xi in COQ. The predicate validate_zpentails Xi (Pi ++ zpexprs_of_meqns Phi) tau checks if tau is indeed represented by Xi using the COQ polynomial ring theory. If the check succeeds, we obtain entails Phi psi by Proposition 5. Otherwise, the predicate entails Phi psi is not established. Note that SINGULAR need not be trusted. If Xi is computed incorrectly, the check validate_zpentails Xi (Pi ++ zpexprs_of_meqns Phi) tau will fail in COQ. Proposition 5 allows us to show entails Phi psi with certification.

5.3 Optimization

Lots of optimizations are needed and verified to make algebraic abstraction feasible for TOYLANG programs with thousands of instructions. For instance, the static single assignment transformation and program slicing algorithms are both specified and verified in COQ. Furthermore, the bit blasting algorithm is extended significantly to check soundness conditions effectively. For example, the soundness condition for the half-multiplication instruction MUL requires *bvmul* (Fig. 8). This could not work well because of complicated non-linear bit-vector computation. To reduce the complexity of overflow checking in half-multiplication, we implement and verify the algorithm from [10]. Last but not least, algebraic abstraction almost surely induces ideals with hundreds of polynomial generators if not thousands. Computing Gröbner bases for such ideals is infeasible. To address this problem, we develop heuristics to reduce the number of generators in ideals through rewriting. Our heuristics are also specified and verified in COQ. These optimizations are essential in our experiments.

6 Evaluation

We have implemented certified algebraic abstraction in the tool COQCRYPTOLINE [1]. COQCRYPTOLINE is built upon OCAML codes extracted from our COQ development. It calls the computer algebra system SINGULAR [13] and certifies answers from the algebraic tool. The certified SMT QF_BV solver COQQFBV [26] is used to verify soundness conditions. We choose two classes of real-world cryptographic programs in experiments. For elliptic curve cryptography, we verify various field or group operations from BITCOIN [27], BORINGSSL [8,12], NSS [20], OPENSSL [23], and PQCRYPTO-SIDH [18]. For post-quantum cryptography, we verify the C reference and optimized Intel avx2 implementations of the Number-Theoretic Transform in the cryptosystem KYBER [6]. Experiments are conducted on an Ubuntu 22.04.1 Linux server with 3.20 GHz 32-core Xeon Gold 6134M and 1TB RAM.

We compare COQCRYPTOLINE with the uncertified CRYPTOLINE [9,24]. Table 1 shows the experimental results. L_{CL} shows the number of instructions. T_{CCL} and T_{CL} give the verification time of COQCRYPTOLINE and CRYPTOLINE in seconds respectively. $\%_{Int}$ shows the percentage of time spent in extracted OCAML programs in COQCRYPTOLINE. $\%_{CAS}$ and $\%_{SMT}$ give the percentages of time spent on SINGULAR and COQQFBV respectively.

Table 1. Experimental Results on Industrial Cryptographic Programs

Function	L_{CL}	$\%_{Int}$	$\%_{SMT}$	$\%_{CAS}$	T_{CCL}	T_{CL}	Function	L_{CL}	$\%_{Int}$	$\%_{SMT}$	$\%_{CAS}$	T_{CCL}	T_{CL}
bitcoin/asm/secp256k1_fe_.*													
mul_inner	167	0.13	99.52	0.34	91.96	2.41	sqr_inner	151	0.28	99.13	0.59	28.30	1.17
bitcoin/field/secp256k1_fe_.*													
mul_inner	132	0.09	98.81	1.11	58.34	1.44	mul_int	6	0.14	95.21	4.65	1.17	0.02
negate	10	0.37	95.60	4.04	0.61	0.02	sqr_inner	119	0.12	98.60	1.28	34.08	0.91
bitcoin/group/													
secp256k1_ge_neg								31	1.82	90.48	7.70	0.24	0.03
secp256k1_gej_double_var.part.14								948	0.53	98.93	0.54	1091.28	25.50
bitcoin/scalar/secp256k1_scalar_.*													
mul	918	1.19	98.26	0.54	167.97	6.28	mul_512	338	0.50	98.51	0.98	36.97	2.20
sqr	929	1.49	97.81	0.70	147.07	5.41	sqr_512	349	0.66	98.10	1.23	27.45	3.11
secp256k1_scalar_reduce								104	2.50	91.18	6.32	1.21	0.09
secp256k1_scalar_reduce_512								580	1.62	97.50	0.88	47.83	1.88
boringssl/fiat_curve25519/fe_.*													
mul_impl	114	0.04	99.67	0.29	70.85	1.65	sqr_impl	96	0.09	99.38	0.53	25.30	0.75
fe_mul121666								54	1.31	95.61	3.08	0.84	0.07
x25519_scalar_mult_generic[a]								1068	0.27	99.55	0.18	1019.43	279.95
boringssl/fiat_curve25519_x86/fe_.*													
mul_impl	375	0.38	99.28	0.34	81.67	1.79	sqr_impl	299	0.52	99.08	0.40	39.89	0.97
fe_mul121666								96	1.96	95.02	3.02	1.07	0.08
x25519_scalar_mult_generic[a]								3287	0.45	99.40	0.15	4454.87	240.00
nss/Hacl_Curve25519_51/													
fmul0	127	0.03	99.67	0.30	136.53	31.11	fmul1	67	0.09	98.85	1.06	12.65	0.26
fsqr0	98	0.03	99.64	0.33	75.10	2.90	fsqr20	196	0.06	99.55	0.38	105.24	3.15
fmul20								238	0.06	99.65	0.29	200.54	35.29
point_add_and_double[a]								1165	0.13	99.65	0.22	2611.51	355.34
point_double								582	0.17	99.49	0.35	975.02	17.06
openssl/curve25519/fe51_.*													
mul	111	0.06	99.66	0.28	57.91	1.20	sq	93	0.08	99.34	0.58	23.06	0.69
fe51_mul121666								55	1.27	95.95	2.78	0.70	0.07
x25519_scalar_mult[a]								1042	0.29	99.54	0.17	912.24	281.26
PQCrypto-SIDH/P434/x86_64/													
fpmul434	266	91.74	0.02	8.24	0.39	0.05	fp2mul434	1161	1.10	98.62	0.29	726.40	42.44
PQCrypto-SIDH/P503/arm64/													
fpmul	553	2.43	96.19	1.39	249.24	5.49	fpmul-fixed	554	2.39	95.75	1.86	250.41	5.46
PQClean/kyber/NTT													
PQCLEAN_KYBER512_CLEAN_ntt								6273	4.78	34.21	61.01	1113.92	46.54
PQCLEAN_KYBER768_AVX2_ntt								8975	5.41	83.63	10.96	433.31	29.63

[a] One (out of three) modular polynomial equation in post-conditions fails to certify due to stack overflow.

6.1 Field and Group Operation in Elliptic Curves

In elliptic curve cryptography, a rational point on a curve is represented by field elements from a large finite field. Rational points on the curve form a group. The group operation in turn is computed by operations in the underlying finite field. In BITCOIN, the finite field is $\mathbb{Z}_{p256k1}$ with $p256k1 = 2^{256} - 2^{32} - 2^{9} - 2^{8} - 2^{7} - 2^{6} - 2^{4} - 1$. The underlying field for Curve25519 is $\mathbb{Z}_{p25519}$ with $p25519 = 2^{255} - 19$. PQCRYPTO-SIDH however uses slightly more complicated fields $\mathbb{Z}_{p434}/\langle x^2+1\rangle$ and $\mathbb{Z}_{p503}/\langle x^2+1\rangle$ with $p434 = 2^{216} \cdot 3^{137} - 1$ and $p503 = 2^{250} \cdot 3^{159} - 1$. Field elements in $\mathbb{Z}_{p256k1}$ and

$\mathbb{Z}_{p25519}$ are represented by multiple *limbs* of 64-bit numbers. Field multiplication, for instance, is implemented by a number of 64-bit arithmetic instructions. Field elements in $\mathbb{Z}_{p434}/\langle x^2 + 1\rangle$ and $\mathbb{Z}_{p503}/\langle x^2 + 1\rangle$ are of the form $u + vx$ where $u, v \in \mathbb{Z}_{p434}$ or $\mathbb{Z}_{p503}$ and $x^2 = -1$. Two moduli are used to specify multiplication for such fields: $p434$, $x^2 + 1$ for $\mathbb{Z}_{p434}/\langle x^2 + 1\rangle$, and $p503$, $x^2 + 1$ for $\mathbb{Z}_{p503}/\langle x^2 + 1\rangle$. Multiplication of PQCRYPTO-SIDH is easily specified by modular equations with multiple moduli.

COQCRYPTOLINE verifies every field operation with certification within 12.1 min. Group operations are implemented by field operations. Their certified verification thus takes more time. The most complicated case x25519_scalar_mult_generic (3287 instructions) from BORINGSSL takes about 1.3 h.[a] In comparison, CRYPTOLINE verifies the same program in 4 min without certification. In almost all cases, a majority of time is spent on COQQFBV. Running time for extracted OCAML programs is negligible. Interestingly, COQCRYPTOLINE finds a bug in the arm64 multiplication code for $\mathbb{Z}_{p503}/\langle x^2 + 1\rangle$ from PQCRYPTO-SIDH. Towards the end of multiplication, the programmer incorrectly stores the register x25 in memory *before* adding a carry. After fixing the bug, COQCRYPTOLINE finishes certified verification in about 5 min.

6.2 Number-Theoretic Transform in KYBER

The United States National Institute of Standards and Technology (NIST) is currently determining next-generation post-quantum cryptography (PQC) standards. In July 2022, Crystals-KYBER (or simply KYBER) was announced to be the winner for key establishment mechanisms.

One of the most critical steps in KYBER is modular polynomial multiplication over the polynomial ring $\mathcal{R}_q = \mathbb{Z}_q[x]/\langle x^{256} + 1\rangle$ with $q = 3329$. In $\mathcal{R}_q$, coefficients are elements in the field $\mathbb{Z}_q$. A polynomial in $\mathcal{R}_q$ is obtained by modulo $x^{256} + 1$ and hence has a degree less than 256. Consider $x^{256} \in \mathbb{Z}_q[x]$. Since $x^{256} \equiv -1 \mod (x^{256} + 1)$, x^{256} is -1 in $\mathcal{R}_q$. Unsurprisingly, polynomial multiplication is one of the most expensive computations in KYBER. An efficient way to multiply polynomials is through a discretized Fast Fourier Transform called the Number-Theoretic Transform (NTT).

Recall the Chinese remainder theorem for integers is but a ring isomorphism between residue systems. For instance, $\mathbb{Z}_{42} \cong \mathbb{Z}_6 \times \mathbb{Z}_7$. For polynomial rings, we have the following ring isomorphism

$$\mathbb{Z}_q[x]/\langle x^{2n} - \omega^2\rangle \cong \mathbb{Z}_q[x]/\langle x^n - \omega\rangle \times \mathbb{Z}_q[x]/\langle x^n + \omega\rangle \qquad (\omega \in \mathbb{Z}_q).$$

Observe that x^n is equal to ω in $\mathbb{Z}_q[x]/\langle x^n - \omega\rangle$ for $x^n \equiv \omega \mod (x^n - \omega)$. Similarly, x^n is equal to $-\omega$ in $\mathbb{Z}_q[x]/\langle x^n + \omega\rangle$. Recall polynomials in $\mathbb{Z}_q[x]/\langle x^{2n} - \omega^2\rangle$ have degrees less than $2n$. We can rewrite any polynomial in $\mathbb{Z}_q[x]/\langle x^{2n} - \omega^2\rangle$ as $f(x) + g(x)x^n$ where degrees of f and g are both less than n. The polynomial $f(x) + g(x)x^n$ is then equal to $f(x) + \omega g(x)$ in $\mathbb{Z}_q[x]/\langle x^n - \omega\rangle$; and it is equal to $f(x) - \omega g(x)$ in $\mathbb{Z}_q[x]/\langle x^n + \omega\rangle$. NTT computes the following ring isomorphism between $\mathbb{Z}_q[x]/\langle x^{2n} - \omega^2\rangle$ and $\mathbb{Z}_q[x]/\langle x^n - \omega\rangle \times \mathbb{Z}_q[x]/\langle x^n + \omega\rangle$ by substituting $\pm\omega$ for x^n in $f(x) + g(x)x^n$:

$$f(x) + g(x)x^n \leftrightarrow (f(x) + \omega g(x), f(x) - \omega g(x)). \tag{1}$$

Multiplication in $\mathbb{Z}_q[x]/\langle x^{2n} - \omega^2\rangle$ can therefore be computed by respective multiplications in $\mathbb{Z}_q[x]/\langle x^n \pm \omega\rangle$ through the isomorphism. That is, a multiplication for polynomials of degrees less than $2n$ (in $\mathbb{Z}_q[x]/\langle x^{2n} - \omega^2\rangle$) is replaced by two multiplications for polynomials of degrees less than n (in $\mathbb{Z}_q[x]/\langle x^n \pm \omega\rangle$).

In KYBER, ring isomorphisms are applied repeatedly until linear polynomials are obtained. That is, KYBER NTT computes the isomorphism

$$\mathcal{R}_q = \mathbb{Z}_q[x]/\langle x^{256} + 1\rangle \cong \mathbb{Z}_q[x]/\langle x^2 - \zeta_0\rangle \times \cdots \times \mathbb{Z}_q[x]/\langle x^2 - \zeta_{127}\rangle \qquad (2)$$

where ζ_j's are the principal 256-th roots of unity. A polynomial of a degree less than 256 is hence mapped via KYBER NTT to 128 linear polynomials, each modulo a different $x^2 - \zeta_j$. In PQCLEAN [25], a reference C implementation and a hand-optimized Intel avx2 assembly implementation of KYBER NTT are provided. In addition to degree reduction, the two implementations utilize signed Montgomery reduction extensively for efficient multiplication over $\mathbb{Z}_q$. We verify whether the two NTT implementations compute the ring isomorphism correctly.

To specify the correctness requirements of KYBER NTT, one could write down modular equations (1) according to its computation. Each equation would require explicit substitution. Thanks to modular equations with multiple moduli, a more intuitive and mathematical specification based on (2) is also expressible. Let $F = \Sigma_{k=0}^{255} f_k x^k$ denote the input polynomial in $\mathcal{R}_q = \mathbb{Z}_q[x]/\langle x^{256} + 1\rangle$ and the coefficients f_k's are input variables with $-q < f_k < q$ ($0 \le k < 256$). Let $G_j = g_{j,0} + g_{j,1}x$ be the j-th final output linear polynomial from the implementations. The modular equations

$$F \equiv G_j \bmod [q, x^2 - \zeta_j], \text{ for all } 0 \le j < 128$$

specify the correctness of the KYBER NTT implementations. Observe that our specification is almost identical to (2). Modular equations with multiple moduli allow cryptographic programmers to express mathematical specification naturally. They greatly improve usability and reduce specification efforts in algebraic abstraction.

COQCRYPTOLINE verifies the C reference implementation in about 18.6 min. The highly optimized avx2 implementation is verified in about 7.2 min. Observe that each layer of ring isomorphism requires 128 signed Montgomery reductions. KYBER NTT therefore has $7 \times 128 = 896$ Montgomery reductions similar to the running example in Fig. 4b. Algebraic abstraction successfully verifies the two KYBER NTT implementations within 20 min. In comparison, CRYPTOLINE verifies both NTT implementations in 1 min without certification.

7 Conclusion

Verification through algebraic abstraction combines both algebraic and bit-accurate analyses. Non-linear computation is analyzed algebraically; soundness conditions are checked with bit-accurate SMT QF_BV solvers. We describe how to verify the technique and certify its results. In the experiments, the hybrid technique successfully verifies non-linear integer computation found in cryptographic programs from elliptic curve and post-quantum cryptography with certification. We plan to explore more applications of algebraic abstraction in programs from post-quantum cryptography in near future.

Acknowledgments. The authors in Academia Sinica are partially funded by National Science and Technology Council grants NSTC110-2221-E-001-008-MY3, NSTC111-2221-E-001-014-MY3, NSTC111-2634-F-002-019, the Sinica Investigator Award AS-IA-109-M01, the Data Safety and Talent Cultivation Project AS-KPQ-109-DSTCP, and the Intel Fast Verified Postquantum Software Project. The authors in Shenzhen University and ISCAS are partially funded by Shenzhen Science and Technology Innovation Commission (JCYJ20210324094202008), the National Natural Science Foundation of China (62002228, 61836005), and the Natural Science Foundation of Guangdong Province (2022A1515011458, 2022A1515010880).

References

1. CoqCryptoLine GitHub repository (2023). https://github.com/fmlab-iis/coq-cryptoline

2. Barrett, C., Fontaine, P., Tinelli, C.: The Satisfiability Modulo Theories Library (SMT-LIB). http://www.smt-lib.org/ (2016)

3. Bernstein, D.J., Schwabe, P.: gfverif. http://gfverif.cryptojedi.org (2015)

4. Bertot, Y., Castéran, P.: Interactive Theorem Proving and Program Development - Coq'Art: The Calculus of Inductive Constructions. Texts in Theoretical Computer Science. Springer, Heidelberg (2004). https://doi.org/10.1007/978-3-662-07964-5

5. Biere, A., Fazekas, K., Fleury, M., Heisinger, M.: CaDiCaL, Kissat, Paracooba, Plingeling and treengeling entering the SAT competition 2020. In: Balyo, T., Froleyks, N., Heule, M., Iser, M., Suda, M.J.M. (eds.) Competition 2020 - Solver and Benchmark Descriptions. Department of Computer Science Report Series B, vol. B-2020-1, pp. 50–53. University of Helsinki (2020)

6. Bos, J., et al.: CRYSTALS - Kyber: a CCA-secure module-lattice-based KEM. In: Smith, M., Piessens, F. (eds.) IEEE European Symposium on Security and Privacy, pp. 353–367. IEEE (2018)

7. Buchberger, B., Winkler, F.: Gröbner bases and applications, vol. 17. Cambridge University Press Cambridge (1998)

8. Erbsen, A., Philipoom, J., Gross, J., Sloan, R., Chlipala, A.: Simple high-level code for cryptographic arithmetic - with proofs, without compromises. In: IEEE Symposium on Security and Privacy, pp. 1202–1219. IEEE (2019)

9. Fu, Y.F., Liu, J., Shi, X., Tsai, M.H., Wang, B.Y., Yang, B.Y.: Signed cryptographic program verification with typed CryptoLine. In: Cavallaro, L., Kinder, J., Wang, X., Katz, J. (eds.) ACM SIGSAC Conference on Computer and Communications Security, pp. 1591–1606. ACM (2019)

10. Gok, M., Schulte, M.J., Arnold, M.G.: Integer multipliers with overflow detection. IEEE Trans. Comput. **55**(8), 1062–1066 (2006)

11. Gonthier, G., Mahboubi, A.: An introduction to small scale reflection in Coq. J. Formalized Reason. **3**(2), 95–152 (2010)

12. Google: BoringsSSL (2021). https://boringssl.googlesource.com/boringssl/

13. Greuel, G.M., Pfister, G.: A Singular Introduction to Commutative Algebra. Springer, Heidelberg (2002). https://doi.org/10.1007/978-3-662-04963-1

14. Harrison, J.: Automating elementary number-theoretic proofs using Gröbner bases. In: Pfenning, F. (ed.) CADE 2007. LNCS (LNAI), vol. 4603, pp. 51–66. Springer, Heidelberg (2007). https://doi.org/10.1007/978-3-540-73595-3_5

15. Hwang, V., et al.: Verified NTT multiplications for NISTPQC KEM lattice finalists: Kyber, SABER, and NTRU. IACR Trans. Cryptograph. Hardware Embedd. Syst. **2022**, 718–750 (2022)

16. Lammich, P.: Efficient verified (UN)SAT certificate checking. In: de Moura, L. (ed.) CADE 2017. LNCS (LNAI), vol. 10395, pp. 237–254. Springer, Cham (2017). https://doi.org/10.1007/978-3-319-63046-5_15

17. Liu, J., Shi, X., Tsai, M.H., Wang, B.Y., Yang, B.Y.: Verifying arithmetic in cryptographic C programs. In: Lawall, J., Marinov, D. (eds.) IEEE/ACM International Conference on Automated Software Engineering, pp. 552–564. IEEE (2019)

18. Microsoft Research: PQCrypto-SIDH (2022). https://github.com/microsoft/PQCrypto-SIDH

19. Montgomery, P.L.: Modular multiplication without trial division. Math. Comput. **44**, 519–521 (1985)

20. Mozilla: Network security services (2021). https://developer.mozilla.org/en-US/docs/Mozilla/Projects/NSS

21. Müller-Olm, M., Seidl, H.: Computing polynomial program invariants. Inf. Process. Lett. **91**, 233–244 (2004)

22. Müller-Olm, M., Seidl, H.: Precise interprocedural analysis through linear algebra. In: Leroy, X. (ed.) POPL, pp. 330–341. ACM (2004)

23. OpenSSL: OpenSSL library. https://github.com/openssl/openssl (2021)

24. Polyakov, A., Tsai, M.H., Wang, B.Y., Yang, B.Y.: Verifying arithmetic assembly programs in cryptographic primitives. In: Schewe, S., Zhang, L. (eds.) International Conference on Concurrency Theory, pp. 1–16. LIPIcs, Schloss Dagstuhl - Leibniz-Zentrum fuer Informatik (2018)

25. PQClean: The PQClean project. https://github.com/PQClean/PQClean (2021)

26. Shi, X., Fu, Y.F., Liu, J., Tsai, M.H., Wang, B.Y., Yang, B.Y.: CoqQFBV: a scalable certified SMT quantifier-free bit-vector solver. In: Silva, A., Leino, K.R.M. (eds.) CAV 2021. LNCS, vol. 12760, pp. 149–171. Springer, Cham (2021). https://doi.org/10.1007/978-3-030-81688-9_7

27. The Bitcoin Developers: Bitcoin source code (2021). https://github.com/bitcoin/bitcoin

28. Tsai, M.H., Fu, Y.F., Shi, X., Liu, J., Wang, B.Y., Yang, B.Y.: Automatic certified verification of cryptographic programs with COQCRYPTOLINE . IACR Cryptol. ePrint Arch. 1116 (2022). https://eprint.iacr.org/2022/1116

29. Tsai, M.H., Wang, B.Y., Yang, B.Y.: Certified verification of algebraic properties on low-level mathematical constructs in cryptographic programs. In: Evans, D., Malkin, T., Xu, D. (eds.) ACM SIGSAC Conference on Computer and Communications Security, pp. 1973–1987. ACM (2017)

Complete Multiparty Session Type Projection with Automata

Elaine Li[1], Felix Stutz[2](✉), Thomas Wies[1], and Damien Zufferey[3]

[1] New York University, New York, USA
ef19013@nyu.edu, wies@cs.nyu.edu
[2] Max Planck Institute for Software Systems,
Kaiserslautern, Germany
fstutz@mpi-sws.org
[3] SonarSource, Geneva, Switzerland
damien.zufferey@sonarsource.com

Abstract. Multiparty session types (MSTs) are a type-based approach to verifying communication protocols. Central to MSTs is a *projection operator*: a partial function that maps protocols represented as global types to correct-by-construction implementations for each participant, represented as a communicating state machine. Existing projection operators are syntactic in nature, and trade efficiency for completeness. We present the first projection operator that is sound, complete, and efficient. Our projection separates synthesis from checking implementability. For synthesis, we use a simple automata-theoretic construction; for checking implementability, we present succinct conditions that summarize insights into the property of implementability. We use these conditions to show that MST implementability is PSPACE-complete. This improves upon a previous decision procedure that is in EXPSPACE and applies to a smaller class of MSTs. We demonstrate the effectiveness of our approach using a prototype implementation, which handles global types not supported by previous work without sacrificing performance.

Keywords: Protocol verification · Multiparty session types · Communicating state machines · Protocol fidelity · Deadlock freedom

1 Introduction

Communication protocols are key components in many safety and operation critical systems, making them prime targets for formal verification. Unfortunately, most verification problems for such protocols (e.g. deadlock freedom) are undecidable [11]. To make verification computationally tractable, several restrictions have been proposed [2,3,10,14,33,42]. In particular, multiparty session types (MSTs) [24] have garnered a lot of attention in recent years (see, e.g., the survey by Ancona et al. [6]). In the MST setting, a protocol is specified as a global

---

E. Li and F. Stutz—equal contribution.

ⓒ The Author(s) 2023
C. Enea and A. Lal (Eds.): CAV 2023, LNCS 13966, pp. 350–373, 2023.
https://doi.org/10.1007/978-3-031-37709-9_17

type, which describes the desired interactions of all roles involved in the protocol. Local implementations describe behaviors for each individual role. The implementability problem for a global type asks whether there exists a collection of local implementations whose composite behavior when viewed as a communicating state machine (CSM) matches that of the global type and is deadlock-free. The synthesis problem is to compute such an implementation from an implementable global type.

MST-based approaches typically solve synthesis and implementability simultaneously via an efficient syntactic *projection operator* [18,24,34,41]. Abstractly, a projection operator is a partial map from global types to collections of implementations. A projection operator proj is sound when every global type $\mathbf{G}$ in its domain is implemented by $\text{proj}(\mathbf{G})$, and complete when every implementable global type is in its domain. Existing practical projection operators for MSTs are all incomplete (or unsound). Recently, the implementability problem was shown to be decidable for a class of MSTs via a reduction to safe realizability of globally cooperative high-level message sequence charts (HMSCs) [38]. In principle, this result yields a complete and sound projection operator for the considered class. However, this operator would not be practical. In particular, the proposed implementability check is in EXPSPACE.

Contributions. In this paper, we present the first practical sound and complete projection operator for general MSTs. The synthesis problem for implementable global types is conceptually easy [38] – the challenge lies in determining whether a global type *is* implementable. We thus separate synthesis from checking implementability. We first use a standard automata-theoretic construction to obtain a candidate implementation for a potentially non-implementable global type. However, unlike [38], we then verify the correctness of this implementation directly using efficiently checkable conditions derived from the global type. When a global type is not implementable, our constructive completeness proof provides a counterexample trace.

The resulting projection operator yields a PSPACE decision procedure for implementability. In fact, we show that the implementability problem is PSPACE-complete. These results both generalize and tighten the decidability and complexity results obtained in [38].

We evaluate a prototype of our projection algorithm on benchmarks taken from the literature. Our prototype benefits from both the efficiency of existing lightweight but incomplete syntactic projection operators [18,24,34,41], and the generality of heavyweight automata-based model checking techniques [28,36]: it handles protocols rejected by previous practical approaches while preserving the efficiency that makes MST-based techniques so attractive.

2   Motivation and Overview

Incompleteness of Existing Projection Operators. A key limitation of existing projection operators is that the implementation for each role is obtained

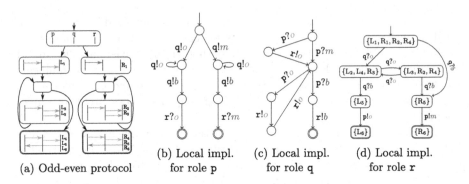

(a) Odd-even protocol

(b) Local impl. for role p

(c) Local impl. for role q

(d) Local impl. for role r

Fig. 1. Odd-even: An implementable but not (yet) projectable protocol and its local implementations

via a linear traversal of the global type, and thus shares its structure. The following example, which is not projectable by any existing approach, demonstrates how enforcing structural similarity can lead to incompleteness.

Example 2.1 (Odd-even). Consider the following global type $\mathbf{G}_{oe}$:

$$+ \begin{cases} p\rightarrow q{:}o.\,q\rightarrow r{:}o.\,\mu t_1.\,(p\rightarrow q{:}o.\,q\rightarrow r{:}o.\,q\rightarrow r{:}o.\,t_1 \;+\; p\rightarrow q{:}b.\,q\rightarrow r{:}b.\,r\rightarrow p{:}o.\,0) \\ p\rightarrow q{:}m.\,\mu t_2.\,(p\rightarrow q{:}o.\,q\rightarrow r{:}o.\,q\rightarrow r{:}o.\,t_2 \;+\; p\rightarrow q{:}b.\,q\rightarrow r{:}b.\,r\rightarrow p{:}m.\,0) \end{cases}$$

A term $p \rightarrow q : m$ specifies the exchange of message m between sender p and receiver q. The term represents two local events observed separately due to asynchrony: a send event $p \triangleright q!m$ observed by role p, and a receive event $q \triangleleft p?m$ observed by role q. The $+$ operator denotes choice, $\mu t.\,G$ denotes recursion, and 0 denotes protocol termination.

Figure 1a visualizes $\mathbf{G}_{oe}$ as an HMSC. The left and right sub-protocols respectively correspond to the top and bottom branches of the protocol. Role p chooses a branch by sending either o or m to q. On the left, q echoes this message to r. Both branches continue in the same way: p sends an arbitrary number of o messages to q, each of which is forwarded twice from q to r. Role p signals the end of the loop by sending b to q, which q forwards to r. Finally, depending on the branch, r must send o or m to p.

Figures 1b and 1c depict the structural similarity between the global type $\mathbf{G}_{oe}$ and the implementations for p and q. For the "choicemaker" role p, the reason is evident. Role q's implementation collapses the continuations of both branches into a single sub-component. For r (Fig. 1d), the situation is more complicated. Role r does not decide on or learn directly which branch is taken, but can deduce it from the parity of the number of o messages received from q: odd means left and even means right. The resulting local implementation features transitions going back and forth between the two branches that do not exist in the global type. Syntactic projection operators fail to create such transitions. ◀

One response to the brittleness of existing projection operators has been to give up on global type specifications altogether and instead revert to model checking

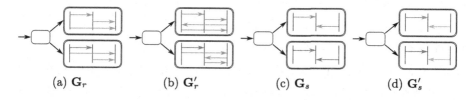

(a) $\mathbf{G}_r$ (b) $\mathbf{G}'_r$ (c) $\mathbf{G}_s$ (d) $\mathbf{G}'_s$

Fig. 2. High-level message sequence charts for the global types of Example 2.2.

user-provided implementations [28,36]. We posit that what needs rethinking is not the concept of global types, but rather how projections are computed and how implementability is checked.

Our Automata-Theoretic Approach. The synthesis step in our projection operator uses textbook automata-theoretic constructions. From a given global type, we derive a finite state machine, and use it to define a homomorphism automaton for each role. We then determinize this homomorphism automaton via subset construction to obtain a local candidate implementation for each role. If the global type is implementable, this construction always yields an implementation. The implementations shown in Figs. 1b to 1d are the result of applying this construction to $\mathbf{G}_{oe}$ from Example 2.1. Notice that the state labels in Fig. 1d correspond to sets of labels in the global protocol.

Unfortunately, not all global types are implementable.

Example 2.2. Consider the following four global types also depicted in Fig. 2:

$$\mathbf{G}_r = + \begin{cases} \mathtt{p} \to \mathtt{q}\!:\!o.\,\mathtt{q} \to \mathtt{r}\!:\!o.\,\mathtt{p} \to \mathtt{r}\!:\!o.\,0 \\ \mathtt{p} \to \mathtt{q}\!:\!m.\,\mathtt{p} \to \mathtt{r}\!:\!o.\,\mathtt{q} \to \mathtt{r}\!:\!o.\,0 \end{cases} \qquad \mathbf{G}_s = + \begin{cases} \mathtt{p} \to \mathtt{q}\!:\!o.\,\mathtt{r} \to \mathtt{q}\!:\!o.\,0 \\ \mathtt{p} \to \mathtt{q}\!:\!m.\,\mathtt{r} \to \mathtt{q}\!:\!m.\,0 \end{cases}$$

$$\mathbf{G}'_r = + \begin{cases} \mathtt{p} \to \mathtt{q}\!:\!o.\,\mathtt{q} \to \mathtt{r}\!:\!o.\,\mathtt{r} \to \mathtt{p}\!:\!o.\,\mathtt{p} \to \mathtt{r}\!:\!o.\,0 \\ \mathtt{p} \to \mathtt{q}\!:\!m.\,\mathtt{p} \to \mathtt{r}\!:\!o.\,\mathtt{r} \to \mathtt{q}\!:\!o.\,\mathtt{q} \to \mathtt{r}\!:\!o.\,0 \end{cases} \qquad \mathbf{G}'_s = + \begin{cases} \mathtt{p} \to \mathtt{q}\!:\!o.\,\mathtt{r} \to \mathtt{q}\!:\!b.\,0 \\ \mathtt{p} \to \mathtt{q}\!:\!m.\,\mathtt{r} \to \mathtt{q}\!:\!b.\,0 \end{cases}$$

Similar to $\mathbf{G}_{oe}$, in all four examples, $\mathtt{p}$ chooses a branch by sending either o or m to $\mathtt{q}$. The global type $\mathbf{G}_r$ is not implementable because $\mathtt{r}$ cannot learn which branch was chosen by $\mathtt{p}$. For any local implementation of $\mathtt{r}$ to be able to execute both branches, it must be able to receive o from $\mathtt{p}$ and $\mathtt{q}$ in any order. Because the two send events $\mathtt{p} \triangleright \mathtt{r}!o$ and $\mathtt{q} \triangleright \mathtt{r}!o$ are independent of each other, they may be reordered. Consequently, any implementation of $\mathbf{G}_r$ would have to permit executions that are consistent with global behaviors not described by $\mathbf{G}_r$, such as $\mathtt{p} \to \mathtt{q}\!:\!m \cdot \mathtt{q} \to \mathtt{r}\!:\!o \cdot \mathtt{p} \to \mathtt{r}\!:\!o$. Contrast this with $\mathbf{G}'_r$, which is implementable. In the top branch of $\mathbf{G}'_r$, role $\mathtt{p}$ can only send to $\mathtt{r}$ after it has received from $\mathtt{r}$, which prevents the reordering of the send events $\mathtt{p} \triangleright \mathtt{r}!o$ and $\mathtt{q} \triangleright \mathtt{r}!o$. The bottom branch is symmetric. Hence, $\mathtt{r}$ learns $\mathtt{p}$'s choice based on which message it receives first.

For the global type $\mathbf{G}_s$, role $\mathtt{r}$ again cannot learn the branch chosen by $\mathtt{p}$. That is, $\mathtt{r}$ cannot know whether to send o or m to $\mathtt{q}$, leading inevitably to deadlocking executions. In contrast, $\mathbf{G}'_s$ is again implementable because the expected behavior of $\mathtt{r}$ is independent of the choice by $\mathtt{p}$.   ◀

These examples show that the implementability question is non-trivial. To check implementability, we present conditions that precisely characterize when the subset construction for **G** yields an implementation.

Overview. The rest of the paper is organized as follows. Section 3 contains relevant definitions for our work. Section 4 describes the synthesis step of our projection. Section 5 presents the two conditions that characterize implementability of a given global type. In Sect. 6, we prove soundness of our projection via a stronger inductive invariant guaranteeing per-role agreement on a global run of the protocol. In Sect. 7, we prove completeness by showing that our two conditions hold if a global type is implementable. In Sect. 8, we discuss the complexity of our construction and condition checks. Section 9 presents our artifact and evaluation, and Sect. 10 as well as Sect. 11 discuss related work. Additional details including omitted proofs can be found in the extended version of the paper [29].

3   Preliminaries

Words. Let Σ be a finite alphabet. Σ^* denotes the set of finite words over Σ, Σ^ω the set of infinite words, and Σ^∞ their union $\Sigma^* \cup \Sigma^\omega$. A word $u \in \Sigma^*$ is a *prefix* of word $v \in \Sigma^\infty$, denoted $u \le v$, if there exists $w \in \Sigma^\infty$ with $u \cdot w = v$.

Message Alphabet. Let $\mathcal{P}$ be a set of roles and $\mathcal{V}$ be a set of messages. We define the set of *synchronous events* $\Sigma_{sync} := \{\mathsf{p} \to \mathsf{q} : m \mid \mathsf{p}, \mathsf{q} \in \mathcal{P} \text{ and } m \in \mathcal{V}\}$ where $\mathsf{p} \to \mathsf{q} : m$ denotes that message m is sent by p to q atomically. This is split for *asynchronous events*. For a role $\mathsf{p} \in \mathcal{P}$, we define the alphabet $\Sigma_{\mathsf{p},!} = \{\mathsf{p} \triangleright \mathsf{q}!m \mid \mathsf{q} \in \mathcal{P}, \ m \in \mathcal{V}\}$ of *send* events and the alphabet $\Sigma_{\mathsf{p},?} = \{\mathsf{p} \triangleleft \mathsf{q}?m \mid \mathsf{q} \in \mathcal{P}, \ m \in \mathcal{V}\}$ of *receive* events. The event $\mathsf{p} \triangleright \mathsf{q}!m$ denotes role p sending a message m to q, and $\mathsf{p} \triangleleft \mathsf{q}?m$ denotes role p receiving a message m from q. We write $\Sigma_{\mathsf{p}} = \Sigma_{\mathsf{p},!} \cup \Sigma_{\mathsf{p},?}$, $\Sigma_! = \bigcup_{\mathsf{p} \in \mathcal{P}} \Sigma_{\mathsf{p},!}$, and $\Sigma_? = \bigcup_{\mathsf{p} \in \mathcal{P}} \Sigma_{\mathsf{p},?}$. Finally, $\Sigma_{async} = \Sigma_! \cup \Sigma_?$. We say that p is *active* in $x \in \Sigma_{async}$ if $x \in \Sigma_{\mathsf{p}}$. For each role $\mathsf{p} \in \mathcal{P}$, we define a homomorphism $\Downarrow_{\Sigma_{\mathsf{p}}}$, where $x \Downarrow_{\Sigma_{\mathsf{p}}} = x$ if $x \in \Sigma_{\mathsf{p}}$ and ε otherwise. We write $\mathcal{V}(w)$ to project the send and receive events in w onto their messages. We fix $\mathcal{P}$ and $\mathcal{V}$ in the rest of the paper.

Global Types – Syntax. Global types for MSTs [31] are defined by the grammar:

$$G ::= 0 \ \mid \ \sum_{i \in I} \mathsf{p} \to \mathsf{q}_i : m_i . G_i \ \mid \ \mu t. \, G \ \mid \ t$$

where p, q_i range over $\mathcal{P}$, m_i over $\mathcal{V}$, and t over a set of recursion variables.

We require each branch of a choice to be distinct: $\forall i, j \in I. \, i \ne j \Rightarrow (\mathsf{q}_i, m_i) \ne (\mathsf{q}_j, m_j)$, the sender and receiver of an atomic action to be distinct: $\forall i \in I. \, \mathsf{p} \ne \mathsf{q}_i$, and recursion to be guarded: in $\mu t. \, G$, there is at least one message between μt and each t in G. When $|I| = 1$, we omit $\sum$. For readability, we sometimes use the infix operator $+$ for choice, instead of $\sum$. When working with a protocol described by a global type, we write **G** to refer to the top-level type, and we use G to refer to its subterms. For the size of a global type, we disregard multiple occurrences of the same subterm.

We use the extended definition of global types from [31] that allows a sender to send messages to different roles in a choice. We call this *sender-driven choice*, as in [38], while it was called generalized choice in [31]. This definition subsumes classical MSTs that only allow *directed choice* [24]. The types we use focus on communication primitives and omit features like delegation or parametrization. We defer a detailed discussion of different MST frameworks to Sect. 11.

Global Types – Semantics. As a basis for the semantics of a global type $\mathbf{G}$, we construct a finite state machine $\mathsf{GAut}(\mathbf{G}) = (Q_\mathbf{G}, \Sigma_{sync}, \delta_\mathbf{G}, q_{0,\mathbf{G}}, F_\mathbf{G})$ where

- $Q_\mathbf{G}$ is the set of all syntactic subterms in $\mathbf{G}$ together with the term 0,
- $\delta_\mathbf{G}$ is the smallest set containing $(\sum_{i \in I} \mathsf{p} \to \mathsf{q}_i : m_i.G_i, \mathsf{p} \to \mathsf{q}_i : m_i, G_i)$ for each $i \in I$, as well as $(\mu t.G', \varepsilon, G')$ and $(t, \varepsilon, \mu t.G')$ for each subterm $\mu t.G'$,
- $q_{0,\mathbf{G}} = \mathbf{G}$ and $F_\mathbf{G} = \{0\}$.

We define a homomorphism $\mathtt{split}$ onto the asynchronous alphabet:

$$\mathtt{split}(\mathsf{p} \to \mathsf{q} : m) := \mathsf{p} \triangleright \mathsf{q}!m. \, \mathsf{q} \triangleleft \mathsf{p}?m \ .$$

The semantics $\mathcal{L}(\mathbf{G})$ of a global type $\mathbf{G}$ is given by $\mathcal{C}^\sim(\mathtt{split}(\mathcal{L}(\mathsf{GAut}(\mathbf{G}))))$ where $\mathcal{C}^\sim$ is the closure under the indistinguishability relation $\sim$ [31]. Two events are independent if they are not related by the *happened-before* relation [26]. For instance, any two send events from distinct senders are independent. Two words are indistinguishable if one can be reordered into the other by repeatedly swapping consecutive independent events. The full definition is in the extended version [29].

Communicating State Machine [11]. $\mathcal{A} = \{\!\!\{A_\mathsf{p}\}\!\!\}_{\mathsf{p} \in \mathcal{P}}$ is a CSM over $\mathcal{P}$ and $\mathcal{V}$ if A_p is a finite state machine over Σ_p for every $\mathsf{p} \in \mathcal{P}$, denoted by $(Q_\mathsf{p}, \Sigma_\mathsf{p}, \delta_\mathsf{p}, q_{0,\mathsf{p}}, F_\mathsf{p})$. Let $\prod_{\mathsf{p} \in \mathcal{P}} s_\mathsf{p}$ denote the set of global states and $\mathsf{Chan} = \{(\mathsf{p}, \mathsf{q}) \mid \mathsf{p}, \mathsf{q} \in \mathcal{P}, \mathsf{p} \neq \mathsf{q}\}$ denote the set of channels. A *configuration* of $\mathcal{A}$ is a pair $(\vec{s}, \xi)$, where $\vec{s}$ is a global state and $\xi : \mathsf{Chan} \to \mathcal{V}^*$ is a mapping from each channel to a sequence of messages. We use $\vec{s}_\mathsf{p}$ to denote the state of p in $\vec{s}$. The CSM transition relation, denoted $\to$, is defined as follows.

- $(\vec{s}, \xi) \xrightarrow{\mathsf{p} \triangleright \mathsf{q}!m} (\vec{s}', \xi')$ if $(\vec{s}_\mathsf{p}, \mathsf{p} \triangleright \mathsf{q}!m, \vec{s}'_\mathsf{p}) \in \delta_\mathsf{p}$, $\vec{s}_\mathsf{r} = \vec{s}'_\mathsf{r}$ for every role $\mathsf{r} \neq \mathsf{p}$, $\xi'(\mathsf{p}, \mathsf{q}) = \xi(\mathsf{p}, \mathsf{q}) \cdot m$ and $\xi'(c) = \xi(c)$ for every other channel $c \in \mathsf{Chan}$.
- $(\vec{s}, \xi) \xrightarrow{\mathsf{q} \triangleleft \mathsf{p}?m} (\vec{s}', \xi')$ if $(\vec{s}_\mathsf{q}, \mathsf{q} \triangleleft \mathsf{p}?m, \vec{s}'_\mathsf{q}) \in \delta_\mathsf{q}$, $\vec{s}_\mathsf{r} = \vec{s}'_\mathsf{r}$ for every role $\mathsf{r} \neq \mathsf{q}$, $\xi(\mathsf{p}, \mathsf{q}) = m \cdot \xi'(\mathsf{p}, \mathsf{q})$ and $\xi'(c) = \xi(c)$ for every other channel $c \in \mathsf{Chan}$.

In the initial configuration $(\vec{s}_0, \xi_0)$, each role's state in $\vec{s}_0$ is the initial state $q_{0,\mathsf{p}}$ of A_p, and ξ_0 maps each channel to ε. A configuration $(\vec{s}, \xi)$ is said to be *final* iff $\vec{s}_\mathsf{p}$ is final for every p and ξ maps each channel to ε. Runs and traces are defined in the expected way. A run is *maximal* if either it is finite and ends in a final configuration, or it is infinite. The language $\mathcal{L}(\mathcal{A})$ of the CSM $\mathcal{A}$ is defined as the set of maximal traces. A configuration $(\vec{s}, \xi)$ is a *deadlock* if it is not final and has no outgoing transitions. A CSM is *deadlock-free* if no reachable configuration is a deadlock.

Finally, implementability is formalized as follows.

Definition 3.1 (Implementability [31]). *A global type* **G** *is* implementable *if there exists a CSM* $\{\!\!\{A_p\}\!\!\}_{p \in \mathcal{P}}$ *such that the following two properties hold:* (i) protocol fidelity: $\mathcal{L}(\{\!\!\{A_p\}\!\!\}_{p \in \mathcal{P}}) = \mathcal{L}(\mathbf{G})$, *and* (ii) deadlock freedom: $\{\!\!\{A_p\}\!\!\}_{p \in \mathcal{P}}$ *is deadlock-free. We say that* $\{\!\!\{A_p\}\!\!\}_{p \in \mathcal{P}}$ *implements* **G**.

4   Synthesizing Implementations

The construction is carried out in two steps. First, for each role $p \in \mathcal{P}$, we define an intermediate state machine $\mathsf{GAut}(\mathbf{G}){\downarrow}_p$ that is a homomorphism of $\mathsf{GAut}(\mathbf{G})$. We call $\mathsf{GAut}(\mathbf{G}){\downarrow}_p$ the *projection by erasure* for p, defined below.

Definition 4.1 (Projection by Erasure). *Let* **G** *be some global type with its state machine* $\mathsf{GAut}(\mathbf{G}) = (Q_{\mathbf{G}}, \Sigma_{sync}, \delta_{\mathbf{G}}, q_{0,\mathbf{G}}, F_{\mathbf{G}})$. *For each role* $p \in \mathcal{P}$, *we define the state machine* $\mathsf{GAut}(\mathbf{G}){\downarrow}_p = (Q_{\mathbf{G}}, \Sigma_p \uplus \{\varepsilon\}, \delta_{\downarrow}, q_{0,\mathbf{G}}, F_{\mathbf{G}})$ *where* $\delta_{\downarrow} := \{q \xrightarrow{split(a){\Downarrow}_{\Sigma_p}} q' \mid q \xrightarrow{a} q' \in \delta_{\mathbf{G}}\}$. *By definition of* $split(\text{-})$, *it holds that* $split(a){\Downarrow}_{\Sigma_p} \in \Sigma_p \uplus \{\varepsilon\}$.

Then, we determinize $\mathsf{GAut}(\mathbf{G}){\downarrow}_p$ via a standard subset construction to obtain a deterministic local state machine for p.

Definition 4.2 (Subset Construction). *Let* **G** *be a global type and* p *be a role. Then, the subset construction for* p *is defined as*

$$\mathscr{C}(\mathbf{G}, p) = (Q_p, \Sigma_p, \delta_p, s_{0,p}, F_p) \text{ where}$$

- $\delta(s, a) := \{q' \in Q_{\mathbf{G}} \mid \exists q \in s, q \xrightarrow{a} \xrightarrow{\varepsilon}{}^* q' \in \delta_{\downarrow}\}$, *for every* $s \subseteq Q_{\mathbf{G}}$ *and* $a \in \Sigma_p$
- $s_{0,p} := \{q \in Q_{\mathbf{G}} \mid q_{0,\mathbf{G}} \xrightarrow{\varepsilon}{}^* q \in \delta_{\downarrow}\}$,
- $Q_p := \mathsf{lfp}_{\{s_{0,p}\}}^{\subseteq} \lambda Q. Q \cup \{\delta(s, a) \mid s \in Q \wedge a \in \Sigma_p\} \setminus \{\emptyset\}$, *and*
- $\delta_p := \delta|_{Q_p \times \Sigma_p}$
- $F_p := \{s \in Q_p \mid s \cap F_{\mathbf{G}} \neq \emptyset\}$

Note that the construction ensures that Q_p only contains subsets of $Q_{\mathbf{G}}$ whose states are reachable via the same traces, i.e. we typically have $|Q_p| \ll 2^{|Q_{\mathbf{G}}|}$.

The following characterization is immediate from the subset construction; the proof can be found in the extended version [29].

Lemma 4.3. *Let* **G** *be a global type,* r *be a role, and* $\mathscr{C}(\mathbf{G}, r)$ *be its subset construction. If* w *is a trace of* $\mathsf{GAut}(\mathbf{G})$, $split(w){\Downarrow}_{\Sigma_r}$ *is a trace of* $\mathscr{C}(\mathbf{G}, r)$. *If* u *is a trace of* $\mathscr{C}(\mathbf{G}, r)$, *there is a trace* w *of* $\mathsf{GAut}(\mathbf{G})$ *such that* $split(w){\Downarrow}_{\Sigma_r} = u$. *It holds that* $\mathcal{L}(\mathbf{G}){\Downarrow}_{\Sigma_r} = \mathcal{L}(\mathscr{C}(\mathbf{G}, r))$.

Using this lemma, we show that the CSM $\{\!\{\mathscr{C}(\mathbf{G},\mathtt{p})\}\!\}_{\mathtt{p}\in\mathcal{P}}$ preserves all behaviors of $\mathbf{G}$.

Lemma 4.4. *For all global types* $\mathbf{G}$, $\mathcal{L}(\mathbf{G}) \subseteq \mathcal{L}(\{\!\{\mathscr{C}(\mathbf{G},\mathtt{p})\}\!\}_{\mathtt{p}\in\mathcal{P}})$.

We briefly sketch the proof here. Given that $\{\!\{\mathscr{C}(\mathbf{G},\mathtt{p})\}\!\}_{\mathtt{p}\in\mathcal{P}}$ is deterministic, to prove language inclusion it suffices to prove the inclusion of the respective prefix sets:

$$\mathrm{pref}(\mathcal{L}(\mathbf{G})) \subseteq \mathrm{pref}(\mathcal{L}\{\!\{\mathscr{C}(\mathbf{G},\mathtt{p})\}\!\}_{\mathtt{p}\in\mathcal{P}})$$

Let w be a word in $\mathcal{L}(\mathbf{G})$. If w is finite, membership in $\mathcal{L}(\{\!\{\mathscr{C}(\mathbf{G},\mathtt{p})\}\!\}_{\mathtt{p}\in\mathcal{P}})$ is immediate from the claim above. If w is infinite, we show that w has an infinite run in $\{\!\{\mathscr{C}(\mathbf{G},\mathtt{p})\}\!\}_{\mathtt{p}\in\mathcal{P}}$ using König's Lemma. We construct an infinite graph $\mathcal{G}_w(V,E)$ with $V := \{v_\rho \mid \mathtt{trace}(\rho) \leq w\}$ and $E := \{(v_{\rho_1}, v_{\rho_2}) \mid \exists x \in \Sigma_{async}.\ \mathtt{trace}(\rho_2) = \mathtt{trace}(\rho_1) \cdot x\}$. Because $\{\!\{\mathscr{C}(\mathbf{G},\mathtt{p})\}\!\}_{\mathtt{p}\in\mathcal{P}}$ is deterministic, $\mathcal{G}_w$ is a tree rooted at v_ε, the vertex corresponding to the empty run. By König's Lemma, every infinite tree contains either a vertex of infinite degree or an infinite path. Because $\{\!\{\mathscr{C}(\mathbf{G},\mathtt{p})\}\!\}_{\mathtt{p}\in\mathcal{P}}$ consists of a finite number of communicating state machines, the last configuration of any run has a finite number of next configurations, and $\mathcal{G}_w$ is finitely branching. Therefore, there must exist an infinite path in $\mathcal{G}_w$ representing an infinite run for w, and thus $w \in \mathcal{L}(\{\!\{\mathscr{C}(\mathbf{G},\mathtt{p})\}\!\}_{\mathtt{p}\in\mathcal{P}})$.

The proof of the inclusion of prefix sets proceeds by structural induction and primarily relies on Lemma 4.3 and the fact that all prefixes in $\mathcal{L}(\mathbf{G})$ respect the order of send before receive events.

5   Checking Implementability

We now turn our attention to checking implementability of a CSM produced by the subset construction. We revisit the global types from Example 2.2 (also shown in Fig. 2), which demonstrate that the naive subset construction does not always yield a sound implementation. From these examples, we distill our conditions that precisely identify the implementable global types.

In general, a global type $\mathbf{G}$ is not implementable when the agreement on a global run of $\mathsf{GAut}(\mathbf{G})$ among all participating roles cannot be conveyed via sending and receiving messages alone. When this happens, roles can take locally permitted transitions that commit to incompatible global runs, resulting in a trace that is not specified by $\mathbf{G}$. Consequently, our conditions need to ensure that when a role $\mathtt{p}$ takes a transition in $\mathscr{C}(\mathbf{G},\mathtt{p})$, it only commits to global runs that are consistent with the local views of all other roles. We discuss the relevant conditions imposed on send and receive transitions separately.

Send Validity. Consider $\mathbf{G}_s$ from Example 2.2. The CSM $\{\!\{\mathscr{C}(\mathbf{G}_s,\mathtt{p})\}\!\}_{\mathtt{p}\in\mathcal{P}}$ has an execution with the trace $\mathtt{p}\triangleright\mathtt{q}!o\cdot\mathtt{q}\triangleleft\mathtt{p}?o\cdot\mathtt{r}\triangleright\mathtt{q}!m$. This trace is possible because the initial state of $\mathscr{C}(\mathbf{G}_s,\mathtt{r})$, $s_{0,\mathtt{r}}$, contains two states of $\mathsf{GAut}(\mathbf{G}_s){\downarrow}_{\mathtt{r}}$, each of which has a single outgoing send transition labeled with $\mathtt{r}\triangleright\mathtt{q}!o$ and $\mathtt{r}\triangleright\mathtt{q}!m$ respectively. Both of these transitions are always enabled in $s_{0,\mathtt{r}}$, meaning that $\mathtt{r}$ can send

$r \rhd q!m$ even when p has chosen the top branch and q expects to receive o instead of m from r. This results in a deadlock. In contrast, while the state $s_{0,r}$ in $\mathscr{C}(\mathbf{G}'_s, r)$ likewise contains two states of $\mathsf{GAut}(\mathbf{G}'_s)\!\downarrow_r$, each with a single outgoing send transition, now both transitions are labeled with $r \rhd q!b$. These two transitions collapse to a single one in $\mathscr{C}(\mathbf{G}'_s, r)$. This transition is consistent with both possible local views that p and q might hold on the global run.

Intuitively, to prevent the emergence of inconsistent local views from send transitions of $\mathscr{C}(\mathbf{G}, p)$, we must enforce that for every state $s \in Q_p$ with an outgoing send transition labeled x, a transition labeled x must be enabled in all states of $\mathsf{GAut}(\mathbf{G})\!\downarrow_p$ represented by s. We use the following auxiliary definition to formalize this intuition subsequently.

Definition 5.1 (Transition Origin and Destination). *Let* $s \xrightarrow{x} s' \in \delta_p$ *be a transition in* $\mathscr{C}(\mathbf{G}, p)$ *and* $\delta_\downarrow$ *be the transition relation of* $\mathsf{GAut}(\mathbf{G})\!\downarrow_p$. *We define the set of* transition origins tr-orig$(s \xrightarrow{x} s')$ *and* transition destinations tr-dest$(s \xrightarrow{x} s')$ *as follows:*

$$\text{tr-orig}(s \xrightarrow{x} s') := \{G \in s \mid \exists G' \in s'.\, G \xrightarrow{x}{}^* G' \in \delta_\downarrow\} \text{ and}$$
$$\text{tr-dest}(s \xrightarrow{x} s') := \{G' \in s' \mid \exists G \in s.\, G \xrightarrow{x}{}^* G' \in \delta_\downarrow\} \ .$$

Our condition on send transitions is then stated below.

Definition 5.2 (Send Validity). $\mathscr{C}(\mathbf{G}, p)$ *satisfies* Send Validity *iff every send transition* $s \xrightarrow{x} s' \in \delta_p$ *is enabled in all states contained in* s:

$$\forall s \xrightarrow{x} s' \in \delta_p.\ x \in \Sigma_{p,!} \implies \text{tr-orig}(s \xrightarrow{x} s') = s \ .$$

Receive Validity. To motivate our condition on receive transitions, let us revisit $\mathbf{G}_r$ from Example 2.2. The CSM $\{\!\{\mathscr{C}(\mathbf{G}_r, p)\}\!\}_{p \in \mathcal{P}}$ recognizes the following trace not in the global type language $\mathcal{L}(\mathbf{G}_r)$:

$$p \rhd q!o \cdot q \lhd p?o \cdot q \rhd r!o \cdot p \rhd r!o \cdot r \lhd p?o \cdot r \lhd q?o \ .$$

The issue lies with r which cannot distinguish between the two branches in $\mathbf{G}_r$. The initial state $s_{0,r}$ of $\mathscr{C}(\mathbf{G}_r, r)$ has two states of $\mathsf{GAut}(\mathbf{G}_r)$ corresponding to the subterms $G_t := q \to r\!:\! o.\, p \to r\!:\! o.\, 0$ and $G_b := p \to r\!:\! o.\, q \to r\!:\! o.\, 0$. Here, G_t and G_b are the top and bottom branch of $\mathbf{G}_r$ respectively. This means that there are outgoing transitions in $s_{0,r}$ labeled with $r \lhd p?o$ and $r \lhd q?o$. If r takes the transition labeled $r \lhd p?o$, it commits to the bottom branch G_b. However, observe that the message o from p can also be available at this time point if the other roles follow the top branch G_t. This is because p can send o to r without waiting for r to first receive from q. In this scenario, the roles disagree on which global run of $\mathsf{GAut}(\mathbf{G}_r)$ to follow, resulting in the violating trace above.

Contrast this with $\mathbf{G}'_r$. Here, $s_{0,r}$ again has outgoing transitions labeled with $r \lhd p?o$ and $r \lhd q?o$. However, if r takes the transition labeled $r \lhd p?o$, committing to the bottom branch, no disagreement occurs. This is because if the other roles are following the top branch, then p is blocked from sending to r until after it has received confirmation that r has received its first message from q.

For a receive transition $s \xrightarrow{x} s_1$ in $\mathscr{C}(\mathbf{G}, p)$ to be safe, we must enforce that the receive event x cannot also be available due to reordered sent messages in the continuation $G_2 \in s_2$ of another outgoing receive transition $s \xrightarrow{y} s_2$. To formalize this condition, we use the set $M^{\mathcal{B}}_{(G...)}$ of *available messages* for a syntactic subterm G of $\mathbf{G}$ and a set of *blocked* roles $\mathcal{B}$. This notion was already defined in [31, Sec. 2.2]. Intuitively, $M^{\mathcal{B}}_{(G...)}$ consists of all send events $q \triangleright r!m$ that can occur on the traces of G such that m will be the first message added to channel (q, r) before any of the roles in $\mathcal{B}$ takes a step.

Available Messages. The set of available messages is recursively defined on the structure of the global type. To obtain all possible messages, we need to unfold the distinct recursion variables once. For this, we define a map $get\mu$ from variable to subterms and write $get\mu_{\mathbf{G}}$ for $get\mu(\mathbf{G})$:

$$get\mu(0) := [] \qquad get\mu(t) := [] \qquad get\mu(\mu t.G) := [t \mapsto G] \cup get\mu(G)$$
$$get\mu(\textstyle\sum_{i \in I} p \to q_i : m_i.G_i) := \bigcup_{i \in I} get\mu(G_i)$$

The function $M^{\mathcal{B},T}_{(-...)}$ keeps a set of unfolded variables T, which is empty initially.

$$M^{\mathcal{B},T}_{(0...)} := \emptyset \qquad M^{\mathcal{B},T}_{(\mu t.G...)} := M^{\mathcal{B},T\cup\{t\}}_{(G...)} \qquad M^{\mathcal{B},T}_{(t...)} := \begin{cases} \emptyset & \text{if } t \in T \\ M^{\mathcal{B},T\cup\{t\}}_{(get\mu_{\mathbf{G}}(t)...)} & \text{if } t \notin T \end{cases}$$

$$M^{\mathcal{B},T}_{(\sum_{i \in I} p \to q_i m_i.G_i...)} := \begin{cases} \bigcup_{i \in I, m \in \mathcal{V}}(M^{\mathcal{B},T}_{(G_i...)}) \setminus \{q_i \triangleleft p?m\}) \cup \{q_i \triangleleft p?m_i\} & \text{if } p \notin \mathcal{B} \\ \bigcup_{i \in I} M^{\mathcal{B}\cup\{q_i\},T}_{(G_i...)} & \text{if } p \in \mathcal{B} \end{cases}$$

We write $M^{\mathcal{B}}_{(G...)}$ for $M^{\mathcal{B},\emptyset}_{(G...)}$. If $\mathcal{B}$ is a singleton set, we omit set notation and write $M^{p}_{(G...)}$ for $M^{\{p\}}_{(G...)}$. The set of available messages captures the possible states of all channels before a given receive transition is taken.

Definition 5.3 (Receive Validity). $\mathscr{C}(\mathbf{G}, p)$ *satisfies* Receive Validity *iff no receive transition is enabled in an alternative continuation that originates from the same source state:*

$$\forall s \xrightarrow{p \triangleleft q_1 ? m_1} s_1, s \xrightarrow{p \triangleleft q_2 ? m_2} s_2 \in \delta_p.$$
$$q_1 \neq q_2 \implies \forall G_2 \in \text{tr-dest}(s \xrightarrow{p \triangleleft q_2 ? m_2} s_2). q_1 \triangleright p!m_1 \notin M^{p}_{(G_2...)}.$$

Subset Projection. We are now ready to define our projection operator.

Definition 5.4 (Subset Projection of G). *The subset projection* $\mathscr{P}(\mathbf{G}, p)$ *of* $\mathbf{G}$ *onto* p *is* $\mathscr{C}(\mathbf{G}, p)$ *if it satisfies Send Validity and Receive Validity. We lift this operation to a partial function from global types to CSMs in the expected way.*

We conclude our discussion with an observation about the syntactic structure of the subset projection: Send Validity implies that no state has both outgoing send and receive transitions (also known as mixed choice).

Corollary 5.5 (No Mixed Choice). *If* $\mathscr{P}(\mathbf{G}, p)$ *satisfies Send Validity, then for all* $s \xrightarrow{x_1} s_1, s \xrightarrow{x_2} s_2 \in \delta_p$, $x_1 \in \Sigma_!$ *iff* $x_2 \in \Sigma_!$.

6   Soundness

In this section, we prove the soundness of our subset projection, stated as follows.

Theorem 6.1. *Let* $\mathbf{G}$ *be a global type and* $\{\!\!\{\mathscr{P}(\mathbf{G},\mathsf{p})\}\!\!\}_{\mathsf{p}\in\mathcal{P}}$ *be the subset projection. Then,* $\{\!\!\{\mathscr{P}(\mathbf{G},\mathsf{p})\}\!\!\}_{\mathsf{p}\in\mathcal{P}}$ *implements* $\mathbf{G}$.

Recall that implementability is defined as protocol fidelity and deadlock freedom. Protocol fidelity consists of two language inclusions. The first inclusion, $\mathcal{L}(\mathbf{G}) \subseteq \mathcal{L}(\{\!\!\{\mathscr{P}(\mathbf{G},\mathsf{p})\}\!\!\}_{\mathsf{p}\in\mathcal{P}})$, enforces that the subset projection generates at least all behaviors of the global type. We showed in Lemma 4.4 that this holds for the subset construction alone (without Send and Receive Validity).

The second inclusion, $\mathcal{L}(\{\!\!\{\mathscr{P}(\mathbf{G},\mathsf{p})\}\!\!\}_{\mathsf{p}\in\mathcal{P}}) \subseteq \mathcal{L}(\mathbf{G})$, enforces that no new behaviors are introduced. The proof of this direction relies on a stronger inductive invariant that we show for all traces of the subset projection. As discussed in Sect. 5, violations of implementability occur when roles commit to global runs that are inconsistent with the local views of other roles. Our inductive invariant states the exact opposite: that all local views are consistent with one another. First, we formalize the local view of a role.

Definition 6.2 (Possible run sets). *Let* $\mathbf{G}$ *be a global type and* $\mathsf{GAut}(\mathbf{G})$ *be the corresponding state machine. Let* p *be a role and* $w \in \Sigma^*_{async}$ *be a word. We define the set of possible runs* $\mathrm{R}^{\mathbf{G}}_{\mathsf{p}}(w)$ *as all maximal runs of* $\mathsf{GAut}(\mathbf{G})$ *that are consistent with* p*'s local view of* w:

$$\mathrm{R}^{\mathbf{G}}_{\mathsf{p}}(w) := \{\rho \text{ is a maximal run of } \mathsf{GAut}(\mathbf{G}) \mid w\!\!\Downarrow_{\Sigma_{\mathsf{p}}} \leq \textit{split}(\textit{trace}(\rho))\!\!\Downarrow_{\Sigma_{\mathsf{p}}}\} .$$

While Definition 6.2 captures the set of maximal runs that are consistent with the local view of a single role, we would like to refer to the set of runs that is consistent with the local view of all roles. We formalize this as the intersection of the possible run sets for all roles, which we denote as

$$I(w) := \bigcap_{\mathsf{p}\in\mathcal{P}} \mathrm{R}^{\mathbf{G}}_{\mathsf{p}}(w) .$$

With these definitions in hand, we can now formulate our inductive invariant:

Lemma 6.3. *Let* $\mathbf{G}$ *be a global type and* $\{\!\!\{\mathscr{P}(\mathbf{G},\mathsf{p})\}\!\!\}_{\mathsf{p}\in\mathcal{P}}$ *be the subset projection. Let* w *be a trace of* $\{\!\!\{\mathscr{P}(\mathbf{G},\mathsf{p})\}\!\!\}_{\mathsf{p}\in\mathcal{P}}$. *It holds that* $I(w)$ *is non-empty.*

The reasoning for the sufficiency of Lemma 6.3 is included in the proof of Theorem 6.1, found in the extended version [29]. In the rest of this section, we focus our efforts on how to show this inductive invariant, namely that the intersection of all roles' possible run sets is non-empty.

We begin with the observation that the empty trace ε is consistent with all runs. As a result, $I(\varepsilon) = \bigcap_{\mathsf{p}\in\mathcal{P}} \mathrm{R}^{\mathbf{G}}_{\mathsf{p}}(\varepsilon)$ contains all maximal runs in $\mathsf{GAut}(\mathbf{G})$. By definition, state machines for global types include at least one run, and the base case is trivially discharged. Intuitively, $I(w)$ shrinks as more events are appended

$x = \text{p} \triangleright \text{q}!m,\ w \in \Sigma^*_{async}$

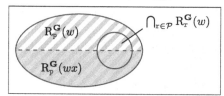

$y = \text{q} \triangleleft \text{p}?m,\ w' = wxu$ with $u \in \Sigma^*_{async}$

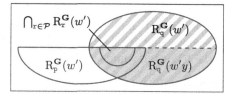

Fig. 3. Evolution of $\text{R}^{\mathbf{G}}_{-}(\text{-})$ sets when p sends a message m and q receives it.

to w, but we show that at no point does it shrink to $\emptyset$. We consider the cases where a send or receive event is appended to the trace separately, and show that the intersection set shrinks in a principled way that preserves non-emptiness. In fact, when a trace is extended with a receive event, Receive Validity guarantees that the intersection set does not shrink at all.

Lemma 6.4. *Let* $\mathbf{G}$ *be a global type and* $\{\!\!\{\mathscr{P}(\mathbf{G},\text{p})\}\!\!\}_{\text{p}\in\mathcal{P}}$ *be the subset projection. Let* wx *be a trace of* $\{\!\!\{\mathscr{P}(\mathbf{G},\text{p})\}\!\!\}_{\text{p}\in\mathcal{P}}$ *such that* $x \in \Sigma_?$. *Then,* $I(w) = I(wx)$.

To prove this equality, we further refine our characterization of intersection sets. In particular, we show that in the receive case, the intersection between the sender and receiver's possible run sets stays the same, i.e.

$$\text{R}^{\mathbf{G}}_{\text{p}}(w) \cap \text{R}^{\mathbf{G}}_{\text{q}}(w) = \text{R}^{\mathbf{G}}_{\text{p}}(wx) \cap \text{R}^{\mathbf{G}}_{\text{q}}(wx) \ .$$

Note that it is not the case that the receiver only follows a subset of the sender's possible runs. In other words, $\text{R}^{\mathbf{G}}_{\text{q}}(w) \subseteq \text{R}^{\mathbf{G}}_{\text{p}}(w)$ is not inductive. The equality above simply states that a receive action can only eliminate runs that have already been eliminated by its sender. Figure 3 depicts this relation.

Given that the intersection set strictly shrinks, the burden of eliminating runs must then fall upon send events. We show that send transitions shrink the possible run set of the sender in a way that is *prefix-preserving*. To make this more precise, we introduce the following definition on runs.

Definition 6.5 (Unique splitting of a possible run). *Let* $\mathbf{G}$ *be a global type,* p *a role, and* $w \in \Sigma^*_{async}$ *a word. Let* ρ *be a possible run in* $\text{R}^{\mathbf{G}}_{\text{p}}(w)$. *We define the longest prefix of* ρ *matching* w:

$$\alpha' := \max\{\rho' \mid \rho' \leq \rho \ \wedge \ \textit{split}(\textit{trace}(\rho'))\!\Downarrow_{\Sigma_{\text{p}}} \leq w\!\Downarrow_{\Sigma_{\text{p}}}\} \ .$$

If $\alpha' \neq \rho$, *we can split* ρ *into* $\rho = \alpha \cdot G \xrightarrow{l} G' \cdot \beta$ *where* $\alpha' = \alpha \cdot G$, G' *denotes the state following* G, *and* β *denotes the suffix of* ρ *following* $\alpha \cdot G \cdot G'$. *We call* $\alpha \cdot G \xrightarrow{l} G' \cdot \beta$ *the unique splitting of* ρ *for* p *matching* w. *We omit the role* p *when obvious from context. This splitting is always unique because the maximal prefix of any* $\rho \in \text{R}^{\mathbf{G}}_{\text{p}}(w)$ *matching* w *is unique.*

When role p fires a send transition $p \triangleright q!m$, any run $\rho = \alpha \cdot G \xrightarrow{l} G' \cdot \beta$ in p's possible run with $\mathrm{split}(l){\Downarrow}_{\Sigma_p} \neq p \triangleright q!m$ is eliminated. While the resulting possible run set could no longer contain runs that end with $G' \cdot \beta$, Send Validity guarantees that it must contain runs that begin with $\alpha \cdot G$. This is formalized by the following lemma.

Lemma 6.6. *Let $\mathbf{G}$ be a global type and $\{\!\{\mathscr{P}(\mathbf{G}, p)\}\!\}_{p\in\mathcal{P}}$ be the subset projection. Let wx be a trace of $\{\!\{\mathscr{P}(\mathbf{G}, p)\}\!\}_{p\in\mathcal{P}}$ such that $x \in \Sigma_! \cap \Sigma_p$ for some $p \in \mathcal{P}$. Let ρ be a run in $I(w)$, and $\alpha \cdot G \xrightarrow{l} G' \cdot \beta$ be the unique splitting of ρ for p with respect to w. Then, there exists a run ρ' in $I(wx)$ such that $\alpha \cdot G \leq \rho'$.*

This concludes our discussion of the send and receive cases in the inductive step to show the non-emptiness of the intersection of all roles' possible run sets. The full proofs and additional definitions can be found in the extended version [29].

7 Completeness

In this section, we prove completeness of our approach. While soundness states that if a global type's subset projection is defined, it then implements the global type, completeness considers the reverse direction.

Theorem 7.1 (Completeness). *If $\mathbf{G}$ is implementable, then $\{\!\{\mathscr{P}(\mathbf{G}, p)\}\!\}_{p\in\mathcal{P}}$ is defined.*

We sketch the proof and refer to the extended version [29] for the full proof.

From the assumption that $\mathbf{G}$ is implementable, we know there exists a witness CSM that implements $\mathbf{G}$. While the soundness proof picks our subset projection as the existential witness for showing implementability – thereby allowing us to reason directly about a particular implementation – completeness only guarantees the existence of some witness CSM. We cannot assume without loss of generality that this witness CSM is our subset construction; however, we must use the fact that it implements $\mathbf{G}$ to show that Send and Receive Validity hold on our subset construction.

We proceed via proof by contradiction: we assume the negation of Send and Receive Validity for the subset construction, and show a contradiction to the fact that this witness CSM implements $\mathbf{G}$. In particular, we contradict protocol fidelity (Definition 3.1(i)), stating that the witness CSM generates precisely the language $\mathcal{L}(\mathbf{G})$. To do so, we exploit a simulation argument: we first show that the negation of Send and Receive Validity forces the subset construction to recognize a trace that is not a prefix of any word in $\mathcal{L}(\mathbf{G})$. Then, we show that this trace must also be recognized by the witness CSM, under the assumption that the witness CSM implements $\mathbf{G}$.

To highlight the constructive nature of our proof, we convert our proof obligation to a witness construction obligation. To contradict protocol fidelity, it suffices to construct a witness trace v_0 satisfying two properties, where $\{\!\{B_p\}\!\}_{p\in\mathcal{P}}$ is our witness CSM:

(a) v_0 is a trace of $\{\!\{B_p\}\!\}_{p \in \mathcal{P}}$, and

(b) the run intersection set of v_0 is empty: $I(v_0) = \bigcap_{p \in \mathcal{P}} R_p^{\mathbf{G}}(v_0) = \emptyset$.

We first establish the sufficiency of conditions (a) and (b). Because $\{\!\{B_p\}\!\}_{p \in \mathcal{P}}$ is deadlock-free by assumption, every prefix extends to a maximal trace. Thus, to prove the inequality of the two languages $\mathcal{L}(\{\!\{B_p\}\!\}_{p \in \mathcal{P}})$ and $\mathcal{L}(\mathbf{G})$, it suffices to prove the inequality of their respective prefix sets. In turn, it suffices to show the existence of a prefix of a word in one language that is not a prefix of any word in the other. We choose to construct a prefix in the CSM language that is not a prefix in $\mathcal{L}(\mathbf{G})$. We again leverage the definition of intersection sets (Definition 6.2) to weaken the property of language non-membership to the property of having an empty intersection set as follows. By the semantics of $\mathcal{L}(\mathbf{G})$, for any $w \in \mathcal{L}(\mathbf{G})$, there exists $w' \in \mathtt{split}(\mathcal{L}(\mathsf{GAut}(\mathbf{G})))$ with $w \sim w'$. For any $w' \in \mathtt{split}(\mathcal{L}(\mathsf{GAut}(\mathbf{G})))$, it trivially holds that w' has a non-empty intersection set. Because intersection sets are invariant under the indistinguishability relation $\sim$, w must also have a non-empty intersection set. Since intersection sets are monotonically decreasing, if the intersection set of w is non-empty, then for any $v \leq w$, the intersection set of v is also non-empty. Modus tollens of the chain of reasoning above tells us that in order to show a word is not a prefix in $\mathcal{L}(\mathbf{G})$, it suffices to show that its intersection set is empty.

Having established the sufficiency of properties (a) and (b) for our witness construction, we present the steps to construct v_0 from the negation of Send and Receive Validity respectively. We start by constructing a trace in $\{\!\{\mathscr{C}(\mathbf{G}, p)_p\}\!\}_{p \in \mathcal{P}}$ that satisfies (b), and then show that $\{\!\{B_p\}\!\}_{p \in \mathcal{P}}$ also recognizes the trace, thereby satisfying (a). In both cases, let p be the role and s be the state for which the respective validity condition is violated.

Send Validity (Definition 5.2). Let $s \xrightarrow{p \triangleright q!m} s' \in \delta_p$ be a transition such that

$$\mathrm{tr\text{-}orig}(s \xrightarrow{p \triangleright q!m} s') \neq s .$$

First, we find a trace u of $\{\!\{\mathscr{C}(\mathbf{G}, p)_p\}\!\}_{p \in \mathcal{P}}$ that satisfies: (1) role p is in state s in the CSM configuration reached via u, and (2) the run of $\mathsf{GAut}(\mathbf{G})$ on u visits a state in $s \setminus \mathrm{tr\text{-}orig}(s \xrightarrow{p \triangleright q!m} s')$. We obtain such a witness u from the $\mathtt{split}(\mathtt{trace}(-))$ of a run prefix of $\mathsf{GAut}(\mathbf{G})$ that ends in some state in $s \setminus \mathrm{tr\text{-}orig}(s \xrightarrow{p \triangleright q!m} s')$. Any prefix thus obtained satisfies (1) by definition of $\mathscr{C}(\mathbf{G}, p)$, and satisfies (2) by construction. Due to the fact that send transitions are always enabled in a CSM, $u \cdot p \triangleright q!m$ must also be a trace of $\{\!\{\mathscr{C}(\mathbf{G}, p)\}\!\}_{p \in \mathcal{P}}$, thus satisfying property (a) by a simulation argument. We then argue that $u \cdot p \triangleright q!m$ satisfies property (b), stating that $I(u \cdot p \triangleright q!m)$ is empty: the negation of Send Validity gives that there exist no run extensions from our candidate state in $s \setminus \mathrm{tr\text{-}orig}(s \xrightarrow{p \triangleright q!m} s')$ with the immediate next action $p \to q : m$, and therefore there exists no maximal run in $\mathsf{GAut}(\mathbf{G})$ consistent with $u \cdot p \triangleright q!m$.

Receive Validity (Definition 5.3). Let $s \xrightarrow{\mathsf{p} \lhd \mathsf{q}_1 ? m_1} s_1$ and $s \xrightarrow{\mathsf{p} \lhd \mathsf{q}_2 ? m_2} s_2 \in \delta_\mathsf{p}$ be two transitions, and let $G_2 \in \text{tr-dest}(s \xrightarrow{\mathsf{p} \lhd \mathsf{q}_2 ? m_2} s_2)$ such that

$$\mathsf{q}_1 \neq \mathsf{q}_2 \text{ and } \mathsf{q}_1 \rhd \mathsf{p}!m_1 \in M^\mathsf{p}_{(G_2\dots)} \ .$$

Constructing the witness v_0 pivots on finding a trace u of $\{\!\{\mathscr{C}(\mathbf{G}, \mathsf{p})\}\!\}_{\mathsf{p} \in \mathcal{P}}$ such that both $u \cdot \mathsf{p} \lhd \mathsf{q}_1 ? m_1$ and $u \cdot \mathsf{p} \lhd \mathsf{q}_2 ? m_2$ are traces of $\{\!\{\mathscr{C}(\mathbf{G}, \mathsf{p})\}\!\}_{\mathsf{p} \in \mathcal{P}}$. Equivalently, we show there exists a reachable configuration of $\{\!\{\mathscr{C}(\mathbf{G}, \mathsf{p})\}\!\}_{\mathsf{p} \in \mathcal{P}}$ in which p can receive either message from distinct senders q_1 and q_2. Formally, the local state of p has two outgoing states labeled with $\mathsf{p} \lhd \mathsf{q}_1 ? m_1$ and $\mathsf{p} \lhd \mathsf{q}_2 ? m_2$, and the channels q_1, p and q_2, p have m_1 and m_2 at their respective heads. We construct such a u by considering a run in $\text{GAut}(\mathbf{G})$ that contains two transitions labeled with $\mathsf{q}_1 \to \mathsf{p} : m_1$ and $\mathsf{q}_2 \to \mathsf{p} : m_2$. Such a run must exist due to the negation of Receive Validity. We start with the split trace of this run, and argue that, from the definition of $M(\text{-})$ and the indistinguishability relation $\sim$, we can perform iterative reorderings using $\sim$ to bubble the send action $\mathsf{q}_1 \rhd \mathsf{p}!m_1$ to the position before the receive action $\mathsf{p} \lhd \mathsf{q}_2 ? m_2$. Then, (a) for $u \cdot \mathsf{p} \lhd \mathsf{q}_1 ? m_1$ holds by a simulation argument. We then separately show that (b) holds for $\mathsf{p} \lhd \mathsf{q}_1 ? m_1$ using similar reasoning as the send case to complete the proof that $u \cdot \mathsf{p} \lhd \mathsf{q}_1 ? m_1$ suffices as a witness for v_0.

It is worth noting that the construction of the witness prefix v_0 in the proof immediately yields an algorithm for computing counterexample traces to implementability.

Remark 7.2 (Mixed Choice is Not Needed to Implement Global Types). Theorem 7.1 basically shows the necessity of Send Validity for implementability. Corollary 5.5 shows that Send Validity precludes states with both send and receive outgoing transitions. Together, this implies that an implementable global type can always be implemented without mixed choice. Note that the syntactic restrictions on global types do not inherently prevent mixed choice states from arising in a role's subset construction, as evidenced by r in the following type: $\mathsf{p} \to \mathsf{q} : l. \mathsf{q} \to \mathsf{r} : m. 0 + \mathsf{p} \to \mathsf{q} : r. \mathsf{r} \to \mathsf{q} : m. 0$. Our completeness result thus implies that this type is not implementable. Most MST frameworks [18,24,31] implicitly force *no mixed choice* through syntactic restrictions on local types. We are the first to prove that mixed choice states are indeed not necessary for completeness. This is interesting because mixed choice is known to be crucial for the expressive power of the synchronous π-calculus compared to its asynchronous variant [32].

8   Complexity

In this section, we establish PSPACE-completeness of checking implementability for global types.

Theorem 8.1. *The MST implementability problem is PSPACE-complete.*

Proof. We first establish the upper bound. The decision procedure enumerates for each role p the subsets of $\mathsf{GAut}(G){\downarrow}_p$. This can be done in polynomial space and exponential time. For each p and $s \subseteq Q_G$, it then (i) checks membership of s in Q_p of $\mathscr{C}(G, p)$, and (ii) if $s \in Q_p$, checks whether all outgoing transitions of s in $\mathscr{C}(G, p)$ satisfy Send and Receive Validity. Check (i) can be reduced to the intersection non-emptiness problem for nondeterministic finite state machines, which is in PSPACE [44]. It is easy to see that check (ii) can be done in polynomial time. In particular, the computation of available messages for Receive Validity only requires a single unfolding of every loop in G.

Note that the synthesis problem has the same complexity. The subset construction to determinize $\mathsf{GAut}(G){\downarrow}_p$ can be done using a PSPACE transducer. While the output can be of exponential size, it is written on an extra tape that is not counted towards memory usage. However, this means we need to perform the validity checks as described above instead of using the computed deterministic state machines.

Second, we prove the lower bound. The proof is inspired by the proof for Theorem 4 [4] in which Alur et al. prove that checking safe realizability of bounded HMSCs is PSPACE-hard. We reduce the PSPACE-complete problem of checking universality of an NFA $M = (Q, \Delta, \delta, q_0, F)$ to checking implementability. Without loss of generality, we assume that every state can reach a final state. We construct a global type G for p, q and r that is implementable iff $\mathcal{L}(M) = \Delta^*$. For this, we define subterms G_l and G_r as well as G_q for every $q \in Q$ and G_*. We use a fresh letter $\perp$ to handle final states of M. We also define $p \leftrightarrow q : m$ as an abbreviation for $p \rightarrow q : m . q \rightarrow p : m$.

$$G := G_l + G_r$$

$$G_l := p \leftrightarrow q : l . p \leftrightarrow r : go . G_{q_0}$$

$$G_q := \begin{cases} \sum_{(a, q') \in \delta(q)} (r \leftrightarrow q : a . G_{q'}) & \text{if } q \notin F \\ r \leftrightarrow q : \perp . 0 + \sum_{(a, q') \in \delta(q)} (r \leftrightarrow q : a . G_{q'}) & \text{if } q \in F \end{cases}$$

$$G_r := p \leftrightarrow q : r . p \leftrightarrow r : go . G_*$$

$$G_* := r \leftrightarrow q : \perp . 0 + \sum_{a \in \Delta} (r \leftrightarrow q : a . G_*)$$

The global type G is constructed such that p first decides whether words from $\mathcal{L}(M)$ or from Δ^* are sent subsequently. This decision is known to p and q but not to r. The protocol then continues with r sending letters from Δ to q, and p is not involved. Intuitively, q is able to receive these letters if and only if $\mathcal{L}(M) = \Delta^*$. From Theorems 6.1 and 7.1, we know that $\{\!\{\mathscr{C}(G, p)_p\}\!\}_{p \in \mathcal{P}}$ implements G if G is implementable.

We claim that $\{\!\{\mathscr{C}(G, p)_p\}\!\}_{p \in \mathcal{P}}$ implements G if and only if $\mathcal{L}(M) = \Delta^*$.

First, assume that $\mathcal{L}(M) \neq \Delta^*$. Then, there exists $w \notin \mathcal{L}(M)$. We can construct the following run of $\{\!\{\mathscr{C}(\mathbf{G}, \mathsf{p})_\mathsf{p}\}\!\}_{\mathsf{p} \in \mathcal{P}}$ that deadlocks. Role p chooses the left subterm G_l and, subsequently, r sends w to q. We do a case analysis on whether w contains a prefix w' such that $w' \notin \mathrm{pref}(\mathcal{L}(M))$. If so, sending the last letter of a minimal prefix leads to a deadlock in $\{\!\{\mathscr{C}(\mathbf{G}, \mathsf{p})_\mathsf{p}\}\!\}_{\mathsf{p} \in \mathcal{P}}$, contradicting deadlock freedom. If not, it holds that w is a prefix of a word in $\mathcal{L}(M)$. Still, role r can send $\perp$, which cannot be received, also contradicting deadlock freedom.

Second, assume that $\mathcal{L}(M) = \Delta^*$. With this, it is fine that r does not know the branch. Role q will be able to receive all messages since $\mathscr{C}(\mathbf{G}, \mathsf{q})$ can receive, letter by letter, $w.\perp$ for every $w \in \mathcal{L}(M)$ from r. Thus, protocol fidelity and deadlock freedom hold, concluding the proof.

Note that PSPACE-hardness only holds if the size of $\mathbf{G}$ does not account for common subterms multiple times. Because every message is immediately acknowledged, the constructed global type specifies a universally 1-bounded [23] language, proving that PSPACE-hardness persists for such a restriction. For our construction, it does not hold that $\mathcal{V}(\mathcal{L}(G_l)\Downarrow_{\Sigma_{\mathsf{q},?}}) = \mathcal{L}(M)$. We chose so to have a more compact protocol. However, we can easily fix this by sending the decision of r first to p, allowing to omit the messages $\perp$ to q. □

This result and the fact that local languages are preserved by the subset projection (Lemma 4.3) leads to the following observation.

Corollary 8.2. *Let* $\mathbf{G}$ *be an implementable global type. Then, the subset projection* $\{\!\{\mathscr{P}(\mathbf{G}, \mathsf{p})\}\!\}_{\mathsf{p} \in \mathcal{P}}$ *is a local language preserving implementation for* $\mathbf{G}$, *i.e.,* $\mathcal{L}(\mathscr{P}(\mathbf{G}, \mathsf{p})) = \mathcal{L}(\mathbf{G})\Downarrow_{\Sigma_\mathsf{p}}$ *for every* p, *and can be computed in PSPACE.*

Remark 8.3 (MST implementability with directed choice is PSPACE-hard). Theorem 8.1 is stated for global types with sender-driven choice but the provided type is in fact directed. Thus, the PSPACE lower bound also holds for implementability of types with directed choice.

9 Evaluation

We consider the following three aspects in the evaluation of our approach: (E1) difficulty of implementation (E2) completeness, and (E3) comparison to state of the art.

For this, we implemented our subset projection in a prototype tool [1,37]. It takes a global type as input and computes the subset projection for each role. It was straightforward to implement the core functionality in approximately 700 lines of Python3 code closely following the formalization (E1).

We consider global types (and communication protocols) from seven different sources as well as all examples from this work (cf. 1st column of Table 1). Our experiments were run on a computer with an Intel Core i7-1165G7 CPU and used at most 100MB of memory. The results are summarized in Table 1. The reported size is the number of states and transitions of the respective state machine, which

Table 1. Projecting Global Types. For every protocol, we report whether it is implementable ✓ or not ×, the time to compute our subset projection and the generalized projection by Majumdar et al. [31] as well as the outcome as ✓ for "implementable", × for "not implementable" and (×) for "not known". We also give the size of the protocol (number of states and transitions), the number of roles, the combined size of all subset projections (number of states and transitions).

Source	Name	Impl.	Subset Proj. (complete)		Size	$\|\mathcal{P}\|$	Size Proj's	[31] (incomplete)	
	Instrument Contr. Prot. A	✓	✓	0.4 ms	22	3	61	✓	0.2 ms
[35]	Instrument Contr. Prot. B	✓	✓	0.3 ms	17	3	47	✓	0.1 ms
	OAuth2	✓	✓	0.1 ms	10	3	23	✓	< 0.1 ms
[34]	Multi Party Game	✓	✓	0.5 ms	21	3	67	✓	0.1 ms
[24]	Streaming	✓	✓	0.2 ms	13	4	28	✓	< 0.1 ms
[13]	Non-Compatible Merge	✓	✓	0.2 ms	11	3	25	✓	0.1 ms
[45]	Spring-Hibernate	✓	✓	1.0 ms	62	6	118	✓	0.7 ms
	Group Present	✓	✓	0.6 ms	51	4	85	✓	0.6 ms
[31]	Late Learning	✓	✓	0.3 ms	17	4	34	✓	0.2 ms
	Load Balancer ($n = 10$)	✓	✓	3.9 ms	36	12	106	✓	2.4 ms
	Logging ($n = 10$)	✓	✓	71.5 ms	81	13	322	✓	10.0 ms
	2 Buyer Protocol	✓	✓	0.5 ms	22	3	60	✓	0.2 ms
[38]	2B-Prot. Omit No	✓	✓	0.4 ms	19	3	56	(×)	0.1 ms
	2B-Prot. Subscription	✓	✓	0.7 ms	46	3	95	(×)	0.3 ms
	2B-Prot. Inner Recursion	✓	✓	0.4 ms	17	3	51	✓	0.1 ms
	Odd-even (Example 2.1)	✓	✓	0.5 ms	32	3	70	(×)	0.2 ms
	$\mathbf{G}_r$ – Receive Val. Violated (§2)	×	×	0.1 ms	12	3	-	(×)	< 0.1 ms
New	$\mathbf{G}'_r$ – Receive Val. Satisfied (§2)	✓	✓	0.2 ms	16	3	35	✓	0.1 ms
	$\mathbf{G}_s$ – Send Val. Violated (§2)	×	×	< 0.1 ms	8	3	-	(×)	< 0.1 ms
	$\mathbf{G}'_s$ – Send Val. Satisfied (§2)	✓	✓	< 0.1 ms	7	3	17	✓	< 0.1 ms
	$\mathbf{G}_{\mathrm{fold}}$ (§10)	✓	✓	0.4 ms	21	3	50	(×)	0.1 ms
	$\mathbf{G}_{\mathrm{unf}}$ (§10)	✓	✓	0.4 ms	30	3	61	✓	0.2 ms

allows not to account for multiple occurrences of the same subterm. As expected, our tool can project every implementable protocol we have considered (E2).

Regarding the comparison against the state of the art (E3), we directly compared our subset projection to the incomplete approach by Majumdar et al. [31], and found that the run times are in the same order of magnitude in general (typically a few milliseconds). However, the projection of [31] fails to project four implementable protocols (including Example 2.1). We discuss some of the other examples in more detail in the next section. We further note that most of the run times reported by Scalas and Yoshida [36] on their model checking based tool are around 1 s and are thus two to three orders of magnitude slower.

10   Discussion

Success of Syntactic Projections Depends on Representation. Let us illustrate how unfolding recursion helps syntactic projection operators to succeed. Consider this implementable global type, which is not syntactically projectable:

$$G_{\text{fold}} := + \begin{cases} p \to q : o.\, \mu t_1.\, (p \to q : o.\, q \to r : o.\, t_1 \; + \; p \to q : b.\, q \to r : b.\, 0) \\ p \to q : m.\, q \to r : m.\, \mu t_2.\, (p \to q : o.\, q \to r : o.\, t_2 \; + \; p \to q : b.\, q \to r : b.\, 0) \end{cases} .$$

Similar to projection by erasure, a syntactic projection erases events that a role is not involved in and immediately tries to *merge* different branches. The merge operator is a partial operator that checks sufficient conditions for implementability. Here, the merge operator fails for r because it cannot merge a recursion variable binder and a message reception. Unfolding the global type preserves the represented protocol and resolves this issue:

$$G_{\text{unf}} := + \begin{cases} p \to q : o.\, \begin{cases} p \to q : b.\, q \to r : b.\, 0 \\ p \to q : o.\, q \to r : o.\, \mu t_1.\, (p \to q : o.\, q \to r : o.\, t_1 \; + \; p \to q : b.\, q \to r : b.\, 0) \end{cases} \\ p \to q : m.\, q \to r : m.\, \mu t_2.\, (p \to q : o.\, q \to r : o.\, t_2 \; + \; p \to q : b.\, q \to r : b.\, 0) \end{cases} .$$

(We refer to [29] for visual representations of both global types.) This global type can be projected with most syntactic projection operators and shows that the representation of the global type matters for syntactic projectability. However, such unfolding tricks do not always work, e.g. for the odd-even protocol (Example 2.1). We avoid this brittleness using automata and separating the synthesis from checking implementability.

Entailed Properties from the Literature. We defined implementability for a global type as the question of whether there exists a deadlock-free CSM that generates the same language as the global type. Various other properties of implementations and protocols have been proposed in the literature. Here, we give a brief overview and defer to the extended version [29] for a detailed analysis. *Progress* [18], a common property, requires that every sent message is eventually received and every expected message will eventually be sent. With deadlock freedom, our subset projection trivially satisfies progress for finite traces. For infinite traces, as expected, fairness assumptions are required to enforce progress. Similarly, our subset projection prevents *unspecified receptions* [14] and *orphan messages* [9,21], respectively interpreted in our multiparty setting with sender-driven choice. We also ensure that every local transition of each role is *executable* [14], i.e. it is taken in some run of the CSM. Any implementation of a global type has the *stable property* [28], i.e., one can always reach a configuration with empty channels from every reachable configuration. While the properties above are naturally satisfied by our subset projection, the following ones can be checked directly on an implementable global type without explicitly constructing the implementation. A global type is *terminating* [36] iff it does not contain recursion and *never-terminating* [36] iff it does not contain term 0.

11 Related Work

MSTs were introduced by Honda et al. [24] with a process algebra semantics, and the connection to CSMs was established soon afterwards [20].

In this work, we present a complete projection procedure for global types with sender-driven choice. The work by Castagna et al. [13] is the only one to present a projection that aims for completeness. Their semantic conditions, however, are not effectively computable and their notion of completeness is "less demanding than the classical ones" [13]. They consider multiple implementations, generating different sets of traces, to be sound and complete with regard to a single global type [13, Sec. 5.3]. In addition, the algorithmic version of their conditions does not use global information as our message availability analysis does.

MST implementability relates to safe realizability of HMSCs, which is undecidable in general but decidable for certain classes [30]. Stutz [38] showed that implementability of global types that are always able to terminate is decidable.[1] The EXPSPACE decision procedure is obtained via a reduction to safe realizability of globally-cooperative HMSCs, by proving that the HMSC encoding [39] of any implementable global type is globally-cooperative and generalizing results for infinite executions. Thus, our PSPACE-completeness result both generalizes and tightens the earlier decidability result obtained in [38]. Stutz [38] also investigates how HMSC techniques for safe realizability can be applied to the MST setting – using the formal connection between MST implementability and safe realizability of HMSCs – and establishes an undecidability result for a variant of MST implementability with a relaxed indistinguishability relation.

Similar to the MST setting, there have been approaches in the HMSC literature that tie branching to a role making a choice. We refer the reader to the work by Majumdar et al. [31] for a survey.

Standard MST frameworks project a global type to a set of *local types* rather than a CSM. Local types are easily translated to FSMs [31, Def.11]. Our projection operator, though, can yield FSMs that cannot be expressed with the limited syntax of local types. Consider this implementable global type: $p \rightarrow q : o.\, 0 + p \rightarrow q : m.\, p \rightarrow r : b.\, 0$. The subset projection for r has two final states connected by a transition labeled $r \triangleleft p?b$. In the syntax of local types, 0 is the only term indicating termination, which means that final states with outgoing transitions cannot be expressed. In contrast to the syntactic restrictions for global types, which are key to effective verification, we consider local types unnecessarily restrictive. Usually, local implementations are type-checked against their local types and subtyping gives some implementation freedom [12,16,17,27]. However, one can also view our subset projection as a local specification of the actual implementation. We conjecture that subtyping would then amount to a variation of alternating refinement [5].

CSMs are Turing-powerful [11] but decidable classes were obtained for different semantics: restricted communication topology [33,42], half-duplex communication (only for two roles) [14], input-bounded [10], and unreliable channels [2,3].

---

[1] This syntactic restriction is referred to as 0-reachability in [38].

Global types (as well choreography automata [7]) can only express existentially 1-bounded, 1-synchronizable and half-duplex communication [39]. Key to this result is that sending and receiving a message is specified atomically in a global type — a feature Dagnino et al. [19] waived for their deconfined global types. However, Dagnino et al. [19] use deconfined types to capture the behavior of a given system rather than projecting to obtain a system that generates specified behaviors.

This work relies on reliable communication as is standard for MST frameworks. Work on fault-tolerant MST frameworks [8,43] attempts to relax this restriction. In the setting of reliable communication, both context-free [25,40] and parametric [15,22] versions of session types have been proposed to capture more expressive protocols and entire protocol families respectively. Extending our approach to these generalizations is an interesting direction for future work.

Acknowledgements. This work is funded in part by the National Science Foundation under grant 1815633. Felix Stutz was supported by the Deutsche Forschungsgemeinschaft project 389792660 TRR 248—CPEC.

References

1. Prototype Implementation of Subset Projection for Multiparty Session Types. https://gitlab.mpi-sws.org/fstutz/async-mpst-gen-choice/
2. Abdulla, P.A., Aiswarya, C., Atig, M.F.: Data communicating processes with unreliable channels. In: Grohe, M., Koskinen, E., Shankar, N. (eds.) Proceedings of the 31st Annual ACM/IEEE Symposium on Logic in Computer Science, LICS '16, New York, NY, USA, 5–8 July 2016, pp. 166–175. ACM (2016). https://doi.org/10.1145/2933575.2934535
3. Abdulla, P.A., Bouajjani, A., Jonsson, B.: On-the-fly analysis of systems with unbounded, lossy FIFO channels. In: Hu, A.J., Vardi, M.Y. (eds.) CAV 1998. LNCS, vol. 1427, pp. 305–318. Springer, Heidelberg (1998). https://doi.org/10.1007/BFb0028754
4. Alur, R., Etessami, K., Yannakakis, M.: Realizability and verification of MSC graphs. Theor. Comput. Sci. **331**(1), 97–114 (2005). https://doi.org/10.1016/j.tcs.2004.09.034
5. Alur, R., Henzinger, T.A., Kupferman, O., Vardi, M.Y.: Alternating refinement relations. In: Sangiorgi, D., de Simone, R. (eds.) CONCUR 1998. LNCS, vol. 1466, pp. 163–178. Springer, Heidelberg (1998). https://doi.org/10.1007/BFb0055622
6. Ancona, D., et al.: Behavioral types in programming languages. Found. Trends Program. Lang. **3**(2-3), 95–230 (2016). https://doi.org/10.1561/2500000031
7. Barbanera, F., Lanese, I., Tuosto, E.: Choreography automata. In: Bliudze, S., Bocchi, L. (eds.) COORDINATION 2020. LNCS, vol. 12134, pp. 86–106. Springer, Cham (2020). https://doi.org/10.1007/978-3-030-50029-0_6
8. Barwell, A.D., Scalas, A., Yoshida, N., Zhou, F.: Generalised multiparty session types with crash-stop failures. In: Klin, B., Lasota, S., Muscholl, A. (eds.) 33rd International Conference on Concurrency Theory, CONCUR 2022, 12–16 September 2022, Warsaw, Poland. LIPIcs, vol. 243, pp. 35:1–35:25. Schloss Dagstuhl - Leibniz-Zentrum für Informatik (2022). https://doi.org/10.4230/LIPIcs.CONCUR.2022.35

9. Bocchi, L., Lange, J., Yoshida, N.: Meeting deadlines together. In: Aceto, L., de Frutos-Escrig, D. (eds.) 26th International Conference on Concurrency Theory, CONCUR 2015, Madrid, Spain, 1–4 September 2015. LIPIcs, vol. 42, pp. 283–296. Schloss Dagstuhl - Leibniz-Zentrum für Informatik (2015). https://doi.org/10.4230/LIPIcs.CONCUR.2015.283

10. Bollig, B., Finkel, A., Suresh, A.: Bounded reachability problems are decidable in FIFO machines. In: Konnov, I., Kovács, L. (eds.) 31st International Conference on Concurrency Theory, CONCUR 2020, 1–4 September 2020, Vienna, Austria (Virtual Conference). LIPIcs, vol. 171, pp. 49:1–49:17. Schloss Dagstuhl - Leibniz-Zentrum für Informatik (2020). https://doi.org/10.4230/LIPIcs.CONCUR.2020.49

11. Brand, D., Zafiropulo, P.: On communicating finite-state machines. J. ACM **30**(2), 323–342 (1983). https://doi.org/10.1145/322374.322380

12. Bravetti, M., Carbone, M., Zavattaro, G.: On the boundary between decidability and undecidability of asynchronous session subtyping. Theor. Comput. Sci. **722**, 19–51 (2018). https://doi.org/10.1016/j.tcs.2018.02.010

13. Castagna, G., Dezani-Ciancaglini, M., Padovani, L.: On global types and multiparty session. Log. Methods Comput. Sci. **8**(1) (2012). https://doi.org/10.2168/LMCS-8(1:24)2012

14. Cécé, G., Finkel, A.: Verification of programs with half-duplex communication. Inf. Comput. **202**(2), 166–190 (2005). https://doi.org/10.1016/j.ic.2005.05.006

15. Charalambides, M., Dinges, P., Agha, G.A.: Parameterized, concurrent session types for asynchronous multi-actor interactions. Sci. Comput. Program. **115-116**, 100–126 (2016). https://doi.org/10.1016/j.scico.2015.10.006

16. Chen, T., Dezani-Ciancaglini, M., Scalas, A., Yoshida, N.: On the preciseness of subtyping in session types. Log. Methods Comput. Sci. 13(2) (2017). https://doi.org/10.23638/LMCS-13(2:12)2017

17. Chen, T., Dezani-Ciancaglini, M., Yoshida, N.: On the preciseness of subtyping in session types. In: Chitil, O., King, A., Danvy, O. (eds.) Proceedings of the 16th International Symposium on Principles and Practice of Declarative Programming, Kent, Canterbury, United Kingdom, 8–10, September 2014. pp. 135–146. ACM (2014). https://doi.org/10.1145/2643135.2643138

18. Coppo, M., Dezani-Ciancaglini, M., Padovani, L., Yoshida, N.: A gentle introduction to multiparty asynchronous session types. In: Bernardo, M., Johnsen, E.B. (eds.) SFM 2015. LNCS, vol. 9104, pp. 146–178. Springer, Cham (2015). https://doi.org/10.1007/978-3-319-18941-3_4

19. Dagnino, F., Giannini, P., Dezani-Ciancaglini, M.: Deconfined global types for asynchronous sessions. In: Damiani, F., Dardha, O. (eds.) COORDINATION 2021. LNCS, vol. 12717, pp. 41–60. Springer, Cham (2021). https://doi.org/10.1007/978-3-030-78142-2_3

20. Deniélou, P.-M., Yoshida, N.: Multiparty session types meet communicating automata. In: Seidl, H. (ed.) ESOP 2012. LNCS, vol. 7211, pp. 194–213. Springer, Heidelberg (2012). https://doi.org/10.1007/978-3-642-28869-2_10

21. Deniélou, P.-M., Yoshida, N.: Multiparty compatibility in communicating automata: characterisation and synthesis of global session types. In: Fomin, F.V., Freivalds, R., Kwiatkowska, M., Peleg, D. (eds.) ICALP 2013. LNCS, vol. 7966, pp. 174–186. Springer, Heidelberg (2013). https://doi.org/10.1007/978-3-642-39212-2_18

22. Deniélou, P., Yoshida, N., Bejleri, A., Hu, R.: Parameterised multiparty session types. Log. Methods Comput. Sci. **8**(4) (2012). https://doi.org/10.2168/LMCS-8(4:6)2012

23. Genest, B., Kuske, D., Muscholl, A.: On communicating automata with bounded channels. Fundam. Inform. **80**(1–3), 147–167 (2007). http://content.iospress.com/articles/fundamenta-informaticae/fi80-1-3-09

24. Honda, K., Yoshida, N., Carbone, M.: Multiparty asynchronous session types. In: Necula, G.C., Wadler, P. (eds.) Proceedings of the 35th ACM SIGPLAN-SIGACT Symposium on Principles of Programming Languages, POPL 2008, San Francisco, California, USA, 7–12 January 2008, pp. 273–284. ACM (2008). https://doi.org/10.1145/1328438.1328472

25. Keizer, A.C., Basold, H., Pérez, J.A.: Session coalgebras: a coalgebraic view on regular and context-free session types. ACM Trans. Program. Lang. Syst. **44**(3), 18:1–18:45 (2022). https://doi.org/10.1145/3527633

26. Lamport, L.: Time, clocks, and the ordering of events in a distributed system. Commun. ACM **21**(7), 558–565 (1978). https://doi.org/10.1145/359545.359563

27. Lange, J., Yoshida, N.: On the undecidability of asynchronous session subtyping. In: Esparza, J., Murawski, A.S. (eds.) FoSSaCS 2017. LNCS, vol. 10203, pp. 441–457. Springer, Heidelberg (2017). https://doi.org/10.1007/978-3-662-54458-7_26

28. Lange, J., Yoshida, N.: Verifying asynchronous interactions via communicating session automata. In: Dillig, I., Tasiran, S. (eds.) CAV 2019. LNCS, vol. 11561, pp. 97–117. Springer, Cham (2019). https://doi.org/10.1007/978-3-030-25540-4_6

29. Li, E., Stutz, F., Wies, T., Zufferey, D.: Complete multiparty session type projection with automata. CoRR abs/2305.17079 (2023). https://doi.org/10.48550/arXiv.2305.17079

30. Lohrey, M.: Realizability of high-level message sequence charts: closing the gaps. Theor. Comput. Sci. **309**(1-3), 529–554 (2003). https://doi.org/10.1016/j.tcs.2003.08.002

31. Majumdar, R., Mukund, M., Stutz, F., Zufferey, D.: Generalising projection in asynchronous multiparty session types. In: Haddad, S., Varacca, D. (eds.) 32nd International Conference on Concurrency Theory, CONCUR 2021, 24–27 August 2021, Virtual Conference. LIPIcs, vol. 203, pp. 35:1–35:24. Schloss Dagstuhl - Leibniz-Zentrum für Informatik (2021). https://doi.org/10.4230/LIPIcs.CONCUR.2021.35

32. Palamidessi, C.: Comparing the expressive power of the synchronous and asynchronous pi-calculi. Math. Struct. Comput. Sci. **13**(5), 685–719 (2003). https://doi.org/10.1017/S0960129503004043

33. Peng, W., Purushothaman, S.: Analysis of a class of communicating finite state machines. Acta Informatica **29**(6/7), 499–522 (1992). https://doi.org/10.1007/BF01185558

34. Scalas, A., Dardha, O., Hu, R., Yoshida, N.: A linear decomposition of multiparty sessions for safe distributed programming. In: Müller, P. (ed.) 31st European Conference on Object-Oriented Programming, ECOOP 2017, 19–23 June 2017, Barcelona, Spain. LIPIcs, vol. 74, pp. 24:1–24:31. Schloss Dagstuhl - Leibniz-Zentrum für Informatik (2017). https://doi.org/10.4230/LIPIcs.ECOOP.2017.24

35. Scalas, A., Yoshida, N.: Mpstk: the multiparty session types toolkit (2018). https://doi.org/10.1145/3291638

36. Scalas, A., Yoshida, N.: Less is more: multiparty session types revisited. Proc. ACM Program. Lang. **3**(POPL), 30:1–30:29 (2019). https://doi.org/10.1145/3290343

37. Stutz, F.: Artifact for "Complete Multiparty Session Type Projection with Automata", April 2023. https://doi.org/10.5281/zenodo.7878493

38. Stutz, F.: Asynchronous multiparty session type implementability is decidable - lessons learned from message sequence charts. In: 37th European Conference on Object-Oriented Programming, ECOOP 2023. LIPIcs (2023). https://arxiv.org/pdf/2302.11272.pdf
39. Stutz, F., Zufferey, D.: Comparing channel restrictions of communicating state machines, high-level message sequence charts, and multiparty session types. In: Ganty, P., Monica, D.D. (eds.) Proceedings of the 13th International Symposium on Games, Automata, Logics and Formal Verification, GandALF 2022, Madrid, Spain, 21–23 September 2022. EPTCS, vol. 370, pp. 194–212 (2022). https://doi.org/10.4204/EPTCS.370.13
40. Thiemann, P., Vasconcelos, V.T.: Context-free session types. In: Garrigue, J., Keller, G., Sumii, E. (eds.) Proceedings of the 21st ACM SIGPLAN International Conference on Functional Programming, ICFP 2016, Nara, Japan, 18–22 September 2016, pp. 462–475. ACM (2016). https://doi.org/10.1145/2951913.2951926
41. Toninho, B., Yoshida, N.: Certifying data in multiparty session types. J. Log. Algebraic Methods Program. **90**, 61–83 (2017). https://doi.org/10.1016/j.jlamp.2016.11.005
42. La Torre, S., Madhusudan, P., Parlato, G.: Context-bounded analysis of concurrent queue systems. In: Ramakrishnan, C.R., Rehof, J. (eds.) TACAS 2008. LNCS, vol. 4963, pp. 299–314. Springer, Heidelberg (2008). https://doi.org/10.1007/978-3-540-78800-3_21
43. Viering, M., Hu, R., Eugster, P., Ziarek, L.: A multiparty session typing discipline for fault-tolerant event-driven distributed programming. Proc. ACM Program. Lang. **5**(OOPSLA), 1–30 (2021). https://doi.org/10.1145/3485501
44. Wehar, M.: On the complexity of intersection non-emptiness problems. Ph.D. thesis, University of Buffalo (2016)
45. Spring and Hibernate Transaction in Java. https://www.uml-diagrams.org/examples/spring-hibernate-transaction-sequence-diagram-example.html

Early Verification of Legal Compliance via Bounded Satisfiability Checking

Nick Feng[1]([✉]), Lina Marsso[1], Mehrdad Sabetzadeh[2], and Marsha Chechik[1]

[1] University of Toronto, Toronto, Canada
{fengnick,lmarsso,chechik}@cs.toronto.edu
[2] University of Ottawa, Ottawa, Canada
m.sabetzadeh@uottawa.ca

Abstract. Legal properties involve reasoning about data values and time. Metric first-order temporal logic (MFOTL) provides a rich formalism for specifying legal properties. While MFOTL has been successfully used for verifying legal properties over operational systems via runtime monitoring, no solution exists for MFOTL-based verification in early-stage system development captured by requirements. Given a legal property and system requirements, both formalized in MFOTL, the compliance of the property can be verified on the requirements via satisfiability checking. In this paper, we propose a practical, sound, and complete (within a given bound) satisfiability checking approach for MFOTL. The approach, based on satisfiability modulo theories (SMT), employs a counterexample-guided strategy to incrementally search for a satisfying solution. We implemented our approach using the Z3 SMT solver and evaluated it on five case studies spanning the healthcare, business administration, banking and aviation domains. Our results indicate that our approach can efficiently determine whether legal properties of interest are met, or generate counterexamples that lead to compliance violations.

1 Introduction

Software systems, such as medical systems, are increasingly required to comply with laws and regulations aimed at ensuring safety, security, and data privacy [1,36]. The properties stipulated by these laws and regulations – which we refer to as *legal properties* (LP) hereafter – typically involve reasoning about actions, ordering and time. As an example, consider the following LP, $P1$, derived from a health-data regulation (s.11, PHIPA [20]): "If personal health information is not accurate or not up-to-date, it should not be accessed". In this property, the accuracy and the freshness of the data depend on how and when the data was collected and updated before being accessed. Specifically, this property constrains the data action *access* to have accurate and up-to-date data values, which further constrains the order and time of *access* with respect to other data actions.

System compliance with LPs can be checked on the system design or on an operational model of a system implementation. In this paper, we focus on the early stage, where one can check whether a formalization of the system

© The Author(s) 2023
C. Enea and A. Lal (Eds.): CAV 2023, LNCS 13966, pp. 374–396, 2023.
https://doi.org/10.1007/978-3-031-37709-9_18

requirements satisfies an LP. The formalization can be done using a descriptive formalism like temporal logic [24,35]. For instance, the requirement (req_0) of a data collection system: "no data can be accessed prior to 15 days after the data has been collected" needs to be formalized for verifying compliance of $P1$. It is important to formalize the data and time constraints of both the system requirements and LPs, such as the ones of $P1$ and req_0.

Metric first-order temporal logic (MFOTL) enables the specification of data and time constraints [3] and has an expressive formalism for capturing LPs and the related system requirements that constrain data and time [1]. Existing work on MFOTL verification focuses on detecting violations at run-time through monitoring [1,19], with MFOTL formulas being checked on execution logs. There is an unmet need for determining the *satisfiability* of MFOTL specifications, i.e., looking for LP violations possible in MFOTL specification. This is important for designing systems that comply with their legal requirements.

MFOTL satisfiability checking is generally undecidable since MFOTL is an extension of first-order logic (FOL). Restrictions are thus necessary for making the problem decidable. In this paper, we restrict ourselves to safety properties. For safety properties, LP violations are finite sequences of data actions, captured via a finite-length counterexample. For example, a possible violation of $P1$ is a sequence consisting of storing a value v in a variable d, updating d's value to v', then reading d again and not obtaining v'. Since we are interested in finite counterexamples, bounded verification is a natural strategy to pursue for achieving decidability. SAT solvers have been previously used for bounded satisfiability checking of metric temporal logic (MTL) [24,35]. However, MTL cannot effectively capture quantified data constraints in LPs, hence the solution is not applicable directly. As an extension to MTL, MFOTL can effectively capture data constraints used in LP. Yet, to the best of our knowledge, there has not been any prior work on bounded MFOTL satisfiability checking.

To establish a *bound* in bounded verification, researchers have predominantly relied on bounding the *size of the universe* [13]. Bounding the universe would be too restrictive because LPs routinely refer to variables with large ranges, e.g., timed actions spanning several years. Instead, we bound the *number of data actions in a run*, which bounds the number of actions in the counterexample.

Equipped with our proposed notion of a bound, we develop an incremental approach (IBS) for bounded satisfiability checking of MFOTL. We first translate the MFOTL property and requirements into first-order logic formulas with quantified relational objects (FOL*). We then incrementally ground the FOL* constraints to eliminate the quantifiers by considering an increasing number of relational objects. Subsequently, we check the satisfiability of the resulting constraints using an SMT solver. Specifically, we make the following contributions: (1) we propose a translation of MFOTL formulas to FOL*; (2) we provide a novel bounded satisfiability checking solution, IBS, for the translated FOL* formulas with incremental and counterexample-guided over/ under-approximation. Note that while our solution to MFOTL satisfibility checking can be applied to a broader set of applications, in this paper we focus on the legal domain. We

$P1 = \square \; \forall d, v(Access(d, v)) \implies (\forall v'(v' \neq v \Rightarrow \neg Update(d, v') \wedge \neg Collect(d, v'))) \; \mathcal{S} \; (Update(d, v) \vee Collect(d, v)))$
If a personal health information is not accurate or not up-to-date, it should not be accessed.

$req_0 = \square \; \forall d, v(Access(d, v)) \implies \blacklozenge_{[360,)} \exists v'. Collect(d, v')$
No data is allowed to be accessed before the data ID has been collected for at least 15 days (360 hours).

$req_1 = \square \; \forall d, v(Update(d, v)) \implies \neg(\blacklozenge_{[1,168]} \exists v'.(Collect(d, v') \vee Update(d, v'))))$
Data value can only be updated after having been collected or last updated for more than a week (168 hours).

$req_2 = \square \; \forall d, v(Access(d, v)) \implies \blacklozenge_{[0,168]} \; Collect(d, v) \vee Update(d, v))$
Data can only be accessed if has been collected or updated within a week (168 hours).

$req_3 = \square \; \forall d, v(Collect(d, v)) \implies \neg(\exists v''.(Collect(d, v'') \wedge v \neq v'') \vee \blacklozenge_{[1,)} \exists v'. Collect(d, v')))$ No data re-collection.

Fig. 1. Example requirements and legal property $P1$ of DCC, with signature $S_{data} = (\emptyset, \{Collect, \; Update, \; Access\}, \iota_{data})$, where $\iota_{data}(Collect) = \iota_{data}(Update) = \iota_{data}(Access) = 2$.

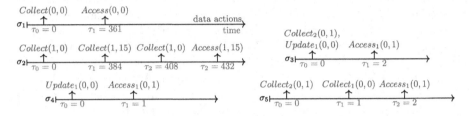

Fig. 2. Five traces from the DCC example.

empirically evaluate IBS on five case studies with a total of 24 properties showing that it can effectively and efficiently find LP violations or prove satisfiability.

The rest of this paper is organized as follows. Sect. 2 provides background and establishes our notation. Sect. 3 defines the bounded satisfiability checking (BSC) problem. Sect. 4 provides an overview of our solution and the translation of MFOTL to FOL*. Sect. 5 presents our solution; proofs of soundness, termination and optimality are available in the extended version [11]. Sect. 6 reports on the experiments performed to validate our bounded satisfiability checking solution for MFOTL. Sect. 7 discusses related work. Sect. 8 concludes the paper.

2 Preliminaries

In this section, we describe metric first-order temporal logic (MFOTL) [3].
Syntax. Let $\mathbb{I}$ be a set of non-empty intervals over $\mathbb{N}$. An *interval* $I \in \mathbb{I}$ can be expressed as $[b, b')$ where $b \in \mathbb{N}$ and $b' \in \mathbb{N} \cup \infty$. A *signature* S is a tuple (C, R, ι), where C is a set of constants and R is a finite set of predicate symbols (for relation), respectively. Without loss of generality, we assume all constants are from the integer domain $\mathbb{Z}$ where the theory of linear integer arithmetic (LIA) holds. The function $\iota : R \to \mathbb{N}$ associates each predicate symbol $r \in R$ with an arity $\iota(r) \in \mathbb{N}$. Let Var be a countable infinite set of variables from domain $\mathbb{Z}$ and a term t is defined inductively as $t : c \mid v \mid t + t \mid c \times t$. We denote $\bar{t}$ as a vector of terms and $\bar{t}_x^k$ as the vector that contains x at index k. The syntax of MFOTL formulas is defined as follows: *(1)* $\top$ and $\bot$, representing values "true" and "false"; *(2)* $t = t'$ and $t > t'$, for terms t and t'; *(3)* $r(t_1...t_{\iota(r)})$ for $r \in R$ and terms $t_1...t_{\iota(r)}$; *(4)* $\phi \wedge \psi, \neg\phi$ for MFOTL formulas ϕ and ψ; *(5)* $\exists x.(r(\bar{t}_x^k) \wedge \phi)$

for MFOTL formula ϕ, relation symbol $r \in R$, variable $x \in Var$ and a vector of terms $\bar{t}_x^k$ s.t. $x = \bar{t}_x^k[k]$; and *(6)* $\phi\, \mathcal{U}_I\, \psi$ (until), $\phi\, \mathcal{S}_I\, \psi$ (since), $\bigcirc_I \phi$ (next), $\bullet_I \phi$ (previous) for MFOTL formulas ϕ and ψ, and an interval $I \in \mathbb{I}$.

We consider a restricted form of quantification (syntax rule *(5)*, above) similar to guarded quantification [18]. Every existentially quantified variable x must be guarded by some relation r (i.e., for some $\bar{t}$, $r(\bar{t})$ holds and x appears in $\bar{t}$). Similarly, universal quantification must be guarded as $\forall x.(r(\bar{t}) \Rightarrow \phi)$ where $x \in \bar{t}$. Thus, $\neg\exists x.\neg r(x)$ (and $\forall x.r(x)$) are not allowed.

The temporal operators $\mathcal{U}_I$, $\mathcal{S}_I$, $\bullet_I$ and $\bigcirc_I$ require the satisfaction of the formula within the time interval given by I. We write $[b,)$ as a shorthand for $[b, \infty)$; if I is omitted, then the interval is assumed to be $[0, \infty)$. Other classical unary temporal operators $\Diamond_I$ (eventually), $\Box_I$ (always), and $\blacklozenge_I$ (once) are defined as follows: $\Diamond_I \phi = \top\, \mathcal{U}_I\, \phi$, $\Box_I \phi = \neg\Diamond_I \neg\phi$, and $\blacklozenge_I \phi = \top\, \mathcal{S}_I\, \phi$. Other common logical operator such as $\vee$ (disjunction) and $\forall$ (universal quantification) are expressed through negation of $\wedge$ and $\exists$, respectively.

Example 1. Suppose a data collection centre (DCC) *collects* and *accesses* personal data information with three requirements: req_0 stating that no data is allowed to be accessed before the data ID has been collected for 15 days (360 hours); req_1: data can only be updated after having been collected or last updated for more than a week (168 hours); and req_2: data value can only be accessed if the value has been collected or updated within a week (168 hours). The signature S_{data} for DCC contains three binary relations (R_{data}): *Collect*, *Update*, and *Access*, such that *Collect(d, v)*, *Update(d, v)* and *Access(d, v)* hold at a given time point if and only if data at id d is collected, updated, and accessed with value v at this time point, respectively. The MFOTL formulas for P1, req_0, req_1 and req_2 are shown in Fig. 1. For instance, the formula req_0 specifies that if a data value stored at id d is accessed, then some data must have been collected and stored at id d at least 360 hours ago ($\blacklozenge_{[360,)}]$).

Semantics. A first-order (FO) structure D over the signature $S = (C, R, \iota)$ is comprised of a non-empty domain $dom(D) \neq \emptyset$ and an interpretation for $c^D \in dom(D)$ and $r^D \subseteq dom(D)^{\iota(r)}$ for each $c \in C$ and $r \in R$. The semantics of MFOTL formulas is defined over a sequence of FO structures $\bar{D} = (D_0, D_1, \ldots)$ and a sequence of natural numbers representing time $\bar{\tau} = (\tau_0, \tau_1, \ldots)$, where (a) $\bar{\tau}$ is a monotonically increasing sequence; (b) $dom(D_i) = dom(D_{i+1})$ for all $i \geq 0$ (all D_i have a fixed domain); and (c) each constant symbol $c \in C$ has the same interpretation across $\bar{D}$ (i.e., $c^{D_i} = c^{D_{i+1}}$). Property (a) ensures that time never decreases as the sequence progresses; and (b) ensures that the domain is fixed (referred to as $dom(\bar{D})$) $\bar{D}$ is similar to timed words in metric time logic (MTL), but instead of associating a set of propositions with each time point, MFOTL uses a structure D to interpret the symbols in the signature S. The semantics of MFOTL is defined over a trace of timed first-order structures $\sigma = (\bar{D}, \bar{\tau})$, where every structure $D_i \in \bar{D}$ specifies the set of tuples (r^{D_i}) that hold for every relation r at time $\tau_i \in \bar{\tau}$. Let $(\bar{D}, \bar{\tau})$ denote an MFOTL trace.

$$
\begin{aligned}
(\bar{D}, \bar{\tau}, v, i) &\models t = t' && \text{iff } v(t) = v(t') \\
(\bar{D}, \bar{\tau}, v, i) &\models t > t' && \text{iff } v(t) > v(t') \\
(\bar{D}, \bar{\tau}, v, i) &\models r(t_1, .., t_{\iota(r)}) && \text{iff } r(v(t_1), .., v(t_{i(r)})) \in r^{D_i} \\
(\bar{D}, \bar{\tau}, v, i) &\models \neg \phi && \text{iff } (\bar{D}, \bar{\tau}, v, i) \not\models \phi \\
(\bar{D}, \bar{\tau}, v, i) &\models \phi \wedge \psi && \text{iff } (\bar{D}, \bar{\tau}, v, i) \models \phi \text{ and } (\bar{D}, \bar{\tau}, v, i) \models \psi \\
(\bar{D}, \bar{\tau}, v, i) &\models \exists x \cdot (r(\bar{t}_x^k) \wedge \phi) && \text{iff } (\bar{D}, \bar{\tau}, v[x \to d], i) \models (r(\bar{t}_x^k)) \wedge \phi \text{ for some } d \in dom(\bar{D}) \\
(\bar{D}, \bar{\tau}, v, i) &\models \bigcirc_I \phi && \text{iff } (\bar{D}, \bar{\tau}, v, i+1) \models \phi \text{ and } \tau_{i+1} - \tau_i \in I \\
(\bar{D}, \bar{\tau}, v, i) &\models \bullet_I \phi && \text{iff } i \geq 1 \text{ and } (\bar{D}, \bar{\tau}, v, i-1) \models \phi \text{ and } \tau_i - \tau_{i-1} \in I \\
(\bar{D}, \bar{\tau}, v, i) &\models \phi \, \mathcal{U}_I \, \psi && \text{iff exists } j \geq i \text{ and } (\bar{D}, \bar{\tau}, j, v) \models \psi \text{ and } \tau_j - \tau_i \in I \\
& && \quad \text{and for all } k \in \mathbb{N} \, i \leq k < j \Rightarrow (\bar{D}, \bar{\tau}, k, v) \models \phi \\
(\bar{D}, \bar{\tau}, v, i) &\models \phi \, \mathcal{S}_I \, \psi && \text{iff exists } j \leq i \text{ and } (\bar{D}, \bar{\tau}, j, v) \models \psi \text{ and } \tau_i - \tau_j \in I \\
& && \quad \text{and for all } k \in \mathbb{N} \, i \geq k > j \Rightarrow (\bar{D}, \bar{\tau}, k, v) \models \phi
\end{aligned}
$$

Fig. 3. MFOTL semantics.

Example 2. Consider the signature S_{data} in the DCC example. Let $\tau_1 = 0$ and $\tau_2 = 361$, and let D_1 and D_2 be two first-order structures with $r^{D_1} = Collect(0,0)$ and $r^{D_2} = Access(0,0)$, respectively. The trace $\sigma_1 = ((D_1, D_2), (\tau_1, \tau_2))$ is a valid trace shown in Fig. 2 and representing two timed relations: (1) data value 0 collected and stored at id 0 at hour 0 and (2) data value 0 is read by accessing id 0 at hour 361.

A *valuation function* $v : Var \to dom(\bar{D})$ maps a set Var of variables to their interpretations in the domain $dom(\bar{D})$. For vectors $\bar{x} = (x_1, \ldots, x_n)$ and $\bar{d} = (d_1, \ldots, d_n) \in dom(\bar{D})^n$, the *update operation* $v[\bar{x} \to \bar{d}]$ produces a new valuation function v' s.t. $v'(x_i) = d_i$ for $1 \leq i \leq n$, and $v(x') = v'(x')$ for every $x' \notin \bar{x}$. For any constant c, $v(c) = c^D$. Let $\bar{D}$ be a sequence of FO structures over signature $S = (C, R, \iota)$ and $\bar{\tau}$ be a sequence of natural numbers. Let ϕ be an MFOTL formula over S, v be a valuation function and $i \in \mathbb{N}$. A fragment of the relation $(\bar{D}, \bar{\tau}, v, i) \models \phi$ is defined in Fig. 3.

The operators $\bullet_I$, $\bigcirc_I$, $\mathcal{U}_I$ and $\mathcal{S}_I$ are augmented with an interval $I \in \mathbb{I}$ which defines the satisfaction of the formula within a time range specified by I relative to the current time at step i, i.e., τ_i.

Definition 1 (MFOTL Satisfiability). *An MFOTL formula ϕ is* satisfiable *if there exists a sequence of FO structures $\bar{D}$ and natural numbers $\bar{\tau}$, and a valuation function v such that $(\bar{D}, \bar{\tau}, v, 0) \models \phi$. ϕ is* unsatisfiable *otherwise.*

Example 3. In the DCC example, the MFOTL formula req_0 is *satisfiable* because $(\bar{D}, \bar{\tau}, v, 0) \models req_0$ (where $\sigma_1 = (\bar{D}, \bar{\tau})$ in Fig. 2). Let req_0' be another MFOTL formula: $\Diamond_{[0,359]} \exists j.(Access(0, j))$. The formula $req_0' \wedge req_0$ is *unsatisfiable* because if data stored at id 0 is accessed between 0 and 359 hours, then it is impossible to collect the data at least 360 hours prior to its access.

3 Bounded Satisfiability Checking Problem

The satisfiability of MFOTL properties is generally undecidable since MFOTL is expressive enough to describe the blank tape problem [31] (which has been shown to be undecidable). Despite the undecidability result, we can derive a bounded version of the problem, *bounded satisfiability checking* (BSC), for which a sound and complete decision procedure exists. When facing a hard instance for satisfiability checking, the solution to BSC provides bounded guarantees (i.e., whether a solution exists within a given bound). In this section, we first define satisfiability checking and then the BSC problem for MFOTL formulas. *Satisfiability checking* [32] is a verification technique that extends model checking by replacing a state transition system with a set of temporal logic formulas. In the following, we define satisfiability checking of MFOTL formulas.

Definition 2 (Satisfiability Checking of MFOTL Formulas). *Let P be an MFOTL formula over a signature $S = (C, R, \iota)$, and let Reqs be a set of MFOTL requirements over S. Reqs complies with P (denoted as Reqs $\Rightarrow P$) iff $\bigwedge_{\psi \in Reqs} \psi \wedge \neg P$ is unsatisfiable. We call a solution to $\bigwedge_{\psi \in Reqs} \psi \wedge \neg P$, if one exists,* a counterexample *to Reqs $\Rightarrow P$.*

Example 4. Consider our DCC system requirements and the privacy data property $P1$ stating that if personal health information is not accurate or not up-to-date, it should not be accessed (see Fig. 1). $P1$ is not respected by the set of DCC requirements $\{req_0, req_1, req_2\}$ because $\neg P1 \wedge req_0 \wedge req_1 \wedge req_2$ is *satisfiable*. The counterexample σ_2 (shown in Fig. 2) indicates that data can be re-collected, and the re-collection does not have the same time restriction as the updates. If a fourth policy requirement req_3 (Fig. 1) is added to prohibit re-collection of collected data, then property $P1$ would be respected (i.e., $\{req_0, req_1, req_2, req_3\} \Rightarrow P1$).

Definition 3 (Finite trace and bounded trace). *Given a trace $\sigma = (\bar{D}, \bar{\tau}, v)$, we use $vol(\sigma)$ (the volume of σ), to denote the total number of times that any relation holds across all FO structures in $\bar{D}$ (i.e., $\sum_{r \in R} \sum_{D_i \in \bar{D}} (|r^{D_i}|)$). The trace σ is* finite *if $vol(\sigma)$ is finite. The trace is* bounded *by volume $vb \in \mathbb{N}$ if and only if $vol(\sigma) \leq vb$.*

Example 5. The volume of trace σ_3 in Fig. 2, $vol(\sigma_3) = 3$ since there are three relations: $Collect(1, 15)$, $Update(1, 0)$, and $Access(1, 15)$. Note that the volume is the total number of tuples that hold for any relation across all time points; multiple tuples can thus hold for multiple relations for a single time point.

Definition 4 (Bounded satisfiability checking of MFOTL properties). *Let P be an MFOTL property, Reqs be a set of MFOTL requirements, and vb be a natural number. The* bounded satisfiability checking *problem determines the existence of a counterexample σ to Reqs $\Rightarrow P$ such that $vol(\sigma) \leq vb$.*

4   Checking Bounded Satisfiability

In this section, we present an overview of the bounded satisfiability checking (BSC) process that translates the MFOTL formula into *first-order logic with relational objects* (FOL*) formulas, and looks for a satisfying solution for the FOL* formulas. Then, we provide the translation of MFOTL formulas to FOL* and discuss the process complexity.

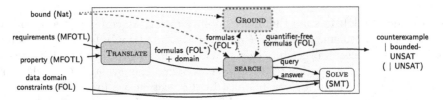

Fig. 4. Overview of the naive and our incremental (IBS) MFOTL bounded satisfiability checking approaches. Solid boxes and arrows are shared between the two approaches. Blue dashed arrow is specific to the naive approach. Red dotted arrows and the additional red output in bracket are specific to IBS. (Color figure online)

4.1 Overview of BSC for MFOTL Formulas

We aim to address the bounded satisfiability checking problem (Definition 4), looking for a satisfying run σ within a given volume bound vb that limits the number of relations in σ. First, we TRANSLATE the MFOTL formulas to FOL* formulas. The considered constraints in the formulas include those of the system requirements and the legal property, and *optional* data constraints specifying the data value constraint for a datatype. The data constraints can be defined as a range, a "small" data set, or the union/intersection of other data constraints. If data constraints are not specified, then the data value comes from the domain $\mathbb{Z}$. Note that the optional data constraints do not affect the complexity of BSC, but they do help prune unrealistic counterexamples. Second, we SEARCH for a satisfying solution to the FOL* formula; an SMT solver is used here to determine the satisfiability of the FOL* constraints and the data domain constraints. The answer from the SMT solver is analyzed to return an answer to the satisfiability checking problem (a counterexample σ, or"bounded-UNSAT").

4.2 Translation of MFOTL to First-Order Logic

In this section, we describe the translation target FOL*, the translation rules and prove their correctness.

FOL with Relational Object (FOL*). We start by introducing the syntax of FOL*. A *signature* S is a tuple (C, R, ι), where C is a set of constants, R is a set of relation symbols, and $\iota : R \rightarrow \mathbb{N}$ is a function that maps a relation to its arity. We assume that the domain of constant C is $\mathbb{Z}$, which matches the one for MFOTL, where the theory of linear integer arithmetic (LIA) holds. Let Var be a set of variables in the domain $\mathbb{Z}$. A *relational object* o of class $r \in R$ (denoted as $o : r$) is an object with $\iota(r)$ regular attributes and two special attributes, where every attribute is a variable. We assume that all regular attributes are ordered and denote $o[i]$ to be the ith attribute of o. Some attributes are named, and $o.x$ refers to o's attribute with the name 'x'. Each relational object o has two special attributes $o.ext$ and $o.time$. The former is a boolean variable indicating whether o exists in a solution, and the latter is a variable representing the occurrence time of o. For convenience, we define a function CLS(o) to return the relational object's class. Let a FOL* *term* t be defined inductively as $t : c \mid v \mid o[k] \mid o.x \mid t+t \mid c \times t$

for any constant $c \in C$, any variable $v \in Var$, any relational object $o : r$, any index $k \in [1, \iota(r)]$ and any valid attribute name x. Given a signature S, the syntax of the FOL* formulas is defined as follows: *(1)* $\top$ and $\bot$, representing values "true" and "false"; *(2)* $t = t'$ and $t > t'$, for term t and t'; *(3)* $\phi_f \wedge \psi_f$, $\neg\phi_f$ for FOL* formulas ϕ_f and ψ_f; *(4)* $\exists o : r \cdot (\phi_f)$ for an FOL* formula ϕ_f and a class r; *(5)* $\forall o : r \cdot (\phi_f)$ for an FOL* formula ϕ_f and a class r. The quantifiers for FOL* formulas are limited to relational objects, as shown by rules (4) & (5). Operators $\vee$ and $\forall$ can be defined in FOL* as follows: $\phi_f \vee \psi_f = \neg(\neg\phi_f \wedge \neg\psi_f)$ and $\forall o : r \cdot \phi_f = \exists o : r \cdot \neg\phi_f$. We say an FOL* formula is in a *negation normal form* (NNF) if negations ($\neg$) do not appear in front of $\neg, \wedge, \vee, \exists$ and $\forall$. For the rest of the paper, we assume that every FOL* ϕ is in NNF.

Given a signature S, a *domain* D is a finite set of relational objects. An FOL* formula *grounded* in the domain D (denoted by ϕ_D) is a quantifier-free FOL formula that eliminates quantifiers on relational objects using the following rules: (1) $\exists o : r \cdot (\phi_f)$ to $\bigvee_{o':r \in D}(o'.ext \wedge \phi_f[o \leftarrow o'])$ and (2) $\forall o : r \cdot (\phi_f)$ to $\bigwedge_{o':r \in D}(o'.ext \Rightarrow \phi_f[o \leftarrow o'])$. An FOL* formula ϕ_f is *satisfiable in D* if there exists a variable assignment v that evaluates ϕ_D to $\top$ according to the standard semantics of FOL. An FOL* formula ϕ_f is *satisfiable* if there exists a finite domain D such that ϕ_f is satisfiable in D. We call $\sigma = (D, v)$ a *satisfying solution* to ϕ_f, denoted as $\sigma \models \phi_f$. Given a solution $\sigma = (D, v)$, we say a relational object o is in σ, denoted as $o \in \sigma$, if $o \in D$ and $v(o.ext)$ is true. The *volume of the solution*, denoted as $vol(\sigma)$, is $|\{o \mid o \in \sigma\}|$.

Example 6. Let a be a relational object of class A with attribute name *val*. The formula $\forall a : A. (\exists a' : A \cdot (a.val < a'.val) \wedge \exists a : A \cdot a.val = 0)$ has no satisfying solutions in any finite domain. On the other hand, the formula $\forall a : A \cdot (\exists a', a'' : A \cdot (a.val = a'.val + a''.val) \wedge \exists a : A \cdot a.val = 5)$ has a solution $\sigma = (D, v)$ of volume 2, with the domain $D = (a_1, a_2)$ and the value function $v(a_1.val) = 5$, $v(a_2.val) = 0$ because if $a \leftarrow a_1$ then the formula is satisfied by assigning $a' \leftarrow a_1$, $a'' \leftarrow a_2$; and if $a \leftarrow a_2$, then the formula is satisfied by assigning $a' \leftarrow a_2$, $a'' \leftarrow a_2$.

From MFOTL Formulas to FOL* Formulas. We now discuss the translation rule from the MFOTL formulas to FOL* formulas. Recall that MFOTL semantics is defined for a time point i on a trace $\sigma = (\bar{D}, \bar{\tau}, v, i)$, where $\bar{D} = (D_1, D_2, \ldots)$ is a sequence of FO structures and $\bar{\tau} = (\tau_1, \tau_2, \ldots)$ is a sequence of time values. The time value of the time point i is given by τ_i, and if i is not specified, then $i = 1$. The semantics of the FOL* formulas is defined for a domain D where the information of time is associated with relational objects in the domain. Therefore, the time point i (and its time value τ_i) should be considered during the translation from MFOTL to FOL* since the same MFOTL formula at different time points represents different constraints on the trace σ. Formally, our translation function TRANSLATE, abbreviated as T, translates an MFOTL formula ϕ into a function $f : \tau \to \phi_f$, where $\tau \in \mathbb{N}$ and ϕ_f is an FOL* formula. The translation rules are stated in Fig. 5.

$$T(t = t', \tau_i) \quad\quad \rightarrow t = t'$$
$$T(t > t', \tau_i) \quad\quad \rightarrow t > t'$$
$$T(r(t_1, .., t_{\iota(r)}), \tau_i) \rightarrow \exists o : r \cdot \bigwedge_{j=1}^{\iota(r)}(o.j = t_j) \wedge (\tau_i = o.time)$$
$$T(\neg\phi, \tau_i) \quad\quad \rightarrow \neg T(\phi, \tau_i)$$
$$T(\phi \wedge \psi, \tau_i) \quad\quad \rightarrow T(\phi, \tau_i) \wedge T(\psi, \tau_i)$$
$$T(\exists x \cdot r(\bar{t}_x^k) \wedge \phi, \tau_i) \rightarrow \exists o : r \cdot T((r(\bar{t}_x^k) \wedge \phi)[x \rightarrow o[k]], \tau_i)$$
$$T(\bigcirc_I \phi, \tau_i) \quad\quad \rightarrow \exists o : \mathrm{TP} \cdot \mathrm{NEXT}(o.time, \tau_i) \wedge T(\phi, o.time) \wedge (o.time - \tau_i) \in I$$
$$T(\bullet_I \phi, \tau_i) \quad\quad \rightarrow \exists o : \mathrm{TP} \cdot \mathrm{PREV}(o.time, \tau_i) \wedge T(\phi, o.time) \wedge (\tau_i - o.time) \in I$$
$$T(\phi \, \mathcal{U}_I \, \psi, \tau_i) \quad \rightarrow \exists o : \mathrm{TP} \cdot (o.time \geq \tau_i \wedge (o.time - \tau_i) \in I \wedge T(\psi, o.time)$$
$$\text{and } \forall o' : \mathrm{TP} \cdot o'.time \cdot (\tau_i \leq o'.time < o.time \Rightarrow T(\phi, o'.time)))$$
$$T(\phi \, \mathcal{S}_I \, \psi, \tau_i) \quad \rightarrow \exists o : \mathrm{TP} \cdot (o.time \leq \tau_i \wedge (\tau_i - o.time) \in I \wedge T(\psi, o.time)$$
$$\text{and } \forall o' : \mathrm{TP} \cdot (\tau_i \geq o'.time > o.time \Rightarrow T(\phi, o'.time)))$$
$$T(\phi) \quad\quad\quad \rightarrow T(\phi, \tau_1)$$

Fig. 5. Translation rules from MFOTL to FOL*. TP is an internal class of relational objects used to represent time values at different time points. The predicate $\mathrm{NEXT}(t_1, t_2)$ ($\mathrm{PREV}(t_1, t_2)$) asserts that t_1 is the next (previous) time value of t_2.

Representing time points in FOL*. Since FOL* quantifiers are limited to relational objects, to quantify over time points (which is necessary to capture the semantics of MFOTL temporal operators such as $\mathcal{U}$), the translated FOL* formulas use a special *internal* class of relational objects TP (e.g., $\exists o : \mathrm{TP}$). Relational objects of class TP capture all possible time points in a trace, and they have two attributes, *ext* and *time*, to record the existence and the value of the time point, respectively. To ensure that every time value in a solution is represented by some relational object of TP, we introduce the *time coverage* FOL* axiom.

Axiom 1 (Time coverage). Let ϕ_f be an FOL* formula and let σ be its solution. For every relational object $o \in \sigma$, there exists an object o' of class TP s.t. o and o' share the same time value. Formally, $\forall o \cdot (\exists o' : \mathrm{TP} \cdot o.time = o'.time)$.

The translation of $\bigcirc_I \phi$ uses function $\mathrm{NEXT}(t_1, t_2)$ to assert that t_1 is the next time value of t_2. Formally, $\mathrm{NEXT}(t_1, t_2) = \forall o : \mathrm{TP} \cdot o.time > t_2 \Rightarrow t_1 \leq o.time$. Function $\mathrm{PREV}(t_1, t_2)$ for translation of $\bullet_I \phi$ is defined similarly.

Definition 5 (Mapping from MFOTL trace to FOL* trace). *Let an MFOTL trace $(\bar{D}, \bar{\tau})$ and a valuation function v be given. A function $M((\bar{D}, \bar{\tau}), v) \rightarrow (D, v')$ is a mapping between an MFOTL trace and an FOL* trace if M satisfies the following rules: (1) for every $\tau_i \in \bar{\tau}$, there exists a relational object $o : \mathrm{TP} \in D$ such that $\tau_i = v'(o.time)$; (2) for every structure $D_i \in \bar{D}$, if a tuple $\bar{t}$ holds for a relation r, (i.e., $\bar{t} \in r^{D_i}$), then there exists a relational object $o : r$ such that for $j \in \iota(r)$, $\bar{t}[j] = v'(o[j])$ and $v'(o.time) = \tau_i \wedge v'(o.ext) = \top$; (3) for every term t defined for v, $v(t) = v'(T(t, \tau_i))$.*

The inverse of M, denoted as M^{-1}, is defined as follows: (1) $\bar{\tau} = \mathrm{SORT}(\{v'(o.time) \mid o : \mathrm{TP} \in D \cdot v'(o.ext)\})$ and (2) for every relational object $o : r$, if $v'(o.ext)$, then $(v'(o[1]) \ldots v'(o[\iota(r)])) \in r^{D_i}$, where i is the index of the time value $v'(o.time)$ in $\bar{\tau}$.

Lemma 1. *Given an MFOTL formula ϕ, an MFOTL trace $(\bar{D}, \bar{\tau})$, a valuation function v, and a time point i, the relation $(\bar{D}, \bar{\tau}, v, i) \models \phi$ holds iff there exists a satisfying trace $\sigma = (D, v')$ for the formula $T(\phi, \tau_i)$.*

Proof Sketch. In the proof, we use M and M^{-1} (see Definition 5) to transform an MFOTL solution into an FOL* trace, and show that it is a solution to the translated FOL* formula (and vice versa).

$\Longrightarrow$: if $(\bar{D}, \bar{\tau}, v, i) \models \phi$, then it is sufficient to show $(D, v') \leftarrow M(\bar{D}, \bar{\tau}, v)$ is an FOL* solution. To prove (D, v') is the solution to $T(\phi, \tau_i)$, we consider all the translation rules in Fig. 5. The translated FOL* matches the semantics (Fig. 3) of MFOTL except for the translation of temporal operators (e.g., $T(\bigcirc_I \phi, \tau_i)$ and $T(\phi \, \mathcal{U}_I \, \psi, \tau_i)$) where instead of quantifying over time points (e.g., $\exists j$ and $\forall k$), internal relational objects of class TP ($o, o' : $ TP) are quantified over. By rule (1) of Dec. 5, every time point and its time value are mapped to some relational object of class TP. Therefore, the quantifiers on time points can be translated into the quantifiers on the relational objects of TP. The mapped solution (D, v') also satisfies Axiom 1 because if a tuple $\bar{t}$ holds for some relation r at some time τ in the MFOTL trace $(\bar{D}, \bar{\tau})$, then there exists a time point $i \in [1, |\bar{\tau}|]$ such that $\tau_i = \tau$. Therefore, by rule (1) of M, τ_i is represented by some $o : $ TP.

$\Longleftarrow$: if $(D, v') \models T(\phi, \tau_i)$, then it is sufficient to show that the MFOTL trace $(\bar{D}, \bar{\tau}, v) \leftarrow M^{-1}(D, v')$ satisfies ϕ at point i (i.e., $(\bar{D}, \bar{\tau}, v, i) \models \phi$). To prove $(\bar{D}, \bar{\tau}, v, i) \models \phi$, we consider all the translation rules in Fig. 5. The translated FOL* formula matches the semantics of MFOTL (Fig. 3) except for the difference between the time points and the relational objects of class TP. By Axiom 1, every relational object's time is captured by some time point, and by rule (2) of M^{-1}, every relational object is mapped onto some structure D_i at some time τ_i by M. Therefore, $(\bar{D}, \bar{\tau}, v, i) \models \phi$. □

Theorem 1 (Translation Correctness). *Given an MFOTL formula ϕ and an MFOTL trace σ, let $M(\sigma)$ be the FOL* solution mapped from σ using function M (Definition 5). Then (1) $\sigma \models \phi$ if and only if $M(\sigma) \models T(\phi)$, and (2) $vol(\sigma) = vol(M(\sigma)) - |\{o : \text{TP} \in M(\sigma)\}|$, where $|\{o : \text{TP} \in M(\sigma)\}|$ is the number of relational objects of the internal class TP in the solution $M(\sigma)$.*

Proof. Statement (1) of Thm. 1 is a direct consequence of Lemma 1. Statement (2) is the result of rule (2) in Definition 5 because every relational object in the FOL* solution, except for the internal ones, i.e., $o : $ TP, has a one-to-one correspondence to tuples that hold for some relation in the MFOTL solution. □

For the rest of the paper, we assume that the internal relational objects of class TP do not count toward the volume of the FOL*, i.e., $vol(\sigma) = vol(T(\sigma))$.

Example 7. Consider a formula $exp = \square \, \forall d \cdot (A(d) \implies \Diamond_{[5,10]} B(d))$, where A and B are unary relations. The translated FOL* formula $T(exp)$ is: $\forall o : \text{TP} \cdot \forall a : A \cdot (o.time = a.time \Rightarrow \exists o' : \text{TP} \cdot b : B \cdot o'.time = b.time \wedge a[1] = b[1] \wedge o.time + 5 \leq o'.time \leq o.time + 10)$. Since $o.time = a.time$ and $o'.time = b.time$, we can substitute $o.time$ and $o'.time$ with $a.time$ and $b.time$ in $T(exp)$, respectively. Then, the formula contains no reference to o and o', and we can safely drop the quantified o and o' (we can drop existential quantified TP relational object because of the time coverage axiom). The simplified formula is: $\forall a : A \cdot \exists b : B \cdot a[1] = b[1] \land a.time + 5 \leq b.time \leq a.time + 10$.

This is important for designing system requirements that comply with LPs.

Given an MFOTL property P and a set $Reqs$ of MFOTL requirements, and a volume bound vb, the BSC problem can be solved by searching for a satisfying solution v' for the FOL* formula $T(\neg P) \bigwedge_{\psi \in Reqs} T(\psi)$ in a domain D with at most vb relational objects.

4.3   Checking MFOTL Satisfiability: A Naive Approach

Below, we define a naive procedure NBS (shown in Fig. 4) for checking satisfiability of MFOTL formulas translated into FOL*. We then discuss the complexity of this naive procedure. Even though we do not use NBS in this paper, its complexity constitutes an upper bound for our approach proposed in Sect. 5.

Searching for a satisfying solution. Let ϕ_f be an FOL* formula translated from an MFOTL formula ϕ, and let vb be the volume bound. NBS solves ϕ_f via quantifier elimination. The number of relational objects in any satisfying solution of ϕ_f should be at most vb. Therefore, NBS grounds the FOL* formulas within a domain of vb relational objects (see Sect. 4.2), and then uses an SMT solver to check satisfiability of the grounded formula. If the domain has multiple classes of relational objects, we can unify them by introducing a "superposition" class whose attributes are the union of the attributes of all classes and a special "name" attribute to indicate the class represented by the superposition.

Complexity. The size of the quantifier-free formula is $O(vb^k)$, where k is the maximum depth of quantifier nesting. Since the background theory used in ϕ is restricted to linear integer arithmetic, solving the formula is NP-hard [29]. Because T (Tab. 5) is linear in the size of the formula ϕ, NBS is NP-complete w.r.t. the size of the grounded formula, vb^k.

5   Incremental Search for Bounded Counterexamples

The naive BSC approach (NBS) proposed in Sect. 4.3 is inefficient for solving the translated FOL* formulas given a large bound n due to the size of the ground formula. Moreover, NBS cannot detect unbounded unsatisfiability, and cannot provide optimality guarantees on the volume of counterexamples which are important for establishing the proof of unbounded correctness and localizing faults [15], respectively. In this section, we propose an incremental procedure IBS, which can detect unbounded unsatisfiability and provide the shortest counterexamples. An overview of IBS is given in Fig. 4.

IBS maintains an under-approximation of the search domain and the FOL* constraints. It uses the search domain to ground the FOL* constraints, and an SMT solver to determine the satisfiability of the grounded constraints. It analyzes the SMT result and accordingly either expands the search domain, refines the FOL* constraints, or returns an answer to the satisfiability checking problem (a counterexample σ, "bounded-UNSAT", or "UNSAT"). The procedure continues until an answer is obtained (σ or UNSAT), or until the domain exceeds the bound vb, in which case a "bounded-UNSAT" answer is returned.

In the following, we describe IBS in more detail. We explain the key component of IBS, computing over- and under-approximation queries, in Sect. 5.1. We discuss the algorithm itself in Sect. 5.2 and illustrate it in Sect. 5.3. We prove its soundness, completeness, and solution optimality in the extended version [11].

5.1 Over- and Under-Approximation

NBS grounds the input FOL* formulas in a fixed domain D (fixed by the bound vb). Instead, IBS under-approximates D to $D_\downarrow$ such that $D_\downarrow \subseteq D$. With $D_\downarrow$, we can create an over- and an under-approximation query to the bounded satisfiability checking problem. Such queries are used to check the satisfiability of FOL* formulas with domain $D_\downarrow$. IBS starts with a small domain $D_\downarrow$ and gradually expands it until either SAT or UNSAT is returned, or the domain size exceeds some limit (bounded-UNSAT).

Over-approximation. Let ϕ_f be an FOL* formula, and $D_\downarrow$ be a domain of relation objects. The procedure GROUND, $G(\phi_f, D_\downarrow)$, encodes ϕ_f into a quantifier-free FOL formula ϕ_g s.t. the unsatisfiability of ϕ_g implies the unsatisfiability of ϕ_f. We call ϕ_g an *over-approximation* of ϕ_f. The procedure G (Algorithm 2) recursively traverses the syntax tree of the input FOL* formula from top to bottom.

To eliminate the existential quantifier in $\exists o : r \cdot \phi'_f$ (L:1), G creates a new relational object o' of class r (L: 2), and replaces o with o' in ϕ'_f (L:3). To eliminate the universal quantifier in $\forall o : r \cdot \phi'_f$ (L: 4), G grounds the formula in $D_\downarrow$. More specifically, G expands the quantifier into a conjunction of clauses where each clause is $o'.ext \Rightarrow \phi'_f[o \leftarrow o']$ (i.e., o is replaced by o' in ϕ'_f) for each relational object o' of class r in $D_\downarrow$ (L: 5). Intuitively, an existentially quantified relational object is instantiated with a new relational object, and a universally quantified relational object is instantiated with every existing relational object of the same class in $D_\downarrow$, which does not include the ones instantiated during G.

Lemma 2 (Over-approximation Query). *For an FOL* formula ϕ_f, and a domain $D_\downarrow$, if $\phi_g = G(\phi_f, D_\downarrow)$ is UNSAT, then so is ϕ_f.*

Under-Approximation. Let ϕ_f be an FOL* formula, and $D_\downarrow$ be a domain. The over-approximation $\phi_g = G(\phi_f, D_\downarrow)$ contains a set of new relational objects introduced by G (L:2), denoted by $NewRs$. Let NONEWR($NewRs$, $D_\downarrow$) be constraints that enforce that every new relational object o_1 in $NewRs$ be semantically equivalent to some relational objects o_2 in $D_\downarrow$. Formally: the predicate NONEWR($NewRs, D_\downarrow$) is defined as $\bigwedge_{o_1 \in NewRs} \bigvee_{o_2 \in D_\downarrow} (o_1 \equiv o_2)$, where the semantically equivalent relation between o_1 and o_1 (i.e., $o_1 \equiv o_2$) is defined as CLS(o_1) $=$ CLS(o_2) and $\bigwedge_{i=1}^{\iota(\text{CLS}(o))} (o_1[i] = o_2[i]) \wedge o_1.ext = o_2.ext \wedge o_1.time = o_2.time$ (where the CLS(o) returns the class of o). Let $\phi_g^\perp = \phi_g \wedge$ NONEWR($NewRs, D_\downarrow$). If $\phi_g^\perp$ has a satisfying solution, then there is a solution for ϕ_f. We call $\phi_g^\perp$ an *under-approximation* of ϕ_f and denote the procedure for computing it by $\text{UNDERAPPROX}(\phi_f, D_\downarrow)$.

Lemma 3 (Under-Approximation Query). *For an FOL* formula ϕ_f, and a domain $D_\downarrow$, let $\phi_g = G(\phi_f, D_\downarrow)$ and $\phi_g^\perp = \text{UNDERAPPROX}(\phi_f, D_\downarrow)$. If σ is a solution to $\phi_g^\perp$, then there exists a solution to ϕ_f.*

Algorithm 1. IBS: search for a bounded (by vb) solution to $T(\neg P) \bigwedge_{\psi \in Reqs} T(\psi)$.

Input an MFOTL formula $\neg P$, and MFOTL requirements $Reqs = \{\psi_1, \psi_2, ...\}$.

Optional Input vb, the volume bound, and data constraints T_{data}.

Output a counterexample σ, UNSAT or bounded-UNSAT.

```
 1:  Reqs_f ← { ψ_f = T(ψ) | ψ ∈ Reqs}
 2:  ¬P_f ← T(¬P)
 3:  Reqs_⊥ ← ∅ //initially empty requirement
 4:  D_⊥ ← ∅ //initially empty domain
 5:  while ⊤ do
 6:      φ_⊥ ← ¬P_f ∧ Reqs_⊥
 7:      φ_g ← G(φ_⊥, D_⊥) //over-approx.
 8:      φ_g^⊥ ← UNDERAPPROX(φ_⊥, D_⊥) //under-
            approx.
 9:      if SOLVE(φ_g ∧ T_data) = UNSAT then
10:          return UNSAT
11:      σ ← SOLVE(φ_g^⊥ ∧ T_data)
12:      if σ = UNSAT then //expand D_⊥
13:          σ_min ← MINIMIZE(φ_g)
14:          //expand based on σ_min
15:          D_⊥ += {o | o ∈ σ_min}
16:          if vol(σ_min) > vb then
17:              return bounded-UNSAT
18:      else //check all requirements
19:          if σ ⊨ ψ_f for ψ_f ∈ Reqs_f then
20:              return σ
21:          else
22:              lesson ← ψ_f for some σ ⊭ ψ_f
23:              Reqs_⊥.add(lesson)
```

Algorithm 2. G: ground a NNF FOL* formula ϕ_f in a domain $D_\downarrow$.

Input an FOL* formula ϕ_f in NNF, and a domain of relational objects $D_\downarrow$.

Output a grounded quantifier-free formula ϕ_g over relational objects.

```
1:  if match (φ_f, ∃o : r · φ'_f) then //process the existential operator
2:      o' ← NEWACT(r) //create a new relational object of class r
3:      return o'.ext ∧ G (φ'_f[o ← o'], D_⊥)
4:  if match (φ_f, ∀o : r · φ'_f) then //process the universal operator
5:      return ⋀_{[o':r]∈D_⊥} o'.ext ⇒ G (φ'_f[o ← o'], D_⊥)
6:  if match (φ_f, φ'_f op ψ'_f where op = ∧ | ∨) then return G(φ'_f, D_⊥) op G(ψ'_f, D_⊥)
7:  return φ_f //case where φ_f is quantifier-free, including ¬φ'_f where φ'_f is atomic (NNF)
```

The proofs of Lemma 2 and 3 are in the extended version [11].

Suppose, for some domain $D_\downarrow$, that an over-approximation query ϕ_g for an FOL* formula ϕ_f is satisfiable while the under-approximation query $\phi_g^\perp$ is UNSAT. Then, the solution to ϕ_g provides hints on how to expand $D_\downarrow$ to potentially obtain a satisfying solution for ϕ_f, as captured in Corollary 1.

Corollary 1 (Necessary relational objects). *For an FOL* formula ϕ_f and a domain $D_\downarrow$, let ϕ_g and $\phi_g^\perp$ be the over- and under-approximation queries of ϕ_f based on $D_\downarrow$, respectively. Suppose ϕ_g is satisfiable and $\phi_g^\perp$ is UNSAT, then every solution to ϕ_f contains some relational object in formula ϕ_g but not in $D_\downarrow$.*

5.2   Counterexample-Guided Constraint Solving Algorithm

Let an MFOTL formula $\neg P$ (to find a satisfiable counterexample to P), a set of MFOTL requirements $Reqs$, an optional volume bound vb, and optionally a set of FOL* data domain constraints T_{data} be given. IBS, shown in Algorithm 1, searches for a solution σ to $\neg P \wedge \bigwedge_{\psi \in Reqs} \psi$ (with respect to T_{data}) bounded by vb, as a counter-example to $\bigwedge_{\psi \in Reqs} \psi \Rightarrow P$ (Definition 2). bounded by vb. If no such solution is possible regardless of the bound, IBS returns UNSAT. If no solution can be found within the given bound, but a solution may exist for a larger bound, then IBS returns bounded-UNSAT. If vb is not specified, IBS will perform the search unboundedly until a solution or UNSAT is returned.

   IBS first translates $\neg P$ and every $\psi \in Reqs$ into FOL* formulas in $Reqs_f$, denoted by $\neg P_f$ and ψ_f, respectively. Then IBS searches for a satisfying solution to $\neg P_f \wedge \bigwedge_{\psi_f \in Reqs_f} \psi_f$ in the domain D of volume, which is at most vb. Instead of searching in D directly, IBS searches for a solution to $\neg P_f \wedge \bigwedge_{\psi_f \in Reqs_f} \psi_f$ in $D_\downarrow$ (denoted by $\phi_\downarrow$) where $Reqs_\downarrow \subseteq Reqs_f$ and $D_\downarrow \subseteq D$. IBS initializes $Reqs_\downarrow$ and $D_\downarrow$ as empty sets (LL:3-4). Then, for the FOL* formula $\phi_\downarrow$, IBS creates an over- and under-approximation query ϕ_g (L:7) and $\phi_g^\perp$ (L:8), respectively (described in Sect. 5.1). IBS first solves the over-approximation query ϕ_g by querying an SMT solver (L:9). If ϕ_g is unsatisfiable, then $\phi_\downarrow$ is unsatisfiable (Lemma 2), and IBS returns UNSAT (L:10).

   If ϕ_g is satisfiable, then IBS solves the under-approximation query $\phi_g^\perp$ (L:11). If $\phi_g^\perp$ is unsatisfiable, then the current domain $D_\downarrow$ is too small, and IBS expands it (LL:12-18). This is because the satisfiability of ϕ_g indicates the possibility of finding a satisfying solution after adding at least one of the new relational objects in the solution to ϕ_g to $D_\downarrow$ (Corollary 1). The domain $D_\downarrow$ is expanded by adding all relational objects o' in the minimum (in terms of volume) solution σ_{min} to ϕ_g (L:13). To obtain σ_{min}, we follow MaxRes [28] methods: we analyze the UNSAT core of $\phi_g^\perp$ and incrementally weaken $\phi_g^\perp$ towards ϕ_g (i.e., the weakened query $\phi_g^{\perp'}$ is an "over-under approximation" that satisfies $\phi_g^\perp \Rightarrow \phi_g^{\perp'} \Rightarrow \phi_g$) until a satisfying solution σ_{min} is obtained for the weakened query. However, if the volume of σ_{min} exceeds vb (L:16), then bounded-UNSAT is returned (L:17). UNSAT core-guided domain expansion has also been explored for unfolding the definition of recursive functions [30,37].

   On the other hand, if $\phi_g^\perp$ yields a solution σ, then σ is checked on $Reqs_f$ (L:19). If σ satisfies every ψ_f in $Reqs_f$, then σ is returned (L:20). If σ violates some requirements in $Reqs_f$, then the violating requirement $lesson$ is added to $Reqs_\downarrow$ to be considered in the search for the next solutions (L:23).

   If IBS does not find a solution or does not return UNSAT, it means that no solution is found because $D_\downarrow$ is too small or $Reqs_\downarrow$ are too weak. IBS then restarts with the expanded domain $D_\downarrow$ or the refined set of requirements $Reqs_\downarrow$. It computes the over- and under-approximation queries (ϕ_g and $\phi_g^\perp$) again, and repeats the steps. See Sect. 5.3 for an illustration of IBS.

Remark 1. IBS finds the optimal solution because it looks for the minimum solution σ_{min} to the over-approximation query ϕ_g (L:13) and uses it for domain expansion (L:15). However, looking for σ_{min} adds cost. If solution optimality is not required, IBS can be configured to heuristically find a solution σ to ϕ_g such that $vol(\sigma) \leq vb$. The *greedy best-first* search (gBFS) finds a solution to ϕ_g that minimizes the number of relational objects that are not already in $D_\downarrow$, and then uses it to expand $D_\downarrow$. We configured a non-optimal version of IBS (nop) that uses gBFS heuristics and evaluated its performance in Sect. 6.

5.3   Illustration of IBS

Suppose a data collection centre (DCC) *collects* and *accesses* personal data information with two requirements: req_1: data value can only be updated after having been collected or last updated for more than a week (168 hours); and req_2: data can only be accessed if has been collected or updated within a week (168 hours). The signature S_{data} for DCC contains three binary relations (R_{data}): *Collect*, *Update*, and *Access*, such that *Collect*(d, v), *Update*(d, v) and *Access*(d, v) hold at a given time point if and only if data at ID d is collected, updated, and accessed with value v at this time point, respectively. The MFOTL formulas for $P1$, req_1 and req_2 are shown in Fig. 1. Suppose IBS is invoked to find a counterexample for property $P1$ (shown in Fig. 1) subject to requirements $Reqs = \{req_1, req_2\}$ with the bound $vb = 4$. IBS translates the requirements and the property to FOL* and initializes $Reqs_\downarrow$ and $D_\downarrow$ to empty sets. For each iteration, we use ϕ_g and $\phi_g^\perp$ to represent the over- and under-approximation queries computed on LL:7-8, respectively.

<u>1st iteration:</u> $D_\downarrow = \emptyset$ and $Reqs_\downarrow = \emptyset$. Three new relational objects are introduced to ϕ_g (due to $\neg P1$): $access_1$, $collect_1$, and $update_1$ such that: (C1) $access_1$ occurs after $collect_1$ and $update_1$;(C2) $access_1.d = collect_1.d = update_1.d$;(C3) $access_1.v \neq collect_1.v \wedge access_1.v \neq update_1.v$; and (C4) either $collect_1$ or $update_1$ must be in the solution. ϕ_g is satisfiable, but $\phi_g^\perp$ is UNSAT since $D_\downarrow$ is an empty set. We assume $D_\downarrow$ is expanded by adding $access_1$ and $update_1$.

<u>2nd iteration:</u> $D_\downarrow = \{access_1, update_1\}$ and $Reqs_\downarrow = \emptyset$. The over-approximation ϕ_g stays the same, but $\phi_g^\perp$ becomes satisfiable since $access_1$ and $update_1$ are in $D_\downarrow$. Suppose the solution is σ_4 (see Fig. 2). However, σ_4 violates req_2, so req_2 is added to $Reqs_\downarrow$.

<u>3rd iteration:</u> $D_\downarrow = \{access_1, update_1\}$ and $Reqs_\downarrow = \{req_2\}$. Two new relational objects are introduced in ϕ_g (due to req_2): $collect_2$ and $update_2$ such that (C5) $collect_2.time \leq access_1.time \leq collect_2.time + 168$; (C6) $update_2.time \leq access_1.time \leq update_2.time + 168$; (C7) $access_1.d = collect_2.d = update_2.d$; (C8) $access_1.v = collect_2.v = update_2.v$; and (C9) $collect_2$ or $update_2$ is in the solution. The new ϕ_g is satisfiable, but $\phi_g^\perp$ is UNSAT because $update_2 \notin D_\downarrow$ and $update_1 \neq update_2$ (C8 conflicts with C3). Therefore, $D_\downarrow$ needs to be expanded. Assume $collect_2$ is added to $D_\downarrow$.

<u>4th iteration:</u> $D_\downarrow = \{access_1, update_1, collect_2\}$ and $Reqs_\downarrow = \{req_2\}$. The over-approximation ϕ_g stays the same, but $\phi_g^\perp$ becomes satisfiable since $collect_2$ is in

$D_\downarrow$. Suppose the solution is σ_3 (see Fig. 2). Since σ_3 violates req_1, req_1 is added to $Reqs_\downarrow$.

<u>5th iteration:</u> $D_\downarrow = \{access_1, update_1, collect_2\}$ and $Reqs_\downarrow = \{req_1, req_2\}$. The following constraints are added to ϕ_g (due to req_1): (C9) $\neg(update_2.time - 168 \leq collect_1.time \leq update_2.time)$. Since (C9) conflicts with (C8), (C7) and (C1), $update_2$ cannot be in the solution to ϕ_g. The over-approximation ϕ_g is satisfiable if $collect_1$ (introduced in the 1st iteration) or $update_2$ (3rd iteration) are in the solution. However, $\phi_g^\perp$ is UNSAT since $D_\downarrow$ does not contain $collect_1$ or $update_2$. Thus, $D_\downarrow$ is expanded. Assume $update_2$ is added to $D_\downarrow$.

<u>6th iteration:</u> $D_\downarrow = \{access_1, update_1, collect_2, update_2\}$, $Reqs_\downarrow = \{req_1, req_2\}$. The following constraints are added to ϕ_g (C10) $update_2.time \geq update_1.time + 168$ (due to req_1) and (C11) $update_2.time \leq update_1.time$ (due to $\neg P$). Since (C10) conflicts with (C11), $update_2$ cannot be in the solution to ϕ_g. Thus, ϕ_g is satisfiable only if $collect_1$ is in the solution. However, $\phi_g^\perp$ is UNSAT because $collect_1 \notin D_\downarrow$. Therefore, $D_\downarrow$ is expanded by adding $collect_1$.

<u>final iteration:</u> $D_\downarrow = \{access_1, update_1, collect_2, update_2, collect_1\}$ and $Reqs_\downarrow = \{req_1, req_2\}$. The under-approximation $\phi_g^\perp$ becomes satisfiable, and yields the solution σ_5 in Fig. 2 which satisfies both req_1 and req_2.

6 Evaluation

To evaluate our approach, we developed a prototype tool, called LEGOS, that implements our MFOTL bounded satisfiability checking algorithm, IBS (Algorithm 1). It includes Python API for specifying system requirements and MFOTL safety properties. We use pySMT [14] to formulate SMT queries and Z3 [8] to check their satisfiability. The implementation and the evaluation artifacts are included in the supplementary material [12]. In this section, we evaluate the effectiveness of our approach using five case studies, aiming to answer the following research question: *How effective is our approach at determining the bounded satisfiability of MFOTL formulas?* We measure effectiveness in terms of the ability to determine satisfiability (i.e., the satisfying solution and its volume, UNSAT, or bounded UNSAT), and performance, i.e., time and memory usage.

Cases studies. The five case studies considered in this paper are summarized below: (1) PHIM (derived from [1,10]): a computer system for keeping track of personal health information with cost management; (2) CF@H[1]: a system for monitoring COVID patients at home and enabling doctors to monitor patient data; (3) PBC [4]: an approval policy for publishing business reports within a company; (4) BST [4]: a banking system that processes customer transactions; and (5) NASA [26]: an automated air-traffic control system design that aims to avoid aircraft collisions.[2] Table 1 gives their statistics. For each case study, we

---

[1] https://covidfreeathome.org/.

[2] The requirements and properties for the NASA case study are originally expressed in LTL, which is subsumed by MFOTL.

record the number of requirements, relations, relation arguments, and properties, denoted as $\#reqs$, $\#rels$, $\#args$, and $\#props$, respectively. Additionally, Table 1 shows initial configurations used in our experiments, with number of custodians ($\#c$), patients ($\#p$), and data ($\#d$) for PHIM; number of users ($\#u$), and data ($\#d$) for CF@H and PBC; number of employees ($\#e$), customers ($\#c$), transactions ($\#t$), and the maximum amount for a transaction (sup) for BST; number of ground-separated ($\#GSEP$) and of the self-separating aircraft ($\#SSEP$) for NASA.

Table 1. Case study statistics.

Names	Case study statistics				Configuration
	$\#reqs$	$\#rels$	$\#args$	$\#props$	
PHIM	18	22	[1 − 4]	6	$\#c = 2$, $\#p = 2$ $\#d = 5$
CF@H	45	28	[2 − 3]	7	$\#u = 2$, $\#d = 10$
PBC	14	7	[1 − 2]	1	$\#u = 5$, $\#d = 10$
BST	10	3	[1 − 3]	3	$\#e = 1$, $\#c = 2$ $\#t = 4$, $sup = 10$
NASA	194	10	[6 − 79]	6	$\#GSEP = 3$ $\#SSEP = 0$ $\#GSEP = 2$ $\#SSEP = 2$

Table 2. Performance comparison between IBS and nuXmv on case study NASA.

NASA	configuration 1						configuration 2					
	IBS			nuXmv			IBS			nuXmv		
	out.	time (sec)	mem (MB)	out.	time (sec)	mem (MB)	out.	time (sec)	mem (MB)	out.	time (sec)	mem (MB)
na_1	U	0.80	154	U	0.88	82	U	0.13	141	U	1.65	90
na_2	U	0.16	141	U	0.47	70	U	0.15	141	U	1.50	90
na_3	U	0.16	141	U	0.49	83	U	0.13	141	U	1.48	90
na_4	U	0.77	80	U	0.54	83	U	0.15	66	U	1.43	91
na_5	U	0.14	140	U	0.52	82	U	0.15	141	U	1.43	90
na_6	U	0.03	62	U	0.57	72	U	0.03	62	U	1.40	90

Case studies were selected for (i) the purpose of comparison with existing works (i.e., NASA); (ii) checking whether our approach scales with case studies involving data/time constraints (PBC, BST, PHIM and CF@H); or (iii) evaluating the applicability of our approach with real-word case studies (CF@H and NASA). In addition to prior case studies, we include PHIM and CF@H which have complex data/time constraints. The number of requirements for the five case studies ranges between ten (BST) and 194 (NASA). The number of relations present in the MFOTL requirements ranges from three (BST) to 28 (CF@H), and the number of arguments in these relations ranges from 1 (PHM, PBC, and BST) to 79 (NASA).

Experimental setup. Given a set of requirements, data constraints and properties of interest for each case study, we measured the run-time (time) and peak memory usage (mem.) of performing bounded satisfiability checking of MFOTL properties, and the volume vol_σ (the number of relational objects) of the solution (σ) with (op) and without (nop) the optimality guarantees (see Remark 1 for finding non-optimal solutions). We conduct two experiments: the first one evaluates the efficiency and scalability of our approach; the second one compares our approach with satisfiability checking. Since there is no existing work for checking MFOTL satisfiability, we compared with LTL satisfiability checking because MFOTL subsumes LTL. To study the scalability of our approach, our first experiment considers four different configurations obtained by increasing the data constraints of the case-study requirements. The initial configuration (small) is described in Table 1 and the initial bound is 10. The medium and large configurations are obtained by multiplying the initial data constraints and volume bound

Table 3. Run-time performance for four case studies and 18 properties. We record the outcome (out.) of the algorithm with (op) or without (nop) the optimal solution guarantee: UNSAT (U), bounded-UNSAT (b-U), or the volume of the counterexample σ (a natural number, corresponding to vol_σ). We consider four different configurations: small (see Tab. 6), medium (x10), big (x100), and unbounded (∞) data domain constraints and volume bound. Volume differences between op and nop are bolded.

case studies		small			medium			big			unbounded		
		out.	Time (sec)	Mem (MB)	out.	Time (sec)	Mem (MB)	out.	Time (sec)	Mem (MB)	out.	Time (sec)	Mem (MB)
		nop | op	nop | op	nop | op	nop | op	nop | op	nop | op	nop | op	nop | op	nop | op	nop | op	nop | op	nop | op
PHIM	ph_1	U	0.04 | 0.03	29 | 29	U	0.03 | 0.03	136 | 136	U	0.04 | 0.04	136 | 136	U	0.06 | 0.05	64 | 64
	ph_2	U	0.03 | 0.03	138 | 138	U	0.03 | 0.03	136 | 137	U	0.03 | 0.04	136 | 136	U	0.05 | 0.06	64 | 61
	ph_3	U	0.03 | 0.03	134 | 137	U	0.03 | 0.03	138 | 138	U	0.05 | 0.05	137 | 138	U	0.06 | 0.06	64 | 64
	ph_4	U	0.04 | 0.04	136 | 138	U	0.04 | 0.04	138 | 135	U	0.05 | 0.05	138 | 138	U	0.06 | 0.07	64 | 64
	ph_5	U	0.02 | 0.02	135 | 135	U	0.02 | 0.02	608 | 608	56 | 56	30.51 | 30.51	390 | 390	56 | 56	21.64 | 21.60	393 | 390
	ph_6	b-U	0.18 | 0.20	139 | 139	U	0.72 | 0.82	144 | 144	U	0.88 | 0.70	142 | 142	U	0.91 | 0.91	70 | 70
	ph_7	U	0.11 | 0.11	139 | 139	29 | 29	13.80 | 1905.40	193 | 599	**30** | 29	20.25 | 682.22	193 | 601	**32** | 29	20.96 | 1035.87	123 | 383
CF@H	cf_1	b-U	4.80 | 6.90	114 | 176	U	2.87 | 3.55	81 | 86	U	2.98 | 1.71	85 | 76	U	1.71 | 0.74	74 | 68
	cf_2	b-U	0.87 | 0.93	70 | 70	14 | 14	3.21 | 425.41	79 | 334	14 | 14	2.40 | 778.36	76 | 80	14 | 14	3.32 | 16.97	80 | 205
	cf_3	b-U	1.38 | 1.31	145 | 145	16 | 16	6.05 | 90.78	168 | 403	16 | 16	3.54 | 371.65	157 | 846	16 | 16	5.35 | 24.07	86 | 164
	cf_4	b-U	1.52 | 0.73	74 | 68	14 | 14	4.54 | 65.59	90 | 261	14 | 14	5.63 | 57.30	95 | 261	14 | 14	5.65 | 1227.02	89 | 294
	cf_5	8 | 8	1.20 | 1.17	146 | 147	8 | 8	0.48 | 0.54	141 | 142	8 | 8	0.69 | 0.57	141 | 141	8 | 8	0.72 | 0.76	69 | 69
	cf_6	8 | 8	1.06 | 1.16	146 | 147	8 | 8	0.52 | 0.61	142 | 142	8 | 8	0.60 | 0.73	141 | 141	8 | 8	0.72 | 0.72	69 | 69
	cf_7	U	0.58 | 0.58	141 | 142	U	0.38 | 0.36	140 | 141	U	0.47 | 0.44	140 | 141	U	0.30 | 0.34	66 | 67
PBC	pb_1	U	0.04 | 0.04	29 | 140	U	0.16 | 0.17	140 | 139	9 | 9	0.28 | 0.29	141 | 141	9 | 9	0.27 | 0.28	67 | 67
BST	bs_1	U	0.04 | 0.03	64 | 63	U	0.29 | 0.24	70 | 68	U	0.31 | 0.30	69 | 68	U	0.25 | 0.25	69 | 69
	bs_2	2 | 2	0.04 | 0.04	62 | 64	2 | 2	0.04 | 0.04	62 | 62	2 | 2	0.04 | 0.04	64 | 64	2 | 2	0.04 | 0.04	64 | 64
	bs_3	U	0.02 | 0.02	62 | 62	5 | 5	0.4 | 0.9	70 | 73	5 | 5	0.39 | 0.85	70 | 74	5 | 5	0.40 | 0.70	70 | 72

by ten and hundred, respectively. The last (unbounded) configuration does not bound either the data domain or the volume. As we noted earlier in Sect. 4, the purpose of adding data constraints is to avoid unrealistic counterexamples. For example, the NASA case study uses a data set for specifying the possible system control modes and uses data ranges to restrict the possible measures from the aircraft (e.g., aircraft's trajectory). In the other case studies, data constraints are realistic data ranges (e.g., a patient's account balance should be non-negative). To study the performance of our approach relative to existing work, our second experiment considers two configurations of the NASA case study verified in [24] using the state-of-the-art symbolic model checker nuXmv [6][3]. We compare our approach's result against the reproduced result of nuXmv verification. For both experiments, we report the analysis outcomes, i.e., the volume of the satisfying solution (if one exists), UNSAT, or bounded UNSAT; and performance, i.e., time and memory usage. The experiments were conducted using a ThinkPad X1 Carbon with an Intel Core i7 1.80 GHz processor, 8 GB of RAM, and running 64-bit Ubuntu GNU/Linux 8.

Results of the first experiment are summarized in Table 3. Out of the 72 trials, our approach found 31 solutions. It also returned five bounded-UNSAT answers, and 36 UNSAT answers. The results show that our approach is effective in checking satisfiability of case studies with different sizes. More precisely,

---

[3] LEGOS solved all configurations from the NASA case study; see the results in [12]. For comparison, we report only on the configurations that are explicitly supported by nuXmv.

we observe that it takes under three seconds to return UNSAT and between .04 seconds (bs_2:medium) and 32 min (ph_7:medium:op) to return a solution. In the worst case, op took 32 min for checking ph_7 where the property and requirements contain complex constraints. Effectively, ph_7 requires the deletion of data stored at id 10, while the cost of deletion increases over time under PHIM's requirements. Therefore, the user has to perform a number of actions to obtain a sufficient balance to delete the data. Additionally, each action that increases the user's balance has its own preconditions, effects, and time cost, making the process of choosing the sequence of actions to meet the increasing deletion cost non-trivial.

We can see a difference in time between cf2 'big' and 'unbounded', this is because the domain expansion followed two different paths and one produces significantly easier SMT queries. Since our approach is guided by counterexamples (i.e., the path is guided by the solution from the SMT solver (Algorithm1-L:13)), our approach does not have direct control over the exact path selection. In future work, we aim to add optimizations to avoid/backtrack from hard paths.

We observe that the data-domain constraint and volume bound used in different configurations do not affect the performance of IBS when the satisfiability of the instances does not depend on them, which is the case for all the instances except for ph_{6-7}:small, cf_{1-3}:small, and bs_3:small. As mentioned in Sect. 4, the data-domain constraint ensures that satisfying solutions have realistic data values. For $ph1 - ph4$, the bound used in the small, medium and large configurations creates additional constraints in the SMT queries for each relational object, and therefore results in a larger peak memory than the unbounded configuration.

Finding the optimal solution (by op), in contrast to finding a satisfying solution without the optimal guarantee (by nop), imposes a substantial computational cost while rarely achieving a volume reduction. The non-optimal heuristic nop often outperformed the optimal approach for satisfiable instances. Out of 31 satisfiable instances, nop solved 12 instances 3 times faster, 10 instances 10 times faster and seven instances 20 times faster than op. Compared to the non-optimal solution, the optimal solution reduced the volume for only two instances: ph_7:large and ph_7:unbounded by one (3%) and three (9%), respectively. On all other satisfying instances, op and nop both find the optimal solutions. When there is no solution, both op and nop are equally efficient.

Results of the second experiment are summarized in Table 2. Our approach and nuXmv both correctly verified that all six properties were UNSAT in both NASA configurations. We observe that the performance of our approach is comparable to nuXmv for the first configuration with .10 to .20 seconds of difference on average. Yet, for the second configuration, our approach terminates in less than 0.20 seconds and nuXmv takes 1.50 seconds on average. We conclude that our approach's performance is comparable to that of nuXmv for LTL satisfiability checking even though our approach is not specifically designed for LTL.

Summary. In summary, we have demonstrated that our approach is effective at determining the bounded satisfiability of MFOTL formulas using case studies with different sizes and from different application domains. When restricted to

LTL, our approach is at least as effective as the existing work on LTL satisfiability checking which uses a state-of-the-art symbolic model checker. Importantly, IBS can often determine satisfiability of instances without reaching the volume bound, and its performance is not sensitive to the data domain. On the other hand, IBS's optimal guarantee imposes a substantial computational cost while rarely achieving a volume reduction over non-optimal solutions obtained by nop. We need to investigate the trade-off between optimality and efficiency, as well as evaluate the performance of IBS on a broader range of benchmarks.

7   Related Work

Below, we compare with the existing approaches that address the satisfiability checking of temporal logic and first-order logic.

Satisfiability checking of temporal properties. Temporal logic satisfiability checking has been studied for the verification of system designs. Satisfiability checking for Linear Temporal Logic (LTL) can be performed by reducing the problem to model checking [35], by applying automata-based techniques [25], or by SAT solving [5,21–23]. Satisfiability checking for metric temporal logic (MTL) [32] and its variants, e.g., mission-time LTL [24] and signal temporal logic [2], has been studied for the verification of real-time system designs. These existing techniques are inadequate for our needs: LTL and MTL cannot effectively capture quantified data constraints commonly used in legal properties. MFOTL does not have such a limitation as it extends MTL and LTL with first-order quantifiers, thereby supporting the specification of data constraints.

Finite model finding for first-order logic. Finite-model finders [7,33] look for a model by checking universal quantifiers exhaustively over candidate models with progressively larger domains; we look for finite-volume solutions using a similar approach. On the other hand, we consider an explicit bound on the volume of the solution, and are able to find the solution with the smallest volume. SMT solvers support quantifiers with quantifier instantiation heuristics [16,17] such as E-matching [9,27] and conflict-based instantiation [34]. Quantifier instantiation heuristics are nonetheless generally incomplete, whereas, in our approach, we obtain completeness by bounding the volume of the satisfying solution.

8   Conclusion

In this paper, we proposed an incremental bounded satisfiability checking approach, called IBS, aimed to enable verification of legal properties, expressed in MFOTL, against system requirements. IBS first translates MFOTL formulas to first-order logic with relational objects (FOL*) and then searches for a satisfying solution to the translated FOL* formulas in a bounded search space by deriving over- and under-approximating SMT queries. IBS starts with a small search space and incrementally expands it until an answer is returned or until the bound is exceeded. We implemented IBS on top of the SMT solver Z3. Experiments using five case studies showed that our approach is effective for identifying errors in requirements from different application domains. Our approach is currently limited to verifying safety properties. In the future, we plan to extend our approach so that it can handle a broader spectrum of property types, including liveness and fairness. IBS's performance and scalability depend crucially on how the domain of relational objects is maintained and expanded. As future work, we would like to study the effectiveness of other heuristics to improve IBS's scalability (e.g., random restart and expansion with domain-specific heuristics). We also aim to study how to learn/infer MFOTL properties during search to further improve the efficiency of our approach.

References

1. Arfelt, E., Basin, D., Debois, S.: Monitoring the GDPR. In: Sako, K., Schneider, S., Ryan, P.Y.A. (eds.) ESORICS 2019. LNCS, vol. 11735, pp. 681–699. Springer, Cham (2019). https://doi.org/10.1007/978-3-030-29959-0_33
2. Bae, K., Lee, J.: Bounded model checking of signal temporal logic properties using syntactic separation. Proc. ACM Program. Lang. 3(POPL), 51:1–51:30 (2019). https://doi.org/10.1145/3290364
3. Basin, D., Klaedtke, F., Müller, S.: Policy monitoring in first-order temporal logic. In: Touili, T., Cook, B., Jackson, P. (eds.) CAV 2010. LNCS, vol. 6174, pp. 1–18. Springer, Heidelberg (2010). https://doi.org/10.1007/978-3-642-14295-6_1
4. Basin, D.A., Klaedtke, F., Müller, S., Zalinescu, E.: Monitoring metric first-order temporal properties. J. ACM **62**(2), 15:1–15:45 (2015). https://doi.org/10.1145/2699444
5. Bersani, M.M., Frigeri, A., Morzenti, A., Pradella, M., Rossi, M., Pietro, P.S.: Constraint LTL satisfiability checking without automata. J. Appl. Log. **12**(4), 522–557 (2014). https://doi.org/10.1016/j.jal.2014.07.005
6. Cavada, R., et al.: The nuXmv Symbolic Model Checker. In: CAV, pp. 334–342 (2014)
7. Claessen, K., Sörensson, N.: New techniques that improve MACE-style finite model finding. In: Proceedings of the CADE-19 Workshop: Model Computation-Principles, Algorithms, Applications, pp. 11–27. Citeseer (2003)
8. de Moura, L., Bjørner, N.: Z3: an efficient SMT solver. In: Ramakrishnan, C.R., Rehof, J. (eds.) TACAS 2008. LNCS, vol. 4963, pp. 337–340. Springer, Heidelberg (2008). https://doi.org/10.1007/978-3-540-78800-3_24
9. Detlefs, D., Nelson, G., Saxe, J.B.: Simplify: a theorem prover for program checking. J. ACM **52**(3), 365–473 (2005). https://doi.org/10.1145/1066100.1066102
10. Feng, N., Marsso, L., Garavel, H.: Health record. Model checking context model (MCC'21), Dept. of Computer Science - University of Toronto (2021). https://mcc.lip6.fr/pdf/HealthRecord-form.pdf
11. Feng, N., Marsso, L., Sabetzadeh, M., Chechik, M.: Early verification of legal compliance via bounded satisfiability checking (2023). https://arxiv.org/abs/2209.04052
12. Feng, N., Marsso, L., Sabetzadeh, M., Chechik, M.: Supplementary material for: early verification of legal compliance via bounded satisfiability checking (2023). https://github.com/agithubuserseva/IBSC
13. Garavel, H., Graf, S.: Formal methods for safe and secure computers systems. Altros (2013)

14. Gario, M., Micheli, A.: PYSMT: a solver-agnostic library for fast prototyping of SMT-based algorithms. In: SMT Workshop 2015 (2015)
15. Gastin, P., Moro, P., Zeitoun, M.: Minimization of counterexamples in SPIN. In: Graf, S., Mounier, L. (eds.) SPIN 2004. LNCS, vol. 2989, pp. 92–108. Springer, Heidelberg (2004). https://doi.org/10.1007/978-3-540-24732-6_7
16. Ge, Y., Barrett, C., Tinelli, C.: Solving quantified verification conditions using satisfiability modulo theories. In: Pfenning, F. (ed.) CADE 2007. LNCS (LNAI), vol. 4603, pp. 167–182. Springer, Heidelberg (2007). https://doi.org/10.1007/978-3-540-73595-3_12
17. Ge, Y., de Moura, L.: Complete instantiation for quantified formulas in satisfiabiliby modulo theories. In: Bouajjani, A., Maler, O. (eds.) CAV 2009. LNCS, vol. 5643, pp. 306–320. Springer, Heidelberg (2009). https://doi.org/10.1007/978-3-642-02658-4_25
18. Hallé, S., Villemaire, R.: Runtime Enforcement of Web Service Message Contracts with Data. IEEE Trans. Serv. Comput. 5(2), 192–206 (2012). https://doi.org/10.1109/TSC.2011.10
19. Hublet, F., Basin, D.A., Krstic, S.: Real-time policy enforcement with metric first-order temporal logic. In: Atluri, V., Pietro, R.D., Jensen, C.D., Meng, W. (eds.) Computer Security - ESORICS 2022–27th European Symposium on Research in Computer Security, Copenhagen, Denmark, September 26–30, 2022, Proceedings, Part II. Lecture Notes in Computer Science, vol. 13555, pp. 211–232. Springer (2022). https://doi.org/10.1007/978-3-031-17146-8_11
20. Legislative Assembly of Ontario: Personal Health Information Protection Act (PHIPA) (2004). https://www.ontario.ca/laws/statute/04p03
21. Li, J., Pu, G., Zhang, L., Vardi, M.Y., He, J.: Accelerating LTL satisfiability checking by SAT solvers. J. Log. Comput. 28(6), 1011–1030 (2018). https://doi.org/10.1093/logcom/exy013
22. Li, J., Pu, G., Zhang, Y., Vardi, M.Y., Rozier, K.Y.: SAT-based explicit LTLf satisfiability checking. Artif. Intell. 289, 103369 (2020). https://doi.org/10.1016/j.artint.2020.103369
23. Li, J., Rozier, K.Y., Pu, G., Zhang, Y., Vardi, M.Y.: SAT-based explicit LTLf satisfiability checking. In: The Thirty-Third AAAI Conference on Artificial Intelligence, AAAI 2019, The Thirty-First Innovative Applications of Artificial Intelligence Conference, IAAI 2019, The Ninth AAAI Symposium on Educational Advances in Artificial Intelligence, EAAI 2019, Honolulu, Hawaii, USA, January 27 - February 1, 2019, pp. 2946–2953. AAAI Press (2019). https://doi.org/10.1609/aaai.v33i01.33012946
24. Li, J., Vardi, M.Y., Rozier, K.Y.: Satisfiability checking for mission-time LTL. In: Dillig, I., Tasiran, S. (eds.) CAV 2019. LNCS, vol. 11562, pp. 3–22. Springer, Cham (2019). https://doi.org/10.1007/978-3-030-25543-5_1
25. Li, J., Zhang, L., Pu, G., Vardi, M.Y., He, J.: LTL Satisfiability checking revisited. In: Proceedings of the 20th International Symposium on Temporal Representation and Reasoning, Pensacola, FL, USA, 2013, pp. 91–98. IEEE Computer Society (2013). https://doi.org/10.1109/TIME.2013.19
26. Mattarei, C., Cimatti, A., Gario, M., Tonetta, S., Rozier, K.Y.: Comparing different functional allocations in automated air traffic control design. In: Formal Methods in Computer-Aided Design (FMCAD'2015), Austin, Texas, USA, pp. 112–119. IEEE (2015)
27. de Moura, L., Bjørner, N.: Efficient E-matching for SMT solvers. In: Pfenning, F. (ed.) CADE 2007. LNCS (LNAI), vol. 4603, pp. 183–198. Springer, Heidelberg (2007). https://doi.org/10.1007/978-3-540-73595-3_13

28. Narodytska, N., Bacchus, F.: Maximum satisfiability using core-guided MaxSAT resolution. In: Proceedings of the 28th International Conference on Artificial Intelligence (AAAI'14), Québec City, Canada, pp. 2717–2723. AAAI Press (2014). http://www.aaai.org/ocs/index.php/AAAI/AAAI14/paper/view/8513

29. Papadimitriou, C.H.: On the complexity of integer programming. J. ACM **28**(4), 765–768 (1981). https://doi.org/10.1145/322276.322287

30. Passmore, G., et al.: The Imandra automated reasoning system (System Description). In: Peltier, N., Sofronie-Stokkermans, V. (eds.) IJCAR 2020. LNCS (LNAI), vol. 12167, pp. 464–471. Springer, Cham (2020). https://doi.org/10.1007/978-3-030-51054-1_30

31. Post, E.L.: Recursive Unsolvability of a Problem of Thue. J. Symb. Log. **12**(1), 1–11 (1947). https://doi.org/10.2307/2267170

32. Pradella, M., Morzenti, A., San Pietro, P.: Bounded satisfiability checking of metric temporal logic specifications. ACM Trans. Softw. Eng. Methodol. **22**(3), 20:1–20:54 (2013). https://doi.org/10.1145/2491509.2491514

33. Reynolds, A., Tinelli, C., Goel, A., Krstić, S., Deters, M., Barrett, C.: Quantifier instantiation techniques for finite model finding in SMT. In: Bonacina, M.P. (ed.) CADE 2013. LNCS (LNAI), vol. 7898, pp. 377–391. Springer, Heidelberg (2013). https://doi.org/10.1007/978-3-642-38574-2_26

34. Reynolds, A., Tinelli, C., de Moura, L.M.: Finding conflicting instances of quantified formulas in SMT. In: Formal Methods in Computer-Aided Design (FMCAD'2014), Lausanne, Switzerland, pp. 195–202. IEEE (2014). https://doi.org/10.1109/FMCAD.2014.6987613

35. Rozier, K.Y., Vardi, M.Y.: LTL satisfiability checking. In: Bošnački, D., Edelkamp, S. (eds.) SPIN 2007. LNCS, vol. 4595, pp. 149–167. Springer, Heidelberg (2007). https://doi.org/10.1007/978-3-540-73370-6_11

36. Shan, L., Sangchoolie, B., Folkesson, P., Vinter, J., Schoitsch, E., Loiseaux, C.: A survey on the application of safety, security, and privacy standards for dependable systems. In: Proceedings of the 15th European Dependable Computing Conference (EDCC'2019), Naples, Italy, pp. 71–72. IEEE (2019). https://doi.org/10.1109/EDCC.2019.00023

37. Suter, P., Köksal, A.S., Kuncak, V.: Satisfiability modulo recursive programs. In: Yahav, E. (ed.) SAS 2011. LNCS, vol. 6887, pp. 298–315. Springer, Heidelberg (2011). https://doi.org/10.1007/978-3-642-23702-7_23

Formula Normalizations in Verification

Simon Guilloud[(✉)] [iD], Mario Bucev, Dragana Milovančević[iD],
and Viktor Kunčak[iD]

School of Computer and Communication Sciences, EPFL, Station 14, 1015 Lausanne,
Switzerland
{simon.guilloud,mario.bucev,dragana.milovancevic,viktor.kuncak}@epfl.ch

Abstract. We apply and evaluate polynomial-time algorithms to compute two different normal forms of propositional formulas arising in verification. One of the normal form algorithms is presented for the first time. The algorithms compute normal forms and solve the word problem for two different subtheories of Boolean algebra: orthocomplemented bisemilattice (OCBSL) and ortholattice (OL). Equality of normal forms decides the word problem and is a sufficient (but not necessary) check for equivalence of propositional formulas. Our first contribution is a quadratic-time OL normal form algorithm, which induces a coarser equivalence than the OCBSL normal form and is thus a more precise approximation of propositional equivalence. The algorithm is efficient even when the input formula is represented as a directed acyclic graph. Our second contribution is the evaluation of OCBSL and OL normal forms as part of a verification condition cache of the Stainless verifier for Scala. The results show that both normalization algorithms substantially increase the cache hit ratio and improve the ability to prove verification conditions by simplification alone. To gain further insights, we also compare the algorithms on hardware circuit benchmarks, showing that normalization reduces circuit size and works well in the presence of sharing.

1 Introduction

Algorithms and techniques to solve and reduce formulas in propositional logic (and its generalizations) are a major field of study. They have prime relevance in SAT and SMT solving algorithms [2,8,31], in optimization of logical circuit size in hardware [25], in interactive theorem proving where propositional variables can represent assumptions and conclusions of theorems [23,35,43], for decision procedures in automated theorem proving [13,26,37,41,42], and in every subfield of formal verification in general [27]. The propositional problem of satisfiability is NP-complete, whereas validity and equivalence are coNP-complete. While heuristic techniques give useful results in practice, in this paper we investigate guaranteed worst-case polynomial-time deterministic algorithms. Such algorithms can serve as building blocks of more complex functionality, without creating an unpredictable dependency.

Recently, researchers proposed the use of certain non-distributive complemented lattice-like structures to compute normal forms of formulas [20]. These results appear to have a practical potential, but they have not been experimentally evaluated. Moreover, the proposed completeness characterization is in

© The Author(s) 2023
C. Enea and A. Lal (Eds.): CAV 2023, LNCS 13966, pp. 398–422, 2023.
https://doi.org/10.1007/978-3-031-37709-9_19

terms of "orthocomplemented bisemilattices" (OCBSL), which have a number of counterintuitive properties. For example, the structure is not a lattice and does not satisfy the absorption laws $x \wedge (x \vee y) = x$ and $x \vee (x \wedge y) = x$. As a consequence, there is no natural semantic ordering on formulas corresponding to implication, with $x \wedge y = x$ and $x \vee y = y$ inducing two different relations.

Inspired by these limitations, we revisit results on *lattices*, which are much better behaving structures. We strengthen the OCBSL structure with the absorption law to consider the class of *ortholattices*, as summarized in Table 1. Ortholattices (OL) have a natural partial order for which $\wedge, \vee$ act as the greatest lower bound and the least upper bound. They also satisfy de Morgan's law, allowing the elimination of one of the connectives in terms of the other two. On the other hand, ortholattices do not, in general, satisfy the distributivity law, which sets them apart from Boolean algebras.

We present a new algorithm that computes a normal form for OL in quadratic time. The normal form is strictly stronger than the one for OCBSL: there are terms in the language $\{\wedge, \vee, \neg\}$ that are distinct in OCBSL, but are equal in OL. Checking equality of OL normal forms thus more precisely approximates propositional formula equivalence. Both normal forms can be thought of as strengthening of the negation normal form.

Table 1. Laws of algebraic structures with signature $(S, \wedge, \vee, 0, 1, \neg)$. Structures satisfying laws L1–L8 and L1'–L8' were called *orthocomplemented bisemilattices* (OCBSL) in [20]. Those OCBSL that additionally satisfy L9 and L9' are *ortholattices* (OL).

L1:	$x \vee y = y \vee x$	L1':	$x \wedge y = y \wedge x$
L2:	$x \vee (y \vee z) = (x \vee y) \vee z$	L2':	$x \wedge (y \wedge z) = (x \wedge y) \wedge z$
L3:	$x \vee x = x$	L3':	$x \wedge x = x$
L4:	$x \vee 1 = 1$	L4':	$x \wedge 0 = 0$
L5:	$x \vee 0 = x$	L5':	$x \wedge 1 = x$
L6:	$\neg\neg x = x$	L6':	same as L6
L7:	$x \vee \neg x = 1$	L7':	$x \wedge \neg x = 0$
L8:	$\neg(x \vee y) = \neg x \wedge \neg y$	L8':	$\neg(x \wedge y) = \neg x \vee \neg y$
L9:	$x \vee (x \wedge y) = x$	L9':	$x \wedge (x \vee y) = x$

Example 1. Consider the formula $x \wedge (y \vee z)$. An OCBSL algorithm finds it equivalent to

$$x \wedge \neg(\neg y \wedge \neg z) \wedge x$$

but it will consider these two formulas non-equivalent to

$$x \wedge (u \vee x) \wedge (y \vee z)$$

The OL algorithm will identify the equivalence of all three formulas, thanks to the laws (L9, L9'). It will nonetheless consider them non-equivalent to

$$(x \wedge y) \vee (x \wedge z)$$

which a complete but exponential worst-case time algorithm for Boolean algebra equalities, such as one implemented in SAT solvers, will identify as equivalent.

A major practical question is the usefulness of such $O(n \log(n)^2)$ (OCBSL) and $O(n^2)$ (OL) algorithms in verification. Are they as predictably efficient as the theoretical analysis suggests? What benefits do they provide as a component of verification tools? To answer these questions, we implement both OCBSL and OL algorithms on directed acyclic graph representations of formulas. We deploy the algorithms in tools that manipulate formulas, most notably verification conditions in a program verifier, as well as combinational Boolean circuits.

Contributions. We make the following contributions:

- We present the first algorithm computing a *normal form* of *ortholattice* (OL) terms. The algorithm preserves the quadratic time for the decision problem of equality in free ortholattices [7]. The quadratic time remains even when the formula is given in a shared (DAG) representation.
- We implement and experimentally evaluate both the new algorithm for the OL normal form and a previously known (weaker) OCBSL algorithm (shown to run in quasilinear time). Our evaluation (Sect. 6) includes:
  - behavior on randomly generated formulas;
  - scalability evaluation on normalizing circuits of size up to 10^8 gates;
  - normalization for simplification and caching of verification conditions when using the Stainless verifier, with both hard benchmarks (such as a compression algorithm) and collections of student submissions for programming assignments.

We show that OCBSL and OL both have notable potential in practice.

1.1 Related Work

The overarching perspective behind our paper is understanding polynomial-time normalization of boolean algebra terms. Given (co)NP-hardness of problems related to Boolean algebras, we look at subtheories given by a subset of Boolean algebra axioms, including structures such as lattices. Lattices themselves have many uses in program abstraction, including abstract interpretation [11] and model checking [14,18]. The theory of the word problem for lattices has been studied already by Whitman [44], who proposed a quadratic solution for the word problem for free *lattices*. Lattices alone do not incorporate the notion of a complement (negation). Whitman's algorithm has been adapted and extended to finitely presented lattices [17] and other variants, and then to free ortholattices by Bruns [7]. We extend this last result to not only decide equality, but also to compute a *normal form* for free ortholattices and to *circuit* (DAG) representation of terms. An efficient normal form does not follow from an efficient equivalence checking, as there are many formulas in the same equivalence class. Normal form is particularly useful in applications such as formula caching, which we evaluate in Sect. 6. For a weaker theory of OCBSL, the normal form algorithm was introduced in [20], without any experimental evaluation. The theory of ortholattices, even if it adds only one more axiom, is notably stronger and better understood. The underlying lattice structure makes it possible to draw on the body of work on using lattices to abstract systems and enable algorithmic verification. The support for graphs (instead of only terms) as a representation is of immense practical relevance, because expanding circuits into trees without the use of auxiliary variables creates structures of astronomical size (Sect. 6).

A notable normal form that decides equality for propositional logic (thus also accounting for the distributivity law) are reduced ordered binary decision diagrams (ROBDDs) [9]. ROBDDs are of great importance in verification, but can be exponential in the size of the initial formula. Circuit synthesis and verification tools such as ABC [6] use SAT solvers to optimize sub-circuits [45], which is an approach to choose a trade-off between the completeness and cost of exponential-time algorithm. Boolean algebras are in correspondence with boolean rings, which replace the least upper bound operation $\vee$ with the symmetric difference $\oplus$ (defined as $(p \wedge \neg q) \vee (\neg p \wedge q)$ and satisfying $x \oplus x = 0$, corresponding to the *exclusive or* in the two-element case). There have been proposals to exploit the boolean ring structure in verification [12]. Polynomials over rings can also be used to obtain a normal form, but the polynomial canonical forms that we are aware of are exponential-sized. SMT solvers [2,34] extend SAT solvers, which makes them worst-case exponential (at best). We expect that our approach and algorithms could be used for preprocessing or representation, especially in non-clausal variants of SMT solvers [24,39]. In our evaluation, we apply formula normal forms to the problem of caching of verification conditions. Caching is often used in verification tools, including Dafny [28] and Stainless [22]. Our caching works on formulas and preserves the API of a constraint solver. It is thus fine grained and can be added to a program verifier or analyzer, regardless of whether it uses any other, domain-specific, forms of caching [29].

2   Preliminaries

We present definitions and results necessary for the presentation of the ortholattice (OL) normal form algorithm. We assume familiarity with term rewriting and representation of terms as trees and directed acyclic graphs [15,20]. We use first-order logic with equality (whose symbol is $=$). We write $A \models F$ to mean that a first-order logic formula F is a consequence of (thus provable from) the set of formulas A.

Definition 1 (Terms). *Consider an algebraic signature S. We use $\mathcal{T}_S(X)$ to denote the set of terms over S with variables in X (typically an arbitrary countably infinite set, unless specified otherwise). Terms are constructed inductively as trees. Leaves are labeled with constant symbols or variables. Nodes are labeled with function symbols. If the label of a node is a commutative function, the children of the node are considered as a set (non-ordered) and otherwise as a list (ordered). We assume that commutative symbols are denoted as such in the signature.*

Definition 2 (The Word Problem). *Consider an algebraic signature S and a set of equational axioms E on S (for example the theory of lattices or ortholattices). The word problem for E is the problem of determining, given two terms t_1 and $t_2 \in \mathcal{T}_S(X)$, whether $E \models t_1 = t_2$.*

Definition 3 (Normal Form). *Consider an algebraic signature S and a set of equational axioms E on S. A function $f : \mathcal{T}_S(X) \mapsto \mathcal{T}_S(X)$ produces a normal form for E iff:* $\forall t_1, t_2 \in \mathcal{T}_S(X)$, $E \models t_1 = t_2$ *is equivalent to* $f(t_1) = f(t_2)$.

For Z an arbitrary non-empty set and $(\sim) \subseteq Z \times Z$ an equivalence relation on X we use a common notation: if $x \in Z$ then $[x]_\sim = \{y \in Z \mid x \sim y\}$. Let $Z_{/\sim} = \{[x]_\sim \mid x \in Z\}$.

We now briefly review key concepts of free algebras. Let S be a signature and E be an equational theory over this signature. Consider an equivalence relation on terms $p \sim_E q \iff (E \models p = q)$, and note that $\mathcal{T}_S(X)_{/\sim_E}$ is itself an E-algebra. A **freely generated E-algebra**, denoted $F_E(X)$, is an algebra generated by variables in X and isomorphic to $\mathcal{T}_S(X)_{/\sim_E}$, i.e. in which *only* the laws of all E-algebra hold. There is always a homomorphism from a freely generated E-algebra to any other E-algebra over X.

The set of terms $\mathcal{T}_S(X)$ is also called the **term algebra** over S. It is the algebra of all terms that contains no identity other than syntactic equality. Given a (possibly free) algebra A over S and generated by X, there is a natural homomorphism κ_A, in a sense an evaluation function, from $\mathcal{T}_S(X)$ to A. The word problem for a theory E then consists in, given $p, q \in \mathcal{T}_S(X)$, deciding if $E \models p = q$, that is, $\kappa_{F_E}(t_1) = \kappa_{F_E}(t_2)$.

In the sequel, we continue to use $=$ to denote the equality symbol inside formulas as well as the usual identity of mathematical objects. We use $==$ to specifically denote the computer-performed operation of *structural* equality on trees and sets, whereas $===$ denotes *reference* equality of objects, meaning that $a === b$ if and only if a and b denote the same object in memory. The distinction between $==$ and $===$ is relevant because $==$ is a larger relation but may take linear or worse time to compute, whereas we assume $===$ is constant time.

Lattices. Lattices [4] are well-studied structures with signature $(\wedge, \vee)$ satisfying laws L1–L3, L9, L1'–L3' and L9' from Table 1. In particular, they do not have a complement operation, $\neg$, in the signature. Lattices can also be viewed as a special kind of partially ordered sets with an order relation defined by $(a \leq b) \iff (a \wedge b = a)$, where the last condition is also equivalent to $(a \vee b = b)$, given the axioms of lattices. When applied to two-element Boolean algebras, this order relation corresponds to logical implication in propositional logic. A **bounded lattice** is a lattice with maximal and minimal elements 1 and 0. The word problem for *lattices* has been solved by Whitman [44] through an algorithm to decide the $\leq$ relation and is based on the following properties of free lattices:

$$
\begin{aligned}
(1) \ & s_1 \vee \dots \vee s_m \leq t && \iff \forall i. s_i \leq t \\
(2) \ & s \leq t_1 \wedge \dots \wedge t_n && \iff \forall j. s \leq t_j \\
(3) \ & s_1 \wedge \dots \wedge s_m \leq y && \iff \exists i. s_i \leq y \\
(4) \ & x \leq t_1 \vee \dots \vee t_n && \iff \exists j. x \leq t_j
\end{aligned}
$$

$$
s \leq t \iff (\exists i. s_i \leq t) \vee (\exists j. s \leq t_j), \\
\text{with } s = (s_1 \wedge \dots \wedge s_m) \text{ and } t = (t_1 \vee \dots \vee t_n)
\tag{w}
$$

where x and y denote variables and s and t terms. The first four properties are direct consequences of the axioms of lattices. (w) above is *Whitman property* and holds in free lattices (not in all lattices). Applying the above rules recursively decides the $\leq$ relation.

Orthocomplemented Bisemilattices (OCBSL). OCBSL [20] are also a weakening of Boolean algebras (and, in fact, a subtheory of ortholattices). They satisfy laws L1–L8, L1'–L8' but not the absorption law (L9, L9'). This implies in particular that OCBSL do not have a canonical order relation as lattices do, but rather have two, in general distinct, relations:

$$a \leq b \iff a \wedge b = a$$
$$a \sqsubseteq b \iff a \vee b = b$$

If we add absorption axioms, $a \wedge b = a$ implies $a \vee b = (a \wedge b) \vee b = b$ (and dually), so the structure becomes a lattice. The algorithm presented in [20] does not rely on lattice properties. Instead, it is proven that the axioms of OCBSL can be extended to a term rewriting system which is confluent and terminating, and hence admits a normal form. Using variants of algorithms on labelled trees to handle commutativity, this normal form can be computed in quasilinear time $\mathcal{O}(n \log^2(n))$. In contrast, in the case of free *lattices*, there exists no confluent and terminating term rewriting system [16].

3 Deriving an Ortholattice Normal Form Algorithm

Ortholattices [3, Chapter II.1] are structures satisfying laws L1–L9, L1'–L9' of Table 1. An ortholattice (OL) need not be a Boolean algebra, nor an orthomodular lattice; the smallest example of such OL is "Benzene" (O6), with elements $\{0, a, b, \neg b, \neg a, 1\}$ where $a \leq b$ [5]. The word problem for free ortholattices, which checks if a given equation is true, has been shown to be solvable in quadratic time by Bruns [7]. In this section, we go further by presenting an efficient computation of *normal forms*, which reduces the word problem to syntactic equality. In addition, normal forms can be efficiently used for formula simplification and caching, unlike equality procedure itself.

Definition 4. *For a set of variables X, we define a disjoint set of the same cardinality X' with a bijective function $(\cdot)' : X \mapsto X'$. Denote by L the theory of bounded lattices and OL the theory of ortholattices. Define F_L, F_{OL} to be their free lattices and $\mathcal{T}_L$ and $\mathcal{T}_{OL}$ to be the sets of terms over their respective signature. Define $\leq_L$ as the relation on $\mathcal{T}_L$ such that $s \leq_L t \iff \kappa_{F_L}(s) \leq \kappa_{F_L}(t)$ and $\leq_{OL}$ analogously by $s \leq_{OL} t \iff \kappa_{F_{OL}}(s) \leq \kappa_{F_{OL}}(t)$, where κ denotes natural homomorphisms as introduced in the previous section.*

Note: $p \leq_{OL} q \iff (E_{OL} \models (p \wedge q = q))$ where E_{OL} is the set of axioms of Table 1.

3.1   Deciding $\leq_{OL}$ by Reduction to Bounded Lattices

We consider $T_L(X \cup X')$ as a subset of $T_{OL}(X)$ via the injective inclusion on variables mapping $x \mapsto x$ and $x' \mapsto \neg x$. We also define a function $\delta : T_{OL}(X) \to T_L(X \cup X')$ as transformation into negation normal form, using laws L6 (double negation elimination), L8 and L8' (de Morgan's laws).

We define a set $R \subseteq T_L(X \cup X')$ of terms reduced with respect to the contradiction laws (L7 and L7'). These imply that, e.g., given a term $a \vee b$, if $\neg b \leq (a \vee b)$, then from as $b \leq a \vee b$, we have $1 = b \vee \neg b \leq (a \vee b)$. The following inductive definition induces an algorithm to check $x \in R$, meaning that such reductions do not apply inside x:

$$0, 1, x, x' \in R \quad (\text{for } x \in X)$$
$$a \vee b \in R \iff a \in R, b \in R, \ \delta(\neg a) \not\leq_L a \vee b, \ \delta(\neg b) \not\leq_L a \vee b$$
$$a \wedge b \in R \iff a \in R, b \in R, \ \delta(\neg a) \not\geq_L a \wedge b, \ \delta(\neg b) \not\geq_L a \wedge b$$

Above, $\leq_L$ is the order relation on lattices, $x \geq_L y$ denotes $y \leq_L x$, and $\not\leq_L$, $\not\geq_L$ are the negations of those conditions: $x \not\leq_L y$ iff not $x \leq_L y$, whereas $x \not\geq_L y$ iff not $y \leq_L x$.

We also define $\beta : T_L(X \cup X') \to R$ by:

$$\beta(0) = 0, \beta(1) = 1, \beta(x) = x, \beta(x') = x' \ (\text{for } x \in X)$$

$$\beta(a \vee b) = \begin{cases} \beta(a) \vee \beta(b) & \text{if } \beta(a) \vee \beta(b) \in R \\ 1 & \text{otherwise} \end{cases}$$

$$\beta(a \wedge b) = \begin{cases} \beta(a) \wedge \beta(b) & \text{if } \beta(a) \wedge \beta(b) \in R \\ 0 & \text{otherwise} \end{cases}$$

Example 2. We have $\beta((x \wedge \neg y) \vee (\neg x \vee y)) = 1$ because $\delta(\neg(x \wedge \neg y)) = \neg x \vee y$ and $\neg x \vee y \leq_L (x \wedge \neg y) \vee \neg x \vee y$.

Note that it is generally not sufficient to check only for $\delta(\neg a) \not\leq_L b$ for larger examples. In particular, if $\delta(\neg a)$ is itself a conjunction, by Whitman's property, the condition $\delta(\neg a) \not\leq (a \vee b)$ is not in general equivalent to having either $\delta(\neg a) \not\leq_L b$ or $\delta(\neg a) \not\leq_L a$.

We next reformulate the theorem from Bruns [7]. A key construction from the proof is the following Lemma.

Lemma 1. $R_{/\sim_L}$ is an ortholattice isomorphic to $F_{OL}(X)$.

Theorem 1. Let $s, t \in T_{OL}(X)$. Then, $s \leq_{OL} t \iff \beta(\delta(s)) \leq_L \beta(\delta(t))$.

Proof. We sketch and adapt the original proof. Intuitively, computing $\beta(\delta(s)) \leq_L \beta(\delta(t))$ should be sufficient to compute the $\leq_{OL}$relation: δ reduces terms to normal forms modulo rules L6 (double negation elimination) and L8, L8' (De Morgan's Law), and then β takes care of rule L7 (contradiction). The only rules left are rules from (bounded) lattices, which should be dealt with by $\leq_L$. From Lemma 1, the fact that β factors in the evaluation function $\kappa_{F_{OL}}$

(i.e. is equivalence preserving) and properties of free algebras, it can be shown that $\kappa_{F_{OL}} = \gamma \circ N_{\sim_L} \circ \beta \circ \delta$, where $N_{\sim_L}(x) = [x]_{\sim_L}$, and $\gamma : R_{/\sim_L} \to F_{OL}(X)$ is an isomorphism. Hence

$$\kappa_{F_{OL}}(s) \leq \kappa_{F_{OL}}(t) \iff \beta(\delta(s))_{/\sim_L} \leq \beta(\delta(t))_{/\sim_L}$$

which is equivalent to $s \leq_{OL} t \iff \beta(\delta(s)) \leq_L \beta(\delta(t))$.

3.2   Reduction to Normal Form

To obtain a normal form for $T_{OL}(X)$, we will compose δ and β with a normal form function for $T_L(X \cup X')$. A disjunction $a = a_1 \lor ... \lor a_m$ (and dually for a conjunction) is in normal form for $\leq_L$ if and only if the following two properties hold [15, p. 17]:

1. if $a_i = (a_{i1} \land ... \land a_{in})$, then for all j, $a_{ij} \not\leq a$
2. $(a_1, ..., a_n)$ forms an antichain (if $i \neq j$ then $a_i \not\leq a_j$)

We now show how to reduce a term in R so that it satisfies both properties using function ζ that enforces property 1, and then η that additionally enforces property 2. The functions operate dually on $\land$ and $\lor$; we specify them only on $\lor$ cases for brevity.

Enforcing Property 1. Define $\zeta : R \to R$ recursively such that:

$$\zeta(a_1 \lor ... \lor a_m) = \begin{cases} \zeta(a_1 \lor ... \lor a_{ij} \lor ... \lor a_m) & \text{if } a_i = (a_{i1} \land ... \land a_{in}) \\ & \text{and } a_{ij} \leq_L a_1 \lor ... \lor a_m \\ \zeta(a_1) \lor ... \lor \zeta(a_m) & \text{otherwise} \end{cases}$$

(dually for $\land$). It follows that $s \sim_L \zeta(s)$ for every term s because $a_{ij} \leq_L a_1 \lor ... \lor a_m$ implies $a_1 \lor ... \lor a_m = a_1 \lor ... \lor a_m \lor a_{ij}$ and $a_i \lor a_{ij} = a_{ij}$ by absorption.

Enforcing Property 2 (Antichain). Define $\eta : R \to R$ such that

$$\eta(a_1 \lor ... \lor a_m) = \begin{cases} \eta(a_1 \lor ... \lor a_{i-1} \lor a_{i+1} \lor ... \lor a_m) & \text{if } a_i \leq_L a_j, i \neq j \\ \eta(a_1) \lor ... \lor \eta(a_m) & \text{otherwise} \end{cases}$$

We have $s \sim_L \eta(s)$ for every term s because $a_i \leq_L a_j$ means $a_i \lor a_j = a_j$.

Example 3. We have: $\eta(\zeta([(a \lor b) \land (a \lor c)] \lor b)) = \eta((a \lor b) \lor b) = a \lor b$. Indeed, the first equality follows from

$$(a \lor b) \leq_L [(a \lor b) \land (a \lor c)] \lor b$$

and the second from $b \leq_L (a \lor b)$.

Denote by R' the subset of R containing the terms satisfying property 1 and R'' the subset of R' of terms satisfying property 2. It is easy to see that ζ is actually $R \to R'$ and η can be restricted to $R' \to R''$. Moreover $s, t \in R''$ and $s \sim_L t$ implies $s = t$. Recall that $\forall w \in \mathcal{T}_{OL}(X).\beta(\delta(w)) \in R$. Since β and δ are equivalence preserving, $\forall w_1, w_2 \in \mathcal{T}_{OL}(X)$

$$w_1 \sim_{OL} w_2 \iff \beta(\delta(w_1)) \sim_{OL} \beta(\delta(w_2))$$

Moreover, since (by Lemma 1) $R_{/\sim_L}$ is an ortholattice, we have

$$\beta(\delta(w_1)) \sim_{OL} \beta(\delta(w_2)) \iff \beta(\delta(w_1)) \sim_L \beta(\delta(w_2))$$

i.e. in R, $\sim_{OL} \equiv \sim_L$. Then,

$$\beta(\delta(w_1)) \sim_L \beta(\delta(w_2)) \iff \eta(\zeta(\beta(\delta(w_1)))) \sim_L \eta(\zeta(\beta(\delta(w_2))))$$

and since both $\eta(\zeta(\beta(\delta(w_1)))) \in R''$ and $\eta(\zeta(\beta(\delta(w_2)))) \in R''$

$$\eta(\zeta(\beta(\delta(w_1)))) = \eta(\zeta(\beta(\delta(w_2))))$$

We finally conclude:

Theorem 2. $NF_{OL} = \eta \circ \zeta \circ \beta \circ \delta$ *is a computable normal form function for ortholattices.*

3.3   Complexity and Normal Form Size

Before presenting the algorithm in more detail, we argue why the normal form function from the previous section can be computed efficiently. We assume a RAM model and hence that creating new nodes in the tree representation of terms can be done in constant time.

Note that the size of the output of each of δ, β, ζ and η is linearly bounded by the size of the input. Thus, the asymptotic runtime complexity of the composition is the sum of the runtimes of these functions. Recall that δ (negation normal form) is computable in linear time and ζ and η are both computable in worst-case quadratic time, plus the time needed to compute $\leq_L$. Then, β, R and $\leq_L$ are each computable in constant time plus the time needed for the mutually recursive calls. While a direct recursive implementation would be exponential, observe that the computation time of R and β is proportional to the total number of times they get called on. If we store (memoize) the results of the functions for each different input, this time can be bounded by the total number of different sub-nodes that are part of the input or which we create during the algorithm's execution. Similarly, $\leq_L$ needs to be applied to, at worst, every pair of such sub-nodes. Consequently, if we memoize the result of each of these functions at all their calls, we may expect to obtain at most quadratic time to compute them on all the sub-nodes of a formula.

The above argument is, however, not entirely sufficient, because computing $R(a \wedge b)$ requires creating the new nodes $\neg a$ and $\neg b$ and then computing their negation normal form, which again creates new nodes. Indeed, note that, for memoization, we need to rely on *reference* (pointer) equality, as *structural* equality would take a linear amount of time to compute (for a total cubic time). Hence, to obtain quadratic time and space, we need to be able to negate a node in negation normal form without creating new nodes too many new nodes in memory. To do so, define $op : \mathcal{T}_L(X \cup X') \to \mathcal{T}_L(X \cup X')$ by

$$op(x) = x' \quad op(a \wedge b) = op(a) \vee op(b)$$
$$op(x') = x \quad op(a \vee b) = op(a) \wedge op(b)$$

$op(a)$ is functionally equal to $\delta(\neg a)$, but has the crucial property that

$$\text{children}(op(\tau)) === op[\text{children}(\tau)]$$

Where τ denotes a formal conjunction or disjunction and $\text{children}(\tau)$ is the set of children of τ as a tree. op can be efficiently memoized. Moreover, it can be bijectively memoized: if $op(a) = b$ we shall also store $op(b) = a$. We thus obtain $op(\text{children}(op(\tau))) === \text{children}(\tau)$. In this approach we are guaranteed to never instantiate any node beyond the n subnodes of the original formula (in negation normal form) and their opposite for a total of $2n$ nodes. Hence, we only ever needed to call op, R and β on up to $2n$ different inputs and $\leq$ on up to $4n^2$ different inputs, guaranteeing a final quadratic running time.

Minimal Size. Finally, as none of δ, β, ζ and η ever increase the size of the formula (in terms of the number of literals, conjunctions and disjunctions), neither does NF_{OL}. Consequently, for any term w, $\text{NF}_{OL}(w)$ is one of the smallest terms equivalent to w. Indeed, let $w_{\min} = w$ such that $w_{\min}$ is a term of smallest size in the equivalence class of w. In particular, $\text{NF}_{OL}(w_{\min})$ cannot be smaller than $w_{\min}$ (because $w_{\min}$ is minimal in the class) nor larger (because NF_{OL} is size non-increasing). Since $\text{NF}_{OL}(w) = \text{NF}_{OL}(w_{\min})$, $\text{NF}_{OL}(w)$ is of minimal size.

Theorem 3. *The normal form from Theorem 2 can be computed by an algorithm running in time and space $\mathcal{O}(n^2)$. Moreover, the resulting normal form is guaranteed to be smallest in the equivalence class of the input term.*

4   Algorithm with Memoization and Structure Sharing

To obtain a practical realization of Theorem 3, we need to address two main challenges. First, as explained in the previous section, we need to memoize the result of some functions to avoid exponential blowup. Second, we want to make the procedure compatible with structure sharing, since it is an important feature for many applications.

By *memoization* we mean modifying a function so that it saves the result of the calls for each argument, so that they can be found without future recomputations. Results of function calls can be stored in a map. For single-argument functions we find it is typically more efficient to introduce a field in each object to hold the result of calling a function on it. Under *structure sharing* we understand the possibility to reuse subformulas multiple times in the description of a logical expression. In case of signature $\land, \lor, \neg$, such expressions can be viewed as combinational Boolean circuits. We represent such terms using directed acyclic graph (DAG) reference structures instead of tree structures.

Circuits can be exponentially more succinct than equivalent formulas, but not all formula rewrites are efficient in the presence of structure sharing (consider for example, rules with substitution such as $x \land F \rightsquigarrow x \land F[x := 1]$, where F may also be referred to somewhere else). Structure sharing is thus non-trivial to maintain throughout all representations and transformations. Indeed, making a naive recursive modification of a circuit will unfold the DAG into a tree, often causing an exponential increase in space. Doing so optimally also requires the use of memoization. Moreover, the choice of representations and datastructures is critical.

We show that it is possible to make both algorithms fully compatible with structure sharing without ever creating node duplicates. The algorithm ensures that the resulting circuits will contain a smaller number of subnodes, preserve equivalence, and enforce that two circuits have the same representation if and only if they describe the same term (by the laws of OL).

Algorithm 1: Datastructure for Formulas

```
1  numberOfFormulas ← 0
2  Datastructure AIGFormula
3      val uniqueId: Int ← numberOfFormulas++    // get fresh ID on node creation
4      var inverse:AIGFormula ← null
5      var normal:AIGFormula ← null
6      var smaller: Set[Int] ← ∅                              // sparse bitset
7      var notSmaller: Set[Int] ← ∅                           // sparse bitset
8  case Variable(id:String, polarity:Bool) of AIGFormula
9  case Literal(polarity:Bool) of AIGFormula
10 case Conjunction(children:List[AIGFormula], polarity:Bool) of AIGFormula
11 val Positive: Bool = True; val Negative: Bool = False
```

Algorithm 2: Computing Negations

```
1  def inverse(τ)                                  // AIGFormula -> AIGFormula
2      if isDefined(τ.inverse) then
3          return τ.inverse
4      else
5          τ̄ ← τ.copy(polarity = !τ.polarity)
6          τ.inverse ← τ̄
7          τ̄.inverse ← τ
8          return τ̄
```

Algorithm 3: Computing $\leq$

```
 1  def ≤(τ, π)                                    // AIGFormula -> AIGFormula -> Bool
 2      if τ.smaller contains π.uniqueId then return True
 3      else if τ.notSmaller contains π.uniqueId then return False
 4      else
 5          r ← match (τ, π) :
 6              case (lhs, Conjunction(children, Positive)) :
 7              |   ∀c ∈ children. τ≤c
 8              case (Conjunction(children, Negative), rhs) :
 9              |   ∀c ∈ children. inverse(c)≤π
10              case (Variable(id), Conjunction(children, Negative) :
11              |   ∃c ∈ children. τ≤inverse(c)
12              case (Conjunction(children, Positive), Variable(id)) :
13              |   ∃c ∈ children. c≤π
14              case (Conjunction(tauCh, Positive), Conjunction(piCh, Negative)) :
                    // would cause exponential explosion without memoization:
15              |   (∃c ∈ tauCh. c≤π) ∨ (∃c ∈ piCh. τ≤inverse(c))
16              case (Variable(id1), Variable(id2)) :
17              |   id1 == id2
18          if r then τ.smaller += π.uniqueId
19          else τ.notSmaller += π.uniqueId
20          return r
```

Pseudocode. Algorithms 1, 2, 3, 4 present pseudocode implementation of the normal form function from Theorem 2. To more easily maintain structure sharing and gain performance, we move away from the *negation normal form* representation and prefer to use a representation of formulas similar to AIG (And-Inverter Graph) where a formula is either a Conjunction, a Variable or a Literal and contains a boolean value telling if the formula is positive or negative (see Algorithm 1). This implies that δ needs to transform arbitrary Boolean formulas into AIGFormulas instead of negation normal forms. Fortunately, AIGFormula can be efficiently translated to NNF (and back) so we can view them as an alternative representation of terms in $T_L(X \cup X')$. For the sake of space, we do not show the reduction from general formula trees on the signature $(\wedge, \vee, \neg)$ and work directly with AIGFormulas, but the implementation needs memoization to avoid exponential duplication in presence of structure sharing.

Recall that computing R requires taking the negation of some formulas, and projecting them back into $T_L(X \cup X')$ with δ. Using *AIGFormula* makes it possible to always take the negation of a formula in constant time and space. The corresponding function *inverse(τ)* is in Algorithm 2, and corresponds to the *op* function from the previous section. The memoization ensures that for all τ, *inverse(inverse(τ))* $===$ τ, and our choice of data structure ensures that *children(inverse(τ))* $===$ *children(τ)*. Those two properties guarantee that any sequence of access to children and inverses of τ will always yield a formula object within the original DAG, or its single inverse copy. In particular, regardless of structure sharing in the input structure, we never need to store in memory more than twice the total number of formula nodes in the input. As explained in Sect. 3.3, a similar condition could be made to hold with NNF, but we believe it is more complicated and less efficient when implemented.

Function $\leq$ in Algorithm 3 is based on Whitman's algorithm adapted to AIGFormula. For memoization, because the function takes two arguments, we store in each node the set of nodes it is smaller than or not using two sets. Note that storing and accessing values in a set (even a hash set) is only as efficient as computing the equality relation on two objects is. Because structural equality $==$ takes linear time to compute, we use referential equality with the *uniqueId* of each formula (declared in Algorithm 1). We found that using sparse bit sets yields the best performances.

The *simplify* function in Algorithm 4 makes a one-level simplification of a conjunction node, assuming that its children have already been simplified. We present the case when τ is positive. It works in three steps. The subfunction *zeta* corresponds to the ζ function from the previous section. It both flattens consecutive positive conjunctions and applies a transformation based on a strengthened version of the absorption law. Then at line 13, we filter out the nodes which are smaller than some other node, for example if $c \leq b$ then $a \wedge b \wedge c$ becomes $a \wedge c$. This corresponds to function η. Finally, line 16 applies the contradiction law, i.e. if $a \wedge b \wedge c \leq \neg a$ then $a \wedge b \wedge c$ becomes 0. Note again that checking only if either $b \leq \neg a$ or $c \leq \neg a$ holds is not sufficient (see for example the case $a = (\neg b \vee \neg c)$). This corresponds to the β function. The correspondence with the three functions ζ, η and β is not exact; all computations are done in a single traversal over the structure of the formula, rather than in separate passes as the composition $\circ$ of functions in Theorem 2 might suggest.

Importance of Structure Sharing. As detailed in Sect. 6, our implementation finished in a few tenths of a second on circuits containing approximately 10^5 And gates, but whose expanded formula would have size over 10^{2000}, demonstrating the compatibility of the algorithm with structure sharing. For this, we must ensure at every phase and for every intermediate representation, from parsing of the input to exporting the solution, that no duplicate node is ever created. This is achieved, again, using memoization. The complete and testable implementation of both the OL and OCBSL algorithms in Scala is available at https://github. com/epfl-lara/lattices-algorithms.

5   Application to More Expressive Logics

This section outlines how we use OCBSL and OL algorithms in program verification. Boolean Algebra is not only relevant for pure propositional logic; it is also the coreof more complex logics, such as the ones used for verification of software.

Algorithm 4: Computing normal form

```
1  def simplify(τ)                              // Conjunction -> AIGFormula
      // Assume τ is positive
      // (In negative cases, some nodes must be inverted and ≤ reversed.)
2     newChildren ← List()
3     def zeta(child)
4        match child :
5           case PositiveConjunction :
6              newChildren.add(child.Children)
7           case child:NegativeConjunction :
8              gc ← child.children.find(gc ↦ τ≤ gc)
9              if isDefined(gc) then zeta(gc)
10             else newChildren.add(child)

11    for child ← τ.children do
12       zeta(child)

13    children' ← // filter out redundant children smaller than another child
14    if children'.size == 0 then return Literal(True)
15    else if children'.size == 1 then return children'.head
16    else if ∃ c ∈ children'. τ≤ inverse(c) then return Literal(False)
17    else return Conjunction(newChildren)

18
19 def NF_OL(τ)                                  // AIGFormula -> AIGFormula
20    if isDefined(τ.normal) then return τ.normal
21    else
22       τ.normal ← match τ :
23          case Variable(id, True): τ
24          case Variable(id, False): inverse( NF_OL( inverse(τ) ))
25          case Conjunction(children, polarity): simplify( children map NF_OL
                 polarity )
26       return τ.normal
```

Propositional terms appear as subexpressions of the program (as members of the Boolean type), but also in verification conditions corresponding to correctness properties. This section highlights key aspects of such a deployment.

We consider programs containing let bindings, pattern matching, algebraic data types, and theories including numbers and arrays. Let bindings typically arise when a variable is set in a program, but is also introduced in program transformations to prevent exponential increase in the size of program trees. Since OCBSL and OL are compatible with a DAG representation—fulfilling a similar role to let bindings—they can similarly "see through" bindings without breaking them or duplicating subexpressions.

If-then-else and pattern matching conditions can be analyzed and used by the algorithms, possibly leading to dead-branch removal or condition simplification. Extending OCBSL and OL to reason about ADT sorts further increases the simplification potential for pattern matching. For instance, given assumptions ϕ, a scrutinee s and an ADT constructor identifier id of sort S, we are interested in determining whether s is an instance of the constructor id. A trivial case includes checking the form of s. Otherwise, we can run OCBSL or OL to check whether $\phi \implies (s$ is $id)$ holds. If $\phi \implies (s$ is $id)$ fails, we instead test whether $\phi \implies \neg(s$ is $id')$ for all $id' \neq id \in S$. We may also negatively answer to the query if $\phi \implies (s$ is $id')$ for some $id' \neq id \in S$.

The original OCBSL algorithm presented in [20] achieves quasi-linear time complexity by assigning codes to subnodes such that equivalent nodes (by the laws of OCBSL) have the same codes. This is not required for the OL algorithm as it is quadratic anyway, but can still be done to allow common subexpression elimination. This is similar to hash-consing, but more powerful, as it also eliminates expressions which are equivalent with respect to OCBSL or OL.

Of particular relevance is the inclusion of underlying theories such as numbers or arrays. OL has an advantage over OCBSL in terms of extensibility. Namely, OL makes it possible to implement more properties of theories through expansion of its $\leq_{OL}$ relation (Algorithm 3) with inequalities between syntactically distinct *atomic* formulas. For example, if $<_I$ and $\leq_I$ are relations on mathematical integers in the theory of the SMT solver, our implementation deduces that $(x <_I y) \leq_{OL} (x \leq_I y)$ using the rule $z + a <_I 0 \implies z + b \leq_I 0$ when $b \leq_I a + 1$, instantiated with $z = x - y$ and $a = b = 0$. In one of our benchmarks, this simple rule led OL to simplify a verification condition (VC) of the form $\neg(x <_I y \land \phi_1 \land x >_I y \land \phi_2)$ to true, which was of interest because ϕ_1, ϕ_2 were large. This simplification is performed at line 16 of Algorithm 4 with $\tau = x <_I y \land x >_I y \land \phi$, where we have $c = x >_I y$ because $\tau \leq_{OL} (x \leq_I y) \impliedby (x <_I y) \leq_{OL} (x \leq_I y)$. In contrast, OCBSL was not able to do the simplification because it is not able to systematically check for inequalities of subterms. For arrays, our implementation also checks for the property $i \neq j \leq_{OL} a[i := v](j) = a(j)$. Combined with two other rules, related to congruence, OL performs particularly well for array-intensive benchmarks such as `SortedArray`. Note that in OCBSL we may encode a weak form of implication by specifying (giving the same code to) $\phi \land \psi = \phi$ or $\phi \lor \psi = \psi$, but unlike the OL encoding, this does not even allow simplifying formulas such as $\phi \land \tau \land \neg\psi$ without a specific check, which would require quadratic time in general.

Other Extensions. Beyond program verification, we suspect OL or OCBSL based techniques to be extendable in applications such as type checkers, interactive and automated theorem provers using first order, higher order, temporal and modal logics, SMT solvers or lattice problems in abstract interpretation. Unidirectional rules which may be particularly relevant for automated theorem proving include $[f(x) = f(y)] \leq_{OL} [x = y]$, $[\forall x, P(x)] \leq_{OL} P(t)$, and $P \leq_{OL} Q$ when $P \to Q$ is a known theorem. In the context of quantified logics and lambda calculus, both algorithms are compatible with de Bruijn index representation of bound variables. Both algorithms can be used as partial simplification before or while applying more powerful but possibly incomplete heuristic simplification methods, such has the simplification rule $x \land F[x] \rightsquigarrow x \land F[x := 1]$ (which, if viewed as an equality axiom, turns OL into Boolean algebra).

6   Evaluation

Our experimental evaluation comprises three parts. First, we analyze the behavior of the OL and OCBSL algorithms on large random formulas, to understand the feasibility of using them for normalization. Second, we evaluate the algorithms on combinatorial circuits [1]. Third and most importantly, we show their impact through a new simplifier for verification conditions of the Stainless [22] verifier. The goal of the simplifier is to avoid the need to invoke a solver for some of the formulas by reducing them to True, as well as to normalize them before storing them in a persistent cache file. The cache avoids the need to repeatedly prove previously proven verification conditions. By improving normalization, we improve the cache hit rate. We conduct all experiments on a server with 2× Intel®Xeon®CPU E5-2680 v2 at 2.80 GHz, 40 cores including hyperthreading and 64 GB of memory.

6.1   Randomly Generated Propositional Formulas

We first evaluate the two algorithms on randomly generated formulas. We measure the running time and the reduction in formula size. We build the random formulas as follows.

Definition 5. *A random formula is parameterized by a size s and a set of available variables $X = \{x_1, ..., x_n\}$. Given a size s, if $s \leq 1$ then pick uniformly at random a variable from X or its negation and return it. Otherwise, pick t such that $0 < t < s - 1$ and generate two formulas ϕ_1 and ϕ_2 of sizes t and $s - 1 - t$. Return uniformly at random $And(\phi_1, \phi_2)$ or $Or(\phi_1, \phi_2)$.*

Running Time. We show in Fig. 1a the approximate running time of both algorithms for various sizes of formulas. We ran the experiment 21 times for each formula size category and took the median. For comparison with a theoretically linear time process, we also give the running time of the corresponding negation normal form transformation. These implementations do not come with low-level optimizations and are intended for demonstrating usability in practice, and do not serve as a competitive indicator.

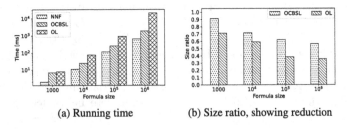

(a) Running time   (b) Size ratio, showing reduction

Fig. 1. (a) Median running time of NNF and the two algorithms (log-log scale). (b) Median size of the normalized formulas relative to the original in NNF. $|X| = 50$ variables.

Size Reduction. For a fairer comparison, we apply a basic simplification (flattening and transformation into negation normal form) to random formulas before computing their size. We compare the number of connectors before and after the simplification for both algorithms. We show the relative improvements of the OL and OCBSL algorithms compared to the original formulas for various sizes of formulas and 50 variables. We have run both algorithms 21 times and report the median results in Figs. 1b.

It is interesting to note that the OL normal form is consistently and significantly smaller than the OCBSL normal form, i.e. the Absorption law actually allows non-trivial reductions in size. This confirms that, in general, there is a trade-off between the two algorithms between speed and simplification strength.

6.2   Computing Normal Forms for Hardware Circuits

Moving towards more realistic formulas, we assess the scalability of OCBSL and OL on the EPFL Combinatorial Benchmark [1] comprising 10 arithmetic circuits designed to challenge optimization tools, with up to 10^8 gates.

Table 2. Results on the EPFL Combinatorial Benchmark. OL times-out for `hyp` after 1h.

	adder	bar	div	hyp	log2	max	mult	sin	sqrt	square
# of gates	50173	72704	10^7	10^8	10^7	10^7	10^7	10^6	10^7	10^7
OCBSL Ratio	1.00	0.703	0.777	0.961	0.700	0.861	0.867	0.652	0.661	0.927
OL Ratio	1.00	0.703	0.777	–	0.697	0.861	0.865	0.647	0.661	0.927
OCBSL Time [s]	0.142	0.182	0.866	2.06	0.564	0.189	0.442	0.255	0.362	0.365
OL Time [s]	0.276	0.338	706	–	339	0.319	73.8	15.7	256	36.0

We run the experiment five times. We report the median running time and the relative size after optimization in Table 2. We observe that the OCBSL algorithm is close to as good as the OL algorithm in all cases, and, moreover, that it is very time-efficient even for problems with hundreds of millions of gates. The OL algorithm sometimes performs slightly better and is pretty much as time-efficient for not too large inputs, but becomes significantly more time-consuming for inputs with more than approximately 10^6 gates. Those results suggest on one hand that OCBSL may be a more suitable reduction technique on some applications with very large formulas, depending on their internal structures. It also suggests that both algorithms work well in practice with Boolean circuits making heavy use of structure sharing. Indeed, the expanded form of, for example, the adder circuit would have about 2^{2000} nodes.

6.3   Caching Verification Conditions in Stainless

We implement the approach described in Sect. 5 by modifying the Stainless verifier [22, 40][1], a publicly available tool for building formally verified Scala programs.

---

[1] https://github.com/epfl-lara/stainless/.

Our implementation adds two new simplifiers to Stainless: OCBSL-backed and OL-backed. They are part of Stainless release v0.9.8[2] and are selectable by the command line options `--simplifier=ocbsl` and `--simplifier=ol` respectively. For the OL simplifier, we have extended the $\leq_{OL}$ relation with 12 simple arithmetic and array rules.

We experimentally compare the two new simplifiers to the existing one (which we denote Old). We use two groups of benchmarks: (1) six Stainless case studies from the Bolts repository[3] that take a significant amount of time to verify, and (2) nine benchmark sets from automated grading of student assignments. Together, this constitutes around 84'000 lines of Scala code, specifications, and auxiliary assertions. We report the following metrics: the size of the VCs after simplification, the number of cache hits, the number of VCs simplified to 1, the wall-clock time and the cumulative solving time. The wall-clock time comprises the full Stainless pipeline, from parsing the program to outputting the result, passing by solver calls and VC simplification.

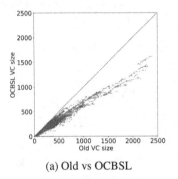 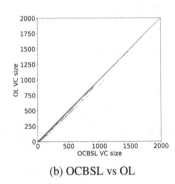

(a) Old vs OCBSL   (b) OCBSL vs OL

Fig. 2. VCs (tree) size scatter plot from all benchmarks for Old, OCBSL and OL.

Evaluation on Bolts Case Studies. We consider the following case studies from the mentioned Bolts repository:

- `LongMap` (9613 VCs, 7091 LOC), a mutable hash map, 64-bit integer keys, open addressing, formalized by Samuel Chassot (EPFL) and proven to behave equivalently to a list of (key, value) pairs.
- A type checker for `System F` [19] (5040 VCs, 2501 LOC) formalized in Stainless by Andrea Gilot and Noé De Santo (EPFL). Among the key properties proven are type judgment uniqueness, preservation and progress.
- `QOI` (4487 VCs, 2812 LOC), an implementation of the Quite OK Image format. Decoding an encoded image is shown to yield the original image [10].
- `RedBlack`, a red-black tree (764 VCs, 796 LOC).
- `SortedArray` (472 VCs, 429 LOC), a mutable array preserving order on insertion. Developed for use in a simplified model of part of a file system [21].

---

[2] https://github.com/epfl-lara/stainless/releases/tag/v0.9.8.
[3] https://github.com/epfl-lara/bolts.

– ConcRope (408 VCs, 621 LOC), a Conc-Tree rope [36], supporting amortized constant time append and prepend operation, based on a Leon formalization [30].

We report the VCs size measurement in Fig. 2, where we aggregate the results from all benchmarks. Figure 2a reveals a couple of VCs with an increased size. Inspection of these VCs shows the reason is due to the new simplifiers always inlining "simple expressions", such as field projection on free variables, instead of having them bound. On average, OCBSL and OL decrease the size of the VCs by 37% compared to Old. OL reduces the size of the VCs slightly compared to OCBSL (Fig. 2b).

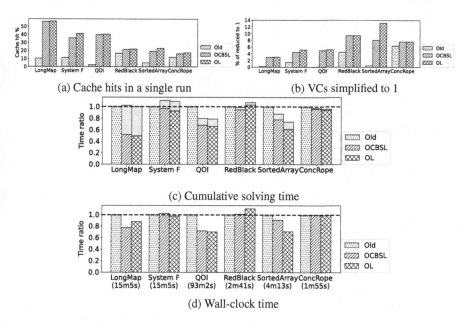

(a) Cache hits in a single run   (b) VCs simplified to 1

(c) Cumulative solving time

(d) Wall-clock time

Fig. 3. Old, OCBSL and OL results for cache hits, VCs reduced to 1, solving and running time. (c), (d) are normalized with respect to Old. In (c), the gray boxes represent the time spared due to extra cache hits and VCs reduced to 1 compared to Old.

In Fig. 3a, we report the cache hit ratio. For the new simplifiers, reducing the formula size has the desired effect of noticeably increasing the hit ratio, especially for 4 out of 6 benchmarks. The additional power of OL helps for System F and SortedArray.

We report in Fig. 3c not only the solving time for the two simplifiers (normalized with respect to Old), but also the solving time saved thanks to additional cache hits and VCs simplified to 1. ConcRope and RedBlack do not benefit from the new simplifiers, while the other benchmarks do in various degrees. For LongMap, adding the two ratios yields a ratio of ≈ 1, implying the reduced solving time is due to extra caching. The solver did not benefit from the new simplifiers for non-cached VCs. The System F benchmark shows a ratio exceeding 1, meaning that OCBSL and OL did not help the solver more than the extra time they took to run. For QOI and SortedArray, the combined ratio is less than 1: the new simplifiers helped the solver for non-cached VCs. OL performs significantly better than OCBSL in the SortedArray benchmark, thanks to the extension of the $\leq_{OL}$ relation with array rules. We note that 25% of QOI VCs have a size of more than 880, against 480 for the second benchmark (SortedArray), and 450 for the third (LongMap).

Turning our attention to Fig. 3d, we note that the time spared to solver calls is essentially compensated for more work on the new simplifiers on three of the benchmarks. Moreover, LongMap, SortedArray and especially QOI have a net benefit over Old.

OCBSL and OL simplifiers show the greatest improvement on large VCs. Note that the outcome of a Stainless run highly depends on user-provided assertions, which were hand-tuned under the Old simplifier. It is thus possible that new simplifiers have a disadvantage because they were not used during the verification process. The additional power provided by the new simplifiers may make writing such intermediate assertions easier and faster, so we expect the full advantage of new simplifiers in newly developed verified software.

Table 3. Results on programming assignments

Benchmark		filter	max	mirror	mem	sigma	nat	uniq	formula	lambda
# Submissions		210	216	96	136	734	381	147	677	782
Cumulative LOC		2367	3452	1165	1987	8347	8950	3648	19226	17958
# VCs		820	844	387	560	1528	2653	1352	9865	5922
Solver Calls	Old	28	81	44	77	75	133	264	1037	1115
	OCBSL	19	**79**	43	75	58	133	**251**	1033	1069
	OL	**18**	**79**	**42**	**74**	**50**	**131**	**251**	**1032**	**1066**
# VCs reduced to 1	Old	211	302	95	151	4	886	381	1322	1320
	OCBSL	211	302	95	151	6	**890**	381	1327	**1322**
	OL	**213**	302	95	151	**794**	**890**	381	**1332**	**1322**
Cache Hits	Old	581	461	248	332	1449	1634	707	7506	3487
	OCBSL	590	463	249	334	1464	1630	720	7505	3531
	OL	589	463	250	335	684	1632	720	7501	3534
VCs (tree) Size	Old	6705	5576	3077	5097	47759	15378	12144	126968	78962
	OCBSL	6479	**5546**	3073	5063	49775	14514	11465	125289	75837
	OL	**6457**	**5546**	**2982**	**5000**	**34173**	14482	**11444**	**125037**	**75307**
Solving Time [s]	Old	2.48	5.61	3.72	5.79	4.17	7.97	14.27	118.61	108.42
	OCBSL	1.91	5.22	3.52	5.75	**3.43**	5.73	14.27	**102.48**	**104.27**
	OL	**1.70**	**4.92**	**3.06**	**5.34**	3.66	**7.03**	**13.57**	134.73	104.60
Total Time [m:s]	Old	**0:27**	**0:36**	**0:16**	**0:21**	**0:59**	14:02	**1:36**	51:01	**115:39**
	OCBSL	0:29	0:38	0:17	0:22	1:04	14:33	1:37	**50:08**	120:48
	OL	0:29	0:38	**0:16**	0:22	1:10	14:43	1:46	58:05	116:09

Evaluation on Programming Assignments. We additionally evaluate our approach on benchmarks consisting of many student solutions for several programming assignments. We consider benchmarks from [32,33], obtained by translation of student solutions in OCaml [38]. In this evaluation, we only prove termination of all student solutions, which is one of the bottlenecks when proving correctness of students solutions. We annotated all benchmarks with explicit decreasing measures. Stainless generates verification conditions that require the measure to decrease in recursive calls. Caching is particularly desirable in this scenario, with many programs and a high degree of similarity. Table 3 shows our evaluation results, comparing the two new simplifiers (OCBSL and OL) to the old one.

First, we note that moving from Old to OCBSL to OL reduces the number of calls to the solver. Furthermore, many new VCs are proven valid by normalization alone (reduced to 1). The largest benefit of OL is in the `sigma` benchmark, where the subsumption of linear arithmetic literals in the simplifier substantially increases the number of formulas proven by normalization: from 6 (0.4%) in OCBSL to 794 (52%) for OL.

The new simplifiers improve the number of cache hits, even if not as much as for the Bolts case studies. The smaller reduction is because there is a high degree of similarity across the submissions, so the Old simplifier already achieves a large percentage of cache hits. Note also that a smaller number of cache hits in the `sigma` benchmark is because many of the VCs are proven valid by the simplifier, avoiding the need to consult the cache or the solver in first place.

Second, we notice a slight reduction in the overall VC size, with a couple of exceptions where OCBSL resulted in a size increase due to inlining. Thanks to formulas proven by normalization and improved cache hits, the overall solving time decreases in several benchmarks. The wall clock running time is approximately unchanged, but we expect such benefits in the future.

7   Conclusion

We proposed a new approach to simplify and reason about formulas, based on algorithms which are sound and complete for the normal form problem (and the word problem) of two subtheories of Boolean algebra. These algorithms are sound but incomplete for Boolean algebras (and thus for the two-element boolean algebra of propositional logic). We introduced and proved the correctness of a new algorithm to compute normal forms in a theory of *ortholattices*, which do not enforce the distributivity law but only its weaker variation, absorption. Our algorithm runs in time $\mathcal{O}(n^2)$. A weaker subtheory, OCBSL, gives up the absorption law. The disadvantage of OCBSL is a weaker normal form, whereas the advantage is that we know of an algorithm running in subquadratic time, $\mathcal{O}(n \log(n)^2)$. We evaluated both algorithms, using them to reduce the size of large random formulas and combinatorial circuits, showing that they work well with structure sharing. We also implemented the algorithms in the Stainless verifier, where computing normal forms reduced the size of formulas given to the solver and improved the cache hit ratio. Our experimental evaluation confirmed that the tradeoff between normal form strength and the asymptotic complexity remains visible in practice. We found both algorithms useful in practice. OCBSL normalization has excellent running time even for very large circuits, so we believe it can replace the simpler negation normal form and syntactic equality checking at low cost in essentially all applications. The quadratic cost of the OL algorithm is too prohibitive on circuits over 10^7 gates. However, this was not a problem for its application to verification conditions in Stainless, where its added precision and the ability to compare atomic formulas made it more effective in normalizing certain formulas to True and increasing cache hits. In some of the most difficult case studies, such as Quite OK Image Format [10], these improvements translated into substantial reduction of the wall clock time. Such measurable improvements, combined with theoretical guarantees, make the OL and OCBSL algorithms an appealing building block for verification systems.

References

1. Amarù, L., Gaillardon, P.E., De Micheli, G.: The EPFL combinational benchmark suite. In: Proceedings of the 24th International Workshop on Logic & Synthesis (IWLS) (2015). https://github.com/lsils/benchmarks
2. Barbosa, H., et al.: cvc5: a versatile and industrial-strength SMT solver. In: Fisman, D., Rosu, G. (eds.) TACAS 2022. LNCS, vol. 13243, pp. 415–442. Springer, Cham (2022). https://doi.org/10.1007/978-3-030-99524-9_24
3. Beran, L.: Orthomodular Lattices (An Algebraic Approach). Springer, Dordrecht (1985). https://doi.org/10.1007/978-94-009-5215-7
4. Birkhoff, G.: Lattice Theory, AMS Colloquium Publications, 3rd edn., vol. 25. AMS (1973)
5. Bonzio, S., Chajda, I.: A note on orthomodular lattices. Int. J. Theor. Phys. **56**, 3740–3743 (2017). https://doi.org/10.1007/s10773-016-3258-6
6. Brayton, R., Mishchenko, A.: ABC: an academic industrial-strength verification tool. In: Touili, T., Cook, B., Jackson, P. (eds.) CAV 2010. LNCS, vol. 6174, pp. 24–40. Springer, Heidelberg (2010). https://doi.org/10.1007/978-3-642-14295-6_5
7. Bruns, G.: Free ortholattices. Can. J. Math. **28**(5), 977–985 (1976). https://doi.org/10.4153/CJM-1976-095-6
8. Bruttomesso, R., Pek, E., Sharygina, N., Tsitovich, A.: The OpenSMT solver. In: Esparza, J., Majumdar, R. (eds.) TACAS 2010. LNCS, vol. 6015, pp. 150–153. Springer, Heidelberg (2010). https://doi.org/10.1007/978-3-642-12002-2_12
9. Bryant, R.E.: Binary decision diagrams. In: Clarke, E., Henzinger, T., Veith, H., Bloem, R. (eds.) Handbook of Model Checking, pp. 191–217. Springer, Cham (2018). https://doi.org/10.1007/978-3-319-10575-8_7
10. Bucev, M., Kunčak, V.: Formally verified quite OK image format. In: Formal Methods in Computer-Aided Design (FMCAD) (2022)
11. Cousot, P., Cousot, R.: Systematic design of program analysis frameworks. In: Aho, A.V., Zilles, S.N., Rosen, B.K. (eds.) Conference Record of the Sixth Annual ACM Symposium on Principles of Programming Languages, San Antonio, Texas, USA, January 1979, pp. 269–282. ACM Press (1979). https://doi.org/10.1145/567752.567778

12. Dershowitz, N., Hsiang, J., Huang, G.-S., Kaiss, D.: Boolean rings for intersection-based satisfiability. In: Hermann, M., Voronkov, A. (eds.) LPAR 2006. LNCS (LNAI), vol. 4246, pp. 482–496. Springer, Heidelberg (2006). https://doi.org/10.1007/11916277_33

13. Duarte, A., Korovin, K.: Implementing superposition in iProver (system description). In: Peltier, N., Sofronie-Stokkermans, V. (eds.) IJCAR 2020. LNCS (LNAI), vol. 12167, pp. 388–397. Springer, Cham (2020). https://doi.org/10.1007/978-3-030-51054-1_24

14. Even-Mendoza, K., Asadi, S., Hyvärinen, A.E.J., Chockler, H., Sharygina, N.: Lattice-based refinement in bounded model checking. In: Piskac, R., Rümmer, P. (eds.) VSTTE 2018. LNCS, vol. 11294, pp. 50–68. Springer, Cham (2018). https://doi.org/10.1007/978-3-030-03592-1_4

15. Freese, R., Jezek, J., Nation, J.: Free Lattices, Mathematical Surveys and Monographs, vol. 42. American Mathematical Society, Providence (1995). https://doi.org/10.1090/surv/042

16. Freese, R., Jezek, J., Nation, J.B.: Term rewrite systems for lattice theory. J. Symb. Comput. **16**(3), 279–288 (1993). https://doi.org/10.1006/jsco.1993.1046

17. Freese, R., Nation, J.B.: Finitely presented lattices. Proc. Am. Math. Soc. **77**(2), 174–178 (1979). https://doi.org/10.2307/2042634

18. Genet, T., Le Gall, T., Legay, A., Murat, V.: A completion algorithm for lattice tree automata. In: Konstantinidis, S. (ed.) CIAA 2013. LNCS, vol. 7982, pp. 134–145. Springer, Heidelberg (2013). https://doi.org/10.1007/978-3-642-39274-0_13

19. Girard, J.Y.: Une extension de L'interpretation de Gödel a L'analyse, et son application a L'elimination des coupures dans L'analyse et la theorie des types. In: Fenstad, J. (ed.) Proceedings of the Second Scandinavian Logic Symposium, Studies in Logic and the Foundations of Mathematics, vol. 63, pp. 63–92. Elsevier (1971). https://doi.org/10.1016/S0049-237X(08)70843-7

20. Guilloud, S., Kunčak, V.: Equivalence checking for orthocomplemented bisemilattices in log-linear time. In: TACAS 2022. LNCS, vol. 13244, pp. 196–214. Springer, Cham (2022). https://doi.org/10.1007/978-3-030-99527-0_11

21. Hamza, J., Felix, S., Kunčak, V., Nussbaumer, I., Schramka, F.: From verified Scala to STIX file system embedded code using Stainless. In: Deshmukh, J.V., Havelund, K., Perez, I. (eds.) NFM 2022. LNCS, vol. 13260, pp. 393–410. Springer, Cham (2022). https://doi.org/10.1007/978-3-031-06773-0_21. http://infoscience.epfl.ch/record/292424

22. Hamza, J., Voirol, N., Kunčak, V.: System FR: formalized foundations for the Stainless verifier. Proc. ACM Program. Lang. **3**, 1–30 (2019). https://doi.org/10.1145/3360592

23. Harrison, J.: HOL light: an overview. In: Berghofer, S., Nipkow, T., Urban, C., Wenzel, M. (eds.) TPHOLs 2009. LNCS, vol. 5674, pp. 60–66. Springer, Heidelberg (2009). https://doi.org/10.1007/978-3-642-03359-9_4

24. Jain, H., Bartzis, C., Clarke, E.: Satisfiability checking of non-clausal formulas using general matings. In: Biere, A., Gomes, C.P. (eds.) SAT 2006. LNCS, vol. 4121, pp. 75–89. Springer, Heidelberg (2006). https://doi.org/10.1007/11814948_10

25. Kojevnikov, A., Kulikov, A.S., Yaroslavtsev, G.: Finding efficient circuits using SAT-solvers. In: Kullmann, O. (ed.) SAT 2009. LNCS, vol. 5584, pp. 32–44. Springer, Heidelberg (2009). https://doi.org/10.1007/978-3-642-02777-2_5

26. Kovács, L., Voronkov, A.: First-order theorem proving and VAMPIRE. In: Sharygina, N., Veith, H. (eds.) CAV 2013. LNCS, vol. 8044, pp. 1–35. Springer, Heidelberg (2013). https://doi.org/10.1007/978-3-642-39799-8_1

27. Kroening, D., Strichman, O.: Decision Procedures - An Algorithmic Point of View. Springer, Heidelberg (2016). https://doi.org/10.1007/978-3-540-74105-3

28. Leino, K.R.M., Wüstholz, V.: The Dafny integrated development environment. In: Dubois, C., Giannakopoulou, D., Méry, D. (eds.) Proceedings 1st Workshop on Formal Integrated Development Environment, F-IDE 2014. EPTCS, Grenoble, France, 6 April 2014, vol. 149, pp. 3–15 (2014). https://doi.org/10.4204/EPTCS. 149.2

29. Leino, K.R.M., Wüstholz, V.: Fine-grained caching of verification results. In: Kroening, D., Păsăreanu, C.S. (eds.) CAV 2015. LNCS, vol. 9206, pp. 380–397. Springer, Cham (2015). https://doi.org/10.1007/978-3-319-21690-4_22

30. Madhavan, R., Kulal, S., Kuncak, V.: Contract-based resource verification for higher-order functions with memoization. In: ACM SIGACT-SIGPLAN Symposium on Principles of Programming Languages (POPL) (2017). https://doi.org/10.1145/3009837.3009874

31. Merz, S., Vanzetto, H.: Automatic verification of TLA$^+$ proof obligations with SMT solvers. In: Bjørner, N., Voronkov, A. (eds.) LPAR 2012. LNCS, vol. 7180, pp. 289–303. Springer, Heidelberg (2012). https://doi.org/10.1007/978-3-642-28717-6_23

32. Milovancevic, D., Kuncak, V.: Proving and disproving equivalence of functional programming assignments (artifact) (2023). https://doi.org/10.5281/zenodo.7810840

33. Milovancevic, D., Kunčak, V.: Proving and disproving equivalence of functional programming assignments. In: ACM SIGPLAN Conference Programming Language Design and Implementation (PLDI) (2023). https://doi.org/10.1145/3591258

34. de Moura, L., Bjørner, N.: Z3: an efficient SMT solver. In: Ramakrishnan, C.R., Rehof, J. (eds.) TACAS 2008. LNCS, vol. 4963, pp. 337–340. Springer, Heidelberg (2008). https://doi.org/10.1007/978-3-540-78800-3_24

35. Naumowicz, A., Korniłowicz, A.: A brief overview of MIZAR. In: Berghofer, S., Nipkow, T., Urban, C., Wenzel, M. (eds.) TPHOLs 2009. LNCS, vol. 5674, pp. 67–72. Springer, Heidelberg (2009). https://doi.org/10.1007/978-3-642-03359-9_5

36. Prokopec, A., Odersky, M.: Conc-trees for functional and parallel programming. In: Shen, X., Mueller, F., Tuck, J. (eds.) LCPC 2015. LNCS, vol. 9519, pp. 254–268. Springer, Cham (2016). https://doi.org/10.1007/978-3-319-29778-1_16

37. Schulz, S.: System description: E 1.8. In: McMillan, K., Middeldorp, A., Voronkov, A. (eds.) LPAR 2013. LNCS, vol. 8312, pp. 735–743. Springer, Heidelberg (2013). https://doi.org/10.1007/978-3-642-45221-5_49

38. Song, D., Lee, W., Oh, H.: Context-aware and data-driven feedback generation for programming assignments. In: Proceedings of the 29th ACM Joint Meeting on European Software Engineering Conference and Symposium on the Foundations of Software Engineering, ESEC/FSE 2021, pp. 328–340. Association for Computing Machinery, New York (2021). https://doi.org/10.1145/3468264.3468598

39. Suter, P.: Non-clausal satisfiability modulo theories. Technical report, M.Sc. thesis, EPFL (2008). http://infoscience.epfl.ch/record/126445

40. Voirol, N., Kneuss, E., Kuncak, V.: Counter-example complete verification for higher-order functions. In: Scala Symposium (2015). https://doi.org/10.1145/2774975.2774978

41. Vukmirović, P., Bentkamp, A., Blanchette, J., Cruanes, S., Nummelin, V., Tourret, S.: Making higher-order superposition work. In: Platzer, A., Sutcliffe, G. (eds.) CADE 2021. LNCS (LNAI), vol. 12699, pp. 415–432. Springer, Cham (2021). https://doi.org/10.1007/978-3-030-79876-5_24

42. Weidenbach, C., Dimova, D., Fietzke, A., Kumar, R., Suda, M., Wischnewski, P.: SPASS version 3.5. In: Schmidt, R.A. (ed.) CADE 2009. LNCS (LNAI), vol. 5663, pp. 140–145. Springer, Heidelberg (2009). https://doi.org/10.1007/978-3-642-02959-2_10

43. Wenzel, M., Paulson, L.C., Nipkow, T.: The isabelle framework. In: Mohamed, O.A., Muñoz, C., Tahar, S. (eds.) TPHOLs 2008. LNCS, vol. 5170, pp. 33–38. Springer, Heidelberg (2008). https://doi.org/10.1007/978-3-540-71067-7_7

44. Whitman, P.M.: Free lattices. Ann. Math. **42**(1), 325–330 (1941). https://doi.org/10.2307/1969001

45. Zhang, H.T., Jiang, J.H.R., Mishchenko, A.: A circuit-based SAT solver for logic synthesis. In: 2021 IEEE/ACM International Conference on Computer Aided Design (ICCAD), pp. 1–6 (2021). https://doi.org/10.1109/ICCAD51958.2021.9643505

Kratos2: An SMT-Based Model Checker for Imperative Programs

Alberto Griggio[1]([⊠]) and Martin Jonáš[1,2]

[1] Fondazione Bruno Kessler, Trento, Italy
griggio@fbk.eu
[2] Masaryk University, Brno, Czechia
martin.jonas@mail.muni.cz

Abstract. This paper describes Kratos2, a tool for the verification of imperative programs. Kratos2 operates on an intermediate verification language called K2, with a formally-specified semantics based on SMT, allowing the specification of both reachability and liveness properties. It integrates several state-of-the-art verification engines based on SAT and SMT. Moreover, it provides additional functionalities such as a flexible Python API, a customizable C front-end, generation of counterexamples, support for simulation and symbolic execution, and translation into multiple low-level verification formalisms. Our experimental analysis shows that Kratos2 is competitive with state-of-the-art software verifiers on a large range of programs. Thanks to its flexibility, Kratos2 has already been used in various industrial projects and academic publications, both as a verification back-end and as a benchmark generator.

1 Introduction

We present Kratos2, a tool for the verification of real-world imperative programs. Kratos2 is a complete rewrite and redesign of Kratos [17], improving and extending it in multiple directions. First, Kratos2 introduces a simple yet expressive intermediate language called K2, with a formally-specified semantics based on Satisfiability Modulo Theories (SMT), which is parametric on the underlying SMT theory. K2 is expressive enough to capture most of the features of real-world C programs, such as pointers, dynamic memory allocation, floating-point data types, and bit-precise semantics of bounded integers, which the old version of the tool could not handle (being limited to C programs without pointers and recursion, and in which C integers were interpreted as mathematical integers). Kratos2 comes with a separate C front-end c2Kratos that can translate C programs to K2. Second, Kratos2 includes a variety of state-of-the-art verification back-ends based on either symbolic model checking or symbolic execution with SAT and SMT solvers. Besides reachability properties, Kratos2 also supports various forms of

A. Griggio has been partly supported by the project "AI@TN" funded by the Autonomous Province of Trento and by the PNRR project FAIR - Future AI Research (PE00000013), under the NRRP MUR program funded by the NextGenerationEU. M. Jonáš has been partly supported by the Czech Science Foundation grant GA23-06506S.

C. Enea and A. Lal (Eds.): CAV 2023, LNCS 13966, pp. 423–436, 2023.
https://doi.org/10.1007/978-3-031-37709-9_20

liveness properties, which can be used to encode termination and more complex linear-time temporal properties. Third, Kratos2 implements an interactive interpreter, which can simulate K2 programs using non-deterministic inputs provided either by the user or by external oracles. Kratos2 also supports counterexample reconstruction, another feature not available in the original Kratos.

The new intermediate language K2 enables modular translation of C programs into various verification languages. Namely, Kratos2 can be used for translating C programs into nuXmv [14], VMT [20], AIGER [9], BTOR2 [31], Constrained Horn Clauses (CHCs) [11], or Boogie [29] formats. Additionally, Kratos2 comes with a Python API for construction and manipulation of K2 programs, which the users can leverage to implement custom front-ends and generators of K2 programs and also additional translators from K2 to other formalisms.

Although Kratos2 has not been described in a publication until now, it has already been successfully used in several research and industrial projects. In particular, Kratos2 has been used as a back-end for the verification of automotive software in the context of the AUTOSAR platform [15,16]; of C code automatically generated from AADL specifications by the TASTE development environment [12]; and for verification of C code for railway interlocking systems automatically generated from the specifications in a controlled natural language [1]. Kratos2 has also been used as a benchmark generator to produce symbolic transition systems from C programs [30].

The rest of the paper is structured as follows. The functionalities offered by Kratos2 from the user perspective are described in Sect. 2; Sect. 3 introduces K2, describing its syntax and formal semantics. The internal architecture of Kratos2, with details about its main components, is presented in Sect. 4; implementation notes and experimental evaluation on C programs from the annual software verification competition SV-COMP are provided in Sect. 5. Finally, Sect. 6 concludes the paper and presents directions for future developments.

2   Functional View

In this section we provide a high-level overview of the functionalities available in Kratos2. More details will then be provided in the following sections.

An Intermediate Language for Imperative Programs. The core of Kratos2 is built around an idealized language for imperative programs called K2. Unlike common high-level real-world programming languages, K2 has a simple and clean semantics based on first-order logic modulo theories that is fully formally specified. The K2 language, similar in spirit to other intermediate verification languages proposed in the literature such as Boogie [29] or Why3 [26] (although less feature rich than the two), is at the same time simple enough to be easily manipulated and translated into formalisms used by SAT-based and SMT-based verification back-ends on one hand, and expressive enough to efficiently capture a significant subset of C on the other, as demonstrated also by our experimental results on standard SV-COMP benchmarks (see Sect. 5).

Verification of Safety and Liveness with Multiple Back-Ends. Kratos2 implements multiple state-of-the-art verification algorithms based on SAT and SMT, supporting both bit-precise reasoning over machine integers and floating-point numbers as well as higher-level reasoning based on, e.g., mathematical integers, real numbers, and uninterpreted functions, depending on the combinations of theories used in the input K2 program under analysis. Moreover, Kratos2 supports not only the verification of safety properties (via a reduction to reachability of designated "error" program locations), but it also supports liveness properties such as proving that a specific program location is reached a finite number of times in all executions, or that it is always visited infinitely often in all infinite executions.

A Python API for Program Manipulations. Kratos2 provides a rich and flexible Python API for parsing, printing, and manipulating K2 programs and expressions, which can be used to implement converters from high-level languages to K2 or to directly generate K2 programs from user-specific applications.

A Customizable C Front-End. Kratos2 comes with a front-end for C programs which supports a wide range of customization options for controlling the translation from C to K2. These range from the choice of theories to use to encode C data types (e.g., bit-vectors or unbounded integers), to the use of customized program transformations or the injection of new built-in functions with special meaning (such as special `assume`, `malloc`, or `memset` built-ins). Thanks to its plug-in architecture, the front-end can be easily customized for domain-specific subsets of C, for example to implement special optimization passes that are safe only in the given context, or to automatically inject properties to the code based on specification files (as is, e.g., the case in SV-COMP [3]).

Encoding into Multiple Formalisms. Kratos2 can be used as an encoder or benchmark generator because it can translate imperative programs written in C or in K2 into other formalisms, including symbolic transition systems in nuXmv [14], VMT [20], AIGER [9] or BTOR2 [31] formats, Constrained Horn Clauses (CHCs) [11], or other intermediate verification languages like Boogie [29].

Simulation and Symbolic Execution. Finally, Kratos2 can be used as an interpreter, allowing an (interactive) simulation of K2 programs and their symbolic execution, as an alternative to the verification back-ends based on model checking.

3   The K2 Language

In this section we introduce K2, the intermediate verification language used by Kratos2. We present its abstract syntax, formally define its semantics, and discuss its support for safety and liveness properties.

$$\begin{aligned}
\langle\text{stmt}\rangle ::= &\ \langle\text{assign-stmt}\rangle \mid \\
&\ \langle\text{assume-stmt}\rangle \mid \\
&\ \langle\text{call-stmt}\rangle \mid \\
&\ \langle\text{havoc-stmt}\rangle \mid \\
&\ \langle\text{jump-stmt}\rangle \mid \\
&\ \langle\text{label-stmt}\rangle \\
\langle\text{assign-stmt}\rangle ::= &\ \textbf{assign}\ \langle\text{symbol}\rangle\ \langle\text{expr}\rangle \\
\langle\text{assume-stmt}\rangle ::= &\ \textbf{assume}\ \langle\text{expr}\rangle \\
\langle\text{call-stmt}\rangle ::= &\ \textbf{call}\ \langle\text{symbol}\rangle \\
&\ \langle\text{expr-list}\rangle \\
&\ \langle\text{symbol-list}\rangle
\end{aligned}$$

$$\begin{aligned}
\langle\text{havoc-stmt}\rangle ::= &\ \textbf{havoc}\ \langle\text{symbol}\rangle \\
\langle\text{jump-stmt}\rangle ::= &\ \textbf{jump}\ \langle\text{symbol}\rangle\ \langle\text{symbol-list}\rangle \\
\langle\text{label-stmt}\rangle ::= &\ \textbf{label}\ \langle\text{symbol}\rangle \\
\langle\text{symbol-list}\rangle ::= &\ \langle\text{symbol}\rangle^* \\
\langle\text{expr}\rangle ::= &\ \langle\text{var-expr}\rangle \mid \langle\text{op-expr}\rangle \\
\langle\text{var-expr}\rangle ::= &\ \textbf{var}\ \langle\text{symbol}\rangle \\
\langle\text{op-expr}\rangle ::= &\ \textbf{op}\ \langle\text{symbol}\rangle\ \langle\text{expr-list}\rangle \\
\langle\text{expr-list}\rangle ::= &\ \langle\text{expr}\rangle^*
\end{aligned}$$

Fig. 1. Abstract syntax of K2 statements and expressions.

$$\begin{aligned}
\langle\text{program}\rangle ::= &\ \langle\text{globals}\rangle\ \langle\text{init}\rangle\ \langle\text{functions-list}\rangle\ \langle\text{entrypoint}\rangle \\
\langle\text{globals}\rangle ::= &\ \textbf{globals}\ \langle\text{var-decl-list}\rangle \\
\langle\text{init}\rangle ::= &\ \textbf{init}\ \langle\text{expr}\rangle \\
\langle\text{functions-list}\rangle ::= &\ \langle\text{function}\rangle^+ \\
\langle\text{function}\rangle ::= &\ \textbf{function}\ \langle\text{symbol}\rangle\ \langle\text{var-decl-list}\rangle\ \langle\text{var-decl-list}\rangle\ \langle\text{var-decl-list}\rangle\ \langle\text{stmt-list}\rangle \\
\langle\text{entrypoint}\rangle ::= &\ \textbf{entry}\ \langle\text{symbol}\rangle \\
\langle\text{stmt-list}\rangle ::= &\ \langle\text{stmt}\rangle^+ \\
\langle\text{var-decl-list}\rangle ::= &\ \langle\text{var-decl}\rangle^* \\
\langle\text{var-decl}\rangle ::= &\ \textbf{var}\ \langle\text{symbol}\rangle\ \langle\text{sort}\rangle
\end{aligned}$$

Fig. 2. Abstract syntax of K2 programs.

Abstract Syntax. We denote lists of elements with an overbar, i.e., $\bar{\cdot}$. If $\bar{a}$ is a list, $|\bar{a}|$ is its length, and if i is a natural number, $\bar{a}_i$ is the i-th element of $\bar{a}$. If e is an element, $\bar{a} \cdot e$ is the list obtained by appending e at the end of $\bar{a}$.

Definition 1 (Variables and Functions). *A* variable *is a symbol with an associated sort, as in the multi-sorted first-order logic. A* function *is a tuple* $\langle f, \bar{a}, \bar{r}, \bar{l}, \bar{\sigma}\rangle$, *where:*

- f, *a symbol, is the name of the function;*
- $\bar{a}$, *a list of variables, are the formal parameters;*
- $\bar{r}$, *a list of variables, are the return variables;*
- $\bar{l}$, *a list of variables, are the local variables;*
- $\bar{\sigma}$, *a list of statements generated by the grammar of Fig. 1, are the body.*

Given a list of variables $\bar{v}$, we define $\mathsf{syms}(\bar{v})$ as the corresponding set of symbols. Given a function $\langle f, \bar{a}, \bar{r}, \bar{l}, \bar{\sigma}\rangle$, we denote with $\mathsf{syms}(f)$ the set $\mathsf{syms}(\bar{a}) \cup \mathsf{syms}(\bar{r}) \cup \mathsf{syms}(\bar{l})$. We extend the definition to lists of statements $\bar{\sigma}$ in the natural way. We now describe K2 programs, whose abstract syntax is shown in Fig. 2.

Definition 2 (Programs). *A program P is a tuple $\langle \overline{g}, F, \iota, e \rangle$, where:*

- *$\overline{g}$, a list of variables, are the global variables;*
- *F is a partial mapping from symbols to functions;*
- *ι, a formula, is the constraint on initial states;*
- *e, a symbol in $\mathrm{dom}(F)$, is the entry point.*

Semantics. We use the standard notions of theory, interpretation, model, and satisfaction from many-sorted first-order logic and SMT [2]. In the following, we assume that we have fixed a theory T with equality that contains at least the sort Bool. Given an interpretation μ that is a model for T, we define the *evaluation* of an expression e (generated by the grammar of Fig. 1) under μ, denoted $\mu[e]$, as $\mu[e] = \mu(v)$ for $e = \mathbf{var}\ v$ and $\mu[e] = \mu(o)(\mu[\overline{p}_1], \ldots, \mu[\overline{p}_n])$ for $e = \mathbf{op}\ o\ \overline{p}$ and $n = |\overline{p}|$. We denote with $\mu[v \mapsto e]$ the interpretation that maps v to e, and that agrees with μ everywhere else, and with $\mu[\backslash v]$ *any* interpretation that agrees with μ on all the symbols *except* v. Finally, if e is of sort Bool, we write $\mu \models e$ to denote that e evaluates to true under μ.

Definition 3 (Program states). *Pairs $\langle f, i \rangle$ where f is a function name and i is a natural number are called* program locations. *A state of a program P is a pair $s = \langle G, \overline{C} \rangle$ where:*

- *G is an interpretation for the global variables of P;*
- *$\overline{C}$ is the current call stack, a list of triples $\langle f, i, L \rangle$, where $\langle f, i \rangle$ is a program location and L is an interpretation of $\mathrm{syms}(f)$, i.e., of parameters, return variables, and local variables of $F(f)$.*

A state s is initial *if and only if $G \models \iota$, $|\overline{C}| = 1$ and $\overline{C}_1 = \langle e, 1, L \rangle$ for some L. Given a state s with $\overline{C}_{|\overline{C}|} = \langle f, i, L \rangle$, we define the* current interpretation μ *for s as $\mu(v) = G(v)$ for $v \in \mathrm{syms}(\overline{g})$ and as $\mu(v) = L(v)$ otherwise.*

We define the semantics for programs as a set of transition rules of the form $s \xrightarrow{\sigma} s'$, where s, s' are states and σ is a statement. We then call a *path* of a program P any sequence of transitions (possibly infinite) $s_0 \xrightarrow{\sigma_0} \ldots \xrightarrow{\sigma_i} s_{i+1} \ldots$ that complies with the transition rules and where s_0 is an initial state.

The rules are shown in Fig. 3. In the definitions, we fix a program $P = \langle \overline{g}, F, \iota, e \rangle$ and use the following convenience functions, where f is a function name and i a natural number: $\mathrm{arg}(f, i)$ returns the variable $\overline{a}_i$ of the function $F(f)$; $\mathrm{ret}(f, i)$ returns the variable $\overline{r}_i$ of the function $F(f)$; $\mathrm{stmt}(f, i)$ returns the statement $\overline{\sigma}_i$ of $F(f)$; $\mathrm{stmts}(f)$ returns the list of statements $\overline{\sigma}$ of $F(f)$.

Reachability and Liveness. We then say that a state s is *reachable* in P iff there exists a finite path $s_0 \xrightarrow{\sigma_0} \ldots \xrightarrow{\sigma_n} s$ that ends in s. Similarly, a *program location* $\langle f, i \rangle$ is reachable iff there exists a path as above in which $\sigma_n = \mathrm{stmt}(f, i)$[1].

---

[1] Note that here we assume w.l.o.g. that all statements in a program are different, even when they are structurally equal, so the above definition is unambiguous.

assign-global: $\langle G, \overline{C} \cdot \langle f, i, L \rangle \rangle \xrightarrow{\text{stmt}(f,i)} \langle G[v \mapsto \mu[e]], \overline{C} \cdot \langle f, i+1, L \rangle \rangle$ if $\text{stmt}(f, i) = $
assign v e and $v \in \text{syms}(\overline{g})$;

assign-local: $\langle G, \overline{C} \cdot \langle f, i, L \rangle \rangle \xrightarrow{\text{stmt}(f,i)} \langle G, \overline{C} \cdot \langle f, i+1, L[v \mapsto \mu[e]] \rangle \rangle$ if $\text{stmt}(f, i) = $
assign v e and $v \in \text{syms}(f)$;

assume: $\langle G, \overline{C} \cdot \langle f, i, L \rangle \rangle \xrightarrow{\text{stmt}(f,i)} \langle G, \overline{C} \cdot \langle f, i+1, L \rangle \rangle$ if $\text{stmt}(f, i) = $ **assume** e and
$\mu \models e$;

havoc-global: $\langle G, \overline{C} \cdot \langle f, i, L \rangle \rangle \xrightarrow{\text{stmt}(f,i)} \langle G[\backslash v], \overline{C} \cdot \langle f, i+1, L \rangle \rangle$ if $\text{stmt}(f, i) = $ **havoc** v
and $v \in \text{syms}(\overline{g})$;

havoc-local: $\langle G, \overline{C} \cdot \langle f, i, L \rangle \rangle \xrightarrow{\text{stmt}(f,i)} \langle G, \overline{C} \cdot \langle f, i+1, L[\backslash v] \rangle \rangle$ if $\text{stmt}(f, i) = $ **havoc** v
and $v \in \text{syms}(f)$;

call: $\langle G, \overline{C} \cdot \langle f, i, L \rangle \rangle \xrightarrow{\text{stmt}(f,i)} \langle G, \overline{C} \cdot \langle f, i, L \rangle \cdot \langle g, 1, L' \rangle \rangle$ if $\text{stmt}(f, i) = $ **call** g $\overline{e}$ $\overline{r}$, where
$L'(v) = \mu[\overline{e}_j]$ if $v = \text{arg}(g, j)$;

return: $\langle G, \overline{C} \cdot \langle f, i, L \rangle \cdot \langle g, k, L'' \rangle \rangle \xrightarrow{\text{stmt}(f,i)} \langle G', \overline{C} \cdot \langle f, i+1, L' \rangle \rangle$ if $\text{stmt}(f, i) = $ **call** g $\overline{e}$ $\overline{r}$
and $k > |\text{stmts}(g)|$, where:

$$G'(v) = \begin{cases} \mu[\text{ret}(g, j)] & \text{if } v = \overline{r}_j \\ G(v) & \text{otherwise} \end{cases} \quad \text{and} \quad L'(v) = \begin{cases} \mu[\text{ret}(g, j)] & \text{if } v = \overline{r}_j \\ L(v) & \text{otherwise} \end{cases}$$

jump: $\langle G, \overline{C} \cdot \langle f, i, L \rangle \rangle \xrightarrow{\text{stmt}(f,i)} \langle G, \overline{C} \cdot \langle f, k, L \rangle \rangle$ if $\text{stmt}(f, i) = $ **jump** $\overline{t}$ and $\text{stmt}(f, k) = $
label l with $l \in \overline{t}$;

label: $\langle G, \overline{C} \cdot \langle f, i, L \rangle \rangle \xrightarrow{\text{stmt}(f,i)} \langle G, \overline{C} \cdot \langle f, i+1, L \rangle \rangle$ if $\text{stmt}(f, i) = $ **label** l.

Fig. 3. Transition rules. In all the rules, μ denotes the current interpretation for the left-hand state of the rule.

Conversely, if no such path exists, then $\langle f, i \rangle$ is *unreachable*. The location $\langle f, i \rangle$ is *infinitely-often reachable* iff there exists an infinite path $s_0 \xrightarrow{\sigma_0} \ldots \xrightarrow{\sigma_i} s_{i+1} \ldots$ in which for all indices j there exists an index $k > j$ such that $\sigma_k = \text{stmt}(f, i)$. If no such path exists, then $\langle f, i \rangle$ is *eventually unreachable*. Finally, we say that $\langle f, i \rangle$ is *live* iff it is infinitely-often reachable *in all infinite paths of* P.

In K2, queries about reachability or liveness of program locations are expressed via *annotations* of **label** statements. Annotations are metadata that are attached to statements, in the form of key-value pairs, which do not affect the semantics of the program, but are meant to provide additional information that can be used by tools that manipulate the K2 program. Specifically, Kratos2 uses the following annotations to define properties:

error <id>: holds iff all labels annotated with the same <id> are unreachable;
notlive <id>: holds iff all labels annotated with the same <id> are eventually
    unreachable;
live <id>: holds iff all labels annotated with the same <id> are live.

These basic properties can be easily used to represent more common higher-level properties of programs, such as assertions and termination. For example, assertions can be reduced to reachability with a combination of **assume** and **jump** statements, whereas termination can be checked by adding a final self loop over a label with an attached `live` annotation. Finally, eventual unreachability can be used to encode arbitrary LTL properties using the standard automata-theoretic approach combined with a symbolic encoding of the accepting automaton such as [22].[2]

3.1   Example

We conclude this section with a simple example of a C program and its equivalent formulation in K2. Both versions are shown in Fig. 4. Most of the code is translated in a fairly direct way (with conditional statements and structured loops translated into nondeterministic jumps constrained by assumptions). However, since in K2, unlike in C, global variables are uninitialized by default, the K2 program contains an additional setup function (called `init_and_main` in the example) that sets `glbl` to zero before calling the original `main`. Another point to highlight is the use of the `:error` annotation (highlighted in bold) to model the C assertion.

4   Architectural View

This section describes the main components of Kratos2 and the flow of information among them. From the high-level point of view, Kratos2 is composed of the front-end c2Kratos, which converts the input C program to the K2 language, and of the core Kratos2, which is responsible for parsing, simplifications, transformations, and verification of K2 code. This separation helps to keep the core Kratos2 simple, as it does not have to handle the complex semantic nuances of C. Moreover, it makes it easy to add front-ends for new languages by writing a separate translator from the language in question to K2.

The front-end c2Kratos reads the input C file, builds its abstract syntax tree (AST) and then builds the corresponding K2 code in two passes. In the first pass, it converts the AST to an *extended* K2. Compared to the standard K2, the extended K2 also has primitives for pointers, records, complex loops, and compound instructions. These are removed in the second pass, by converting pointers to operations over maps, records to multiple variables, complex loops to sequences of assignments, jump instructions, and assumptions, and compound instructions to sequences of basic assignments to auxiliary variables.

The core Kratos2 consists of several components, whose relationships are visualized in Fig. 5:

---

[2] In the case of LTL properties, the question arises as to what to consider as an atomic step of the program. This is both crucial and application-dependent: for example, in embedded software consisting of a "transition function" that is executed periodically, it might make sense to consider each call to such function as one step, whereas in other contexts a more fine-grained notion of step might be needed. K2 (and Kratos2) makes no commitment about this, providing only the support for eventual unreachability of label statements, which can always be defined unambiguously.

C version	K2 version
``int glbl;

int f(int x)
{
    if (glbl > 0) {
        return x - 1;
    } else {
        glbl = 0;
        return x;
    }
}

void main(void)
{
    int y;
    while (y > 0) {
        y = f(y);
    }
    assert(glbl == 0);
}
``` | ```(type cint (sbv 32))
(entry init_and_main)
(globals (var glbl cint))

(function f ((var x cint))
    (return (var ret cint)) (locals)
    (seq
        (jump (label then) (label else))
        (label then)
        (assume (op gt glbl (const 0 cint)))
        (assign ret (sub x (const 1 cint)))
        (jump (label end))
        (label else)
        (assume (op not (op gt glbl (const 0 cint))))
        (assign glbl (const 0 cint))
        (assign ret x)
        (label end)))

(function main () (return) (locals (var y cint))
    (seq
        (label while)
        (jump (label inwhile) (label endwhile))
        (label inwhile)
        (assume (op gt y (const 0 cint)))
        (call f y y)
        (jump (label while))
        (label endwhile)
        (assume (op not (op gt y (const 0 cint))))
        (jump (label then) (label else))
        (label then)
        (assume (op not (op eq glbl (const 0 cint))))
        (! (label err) :error assert-fail)
        (label else)))

(function init_and_main () (return) (locals)
    (seq
        (assign glbl (const 0 cint))
        (call main)))
``` |

Fig. 4. Example C program and its K2 translation.

CFG builder and simplifier reads the input K2 file and builds the corresponding interprocedural control flow graph (CFG). It then performs several simplifications of the CFG, such as constant propagation and lightweight slicing. The result can be used either by the interpreter, symbolic executor, or one of the encoders. The simplified CFG can also be converted back into a K2 representation.

Interpreter interprets the CFG using the externally provided inputs to guide the execution. The inputs contain new values for all havoc commands and also destination labels for all nondeterministic jump commands. The inputs can be provided by the user, a random generator, or by one of the verification engines. The last option is used for counterexample reconstruction and validation.

Transition system encoder encodes the CFG to a symbolic transition system over a suitable theory. The encoder first inlines all function calls in the program. It then encodes the resulting inlined program using *large block encoding* [4], which allows encoding larger acyclic subgraphs of the CFG by a single transition formula. The resulting transition system can be verified by one of the available verification back-ends, or converted to a textual representation in one of the available output formats (VMT [20], nuXmv [14], BTOR2 [31], or AIGER [9]).[3]

---

[3] Depending on the features of the input K2 program, some of the verification back-ends or output formats might not be available. E.g., SAT-based engines are not available if the K2 program contains some infinite-state variables.

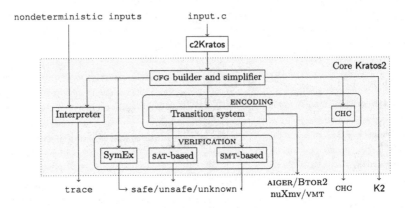

Fig. 5. Architecture of Kratos2.

CHC encoder converts the CFG to a set of Constrained Horn Clauses [11]. In contrast to the transition system encoder, the CHC encoder supports interprocedural analysis and recursive functions, encoded as a set of *non-linear* CHCs as described, e.g., in [28].

Symbolic executor implements a classical symbolic execution algorithm with iterative deepening to avoid getting stuck in long uninteresting branches. It supports (possibly recursive) K2 programs over arbitrary combinations of integers, reals, bit-vectors, floats, and arrays.

SMT-based engines encompass several SMT-based verification algorithms of symbolic transition systems. For reachability properties, Kratos2 implements standard bounded model checking (BMC) [7], k-induction [32], and IC3 with implicit predicate abstraction [18]. For liveness properties, we use a procedure combining liveness-to-safety reduction with ranking functions synthesis [23].

SAT-based engines encompass several verification algorithms of finite-state symbolic transition systems. Namely, for transition systems over the theory of bit-vectors and floats, Kratos2 offers BMC, k-induction, and different variants of IC3 [13], working over the bit-blasted Boolean transition system, for both reachability and liveness properties. Additionally, Kratos2 implements a dedicated engine for reachability properties in transition systems over the theory of bit-vectors, floats, and arrays similar to [10, 30].

5   Implementation and Experimental Evaluation

Implementation. Core Kratos2 is implemented in C++ on top of the Math-SAT5 [19] SMT solver and the nuXmv [14] symbolic model checker. The SAT-based verification engine additionally makes use of the MiniSat [25] and CaDiCaL [8] SAT solvers. The front-end c2Kratos is implemented in Python and relies on pycparser for parsing of the input C program. Kratos2 is freely available for non-commercial purposes from https://kratos.fbk.eu.

Table 1. Solved benchmarks by the three compared tools. Column **U** shows the number of solved *unsafe* benchmarks, **S** of *safe* benchmarks, and **W** of *wrong* results.

Family	CPAchecker			Kratos2			VeriAbs		
	U	S	W	U	S	W	U	S	W
arrays	70	5	0	75	7	0	**106**	**261**	0
bitvectors	13	31	0	13	**33**	0	**14**	31	0
combinations	**295**	36	0	282	47	0	277	**77**	0
controlflow	39	36	0	**40**	37	0	**40**	**47**	0
eca	223	481	0	210	365	0	**467**	**600**	0
floats	41	356	0	**43**	350	0	**43**	**393**	0
heap	**71**	118	1	67	102	0	70	**120**	0
loops	152	334	2	159	307	0	**192**	**427**	0
productlines	**265**	**332**	0	262	315	0	260	322	0
recursive	40	36	1	43	28	0	**46**	**41**	0
sequentialized	347	108	0	**361**	68	0	**361**	**123**	0
xcsp	50	**52**	0	51	51	0	**52**	**52**	0
Total	1606	1925	4	1606	1710	0	**1928**	**2494**	0

Experimental Setup. We performed an experimental evaluation to answer two research questions: Is the K2 language expressive enough to efficiently represent realistic C programs? Do the engines implemented in Kratos2 offer reasonable performance on realistic verification tasks? To this end, we considered all the C programs from the *ReachSafety* category of the 2022 edition of the annual software verification competition SV-COMP [3].The category consists of 5400 C programs divided into 12 benchmark families. We compared Kratos2 with Veri-Abs 1.4.2 [24] and CPAchecker 2.2 [5], respectively the winner and runner-up of the *ReachSafety* category of SV-COMP 2022. Similarly to the approach used by CPAchecker, we executed Kratos2 in *sequential portfolio* mode, which successively runs symbolic execution, SMT-based IC3, SAT-based IC3, and SMT-based BMC with predetermined time-outs for each of the engines.

The experiments were performed on several identical PCs equipped with Intel Core i7-8700 CPU @ 3.20 GHz and 32 GiB of RAM. Each execution was limited to use a single CPU core, 15 min of CPU time, and 8 GiB of RAM. For reliable benchmarking, all experiments were executed using BENCHEXEC [6]. A replication package describing the details of the setup is available at https://doi.org/10.5281/zenodo.7890411.

Results. To answer the first research question, we observe that from the total 5400 benchmarks, only 56 were not converted to K2 by c2Kratos due to unsupported floating point built-ins or features such as variable length arrays.

To answer the second research question, Table 1 shows the numbers of solved benchmarks by the individual tools and quantile plots in Fig. 6 show their running times. The results show that Kratos2 is competitive with CPAchecker on all benchmark families except for eca. It is also competitive with VeriAbs on most benchmark families. There are 23 benchmarks uniquely solved by Kratos2, 48 by CPAchecker, and 1039 by VeriAbs. Moreover, both Kratos2 and VeriAbs produced no wrong results, unlike most other participants of SV-COMP.

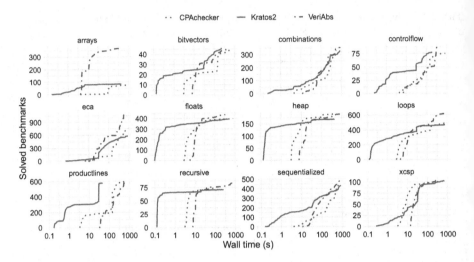

Fig. 6. Quantile plots of solved benchmarks for all three compared tools in individual benchmark families. The plot shows the number of benchmarks (*y*-axis) that were solved within the given number of seconds (*x*-axis).

We remark that CPAchecker is an established and optimized software verifier that regularly scores high in software verification competitions, and that VeriAbs implements algorithm selection heuristics, using both its own custom engines and external state-of-the-art verifiers. As such, it is not surprising that it performs much better than Kratos2 and CPAchecker on some of the families.

We conclude that the K2 language is expressive enough to efficiently capture a significant subset of C used in realistic programs. Furthermore, the verification engines implemented in Kratos2 mostly offer a performance comparable with state-of-the-art software verifiers.

6   Conclusions and Future Work

We have described Kratos2, a mature software verifier for imperative programs written in K2, a new intermediate verification language with a formal semantics based on SMT. Kratos2 is a complete rewrite of the original Kratos tool, offering significant extensions in functionalities and performance. The tool has already been successfully applied in various contexts, both industrial and academic.

As future work, we will consolidate the (currently alpha-quality) implementation of the ESST algorithm of the original Kratos [21] to handle multithreaded programs with cooperative scheduling. We will also investigate a tighter integration with CHC solvers to better handle recursive programs, as well as improved techniques to handle arrays and pointers such as [27,33]. On the language side, we plan to add support for contracts and pre-/post-conditions via annotations.

References

1. Amendola, A., et al.: A model-based approach to the design, verification and deployment of railway interlocking system. In: Margaria, T., Steffen, B. (eds.) ISoLA 2020. LNCS, vol. 12478, pp. 240–254. Springer, Cham (2020). https://doi.org/10.1007/978-3-030-61467-6_16
2. Barrett, C.W., Sebastiani, R., Seshia, S.A., Tinelli, C.: Satisfiability modulo theories. In: Handbook of Satisfiability. Frontiers in Artificial Intelligence and Applications, vol. 336, pp. 1267–1329. IOS Press (2021)
3. Beyer, D.: Progress on software verification: SV-COMP 2022. In: Beyer, D. (ed.) TACAS 2022. LNCS, vol. 13244, pp. 375–402. Springer, Cham (2022). https://doi.org/10.1007/978-3-030-99527-0_20
4. Beyer, D., Cimatti, A., Griggio, A., Keremoglu, M.E., Sebastiani, R.: Software model checking via large-block encoding. In: FMCAD, pp. 25–32. IEEE (2009)
5. Beyer, D., Keremoglu, M.E.: CPACHECKER: A tool for configurable software verification. In: Gopalakrishnan, G., Qadeer, S. (eds.) CAV 2011. LNCS, vol. 6806, pp. 184–190. Springer, Heidelberg (2011). https://doi.org/10.1007/978-3-642-22110-1_16
6. Beyer, D., Löwe, S., Wendler, P.: Reliable benchmarking: requirements and solutions. Int. J. Softw. Tools Technol. Transf. 21(1), 1–29 (2019)
7. Biere, A., Cimatti, A., Clarke, E., Zhu, Y.: Symbolic model checking without BDDs. In: Cleaveland, W.R. (ed.) TACAS 1999. LNCS, vol. 1579, pp. 193–207. Springer, Heidelberg (1999). https://doi.org/10.1007/3-540-49059-0_14
8. Biere, A., Fleury, M., Heisinger, M.: CaDiCaL, Kissat, Paracooba entering the SAT Competition 2021. In: Proceedings of SAT Competition 2021 - Solver and Benchmark Descriptions, volume B-2021-1 of Department of Computer Science Report Series B, pp. 10–13. University of Helsinki (2021)
9. Biere, A., Heljanko, K., Wieringa, S.: AIGER 1.9 and beyond. Technical report 11/2, Institute for Formal Models and Verification, Johannes Kepler University (2011)
10. Bjesse, P.: Word-level sequential memory abstraction for model checking. In: Cimatti, A., Jones, R.B. (eds.) Formal Methods in Computer-Aided Design, FMCAD 2008, Portland, Oregon, USA, 17–20 November 2008, pp. 1–9. IEEE (2008)
11. Bjørner, N., Gurfinkel, A., McMillan, K., Rybalchenko, A.: Horn clause solvers for program verification. In: Beklemishev, L.D., Blass, A., Dershowitz, N., Finkbeiner, B., Schulte, W. (eds.) Fields of Logic and Computation II. LNCS, vol. 9300, pp. 24–51. Springer, Cham (2015). https://doi.org/10.1007/978-3-319-23534-9_2
12. Bombardelli, A., et al.: COMPASTA: extending TASTE with formal design and verification functionality. In: Seguin, C., Zeller, M., Prosvirnova, T. (eds.) IMBSA 2022. LNCS, vol. 13525, pp. 21–27. Springer, Cham (2022). https://doi.org/10.1007/978-3-031-15842-1_2
13. Bradley, A.R.: SAT-based model checking without unrolling. In: Jhala, R., Schmidt, D. (eds.) VMCAI 2011. LNCS, vol. 6538, pp. 70–87. Springer, Heidelberg (2011). https://doi.org/10.1007/978-3-642-18275-4_7
14. Cavada, R., et al.: The NUXMV symbolic model checker. In: Biere, A., Bloem, R. (eds.) CAV 2014. LNCS, vol. 8559, pp. 334–342. Springer, Cham (2014). https://doi.org/10.1007/978-3-319-08867-9_22
15. Cimatti, A., et al.: A comprehensive framework for the analysis of automotive systems. In: MoDELS, pp. 379–389. ACM (2022)

16. Cimatti, A., et al.: EVA: a tool for the compositional verification of AUTOSAR models. In: Sankaranarayanan, S., Sharygina, N. (eds.) TACAS 2023. LNCS, vol. 13994, pp. 3–10. Springer, Cham (2023). https://doi.org/10.1007/978-3-031-30820-8_1

17. Cimatti, A., Griggio, A., Micheli, A., Narasamdya, I., Roveri, M.: KRATOS – a software model checker for SystemC. In: Gopalakrishnan, G., Qadeer, S. (eds.) CAV 2011. LNCS, vol. 6806, pp. 310–316. Springer, Heidelberg (2011). https://doi.org/10.1007/978-3-642-22110-1_24

18. Cimatti, A., Griggio, A., Mover, S., Tonetta, S.: Infinite-state invariant checking with IC3 and predicate abstraction. Formal Methods Syst. Des. **49**(3), 190–218 (2016). https://doi.org/10.1007/s10703-016-0257-4

19. Cimatti, A., Griggio, A., Schaafsma, B.J., Sebastiani, R.: The MathSAT5 SMT solver. In: Piterman, N., Smolka, S.A. (eds.) TACAS 2013. LNCS, vol. 7795, pp. 93–107. Springer, Heidelberg (2013). https://doi.org/10.1007/978-3-642-36742-7_7

20. Cimatti, A., Griggio, A., Tonetta, S.: The VMT-LIB language and tools. In: SMT. CEUR Workshop Proceedings, vol. 3185, pp. 80–89. CEUR-WS.org (2022)

21. Cimatti, A., Narasamdya, I., Roveri, M.: Software model checking with explicit scheduler and symbolic threads. Log. Methods Comput. Sci. **8**(2) (2012)

22. Clarke, E.M., Grumberg, O., Hamaguchi, K.: Another look at LTL model checking. Formal Methods Syst. Des. **10**(1), 47–71 (1997)

23. Daniel, J., Cimatti, A., Griggio, A., Tonetta, S., Mover, S.: Infinite-state liveness-to-safety via implicit abstraction and well-founded relations. In: Chaudhuri, S., Farzan, A. (eds.) CAV 2016. LNCS, vol. 9779, pp. 271–291. Springer, Cham (2016). https://doi.org/10.1007/978-3-319-41528-4_15

24. Darke, P., Agrawal, S., Venkatesh, R.: VeriAbs: a tool for scalable verification by abstraction (competition contribution). In: TACAS 2021. LNCS, vol. 12652, pp. 458–462. Springer, Cham (2021). https://doi.org/10.1007/978-3-030-72013-1_32

25. Eén, N., Sörensson, N.: An extensible SAT-solver. In: Giunchiglia, E., Tacchella, A. (eds.) SAT 2003. LNCS, vol. 2919, pp. 502–518. Springer, Heidelberg (2004). https://doi.org/10.1007/978-3-540-24605-3_37

26. Filliâtre, J.-C., Paskevich, A.: Why3—where programs meet provers. In: Felleisen, M., Gardner, P. (eds.) ESOP 2013. LNCS, vol. 7792, pp. 125–128. Springer, Heidelberg (2013). https://doi.org/10.1007/978-3-642-37036-6_8

27. Garcia-Contreras, I., Gurfinkel, A., Navas, J.A.: Efficient modular SMT-based model checking of pointer programs. In: SAS 2022. LNCS, vol. 13790, pp. 227–246. Springer, Cham (2022). https://doi.org/10.1007/978-3-031-22308-2_11

28. Grebenshchikov, S., Lopes, N.P., Popeea, C., Rybalchenko, A.: Synthesizing software verifiers from proof rules. In: PLDI, pp. 405–416. ACM (2012)

29. Leino, K.R.M., Rümmer, P.: A polymorphic intermediate verification language: design and logical encoding. In: Esparza, J., Majumdar, R. (eds.) TACAS 2010. LNCS, vol. 6015, pp. 312–327. Springer, Heidelberg (2010). https://doi.org/10.1007/978-3-642-12002-2_26

30. Mann, M., Irfan, A., Griggio, A., Padon, O., Barrett, C.W.: Counterexample-guided prophecy for model checking modulo the theory of arrays. Log. Methods Comput. Sci. **18**(3) (2022)

31. Niemetz, A., Preiner, M., Wolf, C., Biere, A.: BTOR2, BtorMC and Boolector 3.0. In: Chockler, H., Weissenbacher, G. (eds.) CAV 2018. LNCS, vol. 10981, pp. 587–595. Springer, Cham (2018). https://doi.org/10.1007/978-3-319-96145-3_32

32. Sheeran, M., Singh, S., Stålmarck, G.: Checking safety properties using induction and a SAT-solver. In: Hunt, W.A., Johnson, S.D. (eds.) FMCAD 2000. LNCS, vol. 1954, pp. 127–144. Springer, Heidelberg (2000). https://doi.org/10.1007/3-540-40922-X_8
33. Vick, C., McMillan, K.L.: Synthesizing history and prophecy variables for symbolic model checking. In: Dragoi, C., Emmi, M., Wang, J. (eds.) VMCAI 2023. LNCS, vol. 13881, pp. 320–340. Springer, Cham (2023). https://doi.org/10.1007/978-3-031-24950-1_15

Making IP = PSPACE Practical: Efficient Interactive Protocols for BDD Algorithms

Eszter Couillard[1] , Philipp Czerner[1]([✉]) , Javier Esparza[1] ,
and Rupak Majumdar[2]

[1] Technical University of Munich, Munich, Germany
{coillar,czerner,esparza}@in.tum.de
[2] Max Planck Institute for Software Systems (MPI-SWS),
Kaiserslautern, Germany
rupak@mpi-sws.org

Abstract. We show that interactive protocols between a prover and a verifier, a well-known tool of complexity theory, can be used in practice to certify the correctness of automated reasoning tools.

Theoretically, interactive protocols exist for all **PSPACE** problems. The verifier of a protocol checks the prover's answer to a problem instance in probabilistic polynomial time, with polynomially many bits of communication, and with exponentially small probability of error. (The prover may need exponential time.) Existing interactive protocols are not used in practice because their provers use naive algorithms, inefficient even for small instances, that are incompatible with practical implementations of automated reasoning.

We bridge the gap between theory and practice by means of an interactive protocol whose prover uses BDDs. We consider the problem of counting the number of assignments to a QBF instance (#CP), which has a natural BDD-based algorithm. We give an interactive protocol for #CP whose prover is implemented on top of an extended BDD library. The prover has only a linear overhead in computation time over the natural algorithm.

We have implemented our protocol in blic, a certifying tool for #CP. Experiments on standard QBF benchmarks show that blic is competitive with state-of-the-art QBF-solvers. The run time of the verifier is negligible. While loss of absolute certainty can be concerning, the error probability in our experiments is at most 10^{-10} and reduces to 10^{-10k} by repeating the verification k times.

This work was supported by an ERC Advanced Grant (787367: PaVeS), by the Deutsche Forschungsgemeinschaft project 389792660 TRR 248—CPEC, and by the Research Training Network of the Deutsche Forschungsgemeinschaft (DFG) (378803395: ConVeY).

C. Enea and A. Lal (Eds.): CAV 2023, LNCS 13966, pp. 437–458, 2023.
https://doi.org/10.1007/978-3-031-37709-9_21

1 Introduction

Automated reasoning tools often underlie our assertions about the correctness of critical hardware and software components. In recent years, the scope and scalability of these techniques have grown significantly.

Automated reasoning tools are not immune to bugs. If we are to trust their verdict, it is important that they provide evidence of their correct behaviour. A substantial amount of research has gone into proof-producing automated reasoning tools [4,14,16,22,23]. These works define a notion of "correctness certificate" suitable for the reasoning problem at hand, and adapt the reasoning engine to produce independently checkable certificates. For example, SAT solvers produce either a satisfying assignment or a proof of unsatisfiability in some proof system, e.g. resolution (see [16] for a survey). Extending such certificates beyond boolean SAT is an active area of current research [3,4,18,24,29].

In the worst case, the size of certificates grows exponentially in the size of the input, even for boolean unsatisfiability (unless NP = coNP). If users have limited computational or communication resources, transferring and checking large certificates becomes a burden. Large certificates are not just a theoretical curiosity. In practice, resolution proofs for complex SAT problems may run to petabytes [15]. Ideally, we would prefer "small" certificates (polynomial in the size of the input) which can be checked independently in polynomial time.

The IP = PSPACE theorem proves that certification with polynomial verification time is possible for any problem in PSPACE, provided one trades off absolute certainty for certainty with high probability [27]. The complexity class IP consists of those languages for which there is a polynomial-round, complete and sound *interactive protocol* [1,2,13,20]—a sequence of interactions between a (computationally unbounded) prover and a (computationally bounded) verifier after which the verifier decides whether the prover correctly performed a computation. The protocol is complete if, whenever an input belongs to the language, there is an *honest prover* who can convince a polynomial-time randomised verifier in a polynomial number of rounds. The protocol is sound if, whenever an input does not belong to the language, the Verifier will reject the input with high probability—no matter what certificates are provided to the Verifier. That is, a "Prover" cannot fool the certification process.

Since every language in PSPACE has an interactive protocol, there are interactive protocols for UNSAT, QBF, *counting* QBF, safety verification of concurrent state machines, etc. Observe that the prover of a protocol may perform exponential time computations (which is unavoidable unless P = PSPACE), but the verifier only requires polynomial time in the original input.

If interactive protocols provide a foundation for small and efficiently verifiable certificates (at least for problems in PSPACE), why are they not in widespread practice? We believe the reason to be the following: for asymptotic complexity purposes, it suffices to use honest provers with best-case exponential complexity that naively enumerate all possibilities. Such provers are incompatible with automated reasoning tools, which use more sophisticated data structures and heuristics to scale to real-world examples. So we need to make *practical algorithms* for automated reasoning *efficiently certifying*. We call an algorithm *efficiently certifying* if, in addition to computing the output, it can execute the steps of an honest prover in an interactive protocol with only polynomial overhead over its running time.

In this paper, we show that algorithms using reduced ordered binary decision diagrams (henceforth called BDDs) [9] can be made efficiently certifying. We consider #CP, the problem of computing the number of satisfying assignments of a *circuit with partial evaluation (CP)*. Besides boolean nodes, a CP contains *partial evaluation* nodes $\pi_{[x:=\mathsf{false}]}$ (resp., $\pi_{[x:=\mathsf{true}]}$) that take a boolean predicate as input, say φ, and output the result of setting x to false (resp., true) in φ. #CP generalises SAT, QBF, and *counting* SAT (#SAT), and has a natural algorithm using BDDs: Compute BDDs for each node of the circuit in topological order, and count the accepting paths of the final BDD.

The theoretical part of the paper proceeds in two steps. First, we present CPCERTIFY, a complete and sound interactive protocol for #CP. CPCERTIFY is similar to the SUMCHECK protocol [20]. It involves encoding boolean formulas as polynomials over a finite field. The prover is responsible for producing certain polynomials from the original circuit and evaluating them at points of the field chosen by the verifier. These polynomials are either multilinear (all exponents are at most 1) or quadratic (at most 2).

Second, we show that an honest prover in CPCERTIFY can be implemented on top of a suitably extended BDD library. The run times of the certifying BDD algorithms are only a constant overhead over the computation time without certification—they depend linearly on the total number of nodes of the intermediate BDDs computed by the prover to solve the #CP instance. We use two key insights. The first is an encoding of multilinear polynomials as BDDs; we show that the intermediate BDDs represent all the multilinear polynomials a prover needs during the run of CPCERTIFY. The second shows that the quadratic polynomials correspond to *intermediate steps* during the computation of the intermediate BDDs. We extend BDDs with additional "book-keeping" nodes that allow the prover to also compute the quadratic polynomials while solving the problem. So computing the polynomials required by CPCERTIFY has *zero* additional cost; the only overhead is the cost of evaluating the polynomials at the field points chosen by the verifier.

We have implemented a certifying #CP solver based on our extended BDD library. Our experiments show that the solver is competitive with state-of-the-art non-certifying QBF solvers, and can outperform certifying QBF solvers based on BDDs. The number of bytes exchanged between the prover and the verifier are an order of magnitude smaller, and Verifier's run time several orders of magnitude smaller, than current encodings of QBF proofs, while bounding the error probability to below 10^{-10}. Thus, our results open the way for practically efficient, probabilistic certification of automated reasoning problems using interactive protocols.

Additional Related Work. Proof systems for SAT and QBF remain an active area of research—both in theoretical proof complexity and in practical tool development. Jussila, Sinz, and Biere [17,28] showed how to extract extended resolution proofs from BDD operations. This is the basis for proof-producing SAT and QBF solvers based on BDDs [6–8]. As in our work, the proof uses intermediate nodes produced in the construction of the BDD operations. We focus on interactive certification instead of extended resolution proofs, which can be exponentially larger than the input formula.

Recently, Luo et al. [21] consider the problem of providing *zero-knowledge* proofs of unsatisfiability, a motivation similar but not equal to ours. Their techniques require the verifier to work in time polynomial in the proof, which can be exponentially bigger than the input formula. In contrast, the verifier of CPCER-TIFY runs in polynomial time in the input. Since any language in PSPACE has a zero knowledge proof [5], our protocol can in principle be made zero knowledge. Whether that system scales in practice is left for future work.

Full Version. Detailed proofs can be found in the full version of the paper [11].

2   Preliminaries

The Class IP. An *interactive protocol* between a *Prover* and a *Verifier* consists of a sequence of interactions in which a Verifier asks questions to a Prover, receives responses to the questions, and must ultimately decide if a common input x belongs to a language. The computational power of the Prover is unbounded but the Verifier is a randomised, polynomial-time algorithm.

Formally, let P, V denote (deterministic) Turing machines.

We say that $(r; m_1, ..., m_{2k})$ is a *k-round interaction*, with $r, m_1, ..., m_{2k} \in \{0,1\}^*$, if $m_{i+1} = V(r, m_1, ..., m_i)$ for even i and $m_{i+1} = P(m_1, ..., m_i)$ for odd i. We think of r as an additional sequence of bits given to Verifier V that is chosen randomly. The *output* $\text{out}(P, V)(x, r, k)$ is defined as m_{2k}, where $(r; m_1, ..., m_{2k})$ is the unique k-round interaction with $m_1 = x$.

A language L belongs to IP if there are V, P_H and polynomials p_1, p_2, p_3, s.t. $V(r, x, m_2, ..., m_i)$ runs in time $p_1(|x|)$ for all $r, x, m_2, ..., m_i$, and, for each x and an $r \in \{0,1\}^{p_2(|x|)}$ chosen uniformly at random:

1. (*Completeness*) $x \in L$ implies $\text{out}(P_H, V)(x, r, p_3(|x|)) = 1$ with probability 1, and
2. (*Soundness*) $x \notin L$ implies that for all P we have $\text{out}(P, V)(x, r, p_3(|x|)) = 1$ with probability at most $2^{-|x|}$.

Intuitively, in an interactive protocol, a computationally unbounded Prover interacts with a randomised polynomial-time Verifier for k rounds. In each round, Verifier sends probabilistic "challenges" to Prover, based on the input and the answers to prior challenges, and receives answers from Prover. At the end of k rounds, Verifier decides to accept or reject the input. The completeness property ensures that if the input belongs to the language L, then there is an "honest" Prover P_H who can always convince Verifier that indeed $x \in L$. If the input does not belong to the language, then the soundness property ensures that Verifier rejects the input with high probability no matter how a (dishonest) Prover tries to convince them.

It is known that IP = PSPACE [20, 27], that is, every language in PSPACE has a polynomial-round interactive protocol. The proof exhibits an interactive protocol for the language QBF of true quantified boolean formulae; in particular, the honest Prover is a polynomial space, exponential time algorithm that uses a truth table representation of the formula to implement the protocol.

Polynomials. Interactive protocols make extensive use of polynomials over some prime finite field $\mathbb{F}$.

Let X be a finite set of variables. We use $x, y, z, \ldots$ for variables and $p, q, \ldots$ for polynomials. When we write a polynomial explicitly, we write it in brackets, e.g. $[3xy - z^2]$. We write $\mathbf{1}$ and $\mathbf{0}$ for the polynomials $[1]$ and $[0]$, respectively. We use the following operations on polynomials:

- *Sum, difference, and product.* Denoted $p + q$, $p - q$, $p \cdot q$, and defined as usual. For example, $[3xy - z^2] + [z^2 + yz] = [3xy + yz]$ and $[x + y] \cdot [x - y] = [x^2 - y^2]$.
- *Partial evaluation.* Denoted $\pi_{[x:=a]} \, p$, it returns the result of setting variable x to the field element a in the polynomial p, e.g. $\pi_{[x:=5]}[3xy - z^2] = [15y - z^2]$.
- *Degree reduction.* Denoted $\delta_x \, p$. It reduces the degree of x in all monomials of the polynomial to 1. For example, $\delta_x[x^3y + 3x^2 + 7z^2] = [xy + 3x + 7z^2]$.

A *(partial) assignment* is a (partial) mapping $\sigma : X \to \mathbb{F}$. We write $\Pi_\sigma \, p$ for $\pi_{[x_1:=\sigma(x_1)]} \cdots \pi_{[x_k:=\sigma(x_k)]} \, p$, where $x_1, \ldots, x_k$ are the variables for which σ is defined. Additionally, we call σ *binary* if $\sigma(x) \in \{0, 1\}$ for each $x \in X$.

Binary and Multilinear Polynomials. A polynomial is *multilinear in x* if the degree of x in p is 0 or 1. A polynomial is *multilinear* if it is multilinear in all its variables. For example, $[xy - y^2]$ is multilinear in x but not in y, and $[3xy - 2zy]$ is multilinear. A polynomial p is *binary* if $\Pi_\sigma \, p \in \{\mathbf{0}, \mathbf{1}\}$ for every binary assignment σ. Two polynomials p, q are *binary equivalent*, denoted $p \equiv_b q$, if $\Pi_\sigma \, p = \Pi_\sigma \, q$ for every binary assignment σ. (Note that non-binary polynomials can be binary equivalent.)

3   Circuits with Partial Evaluation

We introduce circuits with partial evaluation (CP), a compact representation of quantified boolean formulae, and formulate #CP, the problem of counting the number of satisfying assignments of a CP. #CP generalises QBF, the satisfiability problem for quantified boolean formulas. Figure 1 shows an example of a CP. Informally, it is a directed acyclic graph whose nodes are labelled with variables, boolean operators, or *partial evaluation operators* $\pi_{[x:=b]}$. Intuitively, $\pi_{[x:=b]}\varphi$ sets the variable x to the truth value b in the formula φ. In this way, each node of a circuit stands for a boolean function, and the complete circuit stands for the boolean function of the root. Figure 1 shows the formulae represented by each node.

Definition 1. *Let X denote a finite set of* variables *and $S \subseteq X$. A circuit with partial evaluation and variables in S (S-CP) has the form*

- true, false, *or* x, *where* $x \in S$,
- $\neg\varphi$, $\varphi \wedge \psi$, *or* $\varphi \vee \psi$, *where* φ, ψ *are* S-*CPs, or*
- $\pi_{[y:=b]}\,\varphi$, *where* $y \in X \setminus S$, $b \in \{\text{true}, \text{false}\}$, *and* φ *is an* $(S \cup \{y\})$-*CP.*

The set of free variables *of a* S-*CP* φ *is* free$(\varphi) := S$. *The* children *of a CP are inductively defined as follows:* true, false, *and* x *have no children; the children of* $\varphi \wedge \psi$ *and* $\varphi \vee \psi$ *are* φ *and* ψ; *and the only child of* $\neg\varphi$ *and* $\pi_{[y:=b]}\,\varphi$ *is* φ. *The set of* descendants *of* φ *is the smallest set* M *containing* φ *and all children of every element of* M. *The* size *of* φ *is* $|\varphi| := |M|$.

We represent a CP φ as a directed acyclic graph. The nodes of the graph are the descendants of φ. A CP φ encodes a boolean predicate P_φ, which maps assignments $\sigma \colon$ free$(\varphi) \to \{\text{false}, \text{true}\}$ to a truth value $P_\varphi(\sigma) \in \{\text{false}, \text{true}\}$. It does so in the obvious manner, e.g., $P_x(\sigma) := \sigma(x)$, $P_{\varphi \wedge \psi}(\sigma) := P_\varphi(\sigma) \wedge P_\psi(\sigma)$, etc. We use $\pi_{[x:=b]}$ as partial evaluation operator, so $P_{\pi_{[x:=b]}\varphi}(\sigma) := P_\varphi(\sigma \cup \{x \mapsto b\})$. Intuitively, $\pi_{[x:=b]}\,\varphi$ replaces each occurrence of x in φ by b. An assignment σ *satisfies* φ if $P_\varphi(\sigma) = \text{true}$. We define the macros

$$\forall_x \varphi := \pi_{[x:=0]}\,\varphi \wedge \pi_{[x:=1]}\,\varphi$$
$$\exists_x \varphi := \pi_{[x:=0]}\,\varphi \vee \pi_{[x:=1]}\,\varphi$$

Figure 1 shows a CP for the quantified boolean formula $\forall_y(\neg x \vee (x \wedge y))$.

We consider the following problem:

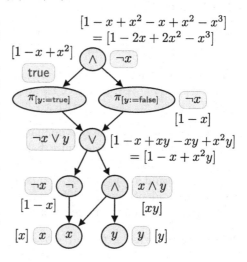

Fig. 1. A CP (Sect. 3), the boolean functions represented by each node (in boxes), and the arithmetisation of the formulae (Sect. 4.1).

#CP   **Input**   CP φ.
Output The number of satisfying assignments of φ.

Given a quantified boolean formula, we can use the macros for quantifiers to construct in linear time an equivalent CP, i.e., a CP with the same satisfying assignments. Similarly, #SAT instances can also be reduced to #CP.

Structure of the Rest of the Paper. In Sect. 4, we give an interactive protocol for #CP called CPCERTIFY. In Sect. 5, we implement an honest Prover for CPCERTIFY on top of an extended BDD-based algorithm for #CP. The prover runs in time polynomial in the size of the largest BDD for any of the subcircuits of the initial circuit. Together, these results yield our main result, Theorem 1, showing that any BDD-based algorithm can be modified to run an interactive protocol with small polynomial overhead. Finally, Sect. 6 presents empirical results.

4   An Interactive Protocol for #CP

In this section we describe an interactive protocol for #CP, following the SUM-CHECK protocol of [20]. Section 4.1 introduces arithmetisation, a technique to transform #CP into an equivalent problem about polynomials. Section 4.2 shows how to transform #CP into an equivalent problem about evaluating polynomials *of low degree*. Finally, Sect. 4.3 presents an interactive protocol for this problem.

4.1   Arithmetisation

We define a mapping $[\![\cdot]\!]$ that assigns to each CP φ a polynomial $[\![\varphi]\!]$ over the variables free(φ), called the *arithmetisation* of φ:

- $[\![\text{true}]\!] := 1$; $[\![\text{false}]\!] := 0$; $[\![x]\!] := [x]$ for every $x \in X$; and $[\![\neg\varphi]\!] := 1 - [\![\varphi]\!]$;
- $[\![\varphi \wedge \psi]\!] := [\![\varphi]\!] \cdot [\![\psi]\!]$; and $[\![\varphi \vee \psi]\!] := [\![\varphi]\!] + [\![\psi]\!] - [\![\varphi]\!] \cdot [\![\psi]\!]$;
- $[\![\pi_{[x:=b]}\,\varphi]\!] := \pi_{[x:=[\![b]\!]]}[\![\varphi]\!]$, with $x \in$ free(φ), $b \in \{\text{true}, \text{false}\}$.

Figure 1 also shows the polynomials corresponding to the nodes of the CP.

Let $\mathbb{F}$ be a fixed prime finite field. Given an arbitrary truth assignment $\sigma \colon X \to \{\text{true}, \text{false}\}$, let $\overline{\sigma} \colon X \to \mathbb{F}$ be the binary assignment given by $\overline{\sigma}(x) = 1$ if $\sigma(x) = \text{true}$ and $\overline{\sigma}(x) = 0$ if $\sigma(x) = \text{false}$, where 0 and 1 denote the additive and multiplicative identities in $\mathbb{F}$. The mapping $[\![\cdot]\!]$ is defined to satisfy the following property, whose proof is immediate:

Proposition 1. *Let φ be an S-CP encoding some boolean predicate P_φ. Then $P_\varphi(\sigma) = \Pi_{\overline{\sigma}}[\![\varphi]\!]$ for every truth assignment σ to S.*

So, intuitively, the polynomial $[\![\varphi]\!]$ is a conservative extension of the predicate P_φ: It returns the same values for all binary assignments. Accordingly, in the rest of the paper we abuse language and write σ instead of $\overline{\sigma}$ for the binary assignment corresponding to the truth assignment σ.

Observe that #CP can be reformulated as follows: given a CP φ, compute the number of binary assignments σ s.t. $\Pi_\sigma[\![\varphi]\!] = 1$.

4.2   Degree Reduction

Given a CP φ, its associated polynomial can have degree exponential in the height of φ. Since we are ultimately interested in evaluating polynomials over binary assignments, and since $x^2 = x$ for $x \in \{0, 1\}$, we can convert polynomials to low degree without changing their behaviour on binary assignments.

For this, we use a *degree-reduction* operator δ_x for every variable x. The operator $\delta_x p$ reduces the exponent of all powers of x in p to 1. For example, $\delta_x[x^2y + 3xy^2 - 2x^3y^2 + 4] = [xy + 3xy^2 - 2xy^2 + 4]$. Observe that $\delta_x p \equiv_b p$. Instead of working on the input CP directly, we first convert it into a *circuit with partial evaluation and degree reduction* by inserting degree-reduction operators after binary operations. This ensures all intermediate polynomials obtained by arithmetisation have low degree.

Definition 2. *A circuit with partial evaluation and degree reduction over the set S of variables (S-CPD) is defined in the same manner as an S-CP, extended as follows:*

- *if φ is an S-CPD and $x \in S$, then $\delta_x\varphi$ is an S-CPD,*
- *$[\![\delta_x\varphi]\!] := \delta_x[\![\varphi]\!]$, and*
- *φ is the only child of $\delta_x\varphi$.*

For an S-CPD φ we define free(φ), $|\varphi|$, children, descendants, and the graphical representation as for S-CPs.

We convert a CP φ into a CPD conv(φ) by adding a degree-reduction operator for each free variable before any binary operation.

Definition 3. *Given a CP φ with free(φ) = $\{x_1, ..., x_k\}$, its associated CPD conv(φ) is inductively defined as follows:*

- conv(false) = false, conv(true) := true,
- conv($\neg\psi$) := $\neg$ conv(ψ), conv($\pi_{[x:=b]} \psi$) := $\pi_{[x:=b]}$ conv(ψ), *and*
- conv($\psi_1 \circledast \psi_2$) := $\delta_{x_1}...\delta_{x_k}$(conv($\psi_1$) $\circledast$ conv(ψ_2)), *for $\circledast \in \{\vee, \wedge\}$.*

Figure 2 shows the CPD conv(φ) for the CP φ of Fig. 1, together with the polynomials corresponding to each node.

We collect some basic properties of CPDs:

Lemma 1. *Let φ be a CP.*

(a) $[\![\text{conv}(\varphi)]\!]$ is a binary multilinear polynomial and $[\![\text{conv}(\varphi)]\!] \equiv_b [\![\varphi]\!]$.
(b) For every descendant ψ of conv(φ), $[\![\psi]\!]$ has maximum degree 2.

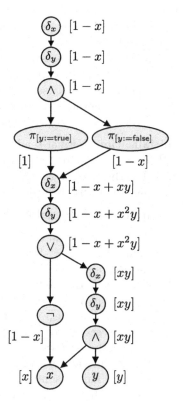

Fig. 2. CPD and polynomials for the CP of Fig. 1.

CPDs have another useful property. Recall that given a CP φ we are interested in its number of satisfying assignments. The next lemma shows that this number can be computed by evaluating the polynomial $[\![\text{conv}(\varphi)]\!]$ on a *single input.*

Lemma 2. *A CP φ with n free variables has $m < |\mathbb{F}|$ satisfying assignments iff $\Pi_\sigma[\![\text{conv}(\varphi)]\!] = m \cdot 2^{-n}$, where σ is the assignment satisfying $\sigma(x) := 2^{-1}$ in the field $\mathbb{F}$ for every variable x.[1]*

---

[1] Any prime field $\mathbb{F}$ with $|\mathbb{F}| > 2$ has an element c such that $2c = 1$.

4.3 CPCertify: An Interactive Protocol for #CP

We describe an interactive protocol, called CPCertify, for a CP φ with n free variables. Let X denote the variables used in φ. Prover and Verifier fix a finite field with at least $m + 1$ elements, where m is an upper bound on the number of assignments (e.g. $m = 2^n$). Prover tries to convince the Verifier that $\Pi_\sigma[\![\mathrm{conv}(\varphi)]\!] = K$ for some $K \in \mathbb{F}$.

In the protocol, Verifier challenges Prover to compute polynomials of the form $\Pi_\sigma([\![\psi]\!])$, where ψ is a node of the CPD $\mathrm{conv}(\varphi)$ and $\sigma \colon \mathrm{free}(\psi) \to \mathbb{F}$ is a (non-binary!) assignment; we call the expression $\Pi_\sigma[\![\mathrm{conv}(\psi)]\!]$ a *challenge*. Observe that all assignments are chosen by Verifier. Prover answers with some $k \in \mathbb{F}$. We call the expression $\Pi_\sigma[\![\mathrm{conv}(\psi)]\!] = k$ a *claim*, or the *answer* to the challenge $\Pi_\sigma[\![\mathrm{conv}(\psi)]\!]$.

CPCertify consists of an initialisation and a number of rounds, one for each descendant of $\mathrm{conv}(\varphi)$. Rounds are executed in topological order, starting at the root, i.e. at $\mathrm{conv}(\varphi)$ itself. The structure of a round for a node ψ of $\mathrm{conv}(\varphi)$ depends on whether ψ is an internal node (including the root), or a leaf.

At each point, Verifier keeps track of a set $\mathcal{C}$ of claims that must be checked.

Initialisation. Verifier sends Prover the challenge $\Pi_\sigma[\![\mathrm{conv}(\varphi)]\!]$, where $\sigma(x) := 2^{-1}$ for every $x \in \mathrm{free}(\varphi)$. Prover returns the claim $\Pi_\sigma[\![\mathrm{conv}(\varphi)]\!] = K$ for some $K \in \mathbb{F}$. (By Lemma 2, this amounts to claiming that φ has $K \cdot 2^n$ satisfying assignments.) Verifier initialises $\mathcal{C} := \{\Pi_\sigma[\![\mathrm{conv}(\varphi)]\!] = K\}$.

Round for an Internal Node. A round for an internal node ψ runs as follows:

(a) Verifier collects all claims $\{\Pi_{\sigma_i}[\![\psi]\!] = k_i\}_{i=1}^m$ in $\mathcal{C}$ relating to ψ, with assignments $\sigma_1, \ldots, \sigma_m \colon \mathrm{free}(\psi) \to \mathbb{F}$ and $k_1, \ldots, k_m \in \mathbb{F}$. (Initially $\psi = \mathrm{conv}(\varphi)$ and the only claim is $\Pi_\sigma[\![\mathrm{conv}(\varphi)]\!] = K$.)

(b) If $m > 1$, Verifier interacts with Prover to compute a unique claim $\Pi_\sigma[\![\psi]\!] = k$ such that very likely[2] the claim is true only if all claims $\{\Pi_{\sigma_i}[\![\psi]\!] = k_i\}_{i=1}^m$ are true. For this, Verifier sends a number of challenges, and checks that the answers are *consistent* with the prior claims. Based on these answers, Verifier then derives new claims. (See "Description of step (b)" below.)

(c) Verifier interacts with Prover to compute a claim $\Pi_{\sigma'}[\![\psi']\!] = k'$ for each child ψ' of ψ. This is similar to (b): if $\Pi_\sigma[\![\psi]\!] \neq k$, i.e. the unique claim from (b) does not hold, then very likely one of the resulting claims will be wrong. Depending on the type of ψ, the claims are computed based on the answers of Prover to challenges sent by Verifier. (See "Description of step (c)" below.)

(d) In total, Verifier removed the claims $\{\Pi_{\sigma_i}[\![\psi]\!] = k_i\}_{i=1}^m$ from $\mathcal{C}$, and replaced them by one claim $\Pi_{\sigma'}[\![\psi']\!] = k'$ for each child ψ' of ψ.

Observe that, since a node ψ can be a child of several nodes, Verifier may collect multiple claims for ψ, one for each parent node.

Round for a Leaf. If ψ is a leaf, then $\psi = x$ for a variable x, or $\psi \in \{\mathsf{true}, \mathsf{false}\}$. Verifier removes all claims $\{\Pi_{\sigma_i}[\![\psi]\!] = k_i\}_{i=1}^m$ from $\mathcal{C}$, computes the values $c_i := \Pi_{\sigma_i}[\![\psi]\!]$, and rejects if $k_i \neq c_i$ for any i.

---

[2] The precise bound on the failure probability will be given in Proposition 2.

Observe that if all claims made by Prover about leaves are true, then very likely Prover's initial claim is also true.

Description of Step (b). Let $\{\Pi_{\sigma_i}[\![\psi]\!] = k_i\}_{i=1}^m$ be the claims in $\mathcal{C}$ relating to node ψ. Verifier and Prover conduct step (b) as follows:

(b.1) While there exists $x \in X$ s.t. $\sigma_1(x), \ldots, \sigma_m(x)$ are not pairwise equal:

    (b.1.1) For every $i \in \{1, \ldots, m\}$, let σ_i' denote the partial assignment which is undefined on x and otherwise matches σ_i. Verifier sends the challenges $\{\Pi_{\sigma_i'}[\![\psi]\!]\}_{i=1}^m$ to Prover. Prover answers with claims $\{\Pi_{\sigma_i'}[\![\psi]\!] = p_i\}_{i=1}^m$. Note that $p_1, \ldots, p_m$ are univariate polynomials with free variable x.

    (b.1.2) Verifier checks whether $k_i = \pi_{[x:=\sigma_i(x)]} p_i$ holds for each i. If not, Verifier rejects. Otherwise, Verifier picks $r \in \mathbb{F}$ uniformly at random and updates $\sigma_i(x) := r$ and $k_i := \pi_{[x:=r]} p_i$ for every $i \in \{1, \ldots, m\}$.

(b.2) If after exiting the loop the values $k_1, \ldots, k_m$ are not pairwise equal, Verifier rejects. Otherwise (that is, if $k_1 = k_2 = \cdots = k_m$), the set $\mathcal{C}$ now contains a unique claim $\Pi_\sigma[\![\psi]\!] = k$ relating to ψ.

Example 1. Consider the case in which $X = \{x\}$, and Prover has made two claims, $\Pi_{\sigma_1}[\![\psi]\!] = k_1$ and $\Pi_{\sigma_2}[\![\psi]\!] = k_2$ with $\sigma_1(x) = 1$ and $\sigma_2(x) = 2$. In step (b.1.1) we have $\sigma_1' = \sigma_2'$ (both are the empty assignment), and so Verifier sends the challenge $[\![\psi]\!]$ to Prover twice, who answers with claims $[\![\psi]\!] = p_1$ and $[\![\psi]\!] = p_2$. In step (b.1.2) Verifier checks that $p_1(1) = k_1$ and $p_2(2) = k_2$ hold, picks a random number r, and updates $\sigma_1(x) := \sigma_2(x) := r$ and $k_1 := p_1(r), k_2 := p_2(r)$. Now the condition of the while loop fails, so Verifier moves to (b.2) and checks $k_1 = k_2$.

Description of Step (c). Let $\Pi_\sigma[\![\psi]\!] = k$ be the claim computed by Verifier in step (b). Verifier removes this claim from $\mathcal{C}$ and replaces it by claims about the children of ψ, depending on the structure of ψ:

(c.1) If $\psi = \psi_1 \circledast \psi_2$, for a $\circledast \in \{\vee, \wedge\}$, then Verifier sends Prover challenges $\Pi_\sigma[\![\psi_i]\!]$ for $i \in \{1, 2\}$, and Prover sends claims $\Pi_\sigma[\![\psi_i]\!] = k_i$ back. Verifier checks the consistency condition $k = \pi_{[x:=k_1]} \pi_{[y:=k_2]} [\![x \circledast y]\!]$, rejecting if it does not hold. If the condition holds, the claim $\Pi_\sigma[\![\psi_i]\!] = k_i$ is added to $\mathcal{C}$, to be checked in the round for ψ_i.

(c.2) If $\psi = \neg\psi'$, then Verifier adds the claim $\Pi_\sigma[\![\psi']\!] = 1 - k$ to ψ'.

(c.3) If $\psi = \pi_{[x:=b]} \psi'$, Verifier sets $\sigma' := \sigma \cup \{x \mapsto b\}$ and adds the claim $\Pi_{\sigma'}[\![\psi']\!] = k$ to $\mathcal{C}$.

(c.4) If $\psi = \delta_x \psi'$, then Verifier sends Prover the challenge $\Pi_{\sigma'}[\![\psi']\!]$, where σ' denotes the partial assignment which is undefined on x and otherwise matches σ. Prover returns the claim $p := \Pi_{\sigma'}[\![\psi']\!]$. Observe that p is a univariate polynomial over x. Verifier checks the consistency condition $\pi_{[x:=\sigma(x)]} \delta_x p = k$, rejecting if it does not hold. If it holds, Verifier picks an $r \in \mathbb{F}$ uniformly at random, conducts the updates $\sigma(x) := r$ and $k := \pi_{[x:=r]} p$, and adds $\Pi_\sigma[\![\psi']\!] = k$ to the set of claims about ψ'.

This concludes the description of the interactive protocol. We now show CPCERTIFY is complete and sound.

Proposition 2 (CPCERTIFY **is complete and sound**). *Let φ be a CP with n free variables. Let $\Pi_\sigma[\![\text{conv}(\varphi)]\!] = K$ be the claim initially sent by Prover to Verifier. If the claim is true, then Prover has a strategy to make Verifier accept. If not, for every Prover, Verifier accepts with probability at most $4n|\varphi|/|\mathbb{F}|$.*

If the original claim is correct, Prover can answer every challenge truthfully and all claims pass all of Verifier's checks. So Verifier accepts. If the claim is not correct, we proceed round by round. We bound the probability that the Verifier is tricked in a single step to at most $2/|\mathbb{F}|$ using the Schwartz-Zippel Lemma. We then bound the number of such steps to $2n|\varphi|$ and use a union bound.

5   A BDD-Based Prover

We assume familiarity with *reduced ordered binary decision diagrams* (BDDs) [9]. We use BDDs over $X = \{x_1, \ldots, x_n\}$. We fix the variable order $x_1 < x_2 < \ldots < x_n$, i.e. the root node would decide based on the value of x_n.

Definition 4. *BDDs are defined inductively as follows:*

- *$\langle\text{true}\rangle$ and $\langle\text{false}\rangle$ are BDDs of level 0;*
- *if $u \neq v$ are BDDs of level ℓ_u, ℓ_v and $i > \ell_u, \ell_v$, then $\langle x_i, u, v\rangle$ is a BDD of level i;*
- *we identify $\langle x_i, u, u\rangle$ and u, for a BDD u of level ℓ_i and $i > \ell_u$.*

The level of a BDD w is denoted $\ell(w)$. The set of descendants *of w is the smallest set S with $w \in S$ and $u, v \in S$ for all $\langle x, u, v\rangle \in S$. The* size *$|w|$ of w is the number of its descendants.*

   The arithmetisation *of a BDD w is the polynomial $[\![w]\!]$ defined as follows: $[\![\langle\text{true}\rangle]\!] := 1$, $[\![\langle\text{false}\rangle]\!] := 0$ and $[\![\langle x, u, v\rangle]\!] := [1 - x] \cdot [\![u]\!] + [x] \cdot [\![v]\!]$.*

Figure 3 shows a BDD for the boolean function $\varphi(x, y, z) = (x \wedge y \wedge \neg z) \vee (\neg x \wedge y \wedge z) \vee (x \wedge \neg y \wedge z)$ and the arithmetisation of each node.

BDDSOLVER: **A BDD-based Algorithm for** #CP. An instance φ of #CP can be solved using BDDs. Starting at the leaves of φ, we iteratively compute a BDD for each node ψ of the circuit encoding the boolean predicate P_ψ. At the end of this procedure we obtain a BDD for P_φ. The number of satisfying assignments of ψ is the number of accepting paths of the BDD, which can be computed in linear time in the size of the BDD.

   For a node $\psi = \psi_1 \circledast \psi_2$, given BDDs representing the predicates P_{φ_1} and P_{φ_2}, we compute a BDD for the predicate $P_\varphi := P_{\varphi_1} \circledast P_{\varphi_2}$, using the Apply$_\circledast$ operator on BDDs. We name this algorithm for solving #CP "BDDSOLVER."

From BDDSOLVER **to** CPCERTIFY. Our goal is to modify BDDSOLVER to play the role of an honest Prover in CPCERTIFY with minimal overhead. In CPCERTIFY, Prover repeatedly performs the same task: evaluate polynomials of the form $\Pi_\sigma[\![\psi]\!]$, where ψ is a descendant of the CPD $\mathrm{conv}(\varphi)$, and σ assigns values to all free variables of ψ except possibly one. Therefore, the polynomials have at most one free variable and, as we have seen, degree at most 2.

Before defining the concepts precisely, we give a brief overview of this section.

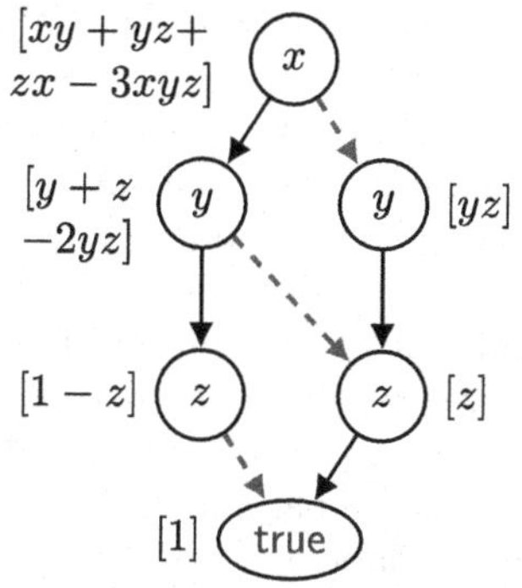

Fig. 3. A BDD and its arithmetisation. For $\langle x, u, v \rangle$, we denote the link from x to v with a solid edge and x to u with a dotted edge. We omit links to $\langle$false$\rangle$.

- First (Proposition 3), we show that BDDs correspond to binary multilinear polynomials. In particular, BDDs allow for efficient evaluation of the polynomial. As argued in Lemma 1(a), for every descendant ψ of φ, the CPD $\mathrm{conv}(\psi)$ (which is a descendant of $\mathrm{conv}(\varphi)$) evaluates to a multilinear polynomial. In particular, Prover can use standard BDD algorithms to calculate the corresponding polynomials $\Pi_\sigma[\![\psi]\!]$ for all descendants ψ of $\mathrm{conv}(\varphi)$ that are neither binary operators nor degree reductions.
- Second (the rest of the section), we prove a surprising connection: the intermediate results obtained while executing the BDD algorithms (with slight adaptations) correspond precisely to the remaining descendants of $\mathrm{conv}(\varphi)$.

The following proposition proves that BDDs represent exactly the binary multilinear polynomials.

Proposition 3. *(a) For a BDD w, $[\![w]\!]$ is a binary multilinear polynomial. (b) For a binary multilinear polynomial p there is a unique BDD w s.t. $p = [\![w]\!]$.*

5.1 Extended BDDs

During the execution of CPCERTIFY for a given CPD $\mathrm{conv}(\varphi)$, Prover sends to Verifier claims of the form $\Pi_\sigma[\![\psi]\!]$, where ψ is a descendant of $\mathrm{conv}(\varphi)$, and $\sigma \colon X \to \mathbb{F}$ is a partial assignment. While all polynomials computed by CPCERTIFY are binary, not all are multilinear: some polynomials have degree 2. For these polynomials, we introduce *extended BDDs* (eBDDs) and give eBDD-based algorithms for the following two tasks:

1. Compute an eBDD representing $[\![\psi]\!]$ for every node ψ of $\mathrm{conv}(\varphi)$.
2. Given an eBDD for $[\![\psi]\!]$ and a partial assignment σ, compute $\Pi_\sigma[\![\psi]\!]$.

Computing eBDDs for CPDs: Informal Introduction. Consider a CP φ and its associated CPD conv(φ). Each node of φ induces a chain of nodes in conv(φ), consisting of degree-reduction nodes $\delta_{x_1}, \ldots, \delta_{x_n}$, followed by the node itself (see Fig. 4). Given BDDs u and v for the children of the node in the CP, we can compute a BDD for the node itself using a well-known BDD algorithm $\text{Apply}_\circledast(u,v)$ parametric in the boolean operation $\circledast$ labelling the node [9]. Our goal is to transform $\text{Apply}_\circledast$ into an algorithm that computes eBDDs *for all nodes in the chain*, i.e. eBDDs for all the polynomials $p_0, p_1, \ldots, p_n$ of Fig. 4.

Fig. 4. A node of a CP ($\circledast$) gets a chain of degree reduction nodes in the associated CPD.

Roughly speaking, $\text{Apply}_\circledast(u,v)$ recursively computes BDDs $w_0 = \text{Apply}_\circledast(u_0, v_0)$ and $w_1 = \text{Apply}_\circledast(u_1, v_1)$, where u_b and v_b are the b-children of u and v, and then returns the BDD with w_0 and w_1 as 0- and 1-child, respectively.[3]

Most importantly, we modify $\text{Apply}_\circledast$ to run in breadth-first order. Figure 5 shows a graphical representation of a run of $\text{Apply}_\vee(u,v)$, where u and v are the two BDD nodes labelled by x. Square nodes represent pending calls to $\text{Apply}_\circledast$. Initially there is only one square call $\text{Apply}_\vee(u,v)$ (Fig. 5, top left). $\text{Apply}_\vee$ calls itself recursively for u_0, v_0 and u_1, v_1 (Fig. 5, top right). Each of the two calls splits again into two; however, the first three are identical (Fig. 5, bottom left), and so reduce to two. These two calls can now be resolved directly; they return nodes true and false, respectively. At this point, the children of $\text{Apply}_\circledast(u,v)$ become $\langle y, \text{true}, \text{true} \rangle = \text{true}$, and $\langle y, \text{true}, \text{false} \rangle$, which exists already as well (Fig. 5, bottom right).

We look at the diagrams of Fig. 5 not as a visualisation aid, but as graphs with two kinds of nodes: standard BDD nodes, represented as circles, and *product nodes*, represented as squares. We call them *extended BDDs*. Each node of an extended BDD is assigned a polynomial in the expected way: the polynomial $[\![u]\!]$ of a standard BDD node u with variable x is $x \cdot [\![u_1]\!] + (1-x) \cdot [\![u_0]\!]$, the polynomial $[\![v]\!]$ of a square $\wedge$-node v is $[\![v_0]\!] \cdot [\![v_1]\!]$, etc. In this way we assign to each eBDD a polynomial. In particular, we obtain the intermediate polynomials p_0, p_1, p_2, p_3 of the figure, one for each level in the recursion. In the rest of the section we show that these are *precisely* the polynomials $p_0, p_1, \ldots, p_n$ of Fig. 4.

Thus, in order to compute eBDDs for all nodes of a CPD conv(φ), it suffices to compute BDDs for all nodes of the CP φ. Since we need to do this anyway to solve #CP, the polynomial certification does not incur any overhead.

---

[3] In fact, this is only true when u and v are nodes at the same level and $\text{Apply}_\circledast(u_0, v_0) \neq \text{Apply}_\circledast(u_1, v_1)$, but at this point we only want to convey some intuition.

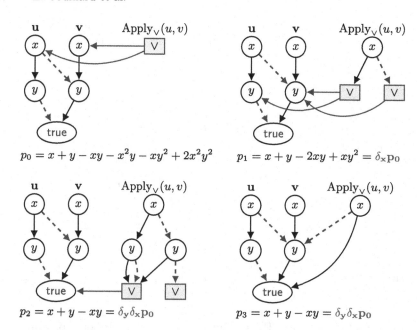

$$p_0 = x + y - xy - x^2y - xy^2 + 2x^2y^2 \qquad p_1 = x + y - 2xy + xy^2 = \delta_{\mathrm{x}}p_0$$

$$p_2 = x + y - xy = \delta_{\mathrm{y}}\delta_{\mathrm{x}}p_0 \qquad p_3 = x + y - xy = \delta_{\mathrm{y}}\delta_{\mathrm{x}}p_0$$

Fig. 5. Run of $\mathrm{Apply}_\vee(u,v)$, but with recursive calls evaluated in breadth-first order. All missing edges go to node false.

Extended BDDs. As for BDDs, we define eBDDs over $X = \{x_1, \ldots, x_n\}$ with the variable order $x_1 < x_2 < \ldots < x_n$.

Definition 5. *Let $\circledast$ be a binary boolean operator. The set of eBDDs (for $\circledast$) is inductively defined as follows:*

- *every BDD is also an eBDD of the same level;*
- *if u, v are BDDs (not eBDDs!), then $\langle u \circledast v \rangle$ is an eBDD of level l where $l := \max\{\ell(u), \ell(v)\}$; we call eBDDs of this form product nodes;*
- *if $u \neq v$ are eBDDs and $i > \ell(u), \ell(v)$, then $\langle x_i, u, v \rangle$ is an eBDD of level i;*
- *we identify $\langle x_i, u, u \rangle$ and u for an eBDD u and $i > \ell(u)$.*

The set of descendants of an eBDD w is the smallest set S with $w \in S$ and $u, v \in S$ for all $\langle u \circledast v \rangle, \langle x, u, v \rangle \in S$ The size of w is its number of descendants. For $u, v \in \{\langle \mathsf{true} \rangle, \langle \mathsf{false} \rangle\}$ we identify $\langle u \circledast v \rangle$ with $\langle \mathsf{true} \rangle$ or $\langle \mathsf{false} \rangle$ according to the result of $\circledast$, e.g. $\langle\langle \mathsf{true} \rangle \vee \langle \mathsf{false} \rangle\rangle = \langle \mathsf{true} \rangle$, as $\mathsf{true} \vee \mathsf{false} = \mathsf{true}$. The arithmetisation of an eBDD for a boolean operator $\circledast \in \{\wedge, \vee\}$ is defined as for BDDs, with the extensions $[\![\langle u \wedge v \rangle]\!] = [\![u]\!] \cdot [\![v]\!]$ and $[\![\langle u \vee v \rangle]\!] = [\![u]\!] + [\![v]\!] - [\![u]\!] \cdot [\![v]\!]$.

Example 2. The diagrams in Fig. 5 are eBDDs for $\circledast := \vee$. Nodes of the form $\langle x, u, v \rangle$ and $\langle u \vee v \rangle$ are represented as circles and squares, respectively. Consider the top-left diagram. Abbreviating $x \oplus y := (x \wedge \neg y) \vee (\neg x \wedge y)$ we get $[\![\mathrm{Apply}_\vee(u,v)]\!] = [\![(x \oplus y) \wedge (x \wedge y)]\!] = [\![x \oplus y]\!] \cdot [\![x \wedge y]\!] = (x(1-y) + (1-x) \cdot y - xy(1-x)(1-y)) \cdot xy$, which is the polynomial p_0 shown in the figure.

Table 1. On the left: Algorithm computing eBDDs for the sequence $[\![w]\!]$, $\delta_{x_n}[\![w]\!]$, $\delta_{x_{n-1}}\delta_{x_n}[\![w]\!]$, ..., $\delta_{x_1}\cdots\delta_{x_n}[\![w]\!]$ of polynomials. On the right: Recursive algorithm to evaluate the polynomial represented by an eBDD at a given partial assignment. $P(w)$ is a mapping used to memoize the polynomials returned by recursive calls.

COMPUTEEBDD(w)

Input: eBDD w

Output: sequence $w_0, ..., w_n$ of eBDDs

$w_0 := w$; output w_0

for $i = 0, \cdots, \ell(w) - 1$ do

  $w_{i+1} := w_i$

  for every node $\langle u \circledast v \rangle$ of w_i

    at level $n - i$ do

  for $b \in \{0, 1\}$ do

    $u_b := \pi_{[x_{n-i} := b]} u$

    $v_b := \pi_{[x_{n-i} := b]} v$

    $t_b := \langle u_b \circledast v_b \rangle$

    $w_{i+1} := w_{i+1}[\langle u \circledast v \rangle / \langle x_{n-i}, t_0, t_1 \rangle]$

output w_{i+1}

EVALUATEEBDD(w, σ) $=: E_\sigma(w)$

Input: eBDD w; assignment $\sigma \colon X \to \mathbb{F}$

Output: $\Pi_\sigma[\![w]\!]$

if $P(w)$ is defined return $P(w)$

if $w \in \{\langle\text{true}\rangle, \langle\text{false}\rangle\}$ return $[\![w]\!]$

if $w = \langle u \wedge v \rangle$

  $P(w) := E_\sigma(u) \cdot E_\sigma(v)$

if $w = \langle u \vee v \rangle$

  $P(w) := E_\sigma(u) + E_\sigma(v) - E_\sigma(u)E_\sigma(v)$

if $w = \langle x, u, v \rangle$ and $\sigma(x)$ undefined

  $P(w) := [1 - x] \cdot E_\sigma(u) + [x] \cdot E_\sigma(v)$

if $w = \langle x, u, v \rangle$ and $\sigma(x) = s \in \mathbb{F}$

  $P(w) := [1 - s] \cdot E_\sigma(u) + [s] \cdot E_\sigma(v)$

return $P(w)$

Computing eBDDs for CPDs. Given a node of a CP corresponding to a binary operator $\circledast$, Prover has to compute polynomials $p_0, \delta_{x_1}p_0, \ldots, \delta_{x_n}\ldots\delta_{x_1}p_0$ corresponding to the nodes of the CPD shown on the right. We show that Prover can compute these polynomials by representing them as eBDDs. Table 1 describes an algorithm that gets as input an eBDD w of level n, and outputs a sequence $w_0, w_1, ..., w_{n+1}$ of eBDDs such that $w_0 = w$; $[\![w_{i+1}]\!] = \delta_{x_{n-i}}[\![w_i]\!]$ for every $0 \le i \le \ell(w) - 1$; and w_{n+1} is a BDD. Interpreted as sequence of eBDDs, Fig. 5 shows a run of this algorithm.

Notation. Given an eBDD w and eBDDs u, v such that $\ell(u) \ge \ell(v)$, we let $w[u/v]$ denote the result of replacing u by v in w. For an eBDD $w = \langle x_i, w_0, w_1 \rangle$ and $b \in \{0, 1\}$ we define $\pi_{[x_i := b]}w := w_b$, and for $j > i$ we set $\pi_{[x_j := b]}w := w$. (Note that $[\![\pi_{[x_j := b]}w]\!] = \pi_{[x_j := b]}[\![w]\!]$ holds for any j where it is defined.)

Proposition 4. *Let ψ_1, ψ_2 denote CPs and u_1, u_2 BDDs with $[\![u_i]\!] = [\![\psi_i]\!]$, $i \in \{1, 2\}$. Let $w := \langle u_1 \circledast u_2 \rangle$ denote an eBDD. Then* COMPUTEEBDD(w) *satisfies $[\![w_0]\!] = [\![\psi_1 \circledast \psi_2]\!]$ and $[\![w_{i+1}]\!] = \delta_{x_{n-i}}[\![w_i]\!]$ for every $0 \le i \le n - 1$; moreover, w_n is a BDD with $w_n = \text{Apply}_\circledast(u_1, u_2)$. Finally, the algorithm runs in time $\mathcal{O}(T)$, where $T \in \mathcal{O}(|u_1| \cdot |u_2|)$ is the time taken by $\text{Apply}_\circledast(u_1, u_2)$.*

Evaluating Polynomials Represented as eBDDs. Recall that Prover must evaluate expressions of the form $\Pi_\sigma[\![\psi]\!]$ for some CPD ψ, where σ assigns values to all variables of ψ except for possibly one. We give an algorithm to evaluate arbitrary expressions $\Pi_\sigma[\![w]\!]$, where w is an eBDD, and show that if there is at most one free variable then the algorithm takes linear time in the size of ψ. The algorithm is shown on the right of Table 1. It has the standard structure of BDD procedures: It recurs on the structure of the eBDD, memoizing the result of recursive calls so that the algorithm is called at most once with a given input.

Proposition 5. *Let w denote an eBDD, $\sigma : X \to \mathbb{F}$ a partial assignment, and k the number of variables assigned by σ. Then* EVALUATEEBDD *evaluates the polynomial $\Pi_\sigma[\![w]\!]$ in time $\mathcal{O}\big(\text{poly}(2^{n-k}) \cdot |w|\big)$.*

5.2   Efficient Certification

In the CPCERTIFY algorithm, Prover must (a) compute polynomials for all nodes of the CPD, and (b) evaluate them on assignments chosen by Verifier. In the last section we have seen that COMPUTEEBDD (for binary operations of the CP), combined with standard BDD algorithms (for all other operations), yields eBDDs representing all these polynomials—at no additional overhead, compared to a BDD-based implementation. This covers part (a). Regarding (b), recall that all polynomials computed in (a) have at most one variable. Therefore, using EVALUATEEBDD we can evaluate a polynomial in linear time in the size of the eBDD representing it.

The Verifier CPCERTIFY is implemented in a straightforward manner. As the algorithm runs in polynomial size w.r.t. the CP (and not the computed BDDs, which may be exponentially larger), incurring overhead is less of a concern.

Theorem 1 (Main Result). *If* BDDSOLVER *solves an instance φ of #CP with n variables in time T, with $T > n|\varphi|$, then*

(a) Prover computes eBDDs for all nodes of $\text{conv}(\varphi)$ in time $\mathcal{O}(T)$,
(b) Prover responds to Verifier's challenges in time $\mathcal{O}(nT)$, and
(c) Verifier executes CPCERTIFY *in time $\mathcal{O}(n^2|\varphi|)$, with failure probability at most $4n|\varphi|/|\mathbb{F}|$.*

As presented above, EVALUATEEBDD incurs a factor-of-n overhead, as every node of the CPD must be evaluated. In our implementation, we use a caching strategy to reduce the complexity of Theorem 1(b) to $\mathcal{O}(T)$.

Note that the bounds above assume a uniform cost model. In particular, operations on BDD nodes and finite field arithmetic are assumed to be $\mathcal{O}(1)$. This is a reasonable assumption, as for a constant failure probability $\log|\mathbb{F}| \approx \log n$. Hence the finite field remains small. (It is possible to verify the number of assignments even if it exceeds $|\mathbb{F}|$, see below.)

5.3   Implementation Concerns

We list a number of points that are not described in detail in this paper, but need to be considered for an efficient implementation.

Finite Field Arithmetic. It is not necessary to use large finite fields. In particular, one can avoid the overhead of arbitrarily sized integers. For our implementation we fix the finite field $\mathbb{F} := \mathbb{Z}_p$, with $p = 2^{61} - 1$ (the largest Mersenne prime to fit in 64 bits).

Incremental eBDD Representation. Algorithm COMPUTEEBDD computes a sequence of eBDDs. These must not be stored explicitly, otherwise one incurs a space-overhead. Instead, we only store the last eBDD as well as the differences between each subsequent element of the sequence. To evaluate the eBDDs, we then revert to a previous state by applying the differences appropriately.

Evaluation Order. It simplifies the implementation if Prover only needs to evaluate nodes of the CPD in some (fixed) topological order. CPCERTIFY can easily be adapted to guarantee this, by picking the next node appropriately in each iteration, and by evaluating only one child of a binary operator $\psi_1 \circledast \psi_2$. The value of the other child can then be derived by solving a linear equation.

Efficient Evaluation. As stated in Theorem 1, using EVALUATEEBDD Prover needs $\Omega(nT)$ time to respond to Verifier's challenges. In our implementation we instead use a caching strategy that reduces this time to $\mathcal{O}(T)$. Essentially, we exploit the special structure of $\text{conv}(\varphi)$: Verifier sends a sequence of challenges $\Pi_{\sigma_0} \delta_{x_1} ... \delta_{x_n} w, \Pi_{\sigma_1} \delta_{x_2} ... \delta_{x_n} w, ..., \Pi_{\sigma_n} w$, where assignments σ_i and σ_{i+1} differ only in variables x_i and x_{i+1}. The corresponding eBDDs likewise change only at levels i and $i + 1$. We cache the linear coefficients of eBDD nodes that contribute to the arithmetisation of the root top-down, and the arithmetised values of nodes bottom up. As a result, only levels $i, i + 1$ need to be updated.

Large Numbers of Assignments. If the number of satisfying assignments of a CP exceeds $|\mathbb{F}|$, Verifier would not be able to verify the count accurately. Instead of choosing $|\mathbb{F}| \geq 2^n$, which incurs a significant overhead, Verifier can query the precise number of assignments, and then choose $|\mathbb{F}|$ randomly. This introduces another possibility of failure, but (roughly speaking) it suffices to double $\log |\mathbb{F}|$ for the additional failure probability to match the existing one. Our implementation does not currently support this technique.

6 Evaluation

We have implemented an eBDD library, blic (BDD Library with Interactive Certification)[4], that is a stand-in replacement for BDDs but additionally performs the role of Prover in the CPCERTIFY protocol. We have also implemented a client that executes the protocol as Verifier. The eBDD library is about 900 lines of C++ code and the CPCERTIFY protocol is about 400 lines. We have built a prototype certifying QBF solver in blic, totalling about 2600 lines of code. We aim to answer the following questions in our evaluation:

RQ1. Is a QBF solver with CPCERTIFY-based certification competitive? If so, how high is the overhead of implementing CPCERTIFY on top of the BDD operations?

RQ2. What is the amount of communication for Prover and Verifier in executing the CPCERTIFY protocol, what is the time requirement for Verifier, and how do these numbers compare to proof sizes and proof checking times for certificates based on resolution and other proof systems?

---

[4] https://gitlab.lrz.de/i7/blic.

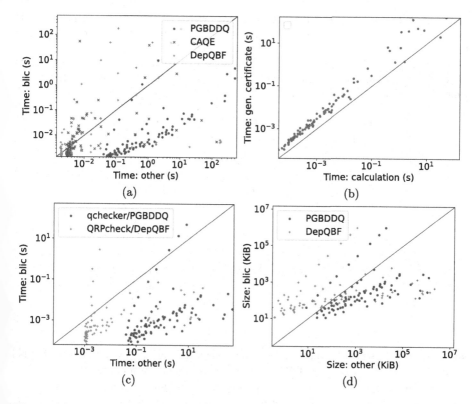

Fig. 6. (a) Time taken on instances (dashed lines are $y = 100x$ and $y = 0.01x$), (b) Cost of generating a certificate over computing the solution, (c) Time to verify the certificate, (d) Size of certificates

RQ1: Performance of blic. We compare blic with CAQE, DepQBF, and PGB-DDQ, three state-of-the-art QBF solvers. CAQE [10,29] does not provide any certificates in its most recent version. DepQBF [12,19] is a certifying QBF solver. PGBDDQ [7,25] is an independent implementation of a BDD-based QBF solver. Both DepQBF and PGBDDQ provide specialised checkers for their certificates, though PGBDDQ can also proofs in standard QRAT format. Note that PGBDDQ is written in Python and generates proofs in an ASCII-based format, incurring overhead compared to the other tools.

We take 172 QBF instances (all unsatisfiable) from the *Crafted Instances* track of the QBF Evaluation 2022.[5] The *Prenex CNF* track of the QBF competition is not evaluated here. It features instances with a large number of variables. BDD-based solvers perform poorly under these circumstances without additional optimisations. Our overall goal is not to propose a new approach for

---

[5] CAQE and DepQBF were the winner and runner-up in this category. The configuration we used differs from the competition, as described in the full version of the paper [11].

Table 2. Comparison of certificate generation, bytes exchanged between prover and verifier, and time taken to verify the certificate on a set of QBF benchmarks from [7]. "Solve time" is time taken to solve the instance and to generate a certificate (seconds), "Certificate" is the size of proof encoding for PGBDDQ, and bytes exchanged by CPCERTIFY for blic, and "Verifier time" is time to verify the certificate (Verifier's run time for blic and time taken by qchecker).

Instance		Solve time (s)		Certificate (MiB)		Verifier time (s)	
n	result	blic	PGBDDQ	blic	PGBDDQ	blic	qchecker
10	sat	0.03	3.67	1.20	8.48	0.01	3.80
10	unsat	0.03	3.66	1.20	8.45	0.01	3.83
15	sat	0.13	18.07	4.12	44.25	0.02	18.45
15	unsat	0.13	18.14	4.11	44.20	0.02	18.55
20	sat	0.54	82.92	11.59	198.54	0.07	80.28
20	unsat	0.53	83.02	11.64	198.76	0.06	79.05
25	sat	1.56	261.16	23.94	566.95	0.14	238.99
25	unsat	1.55	261.25	23.86	565.36	0.15	237.94
40	sat	25.22	4863.71	132.43	7464.96	0.95	5141.08
40	unsat	25.25	4827.06	132.67	7467.84	0.99	5463.54

solving QBF, but rather to certify a BDD-based approach, so we wanted to focus on cases where the existing BDD-based approaches are practical.

We ran each benchmark with a 10 min timeout; all tools other than CAQE were run with certificate production. All times were obtained on a machine with an Intel Xeon E7-8857 CPU and 1.58 TiB RAM[6] running Linux. See the full version of the paper [11] for a detailed description. blic solved 96 out of 172 benchmarks, CAQE solved 98, DepQBF solved 87, and PGBDDQ solved 91. Figure 6(a) shows the run times of blic compared to the other tools. The plot indicates that blic is competitive on these instances, with a few cases, mostly from the Lonsing family of benchmarks, where blic is slower than DepQBF by an order of magnitude. Figure 6(b) shows the overhead of certification: for each benchmark (that finishes within a 10min timeout), we plot the ratio of the time to compute the answer to the time it takes to run Prover in CPCERTIFY. The dotted regression line shows CPCERTIFY has a 2.8× overhead over computing BDDs. For this set of examples, the error probability never exceeds $10^{-8.9}$ ($10^{-11.6}$ when Lonsing examples are excluded); running the verifier k times reduces it to $10^{-8.9k}$.

RQ2: Communication Cost of Certification and Verifier Time. We explore **RQ2** by comparing the number of bytes exchanged between Prover and Verifier and the time needed for Verifier to execute CPCERTIFY with the number of bytes in an QBF proof and the time required to verify the proof produced by DepQBF and PGBDDQ, for which we use QRPcheck [24,26] and qchecker [7,25], respectively. Note that the latter is written in Python.

---

[6] blic uses at most 60 GiB on the shown benchmarks, 5 GiB when excluding timeouts.

We show that the overhead of certification is low. Figure 6(c) shows the run time of Verifier—this is generally negligible for blic, except for the Lonsing and KBKF families, which have a large number of variables, but very small BDDs. Figure 6(d) shows the total number of bytes exchanged between Prover and Verifier in blic against the size of the proofs generated by PGBDDQ and DepQBF. For large instances, the number of bytes exchanged in blic is significantly smaller than the size of the proofs. The exception are again the Lonsing and KBKNF families of instances. For both plots, the dotted line results from a log-linear regression.

In addition to the Crafted Instances, we compare against PGBDDQ on a challenging family of benchmarks used in the PGBDDQ paper (matching the parameters of [7, Table 3]); these are QBF encodings of a linear domino placing game.[7] Our results are summarised in Table 2. The upper bound on Verifier error is $10^{-9.22}$. We show that blic outperforms PGBDDQ both in overall cost of computing the answer and the certificates as well as in the number of bytes communicated and the time used by Verifier.

Our results indicate that giving up absolute certainty through interactive protocols can lead to an order of magnitude smaller communication cost and several orders of magnitude smaller checking costs for the verifier.

7   Conclusion

We have presented a solver that combines BDDs with an interactive protocol. blic can be seen as a self-certifying BDD library able to certify the correctness of arbitrary sequences of BDD operations. In order to trust the result, a user must only trust the verifier (a straightforward program that poses challenges to the prover). We have shown that blic (including certification time) is competitive with other solvers, and Verifier's time and error probabilities are negligible.

Our results show that IP = PSPACE can become an important result not only in theory but also in the practice of automatic verification. From this perspective, our paper is a first step towards practical certification based on interactive protocols. While we have focused on BDDs, we can ask the more general question: which practical automated reasoning algorithms can be made efficiently certifying? For example, whether there is an interactive protocol and an efficient certifying version of modern SAT solving algorithms is an interesting open challenge.

References

1. Arora, S., Barak, B.: Computational Complexity: A Modern Approach. Cambridge University Press, Cambridge (2006). https://theory.cs.princeton.edu/complexity/book.pdf

---

[7] DepQBF only solved 1 of 10 instances within 120 min, and is thus not compared.

2. Babai, L.: Trading group theory for randomness. In: Sedgewick, R. (ed.) Proceedings of the 17th Annual ACM Symposium on Theory of Computing, 6–8 May 1985, Providence, Rhode Island, USA, pp. 421–429. ACM (1985). https://doi.org/10.1145/22145.22192

3. Balabanov, V., Widl, M., Jiang, J.-H.R.: QBF resolution systems and their proof complexities. In: Sinz, C., Egly, U. (eds.) SAT 2014. LNCS, vol. 8561, pp. 154–169. Springer, Cham (2014). https://doi.org/10.1007/978-3-319-09284-3_12

4. Barbosa, H., et al.: Flexible proof production in an industrial-strength SMT solver. In: Blanchette, J., Kovács, L., Pattinson, D. (eds.) IJCAR 2022. LNCS, vol. 13385, pp. 15–35. Springer, Cham (2022). https://doi.org/10.1007/978-3-031-10769-6_3

5. Ben-Or, M., Goldreich, O., Goldwasser, S., Håstad, J., Kilian, J., Micali, S., Rogaway, P.: Everything provable is provable in zero-knowledge. In: Goldwasser, S. (ed.) CRYPTO 1988. LNCS, vol. 403, pp. 37–56. Springer, New York (1990). https://doi.org/10.1007/0-387-34799-2_4

6. Bryant, R.E., Biere, A., Heule, M.J.H.: Clausal proofs for pseudo-boolean reasoning. In: TACAS 2022. LNCS, vol. 13243, pp. 443–461. Springer, Cham (2022). https://doi.org/10.1007/978-3-030-99524-9_25

7. Bryant, R.E., Heule, M.J.H.: Dual proof generation for quantified boolean formulas with a BDD-based solver. In: Platzer, A., Sutcliffe, G. (eds.) CADE 2021. LNCS (LNAI), vol. 12699, pp. 433–449. Springer, Cham (2021). https://doi.org/10.1007/978-3-030-79876-5_25

8. Bryant, R.E., Heule, M.J.H.: Generating extended resolution proofs with a BDD-based SAT solver. In: TACAS 2021. LNCS, vol. 12651, pp. 76–93. Springer, Cham (2021). https://doi.org/10.1007/978-3-030-72016-2_5

9. Bryant, R.: Graph-based algorithms for Boolean function manipulation. IEEE Trans. Comput. **C-35**(8), 677–691 (1986)

10. CAQE (2023). https://github.com/ltentrup/caqe. Accessed 03 Feb 2023

11. Couillard, E., Czerner, P., Esparza, J., Majumdar, R.: Making IP=PSPACE practical: efficient interactive protocols for BDD algorithms. CoRR abs/2305.11813 (2023). https://doi.org/10.48550/arXiv.2305.11813

12. DepQBF (2017). https://github.com/lonsing/depqbf. Accessed 03 Feb 2023

13. Goldwasser, S., Micali, S., Rackoff, C.: The knowledge complexity of interactive proof-systems (extended abstract). In: Sedgewick, R. (ed.) Proceedings of the 17th Annual ACM Symposium on Theory of Computing, 6–8 May 1985, Providence, Rhode Island, USA, pp. 291–304. ACM (1985). https://doi.org/10.1145/22145.22178

14. Henzinger, T.A., Necula, G.C., Jhala, R., Sutre, G., Majumdar, R., Weimer, W.: Temporal-safety proofs for systems code. In: Brinksma, E., Larsen, K.G. (eds.) CAV 2002. LNCS, vol. 2404, pp. 526–538. Springer, Heidelberg (2002). https://doi.org/10.1007/3-540-45657-0_45

15. Heule, M.: Everything's bigger in Texas: "the largest math proof ever". In: Benzmüller, C., Lisetti, C.L., Theobald, M. (eds.) GCAI 2017, 3rd Global Conference on Artificial Intelligence, Miami, FL, USA, 18–22 October 2017. EPiC Series in Computing, vol. 50, pp. 1–5. EasyChair (2017). https://doi.org/10.29007/gdw8

16. Heule, M.J.H.: Proofs of unsatisfiability. In: Biere, A., Heule, M., van Maaren, H., Walsh, T. (eds.) Handbook of Satisfiability - Second Edition, Frontiers in Artificial Intelligence and Applications, vol. 336, pp. 635–668. IOS Press (2021). https://doi.org/10.3233/FAIA200998

17. Jussila, T., Sinz, C., Biere, A.: Extended resolution proofs for symbolic SAT solving with quantification. In: Biere, A., Gomes, C.P. (eds.) SAT 2006. LNCS, vol. 4121, pp. 54–60. Springer, Heidelberg (2006). https://doi.org/10.1007/11814948_8

18. Katz, G., Barrett, C.W., Tinelli, C., Reynolds, A., Hadarean, L.: Lazy proofs for DPLL(T)-based SMT solvers. In: Piskac, R., Talupur, M. (eds.) 2016 Formal Methods in Computer-Aided Design, FMCAD 2016, Mountain View, CA, USA, 3–6 October 2016, pp. 93–100. IEEE (2016). https://doi.org/10.1109/FMCAD.2016.7886666

19. Lonsing, F., Egly, U.: DepQBF 6.0: a search-based QBF solver beyond traditional QCDCL. In: de Moura, L. (ed.) CADE 2017. LNCS (LNAI), vol. 10395, pp. 371–384. Springer, Cham (2017). https://doi.org/10.1007/978-3-319-63046-5_23

20. Lund, C., Fortnow, L., Karloff, H.J., Nisan, N.: Algebraic methods for interactive proof systems. J. ACM **39**(4), 859–868 (1992). https://doi.org/10.1145/146585.146605

21. Luo, N., Antonopoulos, T., Harris, W.R., Piskac, R., Tromer, E., Wang, X.: Proving UNSAT in zero knowledge. In: Yin, H., Stavrou, A., Cremers, C., Shi, E. (eds.) Proceedings of the 2022 ACM SIGSAC Conference on Computer and Communications Security, CCS 2022, Los Angeles, CA, USA, 7–11 November 2022, pp. 2203–2217. ACM (2022). https://doi.org/10.1145/3548606.3559373

22. Namjoshi, K.S.: Certifying model checkers. In: Berry, G., Comon, H., Finkel, A. (eds.) CAV 2001. LNCS, vol. 2102, pp. 2–13. Springer, Heidelberg (2001). https://doi.org/10.1007/3-540-44585-4_2

23. Necula, G.: Proof-carrying code. In: Principles of Programming Languages, pp. 106–119. ACM Press (1997)

24. Niemetz, A., Preiner, M., Lonsing, F., Seidl, M., Biere, A.: Resolution-based certificate extraction for QBF. In: Cimatti, A., Sebastiani, R. (eds.) SAT 2012. LNCS, vol. 7317, pp. 430–435. Springer, Heidelberg (2012). https://doi.org/10.1007/978-3-642-31612-8_33

25. PGBDDQ (2023). https://github.com/rebryant/pgbdd. Accessed 03 Feb 2023

26. QRPcheck (2023). http://fmv.jku.at/qrpcheck/. Accessed 03 Feb 2023

27. Shamir, A.: IP = PSPACE. J. ACM **39**(4), 869–877 (1992). https://doi.org/10.1145/146585.146609

28. Sinz, C., Biere, A.: Extended resolution proofs for conjoining BDDs. In: Grigoriev, D., Harrison, J., Hirsch, E.A. (eds.) CSR 2006. LNCS, vol. 3967, pp. 600–611. Springer, Heidelberg (2006). https://doi.org/10.1007/11753728_60

29. Tentrup, L., Rabe, M.N.: Clausal abstraction for DQBF. In: Janota, M., Lynce, I. (eds.) SAT 2019. LNCS, vol. 11628, pp. 388–405. Springer, Cham (2019). https://doi.org/10.1007/978-3-030-24258-9_27

Ownership Guided C to Rust Translation

Hanliang Zhang[1], Cristina David[1], Yijun Yu[2], and Meng Wang[1(✉)]

[1] University of Bristol, Bristol, UK
{pd21541,cristina.david,meng.wang}@bristol.ac.uk
[2] The Open University, Milton Keynes, UK
yijun.yu@open.ac.uk

Abstract. Dubbed a safer C, Rust is a modern programming language that combines memory safety and low-level control. This interesting combination has made Rust very popular among developers and there is a growing trend of migrating legacy codebases (very often in C) to Rust. In this paper, we present a C to Rust translation approach centred around static ownership analysis. We design a suite of analyses that infer ownership models of C pointers and automatically translate the pointers into safe Rust equivalents. The resulting tool, CROWN, scales to real-world codebases (half a million lines of code in less than 10 s) and achieves a high conversion rate.

1 Introduction

Rust [33] is a modern programming language which features an exciting combination of memory safety and low-level control. In particular, Rust takes inspiration from ownership types to restrict the mutation of shared state. The Rust compiler is able to statically verify the corresponding ownership constraints and consequently guarantee memory and thread safety. This distinctive advantage of provable safety makes Rust a very popular language, and the prospect of migrating legacy codebases in C to Rust is very appealing.

In response to this demand, automated tools translating C code to Rust emerge from both industry and academia [17,26,31]. Among them, the industrial strength translator C2Rust [26] rewrites C code into the Rust syntax while preserving the original semantics. The translation does not synthesise an ownership model and thus is not able to do more than replicating the unsafe use of pointers in C. Consequently, the Rust code must be labelled with the unsafe keyword which allows certain actions that are not checked by the compiler. More recent work focuses on reducing this unsafe labelling. In particular, the tool Laertes [17] aims to rewrite the (unsafe) code produced by C2Rust by searching the solution space guided by the type error messages from the Rust compiler. This is impressive, as for the first time proper Rust code beyond a line-by-line direct conversion from the original C source may be synthesised. On the other hand, the limit of the trial-and-error approach is also clear: the system does not support the reasoning of the generation process, nor create any new understanding of the target code (other than the fact that it compiles successfully).

C. Enea and A. Lal (Eds.): CAV 2023, LNCS 13966, pp. 459–482, 2023.
https://doi.org/10.1007/978-3-031-37709-9_22

In this paper, we take a more principled approach by developing a novel ownership analysis of pointers that is efficient (scaling to large programs (half a million LOC in less than 10 s)), sophisticated (handling nested pointers and inductively-defined data structures), and precise (being field and flow sensitive). Our ownership analysis makes a strengthening assumption about the Rust ownership model, which obviates the need for an aliasing analysis. While this assumption excludes a few safe Rust uses (see discussion in Sect. 5), it ensures that the ownership analysis is both scalable and precise, which is subsequently reflected in the overall scalability and precision of the C to Rust translation.

The primary goal of this analysis is of course to facilitate the C to Rust translation. Indeed, as we will see in the rest of the paper, an automated translation system is built to encode the ownership models in the generated Rust code which is then proven safe by the Rust compiler. However, in contrast to trying the Rust compiler as common in existing approaches [17,31], this analysis approach actually extracts new knowledge about ownership from code, which may lead to other future utilities including preventing memory leaks (currently allowed in safe Rust), identifying inherently unsafe code fragments, and so on. Our current contributions are:

- design a scalable and precise ownership analysis that is able to handle complex inductively-defined data structures and nested pointers. (Section 5)
- develop a refactoring technique for Rust leveraging ownership analyses to enhance code safety. While in this paper we focus on applying our technique to the translation from C to Rust, it can be used to improve the safety of any unsafe Rust code. (Section 6)
- implement a prototype tool (CROWN, standing for C to Rust OWNership guided translation) that translates C code into Rust with enhanced safety. (Section 7)
- evaluate CROWN with a benchmark suite including commonly used data structure libraries and real-world projects (ranging from 150 to half a million LOC) and compare the result with the state-of-the-art. (Section 8)

2   Background

We start by giving a brief introduction of Rust, in particular its ownership system and the use of pointers, as they are central to memory safety.

2.1   Rust Ownership Model

Ownership in Rust denotes a set of rules that govern how the Rust compiler manages memory [33]. The idea is to associate each value with a *unique* owner. This feature is useful for memory management. For example, when the owner goes out of scope, the memory allocated for the value can be automatically recycled.

```
1 let mut v = ...
2 let mut u = v;          // ownership is transferred to u
```

In the above snippet, the assignment of v to u also transfers ownership, after which it is illegal to access v until it is re-assigned a value again.

This permanent transfer of ownership gives strong guarantees but can be cumbersome to manage in programming. In order to allow sharing of values between different parts of the program, Rust uses the concept of *borrowing*, which refers to creating a *reference* (marked by an ampersand). A reference allows referring to some value without taking ownership of it. Borrowing gives the temporary right to read and, potentially, uniquely mutate the referenced value.

This concept of time creates another dimension of ownership management known as *lifetime*. For mutable references (as marked by mut in the above examples), only one reference is allowed at a time. But for immutable references (the ones without the mut marking), multiple of them can coexist as long as there isn't any mutable reference at the same time. As one can expect, this interaction of mutable and immutable references, and their lifetimes is highly non-trivial. In this paper, we focus on analysing mutable references.

2.2 Pointer Types in Rust

Rust has a richer pointer system than C. The primitive C-style pointers (written as *const T or *mut T) are known as *raw pointers*, which are ignored by the Rust compiler for ownership and lifetime checks. Raw pointers are a major source of unsafe Rust (more below). Idiomatic Rust instead advocates *box pointers* (written as Box<T>) as owning pointers that uniquely own heap allocations, as well as *references* (written as &mut T or & T as discussed in the previous subsection) as non-owning pointers that are used to access values owned by others. Rust also offers smart pointers for which the borrow rules are checked at runtime (e.g. RefCell<T>). We aim for our translation to maintain CPU time without additional runtime overhead, and therefore we do not refactor raw pointers into RefCell<T>s.

C-style array pointers are represented in Rust as references to arrays and slice references, with array bounds known at compile time and runtime, respectively. The creation of meta-data such as array bounds is beyond the scope of ownership analysis. In this work, we keep array pointers as raw pointers in the translated code.

2.3 Unsafe Rust

As a pragmatic design, Rust allows programs to contain features that cannot be verified by the compiler as memory safe. This includes dereferencing raw pointers, calling low level functions, and so on. Such uses must be marked with the unsafe keyword and form fragments of *unsafe Rust*. It is worth noting that unsafe does not turn off all compiler checks; safe pointers are still checked.

Unsafe Rust is often used to implement data structures with complex sharing, overcome incompleteness issues of the Rust compiler, and support low-level systems programming [2,18]. But it can also be used for other reasons. For example, c2rust [26] directly translates C pointers into raw pointers. Without unsafe Rust, the generated code would not compile.

3   Overview

In this section, we present an overview of CROWN via two examples. The first example provides a detailed description of the push method for a singly-linked list, whereas the second shows a snippet from a real-world benchmark.

```
1  struct Node {
2      int data;
3      struct Node * next;
4  };
5
6  struct List {
7      Node * head;
8  };
9
10 void push(struct List* list, int
       new_data) {
11     struct Node* new_node = (struct
       Node*) malloc(sizeof(struct
       Node));
12     new_node->data = new_data;
13     new_node->next = list->head;
14     list->head    = new_node;
15 }
16
```

(a) C code

```
1  #[repr(C)]
2  #[derive(Copy, Clone)]
3  pub struct Node {
4      pub data: i32,
5      pub next: *mut Node,
6  }
7
8  #[repr(C)]
9  #[derive(Copy, Clone)]
10 pub struct List {
11     pub head: *mut Node,
12 }
13
14 pub unsafe extern "C" fn push(mut
       list: *mut List, mut
       new_data: i32) {
15     let mut new_node = malloc(::std
       ::mem::size_of::<Node>() as
       libc::c_ulong) as *mut Node;
16     (*new_node).data = new_data;
17     (*new_node).next = (*list).head;
18     (*list).head = new_node;
19 }
20
```

(b) c2rust result

```
1  #[repr(C)]
2  pub struct Node {
3      pub data: i32,
4      pub next: Option<Box<Node>>,
5  }
6
7  #[repr(C)]
8  pub struct List {
9      pub head: Option<Box<Node>>,
10 }
11
12 pub unsafe extern "C" fn push(mut
       list: Option<&mut List>, mut
       new_data: i32) {
13     let mut new_node = Some(Box::new
       (<Node as Default>::default
       ()));
14     (*new_node.as_deref_mut().unwrap
       ()).data = new_data;
15     (*new_node.as_deref_mut().unwrap
       ()).next = (*list.
       as_deref_mut().unwrap()).
       head.take();
16     (*list.as_deref_mut().unwrap()).
       head = new_node;
17 }
18
```

(c) CROWN result

Fig. 1. Pushing into a singly-linked list

3.1   Pushing into a Singly-Linked List

The C code of function push in Fig. 1a allocates a new node where it stores the data received as argument. The new node subsequently becomes the head of list. This code is translated by c2rust to the Rust code in Fig. 1b. Notably, the c2rust translation is syntax-based and simply changes all the C pointers to *mut raw pointers. Given that dereferencing raw pointers is considered an unsafe operation in Rust (e.g. the dereferencing of new_node at line 16 in Fig. 1b), the push method must be annotated with the unsafe keyword (alternatively, it could be placed inside an unsafe block). Additionally, c2rust introduces two directives for the two struct definitions, #[repr(C)] and #[derive(Copy, Clone)]. The former keeps the data layout the same as in C for possible interoperation, and the latter instructs that the corresponding type can only be duplicated through copying.

While c2rust uses raw pointers in the translation, the ownership scheme in Fig. 1b obeys the Rust ownership model, meaning that the raw pointers could be translated to safe ones. A pointer to a newly allocated node is assigned to new_node at line 15. This allows us to infer that the ownership of the newly allocated node belongs to new_node. Then, at line 18, the ownership is transferred from new_node to (*list).head. Additionally, if (*list).head owns any memory object prior to line 17, then its ownership is transferred to (*new_node).next at line 17. This ownership scheme corresponds to safe pointer use: (i) each memory object is associated with a unique owner and (ii) it is dropped when its owner goes out of scope. As an illustration for (i), when the ownership of the newly allocated memory is transferred from new_node to (*list).head at line 18, (*list).head becomes the unique owner, whereas new_node is made invalid and it is no longer used. For (ii), given that argument list of push is an output parameter (i.e. a parameter that can be accessed from outside the function), we assume that it must be owning on exit from the method. Thus, no memory object is dropped in the push method, but rather returned to the caller.

CROWN infers the ownership information of the code translated by c2rust, and uses it to translate the code to safer Rust in Fig. 1c. As explained next, CROWN first retypes raw pointers into safe pointers based on the ownership information, and then rewrites their uses.

Retyping Pointers in Crown. If a pointer owns a memory object at *any point within its scope*, CROWN retypes it into a Box pointer. For instance, in Fig. 1c, local variable new_node is retyped to be Option<Box<Node>> (safe pointer types are wrapped into Option to account for null pointer values). Variable new_node is non-owning upon function entry, becomes owning at line 13 and ownership is transferred out again at line 16.

For struct fields, CROWN considers all the code in the scope of the struct declaration. If a struct field owns a memory object at *any point within the scope of its struct declaration*, then it is retyped to Box. In Fig. 1b, fields next and head are accessed via access paths (*new_node).next and (*list).head, and given ownership at lines 17 and 18, respectively. Consequently, they are retyped to Box at lines 4 and 9 in Fig. 1c, respectively.

A special case is that of output parameters, e.g. list in our example. For such parameters, although they may be owning, CROWN retypes them to &mut in order to enable borrowing. In push, the input argument list is retyped to Option<&mut List> .

Rewriting Pointer Uses in Crown. After retyping pointers, CROWN rewrites their uses. The rewrite process takes into consideration both their new type and the context in which they are being used. Due to the Rust semantics, the rewrite rules are slightly intricate (see Sect. 6). For instance, the dereference of new_node at line 14 is rewritten to (*new_node).as_deref_mut().unwrap() as it needs to be mutated and the optional part of the Box needs to be unwrapped. Similarly, at line 15, (*list).head is rewritten to be ((*list.as_deref_mut()).unwrap()).head.take() as the LHS of the assignment expects a Box pointer.

After the rewrite performed by CROWN, the unsafe block annotation is not needed anymore. However, CROWN does not attempt to remove such annotations. Notably, safe pointers are always checked by the Rust compiler, even inside unsafe blocks.

3.2 Freeing an Argument List in bzip2

We next show the transformation of a real-world code snippet with a loop structure: a piece of code in bzip2 that frees argument lists. bzip2 defines a singly-linked list like structure, Cell, that holds a list of argument names. In Fig. 2, we extract from the source code a snippet that frees the argument lists. Here, the local variable argList is an already constructed argument list, and Char is a type alias to C-style characters. As a note, Cell in Figs. 2b and 2c does not refer to Rust's std::cell::Cell.

```
1  typedef
2  struct zzzz {
3      Char        *name;
4      struct zzzz *link;
5  }
6  Cell;
7  [...]
8  Cell* aa = argList;
9  while (aa != NULL) {
10     Cell* aa2 = aa->link;
11     if (aa->name)
12         free(aa->name);
13     free(aa);
14     aa = aa2;
15 }
16 [...]
17
```
(a) C definition

```
1  #[derive(Copy, Clone)]
2  #[repr(C)]
3  pub struct zzzz {
4      pub name: *mut Char,
5      pub link: *mut zzzz,
6  }
7  pub type Cell = zzzz;
8  [...]
9  let mut aa: *mut Cell = argList;
10 while !aa.is_null() {
11     let mut aa2 = (*aa).link;
12     if !(*aa).name.is_null() {
13         free((*aa).name as *mut libc
               ::c_void);
14     }
15     free(aa as *mut libc::c_void);
16     aa = aa2;
17 }
18 [...]
19
```
(b) c2rust result

```
1  #[repr(C)]
2  pub struct zzzz {
3      pub name: *mut /* owning */ Char
           ,
4      pub link: Option<Box<zzzz>>,
5  }
6  pub type Cell = zzzz;
7  [...]
8  let mut aa: Option<Box<Cell>> =
       argList;
9  while !aa.as_deref().is_none() {
10     let mut aa2 = (*aa.as_deref_mut
           ().unwrap()).link.take();
11     if !(*aa.as_deref().unwrap()).
           name.is_null {
12         free((*aa.as_deref().unwrap
               ()).name as *mut libc::
               c_void);
13     }
14     aa = aa2;
15 }
16 [...]
17
```
(c) CROWN result

Fig. 2. Freeing an argument list

CROWN accurately infers an ownership scheme for this snippet. Firstly, ownership of argList is transferred to aa, which is to be freed in the subsequent loop. Inside the loop, ownership of link accessed from aa is firstly transferred to aa2, then ownership of name accessed from aa is released in a call to free. After the conditional, ownership of aa is also released. Last of all, aa regains ownership from aa2.

Handling of Loops. For loops, CROWN only analyses their body once as that will already expose all the ownership information. For inductively defined data structures such as Cell, while further unrolling of loop bodies explores the data structures deeper, it does not expose any new struct fields: pointer variables and pointer struct fields do not change ownership between loop iterations. Additionally, CROWN emits constraints that equate the ownership of all local pointers at the loop entry and exit. For example, the ownership statuses of aa and aa2 at loop entry are made equal with those at loop exit, and inferred to be owning and non-owning, respectively.

Handling of Null Pointers. It is a common C idiom for pointers to be checked against null after malloc or before free: if `!p.is_null() free(p)`;. This could be problematic since the then-branch and the else-branch would have conflicting ownership statuses for p. We adopt a similar solution as [24]: we insert an explicit null assignment in the null branch if `!p.is_null() free(p); else p = ptr::null_mut();`. As we treat null pointers as both owning and non-owning, the ownership of p will be dictated by the non-null branch, enabling CROWN to infer the correct ownership scheme.

Translation. With the above ownership scheme, CROWN performs the rewrites as in Fig. 2c. Note that we do not attempt to rewrite **name** since it is an array pointer (see Sect. 7 for limitations).

4   Architecture

In this section, we give a brief overview of CROWN's architecture. CROWN takes as input a Rust program with unsafe blocks, and outputs a safer Rust program, where a portion of the raw pointers have been retyped as safe ones (in accordance to the Rust ownership model), and their uses modified accordingly. In this paper we focus on applying our technique to programs automatically translated by c2rust, which maintain a high degree of similarity to the original C ones, where the C syntax is replaced by Rust syntax.

CROWN applies several static analyses on the MIR of Rust to infer properties of pointers:

- **Ownership analysis:** computes ownership information about the pointers in the code, i.e. for each pointer it infers whether it is owning/non-owning at particular program locations.
- **Mutability analysis:** infers which pointers are used to modify the object they point to (inspired by [22,25]).
- **Fatness analysis:** distinguishes array pointers from non-array pointers (inspired by [32]).

The results of these analyses are summarised as type qualifiers [21]. A type qualifier is an atomic property (i.e., ownership, mutability, and fatness) that 'qualifies' the standard pointer type. These qualifiers are then utilised for pointer retyping. For example, an owning, non-array pointer is retyped to `Box` . After pointers have been retyped, CROWN rewrites their usages accordingly.

5   Ownership Analysis

The goal of our ownership analysis is to compute an ownership scheme for a given program that obeys the Rust ownership model, if such a scheme exists. The ownership scheme contains information about whether pointers in the program are owning or non-owning at particular program locations. At a high-level, our analysis works by generating a set of ownership constraints (Sect. 5.2), which are then solved by a SAT solver (Sect. 5.3). A satisfying assignment for the ownership constraints is an ownership scheme that obeys the Rust semantics.

Our ownership analysis is flow and field sensitive, where the latter enables inferring ownership information for pointer struct fields. To satisfy field sensitivity, we track ownership information for *access paths* [10,14,29]. An access path represents a memory location by the way it is accessed from an initial, base variable, and comprises of the base variable and a sequence of field selection operators. For the program Fig. 1b, some example access paths are `new_node` (consists only of the base variable), `(*new_node).next`, and `(*list).head`. Our analysis associates an ownership variable with each access path, e.g. p has associated ownership variable $\mathbb{O}_p$, and `(*p).next` has associated ownership variable $\mathbb{O}_{(*p).next}$. Each ownership variable can take the value 1 if the corresponding access path is owning, or 0 if it is non-owning. By ownership of an access path we mean the ownership of the field (or, more generally, pointer) accessed last through the access path, e.g. the ownership of `(*new_node).next` refers to the ownership of field `next`.

5.1 Ownership and Aliasing

One of the main challenges of designing an ownership analysis is the interaction between ownership and aliasing. To understand the problem, let us consider the pointer assignment at line 3 in the code listing below. We assume that the lines before the assignment allow inferring that q, `(*q).next` and r are owning, whereas p and `(*p).next` are non-owning. Additionally, we assume that the lines after the assignment require `(*p).next` to be owning (e.g. `(*p).next` is being explicitly freed). From this, an ownership analysis could reasonably conclude that ownership transfer happens at line 3 (such that `(*p).next` becomes owning), and the inferred ownership scheme obeys the Rust semantics.

```
1   let p, r, q : *mut Node;
2   // p and (*p).next non-owning; q, (*q).next and r owning
3   (*p).next = r;
4   // (*p).next must have ownership
```

Let's now also consider aliasing. A possible assumption is that, just before line 3, p and q alias, meaning that `(*p).next` and `(*q).next` also alias. Then, after line 3, `(*p).next` and `(*q).next` will still alias (pointing to the same memory object). However, according to the ownership scheme above, both `(*p).next` and `(*q).next` are owning, which is not allowed in Rust, where a memory object must have a unique owner. This discrepancy was not detected by the ownership analysis mimicked above. The issue is that the ownership analysis ignored aliasing. Indeed, ownership should not be transferred to `(*p).next` if there exists an owning alias that, after the ownership transfer, continues to point to the same memory object as `(*p).next`.

Precise aliasing information is very difficult to compute, especially in the presence of inductively defined data structures. In the current paper, we alleviate the need to check aliasing by making a strengthening assumption about the Rust ownership model: we restrict the way in which pointers can acquire ownership along an access path, thus limiting the interaction between ownership and aliasing. In particular, we introduce a novel concept of *ownership monotonicity*. This property states that, along an access path, the ownership values of pointers can only decrease (see Definition 1, where *is_prefix*(a, b) returns true if access path a is a prefix of b, and false otherwise – e.g. *is_prefix*(p, (*p).next) = *true*). Going back to the previous code listing, the ownership monotonicity implies that, for access path (*p).next we have $\mathbb{O}_p \geq \mathbb{O}_{(*p).next}$, and for access path (*q).next we have $\mathbb{O}_q \geq \mathbb{O}_{(*q).next}$. This means that, if (*p).next is allowed to take ownership, then p must already be owning. Consequently, all aliases of p must be non-owning, which means that all aliases of (*p).next, including (*q).next, are non-owning.

Definition 1 (Ownership monotonicity). *Given two access paths a and b, if is_prefix(a, b), then $\mathbb{O}_a \geq \mathbb{O}_b$.*

Ownership monotonicity is stricter than the Rust semantics, causing our analysis to reject two scenarios that would otherwise be accepted by the Rust compiler (see discussion in Sect. 5.4). In this work, we made the design decision to use ownership monotonicity over aliasing analysis as it allows us to retain more control over the accuracy of the translation. Conversely, using an aliasing analysis would mean that the accuracy of the translation is directly dictated by the accuracy of the aliasing analysis (i.e. false alarms from the aliasing analysis [23, 40] would result in CROWN not translating pointers that are actually safe). With ownership monotonicity, we know exactly what the rejected valid ownership schemes are, and we can explicitly enable them (again, see discussion in Sect. 5.4).

5.2   Generation of Ownership Constraints

During constraint generation, we assume a given k denoting the length of the longest access path used in the code. This enables us to capture the ownership of all the access paths exposed in the code. Later in this section, we will discuss the handling of loops, which may expose longer access paths.

Next, we denote by $\mathcal{P}$ the set of all access paths in a program, $base\_var(a)$ returns the base variable of access path a, and $|a|$ computes the length of the access path a in terms of applied field selection operators from the base variable. In the context of the previous code listing, $base\_var((*p).next) = p$, $base\_var(p) = p$, $|p| = 1$ and $|(*p).next| = 2$. Then, we define $ap(v, lb, ub)$ to return the set of access paths with base variable v and length in between lower bound lb and upper bound ub: $ap(v, lb, ub) = \{a \in \mathcal{P}|base\_var(a) = v \land lb \leq |a| \leq ub\}$. For illustration, we have $ap(p, 1, 2) = \{p, (*p).next\}$.

Ownership Transfer. The program instructions where ownership transfer can happen are (pointer) assignment and function call. Here we discuss assignment and, due to space constraints, we leave the rules for interprocedural ownership analysis in the extended version [41]. Our rule for ownership transfer at assignment site follows Rust's Box semantics: when a Box pointer is moved, the

ASSIGN

$$v = base\_var(\mathbf{p}), \quad w = base\_var(\mathbf{q}),$$
$$a \in ap(v, |\mathbf{p}|, k), \quad b \in ap(w, |\mathbf{q}|, k), \quad c \in ap(v, 1, |\mathbf{p}|-1), \quad d \in ap(w, 1, |\mathbf{q}|-1)$$
$$|a| - |\mathbf{p}| = |b| - |\mathbf{q}|, |c| = |d|$$
$$is\_prefix(p, a), \ is\_prefix(q, b), \ is\_prefix(c, p), \ is\_prefix(d, q)$$
$$C' = C \cup \{ \mathbb{O}_a = 0 \wedge \mathbb{O}_{a'} + \mathbb{O}_{b'} = \mathbb{O}_b \ \wedge \mathbb{O}_{c'} = \mathbb{O}_c \wedge \mathbb{O}_{d'} = \mathbb{O}_d \}$$
$$\overline{\rule{0pt}{1em}\quad C \vdash \mathbf{p} = \mathbf{q}; \Rightarrow C' \quad}$$

Fig. 3. Ownership constraint generation for assignment

object it points to is moved as well. For instance, in the following Rust pseudocode snippet:

```
1 let p,q: Box<Box<i32>>;
2 p = q; // ownership transfer occurs
3 // the use of q and *q is disallowed
```

when ownership is transferred from q to p, *q also loses ownership. Except for reassignment, the use of a Box pointer after it lost its ownership is disallowed, hence the use of q or *q is forbidden at line 3.

Consequently, we enforce the following *ownership transfer rule*: if ownership transfer happens for a pointer variable (e.g. p and q in the example), then it must happen for all pointers reachable from that pointer (e.g. *p and *q). The ownership of pointer variables from which the pointer under discussion is reachable remains the same (e.g. if ownership transfer happens for some assignment *p = *q in the code, then q and p retain their respective previous ownership values).

Possible Ownership Transfer at Pointer Assignment: The ownership transfer rule at pointer assignment site is captured by rule ASSIGN in Fig. 3. The judgement $C \vdash \mathbf{p} = \mathbf{q}; \Rightarrow C'$ denotes the fact that the assignment is analysed under the set of constraints C, and generates C'. We use prime notation to denote variables after the assignment. Given pointer assignment $\mathbf{p} = \mathbf{q}$, a and b represent all the access paths respectively starting from p and q, whereas c and d denote the access paths from the base variables of p and q that reach p and q, respectively. Then, equality $\mathbb{O}_{a'} + \mathbb{O}_{b'} = \mathbb{O}_b$ captures the possibility of ownership transfer for all access paths originating at p and q: (i) If transfer happens then the ownership of b transfers to a' ($\mathbb{O}_{a'} = \mathbb{O}_b$ and $\mathbb{O}_{b'} = 0$). (ii) Otherwise, the ownership values are left unchanged ($\mathbb{O}_{a'} = \mathbb{O}_a$ and $\mathbb{O}_{b'} = \mathbb{O}_b$). The last two equalities, $\mathbb{O}_{c'} = \mathbb{O}_c \wedge \mathbb{O}_{d'} = \mathbb{O}_d$, denote the fact that, for both (i) and (ii), pointers on access paths c and d retain their previous ownership. Note that "+" is interpreted as the usual arithmetic operation over $\mathbb{N}$, where we impose an implicit constraint $0 \leq \mathbb{O} \leq 1$ for every ownership variable $\mathbb{O}$.

C Memory Leaks: In the ASSIGN rule, we add constraint $\mathbb{O}_a = 0$ to C' in order to force a to be non-owning before the assignment. Conversely, having a owning before being reassigned via the assignment under analysis signals a memory leak in the original C program. Given that in Rust memory is automatically returned, allowing the translation to happen would change the semantics of the original program by fixing the memory leak. Instead, our design choice is to disallow the ownership analysis from generating such a solution. As we will explain in Sect. 8, we intend for our translation to preserve memory usage (including possible memory leaks).

Simultaneous Ownership Transfer Along an Access Path: One may observe that the constraints generated by ASSIGN do not fully capture the stated ownership transfer rule. In particular, they do not ensure that, whenever ownership transfer occurs from p to q, it also transfers for all pointers on all access paths a and b. Instead, this is implicitly guaranteed by the ownership monotonicity rule, as stated in Theorem 1.

Theorem 1 (Ownership transfer). *If ownership is transferred from p to q, then, by the ASSIGN rule and ownership monotonicity, ownership also transfers between corresponding pointers on all access paths a and b: $\mathbb{O}_{a'} = \mathbb{O}_b$ and $\mathbb{O}_{b'} = 0$. (proof in the extended version [41])*

Ownership and Aliasing: We saw in Sect. 5.1 that aliasing may cause situations in which, after ownership transfer, the same memory object has more than one owner. Theorem 2 states that this is not possible under ownership monotonicity.

Theorem 2 (Soundness of pointer assignment under ownership monotonicity). *Under ownership monotonicity, if all allocated memory objects have a unique owner before a pointer assignment, then they will also have a unique owner after the assignment. (proof in the extended version [41])*

Intuitively, Theorem 2 enables a pointer to acquire ownership without having to consider aliases: after ownership transfer, this pointer will be the unique owner. The idea resembles that of strong updates [30].

Additional Access Paths: As a remark, it is possible for p and q to be accessible from other base variables in the program. In such cases, given that those access paths are not explicitly mentioned at the location of the ownership transfer, we do not generate new ownership variables for them. Consequently, their current ownership variables are left unchanged by default.

Ownership Transfer Example. To illustrate the ASSIGN rule, we use the singly-linked list example below, where we assume that p, q are both of type *mut Node. Therefore, we will have to consider the following four access path p, q, (*p).next, (*q).next. In SSA-style, at each line in the example, we generate new ownership variables (by incrementing their subscript) for the access paths mentioned at that line. For the first assignment, ownership transfer can happen between p and q, and (*p).next and (*q).next, respectively. For the second assignment, ownership can be transferred between (*p).next and (*q).next, while p and q must retain their previous ownership.

```
1  p = q;          // 𝕆_{p_1} = 0 ∧ 𝕆_{p_2} + 𝕆_{q_2} = 𝕆_{q_1} ∧
2                  // 𝕆_{(*p_1).next} = 0 ∧ 𝕆_{(*p_2).next} + 𝕆_{(*q_2).next} = 𝕆_{(*q_1).next}
3  (*p).next = (*q).next;
4                  // 𝕆_{p_3} = 𝕆_{p_2} ∧ 𝕆_{q_3} = 𝕆_{q_2} ∧
5                  // 𝕆_{(*p_2).next} = 0 ∧ 𝕆_{(*p_3).next} + 𝕆_{(*q_3).next} = 𝕆_{(*q_2).next}
```

Besides generating ownership constraints for assignments, we must model the ownership information for commonly used C standard function like `malloc`, `calloc`, `realloc`, `free`, `strcmp`, `memset`, etc. Due to space constraints, more details about these, as well as the rules for ownership monotonicity and interprocedural ownership analysis are provided in the extended version [41].

Handling Conditionals and Loops. As mentioned in Sect. 3.2, we only analyse the body of loops once as it is sufficient to expose all the required ownership variables. For inductively defined data structures, while further unrolling of loop bodies increases the length of access paths, it does not expose any new struct fields (struct fields do not change ownership between loop iterations).

To handle join points of control paths, we apply a variant of the SSA construction algorithm [6], where different paths are merged via ϕ nodes. The value of each ownership variable must be the same on all joined paths, or otherwise the analysis fails.

5.3   Solving Ownership Constraints

The ownership constraint system consists of a set of 3-variable linear constraints of the form $O_v = O_w + O_u$, and 1-variable equality constraints $O_v = 0$ and $O_v = 1$.

Definition 2 (Ownership constraint system). *An ownership constraint system $(P, \Delta, \Sigma, \Sigma_\neg)$ consists of a set of ownership variables P that can have either value 0 or 1, a set of 3-variable equality constraints $\Delta \subseteq P \times P \times P$, and two sets of 1-variable equality constraints, $\Sigma, \Sigma_\neg \subseteq P$. The equalities in Σ are of the form $x = 1$, whereas the equalities in $\Sigma_\neg$ are of the form $x = 0$.*

Theorem 3 (Complexity of the ownership constraint solving). *Deciding the satisfiability of the ownership constraint system in Definition 2 is NP-complete. (proof in the extended version [41]).*

We solve the ownership constraints by calling a SAT solver. The ownership constraints may have no solution. This happens when there is no ownership scheme that obeys the Rust ownership model and the ownership monotonicity property (which is stricter than the Rust model for some cases), or the original C program has a memory leak. In the case where the ownership constraints have more than one solution, we consider the first assignment returned by the SAT solver.

Due to the complex Rust semantics, we do not formally prove that a satisfying assignment obeys the Rust ownership model. Instead, this check is performed after the translation by running the Rust compiler.

5.4   Discussion on Ownership Monotonicity

As mentioned earlier in Sect. 5, ownership monotonicity is stricter than the Rust semantics, causing our analysis to potentially reject some ownership schemes that would otherwise be accepted by the Rust compiler. We identified two such scenarios:

(i) Reference output parameter: This denotes a reference passed as a function parameter, which acts as an output as it can be accessed from outside the function (e.g. `list` in Fig. 1a). For such parameters, the base variable is non-owning (as it is a reference) and mutable, whereas the pointers reachable from it may be owning (see example in Fig. 1c, where `(*node).head` gets assigned a pointer to a newly allocated node). We detect such situations and explicitly enable them. In particular, we explicitly convert owning pointers `p` to `&mut (*p)` at the translation stage.

(ii) Local borrows: The code below involving a mutable local borrow is not considered valid by CROWN as it disobeys the ownership monotonicity: after the assignment, `local_borrow` is non-owning, whereas `*local_borrow` is owning.

```
1   let local_borrow = &mut n;
2   *local_borrow = Box::new(1);
```

While we could explicitly handle the translation to local borrows, in order to do so soundly, we would have to reason about lifetime information (e.g. CROWN would have to check that there is no overlap between the lifetimes of different mutable references to the same object). In this work, we chose not to do this and instead leave it as future work (as also mentioned under limitations in Sect. 7). It was observed in [13] that scenario (i) is much more prevalent than scenario (ii). Additionally, we observed in our benchmarks that output parameter accounts for 93% of mutable references (hence the inclusion of a special case enabling the translation of scenario (i) in CROWN).

6   C to Rust Translation

CROWN uses the results of the ownership, mutability and fatness analyses to perform the actual translation, which consists of retyping pointers (Sect. 6.1) and rewriting pointer uses (Sect. 6.2).

6.1   Retyping Pointers

As mentioned in Sect. 2.2, we do not attempt to translate array pointers to safe pointers. In the rest of the section, we focus on mutable, non-array pointers.

The translation requires a global view of pointers' ownership, whereas information inferred by the ownership analysis refers to individual program locations. For the purpose of translation, given that we refactor owning pointers into box pointers, a pointer is considered (globally) owning if it owns a memory object at any program location within its scope. Otherwise, it is (globally) non-owning.

When retyping pointer fields of structs, we must consider the scope of the struct declaration, which generally transcends the whole program. Within this scope, each field is usually accessed from several base variables, which must all be taken into consideration. For instance, given the List declaration in Fig. 1b and two variables l1 and l2 of type *mut List. Then, in order to determine the ownership status of field next, we have to consider all the access paths to next originating from both base variables l1 and l2.

The next table shows the retyping rules for mutable, non-array pointers, where we wrap safe pointer types into Option to account for null pointer values:

	Non-array pointers
Owning	Option<Box<T>>
Non-owning	*mut T or Option<&mut T>

The non-owning pointers that are kept as raw pointers *mut T correspond to mutable local borrows. As explained in Sects. 5.4 and 7, CROWN doesn't currently handle the translation to mutable local borrows due to the fact that we do not have a lifetime analysis. Notably, this restriction does not apply to output parameters (which covers the majority of mutable references), where we translate to mutable references. The lack of a lifetime analysis means that we also can't handle immutable local borrows, hence our translation's focus on mutable pointers.

6.2   Rewriting Pointer Uses

The rewrite of a pointer expression depends on its new type and the context in which it is used. For example, when rewriting q in p = q, the context will depend on the new type of p. Based on this new type, we can have four contexts: BoxCtxt which requires Box pointers, MutCtxt which requires &mut references, ConstCtxt which requires & references, and RawCtxt which requires raw pointers. For example, if p above is a Box pointer, then we rewrite q in a BoxCtxt.

Then, the rewrite takes place according to the following table, where columns correspond to the new type of the pointer to be rewritten, and rows represent possible contexts[1].

	Option<Box<T>>	Option<&mut T>	*mut T
BoxCtxt	p.take()	⊥	Some(Box::from_raw(p))
MutCtxt	p.as_deref_mut()	p.as_deref_mut()	p.as_mut()
ConstCtxt	p.as_deref()	p.as_deref()	p.as_ref()
RawCtxt	to_raw(&mut p)	to_raw(&mut p)	p

Our translation uses functions from the Rust standard library, as follows:

1. When Option<Box<T>> is passed to a BoxCtxt, we expect a move, and consequently we use take to replace the value inside the option with None;
2. We use as_deref and as_deref_mut in order to not consume the original option, and we create new options with references to the original ones;

---

[1] The cell marked as ⊥ is not applicable due to our treatment of output parameter.

3. `as_mut` and `as_ref` converts raw pointers to references;
4. `Box::from_raw` converts raw pointers into `Box` pointers.

We also define the helper function `to_raw` that transform safe pointers into raw pointers:

```
fn to_raw<T>(b: &mut Option<Box<T>>) -> *mut T {
    b.as_deref_mut().map(|b| b as *mut T).unwrap_or(null_mut())
}
```

Here, we explain `to_raw` for a `Box` argument (the explanation for `&mut` is the same because of the polymorphic nature of `as_deref_mut`):

1. To convert `Option<Box<T>>`, we first mutably borrow the entire option as denoted by the mutable borrow argument of the helper function. This is needed because `Option` is not copyable, and it would be otherwise consumed;
2. `as_deref_mut` converts `&mut Option<Box<T>>` to `Option<&mut T>`;
3. `map` converts the optional part of the reference into an option of raw pointers;
4. Finally, `unwrap_or` returns the `Some` value of the option, or a null pointer `std::ptr::null_mut()` if the value is `None`.

Dereferences: When a pointer `p` is dereferenced as part of a larger expression (e.g. `(*p).next`), we need an additional `unwrap()`.

Box pointers check: Rust disallows the use of `Box` pointers after they lost their ownership. As this rule cannot be captured by the ownership analysis, such situations are detected at translation stage, and the culpable `Box` pointers are reverted back to raw pointers.

For brevity, we omitted the slightly different treatment of struct fields that are not of pointer type.

7   Challenges of Handling Real-World Code

We designed CROWN to be able to analyse and translate real-world code, which poses significant challenges. In this section, we discuss some of the engineering challenges of CROWN and its current limitations.

7.1   Preprocessing

During the transpilation of C libraries, c2rust treats each file as a separate compilation unit, which gets translated into a separate Rust module. Consequently, struct definitions are duplicated, and available function definitions are put in `extern` blocks [17]. We apply a preprocessing step similar to the resolve-imports tool of Laertes [17] that links those definitions across files.

7.2 Limitations of the Ownership Analysis

There are a few C constructs and idioms that are not fully supported by our implementation, for which CROWN generates partial ownership constraints. CROWN's translation will attempt to rewrite a variable as long as there exists a constraint involving it. As a result, the translation is in theory neither *sound* nor *complete*: it may generate code that does not compile (though we have not observed this in practice for the benchmarks where CROWN produces a result – see Sect. 8) and it may leave some pointers as raw pointers resulting in a less than optimal translation. We list below the cases when such a scenario may happen.

Certain Unsafe C Constructs. For type casts, we only generate ownership transfer constraints for head pointers; for unions we assume that they contain no pointer fields and consequently, we generate no constraints; similarly, we generate no constraints for variadic arguments. We noticed that unions and variadic arguments may cause our tool to crash (e.g. three of the benchmarks in [17], as mentioned in Sect. 8). Those crashes happen when analysing access paths that contain dereferences of union fields (where we assumed no pointer fields), and when analysing calls to functions with variadic arguments where a pointer is passed as argument.

Function Pointers. CROWN does not generate any constraints for them.

Non-standard Memory Management in C Libraries. Certain C libraries wrap `malloc` and `free`, often with static function pointers (pointers to allocator/deallocator are stored in static variables), or function pointers in structs. CROWN does not generate any constraints in such scenarios. In C, it is also possible to use `malloc` to allocate a large piece of memory, and then split it into several sub-regions assigned to different pointers. In our ownership analysis, only one pointer can gain ownership of the memory allocated by a call to `malloc`. Another C idiom that we don't fully support occurs when certain pointers can point to either heap allocated objects, or statically allocated stack arrays. CROWN generates ownership constraints only for the heap and, consequently, those variables will be left under-constrained.

7.3 Other Limitations of CROWN

Array Pointers. For array pointers, although CROWN infers the correct ownership information, it does not generate the meta data required to synthesise Rust code.

Mutable Local Borrows. As explained in the last paragraph of Sect. 6.1, CROWN does not translate mutable non-owning pointers to local mutable references as this requires dedicated analysis of lifetimes. Note that CROWN does however generate mutable references for output parameters.

Access Paths that Break Ownership Monotonicity. As discussed in Sect. 5.4, ownership monotonicity may be stricter in certain cases than Rust's semantics.

8   Experimental Evaluation

We implement CROWN on top of the Rust compiler, version `nightly-2023-01-26`. We use `c2rust` with version 0.16.0. For the SAT solver, we rely on a Rust-binding of `z3` [20] with version 0.11.2. We run all our experiments on a MacBook Pro with an Apple M1 chip, with 8 cores (4 performance and 4 efficiency). The computer has 16 GB RAM and runs macOS Monterey 12.5.1.

Benchmark Selection. To evaluate the utility of CROWN, we collected a benchmark suite of 20 programs (Table 1). These include benchmarks from Laertes [17]'s accompanying artifact [16] (marked by * in Table 1)[2], and additionally 8 real-world projects (`binn`, `brotli`, `buffer`, `heman`, `json.h`, `libtree`, `lodepng`, `rgba`) together with 4 commonly used data structure libraries (`avl`, `bst`, `ht`, `quadtree`).

Functional and Non-functional Guarantees. With respect to functional properties, we want the original program and the refactored program to be observationally equivalent, i.e. for each input they produce the same output. We empirically validated this using all the available test suites (i.e. for `libtree`, `rgba`, `quadtree`, `urlparser`, `genann`, `buffer` in Table 1). All the test suites continue to pass after the translation. For nonfunctional properties, we intend to preserve memory usage and CPU time, i.e. we don't want our translation to introduce runtime overhead. We also validated this using the test suites.

Table 1. Benchmarks information

Benchmark	Files	Structs	Functions	LOC	Benchmark	Files	Structs	Functions	LOC
Avl	1	2	11	229	libcsv*	1	6	23	976
binn	1	5	165	4426	libtree	1	18	32	2610
brotli	30	237	867	537723	libzahl*	49	65	108	4655
bst	1	1	6	154	lil*	2	9	136	5670
buffer	2	3	42	1207	lodepng	1	19	236	14153
bzip2*	9	39	126	14829	quadtree	5	14	31	1216
genann*	6	10	27	2410	rgba	2	3	19	1855
heman	24	52	302	13762	robotfindskitten*	1	8	18	1508
ht	1	3	10	264	tulipindicators*	111	18	229	22363
json.h	1	13	53	3860	urlparser*	1	1	21	1379

8.1   Research Questions

We aim at answering the following research questions.

---

[2] We excluded `json-c`, `optipng`, `tinycc` where CROWN crashes because of the uses of unions and variadic arguments as discussed in Sect. 7. Additional programs (`qsort`, `grabc`, `xzoom`, `snudown`, `tmux`, `libxml2`) are mentioned in the paper [17] but are either missing or incomplete in the artifact [16].

RQ1. How many raw pointers/pointer uses can CROWN translate to safe pointers/pointer uses?

RQ2. How does CROWN's result compare with the state-of-the-art [17]?

RQ3. What is the runtime performance of CROWN?

RQ 1: Unsafe pointer reduction. In order to judge CROWN's efficacy, we measure the reduction rate of raw pointer declarations and uses. This is a direct indicative of the improvement in safety, as safe pointers are always checked by the Rust compiler (even inside unsafe regions). As previously mentioned, we focus on mutable non-array pointers. The results are presented in Table 2, where #ptrs counts the number of raw pointer declarations in a given benchmark, #uses counts the number of times raw pointers are being used, and the Laertes and Crown headers denote the reduction rates of the number of raw pointers and raw pointer uses achieved by the two tools, respectively. For instance, for benchmark avl, the rate of 100% means that all raw pointer declarations and their uses are translated into safe ones. Note that the "-" symbols on the row corresponding to robotfindskitten are due to the fact that the benchmark contains 0 raw pointer uses.

The median reduction rates achieved by CROWN for raw pointers and raw pointer uses are 37.3% and 62.1%, respectively. CROWN achieves a 100% reduction rate for many non-trivial data structures (avl, bst, buffer, ht), as well as for rgba. For brotli, a lossless data compression algorithm developed by Google, which is our largest benchmark, CROWN achieves reduction rates of 21.4% and 20.9%, respectively. The relatively low reduction rates for brotli and a few other benchmarks (tulipindicators, lodepng, bzip2, genann, libzahl) is due to their use of non-standard memory management strategies (discussed in detail in Sect. 7).

Notably, all the translated benchmarks compile under the aforementioned Rust compiler version. As a check of semantics preservation, for the benchmarks that provide test suites (libtree, rgba, quadtree, urlparser, genann, buffer), our translated benchmarks pass all the provided tests.

RQ 2: Comparing with state-of-the-art. The comparison of CROWN with Laertes [17] is also shown in Table 2, with bold font highlighting better results. The data on Laertes is either directly extracted from the artifact [16] or has been confirmed by the authors through private correspondence. We can see that CROWN outperforms the state-of-the-art (often by a significant degree) in most cases, with lodepng being the only exception, where we suspect that the reason also lies with non-standard memory management strategies mentioned before. Laertes is less affected by this as it does not rely on ownership analysis.

RQ 3: Runtime performance. Although our analysis relies on solving a constraint satisfaction problem that is proven to be NP-complete, in practice the runtime performance of CROWN is consistently high. The execution time of the analysis and the rewrite for the whole benchmark suite is within 60 s (where the execution time for our largest benchmark, brotli, is under 10 s).

Table 2. Reduction of (mutable, non-array) raw pointer declarations and uses

Benchmark	#ptrs	Laertes	Crown	#uses	Laertes	Crown
avl	8	0.0%	**100.0%**	41	0.0%	**100.0%**
binn	103	46.6%	**65.0%**	247	62.3%	**71.3%**
brotli	846	0.0%	**21.4%**	3686	0.0%	**20.9%**
bst	5	0.0%	**100.0%**	22	0.0%	**100.0%**
buffer	38	0.0%	**100.0%**	56	0.0%	**100.0%**
bzip2*	126	14.3%	**26.2%**	2946	2.2%	**3.7%**
genann*	28	0.0%	**7.1%**	160	0.0%	**15.0%**
heman	360	30.3%	**35.0%**	926	50.2%	**60.2%**
ht	6	33.3%	**100.0%**	28	42.9%	**100.0%**
json.h	128	2.3%	**23.4%**	647	1.2%	**62.1%**
libcsv*	20	65.0%	**70.0%**	141	97.9%	97.9%
libtree	48	29.2%	**39.6%**	227	33.0%	**62.1%**
libzahl*	87	2.2%	**16.1%**	279	4.1%	**16.8%**
lil*	202	9.2%	**18.8%**	1018	51.4%	**69.4%**
lodepng	227	**46.3%**	44.9%	1232	40.4%	37.7%
quadtree	33	0.0%	**42.4%**	117	0.0%	**48.7%**
rgba	6	83.3%	83.3%	12	100.0%	100.0%
robotfindskitten*	1	0.0%	0.0%	0	–	–
tulipindicators*	134	0.0%	**0.7%**	625	0.0%	0.0%
urlparser*	9	0.0%	**11.1%**	40	0.0%	**45.0%**

9   Related Works

Ownership Discussion. Ownership has been used in OO programming to enable controlled aliasing by restricting object graphs underlying the runtime heap [11,12] with efforts made in the automatic inference of ownership information [1,4,39], and applications of ownership to memory management [5,42]. Similarly, the concept of ownership has also been applied to analyse C/C++ programs. Heine et al. [24] inferred pointer ownership information for detecting memory leaks. Ravitch et al. [37] apply static analysis to infer ownership for automatic library binding generation. Giving the different application domains, each of these works makes different assumptions. Heine et al. [24] assumes that indirectly-accessed pointers (i.e. any pointer accessed through a path, like (*p).next) cannot acquire ownership, whereas Ravitch et al. [37] assumes that all struct fields are owning unless explicitly annotated. We took from [24] its handling of flow sensitivity, but enhanced it with the analysis of nested pointers and inductively defined data structures, which we found to be essential for translating real-world code. The analysis in [24] assigns a default "non-owning" status to all indirectly accessed pointers. This rules out many interesting data structures such as linked lists, trees, hash tables, etc., and commonly used idioms such as passing by reference. Conversely, in our work, we rely on a strengthening assumption about the Rust ownership model, which allows handling the aforementioned scenarios and data structures. Lastly, the idea of ownership is also broadly applied in concurrent separation logic [7–9,19,38]. However, these works are not aimed as automatic ownership inference systems.

Rust Verification. The separation logic based reasoning framework Iris [28] was used to formalise the Rust type system [27], and verify Rust programs [34]. While these works cover unsafe Rust fragments, they are not fully automatic. When restricting reasoning to only safe Rust, RustHorn [35] gives a first-order logic formulation of the behavior of Rust code, which is ameanable to fully automatic verification, while Prusti [3] leverages Rust compiler information to generate separation logic verification conditions that are discharged by Viper [36]. In the current work, we provide an automatic ownership analysis for unsafe Rust programs.

Type Qualifiers. Type qualifiers are a lightweight, practical mechanism for specifying and checking properties not captured by traditional type systems. A general flow-insensitive type qualifier framework has been proposed [21], with subsequent applications analysing Java reference mutability [22,25] and C array bounds [32]. We adapted these works to Rust for our mutability and fatness analyses, respectively.

C to Rust Translation. We have already discussed c2rust [26], which is an industrial strength tool that converts C to Rust syntax. c2rust does not attempt to fix unsafe features such as raw pointers and the programs it generates are always annotated as unsafe. Nevertheless it forms the bases of other translation efforts. CRustS [31] applies AST-based code transformations to remove superfluous unsafe labelling generated by c2rust. But it does not fix the unsafe features either. Laertes [17] is the first tool that is actually able to automatically reduce the presence of unsafe code. It uses the Rust compiler as a blackbox oracle and search for code changes that remove raw pointers, which is different from CROWN's approach (see Sect. 8 for an experimental comparison). The subsequent work [15] develops an evaluation methodology for studying the limitations of existing techniques that translate unsafe raw pointers to safe Rust references. The work adopts a new concept of 'pseudo safety', under which semantics preservation of the original programs is no longer guaranteed. As explained in Sect. 8, in our work, we aim to maintain semantic equivalence.

10   Conclusion

We devised an ownership analysis for Rust programs translated by c2rust that is scalable (handling half a million LOC in less than 10 s) and precise (handling inductive data structures) thanks to a strengthening of the Rust ownership model, which we call ownership monotonicity. Based on this new analysis, we prototyped a refactoring tool for translating C programs into Rust programs. Our experimental evaluation shows that the proposed approach handles real-world benchmarks and outperforms the state-of-the-art.

References

1. Aldrich, J., Kostadinov, V., Chambers, C.: Alias annotations for program understanding. In: Proceedings of the 17th ACM SIGPLAN Conference on Object-Oriented Programming, Systems, Languages, and Applications. OOPSLA '02, pp. 311–330. Association for Computing Machinery, New York, NY, USA (2002). https://doi.org/10.1145/582419.582448

2. Astrauskas, V., Matheja, C., Poli, F., Müller, P., Summers, A.J.: How do programmers use unsafe rust? Proc. ACM Program. Lang. **4**(OOPSLA) (2020). https://doi.org/10.1145/3428204

3. Astrauskas, V., Müller, P., Poli, F., Summers, A.J.: Leveraging rust types for modular specification and verification. Proc. ACM Program. Lang. **3**(OOPSLA) (oct 2019). https://doi.org/10.1145/3360573

4. Boyapati, C., Liskov, B., Shrira, L.: Ownership types for object encapsulation. In: Proceedings of the 30th ACM SIGPLAN-SIGACT Symposium on Principles of Programming Languages. POPL '03, pp. 213–223. Association for Computing Machinery, New York, NY, USA (2003). https://doi.org/10.1145/604131.604156

5. Boyapati, C., Salcianu, A., Beebee, W., Rinard, M.: Ownership types for safe region-based memory management in real-time Java. In: Proceedings of the ACM SIGPLAN 2003 Conference on Programming Language Design and Implementation. PLDI '03, pp. 324–337. Association for Computing Machinery, New York, NY, USA (2003). https://doi.org/10.1145/781131.781168

6. Briggs, P., Cooper, K.D., Harvey, T.J., Simpson, L.T.: Practical improvements to the construction and destruction of static single assignment form. Softw. Pract. Exper. **28**(8), 859–881 (1998)

7. Brookes, S.: Variables as resource for shared-memory programs: semantics and soundness. Electron. Notes Theor. Comput. Sci. **158**, 123–150 (2006). https://doi.org/10.1016/j.entcs.2006.04.008

8. Brookes, S.: A semantics for concurrent separation logic. Theor. Comput. Sci. **375**(1–3), 227–270 (2007). https://doi.org/10.1016/j.tcs.2006.12.034

9. Calcagno, C., O'Hearn, P.W., Yang, H.: Local action and abstract separation logic. In: Proceedings of the 22nd Annual IEEE Symposium on Logic in Computer Science. p. 366–378. LICS '07, IEEE Computer Society, USA (2007). https://doi.org/10.1109/LICS.2007.30

10. Cheng, B.C., Hwu, W.M.W.: Modular interprocedural pointer analysis using access paths: design, implementation, and evaluation. In: Proceedings of the ACM SIGPLAN 2000 Conference on Programming Language Design and Implementation. PLDI '00, pp. 57–69. Association for Computing Machinery, New York, NY, USA (2000). https://doi.org/10.1145/349299.349311

11. Clarke, D., Östlund, J., Sergey, I., Wrigstad, T.: Ownership types: a survey. In: Clarke, D., Noble, J., Wrigstad, T. (eds.) Aliasing in Object-Oriented Programming. Types, Analysis and Verification. LNCS, vol. 7850, pp. 15–58. Springer, Heidelberg (2013). https://doi.org/10.1007/978-3-642-36946-9_3

12. Clarke, D.G., Potter, J.M., Noble, J.: Ownership types for flexible alias protection. In: Proceedings of the 13th ACM SIGPLAN Conference on Object-Oriented Programming, Systems, Languages, and Applications. OOPSLA '98, pp. 48–64. Association for Computing Machinery, New York, NY, USA (1998). https://doi.org/10.1145/286936.286947

13. Das, M.: Unification-based pointer analysis with directional assignments. In: Proceedings of the ACM SIGPLAN 2000 Conference on Programming Language

Design and Implementation. PLDI '00, pp. 35–46. Association for Computing Machinery, New York, NY, USA (2000). https://doi.org/10.1145/349299.349309

14. De, A., D'Souza, D.: Scalable flow-sensitive pointer analysis for java with strong updates. In: Noble, J. (ed.) ECOOP 2012. LNCS, vol. 7313, pp. 665–687. Springer, Heidelberg (2012). https://doi.org/10.1007/978-3-642-31057-7_29

15. Emre, M., Boyland, P., Parekh, A., Schroeder, R., Dewey, K., Hardekopf, B.: Aliasing limits on translating c to safe rust. Proc. ACM Program. Lang. **7**(OOPSLA1) (2023). https://doi.org/10.1145/3586046

16. Emre, M., Schroeder, R.: Artifact for "translating c to safer rust", September 2021. https://doi.org/10.5281/zenodo.5442253

17. Emre, M., Schroeder, R., Dewey, K., Hardekopf, B.: Translating C to safer rust. Proc. ACM Program. Lang. **5**(OOPSLA), 1–29 (2021). https://doi.org/10.1145/3485498

18. Evans, A.N., Campbell, B., Soffa, M.L.: Is rust used safely by software developers? In: Proceedings of the ACM/IEEE 42nd International Conference on Software Engineering. ICSE '20, pp. 246–257. Association for Computing Machinery, New York, NY, USA (2020). https://doi.org/10.1145/3377811.3380413

19. Feng, X.: Local rely-guarantee reasoning. In: Proceedings of the 36th Annual ACM SIGPLAN-SIGACT Symposium on Principles of Programming Languages. POPL '09, pp. 315–327. Association for Computing Machinery, New York, NY, USA (2009). https://doi.org/10.1145/1480881.1480922

20. Fitzgerald, N., Hoare, G., Mitchener, B., Puri, S.: Rust bindings to the z3 SMT solver. https://crates.io/crates/z3

21. Foster, J.S., Johnson, R., Kodumal, J., Aiken, A.: Flow-insensitive type qualifiers. ACM Trans. Program. Lang. Syst. **28**(6), 1035–1087 (2006). https://doi.org/10.1145/1186632.1186635

22. Greenfieldboyce, D., Foster, J.S.: Type qualifier inference for java. In: Proceedings of the 22nd Annual ACM SIGPLAN Conference on Object-Oriented Programming Systems, Languages and Applications. OOPSLA '07, pp. 321–336. Association for Computing Machinery, New York, NY, USA (2007). https://doi.org/10.1145/1297027.1297051

23. Hackett, B., Aiken, A.: How is aliasing used in systems software? In: Proceedings of the 14th ACM SIGSOFT International Symposium on Foundations of Software Engineering. SIGSOFT '06/FSE-14, pp. 69–80. Association for Computing Machinery, New York, NY, USA (2006). https://doi.org/10.1145/1181775.1181785

24. Heine, D.L., Lam, M.S.: A practical flow-sensitive and context-sensitive C and C++ memory leak detector. In: Cytron, R., Gupta, R. (eds.) Proceedings of the ACM SIGPLAN 2003 Conference on Programming Language Design and Implementation 2003, San Diego, California, USA, 9–11 June 2003, pp. 168–181. ACM (2003). https://doi.org/10.1145/781131.781150

25. Huang, W., Milanova, A., Dietl, W., Ernst, M.D.: Reim & reminfer: checking and inference of reference immutability and method purity. In: Proceedings of the ACM International Conference on Object Oriented Programming Systems Languages and Applications. OOPSLA '12, pp. 879–896. Association for Computing Machinery, New York, NY, USA (2012). https://doi.org/10.1145/2384616.2384680

26. inc., I.: c2rust. https://github.com/immunant/c2rust

27. Jung, R., Jourdan, J.H., Krebbers, R., Dreyer, D.: Rustbelt: securing the foundations of the rust programming language. Proc. ACM Program. Lang. **2**(POPL) (2017). https://doi.org/10.1145/3158154

28. Jung, R., Krebbers, R., Jourdan, J.H., Bizjak, A., Birkedal, L., Dreyer, D.: Iris from the ground up: a modular foundation for higher-order concurrent separation logic. J. Funct. Program. **28**(e20) (2018). https://doi.org/10.1017/S0956796818000151, https://hal.science/hal-01945446

29. Lerch, J., Späth, J., Bodden, E., Mezini, M.: Access-path abstraction: scaling field-sensitive data-flow analysis with unbounded access paths (t). In: 2015 30th IEEE/ACM International Conference on Automated Software Engineering (ASE), pp. 619–629 (2015). https://doi.org/10.1109/ASE.2015.9

30. Lhoták, O., Chung, K.C.A.: Points-to analysis with efficient strong updates. In: Proceedings of the 38th Annual ACM SIGPLAN-SIGACT Symposium on Principles of Programming Languages. POPL '11, pp. 3–16. Association for Computing Machinery, New York, NY, USA (2011). https://doi.org/10.1145/1926385.1926389

31. Ling, M., Yu, Y., Wu, H., Wang, Y., Cordy, J.R., Hassan, A.E.: In rust we trust - a transpiler from unsafe C to safer rust. In: 44th IEEE/ACM International Conference on Software Engineering: Companion Proceedings, ICSE Companion 2022, Pittsburgh, PA, USA, 22–24 May 2022, pp. 354–355. ACM/IEEE (2022). https://doi.org/10.1145/3510454.3528640

32. Machiry, A., Kastner, J., McCutchen, M., Eline, A., Headley, K., Hicks, M.: C to checked c by 3c. Proc. ACM Program. Lang. **6**(OOPSLA1) (2022). https://doi.org/10.1145/3527322

33. Matsakis, N.D., Klock, F.S.: The rust language. In: Proceedings of the 2014 ACM SIGAda Annual Conference on High Integrity Language Technology. HILT '14, pp. 103–104. Association for Computing Machinery, New York, NY, USA (2014). https://doi.org/10.1145/2663171.2663188

34. Matsushita, Y., Denis, X., Jourdan, J.H., Dreyer, D.: Rusthornbelt: a semantic foundation for functional verification of rust programs with unsafe code. In: Proceedings of the 43rd ACM SIGPLAN International Conference on Programming Language Design and Implementation. PLDI 2022, pp. 841–856. Association for Computing Machinery, New York, NY, USA (2022). https://doi.org/10.1145/3519939.3523704

35. Matsushita, Y., Tsukada, T., Kobayashi, N.: Rusthorn: CHC-based verification for rust programs. ACM Trans. Program. Lang. Syst. **43**(4) (2021). https://doi.org/10.1145/3462205

36. Müller, P., Schwerhoff, M., Summers, A.J.: Viper: a verification infrastructure for permission-based reasoning. In: Jobstmann, B., Leino, K.R.M. (eds.) VMCAI 2016. LNCS, vol. 9583, pp. 41–62. Springer, Heidelberg (2016). https://doi.org/10.1007/978-3-662-49122-5_2

37. Ravitch, T., Jackson, S., Aderhold, E., Liblit, B.: Automatic generation of library bindings using static analysis. In: Hind, M., Diwan, A. (eds.) Proceedings of the 2009 ACM SIGPLAN Conference on Programming Language Design and Implementation, PLDI 2009, Dublin, Ireland, 15–21 June 2009, pp. 352–362. ACM (2009). https://doi.org/10.1145/1542476.1542516

38. Vafeiadis, V., Herlihy, M., Hoare, T., Shapiro, M.: Proving correctness of highly-concurrent linearisable objects. In: Proceedings of the Eleventh ACM SIGPLAN Symposium on Principles and Practice of Parallel Programming. PPoPP '06, pp. 129–136. Association for Computing Machinery, New York, NY, USA (2006). https://doi.org/10.1145/1122971.1122992

39. Wolff, F., Bílý, A., Matheja, C., Müller, P., Summers, A.J.: Modular specification and verification of closures in rust. Proc. ACM Program. Lang. **5**(OOPSLA) (2021). https://doi.org/10.1145/3485522

40. Wu, J., Hu, G., Tang, Y., Yang, J.: Effective dynamic detection of alias analysis errors. In: Proceedings of the 2013 9th Joint Meeting on Foundations of Software Engineering. ESEC/FSE 2013, pp. 279–289. Association for Computing Machinery, New York, NY, USA (2013). https://doi.org/10.1145/2491411.2491439
41. Zhang, H., David, C., Yu, Y., Wang, M.: Ownership guided c to rust translation (2023). https://doi.org/10.48550/arXiv.2303.10515
42. Zhao, T., Baker, J., Hunt, J., Noble, J., Vitek, J.: Implicit ownership types for memory management. Sci. Comput. Program. **71**(3), 213–241 (2008)

R2U2 Version 3.0: Re-Imagining a Toolchain for Specification, Resource Estimation, and Optimized Observer Generation for Runtime Verification in Hardware and Software

Chris Johannsen[1(✉)], Phillip Jones[1], Brian Kempa[1], Kristin Yvonne Rozier[1], and Pei Zhang[2]

[1] Iowa State University, Ames, USA
{cgjohann,phjones,bckempa,
kyrozier}@iastate.edu
[2] Google LLC, Sunnyvale, USA

Abstract. R2U2 is a modular runtime verification framework capable of monitoring sets of specifications in real time and in resource-constrained environments. Such environments demand that a runtime monitor be fast, easily integratable, accessible to domain experts, and have predictable resource requirements. Version 3.0 adds new features to R2U2 and its associated suite of tools that meet these needs including a new front-end compiler that accepts a custom specification language, a GUI for resource estimation, and improvements to R2U2's internal architecture.

1 Tool Overview

R2U2 (Realizable Responsive Unobtrusive Unit) is a modular framework for hardware (FPGA) and software (C and C++) real-time runtime verification (RV). R2U2 runs *online*, during system execution, with minimal overhead. (It also runs *offline*, over simulated data streasms or recorded data logs.) R2U2 is *stream-based*; given a runtime requirement φ and an input computation π of sensor and software values at each timestamp i, R2U2 returns the verdict (`true` or `false`) for all i as to whether $\pi, i \models \varphi$. We call this output stream an *execution sequence* [34]; it is a stream of two-tuples $\langle verdict, time \rangle$ for every time i. R2U2 encodes specifications as *observers* (a set of which we call a *configuration*) via an optimized algorithm with published proofs of correctness, time, and space [18,20,34].

Figure 1 depicts a standard R2U2 workflow. To integrate R2U2 into a target system, we first need a validated set of runtime requirements. Given the system's resource constraints, the Configuration Compiler for Property Organization (C2PO) creates an optimized encoding of the input set of requirements as an R2U2 configuration. Users can

This work was funded by NSF CAREER Award CNS-1552934, NASA-ECF NNX16AR57G, NASA Cooperative Agreement Grant #80NSSC21M0121, and NSF:CPS Award 2038903. Thanks to the NASA Lunar Gateway Vehicle System Manager team for novel feature requests.

C. Enea and A. Lal (Eds.): CAV 2023, LNCS 13966, pp. 483–497, 2023.
https://doi.org/10.1007/978-3-031-37709-9_23

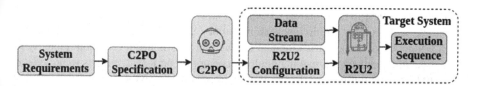

Fig. 1. Workflow for verifying a specification using R2U2. Red shaded boxes denote runtime components and blue shaded boxes denote design-time components. Note that for validation, the runtime components can run offline, e.g., by replacing the data stream with a log file of simulated data. Users formalize their system requirements as MLTL formulas within a C2PO specification, use C2PO to generate an R2U2 configuration, then monitor the verdicts R2U2 outputs based on the configuration and data stream. (Color figure online)

swap configurations monitored by R2U2 at runtime, during system execution, based on system state, mission phase, or to upgrade the specification version – all without recompiling and redeploying the R2U2 engine, a key feature for systems that require onerous code change certifications, or e.g., systems that need to be launched into space and then dynamically updated as their hardware degrades.

R2U2 fills the unique gap in the RV community described by its name [39]:

REALIZABILITY R2U2 analyzes generic, re-usable specifications in Mission-Time Linear Temporal Logic (MLTL) [20,34], a variant of LTL with closed integer-bounded intervals on the temporal operators. MLTL excels at capturing requirements conceptualized as timelines, as is common in aerospace operational concepts, e.g., [1,11,45]. At its core, R2U2 specifications combine either a future-time or past-time MLTL formula with simple signal comparators [34]. New optional extensions provide additional features, such as simple set-level reasoning [5]. R2U2's hardware implementation, written in VHDL, avoids overburdening limited computing resources by utilizing Field Programmable Gate Arrays (FPGAs) to monitor in parallel with the system under absolute timing guarantees. R2U2's two software implementations avoid hardware integration and software instrumentation challenges at the cost of (minimal) compute resources on the host system and are designed to be suitable for different environments. The C version forgoes memory allocation and bounds checking to provide fast deterministic results for real-time controllers under stringent certifiability criteria; alternatively, the C++ version makes full use of dynamic memory, templates, and runtime checks for maximum flexibility without monitor tuning. Additionally, the implementations differ significantly in architecture to provide fault independence. The three monitor implementations enable on-board (embedded) and on-ground execution, integration with multiple human-machine interaction paradigms, cross-validation, or triple modular redundancy voting strategies to increase system trust.

RESPONSIVENESS R2U2 provides two levels of responsiveness. At a system level, runtime reconfiguration of the monitor without a lengthy re-compilation (and re-certification) process keeps R2U2 responsive to the system's needs even as the mission, platform, or requirements evolve. At a specification level, R2U2's asynchronous (event-triggered) observers provably report both true and false verdicts (rather than only reporting property violations) in the first timestamp where there is sufficient information to evaluate $\pi, i \models \varphi$, thus monitoring integrity, safety, and security requirements in real-time. Since the monitor's response time is a function of the specification and known a priori, higher-level autonomous system health and decision-making controllers can rely on R2U2 verdicts to provide a tight bound on mitigation triggering or other reactive behaviors.

UNOBTRUSIVENESS R2U2's multi-architecture, multi-platform design enables effective runtime verification while respecting crucial unobtrusiveness properties of embedded systems, including functionality (no change in behavior), certifiability (bounded time and memory under safety cases), timing (no interference with timing guarantees), and tolerances (respect constraints on size, weight, power, bandwidth, and overhead). R2U2 obeys unobtrusiveness constraints, provably fitting into tight resource limits and operational constraints frequently encountered in space missions. It can operate without code instrumentation or insight into black-box subcomponents such as ITAR, restricted, or closed-source modules [29].

User Base. After an extensive survey of all currently-available verification tools, NASA's Lunar Gateway Vehicle System Manager (VSM) team selected R2U2 for operational verification [8–10]; R2U2 is currently operating in the NASA core Flight System/core Flight Executive (cFS/cFE) [28] VSM environment. R2U2 is embedded in the space left over on the FPGA controlling NASA's Robonaut2's knee to provide real-time fault disambiguation [18], interfacing via the Robot Operating System (ROS) [31]. R2U2 is running on a UAS Traffic Management (UTM) system [5], where it recently detected a flight-plan timing fault. JAXA is running R2U2 on a 2021 autonomous satellite mission with a requirement for a provable memory bound of 200KB [30]. R2U2 recently verified a CubeSat communications system [24], an open-source UAS [16], a sounding rocket [15], and a high-altitude balloon [23]. The CySat-I satellite uses R2U2 for autonomous fault recovery [2]. In the recent past, R2U2 was used in NASA's Autonomy Operating System (AOS) for UAS [22] (where it flew on NASA's S1000 octocopter [21]), the NASA Swift UAS [13,34,36,43], and the NASA DragonEye UAS [41,44]. R2U2 aided in NASA embedded system battery prognostics [42] and a case study on small satellites and landers [35]. R2U2 has also proven useful for monitoring and diagnosis of security threats on-board NASA UAS like the DragonEye [27,40]. R2U2 was cataloged by the user community in a 2018 taxonomy of RV tools [12,39], and appeared in a 2020 Institute of Information Security (ETH Zürich, Switzerland) case study [33]. R2U2 is open-source, dual licensed under MIT[1] and Apache-2.0.[2]

2   Compiler and Specification Language

Specification is a notoriously difficult aspect of RV [37]; verification results are only meaningful if the input specifications are correct and complete with respect to the system requirements. An RV engine is only usable if system engineers can *validate* that it monitors its given requirements as they expect, so they can clearly explain when and why different RV verdicts occur. In consultation with outside groups using R2U2 on

---

[1] https://choosealicense.com/licenses/mit/.

[2] https://choosealicense.com/licenses/apache-2.0/.

Table 1. Overview of changes to the R2U2 specification syntax for a basic temperature limit requirement, where $Temp$ is located at index 0 of the input signal vector. This is not an exhaustive comparison but covers directly equivalent features, while Fig. 2 and the remainder of Sect. 2 detail new capabilities.

Feature	Previous Syntax [39]	C2PO Syntax

Declare Signal	`Temp = 0;`
	Fix name to signal index
		`INPUT`
		`  Temp: float;`
		Declare name/type, signal index handled separately

Define Macro	N/A	`DEFINE`
		`  Temp_Limit = 97;`
		Improves readability and maintenance

Define Struct	N/A	`STRUCT`
		`  Alarm = { T: float; };`
		Enables data organization

Atomic Checker	`OVERTEMP = float(Temp) >`
	`        97;`
	In-lined constants, signal type determined by function name
		`ATOMIC`
		`  OVERTEMP = Temp >`
		`    Temp_Limit;`
		All declared names available, uses known signal types

MLTL Formula	`G[0,3] !OVERTEMP;`	`FTSPEC`
		`  G[0,3] !OVERTEMP;`
		Requires temporal tense declared (FTSPEC or PTSPEC)

real systems [8,14,30], we developed a new specification language and an accompanying formula-set compiler. The language's and compiler's features make specifications easier to read and write, improving user productivity and easing validation to address the challenges of specification in RV.

2.1 New Specification Language

Previous versions of R2U2 used a specification language derived from the implementation of the hardware runtime engine. While sufficiently expressive for the creation of R2U2 configurations, it utilized a restricted syntax that supported only basic MLTL operators and single-operator expressions over non-Boolean data types. Writing specifications that are transparent and easy to validate could be difficult without in-depth knowledge of R2U2's architecture [17].

The new SMV-inspired [26] specification language allows users the option to write specifications more naturally with support for compound expressions over complex data types including sets and C-like structs as well as sections for defining structs, variables, macros, and MLTL formulas. C2PO supports Boolean, struct, and parametric set types

```
1  STRUCT
2    Request: { state: int; time_active: float; };
3    Arbiter: { ReqSet: set<Request>; };
4
5  INPUT
6    st0, st1, st2, st3: int;
7    ta0, ta1, ta2, ta3: float;
8
9  DEFINE
10   WT := 0; GR := 1; RJ := 2;  -- WAIT, GRANT, REJECT
11
12   rq0 := Request(st0, ta0); rq1 := Request(st1, ta1);
13   rq2 := Request(st2, ta2); rq3 := Request(st3, ta3);
14
15   Arb0 := Arbiter({rq0, rq1}); Arb1 := Arbiter({rq2, rq3});
16   ArbSet := {Arb0, Arb1};
17
18 FTSPEC
19   (rq0.time_active - rq1.time_active) < 10.0 &&
20   (rq1.time_active - rq0.time_active) < 10.0;
21
22   foreach(arb: ArbSet)(
23    foreach(rq: arb.ReqSet)(
24     (rq.state == WT) U[0,5] (rq.state == GR || rq.state == RJ)
25    )
26   );
```

Fig. 2. Sample C2PO specification file using structs (lines 2–3, 12–13), sets (lines 3, 15–16), and set aggregation operators (lines 22–23). The specification on lines 19–20 captures the English requirement, "The active times for rq_0 and rq_1 shall differ by no more than 10.0 s," and the specification on lines 22–26 captures the English requirement, "For each request r of each arbiter in *ArbSet*, r's status shall be GRANT or REJECT within the next 5 s and until then shall be WAITING."

with configurable integer and floating point types. To run R2U2 in software, users select a C standard type for each of the integer and float types e.g., an unsigned 16-bit integer (`uint16_t`) and double-precision floating point (`double`). If targeting hardware (FPGA implementation), users can configure integer and float types to a bit-width supported by the target system. Table 1 presents a comparison between the old [39] and new syntaxes and Fig. 2 presents a sample file for monitoring a request-handling system.

To create an R2U2 configuration, C2PO generates an Abstract Syntax Tree (AST) representation of the input, performs type checking, applies optimizations and rewriting rules, then outputs the corresponding R2U2 configuration. R2U2 does not use automata to encode temporal logic observers (as reported erroneously elsewhere [12]); instead C2PO traverses the AST to produce assembly-like imperative evaluation instructions for the R2U2 monitor to executed at runtime.

In order to meet the demands of a wide range of systems, R2U2 Version 3.0 includes many optional features that are specific to one of the three implementations that can be enabled during system integration. For example, the Booleanizer module computes arbitrary non-Boolean expressions in the C implementation of R2U2, but this feature is not an option in the C++ or hardware implementations. C2PO allows users to enable or disable such features according to the capabilities of their target systems and chosen R2U2 implementation.

2.2 Assume-Guarantee Contract Support

Assume Guarantee Contracts (AGCs) provide a template for structuring and validating complex requirements in aerospace operational concepts [3]. AGCs feature a guard or trigger clause called the "assumption" and a system invariant called the "guarantee;" they have been used to structure both English and formal (e.g., temporal logic) requirements by projects including the NASA Lunar Gateway Vehicle System Manager [10]. R2U2 V3.0 now directly supports AGCs with an input syntax for expressing AGCs in C2PO and an output format for R2U2 that provides granular interpretation of verdicts, as presented in [17]. The input syntax for declaring an AGC is `assumption => guarantee` where the semantics for this logical implication provides three distinct cases: the AGC is "inactive" if the assumption is false, "true" if both the assumption and guarantee are true, and "false" otherwise. When the optional AGC feature is enabled, R2U2 produces three-valued verdicts to represent the state of the AGCs in a clear format; otherwise R2U2 interprets logical implications in the standard way (where $false \rightarrow true$ results in the verdict `true` rather than `inactive`).

2.3 Set Aggregation

A common pattern in real-world specifications applies an identical formula to various input signals, such as testing all temperature sensors for an overheat condition. A naive encoding of these specifications in MLTL can be excessively large to the point of obscuring intent while providing ample opportunity for copy-paste errors, typos, or incomplete updates to variables – all of which are difficult for humans to spot during validation. C2PO mitigates this issue by supporting set aggregation operators that compactly encode these expressions as sets of streams with a predicate applied to each element [14].

To illustrate, consider the specification in Fig. 2. The direct encoding of this specification without the "foreach" operator is

```
(rq0.status == W) U[0,5] (rq0.status == G || rq0.status == R) &&
(rq1.status == W) U[0,5] (rq1.status == G || rq1.status == R) &&
(rq2.status == W) U[0,5] (rq2.status == G || rq2.status == R) &&
(rq3.status == W) U[0,5] (rq3.status == G || rq3.status == R)
```

Contrast this with the more compact encoding using the "foreach" operator on lines 22–26 in Fig. 2. The latter retains the intent of the English-level requirement while being semantically equivalent to the direct encoding. This concise representation both eases validation by improving readability and reduces the potential for errors by avoiding replicated values that require simultaneous updates.

2.4 Common Subexpression Elimination

C2PO uses an AST as the intermediate representation of its input and can therefore use optimization techniques common in compiler design such as Common Subexpression Elimination (CSE) [6]. Similarly to applying the isomorphism elimination rule for Binary Decision Trees [4], Common Subexpression Elimination (CSE) prunes all but one instance of any identical AST subtrees, reusing the result from that subtree for monitoring multiple requirements without wasting memory and execution time by representing it redundantly. Analysis of CSE on randomly-generated MLTL requirements resulted in a speed-up of 37% and required 4.3% less memory [18]. We expect larger savings in human-authored requirement specifications, however, due to reuse of both common specification patterns and structures in the underlying system. For example, a non-trivial subexpression might represent a system's confidence in its navigational fix and many specifications might depend on the navigation state, thus re-using this subexpression.

3   Resource Estimation GUI

As R2U2's user base expands, so does the variance in the domain expertise of these specification authors; R2U2 V3.0 therefore enables resource-aware requirements specification by users without experience with the performance trade-offs of syntactically different but semantically equivalent temporal logic encodings. The R2U2 Configuration Explorer is a web application that provides visual feedback from C2PO about the resource costs of specifications, e.g., in the form of MLTL formulas; see Fig. 3. With a short feedback loop on critical parameters like execution time, memory, and relative formula size, all a user needs to understand is what resources are available on their target system (not R2U2 itself) to write performant specifications that fit the available resources.

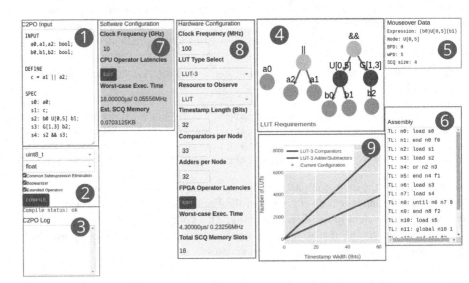

Fig. 3. R2U2 Configuration Explorer web application: 1) C2PO specification input; 2) C2PO options; 3) C2PO output; 4) AST visualization; 5) AST node data; 6) R2U2 instruction; 7) C engine speed and memory calculator; 8) FPGA speed and size calculator; 9) FPGA design size vs maximum timestamp value.

3.1 C2PO Feedback

Feedback from C2PO (elements 1–6 in Fig. 3) allows users to visualize the intermediate representation of a given input specification as well as the effects of optimizations and options on their final R2U2 configurations. Properties such as the memory required to represent specifications with differently-sized temporal intervals, or syntactically different but functionally similar checks, can be unintuitive for users to compute on the fly. The AST visualization provides transparency into this process for users unfamiliar with R2U2's implementation via an interactive web-based interface suited to experimentation with different variations of a possible specification.

3.2 Software Resource Calculator

The software resource calculator (element 7 in Fig. 3) provides users of the R2U2 software implementations with an estimate of the time and memory required to evaluate one time step of a specification in the worst case.

Software Worst-Case Execution Time. The highly optimized nature of R2U2's software implementations makes runtime performance highly dependent on the target platform's architecture, C/C++ compiler version, and make environment factors; e.g., the length of the current working directory name can impact cache alignment. We use a simplified computing model to provide an estimation of the computing speed based on the number of CPU cycles required for each operation on the target platform. Users can edit these clock cycle values in the GUI, e.g., to test for platform-specific latencies. The estimated worst-case execution time (WCET) in software W_{sw} of an AST node g is:

$$W_{sw}(g) = \sum_{c \in \mathbb{C}_g} (W_{sw}(c)) + Cycles(g.type) \qquad (1)$$

where $\mathbb{C}_g$ are the children nodes of g and $Cycles$ is a dictionary mapping AST node types to a corresponding number of clock cycles. For instance, $Cycles(\wedge) = 10$ cycles by default.

Software Memory Requirements. R2U2 uses Shared Connection Queues (SCQs) to store verdict-timestamp pairs for each node in the AST. SCQs are single-writer, many-reader circular buffers that buffer the results of dependent temporal expressions that might not be evaluated at the same timestamp. The total SCQ size for a specification is the total number of SCQ slots required by the specification multiplied by the size of one slot. The required number of SCQ slots for a node g is:

$$size(g.Queue) = max(max\{s.wpd \mid \forall s \in \mathbb{S}_g\} - g.bpd, 0) + 1 \qquad (2)$$

where $g.Queue$ is the output SCQ of g, $s.wpd$ is the worst-case propagation delay of node s, $s.bpd$ is the best-case propagation delay of node s, and $\mathbb{S}_g$ is the set of sibling nodes of g. The propagation delays of a node represent the minimum and maximum number of time steps needed to evaluate the node and are defined recursively in Definition 4 of [18]. Intuitively, a node requires enough memory such that its results will not be overwritten before they are consumed by a parent node. The total SCQ memory of an AST is the sum of the sizes of SCQs of all nodes in the AST.

SCQ memory is an estimation of the actual total memory usage, but is typically the largest and most constraining memory type, e.g., as compared to instruction or pointer memory. The R2U2 C implementation statically fixes all memory sizes in advance to avoid dynamic allocation, so the SCQ sizing feedback is useful for: (1) selecting an initial size based on expected usage and; (2) verifying a configuration will fit on a deployed monitor with a fixed SCQ limit.

3.3 Hardware Resource Calculator

The hardware resource calculator (elements $8 - 9$ in Fig. 3) provides estimations for hardware WCET (W_{hw}), total SCQ memory slots, and a graph for visualizing estimated FPGA resource requirements - Look-Up Tables (LUT) and Block RAMs (BRAM). Required resources depend on the type of FPGA architecture. The GUI accepts clock rate, LUT-type, timestamp length, and node sizing as parameters to better match the estimate to a target platform. This approach was validated on Virtex-5 and Zynq7000 FPGA platforms as well as the ACTEL ProASIC3L used for Robonaut2 in [18].

Hardware Worst-Case Execution Time. The GUI computes the estimated W_{hw} using a more precise method than in Sect. 3.2 by taking into account SCQ usage during execution. The R2U2 hardware implementation's estimated worst-case execution time (W_{hw}) of an AST node g is:

$$W_{hw}(g) = \sum_{c \in C_g} (W_{hw}(c)) + Latency_{init}(g.type)$$
$$+ \, Latency_{eval}(g.type) * \sum_{c \in C_g} (size(c.Queue)) \tag{3}$$

where $Latency_{init}$, $Latency_{eval}$ are dictionaries mapping AST node types to microsecond latencies corresponding to the initial and evaluation times of the node respectively. The multiplication accounts for evaluation of each buffered input from the child node, up to the queue size in the worst case.

Hardware Memory Requirements. The hardware resource calculator provides the explicit number of SCQ slots required for the collection of specifications in the specification set (aka *configuration*) using Formula 2 and summing sizes required for all AST nodes.

FPGAs use BRAMs to implement an R2U2 monitor's SCQ memory, where the size and number of ports of the BRAMs limit the queue depth of the BRAMs. To compute the required number of BRAMs, let d be the total SCQ size, w be the bit width of each verdict-timestamp pair, w_{max} be the widest bit width the BRAM can accommodate, and $D(w)$ be the maximum queue depth of a BRAM with verdict-timestamp pair bit width w. The required number of cascaded BRAMs is:

$$N_{BRAM}(w,d) = \lceil \frac{d}{D(w_{max})} \rceil * mod(w, w_{max}) + \lceil \frac{d}{D(rem(w, w_{max}))} \rceil \quad (4)$$

Hardware LUT Requirements. Each R2U2 operator requires a constant number of comparator and adder/subtractor LUTs, configured by the user in the GUI. The GUI accounts for scaling based on the LUT type and uses the bit width of each verdict-timestamp pair w to estimate total LUT usage. The total number of required comparator LUTs (N_{cmp}) and adder/subtractor LUTs (N_{add}) are:

$$N_{cmp}(w) = \begin{cases} 4*w & \text{if LUT-3} \\ 2*w & \text{if LUT-4} \\ w & \text{if LUT-6} \end{cases} \qquad N_{add}(w) = \begin{cases} 2*w & \text{if LUT-3 or LUT-4} \\ w & \text{if LUT-6} \end{cases}$$

4   Runtime Engine Improvements

To better serve mission-critical systems that must satisfy strict flight certification requirements (such as NASA's VSM [8–10]), we have made a number of improvements to the internal architecture of the C version of R2U2 that provide memory assurances and flexibility as well as extended computational abilities. Figure 4 depicts this updated architecture.

Static Memory Arenas. The R2U2 V3.0 C version uses only statically-allocated memory. This avoids the many pitfalls of allocating memory (slow allocator calls, fragmentation, leaks, out-of-memory errors, etc.) and guarantees the amount of memory required for the entire execution of R2U2 up front. Additionally, many mission-critical systems either do not have or do not permit dynamic memory allocation, e.g., to satisfy requirements for flight certification [32]. R2U2 now runs unmodified on these platforms as well as traditional systems.

Each type of memory (yellow boxes of Fig. 4) has a predefined "arena" with a maximum size set during integration of the monitor with the target platform. When a user loads an R2U2 configuration, R2U2 fills the slots of these arenas in sequence until the arena is full.

Monitor Type Parameterization. Complimentary to the switch to static memory, the internals of the reasoning engine are now fully parameterized. A single header file allows users to adjust maximum values, bit widths, and even internal types. Proper tuning has performance benefits, but crucially allows users to fit R2U2 to use the exact amounts of resources available on a target system. For example, limiting the size of the gaps between timestamps, e.g., in cases where the specification will be either reset frequently or evaluated infrequently, allows more SCQs to fit in the same amount of memory permitting larger formula sets with functionally similar behavior.

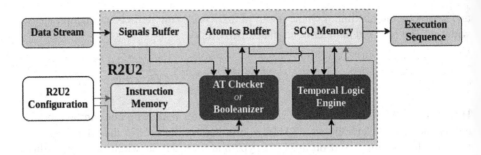

Fig. 4. Internal architecture of an R2U2 monitor. Orange boxes are streams of data, yellow boxes are memory arenas, and blue boxes are modules. Arrows entering and exiting blue boxes denote read and write relationships respectively. The red arrows denote relationships that are only active upon startup i.e., when R2U2 populates instruction memory and configures SCQ memory. (Color figure online)

Arbitrary Data Flow. R2U2 initially worked as a stack of engines, at each timestamp passing results from the Atomic Checker (AT) to the Temporal Logic engine (TL), then passing the TL verdicts through the Bayesian Network (BN) layer to produce that time-stamp's verdict [34]. Now, R2U2 can connect these engines in any order. This simplifies configuration generation from the perspective of C2PO, enabling arbitrary ordering of instructions. Atomic checker properties can now accept results of temporal logic formulas as input, for example, without adding a confusing step delay in the verdict stream.

AT Checker Extended Mode. The C version of the atomic checker has an extended mode allowing for additional comparisons and filters beyond the standard hardware-compatible set. In extended mode, the atomic checker produces Boolean "atomics" from conditionals, where each conditional compares the result of a filter to either a constant or another input signal. Filters are predefined functions such as simple data type casts (bool, int, float, etc.) or mathematical functions like rate, moving average, or absolute angle difference. For example:

- `a5 := abs_diff_angle(s3,105) < 50;` checks if the absolute difference between the data of signal 3 and the value 105 when treated as angles is below 50.
- `a43 := int(s32) == s33;` checks that the values of signals 32 and 33 are in agreement when treated as integers.

Booleanizer. The R2U2 V3.0 C implementation includes a new general-purpose computing module that uses a three-address code representation [7] called the Booleanizer that can take the place of the AT checker. This module enables arbitrary expressions over non-Boolean data types using arithmetic, bitwise, and relational operators as well as extended set aggregation operators such as "forexactlyn" or "foratmostn" operators.

5   Discussion

R2U2's toolchain now provides an effective means by which to formalize, validate, and verify system requirements in real time, giving users control and transparency of the memory and feature set of their target-specific monitors. We have combined the collection of capabilities from previously-published R2U2 case studies into one modular, centralized implementation that we have rigorously evaluated for correctness (e.g., using [19,38]).

C2PO and its new specification language enable higher-level abstractions for users that make the specification development process faster, more transparent, and less reliant on a deep understanding of R2U2's underlying algorithms. The new GUI front-end allows up-front specification design and resource usage estimation by system designers so that users can rapidly prototype specifications before downloading and using R2U2. These improvements make specifying, validating, and monitoring system requirements easier and more accessible to the systems that stand to benefit most from RV. Since specification is the biggest bottleneck to formal methods and autonomy [37], this is an important feature for an RV engine.

It is now much easier to integrate R2U2 into production environments, like NASA cFS/cFE [25,28] or ROS [31], due to the unified front end compiler, expanded engine capabilities, and better user tooling. Recently R2U2 has launched on several real-life, full-scale air and space missions, largely enabled by these advancements. This major upgrade lays a solid foundation for expanded RV capabilities and integration into a wider array of missions and embedded architectures.

References

1. Ryan, J.C., Cummings, M.L., Roy, N., Banerjee, A., Schulte, A.: Designing an Interactive Local and Global Decision Support System for Aircraft Carrier Deck Scheduling. AIAA Infotech (2011)
2. Aurandt, A., Jones, P., Rozier, K.Y.: Runtime verification triggers real-time, autonomous fault recovery on the CySat-I. In: Deshmukh, J.V., Havelund, K., Perez, I. (eds.) NASA Formal Methods. NFM 2022. LNCS, vol. 13260, pp. 816–825. Springer, Cham (2022). https://doi.org/10.1007/978-3-031-06773-0_45
3. Badger, J.M., Strawser, P., Claunch, C.: A distributed hierarchical framework for autonomous spacecraft control. In: 2019 IEEE Aerospace Conference, pp. 1–8. IEEE (2019)
4. Bryant, R.: Graph-based algorithms for Boolean-function manipulation. IEEE TC C–35(8), 677–691 (1986)
5. Cauwels, M., Hammer, A., Hertz, B., Jones, P.H., Rozier, K.Y.: Integrating runtime verification into an automated UAS traffic management system. In: Muccini, H., et al. (eds.) ECSA 2020. CCIS, vol. 1269, pp. 340–357. Springer, Cham (2020). https://doi.org/10.1007/978-3-030-59155-7_26
6. Cooper, K., Eckhardt, J., Kennedy, K.: Redundancy elimination revisited. In: 2008 International Conference on Parallel Architectures and Compilation Techniques (PACT), pp. 12–21 (2008)
7. Cooper, K.D., Torczon, L.: Engineering a Compiler. Elsevier (2011)
8. Dabney, J.B., Badger, J.M., Rajagopal, P.: Adding a verification view for an autonomous real-time system architecture. In: Proceedings of SciTech Forum. p. Online. 2021–0566, AIAA, January 2021. https://doi.org/10.2514/6.2021-0566

9. Dabney, J.B.: Using assume-guarantee contracts in autonomous spacecraft. Flight Software Workshop (FSW), February 2021. https://www.youtube.com/watch?v=zrtyiyNf674

10. Dabney, J.B., Rajagopal, P., Badger, J.M.: Using assume-guarantee contracts for developmental verification of autonomous spacecraft. Flight Software Workshop (FSW), February 2022. https://www.youtube.com/watch?v=HFnn6TzblPg

11. Erzberger, H., Heere, K.: Algorithm and operational concept for resolving short-range conflicts. Proc. IMechE G J. Aerosp. Eng. **224**(2), 225–243 (2010). https://doi.org/10.1243/09544100JAERO546, http://pig.sagepub.com/content/224/2/225.abstract

12. Falcone, Y., Krstić, S., Reger, G., Traytel, D.: A taxonomy for classifying runtime verification tools. In: Colombo, C., Leucker, M. (eds.) RV 2018. LNCS, vol. 11237, pp. 241–262. Springer, Cham (2018). https://doi.org/10.1007/978-3-030-03769-7_14

13. Geist, J., Rozier, K.Y., Schumann, J.: Runtime observer pairs and Bayesian network reasoners on-board FPGAs: flight-certifiable system health management for embedded systems. In: Bonakdarpour, B., Smolka, S.A. (eds.) RV 2014. LNCS, vol. 8734, pp. 215–230. Springer, Cham (2014). https://doi.org/10.1007/978-3-319-11164-3_18

14. Hammer, A., Cauwels, M., Hertz, B., Jones, P., Rozier, K.Y.: Integrating runtime verification into an automated UAS traffic management system (2021). https://doi.org/10.1007/s11334-021-00407-5

15. Hertz, B., Luppen, Z., Rozier, K.Y.: Integrating runtime verification into a sounding rocket control system. In: Proceedings of the 13th NASA Formal Methods Symposium (NFM 2021), May 2021. http://temporallogic.org/research/NFM21/

16. Johannsen, C., et al.: OpenUAS Version 1.0. IEEE, Athens, Greece (Virtual), June 2021

17. Kempa, B., Johannsen, C., Rozier, K.Y.: Improving usability and trust in real-time verification of a large-scale complex safety-critical system. Ada User Journal (2022)

18. Kempa, B., Zhang, P., Jones, P.H., Zambreno, J., Rozier, K.Y.: Embedding online runtime verification for fault disambiguation on Robonaut2. In: Bertrand, N., Jansen, N. (eds.) FORMATS 2020. LNCS, vol. 12288, pp. 196–214. Springer, Cham (2020). https://doi.org/10.1007/978-3-030-57628-8_12 https://research.temporallogic.org/papers/KZJZR20.pdf

19. Li, J., Rozier, K.Y.: MLTL benchmark generation via formula progression. In: Colombo, C., Leucker, M. (eds.) RV 2018. LNCS, vol. 11237, pp. 426–433. Springer, Cham (2018). https://doi.org/10.1007/978-3-030-03769-7_25

20. Li, J., Vardi, M.Y., Rozier, K.Y.: Satisfiability checking for mission-time LTL. In: Dillig, I., Tasiran, S. (eds.) CAV 2019. LNCS, vol. 11562, pp. 3–22. Springer, Cham (2019). https://doi.org/10.1007/978-3-030-25543-5_1

21. Lowry, M., Bajwa, A., Quach, P., Karsai, G., Rozier, K., Rayadurgam, S.: Autonomy Operating System for UAVs, April 2017. https://nari.arc.nasa.gov/sites/default/files/attachments/15%29%20Mike%20Lowry%20SAEApril19-2017.Final_.pdf

22. Lowry, M., Bajwa, A.: Autonomy Operating System (AOS) for UAVs. Proposal Presentation, NASA Ames Research Center, Moffett Field, California, June 2015

23. Luppen, Z., et al.: Elucidation and analysis of specification patterns in aerospace system telemetry. In: In: Deshmukh, J.V., Havelund, K., Perez, I. (eds) NASA Formal Methods. NFM 2022. LNCS, vol. 13260, pp. 527–537. Springer, Cham (2022). https://doi.org/10.1007/978-3-031-06773-0_28

24. Luppen, Z.A., Lee, D.Y., Rozier, K.Y.: A case study in formal specification and runtime verification of a CubeSat communications system. In: SciTech. AIAA, Nashville, TN, USA, January 2021

25. McComas, D.: NASA/GSFC's Flight Software Core Flight System. In: Flight Software Workshop. Southwest Research Institute, San Antonio, Texas, November 2012

26. McMillan, K.L.: The SMV Language. Cadence Berkeley Labs, pp. 1–49 (1999)

27. Moosbrugger, P., Rozier, K.Y., Schumann, J.: R2U2: Monitoring and Diagnosis of Security Threats for Unmanned Aerial Systems, pp. 1–31, April 2017. https://doi.org/10.1007/s10703-017-0275-x

28. NASA: core Flight System (cFS) Background and Overview (2014). https://cfs.gsfc.nasa.gov/cFS-OviewBGSlideDeck-ExportControl-Final.pdf

29. NASA: NASA Export Control Program Operations Manual (2015). https://nodis3.gsfc.nasa.gov/NPR_attachments/N_AII_2190_0001.pdf

30. Okubo, N.: Using R2U2 in JAXA program. Electronic correspondence (November-December 2020). series of emails and zoom call from JAXA to PI with technical questions about embedding R2U2 into an autonomous satellite mission with a provable memory bound of 200KB

31. Open Robotics: Robot Operating System (ROS) (2021). https://www.ros.org/

32. Radio Technical Commission for Aeronautics: DO-333 - formal methods supplement to DO-178C and DO-278A (2011). https://www.rtca.org/content/standards-guidance-materials

33. Raszyk, M., Basin, D., Traytel, D.: Multi-head monitoring of metric dynamic logic. In: Hung, D.V., Sokolsky, O. (eds.) ATVA 2020. LNCS, vol. 12302, pp. 233–250. Springer, Cham (2020). https://doi.org/10.1007/978-3-030-59152-6_13

34. Reinbacher, T., Rozier, K.Y., Schumann, J.: Temporal-logic based runtime observer pairs for system health management of real-time systems. In: Ábrahám, E., Havelund, K. (eds.) TACAS 2014. LNCS, vol. 8413, pp. 357–372. Springer, Heidelberg (2014). https://doi.org/10.1007/978-3-642-54862-8_24

35. Rozier, K.Y.: R2U2 in space: system and software health management for small satellites. In: Spacecraft Flight Software Workshop (FSW), December 2016. https://www.youtube.com/watch?v=OAgQFuEGSi8, https://www.youtube.com/watch?v=OAgQFuEGSi8

36. Rozier, K.Y., Schumann, J., Ippolito, C.: Intelligent Hardware-Enabled Sensor and Software Safety and Health Management for Autonomous UAS. Technical Memorandum NASA/TM-2015-218817, NASA, NASA Ames Research Center, Moffett Field, CA 94035, USA, May 2015

37. Rozier, K.Y.: Specification: the biggest bottleneck in formal methods and autonomy. In: Blazy, S., Chechik, M. (eds.) VSTTE 2016. LNCS, vol. 9971, pp. 8–26. Springer, Cham (2016). https://doi.org/10.1007/978-3-319-48869-1_2

38. Rozier, K.Y.: On the evaluation and comparison of runtime verification tools for hardware and cyber-physical systems. In: Proceedings of International Workshop on Competitions, Usability, Benchmarks, Evaluation, and Standardisation for Runtime Verification Tools (RV-CUBES), Seattle, WA, USA, vol. 3, pp. 123–137. Kalpa Publications, September 2017. https://easychair.org/publications/paper/877G

39. Rozier, K.Y., Schumann, J.: R2U2: tool overview. In: Proceedings of International Workshop on Competitions, Usability, Benchmarks, Evaluation, and Standardisation for Runtime Verification Tools (RV-CUBES), Seattle, WA, USA, vol. 3, pp. 138–156. Kalpa Publications, September 2017. https://easychair.org/publications/paper/Vncw

40. Schumann, J., Moosbrugger, P., Rozier, K.Y.: R2U2: monitoring and diagnosis of security threats for unmanned aerial systems. In: Bartocci, E., Majumdar, R. (eds.) RV 2015. LNCS, vol. 9333, pp. 233–249. Springer, Cham (2015). https://doi.org/10.1007/978-3-319-23820-3_15

41. Schumann, J., Moosbrugger, P., Rozier, K.Y.: Runtime analysis with R2U2: a tool exhibition report. In: Falcone, Y., Sánchez, C. (eds.) RV 2016. LNCS, vol. 10012, pp. 504–509. Springer, Cham (2016). https://doi.org/10.1007/978-3-319-46982-9_35

42. Schumann, J., Roychoudhury, I., Kulkarni, C.: Diagnostic reasoning using prognostic information for unmanned aerial systems. In: Proceedings of the 2015 Annual Conference of the Prognostics and Health Management Society (PHM2015) (2015)

43. Schumann, J., Rozier, K.Y., Reinbacher, T., Mengshoel, O.J., Mbaya, T., Ippolito, C.: Towards real-time, on-board, hardware-supported sensor and software health management for unmanned aerial systems. In: Proceedings of the 2013 Annual Conference of the Prognostics and Health Management Society (PHM2013), pp. 381–401, October 2013
44. Schumann, J., Rozier, K.Y., Reinbacher, T., Mengshoel, O.J., Mbaya, T., Ippolito, C.: Towards real-time, on-board, hardware-supported sensor and software health management for unmanned aerial systems. Int. J. Prognostics Health Manage. (IJPHM) **6**(1), 1–27 (2015)
45. Zhao, Y., Rozier, K.Y.: Formal specification and verification of a coordination protocol for an automated air traffic control system. Sci. Comput. Program. J. **96**(3), 337–353 (2014)

Author Index

A

Abdulla, Parosh Aziz I-184
Akshay, S. I-266, I-367, III-86
Albert, Elvira III-176
Alistarh, Dan I-156
Alur, Rajeev I-415
Amilon, Jesper III-281
Amir, Guy II-438
An, Jie I-62
Anand, Ashwani I-436
Andriushchenko, Roman III-113
Apicelli, Andrew I-27
Arcaini, Paolo I-62
Asada, Kazuyuki III-40
Ascari, Flavio II-41
Atig, Mohamed Faouzi I-184

B

Badings, Thom III-62
Barrett, Clark II-163, III-154
Bastani, Favyen I-459
Bastani, Osbert I-415, I-459
Bayless, Sam I-27
Becchi, Anna II-288
Beutner, Raven II-309
Bisping, Benjamin I-85
Blicha, Martin II-209
Bonchi, Filippo II-41
Bork, Alexander III-113
Braught, Katherine I-351
Britikov, Konstantin II-209
Brown, Fraser III-154
Bruni, Roberto II-41
Bucev, Mario III-398

C

Calinescu, Radu I-289
Češka, Milan III-113
Chakraborty, Supratik I-367

Chatterjee, Krishnendu III-16, III-86
Chaudhuri, Swarat III-213
Chechik, Marsha III-374
Chen, Hanyue I-40
Chen, Taolue III-255
Chen, Yu-Fang III-139
Choi, Sung Woo II-397
Chung, Kai-Min III-139
Cimatti, Alessandro II-288
Cosler, Matthias II-383
Couillard, Eszter III-437
Czerner, Philipp III-437

D

Dardik, Ian I-326
Das, Ankush I-27
David, Cristina III-459
Dongol, Brijesh I-206
Dreossi, Tommaso I-253
Dutertre, Bruno II-187

E

Eberhart, Clovis III-40
Esen, Zafer III-281
Esparza, Javier III-437

F

Farzan, Azadeh I-109
Fedorov, Alexander I-156
Feng, Nick III-374
Finkbeiner, Bernd II-309
Fremont, Daniel J. I-253
Frenkel, Hadar II-309
Fu, Hongfei III-16
Fu, Yu-Fu II-227, III-329

G

Gacek, Andrew I-27
Garcia-Contreras, Isabel II-64

C. Enea and A. Lal (Eds.): CAV 2023, LNCS 13966, pp. 499–502, 2023.
https://doi.org/10.1007/978-3-031-37709-9

Gastin, Paul   I-266
Genaim, Samir   III-176
Getir Yaman, Sinem   I-289
Ghosh, Shromona   I-253
Godbole, Adwait   I-184
Goel, Amit   II-187
Goharshady, Amir Kafshdar   III-16
Goldberg, Eugene   II-110
Gopinath, Divya   I-289
Gori, Roberta   II-41
Govind, R.   I-266
Govind, V. K. Hari   II-64
Griggio, Alberto   II-288, III-423
Guilloud, Simon   III-398
Gurfinkel, Arie   II-64
Gurov, Dilian   III-281

H
Hahn, Christopher   II-383
Hasuo, Ichiro   I-62, II-41, III-40
Henzinger, Thomas A.   II-358
Hofman, Piotr   I-132
Hovland, Paul D.   II-265
Hückelheim, Jan   II-265

I
Imrie, Calum   I-289

J
Jaganathan, Dhiva   I-27
Jain, Sahil   I-367
Jansen, Nils   III-62
Jeż, Artur   II-18
Johannsen, Chris   III-483
Johnson, Taylor T.   II-397
Jonáš, Martin   III-423
Jones, Phillip   III-483
Joshi, Aniruddha R.   I-266
Jothimurugan, Kishor   I-415
Junges, Sebastian   III-62, III-113

K
Kang, Eunsuk   I-326
Karimi, Mahyar   II-358
Kashiwa, Shun   I-253
Katoen, Joost-Pieter   III-113
Katz, Guy   II-438
Kempa, Brian   III-483
Kiesl-Reiter, Benjamin   II-187

Kim, Edward   I-253
Kirchner, Daniel   III-176
Kokologiannakis, Michalis   I-230
Kong, Soonho   II-187
Kori, Mayuko   II-41
Koval, Nikita   I-156
Kremer, Gereon   II-163
Křetínský, Jan   I-390
Krishna, Shankaranarayanan   I-184
Kueffner, Konstantin   II-358
Kunčak, Viktor   III-398

L
Lafortune, Stéphane   I-326
Lahav, Ori   I-206
Lengál, Ondřej   III-139
Lette, Danya   I-109
Li, Elaine   III-350
Li, Haokun   II-87
Li, Jianwen   II-288
Li, Yangge   I-351
Li, Yannan   II-335
Lidström, Christian   III-281
Lin, Anthony W.   II-18
Lin, Jyun-Ao   III-139
Liu, Jiaxiang   II-227, III-329
Liu, Mingyang   III-255
Liu, Zhiming   I-40
Lopez, Diego Manzanas   II-397
Lotz, Kevin   II-187
Luo, Ziqing   II-265

M
Maayan, Osher   II-438
Macák, Filip   III-113
Majumdar, Rupak   II-187, III-3, III-437
Mallik, Kaushik   II-358, III-3
Mangal, Ravi   I-289
Marandi, Ahmadreza   III-62
Markgraf, Oliver   II-18
Marmanis, Iason   I-230
Marsso, Lina   III-374
Martin-Martin, Enrique   III-176
Mazowiecki, Filip   I-132
Meel, Kuldeep S.   II-132
Meggendorfer, Tobias   I-390, III-86
Meira-Góes, Rômulo   I-326
Mell, Stephen   I-459
Mendoza, Daniel   II-383

Metzger, Niklas   II-309
Meyer, Roland   I-170
Mi, Junri   I-40
Milovančević, Dragana   III-398
Mitra, Sayan   I-351

N
Nagarakatte, Santosh   III-226
Narayana, Srinivas   III-226
Nayak, Satya Prakash   I-436
Niemetz, Aina   II-3
Nowotka, Dirk   II-187

O
Offtermatt, Philip   I-132
Opaterny, Anton   I-170
Ozdemir, Alex   II-163, III-154

P
Padhi, Saswat   I-27
Păsăreanu, Corina S.   I-289
Peng, Chao   I-304
Perez, Mateo   I-415
Preiner, Mathias   II-3
Prokop, Maximilian   I-390
Pu, Geguang   II-288

R
Reps, Thomas   III-213
Rhea, Matthew   I-253
Rieder, Sabine   I-390
Rodríguez, Andoni   III-305
Roy, Subhajit   III-190
Rozier, Kristin Yvonne   III-483
Rümmer, Philipp   II-18, III-281
Rychlicki, Mateusz   III-3

S
Sabetzadeh, Mehrdad   III-374
Sánchez, César   III-305
Sangiovanni-Vincentelli, Alberto L.   I-253
Schapira, Michael   II-438
Schmitt, Frederik   II-383
Schmuck, Anne-Kathrin   I-436, III-3
Seshia, Sanjit A.   I-253
Shachnai, Matan   III-226
Sharma, Vaibhav   I-27

Sharygina, Natasha   II-209
Shen, Keyi   I-351
Shi, Xiaomu   II-227, III-329
Shoham, Sharon   II-64
Siegel, Stephen F.   II-265
Sistla, Meghana   III-213
Sokolova, Maria   I-156
Somenzi, Fabio   I-415
Song, Fu   II-413, III-255
Soudjani, Sadegh   III-3
Srivathsan, B.   I-266
Stanford, Caleb   II-241
Stutz, Felix   III-350
Su, Yu   I-40
Sun, Jun   II-413
Sun, Yican   III-16

T
Takhar, Gourav   III-190
Tang, Xiaochao   I-304
Tinelli, Cesare   II-163
Topcu, Ufuk   III-62
Tran, Hoang-Dung   II-397
Tripakis, Stavros   I-326
Trippel, Caroline   II-383
Trivedi, Ashutosh   I-415
Tsai, Ming-Hsien   II-227, III-329
Tsai, Wei-Lun   III-139
Tsitelov, Dmitry   I-156

V
Vafeiadis, Viktor   I-230
Vahanwala, Mihir   I-184
Veanes, Margus   II-241
Vin, Eric   I-253
Vishwanathan, Harishankar   III-226

W
Waga, Masaki   I-3
Wahby, Riad S.   III-154
Wang, Bow-Yaw   II-227, III-329
Wang, Chao   II-335
Wang, Jingbo   II-335
Wang, Meng   III-459
Watanabe, Kazuki   III-40
Wehrheim, Heike   I-206
Whalen, Michael W.   I-27
Wies, Thomas   I-170, III-350

Wolff, Sebastian   I-170
Wu, Wenhao   II-265

X

Xia, Bican   II-87
Xia, Yechuan   II-288

Y

Yadav, Raveesh   I-27
Yang, Bo-Yin   II-227, III-329
Yang, Jiong   II-132
Yang, Zhengfeng   I-304
Yu, Huafeng   I-289
Yu, Yijun   III-459
Yue, Xiangyu   I-253

Z

Zdancewic, Steve   I-459
Zelazny, Tom   II-438
Zeng, Xia   I-304
Zeng, Zhenbing   I-304
Zhang, Hanliang   III-459
Zhang, Li   I-304
Zhang, Miaomiao   I-40
Zhang, Pei   III-483
Zhang, Yedi   II-413
Zhang, Zhenya   I-62
Zhao, Tianqi   II-87
Zhu, Haoqing   I-351
Žikelić, Đorđe   III-86
Zufferey, Damien   III-350

Printed in the United States
by Baker & Taylor Publisher Services